INTERNATIONAL ORGANIZATIONS

The Politics and Processes of Global Governance

MARGARET P. KARNS
KAREN A. MINGST

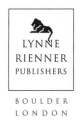

LYNNE
RIENNER
PUBLISHERS

BOULDER
LONDON

Published in the United States of America in 2004 by
Lynne Rienner Publishers, Inc.
1800 30th Street, Boulder, Colorado 80301
www.rienner.com

and in the United Kingdom by
Lynne Rienner Publishers, Inc.
3 Henrietta Street, Covent Garden, London WC2E 8LU

Library of Congress Cataloging-in-Publication Data
Karns, Margaret P.
    International organizations : the politics and processes of global
governance / Margaret P. Karns and Karen A. Mingst.
    Includes bibliographical references and index.
    ISBN 1-55587-987-X (alk. paper)
    ISBN 1-55587-963-2 (pb : alk. paper)
    1. International agencies. 2. International
organization. I. Mingst, Karen A., 1947– II. Title.
  JZ4850.K37   2004
  341.2—dc22
                                           2003026519

British Cataloguing in Publication Data
A Cataloguing in Publication record for this book
is available from the British Library.

Printed and bound in the United States of America

The paper used in this publication meets the requirements
of the American National Standard for Permanence of
Paper for Printed Library Materials Z39.48-1992.

5 4 3

INTERNATIONAL ORGANIZATIONS

To Inis L. Claude Jr. and Harold K. Jacobson

*for their extensive contributions to the study
of international organizations*

Contents

vii

Part 2
Evolving Pieces of Global Governance

3 Foundations of the Pieces of Global Governance   63

4 The United Nations:
Centerpiece of Global Governance   97

5 Regional Organizations   145

Part 4
The Dilemmas of Global Governance

Illustrations

Maps

Preface

When Lynne Rienner calls and invites you to write a book, the invitation is hard to resist, particularly when it comes with passion, enthusiasm, and encouragement. Lynne has been patient through several delays and forebearing as this project grew beyond our collective anticipation. We wish to thank her for the opportunity she provided.

The politics and processes of global governance have become increasingly complex in recent years as the pieces and actors multiplied and challenges mounted. Many of the ideas we have tried to express here have had a long period of gestation. Thus, while work on the book has consumed four years of our lives, it is actually the product of many more years of work. Throughout, we have been inspired by two scholars who have contributed significantly to the study of international organizations, Inis L. Claude Jr. and the late Harold K. Jacobson. It is to them that we dedicate this book, with gratitude for their continuing inspiration.

In the earliest stages of work on this project, we were greatly aided by the lively discussion and feedback from a group of people whom Lynne Rienner helped us convene: Vicki Golich, Valerie Assetto, Paul Wapner, Mary Durfee, Alynna Lyon, and Richard Robyn. Thanks as well to Paul Diehl and Thomas Weiss for insightful suggestions and to two anonymous reviewers who read the manuscript in record time and provided excellent comments and concrete proposals for revisions. To all those who participated in discussions of our ideas but are not named here, we also say thanks.

We have incurred a debt to our students who tested pieces of the book and ideas, gave us feedback on what worked and what did not. To several students we owe special acknowledgement for contributing case material and other pieces, including Laura Rivera, Jason Enia, Jill Marie Gerschutz, Renee Michel, Peter Pergola, Natalie Florea, and Edward Petronzio. Also, special thanks to Jean Poindexter in the Department of Political Science at the University of Dayton and Tony Miller at the Patterson School of Diplomacy, University of Kentucky, for their technical assistance.

Finally, no project like this is possible without the support of families who bear the burden of long hours, weeks, and months of concentrated labor. We are grateful to our husbands, Ralph Johnston and Robert Stauffer, for all the love and encouragement they provided, as well as to Ginger and Brett Stauffer who kept inquiring is it done yet? They, along with Paul and Anna Karns, represent the next generations that must sustain efforts to enhance the pieces of global governance.

PART 1

Understanding Global Governance

1

The Challenges of Global Governance

September 11, 2001, brought home to Americans and to people around the world the threat posed by global networks of terrorists. A variety of other problems pose similarly complex challenges. These include HIV/AIDS and other diseases; weapons of mass destruction—nuclear, chemical, and biological; the continuing conflicts in the Middle East and the Balkans, as well as tensions between India and Pakistan; global financial markets and the increasingly globalized economy; the Internet; the persistence of poverty; environmental threats such as climate change and collapse of global fisheries; ethnic conflicts; and failed states.

None of these problems can be managed by sovereign states acting alone, even by the sole superpower, the United States. All require cooperation of some sort among governments and the increasing number of nonstate actors in the world; many require the active participation of ordinary citizens; some demand the establishment of new, international mechanisms for monitoring or the negotiation of new international rules; and most require the refinement of means for securing states' compliance.

In short, there is a wide variety of international policy problems that require governance. Sometimes the need is truly global in scope as with terrorism, financial markets, HIV/AIDS and other public health threats, climate change, and weapons of mass destruction. In other cases, the governance problem is specific to a region of the world or group of countries, as with the need to manage a major river system such as the Danube, Rhine, or Mekong that flows through several countries, or a regional sea such as the Mediterranean. But what do we mean by governance and is the need for global governance increasing?

■ What Is Global Governance?
In 1995 the Commission on Global Governance, an independent group of prominent international figures, formed to consider what reforms in modes of international cooperation were called for by global changes, and published a report on their five years of deliberations. The group included lead-

3

ers such as Oscar Arias, president of Costa Rica; Barber Conable, president of the World Bank and former U.S. congressman; Olara Otunnu, former foreign minister of Uganda; and Maurice Strong, former Canadian businessman and first executive director of the United Nations Environment Programme (UNEP). The commission defined governance as "the sum of the many ways individuals and institutions, public and private, manage their common affairs. It is a continuing process through which conflicting or diverse interests may be accommodated and cooperative action may be taken. It includes formal . . . as well as informal arrangements that people and institutions have agreed to or perceive to be in their interest" (Commission on Global Governance 1995: 2).

How does governance relate to government? While clearly related, they are not identical. As James Rosenau (1992: 4) put it,

> Both refer to purposive behavior, to goal-oriented activities, to systems of rule; but government suggests activities that are backed by formal authority, by police powers to insure the implementation of duly constituted policies, whereas governance refers to activities backed by shared goals that may or may not derive from legal and formally prescribed responsibilities and that do not necessarily rely on police powers to overcome defiance and attain compliance. Governance, in other words, is a more encompassing phenomenon than government. It embraces governmental institutions, but it also subsumes informal, nongovernmental mechanisms whereby those persons and organizations within its purview move ahead, satisfy their needs, and fulfill their wants.

Thus, global governance is not global government; it is not a single world order; it is not a top-down, hierarchical structure of authority. It is the collection of governance-related activities, rules, and mechanisms, formal and informal, existing at a variety of levels in the world today. We refer to these as the "pieces of global governance."

■ The Pieces of Global Governance

The pieces of global governance are the cooperative problem-solving arrangements and activities that states and other actors have put into place to deal with various issues and problems. They include international rules or laws, norms or "soft law," and structures such as formal international intergovernmental organizations (IGOs) as well as improvised arrangements that provide decisionmaking processes, information gathering and analytical functions, dispute settlement procedures, and operational capabilities for managing technical and development assistance programs, relief aid, and force deployments. In some instances the rules, norms, and structures are linked together in what some scholars refer to as international regimes to govern a particular problem such as nuclear weapons proliferation, whaling, trade, food aid, transportation, ozone, or telecommunications. (See Figure 1.1.)

■ International Law

The scope of what is generally known as public international law has expanded tremendously since the 1960s. Although the Statute of the International Court of Justice recognizes five sources of international law (treaties or conventions, customary practice, the writings of legal scholars, judicial decisions, and general principles of law), much of the growth has been in treaty law. Between 1951 and 1995, 3,666 new multilateral treaties were concluded (Ku 2001). They include the Vienna Convention on Treaties, environmental conventions such as those for ozone, climate change, and whaling, law of the sea, humanitarian law (the Geneva conventions), human rights law, trade law, arms control agreements, and intellectual property law. By far the largest number of new multilateral agreements deals with economic issues. Treaty-based law has been particularly valued because the process of negotiation now involves all affected countries.

Figure 1.1   Pieces of Global Governance

- International rules or laws
    3000+ multilateral agreements
    Customary practices
    Judicial opinions

- Norms or "soft law"
    Some human rights
    Some labor rights
    Framework conventions on climate change and biodiversity

- Structures, formal and informal
    IGOs, global, regional, other
    International courts
    Global conferences
    Group of 8
    NGOs providing humanitarian relief, development aid,
        human rights monitoring
    Ad hoc conferences such as for landmines treaty

- International Regimes
    Linked principles, norms, rules, decisionmaking structures for
        a given issue area such as trade, nuclear nonproliferation,
        food aid, transportation, telecommunications

Nonetheless, customary practice persists as an important source of new law, particularly because of the long time it takes to negotiate and bring into effect agreements involving large numbers of countries.

For purposes of global governance, one major limitation of public international law is that it applies only to states, except for war crimes and crimes against humanity. At present, except within the European Union (EU), multilateral agreements cannot be used directly to bind individuals, multinational corporations, nongovernmental organizations (NGOs), paramilitary forces, terrorists, or international criminals. They can, however, establish norms that states are expected to observe and, where possible, enforce against these nonstate actors.

Another problem in the eyes of many is the absence of international enforcement mechanisms and the role of self-interest in shaping states' decisions about whether or not to accept treaties and other forms of international rules. International law has traditionally left states to use "self-help" means to secure compliance. In reality, the United Nations Charter and European Union treaties, for example, provide enforcement mechanisms, yet the threat of sanctions is not a key motivator for compliance with international rules. Abram Chayes and Antonia Chayes (1995), instead, cite efficiency, interests, and norms as key factors and lack of capability or treaty ambiguity as principal sources of noncompliance. States often value a reputation for law-abiding behavior and desire the benefits of reciprocity (the "golden rule" of "doing unto others as you would have them do unto you"); they are generally inclined to comply with international law. Peer pressure from other states and domestic or transnational pressures from NGOs may induce compliance. For weaker and developing states, failure to comply can be a consequence of inadequate local expertise and governmental capacity to do what is required for compliance. In short, the "force" of international law often comes from the "felt need to coordinate activities . . . and to ensure stable and predictive patterns of behavior" and the reality is "imperfect, varied, and changing implementation and compliance," with many factors affecting the extent to which states meet legal commitments (Jacobson and Weiss 1995: 122).

■ International Norms or "Soft Law"

Many international legal conventions set forth what are not in fact binding obligations for states, but rather norms or standards of behavior, sometimes referred to as "soft law." Some human rights and labor rights, the concept of the global commons applied to the high seas, outer space, and polar regions, as well as the concept of sustainable development are all examples of such "soft law." In environmental law, an initial framework convention often sets forth norms and principles that states agree on, such as those for ozone depletion, loss of biodiversity, and global climate change. As scientific understanding of the problem improves and technology provides possible substitutes for ozone-depleting chemicals, for example, or carbon dioxide-producing energy sources, leading states, key corporations, and other interested actors may later come to agreement on specific, binding steps to be taken. Protocols are used to supplement the initial framework convention, and they are considered to form the "hard" law dealing with the issue.

▪ Intergovernmental Organizations (IGOs)

IGOs are organizations whose members include at least three states, that have activities in several states, and whose members are held together by a formal intergovernmental agreement. In 2003/04, the *Yearbook of International Organizations* identified about 238 IGOs. These organizations range in size from three members (North American Free Trade Agreement [NAFTA]) to more than 190 members (Universal Postal Union [UPU]). Members may come from primarily one geographic region (Organization of American States [OAS]) or from all geographic regions (World Bank). Although some IGOs are designed to achieve a single purpose (Organization of Petroleum Exporting Countries [OPEC]), others have been developed for multiple tasks (United Nations [UN]). Most IGOs are not global in membership, but regional where a commonality of interest motivates states to cooperate on issues directly affecting them. Among the universe of IGOs, most are small in membership and designed to address specific functions. Most have been formed since World War II, and among the different regions, Europe has the densest concentration of IGOs (see Figure 1.2).

IGOs are recognized subjects of international law with separate standing from their member states. In a 1949 advisory opinion, *Reparations for Injuries Suffered in the Service of the United Nations*, the International Court of Justice (ICJ) concluded,

> The Organization [the United Nations] was intended to exercise and enjoy, and is in fact exercising and enjoying, functions and rights which can only be explained on the basis of international personality and the capacity to operate upon an international plane. It is at present the supreme type of international organization, and it could not carry out the intentions of its founders if it was devoid of international personality.

IGOs serve many diverse functions, including collecting information and monitoring trends (United Nations Environment Programme [UNEP]), delivering services and aid (United Nations High Commissioner for Refugees [UNHCR]), providing forums for intergovernmental bargaining (European Union [EU]), and settling disputes (International Court of Justice and World Trade Organization [WTO]). IGOs are instrumental in forming stable habits of cooperation through regular meetings, information

---

Figure 1.2   Classifying Types of IGOs

Geographic Scope	Examples
Global	UN WTO WHO
Regional	ASEAN EU AU
Subregional	Mekong Group Gulf Cooperative Council

Purpose	Examples
General	UN OAS
Specialized	WTO WHO UNICEF ILO

---

gathering and analysis, and dispute settlement as well as operational activities (see Figure 1.3).

Yet how IGOs serve their various functions varies across organizations. Organizations differ in membership. They vary by the scope of the subject and rules. They differ in the amount of resources available and by level and degree of bureaucratization.

Why do states join such organizations? Why do they choose to act and to cooperate through formal IGOs? Kenneth Abbott and Duncan Snidal (1998: 4–5) answer these questions by suggesting that "IOs [intergovernmental organizations] allow for the centralization of collective activities through a concrete and stable organizational structure and a supportive administrative apparatus. These increase the efficiency of collective activities and enhance the organization's ability to affect the understandings, environment, and interests of states." Thus, states join to participate in a stable negotiating forum, permitting rapid reactions in times of crisis. They join IGOs to negotiate and implement agreements that reflect self- and community interests. They participate to provide

Figure 1.3   IGO Functions

- Informational—gathering, analyzing, and disseminating data

- Forum—providing place for exchange of views and decision-making

- Normative—defining standards of behavior

- Rule-creating—drafting legally binding treaties

- Rule-supervisory—monitoring compliance with rules, settling disputes, taking enforcement measures

- Operational—allocating resources, providing technical assistance and relief, deploying forces

mechanisms for dispute resolution. They join to take advantage of centralized organization in the implementation of collective tasks. By participating, they agree to shape international debate on important issues and forge critical norms of behavior. Yet states still maintain their sovereignty and varying degrees of independence of action.

IGOs not only create opportunities for their member states, but they also exercise influence and impose constraints on their member states' policies and processes. IGOs affect member states by setting international and, hence, national agendas and forcing governments to take positions on issues. They subject states' behavior to surveillance through information sharing. They encourage the development of specialized decisionmaking and implementation processes to facilitate and coordinate IGO participation. They embody or facilitate the creation of principles, norms, and rules of behavior with which states must align their policies if they wish to benefit from reciprocity. For example, Chapter 9 explores how China's admission to the World Trade Organization affects its national policies and requires extensive governmental reforms.

The "power" of IGOs is limited in terms of their ability to enforce decisions, except in specific cases such as the EU, which has supranational authority over member states in many policy domains. Most IGO actions are, in fact, recommendations. Their effectiveness lies in actors' willingness to make and comply with commitments. Their suasion is largely moral. Peer pressure can be powerful, however, in pushing states to act in ways that others wish, and IGOs are prime arenas for exercising peer pressure and moral suasion.

Most countries, nevertheless, perceive that there are benefits to being participants in IGOs and international regimes even if they are targets of criticism and condemnation in international forums over long periods, or not receiving as many benefits as they might hope. South Africa never withdrew from the UN over the long years when it was repeatedly condemned for its policies of apartheid. Iraq did not withdraw from the UN in protest over more than a decade of stringent sanctions. China spent fourteen years negotiating the terms of its entry into the international trade system and undertaking changes in laws and policies required to bring itself into compliance with WTO rules. Ten countries joined the EU in 2004, despite the extensive and costly changes required.

Although the earliest IGOs were established in the nineteenth century, there was a veritable explosion of IGOs in the twentieth century, as discussed in Chapter 3. Major power wars (especially World Wars I and II), economic development, technological innovation, and the growth of the state system, especially with decolonization in the 1950s and 1960s, provided impetus for creating many IGOs. Since the 1960s, there has also been a growing phenomenon of IGOs creating other IGOs. One study noted that IGO birthrates "correlate positively with the number of states in the international system," but found death rates of IGOs low (Cupitt et al. 1997: 16). Of thirty-four IGOs functioning in 1914, eighteen were still operational at the end of the twentieth century. The Cold War's end brought the death of the Warsaw Treaty Organization and the Council of Mutual Economic Assistance, both Soviet bloc institutions. The creation of the UN in 1945 led to the demise of the League of Nations. The authoritative source for all data on international organizations, both IGOs and NGOs, is the Union of International Associations (UIA) located in Brussels and UIA's *Yearbook of International Organizations*. Figure 1.4 shows the evolution in numbers of international organizations.

◼ Nongovernmental Organizations

NGOs are private voluntary organizations whose members are individuals or associations that come together to achieve a common purpose. Some organizations are formed to advocate a particular cause such as human rights, peace, or environmental protection. Others are established to provide services such as disaster relief, humanitarian aid in war-torn societies, or development assistance. Some are in reality government-organized groups (dubbed GONGOs). There is a key distinction between not-for-profit groups (the vast majority) and for-profit corporations. NGOs are increasingly active today at all levels of human society and governance, from local or grassroots communities to national and inter-

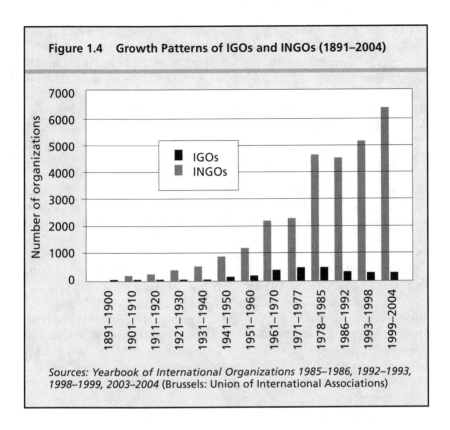

Figure 1.4   Growth Patterns of IGOs and INGOs (1891–2004)

Sources: Yearbook of International Organizations 1985–1986, 1992–1993, 1998–1999, 2003–2004 (Brussels: Union of International Associations)

national politics. National-level groups are often called interest or pressure groups, and many of them are now linked to counterpart groups in other countries through transnational networks or federations. International NGOs, like IGOs, may draw their members from one region or several regions, and they may have very specific functions or be multifunctional.

The estimates of numbers of NGOs vary enormously. The *Yearbook of International Organizations* identifies over 6,500 nongovernmental organizations that have an international dimension either in terms of membership or commitment to conduct activities in several states. Exclusively national NGOs number in the millions. Many large international NGOs (INGOs) are transnational federations involving formal, long-term links among national groups. Examples include the International Federation of Red Cross and Red Crescent Societies, Oxfam, CARE, Médecins Sans Frontières (Doctors Without Borders), World Wildlife Fund, Transparency International (the leading NGO fighting corruption worldwide), Human Rights Watch, Amnesty International, and Save the Children. An example of an INGO that is not a federation of country chapters would be Greenpeace, which claims 4.1 million members worldwide.

NGOs' governance functions parallel many functions provided by IGOs. They create and mobilize global networks, gathering information on local conditions and mobilizing pressures both within states and transnationally. In fact, they have become key sources of information and technical expertise on a wide variety of international issues from the environment to human rights. They participate at least indirectly in IGO-sponsored conferences, raising new issues, submitting documents, and disseminating their expertise. In some instances, such as with the Convention to Ban Landmines, they may be direct contributors of treaty language. They educate delegates, expand policy options, and bring parties together in third-party venues. They play increasingly important governance roles in monitoring implementation of human rights norms and environmental regulations. They enhance public participation, mobilizing individuals and groups to undertake political action, developing networks, monitoring the actions taken and government and corporate behavior.

As a result of global trends to privatize activities previously controlled by governments, NGOs are playing an ever-increasing role. Services once provided by governments or IGOs are being contracted out to private, nongovernmental organizations. They deliver disaster relief; run refugee camps; provide microcredit loans to poor women and men in countries such as Bangladesh; administer development programs; attempt to contain the international spread of disease; and work to clean up the environment. They also have promoted corporate codes of conduct such as the Valdez Principles (a set of environmental principles) and consumer labeling such as "rugmark" (for carpets made with child labor). NGO roles are discussed further in Chapter 6.

■ International Regimes

Scholars have developed the concept of international regimes to understand governance for a given issue area such as nuclear weapons proliferation, whaling, European transboundary air pollution, food aid, trade, telecommunications, and transportation, where principles, norms, rules, and decision-making procedures are linked to one another. Where an international regime exists, participating states and other international actors recognize the existence of certain obligations and feel compelled to honor them. Because this is "governance without government," they comply because they accept the legitimacy of the rules and underlying norms, and the validity of the decisionmaking procedures. They expect other states and actors also to comply and to utilize dispute settlement procedures to resolve conflicts. Key characteristics of international regimes are their association with a specific issue area and the links among the constituent elements.

International regimes encompass rules and norms, as well as the practices of actors that show both how their expectations converge and their acceptance of and compliance with rules. IGO decisionmaking procedures, bureaucracy, budget, headquarters building, and legal personality may be required (or established) within a given issue area, but by themselves, individual IGOs do not constitute a regime. Some issues such as nuclear accidents that trigger widespread nuclear fallout do not need a formal organization that functions regardless of whether there is an accident. Ad hoc arrangements for decisionmaking and action when an accident occurs can be coupled with rules and norms. Nuclear weapons proliferation, however, benefits from the inspection machinery and safeguards systems of the International Atomic Energy Agency (IAEA), as well as the Nuclear Non-Proliferation Treaty, the Comprehensive Test Ban Treaty, and IAEA's technical assistance programs to non-nuclear weapon countries for developing peaceful uses of nuclear energy.

Ad Hoc Arrangements

In situations where an existing IGO does not provide a suitable forum for dealing with a particular problem and a new IGO is not needed, states and other actors may create an ad hoc arrangement. The pattern can be best illustrated with three examples. The Group of 7 (G-7), for example, began in an ad hoc fashion in the mid-1970s when summit meetings of governmental leaders were not yet common practice and major changes in international economic relations suggested the value of periodic, informal gatherings. These later evolved into a regular arrangement, but not a formal IGO.

When Canadian Foreign Minister Lloyd Axworthy decided to negotiate a convention banning antipersonnel landmines in 1996, none of the existing IGO structures such as the UN Conference on Disarmament and the UN General Assembly seemed appropriate for achieving this goal in a short period of time. Instead, Axworthy convened a special conference in Ottawa in December 1997 for the sole purpose of securing agreement on a total ban by the largest possible number of countries. In the mid-1990s, ethnic cleansing in the former Yugoslavia and genocide in Rwanda prompted the UN Security Council to create ad hoc war crimes tribunals to bring those responsible to justice. This gave impetus to the creation of a permanent International Criminal Court.

Global Conferences

During the 1990s, the United Nations convened nine global conferences on economic and social matters, following a similar series in the 1970s and 1980s. Some were designated world summits rather than global conferences because they included meetings of heads of state and government. NGO participation in parallel conferences grew exponentially. Each successive conference exhorted the UN itself and member states to give priority to another set of issues such as environmental protection and sustainable development, women's rights, the rights of the girl child, human settlements, food supply, or the elimination of poverty. As one observer has asked, are these "media events or genuine diplomacy?" (Fomerand 1996) What purposes do they serve? How do they fit into the pieces of global governance?

Conferences like the Summit for Children (1990), the Earth Summit in Rio (1992), or the Fourth World Conference on Women in Beijing (1995) have become an important part of the global political processes for addressing interdependence issues, for seeking ways to improve the lives and well-being of humans, and for strengthening other pieces of governance. They also serve to raise awareness of interdependence issues; galvanize the creation, dissemination, and sharing of knowledge; create new norms and new international law; create new structures; and define global political priorities. Cumulatively, the global conferences have also bolstered understanding of the linkages among issues of environmental protection, equal rights (especially for women), elimination of poverty, improved access to economic resources, sharing of knowledge and technology, and participation of local communities.

Global conferences have spawned complex multilateral diplomacy with NGOs, scientific experts, corporations, and interested individuals trying to influence conference outcomes. They have raised important issues of who gets to participate and in what ways. Often the results are disappointing to those most concerned about the issues because they may represent the least common denominator of agreement among the large number of participants, of whom only states, however, actually have a formal say.

■ Private Governance

Private governance is a growing, but little studied phenomenon. Although the very meaning of the term is controversial, it involves authoritative decisionmaking in areas that once were part of national legal frameworks, the government, the sovereign state, or the public sector (Hall and Biersteker 2002: 203. Examples include international accounting standards; the private bond-rating agencies such as Moody's Investors Service, whose rules can shape government actions through the threatened drop in a country's rating; International Chamber of Commerce rules and actions; private industry governance such as the Worldwide Responsible Apparel Manufacturing Principles and the Forest Stewardship Council, or labor standards within a single multinational firm such as Nike or Ford.

Cyberspace is governed by hybrid institutions, which presently involves a strong dose of private authority. Private firms are attempting to establish enforceable intellectual property rules for music, software, and published materials available on the Internet. Visa and MasterCard have created the Secure Electronic Transaction Protocol to enable bank card transactions to be made securely via the Internet. As Debora Spar (1999: 47) notes about this new electronic environment,

> International organizations lack the power to police cyberspace; national governments lack the authority; and the slow pace of interstate agreement is no match for the rapid-fire rate of technological change. If rules are to emerge along the Internet, private entities will have to create them . . . [including] University consortia and library groups . . . industry associations such as the Electronic Frontier Foundation and the Business Software Alliance.

Private authorities are neither inherently good nor bad. "What is evident, though," Spar (48) says, "is that private entities will play an ever-increasing role in the development and management of electronic interaction. . . . They will assume quasi-governmental functions in many instances, regulating activity in their particular spheres through a combination of formal and informal rules, administrative and technical means." The mix of public and private governance required by the Internet's growth is explored further in Chapter 12.

An interesting hybrid of public and private governance is illustrated by the World Commission on Dams, composed of representatives from government, private industry, and NGOs. Its function is to establish guidelines for decisionmaking on large dam construction.

These various pieces of global governance are not well organized. They vary in scope, effectiveness, and durability. In subsequent chapters we shall be exploring them in more depth and specificity. We turn now, however, to identify the key actors in global governance.

■ Actors in Global Governance

The complexity of global governance is a function not only of many pieces, but also of many actors that are frequently linked in transnational and transgovernmental networks. Such networks have become increasingly dense since the 1970s when Robert Keohane and Joseph Nye (1971) first pointed out the importance of regular interactions across national boundaries of governmental and nongovernmental actors. Such scholars as Anne-Marie Slaughter (1997), Thomas Risse-Kappen (1995), and James Rosenau (1997) have explored the existence of these networks and their policy impact.

States

States continue to be key actors in global governance, creating many of the pieces and carrying out many of the activities. States alone have sovereignty. States create IGOs and determine what actions they can or cannot take; they create international law and norms and determine their effectiveness through their compliance or failure to comply. Because the more than 190 states in the international system vary so dramatically, however, their relative importance in global governance will vary. A large, powerful hegemonic state is more likely to play a greater role in international politics than are smaller, less powerful states. The United States, in particular, used its dominant position after World War II to shape much of the structure and rules of global governance. At that point, IGOs offered a way to create structures compatible with American notions of political order and through which to promote U.S. political and economic interests. Although support for such institutions was not necessarily assured, governmental and public commitment were generally strong. The predominance of Americans in many secretariats and the relatively large share of operating and program funding contributed by the United States reinforced American influence over policies and programs of many IGOs.

Today as the sole superpower, however, the United States cannot shape global governance alone, as even a hegemonic state has to act in coordination with others. In the United Nations system on peace and security issues, that means primarily in coordination with the other four permanent members of the Security Council: Russia, Great Britain, China, and France. In international economic governance, the United States works most closely with the G-7 that includes Germany, Japan, Italy, Britain, France, and Canada. Yet on a number of issues such as the International Criminal Court and the Convention to Ban Landmines, large numbers of other countries have demonstrated a willingness to act even in the face of U.S. opposition. We explore the fluctuations in U.S. support for multilateralism further in Chapter 7.

Middle-power states play a particularly critical role, not as individual states but often acting in concert in the United Nations and other IGOs. Thus, states such as Canada, Australia, Norway, Sweden, Argentina, Brazil, India, and Nigeria are known for their commitment to multilateralism, ability to forge compromises, and support for reform in the international system. The essence of middle-powers' role lies in the importance of secondary players in international politics, as both followers and leaders.

For the large number of less developed, smaller, and weaker states, power and influence generally come only insofar as they are able to form coalitions. IGOs provide arenas for this and also for international recognition and legitimacy. Through their collective efforts, small and developing countries have endeavored to shape the agendas, priorities, and programs of many IGOs over the last forty years, with varying degrees of success.

Although states continue to be major actors in global governance, as Jessica Mathews (1997: 50) so aptly describes, "National governments . . .

are sharing powers—including political, social, and security roles at the core of sovereignty—with businesses, with international organizations, and with a multitude of citizens groups . . . The steady concentration of power in the hands of states that began in 1648 with the Peace of Westphalia is over, at least for a while." Power, indeed, is less concentrated in states and has diffused to the other actors in global governance.

▩ *IGOs*

In considering the significance of IGOs in shaping global governance, we focus not on the structural attributes and programs but on the organizations as actors. This means the IGO officials who play key roles in getting states to act, coordinating the efforts of different groups, providing the diplomatic skills to secure agreements, and ensuring programs' effectiveness. These officials include the UN secretary-general and undersecretaries-general; the directors-general of organizations such as the World Health Organization and World Trade Organization; the UN High Commissioners for Refugees and Human Rights; the UN secretary-general's special representatives for Afghanistan, for child soldiers, or for Kosovo; the president of the World Bank; the executive director of the International Monetary Fund; the president of the European Commission; and the country representatives of the UN Development Programme, to provide just a few illustrations.

Stories are legion about the roles key individuals holding IGO office have played in achieving international trade agreements, ceasefires in wars, and governments' agreement to revise their development strategies to meet international guidelines. Individuals and organizations, then, serve as key actors (or agents) in global governance.

▩ *NGOs*

Like IGOs, NGOs are both pieces of governance and key actors. We have discussed a number of the roles they play. The growth of NGOs and NGO networks in the 1990s has been a major factor in their increasing involvement in governance at all levels from global to local. In addition to the 6,500 or so internationally active NGOs, there are literally millions of small grassroots NGOs in countries around the world. Women have been particularly active in organizing many of these. One group that gained prominence in the late 1970s was the Mothers of the Plaza de Mayo—the mothers of young men and women who disappeared during the period of Argentinian military dictatorship. The majority of such groups are not part of formal networks, but may have informal links, for example, to international human rights or environmental groups from which they may get funding for local programs or training assistance. For governance purposes, these grassroots groups play key roles in activities such as promoting population control, empowerment of women, health care, and environmental protection.

NGOs come in such a variety of forms, with such a variety of emphases, that there is a new group of acronyms that explain subtle differences (see Figure 1.5).

We explore the diversity and activities of NGOs further in Chapter 6. Unlike IGOs, however, NGOs have no legal standing or personality in international law. Thus, it is not surprising that the United Nations system has had difficulty incorporating them into its functioning. Although NGOs operate at the international level in a legal vacuum, in most states NGOs do have legal standing and are subject to national laws and regulations.

Experts

In a world whose problems seem to grow steadily more complex, knowledge and expertise are critical to governance efforts. There is a need to understand the science behind environmental problems such as climate change, ozone depletion, or declining fish stocks in order to consider policy options. Cost-effective alternatives have to be developed for fuels that emit carbon dioxide and ozone-depleting chlorofluorocarbons if there is going to be political support for making policy changes and new rules. Thus, experts from different countries' governmental agencies, research institutes, private industry, or universities have increasingly been drawn into international efforts to deal with different issues. Often these experts may be part of transnational networks and participate in international conferences and negotiations, laying out the state of scientific knowledge, for example, framing issues for debate, or proposing specific solutions. Scholars have

---

Figure 1.5   Varieties of NGOs

AGO	antigovernmental organizations
TRANGO	transnational NGOs
GONGO	government-organized NGOs
GRINGO	government-regulated and initiated NGOs
BINGO	business and industry NGOs
DONGO	donor-organized NGOs
DODONGO	donor-dominated NGOs
ODANGO	ODA-financed NGOs
FLAMINGO	flashy-minded NGOs (representing rich countries)
PO	people's organizations
ONGO	operational NGOs
ANGO	advocacy NGOs
TSMO	transnational social movements
GSM	global social movements

coined the phrase "epistemic communities" to identify networks of knowledge-based experts.

■ *Global Policy Networks*

Experts may also be among the actors in global policy networks that link key individuals in government agencies, IGOs, corporations, professional associations, and NGOs. In 1999, surveys by the World Bank identified about fifty such networks that ranged in focus from fisheries to global climate change to HIV/AIDS. The loose alliances of a broad range of participants "join together to achieve what none can accomplish on its own" (Reincke 1999/2000: 44). Such groups take advantage of the ability to communicate and travel rapidly among distant parts of the globe to promote collaboration, tap expertise, and disseminate new knowledge. The networks have the advantage of flexibility often lacking in traditional governmental, IGO, and corporate bureaucracies. One of the oldest global policy networks is the Consultative Group on International Agricultural Research founded in 1971 to coordinate and finance sixteen agricultural research centers around the world. The UN's leadership has begun to think more strategically about such networks. The secretary-general's Millennium Report points out, "Mobilizing the skills and other resources of diverse global actors . . . may increasingly involve forming loose and temporary global networks that cut across national, institutional and disciplinary lines" (Annan 2000). We shall examine the roles of experts and global policy networks further in Chapter 6.

■ *Multinational Corporations (MNCs)*

MNCs are a particular form of nongovernmental actor organized to conduct for-profit business transactions and operations across the borders of three or more states. Multinational corporations can take many different forms, from licensing local industries to providing foreign suppliers, contract manufacturing, turnkey projects, manufacturing, and assembly operations. What they share in common is that they are companies based in one state with affiliated branches or subsidiaries and activities in other states. They have the ability to invest capital and thus to create jobs, influence political actors, offer incentives to host governments, lobby for changes in state laws, and threaten to move jobs and investment elsewhere should the conditions not be conducive to profitable business.

Since the 1970s, MNCs have been increasingly recognized as significant international actors, controlling resources far greater than those of many states. The world's largest MNCs account for four-fifths of world industrial output. In the 1990s, foreign direct investment grew rapidly, although it was still highly concentrated and distributed unevenly in Europe, the United States, Latin America (particularly Brazil and Mexico), and East and Southeast Asia (especially China). As actors in global governance, MNCs have "profoundly altered the structure and functioning of the global economy" (Gilpin 2001: 290). By choosing where to invest or not to invest, MNCs shape the economic development opportunities of individual communities, countries, and entire regions such as Africa, where little foreign investment takes place compared to East Asia. By moving production from communities such as Peoria, Illinois, or Dayton, Ohio, to Mexico or Malaysia, MNCs' activities can benefit or hurt both developed and developing countries.

Globalization of markets and production in industries such as automobiles challenges corporate leaders and managers to govern these complex structures and challenges states and local governments experiencing a keen loss of connection and control to these larger corporate networks. Corporate choices about investment have changed the landscape of development assistance. Far more funding for development today comes from private investment capital than from bilateral, government-to-government aid, or multilateral aid through the UN and other IGOs. In short, MNCs' activities have raised a number of governance questions: How can MNCs' activities best be regulated—through new forms of international rules or through private mechanisms? How can they be mobilized for economic development in collaboration with international agencies and NGOs? How can less developed countries be assured that powerful MNCs will not interfere in their domestic affairs, challenge their sovereignty, destroy their resources and environment, and relegate them to permanent dependency? MNCs are particularly important actors in addressing trade, labor, and environmental issues. Their participation has been critical, for example, in efforts to address ozone depletion and global warming. They are also targets of NGO activism as discussed further in Chapter 6.

UN Secretary-General Kofi Annan has been a champion of new mechanisms to regulate corporate behavior and to engage MNCs as positive contributors to global governance. In 1999, Annan broke new ground for the UN by convening a meeting with world business leaders and exhorting them to embrace the UN Global Compact whose nine principles cover human rights, labor, and the environment. Companies that participate must submit online updates of their progress for NGOs to scrutinize, thus involving NGOs in policing MNC compliance. This innovation is discussed further in Chapter 9.

The various actors in global governance cannot be analyzed in isolation from each other. Each plays key roles in efforts to deal with various issues and problems. Sometimes, they compete with each other for scarce resources, international standing, and legitimacy. At other times, their activities complement one another. In many instances, they are linked in complex networks. Subsequent chapters will explore the relationships among various actors in global governance.

■ An Increasing Need for Global Governance?

The simple answer to this question is yes, given the necessity of curbing terrorism, blocking the international flow of disease, crime, and drugs, controlling the proliferation of weapons of mass destruction, reducing barriers to trade, alleviating poverty, ensuring environmental protection, keeping the peace after intrastate conflicts, promoting human rights, and other issues of global concern. There is a growing agenda of international challenges and "such globalizing forces as the information and communications revolutions not only propel more challenges to center stage but also rewrite the roles of various protagonists. This profoundly reshapes the ways and means of problem solving" (Simmons and de Jonge Oudraat 2001: vii). Globalization is playing a major role in shrinking the planet, proliferating issues, and changing the roles of key actors. The Cold War's end contributed also to increased needs for governance. The emergence of transnational civil society and the contested nature of state sovereignty likewise factor into the rising need for global governance.

▨ *Globalization*

In the 1970s, many academics identified trends of increasing trade and other links among states as evidence of growing interdependence. But by the 1980s and 1990s, clearly something more fundamental was happening than a mere interconnectedness among states and between states and individuals. International interdependence has been around for centuries and there have been previous periods of globalization. The contemporary form is unprecedented, however, in the degree to which markets, cultures, peoples, and states are being linked together. Globalization is "enabling individuals, corporations and nation-states to reach around the world farther, faster, deeper and cheaper than ever before" (Friedman 1999: 7–8). It has spurred the proliferating networks of NGOs, terrorists, drug traffickers, financial markets, and empowered individuals.

Globalization challenges the assertion by many international relations scholars, most notably by realists and neorealists, that states are still the primary actors in international politics. In its broadest iteration, globalization refers to the "emergence and spread of a supraterritorial dimension of social relations" (Scholte 1996: 36). More specifically,

> It denotes a shift in the spatial form of human organization and activity to transcontinental or interregional patterns of activity, interaction, and the exercise of power. It involves a stretching and deepening of social relations and institutions across space and time such that, on the one hand,

day-to-day activities are increasingly influenced by events happening on the other side of the globe and, on the other, the practices and decisions of local groups of communities can have significant global reverberations (Held 1997: 253).

Globalization affects all spheres of human activity—economic, social, cultural, technological, environmental, and political—but it is not necessarily inevitable; change is not necessarily linear; and not all peoples or areas of the world are equally affected.

Globalization encompasses two simultaneous, yet contradictory patterns in world politics. One involves greater integration and interdependence between people and states, between states and other states, and between states and international bodies. This has been facilitated particularly by the communications revolution and by the preeminence of two core philosophies, economic liberalism and democracy. Economic liberalism emphasizes the role of the private sector over the state (that is, the government) in economic life. The demise of communism in Eastern Europe and the Soviet Union discredited socialist economic systems and brought down many barriers to the movement of goods, communications, and people, while economic difficulties in many less developed countries (LDCs) with state-dominated economies forced them to liberalize and privatize, often under the pressure of International Monetary Fund (IMF) conditions. Consequently, since the mid-1980s, many former socialist states as well as developing countries have changed their economic policies, opened their borders to trade and investment, and become more integrated into the global economic system. Likewise, democratization spread to all regions of the globe in the 1980s and 1990s. From Latin America to Eastern Europe, and from the former Soviet Union to Africa and Asia, many authoritarian governments have been forced to open the political process to competing political parties, to adopt international human rights norms, to hold free elections, and to curb corruption. In many cases democratization and economic liberalism have been linked as integrative forces.

The integrative side of globalization is contradicted by disintegrative tendencies. Globalization "divides, fragments, and polarizes" (Cerny 1996: 8). As James Mittelman (1996: 18) laments,

> Globalization sets in train conflicts among competing capitalisms, generates deeper or reconfigured intraregional disparities, engenders interregional rivalries among neomercantilist coalitions, and has combined with local forces to consign, at the end of this millennium, 265 million people on one continent [Africa] to poverty, with little hope for escape in sight. The foremost contradiction of our time is the conflict between the zones of humanity integrated in the global division of labor and those excluded from it.

Many weak states have been unable to accommodate technological changes and the challenges of more open economies that make them vulnerable to competition and exploitation. Weak states may also be unable to provide the necessary public goods. The resulting disjuncture between the states' persistence as central structures of the international system and an eroding loyalty and confidence of individuals in the institutions of the state has contributed to the resurgence of ethnic and religious identities, ethnic conflicts, and further weakening, if not failure, of some states. The disintegrative tendencies of globalization affect both states' and individuals' perceptions of uncontrollable global processes. No longer are territorial states necessarily the central governing units in the international system. Global financial markets, transnational policy networks, and multinational corporations provide collective goods and elements of governance. Individuals themselves are increasingly alienated as they become further removed from political institutions that lack democratic accountability, or worry about a homogenization of cultures and declining value of labor in global markets.

Measuring the extent and depth of globalization has proven a difficult task. A. T. Kearney has constructed a Globalization Index, breaking down the phenomenon into several components, including level of the flow of goods and services across national boundaries; financial transactions; personal contacts across borders; political engagement; and technology. Of sixty-two countries covered by the index, those with the highest globalization score in 2003 were Ireland, Switzerland, Sweden, Singapore, and Netherlands. The index affirms more global countries have greater income inequality than less global countries. Yet technological and personal integration continue strongly, even when economic integration is low. Kearney (2003: 72) concludes, "Political engagement has expanded because the benefits of multilateral cooperation still outweigh the costs of going it alone." Yet for this measure of globalization, states serve as the basic unit of analysis, and key aspects such as the spread of culture, ideas, and networks cannot be easily quantified.

More important than measuring the levels of globalization are the challenges globalization poses for governance. As scholars Keohane and Nye (2000: 1) note, for example, "Unless some aspects of globalization can be effectively governed, it may not be sustainable in its current form. Complete laissez faire was not a viable option during earlier periods of globalization and is not likely to be now." The 1999 *Human Development Report* (United Nations Development Programme 1999: 2) argues, "Today's globalization is being driven by market expansion—opening national borders to trade, capital, information—outpacing governance of these markets and their repercussions for people. More progress has been made in norms, standards, policies and institutions for open global markets than for people and their rights." The question is not w*ill* globalization be governed, but rather, *how* will globalization be governed? UN Secretary-General Kofi Annan (2000: 6) puts it more bluntly: "The central challenge we face today is to ensure that globalization becomes a positive force for all the world's people, instead of leaving billions of them behind in squalor."

Globalization has both coincided with and contributed to the changed international political environment resulting from the Cold War's end, the growth of transnational civil society, and shifts in the nature of state sovereignty.

■ The Cold War's End

The end of the Cold War was brought about by both political changes toward democratization and economic changes toward liberalization of the economy in the Soviet Union. The fall of the Berlin Wall in 1989 symbolized the end of the Cold War, and two years later the Soviet Union itself disintegrated into fifteen separate, independent states. As Thomas Friedman (1999: 8) has noted, "The Cold War system was characterized by one overarching feature—division . . . symbolized by a single word: the *wall*. . . . The globalization system is a bit different. It also has one overarching feature—integration . . . characterized by a single word: the *Web*." The Cold War's end marked the ending of one historical era and the beginning of another. The international system shifted from a bipolar structure to a post–Cold War structure that was simultaneously unipolar and a nonpolar, networked system of a globalized world.

At the outset, some suggested that history itself was at an end with the triumph of liberal capitalism (Fukuyama 1989) and the end of ideological competition, but those high expectations have not been borne out. Instead, the disintegration of the former Soviet Union and end of the Cold War system revived ethnic rivalries and conflicts in Eastern Europe, Central Asia, the Caucasus, Balkans, and elsewhere, leading some to postulate a clash of civilizations as the new source of enduring conflicts in international politics (Huntington 1993). Although democracy and economic liberalism are now largely unchallenged and the United States is the sole superpower, the Cold War's end produced neither peace nor stability, but a new series of governance challenges. The United Nations and regional IGOs, states, and NGOs have been challenged as never before to deal with ethnic and other intrastate conflicts, weak and failed states, genocide and ethnic cleansing, and the complex humanitarian disasters resulting from these problems.

■ Emergent Transnational Civil Society

Contributing to the Cold War's end and benefiting from both increased democratization and accelerating globalization is the growth of civil society within many countries and transnationally. First, a word about definition. There is a common tendency to equate NGOs with civil society, but the latter is really a broader concept, encompassing all organizations and associations that exist outside of the state and the market (i.e., government and business). It includes not just advocacy groups but also associations of professionals such as doctors, lawyers, and scientists, along with labor unions, chambers of commerce, religious groups, ethnic associations, cultural groups, sporting associations, and political parties. The key distinction between NGOs and civil society groups is their links to citizens. Many NGOs are elite-run groups with tenuous links to citizens on whose behalf they claim to act. Especially in developing and newly democratizing countries, grassroots and national NGOs may depend on international funding. Like NGOs, civil society is neither inherently good nor bad. People work together to advance both nefarious and worthy ends.

The spread of democracy to many corners of the globe has bolstered the growth of civil societies in countries where restrictions on citizens' groups have been lifted. Civil society groups communicate with each other domestically and cross-nationally, creating new coalitions from the local to the global. These "networks of knowledge and action" (Lipschutz 1992: 390) are unconstrained by geographic borders and largely beyond states' control. Transnational civil society groups permeate numerous issue areas, including the environment, human rights, technology, economic development, and security. Their demands for representation in processes of global governance contribute to the increased need to reform existing international institutions and to find new ways to incorporate actors other than states in governance.

◾ Contested Nature of Sovereignty

These trends pose direct challenges to state sovereignty. The norm that states enjoy internal autonomy and cannot be subjected to external authority has been the bedrock of the Westphalian state system that has persisted from 1648 to the present. Some theorists focus on the erosion of sovereignty, suggesting that it may at one time have been absolute, but is compromised by states' own weaknesses, by external influences such as flow from globalization or the development of international human rights norms, or other actors such as MNCs, NGOs, and global financial markets (Jackson 1990; Strange 1996). Others see sovereignty as always having been contested—for example, from within by ethnic groups seeking autonomy or self-determination (their own sovereignty)—and, hence, it varies across time, place, and issues (Krasner 1999; Rosenau 1997).

Over time, then, the nature of sovereignty has changed with the blurring of the lines between domestic and foreign issues, contributing further to the increased need for pieces of global governance. The acceleration of globalization, the rise of powerful nonstate actors, and the emergence of transnational civil society all undermine state sovereignty. Globalization is linking issues and actors together in complex new ways, where economic, humanitarian, health, and environmental problems respect no state boundaries. "Small events in one place can have catalytic effects, so that consequences later and elsewhere are vast" (Keohane and Nye 2000: 11). Viruses like SARS (Severe Acute Respiratory Syndrome) move around the world in a matter of hours, thanks to air travel. "New players, thorny problems, spillover effects, and the magnitude of cross-border flows together inflate the difficulty of coherent action at almost all levels of international affairs. . . . At the same time, these offshoots of escalating interdependence strongly influence the direction in which globalization will move—either toward tighter teamwork in meeting multiple challenges or toward division. . . . the stakes are rising" (Simmons and de Jonge Oudraat 2001: 8). The various processes for dealing with these challenges are predominantly multilateral in character. Therefore we turn now to a brief examination of the nature of multilateral diplomacy and practice.

■ Processes of Global Governance: Multilateralism Matters

Multilateral negotiations have become "management tools in international politics" (Hampson 1995: 6) and a key variable in global governance outcomes. They are "the diplomatic bargaining processes through which the international community confers political legitimacy or comes to accept . . . [generalized] principles" (Hampson 1995: 3). Therefore, understanding the nature of multilateral diplomacy is key to understanding how IGOs function, how NGOs have become involved in governance processes, and how different kinds of outcomes (from degrees of success to failure) come about. What differentiates multilateral diplomacy, however, from traditional bilateral diplomacy other than just the numbers of participants?

John Ruggie (1993: 8) has stated, "At its core, multilateralism refers to coordinating relations among three or more states in accordance with certain principles." Thus relationships are defined by agreed-upon rules, principles, and perhaps by organizations. Participants expect that outcomes will yield "diffuse reciprocity" (Keohane 1984) or roughly equal benefits over time. For example, the principle of nondiscrimination or most-favored-nation (MFN) governing the global trade system prohibits countries from discriminating against imports from other countries that produce the same product. In collective security arrangements, participants must respond to an attack on one as if it were an attack on all. By contrast, bilateralism is expected to provide specific reciprocity and roughly balanced (but not necessarily equal) exchanges by each party at all times.

Complex Diplomacy

Prior to the twentieth century, there was very little multilateralism. As we will discuss in Chapter 3, the nineteenth century was marked by the development of a number of public international unions and river commissions.

The Concert of Europe provided a series of periodic gatherings of great (European) powers. Twentieth-century diplomacy saw the accelerated trend from bilateral to multilateral diplomacy to institutions, especially formal organizations, and the growth of conference diplomacy.

What makes multilateralism at the beginning of the twenty-first century different from multilateralism at the end of World War II is its complexity. There are now literally scores of participants. States alone have almost quadrupled in number since 1945. The first sessions of the UN General Assembly now look like cozy, intimate gatherings. In fact, the UN overall then had fewer members than its Economic and Social Council (ECOSOC) has today! The various other types of actors add to the complexity, as do various coalitions of states. As one observer notes, "Large numbers . . . introduce a qualitatively different kind of diplomacy in international politics. The hallmark of this diplomacy is that it occurs between groups or coalitions of state actors" (Hampson 1995: 4). In addition, a central issue for many IGOs today is how to do a better job of incorporating nonstate actors in processes of global governing since "securing agreement of government officials is not enough to permit the smooth running of these institutions" (O'Brien et al. 2000: 208).

Greater numbers of players (and coalitions of players) mean multiple interests, multiple rules, issues, and hierarchies that are constantly in flux. These all complicate the processes of multilateral diplomacy and negotiation—of finding common ground for reaching agreements on collective action, norms, or rules. Managing complexity has become a key challenge for diplomats and other participants in multilateral settings. For example, UN-sponsored conferences have several thousand delegates from up to 191 countries, speaking through interpreters in English, French, Russian, Chinese, Spanish, and Arabic. There are hundreds of NGOs and numerous private citizens. As one veteran noted, "They are all interested in the subject matter under discussion, all want to be kept informed of every detail, and all have the possibility of being present at almost all of the sessions" (McDonald 1993: 249).

Although the universe of multilateral diplomacy is diverse, there is actually a high degree of similarity in the structures of most IGOs and in the types of decisionmaking processes used. Let us look at key patterns in how decisions get made in IGOs and other settings.

■ How Do Decisions Get Made?

Historically, since IGOs have been created by states, the principle of sovereign equality has dictated one-state, one-vote decisionmaking. Indeed, until well into the twentieth century, all decisions had to be unanimous as states would not accept the concept of majority decisionmaking. This is often cited as one of the sources of failure for the League of Nations.

An alternative principle accords greater weight to some states on the basis of population or wealth and results in weighted or qualified voting. In the IMF and World Bank, for example, votes are weighted according to financial contribution. In the European Union's Council of Ministers, qualified majority voting applies to issues where the EU has supranational authority over member states. The number of votes for each state is based on population; the number of votes required to pass legislation ensures that the largest states must have support of some smaller states; and neither the smaller states alone nor fewer than three large states can block action. Another form of qualified majority voting prevails in the UN Security Council where the five permanent members each possess a veto and all must concur (or not object) for decisions to be taken.

Since the 1980s, much of the decisionmaking in the UN General Assembly, Security Council, and other bodies, as well as in global conferences, the World Trade Organization, and many other multilateral settings has taken the form of consensus. "Pressure toward consensus," Courtney Smith (1999: 173) notes, "now dominates almost all multilateral efforts at global problem solving." The puzzle, he suggests, is "how an organization that is composed of 185 [*sic*] member states, influenced by numerous nongovernmental organizations, lobbied by multinational corporations, and serviced by an international secretariat reconciles all of these potentially diverse interests in search of a consensus on the most pressing issues of the day." Key variables in consensus building are leadership; small, formal negotiating groups; issue characteristics (including issue salience to different actors); various actor attributes such as economic or military power or ability to serve as brokers; the amount and quality of informal contacts among actors; and personal attributes of participants such as intelligence, tolerance, patience, reputation, negotiating skills, creativity, and linguistic versatility. Let us look briefly at two of these: leadership and actor strategies. In Chapter 7, we also explore the role of culture and negotiating style.

■ Leadership

One unique feature of multilateral diplomacy is that leadership can come from diverse sources: powerful and not-so-powerful states, a coalition of states, an NGO or coalition of NGOs, or a skillful individual diplomat. Leadership can involve putting together a winning coalition to secure agreement on a new international trade agreement; it may involve the skill of negotiating a treaty text acceptable to industry, NGOs, and key governments. It may be the efforts of a transnational group of NGOs and college students publicizing an issue such as sweatshops and getting companies to change their behavior. It may involve a government's (or any other actor's) willingness to act first—to commit monetary resources to a program, to change trade laws, or to renounce development of a new weapons system.

Leadership in multilateral diplomacy can also be a UN secretary-general calling attention to an issue and prodding various other actors to do something, as Kofi Annan did in proposing the Global Compact with corporations and other UN responses to the social and economic challenges to globalization.

■ Actor Strategies

The nature of the multilateral arena means that actors cannot just present their individual positions on an issue and then sit down. Delegates must actively engage in efforts to discern the flexibility or rigidity of their respective positions. They must build personal relationships in order to establish the trust essential to working together. Some states (and NGOs) will take a stronger interest in particular topics than others; some will come with specific proposals; some will be represented by individuals with greater familiarity or expertise on a topic than others; some will be represented by individuals with little or no experience in multilateral diplomacy while others have long experience; and some states' positions will matter more than others because of their relative power in the international system, in a given region, or on a particular issue. The face-to-face interactions of the individuals representing participating states are what caucusing is all about. It may take place at the back of the General Assembly hall, in the delegates' dining room, in a hotel lobby bar, at receptions hosted by particular countries, in the restrooms, or in the corridors surrounding the official meeting place.

A hallmark of multilateral diplomacy is the formation of groups or coalitions of states and, increasingly in many contexts, coalitions of NGOs. Coalitions are a way of managing large numbers of participants. States can pool their power and resources to try to obtain a better outcome than they might by going it alone. Just banding together is not enough, however. Group members must negotiate among themselves to agree on a common position; they must maintain cohesion, prevent defections to rival coalitions, and choose representatives to bargain on their behalf. At some point, crosscutting coalitions need to be formed if agreement is to be reached with other parties. Often, it is small states or middle powers that exercise key bridging roles. For example, during the Uruguay Round of international trade negotiations in the early 1990s, a group of countries called the "Cairns Group," led by Canada, Australia, and Argentina, helped to resolve sharp disagreements between the United States and the EU over agricultural trade.

Very early in the UN's history, regional groups formed to elect nonpermanent representatives to the Security Council and other bodies. The Cold War produced two competing groups under the leadership of the Soviet Union and United States as well as a growing group of nonaligned countries. In 1964, Latin American, African, and Asian states formed the Group of 77 (G-77) that remains an active part of UN politics today. Since the mid-1960s, group diplomacy has been pervasive throughout much of the UN system. Other groups are discussed in Chapter 7.

A further actor strategy is the creation of networks to achieve greater policy coherence in the face of the challenges globalization poses. As Ruggie (2003: 301) notes, "Globalization . . . is all about interconnections. . . . The complex interrelatedness of issues and the cumulative, often unforeseen, consequences demand far greater policy coherence than the existing system of national and international institutions has been able to muster." Networks are horizontal associations of diverse actors that operate on the basis of shared normative and conceptual frameworks and the awareness that shared goals cannot be achieved by actors on their own. A network approach is a key strategy for many NGOs. Increasingly, it is being utilized for a variety of issues and problems at the heart of global efforts to address the governance challenges of HIV/AIDS (Human Immunodeficiency Virus/Acquired Immune Deficiency Syndrome) and the Internet as discussed in Chapter 12. It is being used in efforts to promote a common set of Millennium Development Goals (MDGs) across the entire UN system (Ruggie 2003).

■ The Politics and Effectiveness of Global Governance

The politics of global governance reflects "struggles over wealth, power, and knowledge" in the world (C. Murphy 2000: 798). Thus, U.S. power and preferences shaped, and continue to shape, many of the pieces of global governance, especially the liberal international economic system, and ensures that U.S. interests (and often European as well) are accommodated in many regimes.

▒ *Power: Who Gets What?*

Power and influence in global governance, however, does not belong just to powerful states or coalitions of states. Susan Strange (1996: 54), along with others, has noted that "TNCs have come to play a significant role in who-gets-what in the world system." Jessica Mathews (1997), writing about the proliferation of NGOs, refers to a "power shift" to draw attention to their growing influence. The question of how to provide representation in multilateral decisionmaking or some more systematic means of input for key nonstate actors is an important one.

South African Peter Vale (1995), however, argues that economic liberalism and the increased influence of multilateral institutions has only intensified "market-driven poverty" for the vast majority of Africans, Eastern Europeans, and others whose states are failing. The widening inequality between rich and poor, the failure to address growing environmental crises, concerns about labor conditions in many areas of the world, and other shortfalls of contemporary global governance have provoked a lively debate about the politics of global governance and, in particular, the "who gets what" and "who benefits" questions. For many, contemporary pieces of global governance are "Too geographically unbalanced, dominated by the largest economies . . . Most small and poor developing countries are excluded, as are people's organizations . . . The structures and processes for global policy-making are not representative . . . There are no mechanisms for making ethical standards and human rights binding for corporations and individuals, not just governments" (UNDP 1999: 8). For some, then, the politics of global governance is about U.S. power and dominant coalitions. For others, it is about not only who gets included in decisionmaking, but also who gets excluded (and at what price). We borrow from Ronnie Lipschutz (1997: 83) a useful set of questions regarding governance: "Who rules? Whose rules? What rules? What kind of rules? At what level? In what form? Who decides? On what basis?" And, who benefits? Answers to these questions will emerge in subsequent chapters, but first we examine three critical challenges: legitimacy, accountability, and effectiveness.

■ Legitimacy

In the earlier discussion of international law, we touched briefly on the question of why states comply. This question goes to the heart of a fundamental characteristic of power, governance, and rules more generally: namely, how the characteristic of legitimacy leads actors to obey rules without coercion. Thomas Franck in *The Power of Legitimacy Among Nations* (1990: 24) defines legitimacy as "a property of a rule or rulemaking institution which itself exerts a pull toward compliance on those addressed normatively because those addressed believe that the rule or institution has come into being and operates in accordance with generally accepted principles of right process." Some would add that a rule must also be perceived as just to be considered legitimate. As Franck notes, the "compliance pull" of rules and institutions varies widely, meaning that legitimacy "must be a matter of degree" (26). One way this distinction has been expressed internationally is through the concepts of hard and soft law discussed earlier.

A key aspect of legitimacy in the international system is membership in the international community whose system of multilateral, reciprocal interactions helps to validate its members, institutions, and rules. International institutions like the UN, for example, are perceived as legitimate to the extent that they are created and function according to certain principles of right process such as one-state, one-vote. The UN Security Council's legitimacy as the core institution in the international system imbued with authority to authorize the use of force derives from the widespread acceptance of that role, but as we will discuss in Chapter 4, that legitimacy is also under challenge. As political theorists have long noted, flags and rituals are important symbols of legitimate authority. Thus, when peacekeeping forces wear UN blue helmets, they symbolize the international community's desire to preserve a ceasefire in hostilities. Since their coercive power is severely limited, it is their token presence that induces states and other actors to comply. As Franck (1990: 205) explains, "It is because states constitute a community that legitimacy has the power to influence their conduct."

With many nonstate actors and an increasingly vocal civil society demanding a voice, the question of who participates in global governance touches on a fundamental issue of legitimacy. If IGOs' decisionmaking processes exclude civil society or marginalize the voice of small, poor states, does that undermine the legitimacy and viability of these institutions? In Chapters 4 and 6, we explore the issue of NGO participation in particular.

■ *Accountability*

As a result of the diffusion of domestic democratic norms into the international arena, international institutions also have faced growing demands for greater accountability, gender balance in staffing, and transparency. Some of these demands come from NGOs and civil society groups; others from democratic governments. As Keohane and Nye (2000: 27) note, "International bureaucrats are more remote than national bureaucracies. The chain of connection to elections is more indirect." Even if delegates to international conferences and IGO meetings come from democratic governments and are instructed by and accountable to elected officials, the conferences and meetings may well be closed to the public and operate more like private clubs. The World Bank, World Trade Organization, and IMF have particularly been charged with operating in secrecy. Likewise, there is an active debate over the "democratic deficit" in EU institutions. (See Chapter 5.)

Critical to insuring accountability and effectiveness is transparency. Abram Chayes and Antonia Chayes (1995: 22) argue that transparency— "the generation and dissemination of information about the requirements of the regime and the parties' performance under it—is an almost universal element of management strategy . . . [that] influences strategic interactions among parties . . . in the direction of compliance." In some cases, the lack of transparency has been a key to the efficacy of some institutions, usually highly specialized ones such as trade and telecommunications, ensuring that participating governmental ministers could reach decisions absent outside political pressures. But the concerns about legitimacy, accountability, and transparency are not limited to IGOs; they apply equally to many NGOs. A fundamental problem for multilateral cooperation and global governance in the future, then, is how to increase transparency and accountability without undermining the very conditions that made dealmaking possible.

■ *Effectiveness: Measuring Success and Failure*

A third critical challenge involves the effectiveness of governance and the success or failure of different approaches to addressing needs and problems. As Simmons and de Jonge Oudraat (2001: 13–14) note, "Effectiveness goes beyond formal compliance; parties may come into compliance with agreements effortlessly for a time and without undertaking any measures that change behavior or contribute to solving the problem. Agreements themselves may not be ambitious enough to provide more than temporary or cosmetic relief of global problems." The key question is: "What works?" "The complexity of international issues, their overlapping nature, and the turmoil of the arena in which they surface defy tidy theorizing about effective management." There are many points of view and interests to be reconciled, shifting politics, and uncertainties about the efficacies of different policy alternatives.

In assessing effectiveness, several key questions may be asked. Who does what to translate agreements into action, including incorporating norms into domestic laws? Which techniques or mechanisms work best to get targeted actors to change their behavior? And what reactions are there to noncompliance? Who provides incentives or technical assistance to get developing countries to comply with environmental rules? Which actors employ diplomacy or public shaming, impose economic sanctions, or employ military force to punish failure to comply? And what is the outcome? How are people actually affected by the pieces of global governance? The task of assessing effectiveness is one of the central challenges in public policymaking, whether at local, national, regional, or global levels of politics and governance.

The challenges of global governance, then, include a variety of international policy problems and issues that require governance. Many pieces are not necessarily global in scope. Rather, what we see is a multilevel and often very diffuse system of pieces of governance with many different actors playing key roles alongside states. The need for more pieces of governance is clearly rising with globalization and other developments; the processes are complex; the politics, even in a world with a single superpower, is an ongoing struggle to control "who gets what"; and the issues of legitimacy, accountability, and effectiveness require constant attention.

■ Suggested Further Reading

Chayes, Abram, and Antonia Handler Chayes. (1995) *The New Sovereignty. Compliance with International Regulatory Agreements*. Cambridge, Mass.: Harvard University Press.

Commission on Global Governance. (1995) *Our Global Neighbourhood: Report of the Commission on Global Governance*. Oxford: Oxford University Press.

Held, David, and Anthony McGrew, eds. (2002) *Governing Globalization. Power, Authority, and Global Governance*. Cambridge: Blackwell.

Nye, Joseph S., Jr., and John D. Donahue, eds. (2000) *Governance in a Globalizing World*. Washington: Brookings Institution Press.

Simmons, P. J., and Chantal de Jonge Oudraat, eds. (2001) *Managing Global Issues: Lessons Learned*. Washington: Carnegie Endowment for International Peace.

2

The Theoretical Foundations
of Global Governance

Scholars use international relations (IR) theories to describe, explain, and predict various aspects of international relations. Each is based on a set of key ideas about the nature and roles of individuals, conceptions of the state, sovereignty, and interactions among states and other actors, as well as conceptions about the international system. Explicitly or implicitly, international relations theories are also theories of global governance, addressing questions of "who governs," how governance occurs and with what effects, at different points in time. They are also theories of how global change occurs and, hence, how patterns of global governance have changed in the past, may be changing in the present, and might change in the future. In this chapter, we briefly discuss four major theories—liberalism, realism, constructivism, and Marxism—with particular attention to what each has to say about global governance and international cooperation. In addition, we explore some of the most important variants of each theory.

Middle-level theories derived from the major theories often link even more specifically to international law and organization, as well as to core ideas regarding global governance. These include functionalism, integration, international regimes, and collective goods drawn from liberalism; rational choice and hegemonic stability theory drawn from realism; and dependency theory drawn from Marxism. Subsequent chapters refer back to these theories as an aid to understanding and analyzing pieces and processes of global governance.

■ Liberalism

Liberal theory holds that human nature is basically good and that people can improve the moral and material conditions of their existence. Injustice, aggression, and war are, according to liberals, products of inadequate or corrupt social institutions and of misunderstanding among leaders. They are not inevitable, but rather can be eliminated through collective or multilateral action and institutional reform. The expansion of human freedom is a core liberal belief that can be achieved through democracy and market capitalism.

The roots of liberalism are found in the seventeenth-century Grotian tradition, eighteenth-century Enlightenment, nineteenth-century political and economic liberalism, and twentieth-century Wilsonian idealism. The Grotian tradition developed from the writings of Hugo Grotius (1583–1645), an early Dutch legal scholar. Just prior to the European states' challenge to universal religious authority in the peace of Westphalia (1648), Grotius asserted that all international relations were subject to the rule of law—both the law of nations and law of nature. He rejected the idea that states can do whatever they wish and that war is the supreme right of states. Grotius believed that states, like people, are basically rational and law abiding.

The Enlightenment's contribution to liberalism rests on Greek ideas that individuals are rational human beings and have the capacity to improve their condition by creating a just society. If a just society is not attained, then the fault rests with inadequate institutions. The writings of Immanuel Kant (1724–1804) reflect these core Enlightenment beliefs with their extensive treatment of the relationship between democracy and peace. Kant was among the first political thinkers to articulate this connection and the possibility of "perpetual peace" among democratic states. Then as now, the liberal theory of democratic peace did not mean that democratic states would refrain from war in their relations with nondemocratic states, but Kant did argue that in a "pacific union," free, democratic states would retain their sovereignty while working together to avoid war.

Nineteenth-century liberalism linked the rationalism of the Enlightenment and the growing faith in modernization through the scientific and industrial revolutions to promoting democracy and free trade. Adam Smith and Jeremy Bentham believed that free trade would create interdependencies that would raise the cost of war and reward fair cooperation and competition with peace, prosperity, and greater justice. This strand of liberalism forms the basis for economic liberalism. To stimulate individual (and therefore collective) economic growth and to maximize economic welfare, free markets must be allowed to develop and mature, and governments must permit the free flow of trade and economic intercourse.

The beliefs of U.S. President Woodrow Wilson, captured best in the Fourteen Points on which the Versailles Treaty (ending World War I) and the Covenant of the League of Nations were based, formed a core of twentieth-century liberalism. Wilson envisioned that creating a system of collective security, promoting self-determination of peoples, and eliminating power politics could prevent war. The League of Nations illustrated the importance that liberals place on international institutions for collective problemsolving. Early twentieth-century liberals were also strong advocates of international law, arbitration, and courts to promote cooperation and guarantee peace. Because of their faith in human reason and progress, they were often accused of being idealists. With the League of Nations' failure to prevent World War II, the Holocaust, and the Cold War, liberalism and idealism came under intense criticism from realist theorists.

Before examining many of the later contributions to liberalism found among middle-level theories, let us examine the core elements of liberalism further. For liberals, individual human beings are the primary international actors. States are the most important collective actors, but they are pluralistic not unitary actors. That is, moral and ethical principles, elections (in the case of democratic states), power relations and bargaining among domestic and transnational groups, and changing international conditions shape states' interests and policies. There is no single definition of states' national interest; rather, states vary in their goals and their interests change. Liberals place importance on nonstate actors and transnational and transgovernmental groups as well.

Liberals believe that cooperation is possible and will grow over time for two reasons. First, they view the international system as a context within which multiple interactions occur and where various actors "learn" from their interactions, rather than a structure of relationships based on the distribution of power among states and a fixed concept of state sovereignty. Hedley Bull (1977) has also promoted the idea that the system is a society where actors adhere to common norms, consent to common rules and institutions, and recognize common interests. Power matters, but it is exercised within this framework of rules and institutions, which also makes international cooperation possible. Second, liberals expect mutual interests to increase with greater interdependence, knowledge, communication, and the spread of democratic values. This will promote greater cooperation and thereby peace, welfare, and justice.

Liberals are generally supportive of both international organizations and international law. In the latter case, while admitting that law in the international system is different than in a hierarchical domestic system, liberals see law as one of the major instruments for framing and maintaining order in the international system. As Louis Henkin (1979: 22) explains,

> If one doubts the significance of this law, one need only imagine a world in which it were absent. . . . There would be no security of nations or stability of governments; territory and airspace would not be respected; vessels could navigate only at their constant peril; property—within or without any given territory—would be subject to arbitrary seizure; persons would have no protection of law or diplomacy; agreements would not be made or observed; diplomatic relations would end; international trade would cease; international organizations and arrangements would disappear.

For liberals, international organizations play a number of key roles, including contributing to habits of cooperation and serving as arenas for negotiating and developing coalitions. They are a primary means for mitigating the danger of war, promoting the development of shared norms, and enhancing order. They carry out operational activities to help address substantive international problems and may form parts of international regimes. They can be used by states as instruments of foreign policy or to constrain the behavior of others.

Core liberal beliefs in the roots of cooperation and role of international institutions have been challenged since the 1970s by so-called neoliberal institutionalists. Their ideas form an important variant on liberal theory.

▨ *Neoliberal Institutionalism or Neoliberalism*

Liberalism fell into disfavor after World War II, as realism dominated international relations theory. In the 1970s, liberalism experienced a revival centered on an effort to refute many of realism's pessimistic views of world politics, its tenets about states, the anarchic nature of the international system, and the limited possibilities for cooperation. Increasing international interdependence in the 1970s and heightened awareness, especially by Americans, of the sensitivities and vulnerabilities that characterize interdependence were major factors boosting this revival. Robert O. Keohane and Joseph S. Nye's book, *Power and Interdependence (1977)*, which outlined how international institutions constituted an important response to conditions of complex interdependence, also had a major impact. Neoliberal institutionalists argue "even if . . . anarchy constrains the willingness of states to cooperate, states nevertheless can work together and can do so especially with the assistance of international institutions" (Grieco 1993: 117).

The 1970s and early 1980s also presented a puzzle for neoliberals. Given the major international economic dislocations resulting from rising oil prices, collapse of the Bretton Woods arrangements for international monetary relations, increasing third world debt, and the decline in U.S. economic power relative to Europe and Japan, why did the post–World War II institutions for economic cooperation (such as the IMF and GATT) not collapse? Keohane's influential book, *After Hegemony* (1984), answered this question by emphasizing the cooperation states achieved through international institutions and the effects of institutions and practices on state behavior.

Some neoliberal institutionalists, such as Robert Axelrod and Keohane (1986), have drawn on game theory and particularly the prisoner's dilemma (PD) game to illustrate how cooperation is in the individual state's self-interest. PD is the story of two prisoners, each being held and interrogated separately for an alleged crime. The interrogator tells each prisoner that if one of them confesses and the other does not, the one who confesses will go free and the one who kept silent will get a long prison term. If both confess, both will get somewhat reduced prison terms. If neither confesses, both will receive short prison terms based on lack of evidence. In the first play, both prisoners will confess and each will serve a longer sentence than if they had cooperated and kept silent. The self-serving behavior of each player leads to bad outcomes for both players. If the game is repeated, however, or the environment changed—for instance, by allowing communication—the possibility of joint gains provides incentives to cooperate by remaining silent. Neoliberals have drawn a number of conclusions from studying PD games. For example, they have shown that if states use a tit-for-tat strategy of reciprocating each other's cooperation, they are likely to find this mutually beneficial over the long term, especially if the costs of verifying compliance and sanctioning cheaters are relatively low compared to the costs of joint action (Grieco 1993: 122). They have also shown that the applicability of PD varies between economic and security issues, when there are shared norms, and if issues are linked. Finally, use of PD has helped neoliberals demonstrate that states may be independent actors, but their policy choices tend to be interdependent.

Thus, according to neoliberal institutionalists, states that have continuous interactions with each other choose to cooperate, despite the anarchic international environment, because they realize they will have future interactions with the same actors. Continuous interactions also provide the motivation for states to create international institutions, which in turn moderate state behavior, provide a guaranteed framework for interactions and a context for bargaining, provide mechanisms for reducing cheating by monitoring behavior and punishing defectors, and facilitate transparency of the actions of all. International institutions provide focal points for coordination and serve to make state commitments more credible by specifying what is expected, thereby encouraging states to establish reputations for compliance. They are an efficient solution to problems of coordination because they provide information that aids decisionmaking and reduces the transaction costs for achieving agreement among large numbers of states (Keohane and Martin 1995). States benefit because institutions do things for members that cannot be accomplished unilaterally. Thus, for neoliberals, institutions have important and independent effects on interstate interactions, both by providing information and by framing actions, but they do not necessarily affect states' underlying motivations.

Although neoliberals, like liberals, tend to be optimists and see cooperation as generally positive, they also recognize that not all efforts to cooperate will yield good results. Cooperation can aid the few at the expense of the many, accentuate or mitigate injustice. Unlike many earlier liberals, some neoliberals have been more willing to address issues of power, particularly in answering the question of how cooperation emerges initially. To explain the creation, for example, of the post–World War II network of international economic institutions and shared standards for liberalizing trade and capital flows, neoliberal institutionalists such as Robert Keohane (1984) and John Gerard Ruggie (1982) have focused on the role of the United States as a hegemonic state, the particular character of the order it created (embedded liberalism), and the joint gains it offered the Europeans and Japanese for cooperating.

Liberalism and neoliberalism have spawned several middle-level theories that provide additional dimensions for explaining international cooperative behavior. These include functionalism, regime theory, and collective goods theory.

■ *Functionalism*

Functionalism is rooted in the belief that governance arrangements arise out of the basic, or functional, needs of people and states. Thus, it explains the origin and development of many IGOs. Functionalists, however, assert that international economic and social cooperation is a prerequisite for political cooperation and eliminating war, whose causes (in their view) lie in ignorance, poverty, hunger, and disease.

As articulated by David Mitrany (1946: 7) in *A Working Peace System,* the task of functionalism is "not how to keep the nations peacefully apart but how to bring them actively together." He foresaw "a spreading web of international activities and agencies, in which and through which the interests and life of all nations would be gradually integrated" (Mitrany 1946: 14). Not all functionalists share this vision, but they do share a belief that it is possible to bypass political rivalries of states and build habits of cooperation in nonpolitical economic and social spheres by addressing problems requiring international cooperation for solution. Increasing amounts of such cooperation will expand these cooperative interactions and build a base of common values. Eventually, those habits spill over into cooperation in political and military affairs. A key aspect of this process is the role of technical experts and the assumption that these experts will lose their close identification with their own states and develop new sets of allegiances to like-minded individuals around the globe. The form that specific functional organizations take is determined by the problem to be solved and shapes an organization's mandate as well as the scope of its membership. In short, form follows function.

Functionalism is applicable at both regional and global levels and has been important in explaining the evolution of the European Union as a process of economic integration, gradually spilling over into limited political integration. The "father of Europe," Jean Monnet, believed that nationalism could be weakened and war in Europe made unthinkable in the long run by taking practical steps toward economic integration that would ultimately advance European political union. The success of the European Coal and Steel Community, proposed by Monnet, led to the creation of the European Atomic Energy Community (Euratom) to manage peaceful uses of atomic energy and to the European Economic Community, with its common market and many facets of practical cooperation for boosting European economic and social development. Functional theory fell short in its prediction that such cooperation would spill over in a deterministic fashion from the economic area to areas of national security. Although most analysts would credit European integration with making the region a "zone of peace," achieving common foreign and security policy has proved particularly difficult for EU members. (See Chapter 5 for further discussion.) In fact, neofunctionalists theorized that the process and dynamics of cooperation are not automatic. At key points, political decisions are needed and these may or may not be taken (Haas 1964).

Functionalist theory also helps us understand the development of early IGOs such as the International Telegraphe Union, Universal Postal Union, and Commission for Navigation on the Rhine River, as well as the specialized agencies of the UN system such as the World Health Organization (WHO), UN Children's Fund (UNICEF), Food and Agriculture Organization (FAO), and International Labour Organization (ILO). These are discussed further in Chapter 3.

Jacobson, Reisinger, and Mathers (1986) tested key propositions of functionalism as an explanation for the phenomenon of IGO development and found that the overwhelming number of IGOs could be classified as functional. That is, they have specific mandates, links to economic issues, and limited memberships, often related to geographic region. The majority of those created since 1960 have been established by other IGOs and show increasing differentiation of functions, particularly in the social field. This trend toward greater specialization characterizes trends in domestic government as well. Jacobson, Reisinger, and Mathers also found, however, that functionalism did not provide a complete explanation for the trends in IGO development. Historical currents in world politics, particularly the process of decolonization, were important. Finally, they found, "The evolving web of international governmental organizations has modified the global political system, as functionalism argued that it would, but it has not yet radically transformed this system, as functionalism hoped would happen" (1986: 157).

Functionalism fails to address a number of key questions and problem areas. If the ultimate goal is elimination of war and war is not caused just by economic deprivation, illiteracy, hunger, and disease, then how can the other causes of war be alleviated? Another basic flaw is the assumption that political and nonpolitical issues can easily be distinguished. A further problem is the assumption that habits of economic and social cooperation will transfer to political areas. In fact, the European integration process since 1950 has shown the degree to which functionalists underestimated the strength of state sovereignty and national loyalties. Despite these limitations, functionalism has proven a useful theoretical approach for understanding the development of a key piece of global governance—international intergovernmental organizations—and the cooperation many IGOs foster in economic and social issue areas.

■ International Regimes

A second important middle-level theory within liberalism emerged from international law. Beginning in the 1970s, legal scholars began to use the concept of international regimes that we introduced in Chapter 1. They recognized that international law consisted not only of formal authoritative prohibitions, but also of more informal norms and rules of behavior that over time may become codified and sometimes institutionalized. By referring to the totality of these norms and rules of behavior as "regimes," they emphasized the governance provided for specific issue areas. International relations scholars have found regime theory particularly useful for examining many aspects of governance. According to the most widely used definition, a regime includes "sets of implicit or explicit principles, norms, rules, and decisionmaking procedures around which actors' expectations converge in a given issue area" (Krasner 1982: 1).

Unlike functionalism, which is based solely in the liberal tradition, regime theory has been shaped not only by liberalism and especially neoliberalism, but also by realism and neorealism (discussed further on in this chapter). Some regime theorists focus on the role of power relations among states in shaping regimes, particularly the role of a hegemonic state such as the United States (or Great Britain in the nineteenth century). Others recognize how common interests aid states in enhancing transparency and reducing uncertainty in their environment. Regime theorists have also used constructivist approaches (discussed below) to focus on social relations and the ways in which strong patterns of interaction often found in an international regime actually affect state interests (Hasenclever et al. 2000). Explaining how regimes are created and maintained, and how, why, and when they change, are key tasks for regime theorists.

Regime theory has shown how states create these frameworks to coordinate their actions with those of other states, if and when necessary for achieving their national interests. Regimes can provide information to participants and reduce uncertainty. Over time, coordination may lead to a partial convergence of interests and values among the parties in a regime as well as a growing sense of legitimacy.

Regime theorists have focused on IGO roles in the creation and maintenance of regimes, while being careful (as noted in Chapter 1) not to equate an IGO with the existence of a regime. By themselves, IGOs do not constitute a regime, but their charters may incorporate principles, norms, rules, decisionmaking processes, and functions that formalize these aspects of a regime. An IGO's decisionmaking processes may then be used by member states for further norm and rule creation, for rule enforcement and dispute settlement, for the provision of collective goods, and for supporting operational activities. Thus, IGOs are one way that habits of cooperation are sustained and expanded.

Identifying international regimes in different issue areas enables scholars to discuss not only the interaction between states and IGOs, but also between various IGOs, IGOs and NGOs, and among noninstitutionalized rules and procedures that have developed over time. Regimes enable scholars to examine informal patterns and ad hoc groupings that enhance international cooperation. As Hasenclever et al. (2000: 3) succinctly summarize,

> Regimes are deliberately constructed, partial international orders on either a regional or a global scale, which are intended to remove specific issue areas of international politics from the sphere of self-help behaviour. By creating shared expectations about appropriate behaviour and by upgrading the level of transparency in the issue area, regimes help states (and other actors) to cooperate with a view to reaping joint gains in the form of additional welfare or security.

There is now a substantial body of literature explaining the formation, persistence, and decline of international regimes, as well as their specific properties and openness to change (Rittberger 1993; Young 1989; Zacher 1996). Despite inherent ambiguities, the study of international regimes and regime theory has helped link international institutions and governance by establishing that governance and order involve more than just organizational structures.

■ Collective or Public Goods Theory

Still another approach within liberalism to explaining governance and cooperation has involved the application of collective or public goods theory. Biologist Garrett Hardin (1968), in his article, "The Tragedy of the Commons," tells the story of a group of herders who share a common grazing area. Each herder finds it economically rational to increase the size of his own herd, allowing him to sell more in the market and hence return more profits. Yet if all herders follow what is individually rational behavior, then the group loses; too many animals graze the land and the quality of the pasture deteriorates, which leads to decreased output for all. As each person rationally attempts to maximize his own gain, the collectivity suffers, and eventually, all individuals suffer. What Hardin describes—the common grazing area—is a collective good available to all members of the group, regardless of individual contribution.

Collective or public goods may be tangible or intangible. In the global context, they include the "natural commons" such as the high seas, atmosphere, ozone shield, and polar regions. They also include what Kaul (2000: 300) calls "human-made global commons" such as universal norms and principles, knowledge, and the Internet, as well as "global conditions" ranging from peace, health, and financial stability to free trade, environmental sustainability, and freedom from poverty.

The use of collective goods involves activities and choices that are interdependent. Decisions by one state have effects for other states; that is, states can suffer unanticipated negative consequences as a result of the actions of others. In the international case, a decision by wealthy countries in the 1980s to continue the production and sale of chlorofluorocarbons would have affected all countries through further, long-term depletion of the ozone layer. With collective goods, market mechanisms are inadequate and alternative forms of governance are needed. A central concern in collective or public goods theory, therefore, revolves around the question of who provides the public goods. Without some kind of collective action mechanisms, there is a risk that such goods will not be adequately provided. Once they are, however, the goods exist and all can enjoy them, which creates the problem of "free-riding."

Collective goods are easier to provide in small groups than in large. Mancur Olson in *The Logic of Collective Action* (1968: 35) argues "the larger the group, the farther it will fall short of providing an optimal amount of a collective good." Free-riding and defection are harder to conceal and easier to punish if the group is small. With larger groups, the fraction of the group that benefits will decline and organizational costs will increase. Smaller groups can more effectively monitor each other and exert pressure, since violations will be more easily noticed. Small groups can also mobilize collective pressure more effectively and can more easily obtain continuous information necessary for effective allocation. Kahler (1992), however, argues that voting rules, delegation, and other strategies can facilitate cooperation with large numbers.

Another alternative is to force nations or peoples to govern collective goods by establishing organizations with effective police powers that coerce states or individuals to act in a mutually beneficial manner. Such an organization could, for example, force people to limit the number of children they have in order to stop the population explosion. Ostrom (1990), however, suggests that the most effective management may be self-governance, when private agents act as enforcers. Individuals or groups make binding contracts to commit themselves to cooperative strategies and use the enforcer to monitor each other and report infractions.

Finally, public goods theory suggests that those confronted with a collective action problem could seek to restructure actors' preferences through rewards and punishments. For example, mechanisms could be established to offer positive incentives for states to refrain from engaging in the destruction of the polar regions and to tax or threaten to tax those who fail to cooperate.

Collective goods theory can be used to explain the role of international agreements, the UN, and many IGOs, as well as international regimes in producing (or underproducing) various goods. It can also be used to investigate the gaps in international efforts to deal with policy issues. Collective goods theory is especially useful for examining those natural global commons areas such as the high seas or ozone layer where no state can claim sovereignty because these have been designated to be part of the common heritage of humankind.

Thus, collective or public goods theory along with other liberal theories see international organizations, international law, and international regimes playing positive roles in facilitating cooperation and managing public goods. They believe, for example, that the UN has helped to check power politics, create some degree of shared interests in place of national interests, provide a forum for international cooperation, and promote human progress. These views stand in opposition to those of realists who are primarily interested in states' exercise of power and pursuit of national interests.

■ Realism

A product of a long philosophical and historical tradition, realism in its various forms is based on the assumption that individuals are generally power seeking and act in a rational way to protect their own interests. Within the international system, realists see states as the primary actors, entities that act in a unitary way in pursuit of their national interest, generally defined in terms of maximizing power and security. States co-exist in an anarchic international system characterized by the absence of an authoritative hierarchy. As a result, states must rely primarily on themselves to manage their own insecurity through balance of power and deterrence.

To most realists, in the absence of international authority, there are few rules or norms that restrain states, although Hans Morgenthau, generally regarded as the father of modern realism, did include chapters on international morality, international law, and international government in his pathbreaking textbook, *Politics Among Nations*. In his view (1967: 219–220), "the main function of these normative systems has been to keep aspirations for power within socially tolerable bounds. . . . morality, mores, and law intervene in order to protect society against disruption and the individual against enslavement and extinction." Yet Morgenthau suggested there had been a weakening of these moral limitations from earlier times when there was a cohesive international society bound together through elite ties and common morality. Thus, international law and government, in his view, are largely weak and ineffective. For Morgenthau, international organizations are a tool of states to be used when desired; they can increase or decrease the power of states, but they do not affect the basic characteristics of the international system; because they reflect the basic distribution of power among states, they are no more than the sum of their member states. In fact, they are susceptible to great power manipulation. Thus, international organizations have no independent effect on state behavior and will not over time change the system itself. Contemporary realists echo these views. For example, John Mearsheimer (1994–1995: 13) has argued, "The most powerful states in the system create and shape institutions so that they can maintain their share of world power, or even increase it."

Most realist theorists do not claim that international cooperation is impossible, only that there are few incentives for states to enter into international arrangements and they can always exit such arrangements with little difficulty. Hence, since international institutions and agreements have no enforcement power, they will have little independent impact on state actions or world politics in general. They have no authority and hence no power (Gruber 2000). Realists do not acknowledge the importance or strength of nonstate actors such as NGOs and MNCs in international politics and governance, nor do they accept the idea of IGOs as independent actors. To most realists, deterrence and balance of power have proven more effective in maintaining peace than international institutions.

■ *Neorealism or Structural Realism*

Among the variants of realism, the most powerful is neorealism or structural realism, which owes much to Kenneth Waltz's *Theory of International Politics* (1979). The core difference between traditional realists and neorealists lies in the emphasis placed on the structure of the international system for explaining world politics. The system's structure is determined by the ordering principle, namely the absence of overarching authority (anarchy), and the distribution of capabilities (power) among states. What matters are states' material capabilities; state identities and interests are largely given and fixed. Anarchy poses a severe constraint on state behavior. How it is defined, however, and how much of a constraint it imposes on the possibilities for cooperation and international order are matters of dispute and some confusion among both neorealists and neoliberals (Baldwin 1993). This has important implications for theorizing about global governance (Milner 1991) since most definitions involve questions of government, authority, and governance in some way. Likewise, the way in which the power distribution shapes state behavior and provides order in international politics, either through the formation of balances of power or through a hierarchy of relations between states with unequal power, underscores that order is a product less of state actions, much less international institutions, than of system structure.

In neorealist theory, the possibilities for international cooperation are logically slim, though not impossible. As Waltz (1979: 105) posits:

> When faced with the possibility of cooperating for mutual gain, states that feel insecure must ask how the gain will be divided. They are compelled to ask not "Will both of us gain?" but "Who will gain more?" If an expected gain is to be divided, say, in the ratio of two to one, one state may use its disproportionate gain to implement a policy intended to damage or destroy the other. Even the prospect of large absolute gains for both parties does not elicit their cooperation so long as each fears how the other will use its increased capabilities.

In contrast to this neorealist emphasis on relative gains from cooperation, neoliberals stress that actors with common interests try to maximize their absolute gains (Stein 1982: 318). Charles Lipson (1984: 15–18) has pointed out relative gains are more important in security matters than in economic issues. Thus, cooperation is more difficult to achieve, harder to maintain, and more dependent on states' power. Since anarchy fuels insecurity, states are wary of becoming too dependent on others, preferring greater control and increased capabilities.

Many neorealists do recognize the emergence of a plethora of international regimes and institutions, but believe their importance has been exaggerated. Others such as John Mearsheimer are not just skeptical about international institutions, but outright disdainful. In his view, institutions are merely arenas for pursuing power relationships. They have "minimal influence on state behavior and thus hold little promise for promoting stability in the post–Cold War world" (Mearsheimer 1994–1995: 7). In fact, Mearsheimer (49) suggests that the American reliance on such institutions is apt to lead to more failures. While all neorealists would not go as far as Mearsheimer, it is clear that many do not believe that international institutions have independent effects worth studying. Although there are many criticisms of neorealism's inability to explain system change and failure to incorporate variables other than the structure of the international system, it continues to have a strong influence on international relations. One middle-level theory derived from realism that has addressed issues of international cooperation more directly is strategic or rational choice.

Strategic or Rational Choice Theory

Strategic or rational choice theory has enjoyed wide usage in other fields of political science as well as in economics. It assumes that preferences are deduced from objective and material conditions of the state. Predicated on the view that markets are the most efficient mechanism of human behavior, strategic choice theorists often use the language of microeconomic theory to explain state choices. Yet they also acknowledge that market imperfections may arise. There may be incomplete information or too high transaction costs. Then, organizations and institutions can play key roles. They may also act as constraints on choice.

Lloyd Gruber (2000) has paid particular attention to international arrangements. He is intrigued by the fact that states find it rational to take part in international arrangements, even though they would prefer the original, precooperation status quo. He argues that states fear being left behind; they want to join the bandwagon, even when it is not directly in their best interest. States come to believe that the status quo—not participating in such agreements—is not an option and they may be forced to conform to the rules of the game.

Key to rational or strategic choice theory is the assumption that state actions are based on rational calculations about subjective expected utility. Such calculations incorporate estimates of others' capabilities and likely intentions. From this perspective, then, Keohane (1993: 288) suggests, "International institutions exist largely because they facilitate self-interested cooperation by reducing uncertainty, thus stabilizing expectations." Hence, an analysis of rational state action within Europe, for example, must take Europe's many international institutions into account.

Rational choice theorists are also interested in how states use international institutions to further their national goals and how they design institutions to reflect those goals. Thus, they see institutional designs as "rational, negotiated responses to the problems international actors face" (Koremenos, Lipson, and Snidal 2001: 768). For example, U.S., Canadian, and Mexican negotiators made certain that the North American Free Trade Agreement conformed to the rules of the global trading system under GATT. Similarly, participation in the nuclear nonproliferation regime requires states to accept inspections, a deliberate strategy to reduce uncertainty and defection. In short, then, rational choice theory sees decisions on membership rules, scope of issues covered, rules for controlling an institution, and flexibility of arrangements as products of rational design considerations. Unlike other variations on realist theory, power is not a central consideration. The same is not true with hegemonic stability theory.

■ Hegemonic Stability Theory

Middle-level hegemonic stability theory is rooted in the realist tradition, but draws also from neoliberalism, regime, and public goods theories. It was developed in the 1970s and 1980s to answer the question of how an open world economy is created and maintained. The theory's answer is that these happen through the power and leadership of a dominant or hegemonic state that uses its position in particular ways. Some have questioned whether this must be a single state (Krasner 1976); all agree on the relationship between leadership or power and a liberal international economy. As Gilpin (1987: 72) notes, "Hegemony without a liberal commitment to the market economy is more likely to lead to imperial systems and the imposition of political and economic restrictions on lesser powers."

Hegemonic stability theory is based on the premise that an open market economy is a collective or public good (Kindleberger 1973) that cannot be sustained without the actions of a dominant economy. When there is a predominant state with "control over raw materials, control over sources of capital, control over markets, and competitive advantages in the production of highly valued goods" (Keohane 1984: 32), it has the means to exercise leadership over other economies as well as to use its economic power for leverage over other states. If, and it is an important if, such a dominant power is committed to an open, liberal world economy based on nondiscrimination and free markets, it can use its position to guarantee provision of the collective good—an open trading system and stable monetary system. In so doing, it must perform several roles, including the creation of norms and rules, preventing cheating and free riding, encouraging others to share the costs of maintaining the system, encouraging states to remove trade barriers, managing (to some degree) the monetary system, using its own dynamism as an engine of growth for the rest of the system, transferring knowledge and technology, and responding to crises. As strategic choice theorists would argue, the hegemon may also be engaging in behavior that serves to perpetuate its power and position.

There are, to date, only two examples of such hegemonic leadership. The first occurred during the nineteenth century when Great Britain used its dominant position to create an era of free trade among major economic powers. The second occurred after World War II, when the United States established the Bretton Woods international trade and monetary systems, and promoted the reduction of trade barriers, the use of the dollar as a global reserve currency, and the expansion of overseas investment. An important part of its role was the willingness to pay the costs to make its vision of a liberal economic order a reality.

Some have questioned whether a theory based on two cases is sufficient for hegemonic stability theory to explain why a dominant state would undertake a leadership role or be committed to liberal values. These depend, as Ruggie has noted (1982), on the hegemon's "social purpose" and commitment to "embedded liberalism."

The persistence of international economic regimes in the face of the economic dislocations of the 1970s and 1980s led Keohane (1984), in particular, to explore the consequences of declining hegemony. He found that, in a view compatible with the institutionalist position, cooperation may persist, even if the hegemon's power declines and it is not performing a leadership role. A residue of common interests and the norms of the regime help to maintain it, for "regimes are more readily maintained than established" (Kindleberger 1986: 8).

Realism itself, as we have seen, has little to say about the pieces of global governance given its emphasis on power, state interests, and anarchy. Its variants, however, have contributed significantly to understanding the bases of states' choices and the role of power, especially hegemonic power, in the creation of international regimes. Cross-fertilization among different theories clearly strengthens research into different aspects of global governance. This will become even more evident when we look at the development of constructivism.

■ Constructivism: An Alternative Approach

Although a relatively new approach to international relations, constructivism has become important for studying key pieces of global governance, particularly the role of norms. There are many variants of constructivism, however, and some question whether it offers a theory of politics; nonetheless, all constructivists suggest that, in some way, the behavior of individuals, states, and other actors is shaped by shared beliefs, socially constructed rules, and cultural practices. The approach has strong roots in sociology, and while some constructivists place themselves within the liberal tradition, others draw from realism.

At the core of constructivist approaches is a concern with identity and interests and how these can change; a belief that ideas, values, norms, and shared beliefs matter; that how individuals talk about the world shapes practices; that humans are capable of changing the world by changing ideas; and, hence, a determination to show how identities and interests of actors are "socially constructed." Where realists treat states' interests and identity as given, constructivists believe they are socially constructed, that is, influenced by culture, norms, ideas, and domestic and international interactions. Thus, Germany after World War II defined its identity in relation to the North Atlantic Treaty Organization (NATO) and European institutions, while Russia had to redefine its identity after the demise of the Soviet Union. As Peter Katzenstein (1996: 21) puts it, "State interests and strategies are shaped by a never ending political process that generates publicly understood standards for action." Structural forces have only a minor influence. Alexander Wendt (1995), for example, argues that political structure, whether of anarchy or material capabilities, tells us little about state behavior. He has also suggested (1994: 386) that states' ability to cooperate depends in part on whether their identities generate self-interests or collective interests, noting that "the state itself is a testimony to the role of collective identity in human affairs."

Constructivists place a great deal of importance on institutions as embodied in norms, practices, and formal organizations. The most important institution in international society is sovereignty since it determines the identity of states. Constructivists criticize those who see sovereignty as unchanging and point to various transformations in understandings of sovereignty since Westphalia, influenced by both states and nonstate actors (Reus-Smit 1999). To illustrate how sovereignty determines the identity of states, however, one need only consider how so-called failed states such as Somalia retain their statehood and continue to hold their memberships in IGOs.

Among the key norms affecting state behavior is multilateralism. In *Multilateralism Matters*, Ruggie (1993) and others examine how the shared expectations surrounding this norm affect the behavior of states. Several studies have examined the impact of norms and principled beliefs on international outcomes, including the evolution of the international human rights regime (Risse, Ropp, and Sikkink 1999), the end of apartheid in South Africa (Klotz 1995), the spread of weapons taboos (Price and Tannenwald 1996), and humanitarian intervention (Finnemore 1996).

In examining international organizations, constructivists seek to uncover the social content of organizations, the dominant norms that govern behavior and shape interests, and to decipher how these interests in turn influence actors. Martha Finnemore (1996: 5), for example, notes that "States are socialized to accept new norms, values, and perceptions of interest by international organizations." International organizations then may serve as agents of social construction, as norm entrepreneurs, trying to change social understandings (Finnemore and Sikkink 2001). Thus, international organizations can be teachers as well as creators of norms. Finnemore (1996) also examines the ways in which international organizations socialize states to accept political goals and new values. UNESCO, for example, "taught" newly developing states the relevance of establishing science bureaucracies as a necessary component of being a modern state. The International Committee of the Red Cross taught humanitarian rules to states concerning their responsibility for the welfare and protection of wounded soldiers, including enemy soldiers. The World Bank put the concept of poverty alleviation on international and national agendas in the late 1960s. The shift in discourse occurred as the World Bank "sold" poverty alleviation to members through a mixture of persuasion and coercion, redefining in the process what states were supposed to do to ameliorate the situation.

Thus, to constructivists, international organizations have the potential to be purposive actors with independent effects on international relations. Important to the processes of changing understandings and behavior with respect to poverty, humanitarianism, colonialism, slavery, and other problems, Neta Crawford (2002) suggests, are the discussions, persuasion, education, and argument that take place within international organizations and other settings. "State leaders, global businessmen, nongovernmental activists, even the occasional international relations scholar," Craig Murphy (2000: 797) points out, "influence each other's understanding of their own interests' and of the moral and social world in which they live." Although most constructivists have focused on the good outcomes such as decolonization, human rights norms, and poverty alleviation, international organizations may also be dysfunctional, more productive of conflict than cooperation, and contrary to the interests of their constituents (Barnett and Finnemore 1999).

Two further aspects of the constructivist approach that have been important for understanding pieces of global governance concern the development of collective identities and the role of epistemic communities in transmitting ideas and beliefs. Functionalists had earlier raised the possibilities of creating new collective identities "beyond the nation-state." For example, members of the Association of Southeast Asian Nations (ASEAN) have evolved a form of collective identity known as the "ASEAN way." The question for further investigation is the extent to which such an identity is, indeed, shared and shapes states' behavior. Chapter 5 looks at some of this in various regional groupings. Research has also shown how transnational networks of experts can shape understandings of environmental and other issues and, as a result, influence actors' decisions and behavior (Haas 1992). We explore the phenomenon of such epistemic communities further in both Chapter 6 and the issue-related chapters.

■ Critical Theories

Critical theories include a diverse group of overarching theories of international relations that challenge conventional wisdom and provide alternative frameworks for understanding the world. Among the most prominent are Marxist and neo-Marxist theories, their derivatives—dependency and world-systems theories—as well as feminist theories and postmodernism. These challenge realism's focus on the primacy of power and the existing order and liberalism's optimism about the benefits of expanding markets for peace and stability. Those rooted in Marxism share a historicism that drives questions of how the present international order came into being, what forces are at work to change it, and how that change may be influenced or shaped. Understanding how structural changes occur and the role of social forces is central.

■ *Marxist and Neo-Marxist Theory*

Although Marxism was discredited with the demise of the Soviet Union and the triumph of capitalism, it is still an important perspective for describing the hierarchy in the international system and the role of economics in determining that hierarchy. It still influences the thinking of many in the developing world whose colonial past, present weakness, and experience with capitalism is one of poverty and economic disadvantage. Marxist and neo-Marxist critical theories contribute important perspectives to understanding international relations and global governance through the frameworks they provide for linking politics, economics, social forces, and structures of order.

Like realism and liberalism, there is a set of core ideas that unite variants of Marxist theory. These include a grounding in historical analysis, the primacy of economic forces in explaining political and social phenomena, the central role of the production process, the particular character of capitalism as a global mode of production, and the importance of social or economic class in defining actors. The evolution of the production process also is a basis for explaining how new patterns of social relations develop between those who control production and those who execute the tasks of production, therefore explaining the relationship between production, social relations, and power. According to Karl Marx, a clash would inevitably occur between the capitalist class (bourgeoisie) and workers (the proletariat). From that class struggle would come a new social order. Interpreting this in the context of international relations, Robert Cox (1986: 220) notes, "Changes in the organization of production generate new social forces which, in turn, bring about changes in the structure of states and . . . alters the problematic of world order."

Marxist views on the structure of the global system and, hence, on global governance, are rooted in the above set of ideas about the relationships of class, the capitalist mode of production, and power. The hierarchical structure is a by-product of the spread of global capitalism that privileges some states, organizations, groups, and individuals, and imposes significant constraints on others. Thus, developed countries have expanded economically (and in an earlier era politically, through imperialism), enabling them to sell goods and export surplus wealth that they could not absorb at home. Simultaneously, developing countries have become increasingly constrained and dependent on the actions of the developed.

Variants on Marxist theories emphasize the techniques of domination and suppression that arise from the uneven economic development inherent in the capitalist system. An Italian Marxist, Antonio Gramsci (1891–1937) has had considerable influence on critical theorists and some neoliberal institutionalists, however, with his particular interpretation of hegemony as a relationship of consent to political and ideological leadership, not domination by force. Thus Cox (1992: 140) argues that the foundation of hege-monic order "derives from the ways of doing and thinking of the dominant social strata of the dominant state or states . . . [with] the acquiescence of the dominant social strata of other states."

These views have important implications for neo-Marxist theorizing about contemporary global governance. For example, in Murphy's view (2000: 799) global governance is "a predictable institutional response not to the interests of a fully formed class, but to the overall logic of industrial capitalism." Cox (1986) and Gill (1994) have emphasized the importance of "globalizing elites" in the restructuring of the global political economy and, hence, in global governance. These elites are found in the key finan-cial institutions (IMF, WTO, and World Bank), in finance ministries of G-7 countries, in the headquarters of MNCs, in private international relations councils (e.g., the Council on Foreign Relations and Trilateral Commission), and major business schools (Harvard, Wharton, Stanford, and others). True, however, to a classical Marxist dialectical process, transnational social forces backing neoliberalism are increasingly chal-lenged by those resisting globalization, as well as by environmental, femi-nist, and other social movements that in Murphy's view (2000) constitute a new locus for class analysis and potential source of future change.

Marxists and neo-Marxists view international law and organizations as products of a dominant group of states, dominant ideas, and the interests of the capitalist class. Some view them as instruments of capitalist domination imposed on others. The Gramscian view sees international organizations as a means to get others to consent to domination through shared ideas. Murphy (1994) argues that they have been instrumental in the development of the modern capitalist state by facilitating industrial change and the development of liberal ideology. Cox (1992: 3) also sees them concerned with "longer-term questions of global structural change and . . . how inter-national organizations . . . can help shape that change in a consensually desirable direction."

These views on the links between international institutions and the international capitalist order are reflected in many critiques of both the World Bank and the IMF. For example, Cheryl Payer (1982: 20) asserts that the bank "has deliberately and consciously used its financial power to pro-mote the interests of private, international capital in its expansion to every corner of the 'underdeveloped' world."

Marxists and neo-Marxists are almost uniformly normative in their ori-entation. They see capitalism as "bad," its structure and mode of production as exploitative. They have clear positions about what should be done to ameliorate inequities. Thus, they are proponents of major structural change in international relations.

■ Dependency Theory

Dependency theorists, particularly those from Latin America writing in the 1950s such as Raul Prebisch, Enzo Faletto, Fernando Henrique Cardoso, and Andre Gunder Frank, sought to answer the questions why was development benefiting rich Northern countries, rather than the poorer South, and why was that gap widening? They hypothesized that the basic terms of trade were unequal between the developing and developed world, partially as a consequence of the history of colonialism and neocolonialism and partly because multinational corporations and international banks based in developed countries hamstring dependent states. The latter organizations are seen as helping to establish and maintain dependency relations. They are also viewed as agents of penetration, not benign actors, as liberals would characterize them, or marginal actors, as realists would. Dependency theorists argue that public and private international organizations are able to forge transnational relationships with elites in the developing countries (the "comprador class"), linking domestic elites in both exploiter and exploited countries in a symbiotic relationship.

Many dependency theories argued that the solution was to disengage national economies from the international economy, to foster industrial growth in the South through import substitution, to protect internal markets from competition, and to seek major changes in international economic institutions. Only when countries in the South had reached a certain level of development could they participate fully in the international economy. These views had strong appeal and shaped the agenda of developing countries in the UN during the 1960s and 1970s. In essence, dependency theorists argued that development could not take place without fundamental changes in international economic relations in order to redress inequalities of power and wealth.

■ World-System Theory

The world-system version of Marxism elucidated by Immanuel Wallerstein (1980) and others posits three classes of states (or areas) in the evolving world capitalist system—core, periphery, and semiperiphery. At each stage of its evolution, Wallerstein identifies core areas where development is most advanced and the agricultural sector is able to provide sustenance for industrial workers. Peripheral areas are those characterized by cheap, unskilled labor and raw material extraction. They are prevented from developing by the developed core, which maintains its position at the expense of the periphery. In between the core and periphery lies the semiperiphery, characterized today by the newly industrializing countries (NICs) that offer cheap skilled and semiskilled labor to the global economy. The existence of this middle ground indicates that change can occur.

World-systems and dependency theories share the views of other Marxist-derived theories that international organizations are generally the tools of capitalist classes and states (the core). The WTO, for example, perpetuates adverse terms of trade for developing countries in the periphery, to the benefit of core states. Multinational corporations are, likewise, an instrument of capitalist exploitation and a mechanism of domination that perpetuates underdevelopment.

Even with the demise of the Soviet Union, Marxist theory and its variants did not disappear. To be sure, dependency and world-system theory became less popular after the developing countries failed in the 1970s and 1980s to achieve their objectives in the proposed New International Economic Order. Some aspects of these critical theories have resurfaced in the debates over globalization, particularly among opponents of globalization, including those opposing corporate control over the economy and those trying to rewrite the rules of the global economy to strengthen protection for workers, small farmers, poor people, and women (Broad 2002). Worsening economic and social conditions in Latin America and Africa and the widening gap between rich and poor have also fueled renewed interest in the perspectives critical theories offer.

■ Theories of Organizations

International relations theorists are not the only ones who are important for understanding international cooperation and global governance. Organization theorists, especially from sociology, provide insights relevant to studying international organizations as organizations. Organizations are created to solve problems that require collaborative action; they are not just mechanical tools doing what their founders envisioned. Although many organizations have limited capacity to gather and process information and to evaluate alternatives, they do make choices and interact with their environments. Organizations thus develop mechanisms for learning of new developments in the environment; they search for means of action and to decide what problems can and should be solved. In short, organization theorists see organizations as open systems that are continually responding to the environment, developing and changing goals through negotiations among the dominant coalitions, and utilizing various technologies (Perrow 1970; Ness and Brechin 1988; March and Olsen 1989).

Four concepts drawn from organization theory are particularly useful for studying IGOs, NGOs, and MNCs. These are organizational culture, adaptation and learning, interorganizational relations, and networks.

▦ *Organizational Culture*

Over time, organizations tend to develop cultures of their own, independent from and different than the cultures of their individual members. During the

1970s, sociologists and anthropologists began to study these cultures rather than seeing organizations only as technical, rational, impersonal mechanisms. During the 1980s, it became popular to think of organizations as autonomous sites of power, with their own particular cultures, norms, and values. Thus, organizations might become agents themselves, not just structures through which actors operated. Organization theorists, therefore, created typologies of organizational cultures and showed how these change over time (Hawkins 1997).

Some international relations scholars have borrowed the notion of organizational culture, suggesting that national bureaucracies develop cultures that influence state preferences (Legro 1996). This counters the realist view that preferences are exogenously determined.

International organization scholars, particularly constructivists, have also seized upon the notion of organizational culture, believing "the rules, rituals, and beliefs that are embedded in the organization (and its subunits) has [*sic*] important consequences for the way individuals who inhabit that organization make sense of the world" (Barnett and Finnemore 1999: 719). For example, the World Bank has developed a culture based on the fact that its economists, largely trained in U.S. graduate schools, share liberal economic views. Ascher (1983) shows how their technical expertise and control of information allows them to exercise relative autonomy, leading to the illusion that they are making apolitical decisions, and creating a unique organizational culture that is resistant to change from the outside. Different units within an IGO may have distinct cultures also, creating potential cultural clashes. Thus, within the UN High Commissioner for Refugees (UNHCR), one part of the organization takes a legalistic approach toward issues of refugee rights while the other is more concerned with causes of refugee flows and pressures from states to manage those flows.

■ *Organizational Adaptation and Learning*

Organizations also change over time. Organization theorists have been particularly interested in examining how they evolve. Ernst Haas (1990) delineates two such processes. In the first, organizations adapt by adding new activities to their agendas without actually examining or changing underlying bases of the organization and its values. The organization muddles through and change occurs incrementally. Such was the case when the UN took on added peacekeeping tasks in the early 1990s, including election monitoring, humanitarian aid delivery, and protection of populations threatened by ethnic cleansing and genocide. Only with the failures in Somalia and Bosnia did the Secretariat and member states look seriously at the lessons to be learned from the incremental, unplanned changes.

The second kind of change process is based on the premise that organizations can, in fact, learn. With learning, members or staff question earlier beliefs and develop new processes. Thus, learning involves redefinition of organizational purposes, reconceptualization of problems, articulation of new ends, and organizational change based upon new, underlying consensual knowledge. Such has been the case with the evolution of World Bank programs from an initial emphasis on infrastructure projects to basic human needs, structural adjustment, environmental sustainability, and, today, poverty alleviation and good governance. Other examples abound.

▀ *Interorganizational Relations*

The proliferation of international organizations has meant studying what this means for relations among various organizations and with states. Organization theorists have long contended that for many organizations the most important part of the environment is the cooperative and conflictual relations with other organizations. Organizational interdependence emerges from the shared need for resources (money, specialized skills, and markets), overlapping missions, or the desire to add new specialties at reduced cost. In response, organizations may innovate to exclude rivals or increase coordination and cooperation. Thus, interorganizational relations examines how and why organizations, often working within the same environment or on the same type of problems, both clash with each other and cooperate (Mingst 1987).

Interorganization theorists are also interested in the dependency of one organization on another. For example, the UN Security Council needs both resources and information to fulfill its mission. Such dependence limits the organ's autonomy. Similarly, the regional development banks may depend on the World Bank for co-financing large projects, for setting development priorities, and for technical expertise. Karen Mingst (1987: 291) found that the African Development Bank (AfDB) in the 1980s was in such a position as "the newer organization, offering less prestigious employment possibilities; they have had less economic resources, and with that, a less visible presence in the field. They have been 'slower' to innovate, with the World Bank taking the lead in imposing conditionalities and suggesting policy reforms." This dependence was reinforced by the attitude of the African countries themselves who viewed the AfDB as one of the "last lenders" and one of the "last to be repaid."

Coordination problems between and among IGOs such as those among economic and social agencies within the UN system, or among NGOs such as the humanitarian relief groups, form another group of interorganizational problems. Chapter 4 explores how the UN Economic and Social Council (ECOSOC) was intended to play a central, coordinating role for the system but has lacked the resources and clout to do so effectively. The series of humanitarian crises in the late 1990s led to the designation of UN High Commissioner for Refugees (UNHCR) as a lead humanitarian agency coordinating the efforts of other UN system agencies and NGOs in the field.

▪ *Networks*

International organizations do not just interact with each other; they also operate within broader networks. Harold Jacobson titled his pathbreaking textbook *Networks of Interdependence: International Organizations and the Global Political System* (1984) and was the first to identify the relevance of networks for the field. The sociological literature on networks examines the various links between organizations and individuals (both private and public), domestic and international. Often there is a linking-pin organization in the network, an organization able to mobilize coalitions on particular issues or control the process of bargaining. Such organizations have seldom been delegated such authority, but are able to legitimize their actions with respect to the specific issue area (Jönsson 1986).

Transnational advocacy networks have become increasingly important to global governance, as we discussed briefly in Chapter 1 and examine further in Chapter 6. Such networks, note Keck and Sikkink (1998: 2), share "the centrality of values or principled ideas, the belief that individuals can make a difference, the creative use of information, and the employment by nongovernmental actors of sophisticated political strategies in targeting their campaigns." They are "bound together by shared values, a common discourse, and dense exchanges of information and services." These networks also try to set the terms of international and domestic debate, to influence international and state-level policy outcomes, and to alter the behavior of states, international organizations, and other interested parties. The International Campaign to Ban Landmines is one prominent example of a transnational advocacy network from the late 1990s. The human rights, environmental, and women's movements further illustrate the phenomenon. Network analysis encompasses both international and domestic actors and processes, and examines how individuals and groups are linked and what strategies they use to promote their goals.

Organizational theories enable us to probe deeper within specific institutions of global governance by helping us understand the influence of organizational culture, organizational change, interorganizational relations, and networks of organizations.

■ IR Theory and Global Governance

One of the unanswered puzzles is that despite the fact that multilateral diplomacy and institutions became dominant forms of interaction in the twentieth century, multilateralism is generally neglected in international relations theory (Caporaso 1993: 51). As we have seen, neoliberals and neorealists, in particular, have attempted to explain cooperation and the conditions under which cooperation becomes multilateral and institutionalized through international regimes. Constructivist approaches that look at processes of persuasion, discussion, and argumentation contribute further to these understandings. Constructivists have also contributed to our knowledge about how norms, ideas, and beliefs affect outcomes. Critical theories provide perspectives on contemporary structures of global governance; they and neorealist theory share a concern for the role of power and powerful actors. Liberalism and its middle-level derivatives, however, form the foundation for much global governance theorizing.

Subsequent chapters utilize these various theories when appropriate. In Chapters 3 and 5, functionalism explains much of the history of specialized and regional organizations. In Chapters 8, 9, 10, and 11, specific international regimes are examined, along with their major principles, rules, and decisionmaking processes. In Chapter 11, collective goods theory forms a central focus for international efforts to address environmental problems. In Chapter 8, realist theory helps us understand the difficulties that international institutions have in addressing threats to peace and security. Chapter 9 considers how hegemonic stability theory and Marxist and neo-Marxist perspectives have affected efforts to address economic development. Throughout the book, theories of organizations and network analysis help us understand how different organizations function and the connections among different actors and their roles.

■ Suggested Further Reading

Baldwin, David A. (1993) "Neoliberalism, Neorealism, and World Politics." In *Neorealism and Neoliberalism. The Contemporary Debate,* edited by David A. Baldwin. New York: Columbia University Press, pp. 3–28.

Bull, Hedley. (1977) *The Anarchical Society: A Study of Order in World Politics.* New York: Columbia University Press.

Cox, Robert W. (1987) *Production, Power, and World Order: Social Forces in the Making of History.* New York: Columbia University Press.

Haas, Ernst B. (1964) *Beyond the Nation-State: Functionalism and International Organization.* Stanford: Stanford University Press.

Keohane, Robert O. (1984) *After Hegemony. Cooperation and Discord in the World Political Economy.* Princeton: Princeton University Press.

Morgenthau, Hans. (1967) *Politics Among Nations.* 4th ed. New York: Knopf.

Rittberger, Volker, ed. with Peter Mayer. (1993) *Regime Theory and International Relations.* Oxford: Clarendon Press.

Wendt, Alexander. (1995) "Constructing International Politics." *International Security* 20 (summer): 71–81.

PART 2

Evolving Pieces
of Global Governance

3

Foundations of the
Pieces of Global Governance

Political communities throughout history have tried to establish norms and rules for interacting with their neighbors. Many schemes dating as early as ancient Chinese and Indian civilizations were based on principles and methods designed to manage or eliminate conflict among contending parties. For example, Confucius (551–479 B.C.) preached the norm of moderation in interstate relations and condemned the use of violence. The Greeks sought to establish permanent protective alliances among the city-states to address conflict issues. Third-party arbitration proved effective in deflecting conflict and promoting cooperation. United by common culture, the city-states agreed to follow established rules. From these rules, confederations of various city-states grew. Yet each continued to claim sovereignty for itself, while acknowledging the sovereignty of others. None of these arrangements was in actuality either an "international" entity or an "organization," being limited to a specific geographical area and lacking permanent institutionalized relationships.[1]

More than a millennium later, a number of European philosophers began to elaborate structured schemes for international cooperation. The Roman Catholic Church and its head, the pope, provided the impetus. For example, medieval French writer Pierre Dubois (1250–1322) proposed that Christian (at that time, Catholic) leaders should form political alliances against violators of the prevailing norms; the pope could arbitrate any ensuing disputes. Not all such proposals, however, centered on religious foundations. Some were based on common economic interests. The Hanseatic League (1200s–1400s), comprised of 100 to 160 Northern European cities, was formed to facilitate trade and commerce and lasted for two hundred years. It was a system of governance based on the interaction among independent city-states.

Such a system of governance can also be found among the Italian city-states during the fourteenth and fifteenth centuries. The smaller cities and principalities consolidated into five major political units—the Kingdom of Naples and Sicily, the Papal States, and the city-states of Florence, Venice, and Milan. Although they were a mere patchwork of towns whose borders had been frequently redrawn, they established a system of balancing power on the Italian peninsula. Diplomacy was regularized and commercial interaction routinized. Two centuries later these practices were adopted by the state system of governance.

■ The State System and Its Weaknesses

International relations theorists date the contemporary state system from 1648 when the Treaty of Westphalia ended the Thirty Years War. Although most of the more than one hundred articles of the treaty deal with allocating the spoils of war, other provisions proved pathbreaking. Articles 64, 65, and 67 established several key principles of a new state system: territorial sovereignty; the right of the state (prince or ruler) to choose its religion and determine its own domestic policies; and the prohibition of interference from supranational authorities like the Catholic Church or Holy Roman Empire (Bueno de Mesquita 2000). The treaty marked the end of rule by religious authority in Europe and the emergence of secular states. With secular authority came the principle of the territorial integrity of states that were legally equal and sovereign participants in the international system.

Sovereignty was the core concept in this state system. As the French philosopher Jean Bodin (1530–1596) stated, sovereignty is "the distinguishing mark of the sovereign that he cannot in any way be subject to the commands of another, for it is he who makes law for the subject, abrogates law already made, and amends obsolete law" (Bodin 1967: 25). Although there is no supreme arbiter among states, Bodin acknowledged that sovereignty may be limited by divine law or natural law, by the type of regime, or even by promises to the people.

It was during this time frame that Hugo Grotius, as previously discussed, rejected the concept that states have complete freedom to do whatever they wish. Thus, even in the seventeenth century, the meaning of state sovereignty was contested. Krasner (1993: 235) argues, "The actual content of sovereignty, the scope of authority, that states can exercise, has always been contested. The basic organizing principle of sovereignty—exclusive control over territory—has been persistently challenged by the creation of new institutional forms that better meet specific national needs." He asserts that although breaches of sovereignty occur continuously through treaties, contracts, coercion, and imposition, there is no alternative conception of international system organization. Other contemporary scholars such as James Rosenau (1997: 217–236) see states as vulnerable to demands from below—decentralizing tendencies including domestic constituencies and nonstate actors—and from above, including globalization processes and international organizations. They have to contend with a variety of new actors and processes that confound and constrain them, limiting authority and challenging the whole notion of state sovereignty, and hence the state system based on the principle.

The nature of the contemporary state system is a matter of dispute between Westphalians, Grotians, and those who argue that a fundamental transformation has occurred. The weaknesses of the state system became increasingly apparent after the middle of the nineteenth century with increasing international trade, immigration, democratization, technological innovation, and other developments that undermined the capacity of states to govern effectively. These changes gave rise to the earliest international organizations.

■ Governance Innovations in the Nineteenth Century

In the nineteenth century, commerce and trade among the European countries and between European states and their colonies expanded. State-to-state interactions became more frequent and intense. Ideas for a more international approach to governance were proposed. In a pioneering textbook on international organization, *Swords into Plowshares,* Inis L. Claude (1964) describes three major innovations of governance that emerged in the nineteenth century: the Concert of Europe, public international unions, and the Hague conferences.

■ Concert of Europe

The first innovation was a concert of major powers making systemwide decisions by negotiation and consensus, a kind of informal intergovernmentalism. States agreed to coordinate behavior based on certain rights and responsibilities with expectations of diffuse reciprocity. They still operated as separate states and societies, but within a framework of rules and consultation without creating a formal organization.

The Concert of Europe was established in 1815. The concert system involved the practice of multilateral meetings rather than bilateral diplomacy among the leaders of the major European powers for the purpose of settling problems and coordinating actions. Meeting over thirty times in the century preceding World War I, the major powers constituted a club of the like-minded, dictating the conditions of entry for other would-be participants. They legitimized the independence of new European states such as Belgium and Greece in the 1820s. At the last of the concert meetings, which took place in Berlin in 1878, the European powers divided up the previously uncolonized parts of Africa, extending the reach of European imperialism.

Although these concert meetings were not institutionalized and included no explicit mechanism for implementing collective action, they solidified important practices that later international organizations followed.

These included multilateral consultation, collective diplomacy, and special status for great "powers." As Claude (1964: 22) summarizes, "The Concert system was the manifestation of a rudimentary but growing sense of interdependence and community of interest among the states of Europe." Such a community of interest was a vital prerequisite for modern international organizations and broader global governance, even though sovereignty remained intact.

The concert idea of mutual consultations, necessitated by a growing community of interests, can be seen in management of the international gold standard and in the contemporary Group of 7/8. It is also the foundation for the UN Security Council, where the five permanent members have special privileges and responsibilities and continuously consult with each other in a highly institutionalized setting.

■ Public International Unions

Public international unions were another important organizational innovation. Agencies were initially established among European states to deal with problems stemming from the industrial revolution, expanding commerce, communications, and technological innovation. These functional problems involved such concerns as health standards for travelers, shipping rules on the Rhine River, increased mail volume, and the cross-boundary usage of the newly invented telegraph.

Many of these practical problems of expanding international relations among states proved amenable to resolution with intergovernmental cooperation. The International Telegraph Union was formed in 1865 and the Universal Postal Union (UPU) in 1874, each instrumental in facilitating communication, transportation, and hence commerce. With growing levels of interdependence, the European states had found it necessary to cooperate on a voluntary basis to accomplish nonpolitical tasks. The international labor movement provided another model for nonstate groups, organizing in the First International (1864–1872), the Second International (1889–1914), and the Third International (1919–1943). The International Chamber of Commerce was established in 1920, the International Criminal Police Organization (Interpol) in 1923, and the Bank of International Settlements in 1930. The rise of public international unions and specialized organizations dedicated to defined nonpolitical tasks gave rise to functionalism and specialized IGOs helping states deal with practical problems in their international relations, as discussed in Chapter 2.

The public international unions spawned several procedural innovations. International secretariats, composed of permanent bureaucrats hired from a variety of countries, were formed. The public unions also developed the practice of involving specialists from outside ministries of foreign affairs as well as private interest groups in their work. Multilateral diplomacy was no longer the exclusive domain of traditional diplomats. In addition, the public unions began to develop techniques for multilateral conventions, that is, lawmaking or rulemaking treaties.

▨ *The Hague System*

The third governance innovation in the nineteenth century was the emergence of generalized conferences in which all states were invited to participate in problemsolving. In 1899 and 1907, Czar Nicholas II of Russia convened two conferences in The Hague (Netherlands) involving both European *and* non-European states to think proactively about what techniques states should have available to prevent war and under what conditions arbitration, negotiation, and legal recourse would be appropriate (Aldrich and Chinkin 2000). Exploration of such issues in the absence of a crisis was a novelty.

The Hague conferences led to the Convention for the Pacific Settlement of International Disputes, ad hoc international commissions of inquiry, and the Permanent Court of Arbitration. The institutionalization of the latter was the culmination of the widespread practice of inserting clauses into treaties calling for arbitration should disputes arise among parties. The Permanent Court of Arbitration (1899) became a permanent body composed of jurists selected by each country from which members of arbitral tribunals would be chosen. It remains in existence and has been used in recent years for handling claims arising from the 1979–1980 Iran hostage crisis.

The Hague conferences also produced several major procedural innovations. This was the first time that participants included both small and non-European states. The Latin American states, China, and Japan were each accorded an equal voice, thus establishing the twin principles of universality and legal equality of states. What had been largely a European state system until the end of the nineteenth century became a truly international system at the beginning of the twentieth century. For the first time participants utilized such techniques as electing chairs, organizing committees, and taking roll call votes, all of which became permanent features of twentieth-century organizations. The Hague conferences also promoted the novel ideas of common interests of humankind and the codification of international law.

▨ *The Legacy of the Nineteenth Century*

Nineteenth-century innovations served as a vital precursor to the development of modern international organizations and to the broader notion of global governance nascent in the twenty-first century. Governments established new approaches to dealing with problems of joint concern, such as the multilateral diplomacy of the concert system, the cooperative institutions of the public international unions, and the broader legalistic institutions of the Hague system. To implement the new approaches, innovative procedures were developed, participation broadened, and international secretariats established. Each has been extensively utilized during the twentieth century.

Yet the institutional arrangements of the nineteenth century proved inadequate for preventing war among the major European powers. The balance of power among the great powers—so vital to the concert system—broke down into two competing military alliances at the end of the nineteenth century, which, in turn, led to World War I. Interdependence and cooperation in other areas of interest proved insufficient to prevent war when national security was at stake. Hence, the outbreak of World War I pointed vividly to the weaknesses and shortcomings of these arrangements.

■ Multilateralism in the Twentieth Century

The twentieth century was marked by the development of numerous international organizations, both small and large, general purpose and specialized, governmental and nongovernmental, as shown in Figure 1.4. These formal institutions have been created to manage disparate needs. International law has progressively expanded into areas previously not viewed as suitable for public international law, including economic and social issues. Equally as important has been the widespread acceptance of multilateralism as a core practice in international relations.

The League of Nations—Learning from Failure

World War I had hardly begun when private groups and prominent individuals in both Europe and the United States began to plan for the postwar era. NGOs such as the League to Enforce Peace in the United States and the League of Nations in Great Britain were eager to develop more permanent frameworks for preventing future wars. President Woodrow Wilson's proposal to create a permanent international organization through the Versailles Peace Treaty was based on these plans.

League principles.   The League of Nations first and foremost reflected the environment in which it was conceived. Almost one-half of the League covenant's twenty-six provisions focused on preventing war. Two basic principles were paramount: (1) member states agreed to respect and preserve the territorial integrity and political independence of states; and (2) members agreed to try different methods of dispute settlement, but failing that, the League was given the power under Article 16 to enforce settlements through sanctions. The second principle was firmly embedded in the proposition of collective security, namely, that aggression by one state should be countered by all acting together as a "league of nations."

League organs.   The Covenant of the League of Nations established three permanent organs—the Council, Assembly, and Secretariat—as well as two autonomous organizations, the Permanent Court of International Justice (PCIJ), and the International Labour Organization (ILO). Authority within the League rested primarily with the council that was composed of four permanent members (Great Britain, France, Italy, and Japan) and four elected members. The covenant permitted the council and assembly to change both categories of membership. As a result, the membership varied between eight and fifteen states. Germany, for example, gained permanent council membership when it joined the League in 1926. The United States was originally intended to be a permanent member, but its failure to ratify the Versailles Treaty meant that it never assumed that seat. The council was to settle disputes, enforce sanctions, supervise mandates, formulate disarmament plans, approve secretariat appointments, and implement peaceful settlements. Members agreed to submit disputes to arbitration, adjudication, or the council if they could not reach negotiated agreements. They agreed also to respect territorial integrity and political independence of other states and to register all treaties with the League secretariat (thus eliminating secret agreements). If states resorted to war, members of the council had the authority under Article 16 to apply diplomatic and economic sanctions. While the requirement of unanimity made action by the council very difficult to achieve, that requirement clearly institutionalized the special prerogative given to great powers, a lasting remnant of the European concert system.

The League's assembly was a quasi-legislative body that met annually, with membership drawn from all states, about sixty at that time. They were authorized to admit new members, approve the budget, elect the nonpermanent members to the council, and act on matters referred by the council. In addition, the assembly established a number of precedents such as requiring the secretary-general to submit an annual report on the activities of the organization (a practice continued by the UN General Assembly), general debate involving speeches by heads of delegations, and creating six committees to consider important matters between annual sessions. Decisions within committees were by majority in contrast to the assembly itself where decisions required unanimity. Strict unanimity was tempered, however, by special procedures requiring less than majority votes. In practice, states generally preferred to abstain, rather than block action. But the work of the assembly fell short of the anticipated goals; much of its time was spent waiting for the great powers to refer issues to it.

The Covenant of the League of Nations established the secretariat but provided few instructions on its responsibilities. More a clearinghouse for relevant information, the secretariat had little independent authority. Although the first secretary-general, Sir Eric Drummond (1919–1933), was an excellent administrator, he chose not to undertake political initiatives and by playing a limited role avoided the kinds of political pressures to which later UN secretaries-general were subject. The secretariat provided coordination for some twenty organizations that were affiliated with the League to some degree, including the Health Organization, the Mandate Commission, the ILO, and the PCIJ.

Success and failure.   The League did enjoy a number of successes, many of them concerned with European territorial issues. It conducted plebiscites in Silesia and the Saar and then demarcated the German-Polish border. It settled territorial disputes between Lithuania and Poland, Finland and Russia, and Bulgaria and Greece, and guaranteed Albanian territorial integrity against encroachments by Italy, Greece, and Yugoslavia. In the Bulgaria-Greece dispute, for example, the council president requested a ceasefire and withdrawal of troops. Convening in three days, council members agreed to send military observers and establish a commission of inquiry. With such a prompt response, peace was restored with a minimum of hostility. In its first decade, the League also tackled the vexing issue of disarmament.

The League was successful in establishing and administering the mandate system under which former German colonies were entrusted to advanced countries—Great Britain, France, South Africa, Belgium, and Japan—for administration on behalf of the League. The League's Mandate Commission, composed of nongovernmental representatives, reviewed annual reports submitted by the colonial powers about conditions in the mandates.

Most important, the League was the first permanent international organization of a general political nature with continuously functioning machinery. While its origins lay in the nineteenth century, the League embodied the twentieth-century idea that the international community could and should act against international lawbreakers.

Overall, the League fell far short of expectations. The failure to act when Japan invaded Manchuria in 1931 pointed to the organization's fundamental weaknesses: the council's refusal to take decisive action; the unwillingness of either Great Britain or France to institute military action or economic sanctions. A proposal to send a commission of inquiry failed when Japan vetoed the action. The Lytton Commission sent five representatives from the big powers to the area seven months after the Japanese invasion. By that time, Japan had established a puppet government. Too late, the commission rebuked Japan for its aggression, but took no further action. When not supported by the big powers, the League lacked real power to respond to acts of aggression.

The League's response to the Italian invasion of Ethiopia in 1935 further undermined its legitimacy. Ethiopia, a member of the League, appealed to the League council, only to be greeted by stalling actions for nine months. Both France and Great Britain had assured Italian dictator Benito Mussolini that they would not interfere in his operations. The smaller states (plus Russia) were horrified by the lack of support for Ethiopia. Following Italy's invasion, the council, over Italy's objections, identified Italy as the aggressor and called for economic and military sanctions. Fifty of the fifty-four members of the League's assembly concurred with cutting off credit to the Italian economy and stopping arms sales, but these measures were insufficient to make Italy retreat and tighter measures were never instituted. By 1936, all sanctions against Italy were abandoned, having been a case of acting too little and too late. The League neither intervened in the Spanish civil war nor opposed Hitler's remilitarization of the Rhineland and occupation of Austria and Czechoslovakia. With the great powers unwilling to uphold the League's principles, the institution's power and legitimacy deteriorated.

The League of Nations was also unable to respond to the economic depression of the 1930s and the rise of extreme nationalism. Between 1935 and 1939, many members withdrew and efforts to reform the organization were unsuccessful. The League was silent during the six years of World War II from 1939–1945.

While American absence from League membership proved a critical weakness, there are several additional explanations for its failure. The League's close association with the unjust peace of World War I hamstrung the organization from the outset. Not much attention was paid to economic and social issues, although by the late 1930s there were calls for reorganization in that area. The system of collective security was impractical and overly idealistic. And when states failed to respond to overt aggression, as described above, the League was doomed as an instrument of collective security.

Despite these shortcomings, the League represented an important step forward in the process of international organization and in global governance. Thus, early in World War II, many people recognized the need to begin planning for a new organization. This planning began shortly after the United States entered the war and built on the lessons of the League in laying the groundwork for its successor, the United Nations (we turn to its history and functioning in Chapter 4). There was consensus on the importance of such an international organization, albeit one whose scope was far greater than the League's. Hence, planning also proceeded for new functional organizations.

■ The Strengthening of Functional and Specialized Organizations

While the origins of functionally specialized international organizations can be found in the nineteenth-century public international unions, their full development and maturation occurred in the twentieth century. Many now face further adjustments in the twenty-first century.

In a pattern carried over from national governments, single-function organizations have been established to address specific problems. Over time, other organizations often have been created to resolve still more specialized problems in response to changes in the environment. Functional organizations, once perceived to be nonpolitical, in line with functionalist theory, have become increasingly political since the issues they deal with are not merely technical, but can touch at the core of state sovereignty and deeply political concerns. They are important pieces of global governance.

The founders of the UN envisaged that functional agencies would play key roles in activities aimed at economic and social advancement. Indeed, Articles 57 and 63 of the charter call for the affiliation with the UN of various organizations established by separate international agreements to deal with issues such as health (the World Health Organization); food (Food and Agriculture Organization); science, education, and culture (UN Educational, Scientific and Cultural Organization [UNESCO]); and economics (the International Monetary Fund and World Bank). Today, there are seventeen specialized agencies formally affiliated with the UN through agreements with the Economic and Social Council (ECOSOC) and General Assembly. Like the UN itself, they have global, rather than regional, responsibilities, but separate charters, memberships, budgets, and secretariats as well as their own interests and constituencies. They operate largely independent of UN control, despite the ECOSOC's efforts to coordinate their vast areas of activity. Other regionally specific, functional organizations have no formal affiliation with the UN. Figure 3.1 illustrates the variety of functional organizations.

Four major areas of functional activity are discussed below, while others are considered in subsequent chapters.

Evolving economic governance: Origins of the Bretton Woods institutions.   As the industrial revolution expanded, the need for managing increased trade, capital flows, and price fluctuations in raw materials grew. Some initiatives were private, some public. During the 1920s and early 1930s, industry-based cartels emerged as one means of economic gover-

---

**Figure 3.1   Functional Intergovernmental Organizations
(Representative)**

• *Functional Organizations Related to the United Nations*
International Labour Organization
Food and Agriculture Organization
UN High Commissioner for Refugees
International Telecommunications Union
International Civil Aviation Organization
World Health Organization
World Meteorological Organization
Universal Postal Union
International Atomic Energy Agency
International Maritime Organization

• *Other Functional Organizations*
International Whaling Commission
Northwest Atlantic Fisheries Organization
International Coffee Organization
Organization of Petroleum Exporting Countries

• *Regional Functional Organizations*
Organization of Arab Petroleum Exporting Countries
African Development Bank
Pan American Health Organization
Economic Community of West African States
Arab Monetary Fund

---

nance. These cartels sought to coordinate product outputs and hence control prices; many became successful at price fixing and market allocation schemes. Agreements were reached on price controls for industrial products as well as for various commodities, including tin, natural rubber, and wheat. Generally, these were private initiatives, different from the government-organized cartels of the 1960s that are discussed in Chapter 9. Yet these cartel arrangements were sometimes signed by governments, as their promoters realized that secure arrangements could only be enforced through governmental cooperation.

Neither private cartels nor governments were able to control the effects of the worldwide Great Depression of the 1930s. Not only were millions of people out of work and impoverished in the United States and Europe, but the prices of most raw materials plummeted, causing the people in Europe's African and Asian colonies and the independent countries of Latin America also to suffer greatly. Countries adopted "beggar thy neighbor" policies, raising barriers to imports and causing world trade to collapse.

Faced with economic collapse, American and British economists realized that international institutions were needed to help countries with balance of payments difficulties, to provide stable exchange rates and economic assistance, and to promote nondiscrimination in and reciprocal lowering of barriers to trade. The lesson was amplified by the realization in 1944–1945 that recovery and rebuilding after World War II would require more capital than war-ravaged countries alone could expect to raise. Less clear until the 1950s was the need for capital and technical assistance to assist newly independent countries in reducing their colonial ties and boosting growth and stability. The decolonization process and the tripling of the number of states in the 1950s and 1960s would make this the major priority for the World Bank. The dual role envisaged for the World Bank is still reflected in its official name: the International Bank for Reconstruction and Development (IBRD).

Recognizing the importance of reducing barriers to the flow of goods and capital and the value of international economic cooperation for its own well being, the United States furnished the vision of an open international economy, the leadership to establish institutions, and the money to assist others. Henry Dexter White, chief international economist at the U.S. Treasury between 1942 and 1944, and the British economist John Maynard Keynes presented competing plans for economic governance at the conference held in Bretton Woods, New Hampshire, in 1944. In an effort to provide an independent, countervailing balance to American economic power, Keynes proposed a world central bank capable of regulating the flow of credit; he also favored the creation of a new international currency to facilitate lending to countries experiencing liquidity problems. White argued for a weaker agency that would promote the growth of international trade but preserve the central role of the U.S. dollar in the international economy.

White's plan prevailed. The newly formed International Monetary Fund would not be a world central bank, but would promote economic growth by providing financial stability for countries facing short-term balance-of-payments difficulties and thereby stimulating international trade. Over time, the U.S. view about conditionality for assistance would also prevail.

Ideas about how governance of trade should proceed likewise differed. At the Bretton Woods meetings, a comprehensive International Trade Organization (ITO) was proposed. It was expected that the organization would provide a general framework for trade rules and a venue for ongoing trade discussions. One contentious issue concerned the special problem of commodities. The British, under Keynes's influence, argued for international government-controlled buffer stocks of commodities to reduce detrimental price volatility. The United States opposed all such schemes. The details were left to the Havana Conference in 1948, when the charter for the proposed International Trade Organization was to be approved.

At the Havana conference, other major differences surfaced. The United States favored extensive trade liberalization, while the Europeans, including the British, were more concerned with retaining their special preferential arrangements with their colonies and former colonies. Many developing countries, absent from earlier negotiations, took a strong stance in favor of schemes protecting commodity exporters. Cuba, Colombia, and El Salvador each played a key role, advocating such policies as unilateral producer actions. The efforts of the developing countries failed, however, and the industrialized countries won, only agreeing to limited producer and consumer schemes in which voting power was equally balanced. Absent, too, was any discussion of the idea that trading schemes should be used as a way to transfer economic resources from the rich to the poor countries. Such key differences, coupled with major opposition from a coalition of protectionists and free traders in the U.S. Congress and lack of enthusiasm in other industrialized countries, led to the failure of the ITO before it was established. The Havana Charter was never ratified.

Trade governance took on a different character as twenty-three of the participants in the ITO negotiations developed an alternative, the General Agreement on Tariffs and Trade (GATT), envisaged as a temporary arrangement. Despite its lack of organizational character, the GATT became the major venue for trade negotiations from 1949 to 1995, with an interim committee for coordinating international commodity policy and a small secretariat of two hundred persons. The World Trade Organization succeeded it in 1995.

The Bretton Woods institutions were designed to address systemic weaknesses in economic governance and promote a liberal economic order. Their evolving roles are discussed in depth in Chapter 9.

Labor issues and the International Labour Organization (ILO).   The origins of the ILO can be traced to the nineteenth century, when two industrialists, the Welshman Robert Owen and the Frenchman Daniel Legrand, advocated an organization to protect labor from abuses of industrialization, and the labor movement grew in both Europe and the United States. Long factory hours, exploitation of labor, and low wages led to the formation of labor unions to advance the rights of workers. In 1913, the International Federation of Trade Unions was founded to address these grievances on a transnational basis. Labor's growing political importance and Owen and Legrand's ideas led to adoption of the Constitution of the International Labour Organization in 1919 by the Paris Peace Conference, based on the belief that world peace could only be accomplished by attention to social justice. Thus, the ILO became an autonomous organization within the League structure, an institutional model utilized for other functional organizations related to the United Nations.

Important principles articulated in the preamble to the ILO constitution detail the humanitarian, political, and economic motivations for its establishment. The first is based on the humanitarian recognition that "conditions of labour exist involving . . . injustice, hardship and privation to large numbers of people." Such persistent injustices pose a political threat, with the potential to upset international peace and harmony. Second, there is an economic implication that "the failure of any nation to adopt humane conditions of labour is an obstacle in the way of other nations which desire to improve the conditions in their own countries." Yet ironically, organized labor, while agreeing with the general goals, actually opposed the establishment of the ILO, believing that the proposed organization was too weak and lacked the capacity to set labor standards.

Setting standards for treatment of workers is the ILO's major activity. Since 1919, over two hundred labor conventions have been signed and 180 recommendations made. In the first two years alone, sixteen international labor conventions were passed and eighteen recommendations made. In many countries, the international labor codes on such issues as the right to organize and bargain, ban on slavery and forced labor, regulation of hours of work, agreements on wages, and worker compensation and safety are translated directly into domestic law. Among the conventions designated "fundamental" by the ILO are the conventions against forced labor, freedom of association, discrimination, and child labor. Sixty-eight states have ratified all of these conventions; the United States has ratified but two, the forced labor and child labor conventions. Under Article 33, the ILO can take action against states to secure compliance, but in practice, the ILO generally uses less coercive means, promoting compliance by gathering member state reports and hearing complaints of noncompliance. Using peer pressure and persuasion rather than hard sanctions, it makes recommendations to states on how their record can be improved and offers technical assistance programs to facilitate state compliance.

While the ILO processes have not substantially changed over time, the ILO's jurisdiction has broadened. Initially, standards to improve the working conditions of male wage labor were the dominant agenda item. Codes then were expanded to include more general issues of the working person's life: health standards, water treatment, and educational issues. In recent years, the ILO has discussed standards for previously unrepresented workers: women and child laborers, and individuals in the nonorganized labor sector such as home workers and piece workers. This is the platform of action labeled "Decent Work." Although the concept is contested, this agenda is congruent with the interests of the developing country majority, which has pushed also for more technical cooperation and vocational education programs.

The ILO, headquartered in Geneva, Switzerland, became a UN specialized agency in 1946. It accomplishes its work through three major bodies, each of which includes a tripartite representation structure involving government officials, employers, and workers. This integration of governmental and nongovernmental representatives is a unique approach not duplicated in any other IGO. During the Cold War, this tripartite structure was controversial, since in communist states there was no clear differentiation between government, management, and labor. Nonetheless, the arrangement has generally been seen as uniquely suited to represent both governmental and societal interests.

The International Labour Conference meets annually, with each member state represented by four individuals: two government officials, and one each from labor and management. The conference, with each individual voting independently, sets international labor standards. In an important innovation developed in 1926, a Committee of Experts, composed of independent legal authorities, provides a supervisory role by examining government reports detailing adherence to standards and reporting to the conference on compliance.

The Governing Body, the executive arm of the ILO, establishes programs and administers the budget. Twenty-eight government members, fourteen employer members, and fourteen worker members serve on this limited membership body. The most industrialized countries (and often those with the biggest purse) are assured ten governmental seats.

The International Labour Office forms a permanent secretariat under the leadership of the director-general, elected for a five-year renewable term. Both have established strong reputations. The first post–World War II director-general, the American David Morse, was elected in 1948 and served until 1970. During those years, the size of the ILO doubled and its budget increased five times over, with the industrialized countries becoming a minority. While the ILO employs about two thousand officials, more than one-third are located outside of Geneva. In 1969, the ILO was awarded the Nobel Peace Prize for its activities.

At the international level today, ILO responsibility for labor issues intersects with the responsibilities of the WTO for trade. At the founding of the WTO in 1995, a large group of states opposed discussion of labor issues within the WTO, just as most had opposed GATT's involvement in labor issues. Arguing that there is no direct link between trade and labor standards, many developing countries do not want to erode their competitive advantage, namely cheap labor. To them, the proper forum for dealing with labor issues is the ILO. Many in the labor movement believe that it is necessary to give increased power to the ILO, particularly in monitoring and enforcing international labor standards. In contrast, other states and many NGOs argue that trade and labor standards should be linked. Since the WTO has more "teeth" than the ILO, namely, the power to impose sanctions, the WTO should be used for promoting labor standards (Elliott 2000).

The European Union has a long and successful history of addressing labor problems. The founding Treaty of Rome acknowledged in Article 177 the need to improve living and working conditions in member states. Member states agree to align labor policies and collaborate on legislation on working conditions, vocational training, and health and safety standards. Freedom of movement of workers is an integral component, although it was not until 1968 that work permits and preferences for home-country workers were abolished. Rights of workers were augmented in the Single European Act (1985), the Charter on Fundamental Rights for Workers (1989), and the 1992 Treaty of Union. Each agreement broadened community social policy and freedom of movement for labor, aided by provisions for mutual recognition of qualifications. Although the EU has been progressive in covering concerns of labor, the council is not authorized to address directly pay issues and rights of association, including the right to strike or conduct lockouts. Also, not all members have signed labor-related agreements. States with strict safety and environmental protection for workers fear that minimum standard directives may undermine national programs.

NAFTA's involvement in labor issues is less extensive. The NAFTA agreement is supplemented by a side agreement on labor issues, the North American Agreement on Labor Cooperation, which does not impose international or regional standards on the three member states. The agreement provides for trade or economic sanctions for violations of child labor laws or failure to enforce occupational health and safety laws, but on most issues, no such actions are taken and there are no provisions for monitoring (Langille 2001). The lack of a North American regional approach to labor is not surprising. Both the American AFL-CIO and Canada's Congress of Labor opposed NAFTA in the first place, while Mexico's Confederation of Mexican Workers supported NAFTA but opposed cooperation on industrial labor issues (Boswell and Stevis 1997). Without cooperation among groups representing workers across states, regional governance is weakened.

Health care and World Health Organization.   One of the oldest areas of functional activity is health, an issue that respects no national boundaries. In medieval times, as trade expanded between Europe and East Asia, epidemics followed trade routes. With discovery of the Americas came diseases like smallpox, measles, and yellow fever, previously unknown in the Western Hemisphere. Increased trade and travel in nineteenth-century

Europe accelerated the spread of deadly diseases across national borders and populations. Clearly, no one state could solve health problems alone. Cooperation was required.

In response to an outbreak of cholera in Europe, the International Sanitary Conference was convened in Paris in 1851 to develop a collective response based on increased knowledge about public health and medicine and improvements in sanitation. Between 1851 and 1903, a series of eleven such conferences developed procedures to prevent the spread of contagious and infectious diseases.

In 1907, the Office International d'Hygiène Publique (OIHP) was created with a mandate to disseminate information on communicable diseases such as cholera, plague, and yellow fever. More than a decade later, at the request of the League of Nations Council, an International Health Conference met to prepare for a permanent international health organization. OIHP did not become part of this new health organization, but remained a distinct organization with its own secretariat. The United States, for one, was satisfied with this arrangement since it was not a member of the League.

In 1946, a Technical Preparatory Committee met to establish a single health organization, to be known as the World Health Organization, which came into being in 1948 as a UN specialized agency. The basic decision-making body is the World Health Assembly (WHA) comprised of three delegates from each member state, including delegates from the scientific, professional, and nongovernmental communities. Each country, however, has only one vote, unlike the ILO where representatives of each functional group have a separate vote. The executive board is a smaller group of thirty-two members elected by the WHA. By "gentlemen's agreement," at least three of the Security Council members are supposed to be represented. Unlike other functional organizations, but in keeping with Mitrany's ideas of functionalism discussed in Chapter 2, WHO's decisionmaking structures do not privilege the influence of any particular states.

The WHO is close to being a quintessential functionalist organization and is one of the largest of the UN specialized agencies in terms of both membership and budget, a sign of the universality of health concerns. It is also one of the more decentralized functional organizations. The WHO secretariat located in Geneva is highly technical. The director-general, other secretariat officials, and many delegates, are medical doctors, the kind of technical experts that Mitrany advocated. The medical and allied communities form a strong epistemic community based on their technical expertise and training.

Among its major initiatives, WHO has undertaken campaigns to eradicate certain diseases. These included the malaria eradication program and campaigns for eradicating smallpox and polio. The last case of smallpox was reported in 1977, and the eradication program was widely acclaimed as a major WHO success.

With respect to polio, in 2002, there were only 1,918 cases reported in seven countries (www.unicef.org). Rotary International has been actively supporting this campaign, as have other international health groups and the Bill and Melinda Gates Foundation. The goal is expected to become reality by 2005.

Another area of WHO activity involves regulation. One of the most controversial issues was infant formula regulation (Sikkink 1986). In the early 1970s, health workers in the Third World noted an increase in mortality among bottle-fed as compared to breast-fed infants. Research suggested that bottle-fed babies were falling victim to formula mixed with impure water or formula highly diluted to cut costs. The Swiss-based NGO, Third World Action Group, and the U.S.-based Infant Formula Action Coalition organized a highly publicized boycott against Nestlé, one of the largest producers of infant formula, to change marketing practices in developing countries. In 1981, the WHA adopted the Code of Marketing for Breast-Milk Substitutes by a vote of 118 for and one against (the United States), with three abstentions. Although the code was nonbinding, it called for states to adopt regulations banning marketing and advertising of infant formula that discouraged breast feeding while acknowledging a legitimate market for breast-milk substitutes. Three years later, Nestlé agreed not to supply free infant formula to hospitals and to provide written warnings of the product's risks. Credit for the infant formula code owes much to the public health and scientific consensus on the superiority of breast feeding and that improper bottle feeding leads to infant mortality and malnutrition. NGOs, WHO, and the United Nations Children's Fund (UNICEF) played key roles (Sikkink 1986: 840).

A broader area of WHO's regulatory activity concerns pharmaceuticals. Who insures quality control of internationally sold pharmaceuticals? Who sponsors research on drugs for diseases found in the poorer tropical developing countries? The pharmaceutical issues are complex, given the number of products involved. Beginning in 1963, less developed countries sought assurances that imported drugs were of sufficient quality and technical assistance in monitoring quality control. The international drug companies largely opposed these efforts. Yet WHO approved guidelines for drug manufacturing quality control in 1970, covering such issues as labeling, self-inspection, and reports of adverse reactions.

In 1978, the WHA mandated that WHO develop a code of marketing practices under the Action Program on Essential Drugs. Countries were encouraged to develop "national drug lists" deemed essential to health needs, excluding dangerous pharmaceuticals or products such as certain vitamins whose use might represent a misallocation of national and personal health budgets. In the late 1990s, the accessibility and affordability of drugs in developing countries appeared on WHO's agenda. Of particular concern is the antiretroviral "cocktail" of drugs used to treat HIV/AIDs that has been far too costly for use in regions such as Africa where the epidemic is most widespread. WHO has successfully lobbied the pharmaceutical companies for better pricing arrangements for developing countries and been joined by an NGO campaign, as explained in Chapter 12.

Since the 1990s, one major health issue in WHO has been tobacco, a highly contentious lifestyle issue. WHO's campaign against tobacco has encountered stiff opposition from the large tobacco companies. Groups supporting international regulation of tobacco for health reasons have used tactics adapted from the infant formula campaign to convince the tobacco companies to refrain from advertising aimed at the youth market and to stop manipulating public policy in the interest of tobacco profits. In May 2003, the World Health Assembly approved the Framework Convention on Tobacco Control after the United States dropped its major objections. The treaty includes bans on advertising tobacco products, requirements on packaging, and broader liability for manufacturers. At the end of 2003, eighty-six countries had signed the convention, but only five had ratified it. With the economic power of tobacco companies and lobbies, the ratification process is apt to be a contentious one.

Yet at its root, WHO still is concerned with the issues that brought about its establishment—the transmission of infectious diseases. The SARS epidemic of 2003 reminded the international community of the dangers in rapid contagious transmission. WHO issued a global health alert, detailing the disease and its probable method of transmission. Working with public health officials in the United States, Canada, Europe, and Asia, WHO was the conduit through which research was reported and state measures taken. WHO officials visited affected countries, helping to establish national monitoring systems, advising on infection control methods, and providing the necessary technical assistance. Referring to SARS, Gro Harlem Brundtland, the departing director-general of WHO noted, "It has never been clearer than today that a secure healthy future for us all depends on cooperation across borders and between institutions" (quoted in Altman 2003: A6).

Although WHO has expanded the international health agenda well beyond the issues of the nineteenth century, it has not acted alone. Other IGOs, NGOs, and MNCs have become increasingly involved. UNICEF, for example, played a major role in the infant formula controversy and immunization programs against polio and other childhood diseases. In the 1980s, the World Bank emerged as the largest external financier of health programs in developing countries. Since 2000, international funding, however, has increasingly been funneled through major research institutes and foundations such as the Gates Foundation, and administered by NGOs, such as Doctors Without Borders. The increased use of NGOs for aid delivery is also found in the international food regime whose functions are essential to the preservation of health.

The international food regime.   The concept of a regime is a useful way to conceptualize the pieces of governance on food issues. There are a large number of organizations, some global, some regional, some general purpose, many very specialized, which are engaged in activities related to food and agriculture. Among the formal organizations playing key roles are the Food and Agriculture Organization (FAO) established in 1945, the World Food Programme (WFP) created in 1963, the International Fund for Agricultural Development (IFAD) founded in 1977, the International Wheat Council established in 1933, and the Consultative Group on International Agricultural Research (CGIAR) created in 1972. Of these, both FAO and IFAD are UN specialized agencies. Other organizations such as the Organization for Economic Cooperation and Development (OECD)—particularly its committees on Agriculture and Development Assistance—the WTO, and WHO have specific interests and responsibilities that link them to the food regime. Codex Alimentarius sets guidelines and standards relating to food safety and pesticide residues, relying on scientific experts to set international standards and work with authorities to harmonize food safety regulations. In addition, there are private actors such as international and national research institutes and foundations. The multiplicity of organizations in the food regime has produced a good deal of overlap in responsibilities and resulting confusion.

The core organization, FAO, was established at the end of World War II with the objectives of increasing agricultural productivity to eliminate hunger and improve nutrition, addressing problems of surpluses and shortages, establishing common standards, and harmonizing national agricultural policies with free trade principles. Based in Rome, it carries out basic research to enhance technical assistance in agriculture and acts as an information center for agricultural activities, including fishing and forestry. During the 1960s, FAO supported the development and dissemination of high-yield strains of grain and rice that produced the green revolution for developing countries. In the 1980s and 1990s, sustainable agricultural and rural development became the organization's thrust.

The WFP delivers food aid to food-deficit countries. Initially supported largely by the United States and Canada, WFP grew by the mid-1980s to a budget of over $1 billion, more than twenty-five donors, and development projects in over one hundred countries (Hopkins 1990: 180). In 2001, WFP spent $1.74 billion (87 percent on relief, 13 percent on development aid), distributing food to 77 million people in 82 countries, with a staff of over 2,500 employees.

The CGIAR coordinates and oversees the work of research centers such as the International Rice Research Institute. Agricultural research is an essential ingredient for promoting economic development and, hence, an important component of the food regime.

NGOs are an integral part of the food regime also, particularly for the delivery of emergency aid. For example, in Somalia during 1991 and 1992, NGOs such as the International Committee of the Red Cross, CARE, and Doctors Without Borders ran emergency food programs for children and mothers, the most severely affected groups. The food itself was brought in by the World Food Programme, and then delivered by the NGOs.

World Food conferences in 1974, 1996, and 2002 have helped to bring together the various constituencies and forge new principles of cooperation. At the 2002 World Food Summit, for example, many traditional issues filled the agenda: food aid to end hunger; emergencies; food safety and phytosanitary regulations; and securing food under conditions of limited water supplies. Among the new issues were the New Partnership for Africa's Development (NEPAD), discussed in Chapter 9, and the International Treaty on Plant Genetic Resources for Food and Agriculture that engaged the debate on genetic engineering of food crops. Over 650 labor, human rights, and farmers' groups participated in the conference, along with 180 countries. This was a clear signal that collaboration with the NGOs would increase along with partnerships with MNCs. For example, Parmalat, an Italian food giant, joined in funding and providing in-kind support for the summit.

Trends in functional organizations.   In 1973 Robert Cox and Harold K. Jacobson, in their pathbreaking book *The Anatomy of Influence,* compared patterns of influence and decisionmaking within eight functional UN agencies, utilizing criteria of the breadth, technicality, and essentiality of their tasks. Five organizations ranked high regarding technical and functional specificity (GATT, IAEA, IMF, ITU, and WHO); three ranked low (ILO, UNCTAD [UN Conference on Trade and Development], and UNESCO). Only two of eight organizations were relatively immune from political cleavages (WHO and the ITU). Cox and Jacobson (1973: 425) also found "a shift in the dominant ideology for international organizations from functionalism to developmentalism." The North-South conflict of the 1970s and 1980s affected these and other functional organizations. In response to pressures from developing countries plus new issues and evolving ideas about how best to respond to various problems, functional organizations expanded their scope of activity, often moving into more politically controversial issues. Both the ILO and WHO are excellent examples. Furthermore, the trend toward organizing periodic global conferences on key issues that accelerated in the 1970s led to the creation of new organizations, as well as increasing involvement of NGOs and expert groups that laid the foundations for the more complex networks of international organizations we see today.

■ Global Conferences

Multilateral global conferences date back to the period after World War I when the League of Nations convened conferences on economic affairs and disarmament. Such conferences increased in the 1970s with a series of UN-sponsored conferences relating to the environment, food supply, population, women's rights, water supplies, and desertification, as listed in Figure 3.2. The conferences focus international attention on salient issues of the day and bring together diverse constituencies.

Two types of global conferences illustrate the different processes and outcomes possible under this piece of global governance. The first is a traditional intergovernmental conference whose purpose is to negotiate a law-creating treaty for states subsequently to ratify. The Law of the Sea (LOS) negotiations between 1973 and 1982 are illustrative. The latter was a pro-

---

Figure 3.2   Global Conferences

Aging, 1982, 2002
Agrarian Reform and Rural Development, 1984
Children, 1990
Climate, 1979, 1990
Desertification, 1977
Environment, 1972
Environment and Development, 1992
Food, 1974, 1996, 2002
Habitat, Human Settlements, 1976, 1996
Human Rights, 1968, 1993
Law of the Sea, 1958, 1973–1982
New and Renewable Sources of Energy, 1981
Population, 1974, 1984
Population and Development, 1994
Racism, 1987, 2001
Science and Technology for Development, 1979
Social Development, 1995
Sustainable Development, 2002
Sustainable Development of Small Island Countries, 1995
Water, 1972
Women, 1975, 1980, 1985, 1995

tracted political process involving over 160 governments in complex negotiations. This nine-year-long process was triggered by the need to update the law of the sea following the independence of many new states in the 1960s and the endorsement by the UN General Assembly in 1967 of the principle that the high seas and deep seabed were part of the "common heritage of mankind." The Law of the Sea Convention, concluded in 1982, came into effect in 1994 and has been ratified now by more than 120 states (see Figure 3.3 for its provisions).

Participants in the law of the sea negotiations were official representatives of states; there was no formal participation by NGOs. Items were negotiated in committees of the whole, and the outcome was a legal document rather than long statements of goals and aspirations.

In contrast, for other global conferences, preparatory meetings involving NGOs and states are a critical part of the political process where decisions are made on many key agenda items, experts brought in, and NGO roles at the conference itself are determined. By one estimate, at least 60 percent of the final global conference outcomes are determined during the preparatory process (Schechter 2001: 189). The preparatory processes frequently also include in-depth studies that provide background data for the conference and may serve as wake-up calls to the international community.

Figure 3.3   Provisions of the 1982 Law of the Sea Convention

- Delineates internal waters, ports
- Gives states exclusive sovereignty over territorial sea, 12 miles from shore-line baseline
- Allows rights of innocent passage in territorial sea, when not prejudicial to the peace, good order, or security of the coastal state
- Allows rights of transit through international straits
- Permits coastal states to exercise limited jurisdiction in the Contiguous Zone, 24 miles from baseline
- Grants coastal states sovereign rights in the exclusive economic zone, right to explore, exploit, conserve, and manage natural resources of waters to 200 miles from baseline
- Defines high seas as area of ocean floor and its subsoil beyond national jurisdiction; this area and resources are the common heritage of mankind
- Establishes the International Seabed Authority to control deep seabed
- Establishes the Enterprise, the mineral exploration and exploitation organ of the International Seabed Authority

For example, studies prior to the 1982 World Assembly on Aging revealed that developing countries would be confronted by challenges of aging populations comparable to those in industrial countries in less than fifty years (Fomerand 1996: 369). In each case, there were actually two conferences held in the same location—an intergovernmental conference and a parallel NGO conference. This permitted extensive interaction between the two with NGOs proposing measures, governments reacting, and negotiations shaping specific outcomes that had not been previously agreed during the preparatory process. How much NGOs are allowed to participate in the official global conference has varied widely, a topic we discuss further in Chapter 6.

The outcomes of global conferences include a number of goals, sometimes new institutions and programs to meet those goals, calls on states to take action, and, in several cases, charges to NGOs with key roles in implementation. For example, the First World Conference for Women in 1975 led to the creation of the UN Development Fund for Women (UNIFEM) to support projects run by women in developing countries. The International Research and Training Institute for the Advancement of Women (INSTRAW) was formed in 1982, following the second women's conference. Out of the first conference also came the UN Decade for Women (1975–1985) and a charge to ECOSOC and the specialized agencies to gather data on the status of women. The Platform for Action approved by the 1995 Fourth World Conference on Women in Beijing called for the "empowerment of all women" through ensuring "women's equal access to economic resources including land, credit, science and technology, vocational training, information, communication, and markets" (UN 1995: A/Conf.177/20).

Subsequent chapters analyze the outcomes of conferences in various issue areas. Supporters of this approach argue that specific global conferences, such as the Rio Earth Summit in 1992, the Vienna Human Rights Conference in 1994, and the Beijing women's conference in 1995, have been important for articulating new international norms, expanding international law, creating new structures, setting agendas for the UN itself and for governments through programs of action, and promoting linkages among the UN, the specialized agencies, NGOs, and governments. They have contributed to the growth of NGOs and civil society in many parts of the world, raising important questions about who gets to participate in global governance. They have also increased understanding of the links among issues as seemingly disparate as environmental protection, human rights (especially for women), poverty alleviation, development, trade, and technology dissemination. The conferences have served as a counter hierarchy to established international organizations.

Critics have argued that these large conferences are too unwieldy, often duplicate work of other bodies, and are an inefficient way to identify problems and solutions. One critic has asked whether the global conferences are just expensive media events whose declarations and programs of action have little value. The Beijing platform, for example, has 360 articles detailing steps states should take to enhance women's roles (Fomerand 1996). Other critics suggest that specific constituencies have unfairly captured the ears of global conferees. The global conferences are undoubtedly political events, and their outcomes are products of political compromises that merely exhort governments to accept general principles and frameworks to guide their policies. With the combined outputs of all the conferences in the 1990s, the question became how to monitor what was actually being done and how to integrate implementation of those outcomes with the work of the main UN organs, especially ECOSOC.

The bottom line is that conferences must be seen as an integral part of global governance, not as stand-alone events. As part of a broader political process, they mobilize energies and attention in a way that established actors cannot. They have engaged NGOs and pushed IGOs to do the same. According to one analyst, however, the "record of policy and procedural implementation is spotty, varied, and obviously incomplete" (Schechter 2001: 185). Much will depend on NGOs' ability to sustain pressure on governments to live up to commitments they made and to assist the UN in meeting the increased demands placed on it. We return to assess this record in subsequent chapters.

■ *International Courts for Adjudication and Dispute Settlement*

The development of international courts for dispute settlement was another important trend in the twentieth century. It parallels the increasing legalization of issues and the increase in the number and scope of formal interstate treaties. There are now seventeen permanent international courts and almost forty if we include quasi-judicial bodies, tribunals, panels, and commissions. (See Figure 3.4.)

From the PCIJ to the ICJ. The nineteenth-century peace movements and Hague conferences laid foundations for both the Permanent Court of International Justice (PCIJ) and the International Court of Justice (ICJ) and refined such techniques as mediation, inquiry, and arbitration. In 1899, the Hague Convention for the Peaceful Settlement of International Disputes called for commissions to probe the facts of disputes, and in 1907, the Permanent Court of Arbitration was established. They were not courts in the ordinary sense of the term.

The Covenant of the League of Nations in Article 14 established the Permanent Court of International Justice. Judges representing major world legal systems were elected by the League's council and assembly. Unlike

---

Figure 3.4   International and Regional Courts

• *Courts with Universal Scope*
International Court of Justice
International Tribunal for the Law of the Sea
International Criminal Court
World Trade Organization Dispute Settlement Unit (includes the
    Dispute Settlement Body and the Appellate Body)
World Bank Centre for the Settlement of Investment Disputes

• *Ad Hoc Criminal Tribunals*
International Criminal Tribunal for the Former Yugoslavia
International Criminal Tribunal for Rwanda

• *Regional Courts*
Court of Justice of the European Communities, with Court of First
    Instance
Central American Court of Justice
Court of Justice of the Andean Community

• *Specialized Regional Courts*
European Court of Human Rights
Inter-American Court of Human Rights
Court of Justice of the European Free Trade Association
Court of Justice of the Benelux Economic Union
Court of Justice of the Common Market for Eastern and Southern
    Africa
Court of Justice of the Arab Maghreb Union
Judicial Board of the Organization of Arab Petroleum Exporting
    Countries

• *Private International Arbitration*
Arbitration Institute of the Stockholm Chamber of Commerce
International Chamber of Commerce Arbitration
London Court of International Arbitration

---

arbitral tribunals, the PCIJ was permanent, rules were fixed in advance, judgments were binding on parties, and proceedings were public. It could provide advisory opinions as well as binding decisions. The PCIJ, however, was never integrated into the League. States could participate in one and not the other. Between 1922 and 1940, the PCIJ decided twenty-nine contentious cases between states and handed down twenty-seven advisory opinions. Hundreds of treaties and conventions conferred jurisdiction on it to settle disputes among parties. While few in number, many PCIJ decisions helped to clarify key issues of international law and lay a solid foundation for its successor, the International Court of Justice, which refers directly to PCIJ decisions and procedures in conducting its business.

The International Court of Justice, with fifteen justices headquartered in The Hague, The Netherlands, is a major organ of the United Nations. All members of the UN are ipso facto parties to the ICJ Statute. As the judicial arm of the UN, the ICJ shares responsibility with the other major organs for insuring that the principles of the charter are followed. Like the PCIJ, it affords member states an impartial body for settling legal disputes and gives advisory opinions on legal questions referred to it by international agencies.

The ICJ has noncompulsory jurisdiction, meaning that parties to a dispute (only states) must all agree to submit a case to the court; there is no way to force a party to appear before the court and no executive to enforce its decisions. Rather, enforcement of ICJ decisions depends on the perceived legitimacy of the court's actions, the voluntary compliance of states, and the "power of shame" if states fail to comply with an ICJ judgment. The judges are elected by the General Assembly and the Security Council for nine-year terms (five are elected every three years) on the basis of qualifications befitting appointment to the highest judicial body in their home country and recognized competence in international law. Together they represent the major legal systems of the world, but act independently of their national affiliations.

The issue of the court's jurisdiction has been a particularly vexing one. Article 36.2 of the ICJ Statute—the Optional Clause—gives states the opportunity to declare that they recognize ICJ jurisdiction as compulsory. States that sign the Optional Clause agree to accept the court's jurisdiction in all legal disputes, or they may agree to accept the court's jurisdiction as compulsory only for disputes with other states that have also accepted compulsory jurisdiction. The clause was tested in 1984 when Nicaragua initiated proceedings against the United States for mining its harbors and undermining its government and economy (ICJ Case 1984a [Case Concerning Military and Paramilitary Activities In and Against Nicaragua]). The United States disputed the court's jurisdiction on the grounds that Nicaragua had not accepted compulsory ICJ jurisdiction and that even had it done so, the issues were political not legal. The ICJ ruled against the United States. In response, President Ronald Reagan terminated U.S. acceptance of the court's compulsory jurisdiction in October 1985.

The ICJ had 107 contentious cases brought before it between 1946 and 2003, and issued fifty-two judgments. The court has never been heavily burdened, although its caseload is increasing. In the 1970s, it averaged one or two pending cases; between 1990–1997 that number increased to between nine and thirteen pending cases; and since 1998, the number has jumped to over twenty cases on the docket. In addition, between 1946 and 2003, the court issued twenty-four advisory opinions. The increased case-load since 1989 is a result of greater trust in the court by developing countries after the Nicaragua case showed that a small, developing country could win a judicial victory over a major power (the United States). An added factor has been the option of using a chamber of five justices to hear and determine cases by summary procedure, thus speeding up what is often a very lengthy process.

ICJ cases have seldom reflected the major political issues of the day since few states want to trust a legal judgment for settlement of a largely political issue. Only a handful of cases, therefore, were related to the Cold War conflict—and then only indirectly (ICJ Case 1949 [the Corfu Channel Case]). Several cases have addressed decolonization questions (ICJ Case 1971 [Legal Consequences for States of the Continued Presence of South Africa in Namibia]; ICJ Advisory Opinion 1975 [Western Sahara]). The ICJ has helped states to resolve numerous territorial disputes, such as the Case Concerning the Temple of Preah Vihear (ICJ Case 1962) and the Case Concerning the Land and Maritime Boundary between Cameroon and Nigeria (ICJ Case 2002), disputes over delimitation of the continental shelf (ICJ Case 1969 [North Sea Continental Shelf Cases]), and fisheries jurisdiction (ICJ Case 1984b [Gulf of Maine Area Case]; and Fisheries Jurisdiction Case [ICJ Case 1973]). It has also been called upon to rule on the legality of nuclear tests (ICJ Case 1974 [Nuclear Tests Cases]), as well as on hostage taking (ICJ Case 1980 [Case Concerning U.S. Diplomatic and Consular Staff in Tehran]), the right of asylum, the legality of use of force, expropriation of foreign property, and environmental protection and application of treaties (ICJ Case 1997 [Case Concerning the Gabcikovo-Nagymaros Project]).

The ICJ is limited by the fact that only states can bring cases. Furthermore, while judicial decisions are sources of international law under the court's statute, Article 38.1(d) also provides that the "decision of the Court has no binding force except as between the parties and in respect of that particular case." In other words, state sovereignty was intended to limit the applicability of ICJ judgments unlike national courts that use precedents from prior cases to shape future judgments and, hence, the substance and interpretation of law. In reality, however, the ICJ has used many principles from earlier cases to decide later ones. This contributes to greater consistency in its decisions and more respect for the court's ability to contribute to the progressive development of international law. With the creation of other judicial bodies, the ICJ is no longer the only site for adjudicating disputes. In addition, there are many other ways to settle disputes besides resorting to adjudication, as we explore particularly in Chapters 8 and 9.

The growing trend of specialized tribunals.   The ICJ is complemented by a number of other international tribunals—some tied to the specialized agencies, such as the International Labour Organization's Administrative Tribunal or the Law of the Sea Tribunal, and some established to adjudicate specific UN decisions, such as the UN Compensation Commission to deal with claims against Iraq following its invasion of Kuwait.

Of particular note are the International Centre for the Settlement of Investment Disputes (ICSID) within the World Bank and the WTO Dispute Settlement Body. The former is an autonomous bank entity that provides facilities for dispute arbitration between member countries and investors who are citizens of other member countries. Submission of disputes is voluntary, but once the parties agree to arbitration, neither may withdraw its consent. Often agreements between host countries and investors include a provision stipulating that disputes will be sent to the ICSID. In recent years, the number of cases submitted to the center has increased significantly and its activities have expanded to include consultations with governments on investment and arbitration law. The WTO dispute settlement procedures are discussed in Chapter 9.

European Court of Justice (ECJ).   There has also been a proliferation of regional courts and judicial-like bodies, most of which deal with economic or human rights issues. Only one regional court covers multiple issues, is thoroughly institutionalized, and plays a significant role in regional governance, namely, the European Court of Justice (ECJ). The ECJ is a key arm of the most legalized IGO and has the power to interpret the EU's treaty and secondary legislation, as well as to arbitrate disputes between individuals, states, and EU institutions.

What makes the ECJ's role unique among international judicial bodies is that EU treaties are legally enforceable documents, unlike the UN Charter. They create legal obligations that the ECJ may be called upon to interpret and, hence, enforce. All states are obligated to uphold European law, including treaties, subsidiary legislation, and ECJ decisions. If a state fails to comply, infringement proceedings may be brought to the ECJ. This can lead to a fine or imposition of sanctions, measures that other courts do not have the authority to undertake. Furthermore, European law is superior to national law, meaning that state courts are obligated to enforce EU law even when it conflicts with national law (ECJ 1964 [*Flaminio Costa v. Enel*]). National courts, national governments, and individuals may ask for a preliminary ruling on whether national law conflicts with European law, if the national court is unable or unwilling to resolve the dispute based in previous EU case law. This has given the ECJ an ability, in effect, to review national law. Given these unprecedented powers, it is not surprising that Alter (2000: 49) concludes, "The ECJ is perhaps the most active and influential international legal body in existence, operating as a constitutional court of Europe."

The ECJ hears five broad categories of cases: (1) cases brought by the EU commission against governments for infringement of the founding treaties; (2) actions brought by states against decisions of the commission; (3) cases brought by states challenging the EU's jurisdiction; (4) administrative disputes between EU and civil personnel; and (5) complaints from individuals who have been adversely affected by a community action.

The cases also cover many different issue areas. Given the EU's extensive economic role, many cases involve free trade issues, including disputes on customs duties, tax discrimination, and elimination of nontariff barriers. Agricultural policy questions and external trade law (antidumping, countervailing duties) are also litigious topics. Increasingly, ECJ's agenda has included environmental cases, social cases addressing labor issues and freedom of movement for workers, as well as cases on fundamental issues such as EU enlargement and monetary union.

Prior to the 2004 enlargement the ECJ was composed of fifteen judges appointed by member states for six-year, renewable terms plus nine advocates-general who help ease the court's burden by also considering cases and providing what are, in effect, preliminary opinions that may be accepted or rejected by the full court. The court itself may sit *en banc* (the whole) or in smaller chambers. Court rules require that cases brought by member states must be heard by the full court. In the civil law tradition, decisions are generally announced without indicating any dissenting opinions. In 1989, to respond to a rising caseload and allow the judges to concentrate on fundamental tasks, a Court of First Instance was established to deal with all cases brought by individuals and companies, with the exception of cases dealing with trade defense issues such as antidumping. Thus, it hears staff cases, claims for damages, competition cases, and disputes over technical legislation and questions of fact.

As Tsebelis and Garrett (2001: 358) note, "The Court has been remarkably effective in the past forty years, successfully 'constitutionalizing' the EU's treaty base, claiming wide powers of judicial review over this would-be constitution, and exercising judicial activism in the interpretation of secondary legislation." This role is discussed further in Chapter 5.

Ad hoc war crimes tribunals.   The desire to punish individuals responsible for war crimes during World War II led to the establishment of the first war crimes tribunals. Because the Nuremberg and Tokyo trials were the victor's punishment of the vanquished, they were not regarded as precedents for future wartime crimes. In the 1990s, however, the idea of individual responsibility for war crimes and crimes against humanity was revived in the face of the atrocities committed during conflicts in the former Yugoslavia, Rwanda, and Sierra Leone. Frustrated by the international community's inability to bring those responsible for crimes during interstate or civil wars to justice, the UN Security Council established the International Criminal Tribunal for the Former Yugoslavia (ICTFY) in 1993, followed in 1994 by the International Criminal Tribunal for Rwanda (ICTR). Initially, these ad hoc courts lacked established structures or procedures, as well as actual criminals in custody. Yet they recruited prosecutors, investigators, administrators, and judges, devised rules of procedure and evidence, and worked to gain the cooperation of states to carry out their tasks. Deciding whom to indict and getting those individuals into custody has proven to be a time-consuming task.

Employing fourteen judges and three separate proceedings, as well as over six hundred staff members from around the world, the ICTFY now has developed procedures that facilitated the Rwanda tribunal as well. The tribunal has developed answers to questions of authority, jurisdiction, evidence, sentencing, and imprisonment. Thus, by the beginning of 2004, five accused were on trial, including former Serbian President Slobodan Milosevic; sixty-three others had been charged and were undergoing pretrial formalities or were in custody awaiting the beginning of legal proceedings. Forty persons had been sentenced and five had been acquitted. Twenty individuals who had been indicted remain at large. As Sean Murphy (1999: 96–97) concludes, "The real success of the ICTFY lies in the fact that, despite these obstacles, it is a functioning international criminal court that is providing a forum for victims to accuse those who violated civilized norms of behavior; . . . stigmatizing persons . . . and forcing them to relinquish any official power . . . and generating a body of jurisprudence that will undoubtedly continue to build over time."

The ICTR has also met with stern criticism for its slow proceedings (only nine decisions) and high cost ($500 million as of 2002). Some of its inefficiency can be attributed to its location in Arusha, Tanzania. A suitable venue had to be constructed and refurbished, but the location is inconvenient for witnesses from Rwanda who have to travel though four countries, an expensive and time-consuming endeavor. This led Rwanda's attorney general to conclude, "The tribunal was not set up for the people of Rwanda. It was set up to ease the world's guilty consciences, and in everything the court does, this shows" (quoted in Power 2003: 47). Nonetheless, by the beginning of 2004, the Rwandan tribunal had convicted sixteen individuals of genocide and crimes against humanity, including a former prime minister and three media leaders, and had begun the trial of four senior government officials. In addition, there were twenty-four detainees on trial and twenty-two individuals in custody awaiting trial (www.ictr.org).

The International Criminal Court (ICC).   In 1998, in light of the difficulties posed by the ad hoc nature of the Yugoslavia and Rwanda tribunals and a long-standing movement to create a permanent international criminal court, UN members concluded the statute for the International Criminal Court (ICC). In contrast to the ICJ, the ICC has both compulsory jurisdiction and jurisdiction over individuals.

Called by one "the most ambitious initiative in the history of modern international law" (Simons 2003: A9), the new court has jurisdiction over "serious" war crimes that represent a "policy or plan," rather than just random acts in wartime. They must also have been "systematic or widespread," not single abuses. Four types of crimes are covered: genocide (attacking a group of people and killing them because of race, ethnicity, religion); crimes against humanity (murder, enslavement, forcible transfer of population, torture); war crimes; and crimes of aggression (undefined). No individuals (save those under eighteen years) are immune from jurisdiction, including heads of states and military leaders. The ICC will function as a court of last resort in that it can hear cases only when national courts are unwilling or unable to deal with grave atrocities. Prosecution is forbidden for crimes committed before July 1, 2002, when the court came into being, and individuals must be present during the trial. Anyone—an individual, government, group or the UN Security Council—can bring a case before the ICC. In March 2003, eighteen justices were installed, including eleven men and seven women, and a prosecutor appointed. Because the court has to create its procedures, it will be some time before it begins hearing cases.

An umbrella group of over one thousand NGOs, the Coalition for the ICC (CICC), played an important role in mobilizing international support for the ICC and in promoting ratification (Brown 2002). An essential part of their strategy has been promoting public awareness and lobbying nonratifying states. The ICC is also controversial. By 2004, there were 139 signatories to the Rome treaty and ninety-two ratifications. Prominent among the absentees were the United States, China, India, Iraq, and Turkey.

Although the United States has historically supported international accountability for war crimes, it opposes the ICC. One major concern is the possibility that the ICC might prosecute U.S. military personnel or even the president without American approval. Thus, the U.S. Department of Defense has strongly insisted that the U.S. cannot participate, and both the Bush and Clinton administrations as well as Congress have deferred to their judgment. The United States also objects to the aggression clause as undefined and vague. The United States objects more generally on the grounds that the ICC infringes on U.S. sovereignty and the idea that the United States as a world power has a different role to play in international relations. For this reason, the United States has supported an international court whose powers depended upon approval by the UN Security Council where it has veto power.

To protect itself, the United States has negotiated commitments from other states not to send Americans to the court for prosecution, as permitted under Article 98 of the treaty. The United States has signed sixty-two such agreements. As one official defending the action contends, "We are not trying to undermine the court. We're trying to protect American citizens from an unaccountable prosecutor." A supporter of the ICC replies, "For all its huffing and puffing, the U.S. has not been able to blow the house down" (quoted in Marquis 2003: A3). In spite of American objections, the establishment of the ICC moves international adjudication and international law far more in the direction of accepting individuals and nonstate entities such as terrorist and criminal groups as subjects of international law, where only states historically have had such status.

Private International Adjudication.   As economic globalization has broadened and deepened, cross-border trade and investment disputes have become more common. Although there are intergovernmental provisions for settlement of such disputes, like the Centre for the Settlement of Investment Disputes, the growth of such disputes has led to the establishment of private settlement approaches. There are upwards of one hundred different forums, with caseloads doubling every year.

Generally, private arbitration procedures are flexible with rules established for each case. Proceedings are held in private and the awards are confidential. The London Court of International Arbitration is one of the oldest such bodies. Established in 1892, its main function is to select arbitrators for private parties requesting arbitration. The Arbitration Institute of the Stockholm Chamber of Commerce, formed in 1977, likewise appoints arbitral tribunals. Among such groups, the most active is the International Chamber of Commerce Arbitrators. Dating from 1923, its caseload has increased dramatically since the mid-1980s. Some four to five hundred cases are arbitrated annually, most among clients from Europe, though there has been an increase from Latin America and Southeast Asia (Mattli 2001).

Increased international and regional adjudication reflects several trends: (1) international law's expansion into domains previously subject only to state jurisdiction or not the object of multilateral justice; (2) more fluid interactions among states since the Cold War's end; (3) the growth of regional economic arrangements that require adjudication; and (4) massive human rights violations in post–Cold War conflicts that drove creation of arrangements for dealing with war crimes and crimes against humanity. As one legal analyst (Romano 1999: 709) concludes, "The enormous expansion and transformation of the international judiciary is the single most important development of the post–Cold War age."

The foundations of contemporary pieces of global governance have evolved over time from states themselves and a rudimentary set of international rules to an increasingly complex network of international organizations. As we have explored in the chapter, the nineteenth century set a series of precedents for the development of intergovernmental organizations. The twentieth century was marked by the rapid proliferation of multilateral institutions and international adjudicatory institutions. The center of the activity is the United Nations system. It is to that we shall turn in Chapter 4.

■ **Note**

1. Portions of this chapter are drawn from Karen A. Mingst and Margaret P. Karns. (2000) *The United Nations in the Post–Cold War Era,* 2nd ed. Boulder: Westview Press. Reprinted with permission of Westview Press.

■ **Suggested Further Reading**

Alter, Karen. (2001) *Establishing the Supremacy of European Law. The Making of an International Rule of Law in Europe.* Oxford: Oxford University Press.

Claude, Inis L., Jr. (1964) *Swords into Plowshares: The Problems and Progress of International Organization.* 3rd ed. New York: Random House.

Cox, Robert W., and Harold K. Jacobson. (1973) *The Anatomy of Influence. Decision Making in International Organization.* New Haven, Conn: Yale University Press.

Northledge, F. S. (1986) *The League of Nations: Its Life and Times. 1920–1946.* New York: Holmes and Meier.

Romano, Cesare P. R. (1999) "The Proliferation of International Judicial Bodies: The Pieces of the Puzzle," *International Law and Politics* 31: 709–751.

Schechter, Michael, ed. (2001) *United Nations-Sponsored World Conferences. Focus on Impact and Follow-up.* Tokyo: UNU Press.

■ **Internet Resources**

Coalition for an International Criminal Court: www.ICCnow.org

European Court of Justice: www.curia.eu.int/en/index.htm

Food and Agriculture Organization: www.fao.org

INFACT: www.infact.org

International Centre for Settlement of Investment Disputes: www.worldbank.org. icsid/aboutmain.html

International Court of Justice: www.icj-cij.org

International Criminal Court: www.icc-cpi.int/php/index.php

International Criminal Tribunal for Rwanda: www.ictr.org

International Criminal Tribunal for the Former Yugoslavia: www.un.org/icty/index. html

International Labour Organization: www.ilo.org

UN system of organizations (specific functional organizations listed alphabetically): www.unsystem.org

World Food Programme: www.wfp.org

World Health Organization: www.who.org

4

The United Nations: Centerpiece of Global Governance

Since World War II, the United Nations has been the central piece of global governance. It is the only IGO with global scope and nearly universal membership whose agenda encompasses the broadest range of governance issues. The UN is, in fact, a complex system with many pieces. Among its functions are the creation of international law, norms, and principles; it has created other IGOs within the UN system such as the UN Conference on Trade and Development (UNCTAD) and the United Nations Drug Control Programme (UNDCP), as well as countless other committees and programs; it has sponsored global conferences and summits. It serves also as a catalyst for global policy networks and partnerships with other actors. The UN, in short, is the central site for multilateral diplomacy, and the UN General Assembly is center stage. Its three weeks of general debate at the opening of each fall assembly session draw foreign ministers and heads of state from small and large states to take advantage of the opportunity to address all the nations of the world and to engage in intensive diplomacy.

The UN Security Council is the core of the global security system and is the primary legitimizer of actions initiated to deal with threats and aggression. This is what made the 2002–2003 debate over war with Iraq so important. Would the council endorse a U.S.-led war or not? When the Security Council devoted a special session in January 2000 to HIV/AIDS as a security threat, it legitimized this view of the epidemic and the existence of new types of threats. Likewise, the 1999 debate over NATO intervention in Kosovo joined debate over a possible new norm of humanitarian intervention.

The UN's importance, and especially the relative importance of the Security Council and General Assembly, has risen and fallen over the years as world politics affected the organization. At the beginning of the twenty-first century, however, two things symbolized the UN's continuing role as the centerpiece of global governance: the unprecedented Millennium Summit and Declaration and the awarding of the 2001 Nobel Peace Prize to the UN and Secretary-General Kofi Annan. The Norwegian Nobel Committee stated, "Today the Organization is at the forefront of efforts to

achieve peace and security in the world, and of the international mobilization aimed at meeting the world's economic, social and environmental challenges. . . . the only negotiable route to global peace and cooperation goes
by way of the United Nations" (*UN Chronicle* 2001–2002b: 4).

The establishment of the United Nations in the closing days of World
War II was an affirmation of the desire of war-weary nations for an organization that could help them avoid future conflicts and promote international
economic and social cooperation. In many important ways, the structure of
the United Nations was patterned after that of the League of Nations, and
changes were made where lessons had been learned. For example, the
League's council could act only with unanimous agreement; the UN
Security Council, while requiring the support of all five permanent members, requires only a majority of the nonpermanent members to take action.
The UN's charter built on lessons from the League of Nations and earlier
experiments with international unions, conference diplomacy, and dispute
settlement mechanisms. The UN's creation also represented an acceptance
of the necessity for a general international organization.[1]

■ Foundations of the United Nations

▦ From League to United Nations

The Atlantic Charter of August 14, 1941—a joint declaration by U.S.
President Franklin Roosevelt and British Prime Minister Winston Churchill
calling for collaboration on economic issues and a permanent system of
security—was the foundation for the Declaration by the United Nations in
January 1942. Twenty-six nations affirmed the principles of the Atlantic
Charter and agreed to create a new universal organization to replace the
League of Nations. The UN Charter was then drafted in two sets of meet-
ings between August and October 1944 at Dumbarton Oaks in Washington,
D.C. The participants agreed that the organization would be based on the
principle of the sovereign equality of members, with all "peace-loving"
states eligible for membership, thereby excluding the Axis powers—
Germany, Italy, Japan, and Spain. It was also agreed that decisions on security issues would require unanimity of the permanent members of the
Security Council, the great powers. There was also consensus on broadening the scope of the new organization beyond that of the League, and
President Roosevelt early on sought to ensure domestic support for U.S.
participation.

When the United Nations Conference on International Organization
convened in San Francisco on April 25, 1945, delegates from the fifty participating states modified and finalized what had already been negotiated
among the great powers. On July 28, 1945, with Senate approval, the

United States became the first country to ratify the charter. It took only three months for a sufficient number of countries to ratify the document. As one conference participant noted after the charter was signed,

> One of the most significant features was the demonstration of the large area of agreement which existed from the start among the 50 nations. . . . Everyone exhibited a serious minded determination to reach agreement on an organization which would be more effective than the League of Nations. . . . Not a single reservation was made to the charter when it was adopted. . . . The conference will long stand as one of the landmarks in international diplomacy. . . . [Nonetheless] one wonders—will the conversations of men prove powerful enough to curb the might of military power or to harness it to more orderly uses? (Padelford 1945)

■ *The UN Charter and Key Principles*

As the founding legal document of the United Nations, the UN Charter expresses both hopes and aspirations of the founders for a better world and the realities of what the fifty states were able to agree on in 1945. Several key principles undergird the UN's structure and operation and represent fundamental legal obligations of all members. These are contained in Article 2 of the charter as well as in other provisions.

The most fundamental principle is the sovereign equality of member states, which means that states do not recognize any higher governing authority. Equality refers to states' legal status, not their size, military power, or wealth, making Russia, Lithuania, China, and Singapore equals. This is the basis for each state having one vote in the General Assembly. Inequality is also part of the UN framework, embodied in the permanent membership and veto power of five states in the Security Council: the United States, Russia, China, Great Britain, and France.

Closely related to the UN's primary goal of maintaining peace and security are the twin principles that all member states shall (1) refrain from the threat or use of force against the territorial integrity or political independence of any state, or in any manner inconsistent with United Nations purposes, and (2) settle their international disputes by peaceful means. Many times in the last fifty years states have failed to honor these principles and have often failed even to submit their disputes to the UN for settlement. Members also accept the obligation to support enforcement actions such as economic sanctions and to refrain from giving assistance to states that are the objects of UN preventive or enforcement action. They have the collective responsibility to ensure that nonmember states act in accordance with these principles as necessary for the maintenance of international peace and security. A further key principle is the obligation of member states to fulfill in good faith all the obligations assumed by them under the charter. This affirms a fundamental norm of all international law and treaties: *pacta sunt servanda*—treaties must be carried out. One such obligation is payment of assessed annual contributions (dues) to the organization.

The final principle in Article 2 asserts that "nothing in the present charter shall authorize the United Nations to intervene in matters which are essentially within the domestic jurisdiction of any state or shall require the Members to submit such matters to settlement under the present charter . . . [although] this principle shall not prejudice the application of enforcement measures under Chapter VII." This provision underscores the longstanding norm of nonintervention in the domestic affairs of states, but provides a key exception for enforcement actions. But who decides what is an international and what is a domestic problem? Since the UN's founding in 1945, the scope of what is considered "international" has broadened with UN involvement in human rights, development, and environmental degradation. Since the Cold War's end, many UN peacekeeping operations have involved intrastate rather than interstate conflicts, in other words conflicts *within* rather than *between* states. The UN's founders recognized the tension between the commitment to act collectively against a member state and the affirmation of state sovereignty represented in the nonintervention principle. They could not foresee the dilemmas that changing definitions of security, ethnic conflicts, humanitarian crises, failed states, terrorism, and new issues such as the HIV/AIDS epidemic would pose. Human rights might well be seen as a matter of domestic jurisdiction, but the Preamble and Article 1 of the UN Charter both contain references to human rights and obligate states to show "respect for the principle of equal rights and self-determination of peoples." Hence, discussions of human rights have always been regarded as legitimate international, rather than solely domestic, concerns. Actions to promote or enforce human rights norms have been much more controversial.

In Article 51, the charter affirms states' "right of individual or collective self-defence" against armed attack. Thus, states are not required to wait for the UN to act before undertaking measures in their own (and others') defense. They are obligated to report their responses and they may create regional defense and other arrangements. This self-defense principle, not surprisingly, has led to many debates over who initiated hostilities and who was the victim of aggression. For example, in the Middle East conflicts, was it Israel or the Arab states that first used force? In the debate over Iraq, did Iraq possess weapons of mass destruction and did these pose a threat to the United States and other countries to justify war? A special committee labored for many years over the problem of defining aggression before concluding that the UN Security Council has the ultimate responsibility to determine acts of aggression.

■ The Major Organs of the UN

The structure of the United Nations as outlined in the charter includes six major bodies: the Security Council, the General Assembly, the Economic and Social Council, the Trusteeship Council, the International Court of Justice, and the Secretariat. Each organ has changed over time, responding to external realities, internal pressures, and interactions with other organs. Because the United Nations is a complex system of organizations, it extends well beyond these six organs. Among the affiliated organizations are the sixteen, independently established specialized agencies, ranging from the World Health Organization, Food and Agriculture Organization, and UNESCO to the IMF and World Bank (but not the World Trade Organization), which were discussed in Chapter 3. In addition, the General Assembly, Security Council, and ECOSOC have used their powers to create a large number of subsidiary bodies, programs, and funds, illustrating the phenomenon of "IGOs creating other IGOs" (Jacobson 1984: 39). Figure 4.1 captures the complexity of the UN system. In the sections that follow, we shall discuss how the six major UN organs have evolved in practice and some of their political dynamics.

The General Assembly

The General Assembly, like the League's assembly, was designed as the general debate arena where all UN members would be equally represented according to a one-state, one-vote formula. It is the organization's hub, with a diverse agenda and the responsibility for coordinating and supervising subsidiary bodies but with power only to make recommendations to members, except on internal matters such as elections and the budget. It has exclusive competence over the latter, giving it a measure of surveillance and control over all UN programs and subsidiary bodies. The assembly also has important elective functions: admitting states to UN membership, electing the nonpermanent members of the Security Council, ECOSOC, and the Trusteeship Council, appointing judges to the ICJ, and appointing the secretary-general on the recommendation of the Security Council. In many ways, the General Assembly comes closer than any other international body to embodying what is often called the "international community." It is also "the favorite principal organ of weak states . . . because it gives them an influence over decisions that they lack anywhere else in the international system" (Peterson 1986: 2). To paraphrase Shakespeare, if "all the world's a stage," the UN General Assembly is center stage—a stage particularly important for small states such as Malta, Singapore, Zambia, Costa Rica, and Fiji.

The General Assembly can consider any matter within the purview of the UN Charter (Article 10), and the number of items on the assembly's

Figure 4.1 The United Nations System

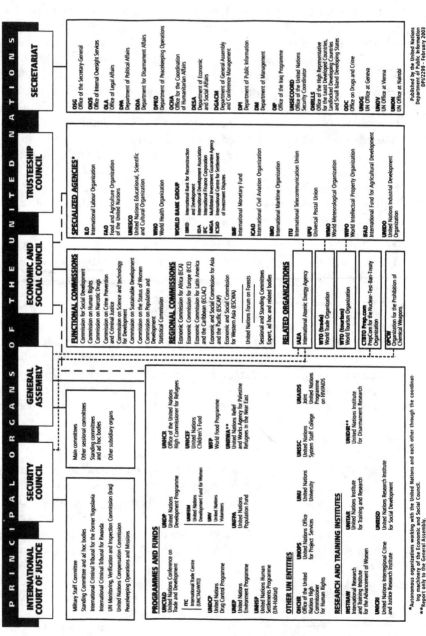

agenda has continually grown over the years from forty-six in 1946 to 165 in 2003. Many items, however, are repeated year after year with no effort at review. They range from various conflict situations to arms control, development, global resource management, human rights, legal issues, the persistence of colonialism, and the UN's finances. Resolutions may be aimed at individual member states, nonmembers, the Security Council or other organs, the secretary-general, or even the assembly itself.

Although the Security Council is the primary organ for dealing with threats to international peace and security, the assembly can make inquiries and studies with respect to conflicts (Articles 13, 14); it may discuss a situation and make recommendations if the council is not exercising its functions (Articles 11, 12); and it has the right to be kept informed by the Security Council and the secretary-general (Articles 10, 11, 12). The "Uniting for Peace Resolution" passed during the Korean War in 1950, however, ignited controversy over the respective roles of the two bodies. Under the resolution, the General Assembly claimed authority to recommend collective measures when the Security Council was deadlocked by a veto. It was subsequently used to deal with crises in Suez and Hungary (1956), the Middle East (1958), the Congo (1960), and the occupied Palestinian territories (1997). In all, ten emergency special sessions of the assembly have dealt with threats to international peace when the Security Council was deadlocked; the most recent in 1997 has reconvened periodically since. In 1962, the ICJ in the *Certain Expenses of the United Nations* case (ICJ Advisory Opinion 1962) was asked to give an advisory opinion on whether the General Assembly had the authority it claimed with respect to authorizing peacekeeping operations. (The opinion was affirmative.) Since the early 1990s, however, the permanent members of the Security Council have tacitly agreed that only the Security Council should authorize the use of armed force. In any case, the General Assembly is a cumbersome body for dealing with delicate situations of peace and security. It is most useful for the symbolic politics of agenda setting and mustering large majorities in support of resolutions.

The UN Charter also entrusted the General Assembly with an important role in the development of international law (Article 13). Although it is not a world legislature, its resolutions may lay the basis for new international law by articulating new principles, such as one that called the seas the "common heritage of mankind," and new concepts such as sustainable development. These then may (or may not) be embodied in multilateral norm- or law-creating treaties and conventions drafted under General Assembly authorization. For example, the "common heritage" principle was incorporated into the 1967 Treaty on Outer Space and 1982 Convention on Law of the Sea. The passage of similar resolutions and declarations over several years is often considered to provide a basis for "soft law"—that is, norms that represent a widespread international consensus but may not (yet) be embodied in "hard" or treaty form. The General Assembly has also produced a large number of multilateral lawmaking treaties, including the 1961 Vienna Convention on Diplomatic Relations, the 1969 Vienna Convention on the Law of Treaties, the 1968 Treaty on the Nonproliferation of Nuclear Weapons, and the 1971 Seabed Arms Control Treaty. Assembly resolutions have promoted all the major international conventions on human rights, although most were drafted in the Commission on Human Rights that functions under ECOSOC.

Finally, the General Assembly shares responsibilities for charter revision with the Security Council. The assembly can propose amendments with a two-thirds majority; two-thirds of the member states, including all the permanent members of the Security Council, must then ratify the changes. The General Assembly and Security Council together may also call a general conference for the purpose of charter review. There have to date, however, been only two instances of charter amendment, both taken to enlarge the membership of the Security Council (1965) and Economic and Social Council (1965 and 1973)

How the General Assembly functions.   Regular annual meetings of the General Assembly are held for three months each fall (or longer) and begin with a "general debate" period when heads of state, prime ministers, and foreign ministers by the score come to New York to speak before the assembly. In addition, there have been twenty special sessions called to deal with specific problems (e.g., Financial and Budgetary Problems in 1963, Development and International Economic Cooperation in 1975, Disarmament in 1978, HIV/AIDS in 2001, and Children in 2002). These special sessions should not be confused with the emergency special sessions convened under a Uniting for Peace resolution, nor with the global conferences the UN has sponsored since the 1970s.

The bulk of the General Assembly's work occurs in six functional committees: the First or Disarmament and International Security Committee; the Second or Economic and Financial Committee; the Third or Social, Humanitarian, and Cultural Committee; the Fourth or Special Political and Decolonization Committee; the Fifth or Administrative and Budgetary Committee; and the Sixth or Legal Committee. All six are committees of the whole, exact duplications of the plenary assembly. The assembly also has created other, smaller committees to carry out specific tasks such as studying a question (e.g., the ad hoc Committee on International Terrorism) or framing proposals and monitoring (e.g., the Committee on Peaceful Uses of Outer Space, the Disarmament Commission, and the Human Rights Committee). The Sixth Committee and the International Law Commission, an elected group of thirty-four jurists nominated by UN member states, have responsibility for drafting international conventions to carry out the assembly's mission of "encouraging the progressive development of international law and its codification" (Article 13).

Each year, the assembly elects a president and seventeen vice presidents who serve for that year's session. By tradition, presidents tend to come from small and middle power states, and often from the third world. Only once (1969) has a woman been elected. The president's powers are limited, but allow much to be accomplished through personal influence and political skills in guiding the work of the assembly, averting crises, bringing parties into agreement, ensuring that procedures are respected, and accelerating the cumbersome agenda.

Key to the assembly's functioning are member states' own delegations. The charter provides that each member can have no more than five representatives in the assembly (Article 9), but assembly rules have permitted five alternates and unlimited advisers and technical experts. The practice of establishing permanent missions and ambassadors began with the League of Nations. Although it is mandatory for Security Council members who must be able to meet immediately in the event of an emergency, the practice became commonplace for almost all member states with the establishment of UN headquarters in New York in 1948. Missions vary in size from about 150 (the United States and Russia) to one or two persons of diplomatic rank. Small and poor states often combine their UN mission with their embassy in Washington to save money; most states' missions grow significantly during the fall assembly sessions, sometimes including a few parliamentarians or legislators. (The U.S. House and Senate alternate in having representatives on the U.S. delegation each year.)

Delegates attend assembly and committee sessions, participate in efforts to shape agendas and debate, and represent national interests. Expertise matters and enables some delegates to be more influential than others. Because almost all states of the world are represented at the annual assembly sessions, there are many opportunities for informal bilateral and multilateral contacts, which countries may use to deal with issues outside the assembly's agenda. UN diplomats have to deal constantly with many different viewpoints and policies; they have to operate under procedures more akin to those of a parliamentary body than to traditional bilateral diplomacy; they have to deal with a huge spectrum of issues; and during the regular assembly sessions, the social obligations of endless receptions, which would be politically incorrect not to attend, can be exhausting.

As discussed in Chapter 1, multilateral diplomacy demands different skills than traditional diplomacy for countries to be effective in their representation at the UN. Former UN ambassadors have often commented that it can take up to eighteen months for a new delegate to learn the ropes and become effective. Thus, it is not uncommon for some delegates to serve a long time. The United States, however, tends to rotate its foreign service officers at the UN mission frequently, demonstrating that skill in multilateral diplomacy is not valued highly.

Ties between UN missions and home governments vary from loose to tight. Some delegations have considerable autonomy in dealing with the various issues on assembly agendas and determining how best to represent their countries' interests. Others operate on a "tighter leash" and must seek instructions from their capitals on what strategies to use and how to vote on given resolutions.

Decisionmaking in the General Assembly.   Early in the UN's history, states from the same geographic region or with shared economic or political interests formed coalitions to shape common positions on particular issues and to control a bloc of votes. Several factors led to the development of such groups. First, the charter itself specified that in electing the nonpermanent members of the Security Council, the General Assembly give consideration to "equitable geographical distribution" but offered no guidance on how to do so or what the appropriate geographic groups should be. The five recognized regional groups of states are: Western European and Other States (includes the United States, Canada, and, as of 2000, Israel under certain circumstances); Eastern European; African, Latin American, and Caribbean; and Asian. Within these regional groups, member states determine whom to champion for Security Council or ECOSOC seats, and which candidates to support for the ICJ or for secretary-general. Israel was long excluded from all regional groups until 2000, for example, which had the effect of precluding it from being a candidate for the Security Council.

A second factor in the emergence of caucusing groups is the one-state, one-vote principle. Because General Assembly decisions are made by a majority (either simple or two-thirds under specified circumstances such as elections and questions of peace and security), a stable coalition of states comprising a majority of members, like a majority political party or coalition of parties in a parliament, can control most decisions. These coalitions within the UN have tended to persist for long periods and to correspond with major substantive issues in the General Assembly. Not surprisingly, one longstanding issue dimension was an East-West one, defined largely by Cold War issues; a second was a North-South dimension related to development issues.

The Cold War led to the formation of two competing coalitions of states aligned with either the United States or the Soviet Union. The Eastern European states could be counted on to vote consistently with the Soviet Union, thus forming a true bloc that voted together against three-quarters of the resolutions passed. Many nominally nonaligned states also regularly voted with the Soviet bloc. The Western European, Latin American, and British Commonwealth states also voted closely with the United States on any issue that involved Cold War competition and also often on human rights, social concerns, and internal UN administration. Colonial and economic questions, however, produced internal tensions and fragmentation in this U.S.-dominated coalition. It held a controlling position in UN voting until 1955, but by 1960 could not muster a simple majority because of the influx of new African and Asian states. Since the Cold War's end, Russia and other East European states have tended to vote with the West Europeans or a larger "Northern" group.

The second longstanding issue dimension was the North-South one centered on economic inequalities and development, colonialism and decolonization, and great-power military capabilities. In the 1950s, developing countries were fragmented into the Afro-Asian group, the Latin American group, and the Non-Aligned Movement (NAM). With the creation of UNCTAD in 1964, the Latin American, African, and Asian states formed the Group of 77 (G-77) and UNCTAD's own system of group negotiation reinforced their growing tendency to operate as a unified bloc that constituted more than two-thirds of the UN's membership. By 1971, the G-77 dominated General Assembly agendas and voting. This then led to several years of very sharp North-South conflict. The G-77 was often supported by the Eastern European states as the Soviet Union took advantage of opportunities to escape its minority position and accuse the West of being responsible for the problems of less developed countries. As scholars Donald J. Puchala and Roger A. Coate (1989: 53) note: "For more than a decade the G-77 could, and did, steer the United Nations in directions that it wanted to move, it could, and did, commit the United Nations to principles that it wanted to legitimize, and it could, and did, demand global actions conducive to its interests. The Group of 77 ultimately could not enforce compliance with its demands, but it could bring attention to them and impressively argue for their rectitude."

In the late 1980s, the G-77's cohesion began to break down with the rapid economic growth of a number of newly industrializing countries, including the so-called Asian tigers such as Singapore, Malaysia, and South Korea. Voting in the General Assembly still clearly shows the North-South divide, but differences in social and economic conditions among Asian, African, and Latin American countries make common policy positions difficult to forge.

The developed countries, however, have never been as cohesive as the South. Many European states have been more supportive of developing countries' concerns than the United States, weakening the North's ability to operate as a coalition in responding to the South.

Other caucusing groups within the UN include the Afro-Asian group, French-speaking and English-speaking African countries, ASEAN, the Arab states, the Non-Aligned Movement, the Islamic Conference, the Nordic Group, and the European Union. (See Figure 4.2.) The level of activity and cohesion within any of these groups depend on the issue, as do the exact processes by which they formulate common positions. The EU has a formalized process of continual consultation and for delegating responsibility for enunciating common policies. Other groups rely on formal and informal meetings of delegates.

Although coalitions and blocs emerged in response to the UN's provisions for elections and voting, more decisionmaking in recent years has been done by consensus, that is, without any formal vote. In the 1990s, only 22 percent of assembly resolutions were being put to a vote (Marin-Bosch 1998: 95). Many of these consensus resolutions are "ritual resolutions," relating either to annual agenda items such as the right to development or the situation in the Palestinian territories, or they concern the budget and other housekeeping matters. Many are formulated in very general terms, thus masking dissent that would become evident if the wording were more specific. Coalitions and blocs are as active in trying to forge consensus as in marshaling votes, but the outcome is less divisive because states' individual positions are not revealed as in a roll call vote. The General Assembly's membership is now so large, however, that it is very unlikely to achieve consensus on precisely defined and specific actions.

Figure 4.2   Caucusing Groups in the United Nations (number of member states)

• *Regional Groups*
African states (43)
Asian states (49)
Latin American and Caribbean states (33)
Western European states and others (20)
Eastern European states (20)

• *Other Multilateral Groups*
Group of 77 (ca. 128)
ASEAN (9)
Non-Aligned Movement (ca. 130)
Islamic Conference (ca. 40)
Nordic Group (4)
European Union (25)

The General Assembly's shifting agendas and relevance.   Politics within the General Assembly mirror world politics, but not always the realities of power given the egalitarian principle of one-state, one-vote. It is *the* place to set the agendas of world politics, to get ideas endorsed or condemned, actions taken or rejected. Any state can propose an agenda item. As membership changed with decolonization in the 1960s, the assembly's agendas and voting patterns changed. They were no longer dominated by Cold War and decolonization issues, but reflected the new majority's interest in economic development. From the early 1960s to the mid-1980s, the G-77 endeavored to use its two-thirds majority in the assembly to achieve a number of third world goals, especially the proposed New International Economic Order (NIEO), which is discussed in Chapter 9. The pattern of lopsided voting and frequent condemnations of U.S. policies led the United States, in particular, to regard the General Assembly, even the UN in general, as a "hostile place" by the mid-1970s. That pattern began to shift in the mid-1980s, however, as a result of the eroding consensus within the G-77 previously noted, changes in Soviet and U.S. policies that increased the Security Council's role, and the increased importance of the IMF and World Bank for dealing with debt and development issues. The result has been a steady decline in the assembly's role.

Today, the North-South divide persists around issues of economic inequality and development, self-determination (particularly for Palestine), and great-power military capabilities. The concept of human security encompasses a set of agenda items that incorporates human rights, development, international security, and the environment. These issues, including most notably neocolonialism resolutions and appeals for action to redress global inequalities, are among the most divisive. Political rights, state sovereignty, and UN intervention, too, have emerged as major, divisive issues. These are all issues where the South and the Non-Aligned Movement still show remarkable voting coherence. As one study concludes, "The North-South division now overwhelmingly defines the terms of political debate in the Assembly. . . . And views of self-determination and economic development . . . reflect the continuing great differences between rich and poor nations" (Kim and Russett 1997: 37, 55).

Many criticisms of the UN are really criticisms of the General Assembly. The number of resolutions passed by the General Assembly steadily increased over time from about 119 annually during the first five years, to a peak of 343 per year during 1981–1985 when efforts to reduce the number began. In the 1990s, the number of resolutions averaged 328 per year (Marin-Bosch 1998). At the 57th General Assembly in 2002, 301 resolutions were approved, many passed with little concern for implementation.

Since the Cold War's end, the General Assembly has been marginalized as the epicenter of UN activity shifted back to the Security Council and Secretariat, much to the dismay of the South, which would like more consultation between the General Assembly and Security Council on peace and security issues. Likewise, with the UN Secretariat forced by its most powerful members (and biggest contributors) to downsize and streamline in the name of efficiency and improved management, the South has worried that its interests are getting short shrift. Unquestionably, the General Assembly needs reform and revitalization. The difficulty lies in accomplishing it despite countless special committees charged with making recommendations. There has been some progress since the mid-1980s in reducing the agenda and number of resolutions as well as requiring explicit renewal of programs or funds based on continuing relevance and effectiveness. Nothing can be done, however, without the political will of a majority of states to reform.

■ The Security Council

Under Article 24 of the UN Charter, the Security Council has primary responsibility for maintenance of international peace and security and the authority to act on behalf of *all* members of the UN. Provisions for carrying out this role are spelled out in Chapters VI and VII. Chapter VI deals with peaceful settlement of disputes, providing a wide range of techniques to investigate disputes and help parties achieve resolution without using force. Chapter VII specifies the Security Council's authority to identify aggressors and commit all UN members to take enforcement measures such as economic sanctions or to provide military forces for joint action. Prior to 1990, the Security Council used its enforcement powers under Chapter VII on only two occasions, relying on the mechanisms in Chapter VI to respond to conflicts during the Cold War years. For example, prior to 1992 all UN peacekeeping forces were authorized under Chapter VI. One dramatic change since the Cold War's end is the Security Council's increased use of Chapter VII, including its provisions for economic sanctions and military enforcement action.

The Security Council was kept small in order to facilitate more efficient (i.e., swifter) decisionmaking in dealing with threats to international peace and security. It is also the only UN body that has both permanent and nonpermanent members. The five permanent members (P-5)—the United States, Great Britain, France, Russia (successor state to the seat of the Soviet Union in 1992), and the People's Republic of China (PRC, replacing the Republic of China in 1971)—are the key to Security Council decisionmaking since each has veto power. The nonpermanent members, originally six in number and expanded to ten in 1965, are elected for two-year terms and participate fully in the council's work. At least four nonpermanent members must vote in favor of a resolution for it to pass. Under current rules, no country may serve successive terms as a nonpermanent member. Five of the nonpermanent seats go to Africa and Asia, two each to Latin America and Western Europe, and one to Eastern Europe.

The designation of permanent members reflected the distribution of military power in 1945 and the desire to ensure the UN's ability to respond quickly and decisively to any aggression. Neither the United States nor the Soviet Union would have accepted UN membership without veto power. It also reflected a realistic acceptance by others that the UN could not undertake enforcement action either against its strongest members or without their concurrence. The veto, however, has always been controversial among small states and middle powers. The current council composition, however, is clearly an anachronism and discussion of "equitable representation" is a major reform issue.

The right to bring issues before the Security Council is not reserved for council members. Any state, including non-UN members, has this right, although there is no guarantee of action. The secretary-general can also bring a matter to the council's attention. This has become more important in recent years with efforts to enhance the secretariat's ability to address problems before they become crises. Nonmembers may attend formal meetings and address the council upon request when they have an interest in a particular issue. This practice has become increasingly routinized, and by 2002, approximately one-third of official meetings involved participation by noncouncil members (Hurd 2002: 42).

The Security Council's functioning and prestige have waxed and waned. The founders envisioned it as the UN's central organ, charged with maintaining international security and participating in key tasks such as election of the secretary-general, justices to the International Court of Justice, and new members in collaboration with the General Assembly. During the 1940s it held approximately 130 meetings a year. The Cold War diminished its use and in 1959 only five meetings were held. The Soviet Union used its veto power frequently during the Cold War, not only to block action on many peace and security issues but also to block admission of Western-supported new members and nominees for secretary-general. The United States did not exercise its veto until the 1970s, reflecting its early dominance and many friends. (See Table 4.1 for a summary of vetoes cast, and note how infrequently the veto has been used since 1990.) In the 1990s, the early precedent that allowed abstentions not to be counted as negative votes (i.e., vetoes) became particularly important. The number of abstentions peaked in 1992 with nineteen abstentions. China abstained a total of twenty-seven times between 1990 and 1996 on a series of enforcement measures (including those against Iraq), thus registering its disagreement but not blocking action. Russia began the same practice in 1995.

In the late 1980s, the Security Council's activity, power, and prestige

Table 4.1   Vetoes in the Security Council, 1946–2003

Period	China[a]	France	Britain	U.S.	USSR/ Russia	Total
1946–1955	1	2			80	83
1956–1965		2	3		26	31
1966–1975	2	2	10	12	7	33
1976–1985		9	11	34	6	60
1985–1996		3	8	24	2	37
1996–2003	2			8		10

Source: Global Policy Forum, http://www.globalpolicy.org/
Notes: a. Between 1946 and 1971, the Chinese seat on the Security Council was occupied by the Republic of China (Taiwan).

increased again following major shifts in Soviet foreign policy. There was a quick succession of breakthroughs in regional conflicts, including the Iran-Iraq war, Afghanistan, Central America, Namibia, and Cambodia. The number of Security Council meetings per year rose dramatically, but the council also began to conduct more informal, private consultations and to reach more decisions by consensus than by formal voting. This practice has drawn criticism from many nonmembers who feel that it exacerbates the exclusivity of the council. Council presidents now play an active role in facilitating discussions and consensus building, determining when the members are ready to reach a decision. The president also confers regularly with the secretary-general, with relevant states, and other actors that are not represented on the council. The presidency rotates monthly among the fifteen members. In addition, the P-5 informally consults, a practice that has enhanced their close cooperation, but also fueled perceptions of great-power collusion.

The confrontation with Iraq in 1990 marked a high point in the Security Council's functioning. The strength of agreement among both the P-5 and the nonpermanent members of the council at that time was extraordinary. Yet, the UN was unable to "make war" itself and had to stand aside while the U.S. and allied forces took the lead without formally reporting to the Security Council as the authorizing organ. Even though the council resumed its lead role with the ceasefire and punitive sanctions imposed on Iraq, the questions raised about its ability to fulfill the mandate of maintaining peace and security would return repeatedly throughout the 1990s.

Since 1987, the Security Council has taken action on more armed conflicts, made more decisions under Chapter VII of the UN Charter, authorized more peacekeeping operations, and imposed more types of sanctions in more situations than ever before. It took the unprecedented step of creating war crimes tribunals to prosecute individuals responsible for genocide and war crimes in Rwanda and the former Yugoslavia. It authorized NATO bombing against Bosnian Serb forces in Bosnia in 1995. It has authorized UN-administered protectorates in Kosovo and East Timor. It expanded definitions of threats to peace to include terrorism following the September 11, 2001, attacks on the World Trade Center and Pentagon. At special sessions in 2000 and 2001, the council identified the HIV/AIDS epidemic and the multifaceted crisis in Africa as security threats. (See Chapters 3, 8, and 12 for further elaboration.)

At the height of post–Cold War optimism about a strengthened Security Council role, the members convened an extraordinary summit meeting of heads of state and government in January 1992. They commissioned then Secretary-General Boutros Boutros-Ghali to do a special report. The resulting *Agenda for Peace*, published in 1992 and revised in 1995, enlarged the debate over the UN, the secretary-general, and the Security Council's roles. This debate about what the UN can and cannot do in dealing with threats to peace has permeated the council's work ever since. The 1990s also revealed again the limits on the UN's role as an independent actor when the United States resumed a posture of ambivalent multilateralism after the 1993 debacle in Somalia. Congress' refusal to authorize full payment of U.S. dues and share of peacekeeping expenses created a financial crisis for the UN. Other members could never be sure what commitments the United States would keep and what it would be willing to contribute in financial, political, and material support for UN-sponsored actions. This made clear how important U.S. willingness to play a role of first among equals, acting collectively with other member states, is to the Security Council's functioning. No one else has the same power to lead. (See Chapter 7 for further discussion of states.)

The decision by the United States and NATO in 1999 to undertake bombing of Yugoslavia (Serbia) without explicit Security Council authorization and in the face of Russian and Chinese opposition signaled the divide within the P-5. Yet the Security Council assumed a major role in Kosovo with the end of NATO bombing. The council unanimously passed Resolution 1441 in November 2002 to compel Iraq's compliance with efforts to destroy its weapons of mass destruction, but there was no agreement on a resolution authorizing war in March 2003, leading the United States and Great Britain to form an ad hoc coalition for military action against Iraq. The fact that war was conducted without Security Council authorization has resulted in a further lively debate. Is the council a "failed and debilitated body"? Has the UN "crashed," as legal scholar Michael Glennon (2003) contends? Or can the council continue to perform vital tasks as Luck and others (2003) suggest?

In short, the charter gives the council enormous formal power, but does not give it direct control over the means to use that power. It depends upon the voluntary cooperation of states willing to contribute to peacekeeping missions, to enforce sanctions, to pay their dues, and to support enforcement actions either under UN command or by a coalition of the willing. Most important, states' voluntary compliance depends on their perceptions of the legitimacy of the council and its actions—its symbolic power (Hurd 2002: 35).

The increase in Security Council activity in the 1990s, however, led many members to push strongly for reform in the council's membership in order that it reflect the world of the twenty-first century, not the world of 1945. This debate, which we take up later in the chapter, is very much about how to ensure the continuing legitimacy of the council's authority and, secondarily, how to make the council function more effectively.

■ *The Economic and Social Council (ECOSOC)*

Although the sections of the UN Charter (Chapters IX and X) dealing with ECOSOC are short and very general, this is the most complex part of the UN system, covering the broadest areas of activity, the majority of expenditures, and greatest number of programs. The founders of the UN envisaged that the various specialized agencies, ranging from the ILO, WHO, and FAO to the World Bank and the IMF, would play primary roles in operational activities devoted to economic and social advancement, with ECOSOC responsible for coordinating those activities. Hence, the charter speaks of ECOSOC's functions in terms of that coordination, as well as undertaking research and preparing reports on economic and social issues, making recommendations, preparing conventions (treaties), and convening conferences. Of those tasks, coordination has proven the most problematic since a myriad of activities lie outside the effective jurisdiction of ECOSOC. Articles 61–66 of the charter empower ECOSOC only to issue recommendations to the specialized agencies, for example, and to receive reports from them. It has no control over the agencies' budgets or secretariats. Recommendations and multilateral conventions drafted by ECOSOC require General Assembly approval (and, in the case of conventions, ratification by member states). The steady expansion of UN economic and social activities has left ECOSOC with an unmanageable task—one that has led to persistent, but largely unsuccessful calls for reform since the late 1940s. As early as 1969 the Jackson Report warned that "the machine as a whole has become unmanageable. . . . It is becoming slower and more unwieldy like some prehistoric monster" (quoted in Fomerand 1990: 2).

ECOSOC's membership has been expanded through two charter amendments. The original eighteen members were increased to twenty-seven in 1965 and to fifty-four in 1973. Members are elected by the General Assembly to three-year terms based on nominations by the regional blocs. Motivated by recognition that states with the ability to pay should be continuously represented, four of the five permanent members of the Security Council (all but China) and major developed countries have been regularly reelected. Through consultative status with ECOSOC many NGOs have official relationships with the UN and its activities. (See Chapter 6 for further discussion.) ECOSOC meetings are held once a year and alternate between UN headquarters in New York and Geneva, where several of the specialized agencies and other programs are headquartered. Decisions are reached by simple majority votes (or consensus).

The economic and social activities that ECOSOC is expected to coordinate are spread among subsidiary bodies, functional commissions, regional commissions, and the seventeen specialized agencies. A number of entities created by the General Assembly, such as the UN Development Programme (UNDP), UN Fund for Population Activities (UNFPA), UN Children's Fund, and World Food Programme, report to both the General Assembly and ECOSOC, compounding the complexity and confusion. The scope of ECOSOC's agenda includes such diverse topics as housing, narcotic drug control, water resources, desertification, population, trade, rights of children, industrial development, literacy, refugees, science and technology, the status of women, the problems of the disabled, the environment, and rights of indigenous peoples. Human rights and development form the two largest subject areas.

The specialized agencies and their relationship to ECOSOC.   Several of the specialized agencies, including the ILO, UPU, and WMO (World Meteorological Organization), predate the UN itself, as discussed in Chapter 3. Article 57 laid out the broad terms under which these agencies were to be brought into relationship with the UN. The first agreement, with the ILO, provided a model for others, although the system of weighted voting in the Bretton Woods institutions distinguishes them from other agencies. The agreements cover such things as exchange of information and documents, treatment to be given by agencies to recommendations from the UN organs, and cooperation in personnel, statistical services, and budgetary arrangements. One of the factors that has complicated the relationship of specialized agencies to ECOSOC is geographical dispersal. ILO, ITU, WIPO (World Intellectual Property Organization), and WHO are headquartered in Geneva, but FAO is in Rome, UNESCO in Paris, ICAO (International Civil Aviation Organization) in Montreal, the IMF and World Bank in Washington, IMO (International Maritime Organization) in London, UNIDO (United Nations Industrial Development Organization) in Vienna, and UPU in Berne (Switzerland). The same pattern has held true in the agency offices in the field with agencies having their own separate buildings and staffs. This dispersal affects efficiency, budgets, and coordination.

Historically, despite their links to the UN, the specialized agencies have operated quite independently. Since directors-general of the agencies have the same diplomatic rank as the UN's secretary-general, they have often perceived themselves as operating their own fiefdoms. How can one achieve an integrated international program when different agencies, each with its own administration and objectives, are carrying out similar activities? The ILO is illustrative. Its activities include employment promotion, vocational guidance, social security, safety and health, labor laws and relations, and rural institutions. These overlap with FAO's concern with land reform, UNESCO's mandate in education, WHO's focus on health standards, and UNIDO's concern with manpower in small industries. The result is constant coordination problems.

The Bretton Woods institutions, in particular, have operated quite independently of ECOSOC and the rest of the UN system. Beginning in 1998, this began to change, however, with ECOSOC hosting annual meetings of finance ministers and the active participation of the World Bank, the IMF, and the WTO in the 2002 International Conference on Financing for Development organized by the UN in Monterrey, Mexico. Likewise, in the late 1990s, resident directors of the World Bank and IMF began cooperating more with other UN agency personnel working in developing countries.

Functional commissions.   Part of ECOSOC's work is done in a set of ten functional commissions: Social Development, Human Rights, Narcotic Drugs, the Status of Women, Science and Technology for Development, Sustainable Development, Population and Development, Crime Prevention and Criminal Justice, Statistics, and Forests. The Commission on Statistics reflects the importance of statistical studies and analysis to economic and social programs and the major contribution the UN system makes annually to governments, researchers, and students worldwide through its statistical studies. The wide range of data on social and economic conditions that has been gathered over the years is vital to dealing with various world problems. For example, when the General Assembly inaugurated the First Development Decade in 1961, women were among the groups singled out for development funds, even though there were then no data on the economic status of women. Only with the publication in 1991 of the first edition of *The World's Women*, compiled under the auspices of the Commission on the Status of Women, were there finally data to inform policymaking on issues relating to women around the world.

The Commission on the Status of Women was established in 1946 to prepare recommendations and reports concerning the promotion of women's political, economic, social, and educational rights and on any problems requiring immediate attention. It drafted a series of early conventions on women's political and marital rights as well as the Declaration on the Elimination of Discrimination against Women adopted by the General Assembly in 1967 and the Convention on the Elimination of All Forms of Discrimination Against Women that was approved in 1979 and entered into force in 1981. After the 1995 Fourth World Conference on Women in Beijing, the commission was given a central role in monitoring implementation of the Platform for Action. Its work through 2005–2006 will continue to relate to these tasks and follow up to the 2000 Review Conference. The commission has forty-five members elected by ECOSOC for four-year terms and meets annually for ten days.

Regional commissions.   In addition to the functional commissions, ECOSOC created a series of regional commissions beginning in 1947 with the Economic Commission for Europe and the Economic Commission for Asia and the Far East (renamed in the 1970s the Economic and Social Commission for Asia and the Pacific, following the formation of the Commission for Western Asia). In 1948, the Economic Commission for Latin America (ECLA) convened, and in 1958, the Economic Commission for Africa was established. These regional commissions were designed to stimulate regional approaches to development with studies and initiatives to promote regional projects.

Field activities.   One of the major factors in the proliferation of economic and social activities, beyond the increase in programs and activities of different agencies, has been the growth of operational field activities, especially technical assistance. Unlike the League of Nations, the UN and other post–World War II international organizations have become heavily involved in disbursing funds and expertise to member governments, most notably developing countries. This has required changes in staffing and organization and posed additional challenges for coordinating what is happening in the field.

Technical assistance has been a core part of UN system development activities. Leaving the mobilization of capital and help with infrastructure to the World Bank institutions, the UN's own programs train people and introduce new technologies, often with specialized agencies such as WHO, FAO, UNESCO, or one of the regional economic commissions. UNDP, established in 1965 by the General Assembly, is the lead organization for technical assistance programs. Its resident representatives in recipient countries coordinate all UN agency programs and link the UN with the recipient government. Some of these activities relating to field activities are explored further in Chapter 9, but as one observer noted, "The UN's thoroughly fragmented and feudal nature is a big liability for critical programmes in the field" (quoted in Weiss and Pasic 1997: 41). Hence, it is not hard to see why ECOSOC's mandate for coordination has been almost impossible to fulfill. Coordination is inherently difficult within any complex organization, and national governments have their own problems in this regard. Indeed, one analyst argues that ECOSOC's problems are attributable in part to "the absence of coordination at the national level in regard to international policies and programmes. . . . different ministries and divisions were involved in different countries and initiatives varying slightly in approach but having very similar objectives could well be launched and carried through simultaneously in two or more international agencies" (Taylor 2000: 108). ECOSOC reform efforts are discussed below.

■ The Secretariat

This body of about 7,500 professional and clerical staff based in New York, Geneva, Vienna, Nairobi, and elsewhere around the world are international civil servants, individuals who, though nationals of member countries, represent the international community. Early IGO secretariats were established by the Universal Postal Union and International Telegraph Union in the 1860s and 1870s, but their members were not independent of national governments. The League of Nations established the first truly international secretariat, responsible for carrying out the will of the League's members, impartial or neutral in serving the organization as a whole and dedicated to its principles. A complementary principle of an international civil service is for member states to respect the international character and responsibilities of the staff, regardless of their nationality. This practice carried over to the United Nations and the specialized agencies, with secretariat members recruited from an ever-broader geographic base as the membership expanded. Secretariat members are not expected to give up their national loyalty, but to refrain from promoting national interests—a difficult task at times in a world of strong nationalisms.

Secretary-General.   The secretary-general's position has been termed "one of the most ill-defined: a combination of chief administrative officer of the United Nations and global diplomat with a fat portfolio whose pages are blank" (Hall 1994: 2). The secretary-general is manager of the organization, responsible for providing leadership to the secretariat, preparing the UN's budget, submitting an annual report to the General Assembly, and overseeing studies conducted at the request of the other major organs. Article 99 of the charter authorized the secretary-general "to bring to the attention of the Security Council any matter which in his opinion may threaten the maintenance of international peace and security." All seven secretaries-general have drawn on the charter's spirit as the basis for political initiatives. Yet, the secretary-general must simultaneously meet the demands of two constituencies—member states and the secretariat. States elect the UN's chief administrator and do not want to be either upstaged or publicly opposed by the person in that position. The secretary-general also has to answer to the secretariat personnel working in programs and specialized agencies across the UN system. The balancing act is not always easy.

By practice, the secretary-general holds office for a five-year renewable term on recommendation by the Security Council and election by two-thirds of the General Assembly. The process of nomination is an intensely political one, with the five permanent members having key input. For example, the United States strongly opposed the reelection of Boutros Boutros-Ghali in 1996, forcing member states to agree on an alternate candidate, Kofi Annan. Efforts to establish a better means of selecting this global leader have not born fruit. Not surprisingly, those elected have tended to come from relatively small and neutral states. (See Figure 4.3.)

The UN secretaries-general have been a key factor in the emergence of the UN itself as an autonomous actor in world politics. Through the secretary-general's leadership "an international organization is transformed from being a forum of multilateral diplomacy into something which is more than the sum of its inputs . . . and make[s] more decisions on behalf of the whole community of nation-states" (Cox 1969: 207). Since 1945, a pattern of leadership has evolved that has taken advantage of opportunities for initiatives, applied flexible interpretations of charter provisions, and sought mandates from UN policy organs as necessary. Successive secretaries-general have developed their own political roles and that of the institution. Their personalities and interpretation of the charter, as well as world

Figure 4.3 UN Secretaries-General (1946–2003)

Secretary-General	Nationality	Dates of Service
Trygve Lie	Norway	1946–1953
Dag Hammarskjöld	Sweden	1953–1961
U Thant	Burma	1961–1971
Kurt Waldheim	Austria	1972–1981
Javier Pérez de Cuéllar	Peru	1982–1991
Boutros Boutros-Ghali	Egypt	1992–1996
Kofi Annan	Ghana	1997–present

events, have combined to increase the power, resources, and importance of the position. More than just a senior civil servant, the UN secretary-general has become an international political figure.

The UN secretary-general is well placed to serve as a neutral communications channel and intermediary for the global community. Although he represents the institution, he can act independently of the policy organs even when resolutions have condemned a party to a dispute, maintaining lines of communication and representing the institution's commitment to peaceful settlement and alleviation of human suffering. While these tasks call for diplomatic skills, it has become essential for the secretary-general also to have strong managerial and budgetary skills.

A key resource for UN secretaries-general is the power of persuasion. The "force" of majorities behind resolutions may lend greater legitimacy to initiatives, though it may not ensure any greater degree of success. Autonomy is also key to the secretary-general's influence. For example, during the Security Council's 2002–2003 debate over Iraq's failure to disarm and cooperate with UN inspections and whether to authorize a U.S.-led war, Kofi Annan steered an independent course by pushing for Iraqi compliance, council unity, and peace. This facilitates a secretary-general's ability to serve as a neutral intermediary. U Thant stated, "The Secretary-General must always be prepared to take an initiative, no matter what the consequences to him or his office may be, if he sincerely believes that it might make the difference between peace and war" (quoted in Young 1967: 284). Annan put it more bluntly in saying, "I know some people have accused me of using diplomacy. That's my job" (quoted in Crossette 1999: A8).

Dag Hammarskjöld, the second secretary-general, played a key part in shaping the role and the UN during the critical period 1953–1961. Hammarskjöld articulated principles for UN involvement in peacekeeping. He demonstrated the secretary-general's efficacy as an agent for peaceful settlement of disputes, beginning with his successful 1954–1955 mediation of the release of eleven U.S. airmen under UN command in Korea who had been imprisoned by the Communist Chinese. This accomplishment was particularly notable because the People's Republic of China was then excluded from the UN. Hammarskjöld also oversaw the initiation of UN peacekeeping operations with the creation of the United Nations Emergency Force (UNEF) at the time of the 1956 Suez crisis.

Javier Pérez de Cuéllar, the fifth secretary-general, presided over the UN's transformation from the brink of irrelevance in the 1980s to an active instrument for resolving conflicts and promoting international peace at the end of the Cold War. In his persistent, patient, low-key approach to Israel's 1982 invasion of Lebanon, the Falklands/Malvinas War, the Iran-Iraq War, and the ongoing problems in Cyprus, Namibia, Afghanistan, and elsewhere, he epitomized the ideal intermediary. He also noted that Article 99 "contains the three elements of right, responsibility, and discretion . . . [that have led] the Secretary-General himself to help to moderate conflicts or negotiate solutions" (Pérez de Cuéllar 1993: 129–130).

Secretary-General Boutros Boutros-Ghali pushed the boundaries of the office further with the benefit of independent UN information gathering and analytical capability. As one commentator describes, "He saw an opening for the UN in the post–Cold War disarray and plunged: prodding the United States to send thousands of American soldiers to rescue Somalis from famine; urging the United Nations into new terrain in Cambodia, Bosnia and Haiti; and, more recently, making a rare journey to North Korea to help solve an impasse over the nuclear program of the isolated Communist nation" (Preston 1994: 10–11).

Boutros-Ghali's activism and his antagonistic relationship with the United States led to his defeat for a second term in 1996. Instead, Kofi Annan, a Ghanaian national, became the seventh secretary-general and the first from within the UN bureaucracy. Among his previous posts were undersecretary-general for peacekeeping operations, special representative to the secretary-general to the former Yugoslavia, and special envoy to NATO. A much quieter individual, Annan pledged change, yet has proven even more activist than his predecessor, earning the 2001 Nobel Peace Prize for himself and the organization. He has carried out extensive administrative and budgetary reforms within the UN, including structural changes within the secretariat, to use the UN's limited resources more efficiently. He initiated steps to strengthen liaison between various departments and NGOs, and dialogue with business leaders. Annan is the first secretary-general to make a special effort to build a better relationship with the U.S. Congress, an important step given American predominance and Congress' refusal to appropriate full funding for U.S. dues to the UN for much of the 1990s. In fact, he helped persuade U.S. Senator Jesse Helms, a major critic of the UN, to accept a deal for paying U.S. arrears over a three-year period. As Annan put it, "The United Nations needs the United States to achieve our goals, and I believe the United States needs the United Nations no less" (quoted in Gourevitch 2003: 54).

Annan has been widely respected and was reelected by acclamation in 2001. He has used his "bully pulpit" as UN head, including his annual reports to the General Assembly, to speak out on many issues and to take a wide variety of initiatives from HIV/AIDS to the Global Compact with private corporations. Following NATO's intervention in Kosovo in 1999 without explicit Security Council authorization but in support of an emerging norm of humanitarian intervention, Annan chose to speak directly to the meaning of state sovereignty, saying (UN 1999: GA/9596), "Nothing in the charter precludes a recognition that there are rights beyond borders." He took the unprecedented step of publishing independent reports on the UN's failures in the disastrous massacre in the UN-declared safe area of Srebrenica, in the Rwandan genocide, and in security for UN personnel in Iraq. He has not been afraid to publicly accept blame. A former Canadian ambassador called this "nothing short of revolutionary at the United Nations" (quoted in Crossette 1999: A8).

The end of Cold War tensions contributed to a renewed interest in the role of the UN secretary-general as broker, mediator, and world figure and underscored the importance of the international context to that role. The increased demands on the UN system, however, and the persistent problems with lack of coordination made attention to the organizational shortcomings of the UN critical. Hence, the job now requires top managerial skills, most particularly creativity in making the most of the UN's very modest budgetary resources.

Functions of the Secretariat.   The UN Secretariat is subject to many problems common to other complex organizations. It has been criticized for lapses in its neutrality, duplication of tasks, and poor administrative practices. Member states share blame with UN secretaries-general and staff for the problems. General Assembly and Security Council resolutions may be vague and unrealistic; objectives often depend on member governments' actions and other factors to be fulfilled; and, since the UN is a political organization, the secretariat is subject to interference from member states. Indeed, many member states do not necessarily want the UN to have an effective secretariat and secretary-general since that could diminish their own ability to control what the UN does.

Only about a third of secretariat members are at UN headquarters in New York and Geneva. Many are involved in field operations in more than 140 countries. Their work often has little to do with the symbolic politics of the General Assembly, or even the high politics debates of the Security Council. It involves the implementation of the economic and social programs that represent much of the UN's tangible contribution to fulfilling the charter promises. The secretariat is also responsible for gathering statistical data, issuing studies and reports, servicing meetings, preparing documentation, and providing translations of speeches, debates, and documents in the UN's six official languages.

Secretariat reform.   The secretariat grew almost constantly until the 1990s: from 300 persons in 1946 to 3,237 in 1964, rising to 11,303 in 1974, and reaching a peak of 14,691 in 1994. This growth stemmed from both the expansion of the UN's membership and the proliferation of programs and activities, ranging from peacekeeping missions to technical assistance. As the UN bureaucracy expanded, charges of political bias and administrative inefficiency surfaced. The United States has been particularly vocal in this regard. During the 1950s and early 1960s, Soviet secretariat personnel were charged with maintaining too close a relationship with their government. During the 1970s, the charge was that heads of some specialized agencies, particularly UNESCO's Amadou-Mahtar M'Bow, FAO's Edouard Saouma, and WHO's Halfdan Mahler, were spokespersons for the third world. In the 1980s, the United States focused on the bloated size of the secretariat. As Sir Brian Urquhart (1991: 352), former UN undersecretary-general, observed, "Too many top-level officials, political appointments, rotten boroughs, and pointless programs had rendered the secretariat fat and flabby over the years."

The first five secretaries-general paid little attention to internal management of the secretariat and also had little incentive for change until the 1990s. Thus, it took the UN over fifty years to implement management systems such as program reviews, internal audits, performance evaluations of staff, and effective recruitment and promotion practices. Even then, developed countries were more concerned about effective management, financial control, and clear objectives than many developing countries. As Julius K. Nyerere, former president of Tanzania, said in 1995, "We all want to see the United Nations well managed. But it is not a business; its operations cannot be judged solely by 'efficiency' in money terms" (quoted in Beigbeder 2000: 207).

When Kofi Annan became secretary-general in January 1997, he was pressured by the United States in particular to undertake the task of reducing the size of the secretariat by 25 percent and implementing other reforms. These included merging departments, cutting administrative costs, strengthening the UN resident coordinators' roles as leaders of UN country teams, preparing a code of conduct for the staff, and reducing documentation by 25 percent. In addition, Annan's "quiet revolution" involved a number of important structural changes such as grouping thirty departments into four sectoral areas (peace and security, humanitarian affairs, development, and economic and social affairs); creating an executive committee to coordinate the work of each; establishing a senior management group to bring coherence to the UN's work and serve as a cabinet; inaugurating the post of deputy secretary-general; setting up a kind of think tank for the secretariat to provide analytical and research capacity independent of member governments; centralizing development administration in the UN Development Group; reorganizing the Department of Humanitarian Affairs into a new Office for the Coordination of Humanitarian Affairs; and consolidating human rights bodies under the Office of the High Commissioner for Human Rights. He could implement these changes because they did not require charter amendments.

At the beginning of the new millennium, it was clear that steps were being taken in the direction of secretariat reform, including the creation of a UN System Integrated Plan on AIDS in 2001 that linked AIDS-related budgets and work plans of twenty-nine UN funds, programs, and agencies. In the area of peacekeeping, the Brahimi Report of 2000 called for strengthening the secretariat's ability to support operations, and the General Assembly approved a 50 percent increase in staff for the Department of Peacekeeping Operations and more flexibility in administration. In 2002, a new system went into effect for recruiting, placing, and promoting staff that gave more emphasis to merit, competence, and accountability for results than tenure and precedent.

Although concern about the secretariat's efficiency is widespread, no country has been as adamant in demanding reforms and staff reductions as the United States. Ironically, the United States has limited the scope of secretariat reform through its insistence on budget cuts that reduce resources, create uncertainty, and lower staff morale (Paul 1997: 2).

Whereas the Secretariat, ECOSOC, the General Assembly, and Security Council have all experienced proliferating demands for action and, as a result of the inevitable growth of agendas, programs, and activities, provoked urgent calls for greater coordination, efficiency, and reform, the International Court of Justice has been underutilized for much of its history. Its role is much more narrowly defined, but no less important within the UN system.

■ The International Court of Justice (ICJ)

As the judicial arm of the UN, the International Court of Justice shares responsibility with the other major organs for insuring that the principles of the charter are followed. Its special role is providing states with an impartial body for settling legal disputes in accordance with international law and giving advisory opinions on legal questions referred to it by international agencies.

The General Assembly and Security Council play a joint role in electing the fifteen judges who serve nine-year terms (five are elected every three years). On twenty-two occasions, they have also sought advisory opinions from the ICJ on legal issues relating to the functioning of the UN. Among the more prominent of these are the *Reparation for Injuries Suffered in the Service of the United Nations* opinion (ICJ Advisory Opinion 1949) in which the UN's international legal personality was clarified; the *Certain Expenses of the United Nations* (ICJ Advisory Opinion 1962), which declared peacekeeping expenses part of the fiscal obligations of member states; and the *Reservations to the Convention on the Prevention and Punishment of the Crime of Genocide* that provided an opinion on the issue of reservations to multilateral treaties (ICJ Advisory Opinion 1951). In the first, the UN was accorded the right to seek payment from a state held responsible for the injury or death of a UN employee. With this case, the ICJ also established that it had the power to interpret the charter, although no such power was expressly conferred upon it either by the charter or by the court's own statute or rules.

Assessments of the court frequently dwell on its relatively light case load due to the reluctance of states to submit disputes, but other opinions stress its contributions to "the process of systematizing, consolidating, codifying and progressively developing international law" (Ramcharan 2000: 177). In this regard, the ICJ has been important to the constitutional development of global governance and complementary in its role to the UN's political organs. As former court president Sir Robert Jennings noted on the fiftieth anniversary of the court, "the International Court of Justice . . . needs to be envisaged not in isolation, but as one major partner in a general complex of different kinds of decision-making . . . Judicial decision-making and political decision-making are very different from each other. . . . their functions are not rival but complementary" (Peck and Lee 1997: 79–80). Thus, the ICJ has contributed to peaceful settlement of disputes of several different kinds, most particularly those involving land and maritime boundaries, and to restoring peace between parties, although governments still prefer to use political methods in many cases. When dealing with the UN Charter and the legality of acts of other UN organs, the court, in the words of Justice Mohammed Bedjaoui, has shown "discretion, measure, modesty, restraint, caution, sometimes even humility" (quoted in Ramcharan 2000: 183). Thus, in the *Reparation for Injury* case cited above, the court took an activist approach to its powers, but in its 1971 advisory opinion on Namibia, it took a narrower view that it did not have power to review the actions by the General Assembly and Security Council (ICJ Advisory Opinion 1971 [*Legal Consequences for States of the Continued Presence of South Africa in Namibia*]). In 1992, the court also took a narrow view of its role when asked to authorize provisional measures requested by Libya after the Security Council threatened it with sanctions unless it extradited nationals accused of participation in the Lockerbie bombing of Pan Am Flight 103 (ICJ 1992 [*Questions of Interpretation and Application of the 1971 Montreal Convention arising from the Aerial Incident at Lockerbie*]). Some would suggest the court abdicated its authority in this situation (Ramcharan 2000: 189). Others see the ICJ moving toward a broader judicial review role.

■ The Trusteeship Council
This council was originally established to oversee the administration of the non-self-governing trust territories that carried over from the League of Nations' mandate system. These were former German colonies, mostly in Africa, that were placed under the League-supervised control of other pow-

ers (Great Britain, France, Belgium, South Africa, and Japan) because they were deemed unprepared for self-determination or independence. The mandates for Lebanon, Syria, Jordan, and Iraq were terminated and each country granted independence after World War II. Great Britain turned the Palestine mandate over to the UN in 1947 when it was no longer able to cope with rising conflict between Arabs and Jews. The eleven UN trust territories also included Pacific islands that the United States had liberated from Japan during World War II. The council's supervisory activities included reporting on the status of the people in the territories, making annual reports, and conducting periodic visits to the territories.

At the initial Trusteeship Council session in 1947, the first secretary-general, Trygve Lie, stated that the "ultimate goal is to give the Trust territories full statehood," and, hence, the council would be working for its own demise (quoted in Groom 2000: 142). Over the years, it did just that and more. The council terminated the last trusteeship agreement when the people of the Trust Territory of the Pacific Islands voted in November 1993 for free association with the United States. The Trusteeship Council and system of supervision also provided a model for the peaceful transition to independence for other colonial and dependent peoples, thus playing a role in the remarkable process of decolonization during the 1950s and 1960s.

The council continues to exist in large part because of the difficulties of amending the UN Charter, but it no longer meets in annual sessions. In recent years, there has been discussion of new functions for the Trusteeship Council. One proposal calls for giving the Trusteeship Council responsibility for monitoring conditions affecting the global commons (seas, seabed, and outer space) and for providing policy guidance in view of long-term global trends. Another calls for using it to assist "failed states." A third proposal would transform the council into a forum for minority and indigenous peoples.

■ World Politics and the Evolution of the United Nations

The United Nations has always mirrored what was happening in the world, and world politics has, in turn, shaped the evolution of the UN and its organs. In this short section, we look briefly at a number of key political developments and how they affected the UN and its functioning over time.

▨ Politics in the Cold War World

The World War II coalition of great powers (the United States, the Soviet Union, Great Britain, France, and China), whose unity had been key to the UN's founding, became a victim of rising tensions almost before the first General Assembly session in 1946. Developments in Europe and Asia between 1946 and 1950 soon made it clear that the emerging Cold War would have fundamental effects on the UN. How could a collective security system operate when there was no unity among the great powers upon whose cooperation it depended? Even the admission of new members to the UN was affected between 1950 and 1955, as each side vetoed applications from states that were allied with the other.

The Cold War made Security Council actions on peace and security threats extremely problematic. It resulted in some conflicts, such as the French and American wars in Vietnam and Soviet interventions in Czechoslovakia and Hungary, not being brought to the UN at all. A UN response to the North Korean invasion of South Korea in 1950 was possible only because the Soviet Union was boycotting the Security Council at the time. To deal with many regional conflicts, the UN developed something never mentioned in the charter, namely, peacekeeping. This has involved the prevention, containment, and moderation of hostilities between or within states through the use of multinational forces of soldiers, police, and civilians. It was a creative response to the breakdown of great-power unity and illustrates that the Cold War "repealed the proposition that the organization should undertake to promote order by bringing the great powers into troubled situations . . . Henceforward, the task of the United Nations was to be defined as that of keeping the great powers *out* of such situations" (Claude 1965: 32).

The effects of the nuclear revolution. The UN Charter had just been signed when the use of two atomic bombs on Japan on August 6 and 10, 1945, unveiled a scientific and technological revolution in warfare that would have far-reaching effects on the post–World War II world. At the United Nations, the earliest and most obvious effect of nuclear weapons was to restore the issue of disarmament (and its relative, arms control) to the agenda. Disarmament as an approach to peace had been discredited during the period between World Wars I and II. The UN, almost from its inception in early 1946, became a forum for discussions and negotiations on arms control and disarmament. Hence, the nuclear threat not only transformed world politics itself, but it also made the UN the key place where diplomats sought to persuade each other that war had become excessively dangerous, that disarmament and arms control were imperative, and that they were devoted to peace and restraint.

The UN's role in decolonization and the emergence of new states. At the close of World War II few predicted the end of colonial rule in Africa and Asia. Yet twenty-five years after the UN Charter's signing, most of the former colonies had achieved independence with relatively little threat to international peace and security. Membership in the UN increased dramatically and the United Nations played a significant role in this remarkably peaceful transformation, much of which took place during the height of the

Cold War. Thirty new states were later seated in the UN after the Cold War's end, most the results of the Soviet Union and Yugoslavia's dissolution. (See Figure 4.4.)

The UN Charter endorsed the principle of self-determination for colonial peoples. Already independent former colonies such as India, Egypt, Indonesia, and the Latin American states used the UN as a forum to advocate an end to colonialism and independence for territories ruled by Great Britain, France, the Netherlands, Belgium, Spain, and Portugal. Success added new votes to the growing anticolonial coalition.

By 1960 a majority of the UN's members favored decolonization. General Assembly Resolution 1514 condemned the continuation of colonial rule and preconditions for granting independence (such as lack of preparation for self-rule) and called for annual reports on the progress toward independence of all remaining colonial territories. During this time the UN provided an important forum for the collective legitimation of a change in

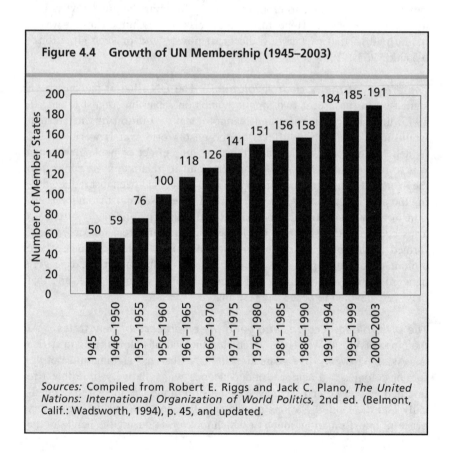

Figure 4.4   Growth of UN Membership (1945–2003)

Sources: Compiled from Robert E. Riggs and Jack C. Plano, *The United Nations: International Organization of World Politics,* 2nd ed. (Belmont, Calif.: Wadsworth, 1994), p. 45, and updated.

international norms (i.e., colonialism and imperialism were no longer acceptable patterns of state behavior) and the full internationalization of the international system.

The consequences of decolonization and the expanded number of independent states were manifold. Where the Cold War had shaped politics in the UN until 1960, the G-77 and what became known as North-South issues shaped much of the politics thereafter, particularly in the General Assembly, by opening a new conflict in world politics between the more developed states of Western Europe and North America (plus Japan and Australia) and the less developed states of Africa, Asia, and Latin America.

The North-South conflict.   By the late 1960s, the agenda of the UN and its subsidiary agencies was heavily tilted toward issues of economic development and relations between the developed countries of the industrial North and the less developed countries of the South. The ideological leaning of the G-77 toward a heavy government role in economic development and redistribution of wealth shaped many UN programs and activities. In the 1970s, the G-77 pushed for a New International Economic Order (NIEO), marshaling support in the UN General Assembly for a Declaration on the Establishment of a New International Economic Order and a Charter of Economic Rights and Duties of States. The NIEO debates dominated and polarized the UN system during the 1970s. The deep divide between North and South at times made agreement on both economic and security issues impossible to achieve.

The North-South conflict continues to be a central feature of world politics and, hence, of the UN, although the rhetoric and issues of the NIEO sharply diminished in the late 1980s and 1990s. Environmental issues, which first emerged on the agenda at the Stockholm Conference on the Human Environment in 1972, for example, have been permeated by North-South differences. And at the 1997 Kyoto Conference on Climate Change, there were echoes of the North-South conflict in developing countries' insistence that industrial countries make the first reductions in carbon dioxide emissions.

▪ Post–Cold War World Politics

The Cold War's end meant new cooperation among the five permanent members of the Security Council and also a resurgence of nationalism, civil wars, and ethnic conflicts, the new phenomenon of failed states, and a related series of humanitarian crises. The consequence was greater demands than ever before on the United Nations to deal with threats to peace and security as well as environment and development issues, democratization, population growth, humanitarian crises, and other problems. UN peacekeepers were called on to rebuild Cambodia, create peace in Bosnia, organize and monitor elections in Nicaragua and Namibia, monitor human rights violations in El Salvador, and oversee humanitarian relief in Bosnia, Somalia, Rwanda, Kosovo, Congo, East Timor, and Afghanistan. Beginning with Iraq's invasion of Kuwait, the UN's enforcement powers were used more in the post–Cold War era than at any previous time.

Democracy spread to all regions of the globe, from Latin America, Eastern Europe, and states created from the former Soviet Union to Africa and Asia, and many authoritarian governments in the late 1980s and 1990s were forced to open the political process to competing political parties, to adopt more stringent human rights standards, and to hold free elections. The UN has been in heavy demand to provide observers for elections in countries around the world. UN-sanctioned intervention in Haiti in 1993 marked the first time the UN took action to restore a democratically elected government. In Namibia and East Timor, the UN was called upon to assist with organizing the elements of independent states, including the provision of transitional administrations, the writing of constitutions, and the organization of elections.

By 1995, however, the early post–Cold War optimism about the United Nations had diminished substantially. The peacekeepers in Somalia, Bosnia, and Rwanda found little peace to be kept, although their presence did alleviate much human suffering. Despite almost continuous meetings of the UN Security Council and numerous resolutions, the UN's own members lacked the political will to provide the military, logistical, and financial resources needed to deal with these complex situations. In addition, the UN faced a deep financial crisis because of the increased cost of peacekeeping and other activities and the failure of many members, including the United States, to pay their assessed contributions. The UN celebrated its fiftieth anniversary in 1995, but failed to use the occasion to enact necessary reforms in its administration, financing, and structure.

■ *Globalization and World Politics in a New Millennium*

Because the Bretton Woods institutions have always operated largely independently, the UN has never played a central role in international economic relations. This became even clearer in the 1990s with rising globalization. Although topics related to globalization appeared on General Assembly, ECOSOC, and other agendas, the major decisionmaking was clearly taking place elsewhere: in the World Bank, the IMF, the WTO, and the G-7, as well as in Washington, Tokyo, Berlin, London, and the headquarters of major corporations. One indicator of the UN's marginal importance to globalization issues was the antiglobalization movement's focus on the other institutions. To be sure, some of the specialized agencies such as the ILO, WHO, and WIPO became very much involved in globalization-related issues of labor, health, and intellectual property rights. Still, globalization's role in fueling the growth of NGOs was felt within the UN system in the pressures for a greater voice for global civil society.

Globalization's effects on a nexus of interdependence issues have also played a role in pressures within the UN for the series of global conferences and summits on the environment, human rights, population and development, women, and social development discussed in Chapter 3. Each of these conferences has been important for articulating new international norms, expanding international law, setting agendas for the UN itself and governments through programs of action, and promoting linkages among NGOs, the UN, and governments.

A related aspect of world politics and the era of globalization is the clear emergence of the United States as the world's sole superpower. Many have worried that this development would result in the UN's marginalization, particularly if or when the United States chose to act unilaterally. An alternative view is that the UN could become a puppet of the sole superpower, dependent upon its goodwill for funding, subservient in authorizing U.S. actions. (See Chapter 7 for further discussion.)

The UN used the occasion of the new millennium to convene a Millennium Summit in 2000 with a special report from the secretary-general, *We the Peoples,* providing his views of the state of the world, the major global challenges, and need for structural reform. In suggesting the special gathering, Kofi Annan hoped "to harness the symbolic power of the millennium to the real and urgent needs of people everywhere" (Wren 2000). The three days of meetings drew the largest gathering of world leaders ever: 147 heads of state or government, plus representatives of forty-four other countries.

The Millennium Declaration adopted by consensus at the close of the extraordinary summit reflected the high degree of consensus on two priorities: peace and development. Different leaders had stressed different aspects of the issues ranging from globalization to nuclear weapons, fairer economic systems, ethnic tolerance, and HIV/AIDS; they had disagreed about how to restructure the UN, but not about the importance of a world organization; they concurred with lofty language about values and principles, but they also committed themselves to a series of specific objectives known as the Millennium Development Goals (MDGs) that include halving the number of people living on less than one dollar a day by the year 2015 and reversing the spread of HIV/AIDS, malaria, and other major diseases. The MDGs are discussed further in Chapter 9, along with the partnerships that are being created to implement them. The declaration outlined special measures to meet the needs of Africa and intensified efforts to reform the Security Council, to strengthen ECOSOC and the ICJ, to make the General

Assembly a more effective deliberative and policymaking body, and to ensure that the UN is provided the resources needed to carry out its mandates.

The test of whether the Millennium Summit and Declaration did, in fact, serve to mobilize new energy and impetus will lie in efforts to meet the goals set, rise to global challenges, and restructure the organization. One year after the summit, the secretary-general issued a report, *Road Map towards the Implementation of the United Nations Millennium Declaration* (UN 2001b), that examined what member states, UN bodies, NGOs, regional organizations, and the private sector were doing and identified strategies for moving forward toward each goal. A website charts progress on an ongoing basis. As Annan noted, "What is needed is not more technical or feasibility studies" (*UN Chronicle* 2001–2002a: 39). The question is whether persistent problems plaguing the UN system will make the Millennium Declaration yet another set of empty promises.

Because the attacks of September 11, 2001, took place in New York City just as the General Assembly was about to convene for its annual session, the UN was powerfully affected by these terrorist actions. The attacks made clear the nature of the global threat posed by Al-Qaeda and other global networks of terrorist organizations. This was a new type of threat to international peace and security, not just an attack on the United States, and one that took advantage of globalization's impact on the ease of moving people, money, communications, and arms across borders. It also made clear that responses would require major new efforts, some of which could be taken through the United Nations system (such as the resolution passed by the Security Council committing members to several new requirements), and others that involve many other actors.

■ **Persistent Organizational Problems and the Need for Reform**

Like any organization, the UN has had institutional problems. The most persistent of these involve financing, coordination, management, and structural weaknesses. The first two can be linked to the proliferation of issues addressed by the organization and the corresponding challenges to the system's capacity for effective response. The last is linked to major changes in the international system and the need to reflect new political and social realities to ensure the UN's continuing legitimacy through structural reform. Each also reflects deep political disagreements among the UN's members and efforts by strong and weak states to influence and steer the organization in directions that are congruent with their objectives or to prevent it from infringing on their interests.

Everyone agrees that the UN needs reform, but there are sharp disagreements over what kind of reform is needed and for what purpose.

Developed countries want more productivity and efficiency from the UN's staff, reduction in programs and activities, elimination of overlap, improved management, and better coordination. They also want to maintain their power within the system. The developing countries tend to be concerned with greater economic and political equity through redistribution of resources and enhanced participation in key decisionmaking. They want more power within the system and more programs and activities oriented toward development. NGOs want a UN that is more open and accountable to civil society, allowing them greater input and participation. Most reform proposals, in short, have hidden political agendas and policy goals. As one observer notes (Paul 1997: 1–2), "In a world divided by chasms between rich and poor, powerful and powerless, differences of interest are certain to shape all reform efforts and keep the UN a contradictory and divided institution." Financing is one area where all agree reform is needed.

■ Financing

Like the UN system itself, the UN's budget is complex. The UN's regular budget covers its administrative machinery, major organs, and their auxiliary agencies and programs. It has grown from less than $20 million in 1946 to $1.25 billion in 2001. Peacekeeping expenses constitute a separate budget, and each of the specialized agencies also has a separate budget. In 2001, total budgets for the specialized agencies were $1.77 billion for a total UN system budget of $3.0 billion. The three types of budget expenditures are funded by contributions assessed among member states according to a formula based on ability to pay. Many economic and social programs (such as UNICEF, UNDP, WFP, and UNHCR) are funded by states' voluntary contributions, which frequently exceed the amounts of their assessments. Table 4.2 illustrates the relative size of each of these categories of budget expenditure based on assessed and voluntary contributions and changes between 1986 and 2000. The fluctuation of peacekeeping costs

Table 4.2   UN System Expenditures (in $US millions)

Year	Assessed Contributions				Voluntary Contributions		
	Regular	Peace- keeping	Agencies	Total Assessed	Organs	Agencies	Total Voluntary
1986	725	242	1,142	2,109	3,075	951	4,026
1990	838	379	1,495	2,712	4,436	1,346	5,782
1995	1,181	3,281	1,847	6,309	5,778	1,159	6,937
2000	1,090	2,139	1,766	4,995	4,023	955	4,978

Source: http://www.globalpolicy.org/finance/tables/tabsyst.htm, http://www.globalpolicy.org/finance/tables/finvol.htm.

since 1990 is particularly notable. Also evident are the effects of the major powers' insistence on "no growth" in the UN's regular budget since the early 1990s, despite developing countries' interests in increased UN social and economic activities. Prior to that time, UN budgets had grown with the membership increases, new programs and agencies, inflation, and currency rate fluctuations.

The formulas for member states' assessed contributions for both the regular budget and peacekeeping operations are reevaluated every three years. The General Assembly's Committee on Contributions considers national income, per capita income, any economic dislocations (such as from war), and members' ability to obtain foreign currencies. Initially, the highest rate (for the United States) was set at 40 percent. The minimum rate was 0.04 percent for states with the most limited means. Over time, these have been adjusted, with the U.S. share reduced to 25 percent, and now 22 percent, and the minimum dropping to 0.01 in 1978 and 0.0001 in 1997. Between 1985 and 2002, for example, Japan's share increased significantly from 11.82 percent to 18.9 percent, while the Soviet/Russian figure declined from 11.98 percent to 1.15 percent, reflecting Russia's reduced size and economic difficulties. Its contribution is now lower than Brazil, South Korea, and China. Figure 4.5 shows the scale of assessments for major contributors and the majority of UN members for the three-year period 2000–2003. Particularly striking is that all but eighteen UN members contribute less than one percent of the budget each while the top five contributors, representing just five out of 191 votes, are assessed 64 percent of the UN's costs.

Not surprisingly, however, the UN has frequently experienced difficulties in getting states to pay their assessments. The reasons for states' failure to pay range from budget technicalities to poverty to politics or unhappiness with the UN in general or with specific programs and activities. The result has been periodic financial crises. The only sanction provided by the charter in Article 19 is denial of voting privileges in the General Assembly if a member falls more than two years in arrears.

In the early 1960s, the first financing crisis arose over UN peacekeeping operations in the Congo and Middle East, with the Soviet Union, other communist countries, and France refusing to pay because in their view peacekeeping authorized by the General Assembly was illegal. The ICJ *Certain Expenses* opinion of 1962 confirmed the legality of the General Assembly's action and the obligation of members to pay. The second crisis arose in the 1980s when the U.S. began withholding part of its dues. The Congress and Reagan administration were unhappy with specific policies and politicization of many agencies, the General Assembly's procedures that gave the U.S. as the largest contributor so little weight in budget decisions, UN administration and management, and the size of the U.S. assess-

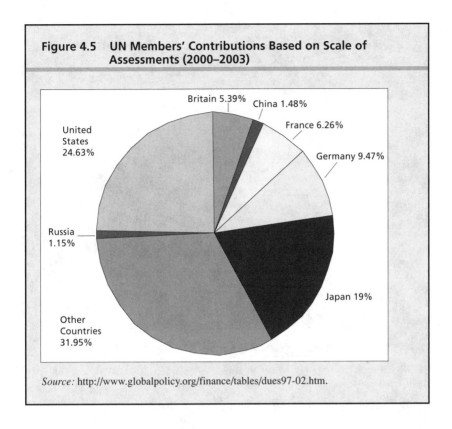

Figure 4.5 UN Members' Contributions Based on Scale of Assessments (2000–2003)

Britain 5.39%
China 1.48%
France 6.26%
United States 24.63%
Germany 9.47%
Russia 1.15%
Japan 19%
Other Countries 31.95%

Source: http://www.globalpolicy.org/finance/tables/dues97-02.htm.

ment relative to that of other wealthy states, specifically Japan and Germany. The Group of Eighteen High-Level Intergovernmental Experts, appointed by the General Assembly, recommended cuts in UN staffing, simplified procedures, and a key compromise that gave the major donors increased power to review programs and establish priorities for use of financial resources through the Committee for Programme and Coordination (CPC), which operates by consensus voting. This became the model followed by almost all UN agencies.

In the late 1990s, the UN faced by far its most serious financial crisis. Member states owed the UN over $2.5 billion for current and past assessments to cover both regular and peacekeeping expenses. Only one hundred of 185 members had paid in full. The United States was by far the biggest debtor, owing $1.6 billion or two-thirds of the total due. (See Figure 4.6.) Many members, including Russia, had major economic problems that made UN payments difficult. The financial crisis prompted by these arrearages (i.e., unpaid assessments or debts) threatened the organization's ability to fulfill the various mandates given it by member states and illustrated the

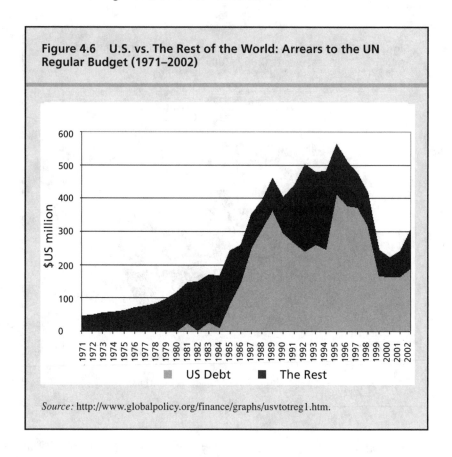

Figure 4.6   **U.S. vs. The Rest of the World: Arrears to the UN Regular Budget (1971–2002)**

Source: http://www.globalpolicy.org/finance/graphs/usvtotreg1.htm.

tension between demands for governance and institutional weakness arising from states' unwillingness (in the case of the United States) or inability (in the case of many states in economic crisis) to pay their assessed contributions.

This most recent crisis was partially resolved by an agreement struck in the U.S. Congress and with the UN General Assembly to reduce the U.S. assessments for the regular budget and peacekeeping and for payment of all arrears by 2003, subject to certain conditions (Mingst and Karns 2002). Nonetheless, in March 2004, arrearages still stood at $1.14 billion and the United States still owed 42 percent of that total.

There has been no shortage of proposals for changes to deal with the UN's financing crisis. The purpose of all proposals on UN financing is to provide a steady and predictable flow of resources for peacekeeping and the range of other economic and social activities. Among the ideas that have been mentioned are international taxes on arms sales, international air travel, and financial transactions. Yet financing problems are not necessarily about money; they are also about political influence. The United States, for example, has flatly opposed all proposals for independent funding sources.

Beyond states' assessed and voluntary contributions, the UN is limited in finding ways to finance its activities and programs. It has no authority to borrow money, nor any history of private fund-raising, but Secretary-General Kofi Annan has been creative in exploring partnerships with the corporate community. Ted Turner, Bill Gates, and other philanthropists may provide resources for specific needs. Fundamentally, however, states are reluctant to see the UN's dependence on them for its financing reduced too much because that would reduce their ability to control what the UN does. This leaves the organization with a persistent funding problem. As Kofi Annan noted in his millennial report, *We the Peoples* (2000), "When the scope of our responsibilities and the hopes invested in us are measured against our resources, we confront a sobering truth. The budget for our core functions . . . is about 4 percent of New York City's annual budget and nearly a billion dollars less than the annual cost of running Tokyo's fire department. Our resources are simply not commensurate with our global tasks."

▓ Coordination and Management

The problem of multiple agencies engaged in similar tasks with no coordination has plagued the UN system. Yet, ironically, the founders designed the organization to be decentralized, as this would increase the capacity of different groups to participate while minimizing the potential for politicization. As Ruggie (2003: 303) notes, "It is not designed as a matrix at all but as a set of deeply rooted columns connected only by thin and tenuous rows. Nothing that has transpired since 1945 has transformed that fundamental reality." And increasingly, as a result of globalization, issues do not fit into clear sectoral or regional boundaries. Hence, there has been a persistent call for better coordination and management of the UN system.

There are a plethora of reports and recommendations for improving ECOSOC's effectiveness as the main coordinating agency for economic and social programs and for reform of the UN's development activities. Three prominent ones are UNDP's 1969 Jackson Report, the 1991 Nordic UN Project, and the 1995 Commission on Global Governance proposal for an Economic Security Council to provide a coherent economic policy framework across the range of UN organizations and the private sector. In 1997, Secretary-General Kofi Annan merged three departments into one Department of Economic and Social Affairs and all of the Geneva-based human rights programs into the single Office of the High Commissioner for Human Rights. Incremental changes are easier to effect than revolutionary ones. The coordination problems have been compounded, however, by the global conferences of the 1990s. Each conference spawned a special commission to follow up on the program of action, yet because of zero-growth budgets, there have been fewer resources to meet greater demands. Recent changes have involved refocusing ECOSOC's activities around crosscutting issues and strengthening its authority to ensure implementation of resources, decisions, and agreed conclusions (Taylor 2000:125–129).

Coordination for economic and social development, however, also involves dialogues with the World Bank and IMF, more effective relationships with the specialized agencies, funds, and programs, as well as greater involvement of NGOs in policymaking processes (Fomerand 2002: 390). The various reforms of the late 1990s have had the effect of making it politically in the interest of specialized agencies to become more oriented to the whole UN system. Ruggie (2003: 305) describes the common set of Millennium Development Goals as "unprecedented for the UN and its agencies, let alone also the Bretton Woods institutions to align their operational activities behind a unifying substantive framework." While implementation of the Millennium Development Goals has just begun and success is not guaranteed, they represent a major shift toward greater coordination. With shared goals, there should be a more effective relationship among the various actors, including those within the UN system and those outside.

Coordination and management issues have also plagued UN efforts to deal with humanitarian crises since the early 1990s. Typically, there is a functional division of responsibilities: UNHCR manages refugee camps; UNICEF handles water and sanitation; WFP is responsible for food supplies; and WHO handles the health sector. In a number of situations, peacekeeping forces were mandated to safeguard relief workers and supplies. Yet, as one observer notes, "the United Nations did not respond as a system but rather as a series of separate and largely autonomous agencies. Each had its own institutional dynamics, formulated its own priorities, and moved according to a timetable of its own devising" (Minear 1994: 28). Complaints about uncoordinated emergency responses became increasingly frequent. Donor countries pushed the General Assembly in 1991 to appoint a humanitarian coordinator and Department of Humanitarian Affairs to remedy the problems, but neither was given power over other agencies nor staff and resources. An ad hoc solution was adopted for the former Yugoslavia where UNHCR was the lead agency responsible for coordination of UN agencies, NGOs, and NATO military personnel. In 1997, a further reorganization produced the Office for the Coordination of Humanitarian Affairs, while UNHCR has continued to play the lead role in the field.

Globalization issues such as the HIV/AIDS epidemic particularly demand better coordination and management. The UN system's adaptations since the mid-1980s to deal with the epidemic illustrate a model of better coordination. Although WHO was the logical agency for the initial responses, various other agencies such as UNDP, UNESCO, UNICEF, and UNFPA gradually became involved. As awareness grew of the multifaceted character of the epidemic's effects—social, political, economic, security, health—a consolidated approach was adopted by creating the Joint Programme on HIV/AIDS, or UNAIDS, in 1996. Eight UN agencies are now involved directly in UNAIDS. In 2001, the UN System Integrated Plan on AIDS was drawn up to link AIDS-related budgets and work plans of twenty-nine UN funds, programs, and agencies. This creates a model for future coordination across the UN system.

Efforts to address the coordination and management issues have led to greater centralization of activities. These steps are controversial, as any proposal to bring agencies under more effective centralized control conflicts with the deliberately decentralized nature of the system. In addition, each proposal for change advantages some agencies, states, and NGOs while disadvantaging others. Since the General Assembly has to approve many of these changes, including creating a new office or department or eliminating overlapping programs or agencies, these are controversial reforms. As one observer notes (Paul 1997: 1–2), "Reforms are possible and needed, but they must proceed by complex bargaining, so that all member states feel they are winning at least something in the process."

■ Structural Reform of the Security Council

Of all the issues on the UN reform agenda, none is as urgent or as controversial as Security Council reform. Given the UN's enlarged membership, virtually all groups agree that more states should be added to the Security Council. The permanent members underrepresent the majority of the world's population; Europe is overrepresented at the expense of Latin America, Africa, and Asia; China is the only third world and Asian country among the permanent members; both Germany and Japan contribute more financially than Russia, China, Great Britain, and France, yet have no guaranteed role. Thus, the first key issue is to increase the number of members for geographic representation and enhanced legitimacy, while maintaining a small enough size to ensure efficiency (Wallensteen 1994).

A second issue concerns whether or not to continue the distinction between permanent and nonpermanent members. Closely related is the question of whether new permanent members will have veto power. Some proposals would give no veto power to the new permanent members; others would limit veto power of all permanent members to Chapter VII decisions; still others would grant veto power comparable to what the P-5 currently enjoy; others would eliminate the veto entirely on the grounds that it is undemocratic. The latter is a nonstarter for all permanent members, and Britain and France are hardly eager to give up their seats. "New veto-wielding permanent members would only increase the likelihood of blockage and still further paralyze the organization" (Paul 1995).

Resolving the representation and permanent member issues has proven impossible thus far. There is no agreement on what process or formula should be used to determine who would get new permanent seats. There are three likely African candidates, for example (Nigeria, Egypt, and South Africa). Countries that know a rival is more likely to be a candidate, such as either India or Pakistan, tend to oppose adding permanent seats. The G-77 wants change, but is divided. The United States supports granting permanent seats to Germany and Japan as well as one each to Africa, Latin America, and Asia, with regional groups deciding if their seat would be given to a single state or filled on a rotating basis. The United States has not taken a position on the veto for any new members, suggesting the issue should be discussed once the council is expanded. Deliberations on the issue continue in the Open-ended Working Group established by the General Assembly in 1994.

In addition to the question of representation, there have been demands to increase the openness (transparency) and efficiency of the council's work. Here, there has been progress. Council members consult with countries contributing troops and materiel to peacekeeping operations prior to making decisions. They have invited NGO representatives to participate in some discussions. They have opened up more meetings, especially at early stages of deliberation and now provide more information on the nature of discussions and what resulted. In 2000, the council decided to make draft resolutions and presidential statements available to nonmembers as soon as they were introduced, thus facilitating input; it also has increased the number of formal, public meetings. An additional strategy for involving states that are not necessarily council members in peacemaking efforts have been informal, ad hoc small groups called "Friends of the Secretary-General," discussed in Chapter 7. The issues in the debate over Security Council reform are summarized in Figure 4.7.

Even with representation issues unresolved, the Security Council retains a high degree of legitimacy. States want to become nonpermanent members. Participation is seen as a mark of status and prestige for a state and its diplomats. States attach symbolic importance to Security Council endorsement of regional peacekeeping operations such as by Nigeria in Liberia or Russia in Georgia, Moldova, and Tajikistan, and enforcement actions by coalitions of the willing such as Australia in East Timor or the United States in Iraq. States may expend considerable efforts to delegitimate council actions as Libya did in trying to show that sanctions for its suspected role in the Pan Am Flight 103 bombing were being imposed

Figure 4.7   The Debate Over Security Council Reform

ISSUE

• *Representation*
Council needs greater representation of Africa, Asia, Latin
    America
Permanent members should better reflect geopolitics and
    economics
    Proposed additions: Germany and Japan
    One member each from Africa, Asia, and Latin America, but
    who and how to select?
No permanent members
No new permanent members
Veto power
    Eliminate entirely
    Reduce scope for its use in Chapter VII decisions
    Keep current P-5, but not give new permanent members veto
    power
    Give all permanent members veto power

• *Openness*
More open council meetings
More information on when council meets, nature of discussions,
    draft resolutions, presidential statements, actions
More consultations with interested states and NGOs

• *Efficiency*
Size should be large enough to allow greater representation, but
    small enough to preserve the ability to act
    Proposed size: 20–24 members

WHO DECIDES
Reform of council membership requires Charter amendment,
which takes a vote of two-thirds of the General Assembly members and must be ratified in accordance with their respective constitutional processes by two-thirds of the members of the UN,
including all permanent members of the Security Council (Chapter
XVIII, Article 108)

Reforms in methods of work may be made by the Security Council
itself

without any judicial finding. Thus, the Security Council continues to be
seen as the most authoritative body within the UN and to retain considerable legitimacy in spite of its obvious unrepresentative composition and in
spite of the 2003 Iraq crisis. As Hurd (2002: 205) explains, "The power that

the council wields over the strong comes not from its ability to block their military adventures (which it is not empowered to do) but rather from the fact that the council is generally seen as legitimate. This legitimacy functions by raising the costs of unilateral action in the eyes of many countries and their citizens." Yet to maintain its legitimacy, the Security Council will have to be reformed; on that, there is no debate.

■ Integrating Nonstate Actors

The increasing involvement of NGOs and private businesses with UN programs and activities demonstrates another area of needed reform: how to better integrate nonstate actors into the UN system of operations. Some of the initiatives that were undertaken in the 1990s in this regard are discussed elsewhere, such as changes in NGO participation discussed in Chapter 6 and the Global Compact Kofi Annan initiated in 2000 with corporate leaders that is discussed in Chapter 9. Prior to the Millennium Summit in 2000, a Millennium Forum brought together more than one hundred NGOs. Its participants resolved to create a global civil society forum to deal with UN institutions, member states, and other institutions (Alger 2002). Annan himself noted in a 1997 speech, "The United Nations once dealt only with governments. By now we know that peace and prosperity cannot be achieved without partnerships involving the governments, international organizations, the business community and civil society" (quoted in Hocking and Kelly 2002: 209).

Nonstate actors now play a substantial role in supplementing the limited financial resources of the UN system. Increasingly, Alger notes (2002: 116), "they are being asked to substitute for the UN in a variety of ways because of UN Secretariat, and UN peacekeeping, shortages of people and money." The UN Fund for International Partnerships was established in 1998 as a result of the $1 billion pledge by Ted Turner to advance UN goals. Likewise, the Global Fund to Fight HIV/AIDS, Tuberculosis and Malaria created in 2001 was specifically conceived as a way of mobilizing the resources of governments, NGOs, and private business. Thus, addressing the issue of greater participation by nonstate actors is a persistent and increasingly urgent one for the UN. While the UN is the central piece of global governance, as noted at the beginning of this chapter, there are many other pieces, among them regional organizations. But what is the relationship between the UN as a global IGO and various regional IGOs?

■ The UN's Relationship to Regional Organizations

When the UN was created in 1945, there were virtually no regional IGOs in existence. The Organization of American States, Council of Europe, NATO, and Arab League were all created between 1945 and 1950, for example. Nonetheless, among the UN's founders there was a tension between the principles of globalism and regionalism, as mentioned in Chapter 1. The British Foreign Office was more interested in regional spheres of influence and order, while U.S. President Roosevelt was an advocate of a universal or global organization. The debate was framed almost exclusively in terms of security and, as a result, the provisions of the charter's Chapter VIII refer to regional security arrangements. The charter is silent on broader roles for regional organizations such as in promoting economic and social cooperation and on how these might be linked to UN activities.

Although Article 52 legitimizes the existence and operation of regional alliances and encourages regional efforts to settle local disputes peacefully, it is very clear that the UN Security Council under Articles 24, 34, and 35 has primary responsibility for maintenance of international peace and security. The council has sole authority to authorize the use of force and to obligate member states to undertake sanctions, except in situations where states may exercise their right of self-defense, either individually or collectively (Article 51). It may also utilize regional security agencies for enforcement action under its authority, but "no enforcement action shall be taken under regional arrangements or by regional agencies without the authorization of the Security Council" (Article 53). Regional organizations are to inform the Security Council of any activities planned or undertaken to maintain international peace and security (Article 54).

The charter does not define the regional entities referred to in Chapter VIII, nor does it indicate how such entities are to interrelate with the UN, thus leaving issues of responsibility and legitimacy unresolved. For much of the Cold War, this was unimportant. It changed dramatically with the Cold War's end when the Security Council became more active and regional, intrastate, and ethnic conflicts, as well as collapsing states, presented a series of complex problems in the Balkans, the former Soviet Union, and Africa (Job 2000). Secretary-General Boutros-Ghali's 1992 *Agenda for Peace* (pars. 64–65) states that "regional action as a matter of decentralization, delegation, and cooperation with the United Nations could not only lighten the burden of the council but also contribute to a deeper sense of participation, consensus and democratization in international affairs. . . . Today a new sense exists that they have contributions to make." A more detailed division of labor is set out in his 1995 *Supplement to An Agenda for Peace*. We discuss further the nature of the relationship between the UN and regional IGOs in dealing with post–Cold War conflicts in Chapter 8.

Beyond these security-related provisions of the UN Charter, ad hoc arrangements were created for coordinating the work of the regional development banks with UN development agencies and the World Bank. Recognizing the necessity of approaching many economic and social problems within regional contexts, as noted, ECOSOC early on created regional economic commissions and arrangements to mesh their work with that of other programs. Some of these arrangements are discussed further in Chapter 9. Today, regionalism and globalism coexist with minimal friction outside the security area, and regional organizations have proliferated even more rapidly than global ones. They have become increasingly important pieces of the global governance puzzle.

■ Note

1. Portions of this chapter are drawn from Karen A. Mingst and Margaret P. Karns. (2000) *The United Nations in the Post–Cold War Era,* 2nd ed. Boulder: Westview Press. Reprinted with permission of Westview Press.

■ Suggested Further Reading

Annan, Kofi A. (2000) *We The Peoples: The Role of the United Nations in the 21st Century.* Available at http://www.un.org/millennium/sg/report/full.htm.

Mingst, Karen A., and Margaret P. Karns. (2000) *The United Nations in the Post–Cold War Era,* 2nd ed. Boulder, CO: Westview Press.

Newman, Edward. (1998) *The UN Secretary-General from the Cold War to the New Era: A Global Peace and Security Mandate?* New York: St. Martin's Press.

Taylor, Paul, and A. J. R. Groom, eds. (2000) *The United Nations at the Millennium: The Principal Organs.* New York: Continuum.

Weiss, Thomas G., David P. Forsythe, and Roger A. Coate. (2003) *The United Nations and Changing World Politics,* 4th ed. Boulder, CO: Westview Press.

Ziring, Lawrence, Robert Riggs, and Jack Plano. (2000) *The United Nations: International Organization and World Politics,* 3rd ed. New York: Harcourt College Publishers.

■ Internet Resources

Academic Council on the UN System: www.acuns.wlu.ca
Global Policy Forum: www.globalpolicy.org
International Court of Justice: www.icj-cij.org
UN Charter: www.un.org/aboutun/charter/index.html
UN Home Page: www.un.org
UN Millennium Development Goals: www.un.org/millenniumgoals/
UN Reform Home Page: www.un.org/reform
UN System: www.unsystem.org
United Nations Association (USA): www.unausa.org

5

Regional Organizations

Regionalism and globalism have both been evident in the processes of developing international organizations and institutions for governance. Whereas the United Nations is the primary global, general-purpose organization, there is a great deal of variation across different regions of the world in the nature, scope, degree of development, and effectiveness of regional organizations. The European Union represents by far the most extensive regional governance institution. Its institutions have supranational powers over the member states in several policy domains, and the processes of creating common community policies have substantially advanced the political and economic integration of the members. Organizations in Asia, Africa, the Middle East, and Latin America are far less developed, although a few predate the EU's predecessor institutions. (See Map 5.1 for details.)

Historically, there has been some question whether regionalism complemented or competed with globalism. Chapter VIII of the UN Charter envisaged the creation of regional security arrangements. Although there is no similar charter provision with respect to economic and social cooperation, ECOSOC very early created regional economic commissions and regional development banks were established in the 1950s and 1960s. Supporters of the GATT-based multilateral trade system, however, have always viewed regional trade arrangements with some suspicion, fearing that they might undermine efforts to create a global system by promoting competing regional trade blocs. Since the Organization of American States (OAS) approved the American Declaration of the Rights of Man seven months before the UN General Assembly passed the Universal Declaration of Human Rights in December 1948, there has never been much argument about competing regional and global frameworks for human rights norms.

Cold War competition between the United States and Soviet Union involved the establishment of regional security arrangements (alliances). In Europe, the creation of the North Atlantic Treaty Organization (NATO) in 1949 was very quickly countered by the Warsaw Treaty Organization. The Western European Union (WEU) was created to monitor West Germany's

Map 5.1   Selected Regional Organizations

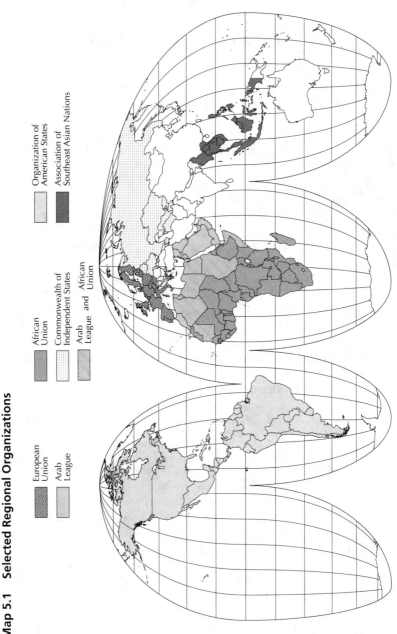

rearmament. In the 1950s, the United States also created alliances in Southeast Asia with the Southeast Asian Treaty Organization (SEATO) and in West Asia with the Central Treaty Organization (CENTO). Neither of these two arrangements lasted. CENTO collapsed with revolutions and coups in Iraq and Pakistan in the late 1950s. SEATO died with U.S. withdrawal from Vietnam in the 1970s.

Regional organizations can be categorized along the same lines as global organizations: general purpose, peace and security, economic, functional and technical. On the political side, they promote goals of security, peace, a stable security community, democracy, and, in the case of the European Union, integration. On the economic side, regional organizations are created to improve economic growth, development, and well-being through the lowering of barriers to trade, flow of goods, services, and capital; aims are to foster greater economic efficiency and consumer welfare through the resources of larger markets.

Some regions (most notably Europe) have evolved formal organizational structures with budgets, secretariats and headquarters, courts, voting procedures, elaborate patterns of meetings, extensive transparency and monitoring, formal rules and agreements duly ratified, and hence, binding commitments by member states. Regionalism in Asia, for example, is more informal, involving periodic meetings, consensus decisionmaking, informal agreements, and limited commitments by states. Like other kinds of IGOs, regional organizations can be analyzed in terms of their scope, organizational form, allocational mode, and strength.

Not all attempts at regionalism have been successful. Hence, it is valuable to assess failed attempts as well as the relative success (or at least persistence) of others. Longevity is not a measure of success, nor is degree of bureaucratic or organizational complexity. The relative success and failure of regionalism, like governance in general, rests on assessments of the degree to which objectives were achieved and problems managed or solved. Did trade patterns change or economic well-being increase? Were conflicts averted and disputes resolved? Were institutions able to weather crises, to adapt organizational structures to meet new challenges, and to develop new ways of doing things?

This chapter examines some of the major factors and theories that are thought to explain the roots and dynamics of regionalism. Because the European experience with regionalism is the most extensive and is often seen as a model for other regions, we look at this in some detail. Examining regional variation helps us understand the range of governance arrangements in the world today. Regional organizations' activities with respect to security, economic well-being and development, human rights, and the environment are discussed in the chapters dealing with each of those issue areas.

■ The Roots and Dynamics of Regionalism

The rationale for regionalism is that states within a given geographic area can more easily and effectively address common problems because they are closer to the problems and are presumed to share some background and approaches. Thus, most definitions of regionalism assume that the participating states share geographical proximity and a degree of mutual interdependence. But what defines the scope of a region?

▓ *Defining a Region*

Traditionally, regionalism has involved the formation of interstate groupings that are less than global in scope. Recognizing the increased importance of nonstate actors, however, regionalism is better defined as "sustained cooperation, formal or informal, among governments, nongovernment organizations, or the private sector in three or more countries for mutual gain" (Alagappa 1994: 158). The essentialist approach is based on the premise that there is a natural, essential core of economic, security, religious, or cultural links between states and peoples that define a region (Jayasuriya 1994: 411). An alternative constructivist approach posits that a region is a social and political construction with various concepts, metaphors, and practices determining how the region is defined and who is included and excluded (Acharya 1997).

There is no clear guide to identifying the boundaries of regions, however. Rather, decisions as to what constitutes a particular region reflect the perceptions, prejudices, or desires of those states that constitute a core group for regional initiatives. They form in effect an "in group" that subsequently determines whether to accept any "outsiders." What is now the EU began with six members. Today it has twenty-five members. Turkey's application for membership, however, is controversial, in part because it is a predominantly Muslim country with a weak democratic system and human rights record. Where does Europe end and Western Asia begin? How should the region be defined?

Many regions are marked by multiple organizations, whose memberships and mandates overlap or coincide. Where several organizations coexist in the same geographic and political space, they may be viewed as concentric circles and/or nested regimes. The networks of regional organizations are most dense in Western Europe and least dense in Asia for reasons that will emerge later when we explore the roots and dynamics of regionalism.

▓ *Political Factors Driving Regionalism*

Several political factors are linked to the development of regionalism. Among them are identity (or shared perception of a definable region), internal or external threats, domestic politics, and leadership. Regionalism does not just happen. Deliberate policy choices by states' leaders are key to increasing the flow of economic or political activity among a group of states in order to reap anticipated benefits.

Identity. Several recent studies have focused on identity or shared perception of being part of a definable region as a key factor in the definition of region. Hurrell (1995b) suggests that such perceptions can be based on either internal or external factors. Internal factors might include common culture and religion; external factors could include a common security or economic threat. Historical experiences of extensive interaction and cooperation in trade or in uniting against a common enemy can create shared identity (and the readiness to cooperate more in the future). Acharya (1997) has analyzed how the ASEAN states constructed their sense of regional identity through the elaboration of key ideas and processes often described as the "ASEAN Way." Since the mid-1990s, however, ASEAN has added four new members (Myanmar, Laos, Cambodia, and Vietnam) whose political systems and economic development differ significantly from the core six states. This diversity is straining the sense of regional identity and the organization's effectiveness. By contrast, the first leaders of independent African states won early support for the idea of African unity and the creation of the Organization of African Unity in 1963. Regional awareness rarely exists naturally, however, and even if it does, may not lead to regional cooperation unless states work to make the best of their regional environment (Fawcett and Hurrell 1995: 10).

Internal and external threats. A shared sense of external or internal threat can be a key political factor driving states toward closer regional cooperation. The threat of communism and especially of Soviet expansion was a powerful impetus to regionalism in Western Europe in the 1950s and 1960s. It was directly responsible for the creation of NATO and part of the rationale behind the European Community's formation. European integration, however, was also driven by the desire to contain German nationalism and expansionism by enmeshing that country in tight links with France and other neighboring states. External threats from China, the heightened U.S. presence during the Vietnam War, and later from Vietnam's invasion of Cambodia played a major role in the formation and evolution of ASEAN. For the Arab League, shared hostility to the state of Israel has been the most powerful source of unity.

Security threats are the most common form of external threat for regional integration, but in the 1990s, two others were also prominent: fear that creation of rival trade blocs would limit market access and fear of marginalization in a world minus the East-West rivalry for power and influence.

Domestic politics.   Domestic politics frequently becomes a significant variable affecting regional governance initiatives. It can take a strong domestic political coalition, including strong export-oriented manufacturing industries, to support closer economic integration, for example, and to take the often tough decisions to open borders to trade and subject locally owned companies to outside competition (Solingen 1998). This was the case with South America's Common Market of the South (Mercosur). By the same token, opposition to regional initiatives may come from trade unions, farmers, key companies, or political groups, as has been the case with NAFTA.

International agreements and regional arrangements can also affect domestic politics, creating constraints on governments that may find this helpful in resisting demands of domestic groups. They may also change the balance of power between branches of a government or give a federal government enhanced power over its subnational units (such as states and provinces), as NAFTA has done in the United States.

International relations scholars have also studied the role that similarities in types of political systems can play in regional governance. In particular, they have focused on how democratic political systems in a group of countries may be a necessary basis for building a stable security community (Deutsch et al. 1957; Adler and Barnett 1998).

Leadership.   Regionalism, like other global governance initiatives, also requires leadership from key individuals, one or more states, or an energetic secretariat to give it direction and impetus. Jean Monnet, France, and Germany were key to the birth of post–World War II European regionalism, while the European Commission and Court of Justice have been important engines of European integration since the late 1950s. Indonesia played a lead role for ASEAN, while Australia and Japan did so for APEC (Asia-Pacific Economic Cooperation), and Egypt for the Arab League. The United States provided leadership for both NATO and the OAS, but it was Canada, not the United States, that proposed the Canada-U.S. Free Trade Agreement that preceded NAFTA.

■ Economic Factors Driving Regionalism

High levels of economic interdependence, most notably trade flows, the complementarity of economies and policies, the availability of compensatory mechanisms for integration in developing countries, and the desire to attract foreign investment through creation of a larger market are commonly linked to regional economic initiatives. Interdependence increases the costs generated by lack of coordinated national policies because it raises the sensitivity of economic events in one country to what is happening with trading partners. Economic interconnectedness, however, does not necessarily lead countries within a geographical area to see themselves as part of a region or to think in terms of regional cooperation. After reviewing the literature on how interdependence may affect states' perceptions of their identity, sense of community, and shared interests, Ravenhill (2001: 14–15) concludes, "No clear correlation exists between levels of interdependence between specific economies, measured by the relative importance of bilateral trade flows, and the emergence of economic regionalism . . . [and] no critical threshold of regional economic interdependence exists below which regionalism never occurs and beyond which such collaboration always takes place. At best, then, the evidence suggests that growing interdependence may generate increasing pressures for governments to collaborate, but such collaboration does not result automatically."

Until the 1980s, for example, interdependence was low among Asian countries. Solingen (1998) argues that it has, in fact, followed (not preceded) regionalism in East and Southeast Asia. Although Asian intraregional trade has grown exponentially in the last twenty years, most Asian countries, including Japan, depend on North American markets for their exports. Consequently, they have insisted on "open regionalism" to keep regional trade arrangements open to outsiders (and preserve their own freedom to participate in other trade arrangements). This contrasts with the more closed regionalism of the European Union, NAFTA, or Mercosur where trade advantages are limited to members.

Yet, economic factors alone have rarely sufficed as a basis for successful regional cooperation. The primary goal of regional economic cooperation, in fact, has often been the political and security benefits of cooperation.

▇ Two Waves of Regionalism

There have been two waves of regionalism over the last fifty years. (See Figure 5.1.) The old or first wave accompanied the initial stages of European integration in the 1960s. Countries in several other parts of the world tried, often unsuccessfully, to emulate Europe by initiating regional economic integration schemes. Interest in regionalism and integration waned as relatively few economic gains were realized and as the economic crises of the 1970s led many countries to adopt protectionist policies.

The second wave of regionalism began in the late 1980s, accompanying the European moves toward the single internal market and European Union in 1992 and the new regionalism in North America with the Canada-U.S. Free Trade Agreement and its later conversion to NAFTA. Among the complex factors fueling this so-called new regionalism were global economic changes, the transformation of the Soviet Union and Eastern Europe, uncertainty over the outcome of the Uruguay Round of world trade negotiations, the European Union's deepening and enlargement, fear that a set of

---

Figure 5.1   Two Waves of Regionalism

FIRST WAVE: 1950s–1960s

Europe and Soviet Bloc	*Latin America*
NATO (1949–)	OAS (1948–)
WEU (1955–)	RIO Pact (1947–)
Warsaw Treaty Organization	Central American Common
(1955–1991)	Market (1961–)
Council of Europe (1948–)	Andean Community (1969–)
ECSC (1952–)	CARICOM (1973–)
Euratom (1958–)	LAFTA (1969–1980)
EEC (1958–)	
COMECON (1948–1991)	*Middle East*
	Arab League (1947–)
West and East Asia	
CENTO (1950s)	*Africa*
SEATO (1954–1975)	OAU (1964–2002)
ASEAN (1967–)	AU (2002–)

SECOND WAVE: 1980s–1990s

Europe	*Latin America*
CSCE (1975–)	Mercosur (1991–)
EEC-EU (1992–)	FTAA (1994–)
CIS (1991–)	NAFTA (1993–)
Asia and Asia-Pacific	*Africa*
APEC (1989–)	ECOWAS (1975–)
ARF (1994–)	SADC (1992–)
	COMESA (1994–)
Middle East	
Gulf Cooperation Council (1981–)	

---

trade blocs was emerging, and new attitudes toward international cooperation. The Cold War's end opened political space for international cooperation by freeing many countries, particularly those of the old Soviet bloc, to reshape their alignments and policies. In a globalizing world, regionalism also has become a means to forestall states' isolation or marginalization. In the economic sphere, the triumph of liberal market economic theories encouraged eliminating barriers to trade and creating larger markets through regional trade agreements in hopes of emulating strong economic growth in Europe and North America.

NAFTA and APEC both span the North-South divide, underscoring that regionalism in the second wave is not just for countries whose economies are of similar size and capability. As Ravenhill (2001: 35) notes, "The philosophy underlying more recent regional schemes . . . is much closer to the idea of bandwagoning—linking up with the more powerful . . . driven by fears of . . . increased protectionism by their main industrialized economy trading partners." Contemporary regional initiatives are also more multidimensional. Although economic concerns remain predominant along with underlying broad security and political goals, transnational interdependence issues such as drug trafficking, environmental degradation, and refugees pose demands for collective management.

■ Europe's Regional Organizations

Since the end of World War II, European states have established a dense network of regional organizations to address security, economic, and other needs. In the Cold War years, the Iron Curtain formed a sharp boundary line between two sets of such organizations. In Eastern Europe, states under Soviet domination joined together in the Warsaw Pact for common defense and the Council of Mutual Economic Assistance (COMECON) to manage their economic relations. In Western Europe, with strong influence and encouragement from the United States, the Organization for European Economic Cooperation (OEEC) was established in 1948 to administer U.S. Marshall Plan aid and to lower trade and currency barriers; NATO was established in 1949. The Europeans themselves created the Council of Europe in 1949, a multipurpose organization "to achieve a greater unity among its Members for the purpose of safeguarding and realizing the ideals and principles which are their common heritage and facilitating their economic and social progress" (Council of Europe Statute 2[Art.1]).

Very shortly, however, the perceived OEEC and Council of Europe's shortcomings led six countries (France, West Germany, the Netherlands, Belgium, Luxembourg, and Italy) to begin a process of deeper integration through a new set of institutions, starting with the European Coal and Steel Community (ECSC) established in 1952. The six countries then established the European Atomic Energy Community (Euratom) and European Economic Community (EEC, or Common Market) in 1958. The integration process they initiated continues today through what is now known as the European Union. Groups of Western European states also created the Western European Union in 1954 to provide a framework for German rearmament and the European Free Trade Association (EFTA) in 1960 for states that chose not to join the Common Market. During the period of detente between East and West in the 1970s, the Conference on Security and Cooperation in Europe (CSCE, or Helsinki Conference) was established, bringing together countries from both East and West Europe (plus the two superpowers).

The Warsaw Pact and COMECON disbanded in 1991 with the collapse of communist governments and dissolution of the Soviet Union itself. Nine former members are now members of NATO and eight have joined the EU. The Cold War's end transformed Europe's landscape and regional organizations. (See Figure 5.2.)

■ *NATO*

NATO is the most highly organized regional security organization in the world. Although it began as a Cold War military alliance, it has now evolved into far more than just a treaty of alliance. Since 1991, it has enlarged its membership and taken on new roles in the conflicts generated

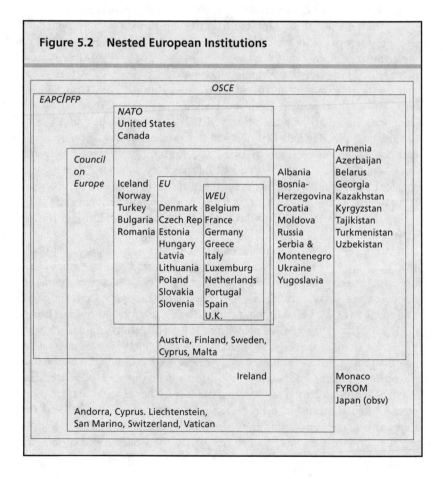

Figure 5.2   Nested European Institutions

by Yugoslavia's breakup and, beyond Europe, in Afghanistan. Still, debate persists about its role in the post–Cold War world.

At the core of the 1948 North Atlantic Treaty is the agreement in Article 5 "that an armed attack against one or more of them [the parties to the treaty] in Europe or North America shall be considered an attack against them all," obligating all member states to assist the member attacked. State sovereignty is protected by the proviso that each need take only such action "as it deems necessary." Nonetheless, NATO's members evolved an elaborate integrated command structure, a complex structure of civilian and military consultation, cooperation, and coordination, as well as agreements on levels of forces and defense expenditure. Forces are maintained in Western Europe, the Atlantic, and Mediterranean, and efforts have been made over many years to coordinate equipment specifications and training to ensure their interoperability (e.g., that Dutch, French, or German artillery can use American ammunition). Despite the integrated command structure, military forces remain under command of their national officers.

NATO now has twenty-six members (see Figure 5.2 for a listing). Since 1966, French participation has been limited, however, because then President Charles de Gaulle withdrew France from NATO's integrated command structure and requested that NATO troops and headquarters be removed from French territory.

Structures. NATO's principal organ is the North Atlantic Council, which meets at the ministerial level (i.e., ministers of foreign affairs or defense) at least twice a year and weekly at the ambassadorial level at its headquarters in Brussels. The NATO secretary-general chairs the council, as well as preparing budgets, arranging meeting agendas, supervising the secretariat, and representing the organization in relations with governments and other international organizations. A large number of committees handle defense planning, political affairs, armaments, air space, and communications. In recent years, members have also held several summit meetings (i.e., heads of government and state) to discuss NATO's post–Cold War role and enlargement.

The NATO Military Committee, composed of chiefs of staff or their representatives from all members except France, oversees the integrated military command structure. The defense area is divided into three command areas: Southern Europe, Northern Europe, and the Atlantic. Over all is the Supreme Allied Commander Europe, known as SACEUR, a position first held by General Dwight Eisenhower (prior to his becoming U.S. president in 1952). Supreme Headquarters Allied Powers Europe (SHAPE) is located in Mons, Belgium.

NATO experienced a variety of stresses during its first forty years. America's commitment to European defense, particularly to maintaining large numbers of troops in Europe during peacetime, has periodically been called into question. The U.S. tendency to inform allies of policy changes only after decisions have been made, rather than consulting with them beforehand, has been a recurring source of tension. Burden sharing has been a persistent debate. The United States has frequently complained about the Europeans paying and doing too little to maintain their own defense capabilities. Defense doctrines, particularly for use of nuclear weapons (massive retaliation) versus reliance on conventional forces (flexible response), have also sparked heated debates.

The Cold War's end posed a dilemma: Was NATO, like its counterpart the Warsaw Pact, an anachronism? In the first part of the 1990s, NATO was an organization in search of a new role. The United States pushed to transform NATO from a collective defense alliance to an organization contributing to overall European security. Key issues have concerned NATO's enlargement, its relationship with Russia, and the scope and nature of its mission.

Post–Cold War enlargement.   Behind the issue of NATO enlargement is the belief that the values uniting the alliance for fifty years, namely democracy, the rule of law, and individual liberties, are keys to lasting peace and security in the Euro-Atlantic region stretching from Vladivostok to Vancouver. The goal, therefore, is to extend the zone of peace and stability eastward and to provide incentives for political and economic change in former Soviet bloc countries. There has been fierce debate, however, over the desirability of enlarging NATO versus strengthening other European security arrangements, particularly the Conference on Security and Cooperation in Europe that was itself transformed in 1995 into the Organization for Security and Cooperation in Europe (OSCE). That debate raged in the United States, among the Europeans, and most particularly with Russia, which fiercely opposed NATO's enlargement. Despite efforts to establish mechanisms for consultation and cooperation with Russia, there is a continuing perception by Russians that NATO is still an anti-Russian military alliance and, hence, potentially threatening. NATO's interventions in Bosnia and Kosovo in 1995 and 1999 over Russia's opposition (and without UN Security Council sanction in the case of Kosovo) heightened Russian fears.

In 1994, NATO took the initial step toward enlargement with the establishment of the Partnership for Peace (PFP) that associated twenty-five countries in Central Europe and Central Asia, with NATO's then sixteen members. At its 1997 Madrid Summit, NATO launched formal enlargement with a decision to admit Poland, the Czech Republic, and Hungary. In 2004, seven other Eastern European countries were admitted. The remaining partnership countries, including Russia, Ukraine, Kazakhstan, and

Belarus, have pledged to bring themselves into line with Western standards for democracy, market principles, and military organization, but most have a long way to go.

New post–Cold War roles.   NATO's transformation has also involved new contributions to European and international security. First, it took a role in stabilizing the Balkans. Indeed, NATO's actions in Bosnia and Kosovo represent its very first military actions ever. In 1995, with Security Council authorization, NATO planes bombed Bosnian Serb installations, an action that helped shift the military balance in Bosnia and lead to the Dayton peace negotiations. NATO then undertook major peacekeeping and peacebuilding responsibilities in conjunction with implementation of the Dayton peace accord. NATO members provided the majority of Implementation Force (IFOR) troops, although a number of other countries, including Russia, were also contributors. Then, in 1999, NATO's seventy-eight-day bombing campaign against the Federal Republic of Yugoslavia (Serbia) and intervention in Kosovo marked yet another step in carving out a new, post–Cold War role. Continuing ethnic tensions in both Bosnia and Kosovo make it doubtful that NATO forces will be significantly reduced or withdrawn for some time.

Since the global war against terrorism began in September 2001, NATO has moved to adapt to this new security environment. It is enhancing its operational capabilities to act quickly and in different modes with the 9,000-member NATO Response Force. In August 2003, NATO assumed control of the 5,000-member, UN-sanctioned international force keeping peace in Afghanistan. This marked the first time that NATO had undertaken an operation outside of Europe.

Relations with Russia.   An important corollary to NATO's enlargement and expanding mission is its efforts to build constructive relations with Russia. Alongside the 1997 decision on enlargement, the Founding Act on Mutual Relations, Cooperation and Security between NATO and the Russian Federation was signed. This created the Permanent Joint Council, a mechanism for regular consultations and cooperation regarding a wide range of issues such as joint peacekeeping operations, transparency of military doctrines, defense conversion, and nuclear safety. In the West, the Council was seen also as a mechanism for influencing Russian military reform and perceptions of NATO. In Russia, it was viewed as an institutionalized means of limiting the impact of NATO enlargement and ensuring Russian influence on NATO policies. Yet, the problem for Russia is that "Europe is about something more than geography; it is also a set of values" (Daalder and Goldgeier 2001: 83).

Russia is understandably leery of NATO enlargement, seeing expansion as a threat, while the United States sees it as a natural consequence of winning the Cold War and creating a new security order. Realists see NATO expansion as a means to achieve relative gains against Russia and further enhance Western security. Liberals view it as a means to strengthen democracy in former communist states and bring stability to crisis areas. NATO members have worked hard to convince Russia that NATO expansion is not a threat, and to institutionalize dialogue with Russia on issues that pertain to Russia's own security.

■ Organization for Security and Cooperation in Europe (OSCE)

The OSCE is the broadest organization in the European security architecture, covering the entire Eurasian region. It is currently composed of fifty-five member states in Europe, plus the United States, Canada, and all the states of the former Soviet Union. As the successor to the Conference on Security and Cooperation in Europe, it has evolved into an important instrument for broadly defined security cooperation and coordination, conflict prevention and resolution since 1990.

The predecessor CSCE was the product of a Soviet/Warsaw Pact proposal in the early 1970s to convene an all-European conference to resolve the outstanding issues from World War II, particularly territorial boundaries and the division of Germany. The Helsinki Final Act of 1975 contains a set of ten principles that should govern interstate relations: (1) sovereign equality of states, (2) refraining from the threat or use of force, (3) inviolability of frontiers, (4) territorial integrity of states, (5) peaceful settlement of disputes, (6) nonintervention in internal affairs, (7) respect for human rights and fundamental freedoms, (8) self-determination of peoples, (9) cooperation among states, and (10) fulfillment of obligations under international law. These principles form the normative core of what is now the OSCE-based European security regime. During the Cold War years, however, they produced several controversies, particularly surrounding the organization's right to intervene on behalf of human rights. The Cold War's end and pressures for independence from groups and regions within the Soviet Union and Yugoslavia highlighted the potential conflicts between principles 4 and 8. The rapidly evolving security environment in Europe between 1988 and 1994 led to strengthening of CSCE-supported confidence-building measures, transparency, democratization, and minority rights protections.

Following approval of the Charter of Paris for a New Europe in November 1990, CSCE was gradually transformed into the OSCE. A secretariat was established along with a Conflict Prevention Center, Office for Democratic Institutions and Human Rights, a parliamentary assembly composed of parliamentarians from all member states, annual ministerial meetings, biannual summits, and a permanent Committee of Senior Officials.

(Different parts of the organization are headquartered in different European cities.) In 1992, the Office of the High Commissioner on National Minorities was established to address ethnic conflicts. A further step toward formalizing the organization was taken in 1993 with the creation of the Permanent Council to carry on the work of the organization between the ministerial and summit conferences.

OSCE's post–Cold War tasks include monitoring elections in Bosnia and Albania; negotiating a ceasefire in Chechnya; mediating agreements between governments and secessionist regions in Moldova, Azerbaijan, Georgia, and Tajikistan; monitoring missions to potential trouble spots such as Kosovo and Vojvodina; preventive diplomacy in Crimea in Ukraine; and postconflict security building in Albania. Despite its large membership, the OSCE has been able "to respond more rapidly than most other institutions and to adapt its responses more appropriately to the specific issues arising in particular cases" (Hopmann 2000: 601). Although it has largely failed to resolve deep-seated ethnic conflicts, it has helped stop violence and prevent it from re-igniting. OSCE's roles in several conflict situations are discussed in Chapter 8.

▣ The European Union (EU)

The EU is a unique entity, involving much more commitment than any other regional organization. Where the initial steps involved only six Western European states, today twenty-five states are full members. The EU's development embodies a process of integration, where steps taken in one area have spilled over into others over time. It has exemplified both functionalism and neofunctionalism. It encompasses aspects of both supranationalism (sometimes also referred to as federalism) and intergovernmentalism. It has involved both the widening of membership and the deepening of ties among the member states, integrating their economies and societies more closely, expanding the authority of the community institutions over the member states. Much of the policymaking in Europe today is common or EU policy, made in Brussels through the institutions of the community. The EU affects the daily lives of its 450 million citizens who can now move freely between most of the member states and carry burgundy EU passports. The EU commands more than a third of the world's trade (both exports and imports), and citizens in eleven member countries use a common currency, the euro, launched in January 2002.

The EU's development has transformed governance in Europe, influencing everything from regulations on the habitat of birds to voting in the World Trade Organization; its complex institutions resemble those of nation-states with its own legal system, parliament, bureaucracy, currency, and court. It has also altered global politics and governance. The process of European integration is attributable to a complex set of factors.

Historical overview of European integration.   Regional political and economic integration in (Western) Europe began in part as an effort by European leaders to find ways to overcome the national rivalries that had led to two devastating world wars in the first half of the twentieth century. The United States was committed to promoting democracy and a more open international economic system to replace the protectionism, competitive currency devaluations, and other policies that had marked the rivalries among European powers (and excluded American businesses from European markets). The Soviet threat added impetus to strengthening the war-weakened countries, as did internal threats from strong communist parties in France and Italy. A desire to enmesh the Germans in international agreements that would prevent them from posing future threats to European security was another motivating factor. The United States added incentives through Marshall Plan requirements that the European governments cooperate in developing a plan for utilizing aid, formulate a joint effort rather than submit a series of national requests, and create an international organization to administer the aid to the sixteen participating countries. There were also Europeans such as Jean Monnet and Alcide De Gasperi who dreamed of the possibilities of a United States of Europe. Security threats, economic incentives, and visions all played a part. So, too, did economic interests of powerful sectors particularly in the French and German economies (notably heavy industry and agriculture), along with trends in the post–World War II international economy (notably rising trade and capital flows among the industrialized countries) that led governments to look for ways to respond to new opportunities for promoting economic gains.

The European Coal and Steel Community.   The birth of European integration occurred in May 1950 with a proposal by then French Foreign Minister Robert Schuman to place Franco-German coal and steel production under a common "High Authority." Schuman was proposing to accept recently defeated Germany as an economic equal and to hand over authority for both countries' key coal and steel industries to a supranational authority. He provided a concrete step for turning vague dreams into reality, but doing so in the key economic sector supporting warmaking capability (arms industries)—a strategy that accorded well with neofunctionalist theory. Schuman's declaration took shape in the European Coal and Steel Community (ECSC) established in 1951 with six member states (France, Germany, Italy, Belgium, Luxembourg, and the Netherlands). Great Britain rejected an invitation to join because of strong sentiments in both major political parties against loss of sovereignty and national control over coal and steel.

Illustrating the classic dynamic of functionalism, the ECSC was successful enough in boosting coal and steel production that the six member states agreed in 1958 to expand their cooperation under the European Atomic Energy Community (Euratom) and the European Economic Community (EEC). The founding documents of these three organizations form the constitutional basis of the EU. The governing institutions of the three have been merged. Two other integrating organizations were proposed in the 1950s but rejected, namely a European Defence Community and a European Political Community.

The Treaties of Rome: Euratom and the Common Market.   The Treaties of Rome represented recognition that the community could not develop the coal and steel sectors in isolation from other economic sectors. One treaty committed members to creating a common market over a period of twelve years through removal of all restrictions on internal trade; a common external tariff; reduction of barriers to free movement of people, services, and capital; the development of common agricultural and transport policies; and through the establishment of a European Social Fund and European Investment Bank. The second treaty created Euratom to establish a common market for atomic energy.

Although there were certainly tensions among the members and between governments and the community institutions, there was remarkably rapid progress in taking significant steps toward achieving the desired common market. In 1968, two years ahead of schedule, the six members completed an industrial customs union and had removed enough internal barriers to trade to agree on a common external tariff with nonmember countries and to form a single negotiating party in international trade talks.

Common policies.   Trade represented the first area in which the EEC members agreed on common policy. Also in 1968, the Common Agricultural Policy (CAP) came into existence with a single market for farm products and guaranteed prices for farmers. Beginning in the 1960s, the six members began the arduous process of harmonizing various health, safety, and consumer protection standards and regulations as well as easing the barriers to movement of workers among member countries. In 1969, governments agreed on the principle of economic and monetary union, both of which were regarded as essential to achieving political union, although the sovereignty lost with monetary union was particularly difficult for them to contemplate. Despite disagreement over whether economic or monetary union should come first, they did agree to begin efforts toward controlling exchange rate fluctuations and coordinate their national economic policies. Common policies have been created in a variety of areas as discussed below.

Enlargement.   Slow economic growth in the 1970s stalled any deepening of European integration, but there was movement on another front. In 1973, the community's first enlargement took place with accession of Great Britain, Ireland, and Denmark. (Norwegian voters rejected the accession agreement their government had signed.) Later in the 1970s, decisions were made that led to the accession of Greece, Spain, and Portugal. The addition of Ireland and the three Southern European countries introduced a much wider disparity among members' levels of economic development than existed with the original six or with the UK and Denmark. For Greece, Spain, and Portugal, however, a strong desire to bolster the new democracies in these countries provided political impetus to their membership. In 1994, the decision was made to admit Finland, Sweden, and Austria and in 2004, ten more countries joined. Table 5.1 details some of the consequences of these five enlargements, which have quadrupled membership and complicated the community's decisionmaking processes, but increased its influence as the world's largest economic bloc.

Single European Act. In 1987, EC members took their most important step since the Treaty of Rome with the Single European Act (SEA) that established the goal of completing a single market by December 1992. This

Table 5.1   EU Enlargements

	Original Members (1958)	First Enlargement (1973)	Second Enlargement (1981)	Third Enlargement (1986)	Fourth Enlargement (1995)	Fifth Enlargement (2004)
Member states	Belgium France Germany Italy Luxembourg Netherlands	Britain Ireland Denmark	Greece	Spain Portugal	Austria Finland Sweden	Cyprus Czech Rep. Estonia Hungary Latvia Lithuania Malta Poland Slovakia Slovenia
Population	185m	273m	287m	338m	370m	450m
Members of the European Parliament	142	273	287	338	370	TBA
Qualified majority voting	12/17	41/58	45/63	54/76	62/87	TBA
Number of member states	6	9	10	12	15	25

meant a complicated process of removing all remaining physical, fiscal, and technical barriers to trade, harmonizing different national health, food processing, and other standards, varying levels of indirect taxation such as value-added taxes (VAT), and barriers to movement of peoples such as professional licensing requirements. (See Chapter 9 for further discussion.) The changes, however, allowed banks and companies to do business throughout the community; EC residents to live, work, and draw pensions anywhere in the EC; and an end to monopolies in sectors such as electricity and telecommunications. The SEA also incorporated a number of important institutional changes such as greater power for the European Parliament.

Maastricht, Amsterdam, and closer union.   Even before the SEA 1992 deadline, the twelve members signed the Maastricht Treaty on European Union calling for "an ever closer union among the peoples of Europe," language first used in the 1957 Treaty of Rome's Preamble. With Maastricht, the European Community became the European Union. The original European Community became one of three pillars of the new EU. A second pillar was Common Foreign and Security Policy (CFSP), while the third pillar included home affairs and justice—new sets of issues for common policy. In fact, both the second and third pillars remain largely matters for individual governments or, at best, intergovernmental agreement. Maastricht also gave impetus to European monetary union with agreement to institute a single European currency by January 1999 and create European citizenship with a common passport and rights to live and vote wherever citizens liked. It included further institutional changes as well. The transition to the EU that Maastricht incorporated was briefly set back when Danish voters rejected the treaty in a referendum; the treaty was also put to a referendum in France where it narrowly passed. Following agreement that Denmark could opt out of certain provisions in the treaty, Danish voters passed a second referendum. This, however, was a wakeup call to EU leaders that deepening integration was not accepted by all of Europe's citizens and prompted debate about the "democratic deficit" within the EU whereby most decisions have been made by governmental leaders and bureaucrats without direct input from voters.

The prospect of still further enlargement to include countries of Eastern Europe and the Mediterranean lent urgency to institutional reform. These issues have been addressed through a series of intergovernmental conferences convened periodically since 1990. The Treaty of Amsterdam that was signed in October 1997 and came into force in May 1999 gave a green light to further enlargement and to issues such as social policy, immigration, asylum, the environment, and consumer protection. Governments failed to reach agreement, however, on necessary changes in the structure of EU institutions, such as the size of the commission and modifications in the voting procedures. Discussions on constitutional changes are focused on the draft Convention on the Future of Europe that is intended to resolve structural problems arising out of the 2004 enlargement. Figure 5.3 summarizes key parts of the European integration process.

Structure.   The basic structure of EU institutions, including the commission, Council of Ministers, council, parliament, and Court of Justice, is shown in Figure 5.4. The discussion that follows is based on the arrangements in effect at the beginning of 2004, subject to change if a new constitution is adopted.

European Commission.   The European Commission, generally known as "the commission" is the supranational, executive body of the EU and the

---

Figure 5.3   Timeline of European Integration

1951	Establishment of European Coal and Steel Community (6 members)
1957	Treaties of Rome establish European Economic Community and European Atomic Energy Community (6 members)
1962	Common Agricultural Policy (CAP) launched
1968	Completion of Customs Union
1970	Launch of European Political Cooperation (foreign policy coordination)
1973	First Enlargement (3 countries)
1979	Launch of European Monetary System
	First direct elections for European Parliament
1981	Second Enlargement (1 country)
1986	Single European Act launches single market program and adds environmental and social policy
	Third Enlargement (2 countries)
1992	Maastricht Treaty on European Union sets goals for economic and monetary union, establishes Common Foreign and Security Policy, launches cooperation on Justice and Home Affairs (3 pillars)
1995	Fourth Enlargement (3 countries)
1997	Treaty of Amsterdam extends competence over Justice and Home Affairs
1999	Launch of common monetary policy and single currency (euro)
2002–2003	Draft Convention on the Future of Europe
2004	Fifth Enlargement (10 countries)

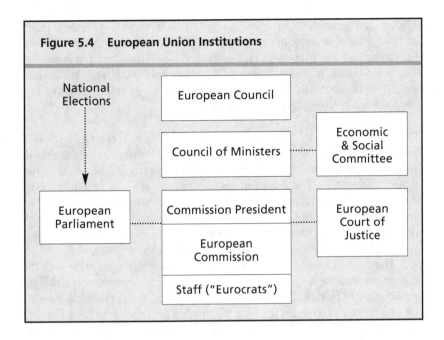

Figure 5.4   European Union Institutions

engine for integration, in keeping with neofunctionalist theory, although it has not always acted as such. It has the exclusive power to initiate community legislation and the responsibility to advance the goals of the treaties. It works with states to implement policies and legislation, represents the EU in international trade negotiations, draws up the budget and spends funds approved, and can promulgate regulations on technical matters that are binding on states. The commission also plays a key role in the enforcement of EU law with the right to warn states when they are violating treaty obligations and the power to initiate legal action in the European Court of Justice against them.

The twenty members of the commission are drawn from each of the member states, with the five largest states currently naming two commissioners each. Although nominated by national governments, the commissioners are not national representatives and may not be removed by their national governments; they are expected to take an impartial view, based on the interests of the union as a whole and the letter and spirit of the founding treaties. They serve for four-year, renewable terms. Commissioners are approved by the European Parliament, which may also censure and thereby remove the entire commission, which the parliament came close to doing in March 1999. The threat of censure alone led the commission to resign at the time. The twenty commissioners are responsible for particular policy areas (known as directorates-general) and for supervising the work of some

17,000 civil servants ("Eurocrats"), aided by their respective personal staffs or cabinets. The directorates range from Agriculture, to Competition Policy, Economic and Monetary Affairs, Regional Policy, Trade, and Environment. The commission, however, makes decisions as a whole, usually by consensus. The president of the commission functions as its chief executive and can veto nominations for commissioners.

Council of Ministers/Council of the European Union.   The EU's Council of Ministers, now the Council of the European Union, represents both supranationalism and intergovernmentalism. Formally, the commission reports to the council, which must approve the commission's policy proposals. It is, in effect, the primary legislative body for the EU—far more powerful than the European Parliament. In reality, for much of the EU's history, the commission has played the engine role described above, with the council ratifying, modifying, or vetoing proposals.

The council is made up of one government minister per state with the composition changing based on the issues under consideration (foreign, economic, agriculture, finance, or transport policy, etc.). Thus, the particular individuals making up the Council of Ministers vary from one meeting to the next. The frequency and importance of council meetings depend upon the degree to which member states have transferred policymaking authority to the EU. Agriculture ministers, for example, meet monthly to deal with issues of commodity prices and subsidy levels since agricultural policy is primarily made in Brussels, not national capitals. Transport, education, and environment ministers meet only a few times a year since these areas are still largely under national governments. With efforts to increase common foreign and security policy since 1992, the members' foreign ministers have met more frequently.

The presidency of the Council of Ministers rotates every six months, and along with the commission president, the council president represents the EU at many major international meetings. There has been a growing tendency for council presidents also to articulate a set of priorities for their terms.

The Council of Ministers has a weighted voting system intended to facilitate more efficient community decisionmaking for all but policy areas of greatest political sensitivity. The system is known as qualified majority voting or QMV. It was designed to ensure that big countries could not act without the cooperation of at least some of the smaller countries (or vice versa) and that decisions could not be blocked by one or more states. Between 1965 and the early 1980s, however, the French government refused to permit the use of qualified weighted majority in any policy areas, which meant the council could act only when there was unanimity among the members. Qualified majority voting, van Oudenaren (2000: 74) notes, "is a device for balancing the requirements of efficiency and supranationality with respect for sovereignty and the distinctive economic and political circumstances of the member states." Supporters of a strong Europe favor extending it, while the UK and others who are reluctant about further integration oppose such extension. Foreign and security policy decisions, along with immigration and taxation, remain firmly intergovernmental and, hence, require unanimous support for action.

The European Parliament. The only EU body that is directly elected by voters in the member states is the European Parliament (EP). The members of the European Parliament (MEPs) have worked over time to increase the institution's power. Since the mid-1980s, they have succeeded in gaining substantially greater legislative and supervisory responsibility as part of the different treaty reforms.

The EP consists currently of 626 MEPs elected for five-year terms. This makes it one of the largest legislative bodies in the world and unwieldy because of its size, the equal status of eleven languages, and its cycle of perpetual motion between three venues: Strasbourg for plenary sessions, Brussels for committee meetings, and Luxembourg where staff have their offices. Seats in the parliament are distributed among member states, but not according to the same member-to-population ratio, resulting in substantial variation. For example, the current ratio for Germany is one MEP for every 805,000 Germans; the ratio for Luxembourg is 1:66,000. Historically, election procedures differed among member states, including the way candidates are nominated, voter eligibility, and the electoral system itself (all continental countries and Ireland using proportional representation and Britain using a winner-take-all system). The 2004 EP election inaugurates a common electoral system, but one that still leaves room for national differences. Prior to the initiation of direct elections in 1979, many MEPs were also members of their national parliaments and thus held what were called "dual mandates." Some countries and political parties now ban individuals from holding a dual mandate.

EP members are seated by political group, not by national delegations. The rules of procedures strongly encourage them to join transnational political groups that correspond to the main European political parties. The two largest groups are the Party of the European Socialists on the left and the European People's Party (or Christian Democrats) on the right. Both groups include political parties or individual politicians from all member states. The strength of these transnational party groups has increased along with the growing scope of European integration. A third center-right group—the Liberals—experienced decline with the successive EU enlargements and splintering of various national party members. The growth of Green and extreme right parties in various European countries has been mirrored by their appearance in the EP since the mid-1980s. Despite ideological differences, however, party groups frequently share common interests on particular issues and in promoting the EP's influence in the EU legislative process.

The EP's role has evolved considerably over time, and especially since the Single European Act in the mid-1980s, as its members have used arguments about democratic accountability to gain greater responsibilities and to be taken more seriously. Because the Council of Ministers is the EU's primary legislative body and the commission has the sole power to propose new laws and policies, the parliament's role in this regard is circumscribed and complex. It cannot initiate any legislation. Nor can it enact laws on its own or raise revenues. Thus, while it looks like a legislative body, it lacks the powers that normally define such bodies.

EU decisionmaking.   Initially, the Council of Ministers was required to solicit parliament's opinion regarding directives and regulations, but was free to ignore them. Under the SEA, parliament began to share legislative responsibilities with the council and could reject council-proposed legislation by a majority vote, which the council could only override if it acted unanimously. Maastricht introduced a procedure of co-decision under which parliament and council must agree on legislation. It also added a procedure of simple yes or no votes (assent) by parliament for decisions taken on a unanimous basis by the Council of Ministers. The latter would include international agreements and admission of new member states. Finally, the Amsterdam Treaty simplified most of the procedures.

In effect, the Council of Ministers and the European Parliament now constitute a bicameral (two-house) legislature. The council must take parliament's opinions more seriously. Party groups in parliament now work more closely together because what the EP does matters more. Lobbyists from interest groups, corporations, and foreign governments pay more attention to the EP to influence the shape of legislation where once they directed most of their efforts at the commission. The parliament also shares joint budgetary authority with the council. It may offer amendments and may ask for appropriations for programs of special interest to MEPs, such as research and development. It can reject the budget with a two-thirds majority, which it did on two occasions in 1979 and 1984. Parliament's power is constrained, however, by its inability to affect EU revenues and, hence, the overall size of the budget. Furthermore, much of EU spending is mandated by policies such as the Common Agricultural Policy and cannot be altered by parliament.

Finally, the parliament has certain powers with respect to other EU institutions, particularly the commission. In addition to its ability to debate legislation proposed by the commission, the EP since 1994 has had the responsibility of approving the appointment of the president and College of Commissioners (but not individual commissioners) and the power to force their resignation through a vote of censure. Because the latter would provoke a major political crisis, it is primarily used as a deterrent tool—threatened but not used. Only once, thus far, has parliament come close to censure. In January 1999, charges of fraud and corruption among the commissioners led 232 MEPs to vote for removal. A committee of inquiry was appointed and in March 1999 the commission resigned. Indeed, EP has used committees of inquiry with increasing frequency to influence community policy. Genetically altered foods were among topics such committees were formed to investigate.

From a weak advisory assembly whose members were appointed by national parliaments, the European Parliament has evolved into the only directly elected and accountable institution in the EU. It has steadily increased its powers over legislation and other EU institutions, especially since the mid-1980s. While it has narrowed the EU's democratic deficit and become a co-legislature with the Council of Ministers, EP still is not a true legislature. Voter turnout in the EP direct elections has slipped, mirroring voters' sense that it still doesn't affect their lives very much. The traveling road show drains time and resources as long as MEPs and the secretariat have to continue to shuttle between three locations. Still, there is no other such directly elected international legislative body in the world.

The European Council. Easily confused with the Council of Ministers, the European Council came into existence in 1974 when European heads of government (prime ministers and, for France and Finland, presidents) agreed to hold regular summit meetings on community matters and thereby to give greater political impetus to the integration process. The council convenes twice a year (usually June and December), and the country holding the presidency of the Council of Ministers also chairs the European Council and hosts the meeting. Although it generally does not get involved in details of legislation and policymaking, it has become the key body for major EU initiatives such as concluding the single market, monetary union, and enlargement. At Maastricht (1991) and Amsterdam (1997) the respective treaties were approved.

The European Court of Justice. The European Court of Justice is a key institution, as discussed in Chapter 3, with responsibility to interpret and enforce EU law from its seat in Luxembourg. The ECJ has the power to rule on the constitutionality of all EU law, interpret the EU treaties, to provide advisory opinions to national courts in cases where there are questions about EU law, and to settle disputes involving other EU institutions, member states, individuals, or corporations. Since the various EU treaties are not ordinary international agreements, the ECJ's work "coincides with the making of a constitution for Europe," in the words of a member of the court (quoted in Dinan 1999: 302).

In Chapter 3, we discussed the ECJ's structure and mode of functioning. Here, we focus on its role in promoting European regional integration and governance. Since 1954, it has heard over 9,000 cases and issued more than 4,000 judgments. The cases fall into one of two categories: preliminary rulings in which the court is advising national courts and tribunals on how points of national law relate to EU law, and direct actions that apply to the parties in a given case (for example, the commission, a member state, or a corporation). Several landmark cases, most of which were requests for preliminary rulings, established the supremacy of EU law over national law and the direct effect of EU legislation.

The ECJ's success (and the corresponding development of community law) has hinged on the willingness of national courts to seek and abide by preliminary rulings under Article 234 of the Treaty of Rome. Through direct actions, the court plays an important role in efforts to get member states, EU institutions, corporations, and individuals to fulfill their legal obligations under the treaties. For example, in carrying out its own role as "guardian of the treaties," the commission may bring an action against a member state for infringement of obligations and has regularly done so over the years. Although no member state has refused to accept a major court ruling, there are many instances of delayed implementation. To address the problem of enforcement, the Maastricht Treaty gave the ECJ power to impose fines on states for refusing to act on a court ruling (Article 228).

Because of the nature of its rules, the court has a unique relationship with the other EU institutions. It has ruled against the commission, especially when the latter tried to extend its competence in the area of external economic relations, but it also works closely with the commission in promoting economic integration. The court shares an integrationist and supranationalist outlook with the parliament and has, in fact, also ruled that the EP could bring community acts for judicial review. The court and the council, on the other hand, are often at odds since the council represents national interests and intergovernmentalism and rarely supranationalism. Almost all states have been taken to the ECJ at some time, some far more than others, and they have often criticized court rulings that they viewed as hostile to national interests. For example in the early 1990s, the court overruled a British act of Parliament and issued a preliminary ruling protecting the rights of migrant workers that angered the British and German governments respectively (Dinan 1999: 311). One could argue that the ECJ is currently the single most powerful international court in the world. Certainly, it is a

key institutional part of European regionalism and the development of the
new legal order that EU law represents.

EU law. The various EU treaties form the EU's primary law and collectively form an informal constitution. EU legislation approved by the
Council of Ministers and European Parliament is a secondary form of EU
law. In addition, there are laws in the form of regulations issued by the
Council of Ministers alone, council and parliament, or commission alone
(depending upon the applicable section of the treaties) that have direct
effect; directives issued by the commission specify results to be achieved,
such as competition policy or air pollution standards, but leave the means
to member states; and finally, decisions are binding measures issued to specific parties, such as to block a merger between two companies.

The supranational and integrationist character of the EU can best be
understood by examining the development of EU law, which unlike international law has direct effect on individuals and other legal persons and
must be obeyed by the sovereign states that are members of the union.
Court preliminary rulings or decisions firmly established the principles of
EU law discussed in Chapter 3: its primacy or supremacy over national law
and its direct effect on states, citizens, and corporations. Court rulings, such
as the Cassis de Dijon case (ECJ 1979), have played a key role in achieving
the EU's goals by providing an ever-expanding body of case law. The court
has promoted equal treatment for women through decisions dealing with
equal pay for men and women, pensions, training, promotions, part-time
work, and so on. It has upheld community authority to govern trade by ruling that member states could no longer enter into obligations with third
countries affecting common rules. In one of its most public cases, the court
also upheld freedom of movement for workers by throwing out the Belgian
soccer club's rules that made it difficult for a Belgian player to transfer to a
French club (ECJ 1995 [Union Royale belge des sociétés de football asso-
ciation]).

Clearly, EU law forms a core component of evolving regional governance and integration. It is a distinctive legal system, lying between traditional national (or municipal) legal systems and international law, with a
powerful court to interpret the law and enforce judgments against member
states. It represents the pooled sovereignty that increasingly characterizes
the EU. Much the same can be said for many areas of common EU policy.

EU common policies. Beginning with trade and agriculture, the EU has
moved progressively into more and more areas of policy, ranging from fisheries to transport, competition, social policy, regional policy, monetary policy and common currency, environment, justice and home affairs, and

external relations. Three different approaches have been used to advance common policies: mutual recognition of different national standards, community directives establishing standards frameworks, and harmonization of standards (the most difficult since it requires agreeing on a new, common set of standards). Chapter 9 addresses policies associated with the single market, agriculture, and monetary union. EU environmental policy is discussed in Chapter 11. We focus here, then, on social policy and the efforts to create common foreign and security policy.

Social policy.   The EU's involvement in social policy is a consequence of the long history of social welfare policies in most member countries. It encompasses issues of workers' rights, women, and working and living conditions. The most active proponents have been European labor unions, social democratic parties, and the commission. Opposing common social policy have been businesses and conservative political parties who argue that social policy makes European companies less competitive in the global market because it keeps labor costs high.

Serious attention to common social policy began in the 1980s and became a key part of the Single European Act. A separate Charter of Social Rights was adopted in 1989 by eleven of the then twelve members. Great Britain's Conservative government at the time opposed what was seen as a socialist document, arguing that it was inappropriate for the community to have laws on working conditions and welfare benefits. Yet, a key objective was lessening the variations in such regulations across the member countries because of their effects on the single market. The charter incorporates twelve principles ranging from freedom of movement and vocational training to gender equality and protection for children, the elderly, and handicapped. It was subsequently incorporated into the Maastricht Treaty with an opt-out provision for Great Britain. Social policy illustrates an area of policy where the EU's supranational powers are evident, while common foreign and security policy illustrates weaker EU power and more intergovernmentalism.

Common foreign and security policy.   After achieving the initial customs union and common external tariff in 1968, the European Community began negotiating as one entity in GATT and initiated foreign policy coordination in 1970 under the guise of European Political Cooperation (EPC). During the 1970s, the community spoke out on behalf of Palestinian rights and against South Africa's apartheid. It imposed sanctions on the Soviet Union after the latter's invasion of Afghanistan in 1979 and expressed solidarity with Great Britain over the 1982 Falklands/Malvinas dispute, imposing sanctions against Argentina. The Single European Act and the Maastricht Treaty strengthened the bases for formulating and implementing common foreign and security policy, but the EU failed to act effectively to stop war in Yugoslavia in 1991–1992, despite having assumed primary responsibility for dealing with the situation. Although it is taking greater responsibility for building peaceful conditions in the Balkans, the division between France and Germany on one side and Great Britain and Spain on the other over the 2003 Iraq war demonstrates the impediments to common policy.

To date, efforts to formulate a common European foreign and security policy have been long on rhetoric and short on results. The larger countries (Great Britain, France, and Germany) have been reluctant to give up their individual voices in world politics (let alone their Security Council permanent seats) and, thus, diminished the EU's potential influence as a collective entity. The absence of an EU defense force is a serious liability, for military capabilities still count in international politics. Efforts to create some EU defense identity, such as the 2001 decision to create a rapid reaction force, have encountered opposition from neutral Ireland and pacifist Denmark, as well as serious U.S. concerns about the relationship between an EU force and NATO.

Still, the EU has developed an extensive web of relationships with individual countries and other regional groupings. The commission has missions in many capitals and at the United Nations and has created the posts of High Representative and Commissioner of External Relations. Other countries maintain diplomatic representatives in Brussels. The commission's president participates in G-7/8 summits, and the EU has been a member of several "contact groups" such as those for the former Yugoslavia and the Israeli-Palestinian conflict. Extensive meetings are held at the UN, global conferences, and in other settings to coordinate a common policy. The Lomé Convention, a trade and aid agreement with seventy-one African, Caribbean, and Pacific countries, many of which are former colonies, is a cornerstone of EU development assistance programs, but some individual member states contribute more aid than the EU does, showing their reluctance to give up national instruments of influence. The EU Humanitarian Office dispenses humanitarian and food aid through NGOs and UN agencies in the Balkans, Africa, and Afghanistan. In short, while members have set up an elaborate system for coordinating their policies more closely, foreign and security policy remains primarily a responsibility of members, not of the EU.

Future directions of European integration: The challenges of widening and deepening.   In December 2002, the fifteen EU members agreed to admit ten new members: two Mediterranean island states and eight Central European and Baltic, former communist states. The result is a "mega-Europe" of twenty-five countries, 450 million people, and an economy of more than $9 trillion—more people and almost as large an economy as that of the United States. For the ten new members, EU membership means adhering to 80,000 pages of EU laws and regulations accumulated over forty-five years of the integration process. Although all won special concessions and extra time to phase in the EU's now extensive environmental legislation, they must wait seven to ten years before getting full benefits such as free movement of labor and agricultural subsidies. All of the new countries are poorer than the rest of the members, however, which will increase the disparities and tensions.

The implications for the EU itself are enormous. The most difficult question is how this bigger EU will be governed. Enlargement makes reform of the current institutional structures imperative, and former French President Valéry Giscard d'Estaing has chaired Europe's "constitutional convention" or Convention on the Future of Europe since early 2002. There is substantial disagreement on what shape the reforms should take. Possibilities include a federation or confederation, more powerful parliament, a president elected by member states for up to two thirty-month terms, and enhanced executive powers for a smaller commission. Under proposed changes, the council would make most decisions by qualified majority voting (Rakove 2003). Yet, smaller states worry about arrangements that favor larger states; Germany and France do not want to lose their leadership positions; ordinary citizens want to remedy the democratic deficit that has allowed government leaders and Eurocrats in Brussels to run the EU with little direct accountability. Taxpayers worry about the cost of enlargement.

The challenges of enlargement or widening of the community are matched by the challenges of deepening. As integration has reduced the latitude of member states, opposition to further integration has grown. Moravcsik (1998) stresses that the process of integration has been largely driven by conscious governmental choices based on economic interests, relative power on different issues under conditions of asymmetric interdependence, and desire to lock in commitments of other governments and future domestic governments through giving up or pooling sovereignty in EU institutions. Yet, strong differences in states' positions persist. For example, Denmark and Great Britain oppose more supranationalism or federalism and the European Monetary Union (EMU) (which both opted out of). They constitute the "Euroskeptics." The ten new members will only increase the probabilities of disagreement and the difficulties of deepening integration. Although the EU constitutes an extraordinary achievement in regional integration, its further development cannot be taken for granted since much will depend on the outcome of the constitutional reforms. We look next at a much newer and more tentative regional initiative on Europe's eastern fringe.

The Commonwealth of Independent States (CIS)

The Commonwealth of Independent States was created simultaneously with the dissolution of the former Soviet Union in late 1991. Russia, Ukraine, and Belarus signed an agreement calling for the creation of an economic trading bloc with eventual implementation of common communications, immigration, crime, and environmental policies. The protocol signed in Alma-Ata on December 21, 1991, admitted Armenia, Azerbaijan, Moldova, Uzbekistan, Kazakhstan, Turkmenistan, Kyrgyzstan, and Tajikistan. Georgia joined in 1993, completing membership in the CIS. The Baltic states of Lithuania, Latvia, and Estonia refused to join, preferring to look to Western Europe for economic assistance and political guidance.

From its genesis, the CIS lacked a clear direction and faced a number of important conflicts because it formed so quickly after its members became sovereign states. There were concerns over potential Russian domination and disagreements over the degree of integration desired. Among the most important early consultations were acceptance of Russia as the successor state to the Soviet Union and the disposition of nuclear weapons in Russia, Ukraine, Belarus, and Kazakhstan. The latter led to agreement to return all weapons to Russia with a promise of future consultations about Russia's weapons capabilities, but only after the United States stepped in to provide security guarantees and development assistance to Ukraine. Another issue concerned whether to have a common, supranational CIS defense force or national armies. Russia itself abandoned the former approach when in 1992 it seized control of Soviet navy and air force assets and formed its Ministry of Defense. In June 1993, the CIS High Command was abolished and replaced with a small staff for military cooperation and coordination. A 1995 agreement on collective security provides for common defense against external threats but does not address conflicts within the CIS, nor has a planned CIS rapid deployment force been implemented. Similarly, although there have been attempts at economic integration beginning with a 1993 Economic Union Treaty, the reality has been a drop in intraregional trade despite high historic interdependence, common problems in shifting to market economies, and low volumes of trade with outside countries. The major difficulty for CIS is the desire of many of the Soviet Union's successor states to foster ties with other European institutions, rather than developing their own region. It also illustrates the degree to which Europe is a magnet if not a model for others.

Is Europe a Model for Other Regions?

There is no question that countries in other regions of the world have viewed developments in Europe as a potential model to follow. As one scholar has noted, "The EC is a laboratory in which to investigate a series of common political phenomena developed further in Europe than elsewhere on the globe" (Moravscik 1998: 500). Yet, the circumstances that supported the development of European regional governance, and particularly European integration from the ECSC to the EU, are unlikely to be duplicated elsewhere. In fact, many Asian leaders strongly reject the European model as inappropriate because of its roots in Western political culture and traditions. They have particularly taken issue with Europe's reliance on formal institutions, rules, and legalism because it is at odds with cultural patterns in much of Asia. Nonetheless, people in many regions of the world continue to use the European experience as a benchmark and guide to one model of regional governance.

■ Regional Organizations in the Americas

▨ *Evolution of Regionalism in the Americas*

Some of the oldest regional initiatives took place in the western hemisphere in the nineteenth century. Simón Bolívar, who liberated many Latin American countries from Spanish colonialism, convened the Congress of Panama in 1826 with the hope of creating an association of newly independent Latin American states. Early moves toward regional unions gained strength primarily during periods of external danger and failed when those declined and interstate disputes dominated relations. In 1889, the first of nine International Conferences of American States (including the United States) created the International Union of American Republics (renamed the Pan American Union in 1910). The last of these conferences in 1948 produced the Organization of American States (OAS). In a separate initiative, the Inter-American Treaty of Reciprocal Assistance (Rio Treaty) for regional collective defense was signed in 1947. The OAS was to be the primary forum for inter-American cooperation while the Rio Treaty was to deal with military actions or aggression initiating from outside or within the region, which was defined in detail in the treaty. This collective defense arrangement was far more limited than NATO, however, because the Latin American governments refused to accept joint command of military forces or any binding obligation to use force without their explicit consent (Article 20). Beginning in the 1950s, there were also a variety of initiatives for subregional economic integration among groups of Central American, South American, and Caribbean states to promote development.

Two approaches: Hemispheric regionalism and subregional integration. These various initiatives embodied two approaches to Latin American regionalism. One is the idea of hemispheric regionalism or pan-Americanism, encompassing the entire Western Hemisphere. The other approach has promoted regional cooperation and economic integration among Latin American countries as a strategy for development and has involved a large number of subregional initiatives. Both approaches have eschewed EU-style supranationalism in favor of intergovernmentalism. Both, however, also are marked by the differing visions of the United States and Latin American states. Where the United States has historically been interested in the security of its backyard, Latin Americans have seen unity as the most effective way to secure their interests, including protection against U.S. dominance. Many Latin American nations, especially Mexico, historically opposed ceding any authority to an organization in which the United States was a member.

The coexistence of these two approaches reflects the most significant characteristic of the Americas: the enormous disparity in size, power, and economic wealth between the United States and all other states. This has inevitably affected the dynamics of hemispheric regionalism in particular. U.S. hegemony and the history of frequent U.S. unilateral interventions, especially in the Caribbean and Central America, have made it difficult to define a regional identity except in geographic terms. Although there are extensive economic ties among countries in the region, they have long reflected classic dominance-dependency patterns, and while the Latin American countries have placed development cooperation at the top of their list of priorities, the same has not generally been true for the United States.

The alternative "integration as road to development" approach emerged from initiatives by the UN-based Economic Commission for Latin America (ECLA, and later, ECLAC after the inclusion of the Caribbean countries, but known also by the Spanish acronym, CEPAL) and its first secretary-general, the Argentinian economist Raul Prebisch. Both were closely associated with dependency theories of underdevelopment that attributed the lack of development to structural factors in the international system, most notably the dominance of the "center" in production of manufactured goods and unequal exchange of manufactured goods and raw materials. Since many national markets are small and a strategy of industrialization through import substitution had its limits, regional integration was seen as a means to providing larger markets and economies of scale for industrialization. Regional integration in this case was not associated with liberalization in other respects, however, for dependency theory advocated import substitution, state regulation, and intervention to boost modernization.

Based on these ideas, regional integration efforts in Central and South America proliferated in the 1950s and 1960s. The schemes varied significantly from loose trade arrangements (as in the Latin American Free Trade Association, or LAFTA) to more interventionist integration systems (Andean Group), but most were little more than empty shells. The

1973–1974 oil crisis and severe economic difficulties in most Latin American countries, including huge debt burdens, ended much of the effort at regional integration and reinforced inward-looking attitudes from the early 1970s until the 1990s.

Regionalism in Latin America made a strong comeback with the Cold War's end, settlements of the Central American conflicts, and the end of ideological conflict. Key factors included the move toward democracy in all Latin American countries except Cuba; the acceptance by most governments of neoliberal market capitalism; the effects of globalization including Latin American countries' fear of being marginalized in the world economy; and a new security agenda of transnational problems including drug trafficking and environmental concerns. Mexico's policy shifts that brought about the North American Free Trade Agreement (NAFTA) with the United States and Canada separated it from other Latin American countries but also opened the possibilities for them of negotiating accession after President George H. W. Bush's Enterprise for the Americas speech in June 1990 that revived the idea of a hemisphere-wide free trade area. These developments opened the way to better relations between the United States and Latin America.

The second wave of Latin American regionalism, then, involves both hemispheric initiatives as well as five subregional integration efforts. The subregional include the Common Market of the South known as Mercosur (Argentina, Brazil, Uruguay, and Paraguay), the Group of Three (Mexico, Colombia, and Venezuela), the Andean Community (Venezuela, Ecuador, Peru, Colombia, and Bolivia), the Central American Common Market (CACM), and the Caribbean Community (CARICOM), in addition to NAFTA.

United States influence.   Key to inter-American hemispheric regionalism, however, has been the amount and type of attention the United States gave to Latin America. Historically, periods of U.S. interest in the region have been followed by periods of neglect when the United States "subordinated its Latin American policy to its global interests" (Thérien, Fortmann, and Gosselin 1996: 233). Neglect, however, is not necessarily all bad as it can allow the Latin Americans more autonomy in dealing with different issues. U.S. hegemony and dominance were greatest during the 1950s and early 1960s, when the United States got the Latin Americans to accept its anticommunist agenda and used the Rio Treaty to legitimize actions against suspected communist subversion in Guatemala, Cuba, and the Dominican Republic.

Beginning with the Cuban revolution in 1959, however, U.S. influence in the region declined as interests diverged. The United States supported many Latin military regimes in the 1960s and 1970s (including the 1971 coup that overthrew the democratically elected government of Chile). After the brief flurry of interest surrounding President Kennedy's Alliance for Progress initiative, U.S. attention was diverted to Vietnam and other global concerns. In addition, Latin America's involvement in the North-South conflict during the 1960s and 1970s led to sharp differences in visions of the international system and inter-American affairs, differences that still mark OAS debates on economic issues. The Reagan administration tried to reimpose American dominance in the early 1980s, especially in dealing with Nicaragua, but its interventionist policies antagonized major Latin American nations.

Political and economic changes in Latin America and the Caribbean in the 1980s, including the 1980s debt crisis, transitions from military dictatorships to democracies in several countries, and the region-wide movement toward economic liberalization were seen as positive developments by the United States, leading to new hemispheric initiatives.

In short, U.S. foreign policy has been pivotal in shaping the responses of other countries—at times encouraging and aiding multilateral initiatives, at others either ignoring the region entirely or using its dominance in ways that precluded cooperation. To understand Latin American regionalism further, we look briefly at the hemispheric approach embodied in the OAS and summit process as well as the integrationist approach associated with subregional initiatives such as NAFTA, Mercosur, and CARICOM.

Hemispheric Regionalism: The Organization of American States (OAS)

The OAS is the most comprehensive IGO in the Americas, a multifaceted institution that has become far more active since the Cold War's end than during in its earlier history. It was established in 1948, when twenty-one countries in the hemisphere adopted the Charter of the Organization of American States. At the same time, participants signed the American Declaration of the Rights and Duties of Man, the first international document devoted to human rights principles, and the Rio Treaty. The OAS subsequently expanded to include fourteen other nations, including the Caribbean island states and Canada, which joined only in 1991. No other regional organization in the world includes as strong a North-South dimension as the OAS, nor the same combination of collective defense, political, economic, and social purposes.

The OAS Charter has been amended four times and includes provisions for strengthening regional peace and security, common action against aggression, and limiting conventional weapons. It also calls for promoting representative democracy, seeking solution of political, juridical, and economic problems, and promoting economic, social, and cultural cooperation, as well as for eradication of extreme poverty.

Organs.   The primary organs of the OAS include the General Assembly, the Permanent Council, the Inter-American Council for Integral Development, and the Secretariat. There are numerous special commissions and committees, two of which are specifically mentioned in the charter as it has been amended over the years: the Inter-American Juridical Committee and the Inter-American Commission on Human Rights. The system also includes the Inter-American Court of Human Rights, which is further discussed in Chapter 10, and the Inter-American Development Bank, which is examined in Chapter 9. All members are represented in the General Assembly, Permanent Council, and Inter-American Council for Integral Development with one vote each.

The General Assembly that meets annually and, when requested, in special session, is considered the OAS's highest decisionmaking body. Like the UN General Assembly, it may consider any matter relating to friendly relations among American states. It is also specifically charged with strengthening cooperation with the UN and its specialized agencies. The Permanent Council is alternately known as the Organ of Consultation under the Rio Security Treaty and is analogous to the UN Security Council in that its primary functions relate to peace and security matters. When it meets in this mode, its members are usually the foreign ministers. Decisions are made by a two-thirds majority, excluding the parties to a dispute.

The Inter-American Council for Integral Development was created with a charter amendment in 1996 after years of discussions about the ineffectiveness of OAS's approaches to development. It is intended to promote a partnership approach to development. Reporting to the OAS General Assembly, the council reviews and makes decisions on competing proposals for multicountry activities in eight priority areas as well as serving as a forum for policy dialogue. The United States, however, expressed reservations about creating the council, leaving doubt about how much would change.

Reflecting the longstanding Latin American interest in international law, the Inter-American Juridical Committee is an advisory body on juridical matters with a mandate to promote development of international law and to study juridical problems relating to the integration of developing countries in the hemisphere, including uniformity in legislation. It is composed of eleven jurists elected by the General Assembly for four-year terms.

The Inter-American Commission on Human Rights was created in 1959 and was a significant player in the struggle against repressive regimes during the 1970s and 1980s. It is composed of seven members elected by the General Assembly who serve independently and do not represent particular countries. The commission's purposes are to promote and protect human rights by assessing the general human rights situation or investigating a specific situation as discussed in Chapter 10. With the Inter-American

Court of Human Rights established in 1978, it forms the regional human rights regime that one human rights expert has called "the second best regional regime" after that in Europe (Forsythe 1991: 87).

The OAS Secretariat, located in Washington, D.C., supports the work of the organization and is headed by the secretary-general, who has traditionally come from one of the Latin American states. In addition to servicing meetings and conferences, the secretariat plans and administers technical assistance projects. Since the mid-1990s, it has also served as secretariat for the Summit of the Americas process. César Gaviria, who became secretary-general in 1995, played a major role both in promoting the OAS's role with respect to democracy and in its restructuring and revitalization.

The OAS, like the UN, has several specialized organizations. These include the Pan American Health Organization, the Inter-American Drug Abuse Control Commission, the Inter-American Indigenous Institute, and the Inter-American Institute for Cooperation on Agriculture. The Inter-American Commission on Women, established in 1928, was the first IGO in the world to work for women's political and civil rights and support women's participation in governance. Today, it continues to support women's movements at the governmental level, through NGOs, and at grassroots level with a focus on the full range of women's rights.

Mutual security and collective defense. The OAS's roles with respect to peace and security involve both collective defense against aggression from outside the region and peaceful settlement of disputes and interventions among the American states themselves. During the Cold War, the United States was primarily interested in using the OAS to counter communist subversion and, after 1960, the spread of Cuba's communist revolution. In 1962, the Cuban government was excluded from participation and sanctions imposed. Cuba is still an OAS member but may not vote or participate in any activities. (A 1975 resolution released OAS members from their obligation to enforce the sanctions.) After the U.S. 1965 intervention in the Dominican Republic, the Latin American members were less willing to support the U.S. anticommunist agenda. In 1979, the United States failed to get OAS support for action to block the leftist Sandinistas from taking power in Nicaragua. It also failed to get the OAS to oppose Argentina's invasion of the Falkland/Malvinas Islands in 1982, and in 1983, the United States invaded Grenada without consulting the OAS, but under the pretext of the Eastern Caribbean Defense Treaty.

The OAS has played a role in numerous regional border and other disputes, mostly in the Caribbean and Central America. Ad hoc groups such as the Contadora (Mexico, Venezuela, Panama, and Colombia) and Rio Group (Mexico, Venezuela, Panama, Colombia, Brazil, Argentina, Peru, and

Uruguay) that sought to secure peace in Central America's conflicts have been more effective than the OAS in dealing with mutual security issues (Tulchin 1997: 39). The OAS, however, pioneered joint peacekeeping and peacebuilding missions with the UN in Haiti, El Salvador, and Nicaragua in the early 1990s, and with its heightened priority on countering antidemocratic developments has become actively involved in "collective defense of democracy" (Bloomfield 1994).

Promoting democracy.   Democratic government has been a goal of peoples in the Americas almost since independence. It was endorsed in declarations of inter-American conferences beginning in 1936 and incorporated in the OAS Charter and American Convention on Human Rights, yet the OAS was largely silent during the 1960 and 1970s when dictatorships became the norm in most Latin American countries. The trend toward democratization throughout the region in the late 1980s and 1990s brought a marked shift, with "growing recognition . . . that democracy can and must be defended through collective, peaceful means" (Munoz 1998: 2). It has become the issue that will determine the OAS's future.

The first step toward this new role occurred in 1979 with a resolution condemning the human rights record of the Somoza regime in Nicaragua. Then in 1985, the Protocol of Cartagena de Indias was approved, revising the OAS Charter to give the organization the mission of promoting democracy as "an indispensable condition for the stability, peace, and development of the region" (Article 26). The Unit for the Promotion of Democracy, established in 1990, assists with elections. In 1991, the General Assembly set up procedures for dealing with threats to democracy in the region. This has been invoked eight times: Haiti (1991, 2002), Peru (1992, 2000), Guatemala (1993), Paraguay (1996, 1999), and Venezuela (2002). The 1997 Protocol of Washington gave the organization the right to suspend a member whose democratically elected government is overthrown by force. Then in 2001, a special session of the General Assembly adopted the Inter-American Democratic Charter that proclaims the peoples' right to democracy and their governments' obligation to promote and defend it (Article 12). Members may call upon the secretary-general or Permanent Council when their democratic institutions are at risk (Article 17). Finally, the charter affirms that steps impairing a democratic order are "an insurmountable obstacle" to a government's participation in any organs or meetings of the OAS (Article 19) and may lead to suspension by the General Assembly and also to action by the Permanent Council to restore democracy.

The Unit for Promotion of Democracy provides the institutional mechanism to carry out the OAS' role in fostering democracy through electoral observation and technical assistance, information dissemination, and dialogue. The Permanent Council and General Assembly have also appointed special missions to countries where democratically elected governments are under threat, such as Peru in 2000 and Venezuela after the 2002 coup. The overthrow of democratic government in Haiti in 1991 established a precedent for applying economic sanctions and also UN-authorized military force.

The OAS' effectiveness with respect to its democracy goals is open to question. Haiti long resisted pressure before military action was taken; the long crises in Peru and Venezuela demonstrate that normative consensus does not necessarily translate into consensus on enforcement action. Indeed, the commitment to safeguard democracy conflicts with longstanding opposition to any outside interference in internal politics, especially intervention involving military force. For example, Chile, Colombia, Ecuador, Peru, and Mexico refused to participate in the U.S.-led UN force that restored President Aristide to power in Haiti. Finally, the OAS is frequently slow to act. Weak resources further limit what it can do just as limited finances have always constrained the OAS' role in fostering economic and social development.

Fostering economic and social development. This aspect of the OAS mission has been a traditional source of friction and one where the North-South division is most evident. The Latin American countries have long sought more attention to development needs and preferential treatment in trade and finance, while the United States maintains that development is a national responsibility (Thérien, Fortmann, and Gosselin 1996: 230). Sharp differences in economic policies combined with the asymmetry in power and wealth aggravated tensions. The changes in most Latin American countries' economic policies in the 1980s, however, produced new consensus. Between 1980 and 1994, sixteen Latin American countries embraced market-opening policies and joined GATT. These changes led to creation of the Council for Integral Development and the Inter-American Agency for Cooperation and Development, established to promote new and better cooperation among members and partnerships with the private sector and civil society to overcome poverty, benefit from the digital revolution, and advance social and economic development.

Whether these steps succeed better than previous hemispheric development initiatives remains to be seen. The alternative integration approach is still the dominant one for promoting development, not only through subregional efforts, but also through the summit process and FTAA negotiations.

▨ *Hemispheric Regionalism: The Summit of the Americas Process*

President Clinton's invitation to the leaders of thirty-three other countries in the Americas to the first hemispheric summit since 1967 set in motion a new process of multilateralism known as the Summit of the Americas process whose relationship to the OAS continues to evolve. Beginning with the Miami Summit in 1994, there have been three subsequent summits: in 1996, 1998, and 2001. Like the G-7/8 summit process, preparation and follow-up involve large numbers of ministerial and high-level working group meetings, as well as inputs from civil society organizations. Indeed, in this area as well as others, the summit process "has become the most important force for reform of the OAS" (Robin Rosenberg 2001: 80).

Taking advantage of the "new moment in the Americas" (Gore 1994), the Miami Summit had a broad agenda ranging from consolidating and strengthening democracy, drug trafficking, trade, environmental protection, poverty, health, education, and job creation. It produced a Declaration of Principles and a Plan of Action with initiatives in twenty-three different areas, including the agreement to create a Free Trade Area of the Americas (FTAA) by 2005. The subsequent three summits have each added new initiatives. The Santiago Summit in 1998 gave the OAS a major role in implementation and technical support. The Quebec City Summit in 2001 laid the groundwork for the Inter-American Democratic Charter discussed above. Both reiterated the importance of strengthening civil society participation for consolidating democracy and development and called for better coordination in implementing summit initiatives.

There is, nevertheless, an implicit challenge to the OAS as the center of hemispheric regionalism with the possibility that the summit process and action items will divert resources and attention. Still, "there is a growing recognition . . . of the new opportunities for reform that adaptation and integration of summitry into the operations and deliberations of the organization can provide" (Robin Rosenberg 2001: 80–81).

▪ *Subregional Integration*

The second wave of subregional integration efforts in Latin America thus far appears to be a far different story from the first—the consequence of learning, domestic political and economic changes, and changes in the global environment. Although much of the impetus for subregional integration is economic, agendas appear to be broadening in many cases. Several groups have responded to political crises that threatened democratic governments in member states, demonstrating that responsibility for upholding democracy is not limited to the OAS. We will briefly examine NAFTA, Mercosur, CARICOM, and the Andean Community to illustrate subregional integration.

NAFTA.   Where the EU's founding Treaty of Rome is the model for common markets, NAFTA is a model for free trade areas. Mexico's decision to enter into negotiations for a free trade area with the United States and

Canada marked not only a major shift in Mexican foreign and economic policies, but also had a major impact on hemispheric regionalism.

The text of NAFTA is extremely broad in scope, long and detailed (some seven hundred pages), including 295 articles and ninety annexes, plus two parallel agreements concerning labor and the environment, a five-volume, fifteen-pound document. One explanation for such precision and thoroughness is to clarify commitments and minimize misinterpretations in the absence of common institutions such as those in the EU where disagreements might be resolved (Bernier and Roy 1999: 72). While there was no desire to create governance institutions, one body was established. The Free Trade Commission oversees implementation of the agreement, makes recommendations, and provides mechanisms for dispute settlement. The commission, operating under the principle of consensus, has no power to adopt legislative measures or promulgate binding commitments on parties. An important aspect of NAFTA's approach to economic integration is the procedure for dispute settlement by special bilateral panels—a procedure very similar to that in the WTO. NAFTA's panels convened for dispute settlement do not require compliance. They refer decisions to the political arenas for further consideration. In fact, noncompliance does occur. The United States has refused to open its borders to cross-border truck traffic and Mexico has delayed access for U.S. express courier services. Because NAFTA is discussed further in Chapter 9, we focus here on its significance for Latin American regionalism.

As one recent study notes, NAFTA is "a complex set of bargains about trade and nontrade issues that advances North America toward closer economic ties" and toward actually "inventing North America" (Poitras 2001: 105). Several studies have questioned how far this process can proceed without some form of regional governance. Currently, the three members have to deal with common problems such as drugs and immigration that are not covered by NAFTA either through bilateral or ad hoc consultations. And, unlike other regional groups, NAFTA members do not necessarily try to speak with a single voice. Because of the asymmetries of power, then, this nascent region might best be characterized as "a U.S. enterprise" (Poitras 2001: 169) or perhaps "the sum of two bilateral relationships" (Pastor 2001: 99), its long-term future as a regional enterprise uncertain. In fact, the treaty makes no reference to the Americas and does not limit future accessions to countries in the Americas.

Mercosur. Mercosur is an interesting illustration of what can happen in a region when longstanding interstate rivalries are reduced. Reconciliation between Brazil and Argentina during the 1980s led to a set of bilateral agreements on nuclear issues and energy cooperation, arms control, trade, integration, and development. In 1990, both renounced their nuclear programs, and in 1991, they signed the Treaty of Asunción with Paraguay and Uruguay, creating Mercado Comun del Sur (Common Market of the South) or Mercosur. As Hirst (1999: 36) notes, "Regional integration was then sought as a political tool to consolidate broader goals aimed at reversing the dark ages of authoritarianism, intraregional antagonism, economic crisis, and international marginalization." At the heart of this new endeavor is the relationship between Argentina and Brazil and the close connection between economic integration goals and domestic and foreign politics. Brazil, for example, supports strengthening Mercosur to counter U.S. strength in the FTAA.

Mercosur is very different from NAFTA and, in fact, represents an approach somewhere between a common market along the lines of the EU and a free trade area such as NAFTA. Although economic integration is a central part of Mercosur, stimulating broad regional cooperation is also important, along with enlarging the political voice of these countries in a globalizing world. In contrast to NAFTA's detailed legal framework, Mercosur is a much simpler agreement with a loose, evolving structure and rules. The original agreement has been supplemented by three protocols and the institutional bodies (which include the Common Market Council, Common Market Group, and Trade Commission) have issued decisions, resolutions, and directives adding to the legal foundations. Much like the EU, there are issues of both broadening and deepening Mercosur over time, although none of its institutions have supranational authority. Also like the EU, Mercosur's initial goal was the graduated achievement of a customs union and common external tariff, which were achieved by 1994 and 1995 respectively. Similarly, Mercosur stimulated a substantial growth in intraregional trade and investment so that by 1995 it was the fourth largest trade bloc after the EU, NAFTA, and ASEAN. It also stimulated growth of a variety of private, nongovernmental networks among business, labor, and other groups, as well as supportive public opinion, creating conditions of more complex interdependence (Pena 1999; Solingen 1998).

Another important feature of Mercosur is the connection between the process of economic integration and domestic political processes. In short, expanded regionalism in the Southern Cone, as it is known, has deepened democratization in the member countries and consensus among political elites. Thus, Hirst notes (1999: 40), "the positive correlation between economic reform, democratization, and regional integration became the essence of Mercosur politics." Indicative of this is Mercosur's quick intervention in Paraguay's political crises in 1996 and 1999. Indeed, following the 1996 crisis, Mercosur members adopted a democracy clause similar to that of the OAS.

The Caribbean Community, Central American Common Market, and the Andean Community.   Indicative of the distinctive subregions within the Western Hemisphere is the persistence of efforts by the many small countries in different areas to join together for both political and economic reasons. Their shared interests stem from a "common sense of *vulnerability*" by what are in most cases fragile democracies with small economies, vulnerable to financial crises, instability, subversion, and drug trafficking (Hurrell 1995a: 257).

The Caribbean Community or CARICOM, established in 1973 as the successor to the Caribbean Free Trade Association (CARIFTA), includes fifteen states in the Caribbean region, many of them tiny island states. Its broad objectives relate to economic development, trade expansion, labor standards, functional cooperation in areas such as education, disaster emergency response, agricultural development, and health, as well as gaining greater leverage in dealing with other states and groups of states. Foreign policy coordination and support for democracy are also among its goals. It has an extensive set of institutions, including the Conference of Heads of Government, the Community Council of Ministers, four ministerial councils, and large numbers of functional entities, among them the Caribbean Development Bank. CARICOM is a customs union and common market whose members negotiate as a bloc with other states and groups. Members have eschewed further integration, however, preferring to retain separate voting power in the UN, OAS, and other bodies. Perhaps more than in any other part of the Americas, the Caribbean states accept a broadened definition of security, given their vulnerability to drug trafficking, money laundering, crime, outward migration, and environmental threats including hurricanes, oil spills, overfishing, and rising sea level. With respect to security policy, however, CARICOM is highly dependent on the hemispheric hegemon, the United States, whose interests and perceptions differ from those of the "marginally sovereign and highly dependent" Caribbean states (Knight and Persaud 2001: 50).

The Central American Common Market (CACM) was originally established in 1960 by Nicaragua, Guatemala, Honduras, and El Salvador (who were later joined by Costa Rica). Like other Latin American subregional initiatives in the 1960s, it was based around the use of regional integration as a means to expand market size while protecting local manufacturers from outside competition through import-substitution policies. Although CACM did stimulate substantial growth in intraregional trade in the 1960s and 1970s, it entered a long period of stagnation after Honduras's withdrawal at the time of its "soccer war" with El Salvador in 1969. Development among its members was uneven, making cooperation difficult, compounded by the debt crisis and civil wars in El Salvador and

Nicaragua in the 1980s. The Central American Peace Agreement (Esquipulas II) in 1987 opened the way to reactivating economic integration. A series of summits and agreements marked progress toward this goal, which emphasizes the region's insertion into the global economy through export-led growth, free trade within the region, reduction in the common external tariff, and incorporation of political and economic efforts. The permanent secretariat is based in Guatemala.

The Andean Community also dates from the early wave of subregional inward-looking integration initiatives when it was known as the Andean Pact. It was established in 1969 by Bolivia, Colombia, Ecuador, Peru, and Venezuela to promote development through a common external tariff, common economic policies, and liberalization of trade within the region, and to reduce their external vulnerability and improve their position in the international economy. Three protocols concluded in the late 1980s and 1990s instituted policy and institutional reforms, including a conversion to more open regionalism. The Andean Community forms part of what is now the Andean Integration System of institutions, including the Andean Presidential Council, Council of Foreign Ministers, Court of Justice, Commission, Parliament, social conventions, and business and labor advisory councils. The group achieved a common external tariff in 1994 and agreement on common foreign policy guidelines in 1995. The ministers of foreign affairs and defense moved to formulate common security policy and arms control through the Andean Charter for Peace and Security approved in 2002. The community has also adopted its own Charter for the Promotion and Protection of Human Rights (2002).

These three subregional groupings—the Caribbean Community, Central American Common Market, and the Andean Community—are all extensively institutionalized and have entered into agreements with each other and with groups outside the hemisphere such as the EU to broaden their linkages and the possibilities for interregional cooperation in areas of common interest. These links demonstrate some of the limits of subregional cooperation, especially when the economies of members are very small. They also demonstrate the increasing complexity of multilateralism both regionally and globally.

As one observer has noted, the European experience teaches us that "regional integration is a long-term enterprise marked by waves and undercurrents. Although scholars of regionalism take notice of the waves . . . often ignored are the undercurrents, the daily actions of the countless smaller actors who keep the project moving forward in response to the waves" (Mace et al. 1999: 36). Such is certainly the case with the undercurrents of both the inter-American hemispheric approach and the various subregional initiatives. The scope and direction of both processes is still difficult to ascertain, yet the continuing efforts, albeit of varying intensity, to make progress signal persistent perceived needs for regional cooperation and commitment to its advancement. Furthermore, there is widespread agreement that "the spread of democracy, free trade, and complex interdependence are making the inter-American system fundamentally more cooperative," despite persistent mistrust of the United States (Peceny 1994: 200–201).

■ Asia's Regional Organizations

In contrast to Latin America, Asian regionalism has been both belated and limited. This is attributed to the persistence of Cold War divisions on the Korean peninsula and communist states in the region (China, Vietnam, and North Korea); the diversity of cultures and levels of development; an absence of experience with cooperation; low levels of interdependence; and the absence of the idea that Asia-Pacific (or East Asia or the Pacific) might constitute a region. Since many Asian countries were European colonies and only gained their independence after World War II, this has left them strongly attached to state sovereignty and suspicious of new forms of dependency or perceived domination (or even of external influences). Japanese imperialism prior to World War II left a further legacy of wariness of regional cooperation that might involve new forms of Japanese domination. There is no single country to provide leadership, but two potential competitors—China and Japan. There is a superpower—the United States—that continues to play a major role in shaping regional relationships and dynamics. In contrast to its encouragement of European regional cooperation, however, the United States never promoted multilateralism in Asia and the Pacific. It preferred a more conventional great-power approach of bilateral relationships, and never intended SEATO to mirror NATO as a collective defense arrangement (Hemmer and Katzenstein 2002).

Regionalism in Asia and Asia-Pacific has proceeded along two overlapping tracks. It first emerged when five countries of Southeast Asia formed the Association of Southeast Asian Nations (ASEAN) in 1967. In the 1990s, Australia and Japan provided leadership for Asia-Pacific Economic Cooperation (APEC) that includes several countries of North and South America, along with Australia, New Zealand, China, Russia, seven ASEAN members, South Korea, Hong Kong, and Taiwan. ASEAN itself grew in the 1990s to ten members, expanded dialogues with nonmember countries (ASEAN Plus 3, for example, includes China, Japan, and South Korea), and convened the ASEAN Regional Forum as a multilateral security dialogue for Asia-Pacific. APEC grew from its original twelve to twenty-one members and from annual ministerial-level gatherings to summits and numerous working groups. The coexistence of ASEAN and APEC has been viewed metaphorically as two concentric circles and a set of nested regimes (Soesastro 1995; Aggarwal 1998), as illustrated in Figure 5.5.

Asian and Asia-Pacific regional institutions tend to be informal with few specific rules, no binding commitments, small secretariats, and an emphasis on consensus decisionmaking. There is a long history of second-track interactions involving business leaders, economists, and security specialists from university centers and think tanks along with government officials acting in their private capacity (Woods 1993). These have played an important role in building confidence among countries with little history of

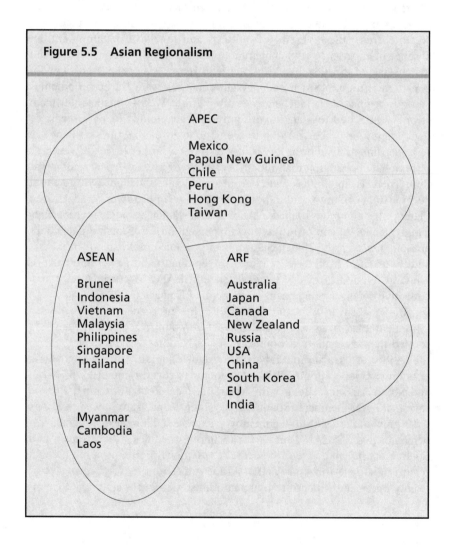

Figure 5.5   Asian Regionalism

APEC

Mexico
Papua New Guinea
Chile
Peru
Hong Kong
Taiwan

ASEAN

Brunei
Indonesia
Vietnam
Malaysia
Philippines
Singapore
Thailand

Myanmar
Cambodia
Laos

ARF

Australia
Japan
Canada
New Zealand
Russia
USA
China
South Korea
EU
India

intergovernmental cooperation and in creating an epistemic community for regional cooperation.

◼ *ASEAN*

ASEAN was established in 1967 by Indonesia, Singapore, Malaysia, Philippines, and Thailand, at the height of U.S. involvement in Vietnam, to promote regional security and economic development. External threats played a prominent role in ASEAN's creation and survival since the founding states wanted to minimize manipulation and domination by major powers, most notably the United States and China. They were also concerned about Chinese-supported communist insurgencies and about separatist movements, but deliberately chose not to create a military alliance. ASEAN's founders were well aware of the profound historical, cultural, and economic circumstances that divided them, but also recognized the advantages of regular consultation and cohesion.

The core principle of ASEAN is nonintervention in the internal affairs of other members. This derived not just from the international norm but also from the series of Asian conferences held between 1947 and the 1955 Asia-African Conference at Bandung where the ideas of the third world and nonalignment were born (Acharya 2003). Nonintervention does not necessarily mean no involvement in others' affairs, but it does mean refraining from open criticism and providing no support to opposition movements. It has also meant there was little interest in integration. One of ASEAN's most distinctive characteristics is the so-called ASEAN Way, which is the process of informal consultation and consensus building (rather than majority voting), through which decisions are made. It involves avoiding legalistic procedures, a preference for nonbinding resolutions, and an emphasis on "process over product" (Acharya 2001). If there is no consensus, the members agree to disagree. If there is an intractable dispute, members set it aside and focus on cooperation in other areas. This is clearly a recipe for conflict avoidance rather than conflict resolution.

For most of its first twenty years, ASEAN's primary focus was regional peace and stability. The communist victory in Vietnam and U.S. withdrawal in 1975 prompted the first summit meeting and the Treaty of Amity and Concord. This made political cooperation a formal part of the ASEAN agenda and codified rules of conduct, including the nonuse of force, peaceful settlement (or deferral) of disputes, and regional solutions for regional problems. The 1978 Vietnamese invasion of Cambodia posed a major threat and members disagreed over how to respond. Thailand's concerns as a frontline state prevailed, and ASEAN organized opposition to Vietnam in the UN and opposed the Vietnamese-backed Cambodian regime. It could do little more until the late 1980s when U.S., Chinese, and UN initiatives allowed ASEAN to play a role in the Cambodian peace process. Narine

(1999: 360) notes, "Despite its junior role in these events, ASEAN emerged . . . with a much higher international profile and an inflated sense of its own capability."

The 1989 Manila Declaration marked a significant change by setting up the ASEAN Plan of Action for economic cooperation. Moving forward with this plan in 1992, member countries agreed to create the ASEAN Free Trade Area (AFTA) within fifteen years, a timetable that was shortened in 1994 to 2003. (See Chapter 9 for further discussion.) In 1994, the ASEAN Regional Forum (ARF) was established to promote multilateral security dialogue, which we examine below. The 1995 Bangkok Treaty created the Southeast Asian Nuclear Weapons Free Zone. In addition, following its decision to participate in APEC, ASEAN initiated a series of dialogue programs with outside powers, including the EU member countries, South Korea, China, India, and Japan. This was an ambitious set of new challenges that over time would raise questions about whether ASEAN's informal structures were adequate to support them.

Structures.   Although the Treaty of Amity and Accord provided for a High Council of ministers to deal with disputes, this mechanism has never been used. In fact, there are few structures in the usual organizational sense of that word. Instead, ASEAN has evolved an extremely dense pattern of formal and informal meetings. The core structures are the various ministerial-level meetings that now extend well beyond the foreign and trade ministries. With the 1997–1998 Asian financial crisis, for example, members' finance ministers began to meet regularly for the first time. Similarly, the haze generated by forest fires in Indonesia in the late 1990s (see Chapter 11) prompted environmental ministers to initiate meetings. There are also regular summits of heads of government, frequent informal gatherings, meetings of senior officials, and numerous ad hoc and permanent committees. Singaporean scholar Chin Kin Wah (1997: 148) has suggested, in fact, that "ASEAN . . . can lay claim to being the most extensively institutionalized (but not supranationalized) regional association besides the European Union." In 1976, a small permanent secretariat based in Jakarta (Indonesia) was created to coordinate activities. Later, the post of secretary-general was added, but both of these have limited powers and capabilities.

Broadening and deepening.   ASEAN's role in the Cambodian settlement and the Cold War's end paved the way for expansion from six to ten members, with Vietnam joining in 1995, Laos and Myanmar (Burma) in 1997, and Cambodia in 1999. This accomplished the goal of becoming "the ASEAN 10." Enlargement has increased ASEAN's political and economic diversity and magnified the challenges of consensus decisionmaking. All four new members are less developed than the others; two have communist regimes; all have major human rights problems with Myanmar being the worst; one (Cambodia) is highly unstable. The United States and the EU along with NGOs actively opposed Myanmar's membership. Still, ASEAN set no conditions other than adherence to the agreement on political cooperation and to economic reforms so that they could join AFTA within ten years. In effect, however, ASEAN is now a two-tiered organization where accommodating differences may require allowing countries to opt out or push ahead on certain issues.

In addition to broadening its membership, ASEAN has expanded its agenda to virtually all areas of public policy, including human rights and the environment. Whether this amounts to deepening remains to be seen. Historically, ASEAN has never been a regional integration project, but in 2003, Singapore and Thailand, two of the economically strongest members, proposed creating a common market

In matters of security, ASEAN's predominant approach has been conflict management by avoidance. Yet in a region marked by a plethora of territorial disputes, ASEAN has created a framework for improving bilateral relations toward the end of dispute resolution. There have been a few cases of mediation, for example, Thailand's involvement in the Malaysian-Philippine conflict over Sabah. With respect to the South China Sea disputes that affect many members, ASEAN reached consensus in 1992 on the Declaration on the South China Sea and in 2002 concluded an agreement with China. Where nonintervention precluded ASEAN from playing any role was in the East Timor crisis in 1999, leaving initiative to Australia and the United Nations.

The framework that ASEAN provided enabled its members to concentrate on building their economies. It also shaped the manner in which outside powers dealt with the region. And since 1994, ASEAN has promoted broader regional security through its sponsorship of the ASEAN Regional Forum, which we discuss below.

With respect to economic cooperation, unlike regional groupings in Latin America, the ASEAN members adopted an outward orientation of integration into the global economy rather than subregional integration as their strategy for growth. They were among the first developing countries to embrace export-led growth and to liberalize trade and investment. Four members (Indonesia, Malaysia, Singapore, and Thailand) made great economic and social strides, and ASEAN itself was "widely regarded as the developing world's most successful subregional institution. . . . Growth, association, and stability reinforced each other in a virtuous circle" (Soesastro and Morrison 2001: 58). AFTA was an outgrowth of this success. If it is fully implemented, it will make ASEAN a more institutionalized economic regime. (See Chapter 9 for further discussion.)

As Jeannie Henderson (1999: 11) notes, "For an association of predominantly small- and medium-sized developing countries, ASEAN's capacity to engage the interest and cooperation of major powers was striking. The distinct 'ASEAN Way' became a model for other experiments in international cooperation." Whether ASEAN can sustain these processes and other parts of its ambitious agenda remains to be seen. Enlargement, environmental problems, and the 1997–1998 financial crisis stalled many of ASEAN's plans. The press and scholarly journals have been filled with articles about ASEAN's loss of self-confidence, disarray, failure, loss of direction, and challenges. Significant political and economic resources will be required to meet its goals, and modifications in the ASEAN Way and structures may also be necessary.

Asia-Pacific Economic Cooperation (APEC)

Asia-Pacific Economic Cooperation was established in 1989 to facilitate intergovernmental dialogue on economic policy issues with the goal of sustaining growth and development. An important unstated purpose, especially for the Asian members, is to support a process of confidence building among countries of the region that have no tradition of multilateral cooperation and were reluctant to create a regional organization that might compete with ASEAN or lead to domination by the United States and Japan (Ravenhill 2001: 97). Hence, the name; because the twenty-one members include not only states but also Taiwan and Hong Kong, members are referred to as "economies" not countries. The diversity of size, economies, political systems, and policies is greater than in any other regional grouping—a source of both strength and weakness.

The basic ideas for an Asia-Pacific regional organization were laid out by Japanese and Australian economists in the late 1960s. They initiated informal gatherings, but it took two decades before governments were ready to act. Neither the U.S. nor Japanese governments were willing to take the lead. Some ASEAN governments were also wary of another organization in the region, of trade liberalization that might advantage the region's industrial countries, of excluding the centrally planned economies of the Soviet Union, Vietnam, and China, and of compromising their nonaligned status. Thus, the idea of Asia-Pacific collaboration was promoted for twenty years by a group of economists through several organizations. The most prominent of these was the Pacific Trade and Development (PAF-TAD) conferences of government, academic, and IGO economists initiated in 1968. This group became an epistemic community and an important agency of socialization, especially for economists from the less developed and nonmarket economies (Ravenhill 2001: 62–65). The Pacific Economic Cooperation Council (PECC), with representatives from academe, business, and governments, first put forward a blueprint of an intergovernmental organization for managing regional interdependence in the early 1980s (Harris 1994).

What moved Asia-Pacific regionalism from idea to APEC were a series of developments in the 1980s that changed the international context, the nature of several countries' economies, and countries' perceptions of their interests (Ravenhill 2001: 66–79). These included proliberalization economists assuming influential positions in many Asian and Latin American governments; the United States, IMF, and World Bank pushing liberalization; divisions within the G-77 that made it easier for ASEAN members to consider new alternatives; and growing interdependence among the economies of the Pacific Rim countries. Increased intraregional foreign direct investment by Japanese, South Korean, Singaporean, and Hong Kong companies created transnational production networks. Also, most ASEAN countries had shifted from primary product exports to manufactured goods as the largest share of exports, increasing confidence in their ability to compete.

This confluence of factors helped change many countries' perceptions of their economic interests and persuade them in 1989 to support the Japanese and Australian initiative to create APEC. It was conceived as a defense against a "Fortress Europe" when both Asians and Americans were concerned about the consequences of the EU's single market (Garnaut 1996: 1); as insurance against protectionism in North America with the creation of NAFTA, U.S. restrictions on imports, and rising U.S.-Japan and U.S.-EC trade disputes; and as a hedge against a fracturing of the global trade system into rival blocs when successful completion of GATT negotiations was in doubt. APEC's key principle of "open regionalism" reflected the commitment to advance regional economic integration without enacting discriminatory trade measures against outsiders.

Structure.   APEC was intended to operate informally with consensus decisionmaking. The core structure initially consisted of the informal meetings of trade and foreign ministers. This changed when President Clinton convened the first summit meeting of heads of government in 1993. Now, in addition to the annual summits, there are dozens of specialized meetings, committees, and working groups convened each year. Initially, national bureaucracies provided support services for the organization, as they had for ASEAN, but a secretariat of twenty-one professionals seconded by their governments and based in Singapore was established in 1992. It services the various gatherings but is not authorized to take any initiatives.

The annual summits have raised APEC's profile and reinforced the idea of Asia-Pacific as a region. As the only institutionalized forum for heads of government from all Pacific Rim countries, they have some value just as a means of facilitating intergovernmental communications at the highest level, for example, during periods of tension between the United States and China when bilateral summits were inconceivable. It has also been valuable to leaders of smaller countries who get the opportunity to talk with counterparts from all countries.

A trade bloc or what?   Even after more than a decade, APEC is shrouded in ambiguity over its goals and how those should be realized and does not fulfill a key criterion for the existence of an international regime: agreement on core principles. There is no agreement among the member economies over priorities among the three pillars of the organization: liberalization of trade and investment, facilitation of trade, and economic and technical cooperation.

The 1994 Bogor Declaration envisioned free trade and investment in the region by 2010 for the industrialized economies and 2020 for developing economies. The plan required individual and collective actions by members. Subsequent summits established a framework for liberalization, a program for coordination and harmonization of economic policies, and joint activities for economic and technical cooperation. Many East Asian members, however, preferred loose coordination of unilateral trade policies and economic and technical cooperation rather than an agenda of trade negotiations (Ravenhill 2001: 155–156). By the 1998 summit, the trade liberalization priority disappeared. A 2000 World Bank survey of regionalism concluded, "There has not yet been any APEC liberalization" (World Bank 2000a).

Economic and technical cooperation is of primary interest to Asian members, but Western governments initially viewed it as development assistance and only slowly realized the value of activities such as developing human capital, strengthening economic infrastructure, harnessing future technologies, and promoting small enterprises. Although a large number of projects were underway in 2000, there was very little coordination among them, few specific objectives, limited financing, and little attention to measurable performance criteria. Many of them involved surveys, research, and seminars, not substantive outputs.

APEC's working groups provide information exchange on subjects ranging from trade and investment data, energy, telecommunications, and marine resource conservation to transportation and tourism. These have been helpful to business and other governments. Still, there is no assurance that information will be made available. As of the end of 2000, Malaysia, Vietnam, Russia, and Thailand had all failed to provide data on tariffs to the APEC Secretariat for an online database (Ravenhill 2001: 170).

APEC illustrates the tension between Asian and Western views on regional cooperation. Asian members want a process of dialogue and socialization that at most produces a general framework for regional economic cooperation and other activities through consensus decisionmaking. They wish to preserve maximum flexibility for unilateral determination of economic and trade policies, to avoid a precise timetable for actions, and to limit any monitoring of compliance. They fear (with some basis, especially in the mid-1990s) that Western members prefer a formal organizational structure and contractual framework of rules achieved through negotiations on specific trade and investment questions. Although initially it appeared that APEC was successfully promoting an Asia-Pacific regional identity, by the end of its first decade the tensions between Western and Asian members were weakening that perception. U.S.-led efforts to make trade liberalization a principal objective with little regard for Asian concerns, combined with the consequences of the 1997-1998 financial crisis, fueled greater collaboration among Asian governments and a growing sense of Asian identity.

Effects of the 1997-1998 financial crisis. Neither ASEAN nor APEC was set up to deal with financial and monetary relations, and the Asian countries had few expectations that they would offer solutions. The crisis was primarily a matter for global institutions, particularly the IMF as is discussed in Chapter 9. At the 1997 APEC summit, the United States vetoed a Japanese proposal, supported by many ASEAN members, for an Asian Monetary Fund to which Japan intended to contribute $50 billion or one-half the proposed capital. The idea resurfaced in 1998 as a $15 billion Japanese bilateral support package, the Miyazawa Initiative. Following the initial crisis in 1997, ASEAN finance ministers began meeting regularly, and ASEAN and APEC fostered agreement on a set of principles for surveillance of capital flows and financial management that effectively put the Asian Development Bank in charge of monitoring the region (Enia and Karns 1999: 18–20).

Western governments' analysis of the causes of the crisis differed from that of many Asian governments. They strongly supported the IMF's push for greater liberalization and dismantling the close relationships between many Asian governments and businesses (sometimes dubbed "crony capitalism"), where the Asian governments wanted rapid international assistance and curbs on short-term capital flows. The behavior of Western governments and IMF officials, combined with policy differences, created a backlash among many Asian governments (Higgott 1998). One result was ASEAN Plus Three, which reflected strengthened perceptions of mutual economic interdependence and vulnerability between Southeast and Northeast Asia (Webber 2001: 356–359). Western members of APEC and especially the United States no longer identify as closely with Asia and have lost interest in APEC. This leaves the question of APEC's future and its identity uncertain.

ASEAN was also greatly weakened by the financial crisis. First, ASEAN's confidence was shattered in the wake of sharp economic decline in so many member states, particularly since the organization had been nurtured by the success of many Asian economies. Second, the crisis highlighted the limits of the ASEAN Way as an institutional method of interaction that revolved around the practice that ASEAN states do not intervene in each other's domestic affairs and do not even comment on or criticize each other's domestic policies. As Narine (2002: 188) notes, the crisis revealed that "ASEAN is not a strongly unified regional body but a loose arrangement that lacks the institutional structures necessary to coordinate regional action."

Lessons from APEC's experience.   Because APEC has been a unique experiment in regionalism, it is valuable to look at what can be learned from it. Its flexibility and ambiguity were consistent with Asian members' preferences, but contributed to lack of agreement on objectives and substantive governance activities. Despite its hegemonic position, the United States failed to change their commitment to "open regionalism" and flexible agreements and, increasingly, found that it still had more in common with Europe than with Asia. In contrast, Japan has identified increasingly with Asia. The diversity of APEC's twenty-one members has made effective cooperation on trade and investment issues difficult. Finally, many of the contextual factors that made APEC's creation fortuitous in 1989 had changed a decade later. Still, APEC's existence is an achievement, even if its contributions to regional governance are modest at best. It links countries of great diversity and longstanding rivalry and hostility. It helped make some countries more comfortable dealing with each other, building confidence where the past offered little experience of constructive interaction. As a long-time Indonesian participant noted, "APEC . . . is first and foremost about community building" (Soesastro 1998: 95).

▓ Asia-Pacific Security Dialogue in the ASEAN Regional Forum (ARF)

The creation of APEC made the establishment of a counterpart forum for discussion of Pacific Rim security issues a logical next step. Still, Simon (1998: 205) notes, "Washington, Tokyo, and Beijing had to be convinced that security multilateralism was in their best interests." Of these, China was the most difficult (and arguably, most important) to persuade as it was the source of the most uncertainty and greatest potential threat in the region. Its power in the mid-1990s was growing rapidly. Yet, China was wary of multilateral institutions, especially any security organization, partly for fear that they might lead to discussion of the Taiwan issue and partly because the Chinese military was hostile to sharing information on its doctrine and deployment. ASEAN members were also initially reluctant to participate in security dialogue. Their reversal reflected a conscious decision to take the lead in order to dominate such a dialogue, but by doing so and by proposing that it adopt the ASEAN Way as its modus operandi, they were instrumental in persuading China to participate (Leifer 1996: 28–29; Johnston 1999: 295–297). Thus, the ASEAN Regional Forum (ARF) began annual meetings in 1994 with twenty-one countries in Asia and around the Pacific participating. (There is no formal membership.) At the outset, there was no agreement on what the primary security issues were, with the exception of the South China Sea. Other concerns included China itself, Korea, weapons of mass destruction, piracy, and many others.

In keeping with the ASEAN Way, ARF relies on consensus decision-making and is weakly institutionalized. Its core is a complex set of official and unofficial (track I and II) processes, including four working groups that address issues of confidence building, peacekeeping operations, and maritime search and rescue. One unique track II feature is the role played by associated Institutes for Strategic and International Studies (known as ASEAN-ISIS) in setting the agenda for discussion of security issues and urging ASEAN's member governments to take the initiative. Many ISIS specialists traditionally had close ties with senior government officials and they continue to prepare studies on key problems that are too sensitive to raise at the official level (Simon 1998: 208). A second track II part of ARF is the Council for Security Cooperation in the Asia Pacific (CSCAP), a federation of national security research organizations that "has become the most comprehensive, regular, nongovernmental forum on Pacific security in history" (Simon 1998: 208). Its working groups create a research base for ARF security dialogues.

ARF has generated a degree of trust among countries with long histories of mutual suspicion and conflict. Like ASEAN itself, ARF has not addressed the many bilateral border and territorial disputes in the region, nor has it dealt with problems of piracy, illegal migration, and smuggling. It contributes to conflict prevention "by facilitating communication, providing information, increasing transparency, and reducing uncertainty" (Simon 1998: 210). How long countries such as the United States, Australia, Canada, and Japan, which would prefer more concrete action and institutionalization (as they also prefer in APEC), will tolerate the informal and general nature of ARF's discussions remains to be seen. This approach prevails and ASEAN continues to lead because that is China's preference.

The Asian experience with regionalism has a lot to do with identity construction and community building, a process that is still incomplete.

Hence, the precise definition of the region remains uncertain. The same is not true about regional governance and cooperation efforts in the continent of Africa where identity construction has not been as problematic, but many other factors have impeded effective efforts.

■ Africa's Regional Organizations

The ideal of unity among the inhabitants of the African continent was one prominent reaction to the enslavement, imperialism, and colonialism of Africa by Western European powers from the sixteenth through early twentieth century. In the nineteenth century, the call for unity was largely based on racial grounds, while in the twentieth century, it was based on the notion that Africans should throw off domination by outside powers and receive independence. This ideal was expressed at the 1945 meeting of the Pan-African Congress, held in Manchester, England, in 1945. With the "Declaration to the Colonial Peoples," participants supported the right of political freedom and self-government, expressed in continent-wide terms.

In the late 1950s, under the initiative of Kwame Nkrumah, president of newly independent Ghana, a pan-African forum for independent countries began to take shape based on an underlying sense of continental unity. There were differences of opinion, however, among pan-Africanists and supporters of subregional approaches. Among pan-Africans, there were disagreements about how to achieve the pan-African ideal. Some saw a very minimalist approach, with states agreeing to cooperate but not much more; others sought real political union among the independent states. The group that finally won this disagreement opted for a loose, continent-wide organization of African states.

■ *From the Organization of African Unity (OAU) to the African Union (AU)*

Meeting in May 1964, the leaders of thirty-one newly independent African states established the Organization of African Unity. It was conceived as a loose association based on voluntary cooperation, whose resolutions would carry moral rather than legal obligations. Three overriding principles guided the organization for thirty-nine years. First, all states were sovereign equals. Thus, within the OAU, there was no formal provision for weighted decisionmaking power for dominant continental powers. Second, states agreed not to interfere in the domestic affairs of fellow members. Third, territorial borders were sacrosanct with no room for alteration in the status quo. Adoption of these principles reflected the bitter colonial experience. No longer did states want to be dominated by outsiders or risk border changes that would unleash ethnic rivalries and invite outside intervention. So at the outset the OAU was designed as a voluntary organization limited by its founding principles.

Over time each of these principles has been violated. Although all states are theoretically equal, there was implicit recognition that some states are able to provide stronger leadership—be it a Nigeria or Ivory Coast in the west or Kenya in the east, or even Libya, Algeria, or Egypt in the north, or South Africa in the south. The principle of noninterference in domestic affairs was also violated, most often during the 1990s when human rights violations were condemned by other states. On a few occasions the OAU also supported changes in state boundaries, for example when Eritrea gained independence from Ethiopia. Then, in July 2002, after two years of negotiations, the OAU was replaced by the African Union. Recognizing that because of the OAU's weakness Africa was increasingly marginalized in international politics, the new organization was designed to meet the challenges that lay ahead and address African problems with renewed African leadership.

Many of the overarching principles of the new African Union are the same as its predecessor, including the principles of domestic sovereignty, territorial integrity, and noninterference by any state in the internal affairs of another. The AU also reasserts the principle of respect for existing national borders. Yet, in other areas new principles are designed to make the AU a stronger and more relevant organization. Among them are a commitment to democracy and respect for human rights. The objectives are much broader, involving the promotion of sustainable development and good governance, social justice, gender equality, and good health. More specifically, while intervention by a member state is prohibited, intervention by the AU is acceptable in situations of war crimes, genocide, and crimes against humanity. The AU's Constitutive Act further provides for the condemnation of governments whose regimes have been changed through unconstitutional methods. Leaders pledge to hold free elections and to allow opposition parties to campaign freely. The union has the power to expel illegitimate governments, something the OAU never had. No longer can sovereignty be a shield to hide gross misconduct. "Our peoples," said South Africa's President Thabo Mbeki, "need democracy, good governance, the eradication of corruption, human rights, peace and stability" (quoted in Swarns 2002: A3). Several new organs have been established to meet the new objectives and to give added teeth to this very ambitious experiment whose architects used the EU as a model (Babarinde 2003: 12).

Organs. Consistent with the sovereign equality principle, the annual Assembly of the Heads of State and Government is the supreme organ that debates, decides issues, and adopts resolutions, just as under the OAU. It is this body that must approve calls for union intervention and give directives to the new Executive Council that was established to execute the decisions of the assembly. The OAU's General Secretariat has been replaced by the commission, which is headed by a chairman rather than a secretary-general. Its functions remain much the same, although there is the presumption that the chairman will assume a more expanded role. As in the OAU, the effectiveness of the commission depends in large part on adequate financing. Also new to the African Union are a Court of Justice, a Pan-African Parliament, a Peace and Security Council, an Economic, Social and Cultural Council, and financial institutions (the African Central Bank, the African Monetary Fund, and the African Investment Bank). These represent the most innovative part of the African Union, and while they are very poorly specified in the founding charter (Packer and Rukare 2002) the AU is gradually taking specific steps to bring them into being and establish rules of procedure. The structure of the African Union, thus, is designed to create a strengthened union with more responsibilities in economic governance, greater ability to intervene in domestic affairs of member states when extraordinary circumstances arise, and an ability to implement decisions. The hope is that the union will become a more legitimate successor organization in the eyes of outsiders than the OAU whose weaknesses and accomplishments are described below.

Approaches to resolving disputes.   Because the OAU had little authority to intervene in states' affairs, the annual Assembly of Heads of State became an informal venue for dispute settlement, where leaders tried to influence other leaders. The rotating presidents of the assembly have often played a mediating role. Given the myriad conflicts in the region, such informal dispute resolution will likely continue under the AU.

Although a multinational military force under OAU auspices was proposed, it was never implemented. The AU agreed in 2004, however, to create a joint force to intervene in civil wars or prevent genocide. The OAU previously had sponsored ad hoc, all-African military forces, most notably for use in Chad in 1981. At other times, the OAU turned to the UN or to subregional organizations like the Economic Community of West African States to organize regional military forces for a specific action; it even authorized a particular country to take such action.

Overall, the OAU record with regard to peace and security is quite positive, including successful resolution of disputes in the Comoros Islands, Sierra Leone, and Lesotho. As Mark Zacher (2001: 231) concludes, "In nine of the eleven territorial wars since 1963, the OAU has been a major influence in securing troop withdrawals, and it could succeed eventually in the Morocco-Western Sahara conflict. When the OAU was founded in 1963, few thought that the society of African states would be such an important force in securing the stability of African boundaries. The OAU members have exerted significant diplomatic pressure on aggressing states, and they have influenced outside powers to back OAU positions against territorial aggressions."

Because of its legal restrictions, the OAU was prohibited from addressing civil strife or even illegitimate regime change. These are areas where the AU has potential for major impact.

Fostering economic development.   Fostering the conditions for continent-wide economic development has always been on the OAU agenda, reiterated in numerous declarations, and culminating in the 1991 treaty establishing the African Economic Community. The goal was a highly ambitious one, namely, creation of an eventual continent-wide common market and of structures and institutions to govern the market, similar to initial plans for the European common market, minus the goals of political integration. Yet, the OAU's work in this area was largely unsatisfactory, although some incremental steps were taken that are consistent with the approach of the new African Union.

In 1987, the OAU took an initiative that set it apart from other regional groups when it recognized health as one of the foundations for development. The growing HIV/AIDS epidemic in Africa with its attendant economic, social, political, and security consequences could not be ignored. HIV/AIDS has been addressed in numerous conferences of African ministers of health. In 2001, it was the subject of the African Summit on HIV/AIDS, Tuberculosis and Other Related Infectious Diseases, held in Abuja, Nigeria. The fact that this issue was finally brought into the most visible OAU forum suggests that it will be high on the AU agenda.

The African Union has a difficult task ahead. It has adopted a holistic approach to encourage economic development, democratic government, and human rights. With respect to economics, the needs of the member states and its peoples are infinite. Africa is on the periphery of the global economy with 2 percent of total trade and 1.2 percent of direct foreign investment. Intra-African trade comprises only 10 percent of total volume. Two of the states with the strongest economies on the continent are Egypt and South Africa. Can either of these countries assume a role in contributing to the economic development of others? Egypt has maintained a quiet profile during discussions due to its priorities in the Middle East, while South Africa has tremendous domestic needs stemming from its continuing transition out of apartheid and high rate of AIDS infections. The New Partnership for Africa's Development (NEPAD) discussed in Chapter 9 offers some promise, but requires cooperation among the African states themselves and with the donor community. With respect to democratization, which states can legitimately take the lead? Two of the AU's strongest supporters, Libya and Uganda, are not themselves democracies, yet the AU's charter calls for promoting democratization across the continent and suspending governments that achieve power unconstitutionally. On a hopeful note, on both of these issues, the AU is according important roles to women and to civil society and NGOs (Babarinde 2003).

■ Subregional Integration Initiatives

Subregional groups have been active in both the economic and political realms in several parts of Africa. They confront many of the same limitations as the OAU and AU, including a wide variety of governments, overwhelming problems to be addressed, and lack of financial resources to make a real difference. We look at three examples.

Economic Community of West African States (ECOWAS).   Of the African subregional groupings, ECOWAS is the largest and most ambitious undertaking. Established in 1975 with the explicit goal of becoming a common market, ECOWAS adopted the EU approach of moving from a freeze on tariffs and ending import duties to creation of a common external tariff and free movement of labor among the sixteen West African states. From the beginning, however, ECOWAS was seen by others as a Nigerian initiative, intended as a way for that country to expand its markets in the region. Nigeria was one of the few countries that produced both primary products and manufactured goods. Absent Nigeria, there was very little intraregional trade. Other countries' major trading partners were located outside of the ECOWAS area (in Europe or the United States); many of the states produced the same primary products and there was no viable transportation infrastructure linking the member states. Progress has been made in the construction of interstate roads and telecommunication links, which are widely acknowledged as critical to the beginning stages of integration.

ECOWAS has proceeded slowly, too slowly, by its own admission. Even though it has barely moved beyond the first stages, reforms have been introduced and new institutions established, including a court of justice, parliament, and economic and social council. Creating more structures, however, does not guarantee that economic progress will occur any faster or more efficiently. Mistrust among members, fears of Nigerian domination, continuing armed conflicts, and the small size of the regional economy impede development.

Since 1990, absent progress on the economic dimension, ECOWAS has assumed more of a political dimension, with meetings devoted to reducing regional tensions and dealing with civil conflicts. Under the standing mediation committee, a 4,000-person multinational force known as ECOMOG (ECOWAS Cease-fire Monitoring Group) was formed to intervene in the Liberian and Sierra Leonean civil wars. The force was largely Nigerian run and financed, with contributions also from Ghana, Guinea, Sierra Leone, and Gambia. It remained in place until 1998 and then redeployed in 2003 after international mediation secured a ceasefire and the departure of Liberia's president. ECOMOG's Nigerian-led forces have been viewed as active participants in the civil strife, rather than peacekeepers, and Nigeria itself is perceived as acting out of national interest rather than collective regional interest. Yet, despite the criticisms, ECOMOG provided a buffer and some semblance of order. Late in 2003, the ECOMOG force became a United Nations operation with an enhanced capacity to increase the number of personnel up to 20,000. ECOMOG has not only been involved in Liberia and Sierra Leone, but also in 1999 in Guinea-Bissau and in 2002 in Ivory Coast. With this expansion of ECOWAS's mandate to include regional security operations, the organization has become known more for this activity than for its economic programs.

Southern African Development Community (SADC).   The Southern African Development Community is a successor to the Southern African Development Coordination Conference that was originally established to reduce economic dependency on South Africa when the latter was still ruled by a white minority regime. The 1994 change in political leadership in South Africa had a major impact on subregional groupings. Previously excluded from many African organizations, South Africa has since become a regional leader in SADC.

With fourteen members, SADC has adopted a broad economic, social, and environmental agenda. Originally organized to expand economic development opportunities by improving regional transportation networks and eliminating trade barriers, SADC now addresses issues from food, forestry practices, and mining activities to refugees and environmental conservation. Many of its members, including Angola, Mozambique, Tanzania, Namibia, and South Africa, have only recently become democratic, and hence they are now united not only by their economic and social objectives, but also by promotion of their political objectives.

Common Market for Eastern and Southern Africa (COMESA).   COMESA Free Trade Area, a larger regional organization than SADC, consists of twenty members, ranging from Egypt, Eritrea, Sudan, and Ethiopia in the north, to Swaziland, Namibia, and Angola in the south, as well as the island countries of the Comoros and Mauritius. Established in 1994 to replace the Preferential Trade Area for Eastern and Southern Africa, which had functioned since 1981, COMESA's goal for its members is to take advantage of larger market size and foster economic and social cooperation. Like SADC, its goals are wide ranging, including trade, customs and monetary affairs, transport, communication, technology, industry, energy, agriculture, environment, and natural resources. The goals are ambitious and comprehensive; its approach is a consultative one, utilizing a variety of subregional institutions designed to promote the goals. At this point, however, the stages are very futuristic and the obstacles considerable.

▨ Regional Bottlenecks

The African states have established a large number of overlapping regional and subregional arrangements, mostly for economic purposes. They have approved grandiose agreements, often modeled after the European experience, but they lack most of the factors that brought the European states together, such as a high level of economic interaction, multiple products in commerce, and relatively advanced transportation and infrastructure networks. Nor have the African states had regional economic or even political hegemons that are widely respected and admired and could play a key role in supporting and sustaining regional arrangements. In short, Africa lacks many of the requisite conditions for successful regional cooperation.

■ Middle East Regional Organizations

Of all the regions of the world, the Middle East probably has the weakest regional organizations and the fewest attempts to create structures for cooperation and coordination of policies.

▨ The League of Arab States

Although it was formed in March 1945, three months before the UN, the League of Arab States, or Arab League, has drawn limited scholarly attention since its inception. Nonetheless, the Arab League is an important player in the Middle East as much for what it does not do as for what it has accomplished. The league was created as a manifestation of Arab unity, in a period when Arab states had recently gained independence and were eager to assert themselves against the great powers of the time. Member states feared foreign influence if they remained completely separate, but the league charter emphasizes state sovereignty. Although the form of pan-Arab nationalism that helped to form the league has waned, the organization remains an important forum in the conflict with Israel, as well as an institution of Arab unity, which is still a popular concept among citizens of the twenty-one member states.

Institutionally, the Arab League is led by its council, which is composed of the foreign ministers of each member state. It meets twice a year, but any two countries can call it into special session. Although not mentioned in its charter, the Arab League also has periodic summits of heads of state that then function in place of the council. The Arab League also has a secretary-general and several permanent committees that consider topics such as culture, communications, and politics. All member states have equal voice in all of the Arab League's bodies, and most resolutions must pass by only a simple majority. A resolution is binding, however, only if a state votes for it. This provision has limited the power of the organization over its members. Because Arab League membership is based strictly on

Arab nationality, it excludes important regional powers such as Turkey and Iran, thereby limiting its effectiveness.

The Arab League's primary focus has historically been its hostility to the state of Israel and its support for the Palestinian cause. (See Chapter 8 for further discussion.) On these issues and on decolonization issues, members have spoken with one voice in the United Nations. Because of internal disputes among members, however, the league did not coordinate the wars with Israel in 1948, 1967, or 1973. Joint military action was taken only in 1961 to prevent Iraq from taking over Kuwait at the time of the latter's independence, and again in 1976 in the Lebanese civil war. The league, however, was unsuccessful in dealing with other disputes in the region. Algeria and Morocco, in fact, turned to the OAU to settle their border dispute. The Arab League failed to act in Yemen's civil war or the Iran-Iraq War, but it condemned Iraq's 1990 invasion of Kuwait. League members were divided over how to avert a U.S. war with Iraq in March 2003, with some members eager to pressure Saddam Hussein to disarm. This confirmed that "the Arab League has never been a model of harmony" (Sachs 2003: A11).

The 1991 Gulf War demonstrated the security weakness of many Arab states and their dependence on outside help. Notably, Saudi Arabia chose to accept American troops on its soil after the war instead of taking offers from Egypt and Syria for defense. This alliance went against everything the Arab League represents, thus demonstrating the weakness of the organization's ideology and purpose in light of the practical realities of international politics.

The Arab League is extensively institutionalized. In addition to the council, committees, and secretariat, there is a joint defense council, permanent military committee, and economic council as well as other agencies. Economic, social, and cultural cooperation has been notably more successful than political and security cooperation, despite the league's higher visibility on these issues. Its economic initiatives have included steps toward creation of a common market (Arab Economic Union) and the Arab Development Bank.

■ The Gulf Cooperation Council

Economically, politically, and culturally, Bahrain, Kuwait, Oman, Qatar, Saudi Arabia, and United Arab Emirates are among the most homogeneous nations in the world. Despite these similarities, the Cooperation Council for the Arab States of the Gulf or Gulf Cooperation Council (GCC) has been plagued by discord and competing visions that have hindered its effectiveness. According to Abdul Abdulla (1999), Kuwait envisioned a common market among the six gulf states, Oman sought a military alliance modeled after NATO, and Saudi Arabia sought an organization to provide a loose sense of collective security while allowing states to follow their own interests. These ideas merged, and the GCC was created in 1981 in response to several new threats in the region including the Iranian Revolution of 1979, the Soviet invasion of Afghanistan, and the war between Iran and Iraq. The council's mandate involves cooperation in economics, finance, trade, customs, tourism, legislation, scientific progress, and foreign investment. The charter of the GCC does not specifically mention security or defense as an area of cooperation, but members conducted joint exercises in 1983 and 1984, leading to the creation of a 7,000-member-strong Peninsula Shield force.

Institutionally, the primary organ of the GCC is the Supreme Council, which meets annually and is composed of the heads of state of the six member countries. Like ASEAN and the OAU, all substantive decisions in the Supreme Council must be unanimous. While the Supreme Council finalizes decisions for the body, much of the work of the organization is handled by the Ministerial Council, which meets every three months and includes the foreign ministers. To enhance citizen participation in the GCC, the Supreme Council created the Consultative Commission in 1997. Five citizens from each country make up this body, and it is charged with enacting the decisions of the Supreme Council. Additionally, the GCC has a Secretariat General that coordinates policies including political, economic, military, human and environment, legal, finance, and administrative affairs.

Although the GCC has outlasted initial pronouncements of failure, its effectiveness as a regional organization is debatable. Despite professed nonalignment during the Cold War, strong anti-American sentiment among citizens, and high military spending, the GCC has always relied on the United States for defense. Both Saudi Arabia and Qatar have granted the United States base rights, Saudi Arabia's used during the Gulf war and Qatar's during the 2003 Iraq war. Economically, the GCC has had duty-free trade among members since 1983, but it has yet to enact common external tariffs toward outsiders, which would complete its eventual goal of becoming a customs union. Although common citizenship allows citizens among the six states to move freely, huge populations of foreigners in each country prevent actual free movement of peoples across borders. Politically, the GCC was ineffective in responding to the Iran-Iraq war and the Iraqi invasion of Kuwait, except in formally requesting U.S. help in the latter case. While the GCC has potential to be a prominent regional actor, and the economic importance of its oil-producing members cannot be overlooked, lack of integration and conflict over the nature of the GCC have caused it to be little more than a convenient label for the six states that are members.

■ Assessing the Consequences of Regionalism

Regional organizations are among the key pieces of global governance. Although in some quarters there is a tendency to see regionalism in competition with global efforts to address issues and problems, in most areas of governance, regional organizations and activities complement global ones through either shared or overlapping responsibilities. To be sure, regional free trade initiatives give rise to a fear of trade blocs and barriers to wider trade patterns. Indeed, the EU has eliminated internal barriers to trade among its members and favored partners, but raised barriers to trade with others. Its common policies, particularly in agriculture, for example, have provoked fierce trade wars, especially with the United States, and blocked efforts to open agricultural trade on a global basis. A regional human rights regime could compromise norms of universal human rights if it adopted a more restrictive view, say, of women's rights.

Frequently, issues and problems may require coordination of global and regional (or subregional) governance activities. Such is certainly true of efforts to deal with terrorism, drug trafficking, certain types of environmental degradation, and security. For example, among the early environmental programs were those dealing with regional seas such as the Mediterranean and Baltic initiated through the UN Environment Programme. In the 1990s, as we shall explore in Chapter 8, there have been increasing efforts to coordinate UN and regional organizations' responses to the conflicts in the former Yugoslavia, Central Africa (Rwanda and Congo), and West Africa (Sierra Leone and Liberia).

Regional organizations vary widely in the nature of their organizational structures, the types of obligations they impose on member states, and the scope of their activities from the formality and supranationalism of the EU to the loose, informal political concertization of policies found in APEC and ASEAN. In many instances, nongovernmental and civil society groups have been key actors in the development of regional as well as global governance pieces. It is to them we turn in Chapter 6.

■ Suggested Further Reading

Acharya, Amitav. (2001) *Constructing a Security Community in Southeast Asia: ASEAN and the Problem of Regional Order.* New York: Routledge.

Adler, Emanuel, and Michael Barnett, eds. (1998) *Security Communities.* Cambridge, UK: Cambridge University Press.

Dinan, Desmond. (1999) *Ever Closer Union: An Introduction to European Integration,* 2nd ed. Boulder, CO: Lynne Rienner Publishers.

Fawcett, Louise, and Andrew Hurrell, eds. (1995) *Regionalism in World Politics: Regional Organization and International Order.* New York: Oxford University Press.

Mace, Gordon, Louis Belanger, and contributers. (1999) *The Americas in*

Transition: The Contours of Regionalism. Boulder, CO: Lynne Rienner Publishers.

Moravcsik, Andrew. (1998) *The Choice for Europe: Social Purpose and State Power from Messina to Maastricht.* Ithaca: Cornell University Press.

Ravenhill, John. (2001) *APEC and the Construction of Pacific Rim Regionalism.* Cambridge, UK: Cambridge University Press.

Schraeder, Peter J. (2004) *African Politics and Society. A Mosaic in Transformation,* 2nd ed. Belmont, CA: Wadsworth/Thomson Learning.

Thomas, Kenneth P., and Mary Ann Tetreault, eds. (1999) *Racing to Regionalize: Democracy, Capitalism, and Regional Political Economy.* Boulder. CO: Lynne Rienner Publishers.

■ Internet Resources

Africa
African Union: www.africa-union.org/
Common Market for Eastern and Southern Africa: www.comesa.int
Economic Community of West African States: www.ecowas.int/
Southern African Development Community: www.sadc.int

Asia
Asia-Pacific Economic Cooperation: www.apecsec.org.sg/
Association of Southeast Asian Nations: www.aseansec.org/

Europe
Commonwealth of Independent States: www.cis.minsk.by/
Council of Europe: www.coe.int/
European Union: www.europa.eu.int/
North Atlantic Treaty Organization: www.nato.int/
Organization for Security and Cooperation in Europe: www.osce.org

Latin America
Andean Community: www.comunidadandina.org
Caribbean Community: www.caricom.org
Central American Common Market: http://memory.loc.gov/frd/cs/honduras/hn_appnb.html
Free Trade Area of the Americas: www.ftaa-alca.org
Mercosur: www.mercosur.org
North American Free Trade Agreement: www.nafta-sec.alena.org
Organization of American States: www.oas.org
Summit of the Americas: www.summit-americas.org

Middle East
Gulf Cooperation Council: www.gcc-sg.org
League of Arab States: www.arableagueonline.org

6

Nonstate Actors: NGOs, Networks, and Social Movements

■ Nonstate Actors in Action

▨ *Take One: Expanding and Limiting the Scope of Global Governance*

In the space of three months in 1998 and 1999, an international treaty to ban landmines entered into effect and negotiations on the Multilateral Agreement on Investment (MAI) were permanently halted. Both events underscored the emergence of transnational political processes in which the activities of international NGOs played key roles. In the case of the landmine treaty, a network of NGOs (composed of more than one thousand organizations in sixty countries, from Germany's Medico International, the Vietnam Veterans of America Foundation, and the Landmine Survivors Network, to Human Rights Watch and the International Committee of the Red Cross), uniting in the International Campaign to Ban Landmines (ICBL), used an array of electronic media tools, including the Web, to send messages, support activities in distant places, and to disseminate the message that landmines have indiscriminate and devastating effects on civilians. In the case of MAI, a diverse group of more than six hundred organizations in seventy countries, ranging from the AFL-CIO and United Steelworkers of America, to Amnesty International, Friends of the Earth, Oxfam, and World Development, used the Web as well as traditional letter-writing campaigns, petitions, and demonstrations to protest the draft agreement.

In both cases, NGOs were successful in reframing the issue discourse. The International Campaign to Ban Landmines successfully defined the landmines issue as a humanitarian or human security issue, instead of an arms control or national security issue (Thakur and Maley 1999). NGOs opposed to the MAI were able to appeal to concerns over globalization, loss of democratic control over political processes, environmental degradation, and mistreatment of the poor (Kobrin 1998).

The network of NGOs forming the International Campaign to Ban Landmines was created in 1993 and celebrated the successful conclusion of a treaty six years later. In the case of the MAI, an effort by twenty-nine states working within the OECD to create a new set of more enforceable rules dealing with multilateral investment came to a halt. Negotiations had been underway for almost two years when the Washington-based public interest group founded by Ralph Nader, Public Citizen, acquired a leaked version of the draft text and published it on the Web in early 1997. Less than two years later, the OECD announced that negotiations would not resume.

NGOs clearly were primary players in both cases and able to accomplish their goals more quickly and effectively thanks to the ways in which the Web permitted them to gather and disseminate information to private citizens and government officials around the world, as well as to build transnational coalitions in support of their goals. As Warkentin and Mingst note (2000: 253): "Technological developments . . . have collapsed political time. . . . in the landmine case, norms of prohibition were developed and reproduced with relative speed, in years rather than the decades or centuries of the past. . . . traditional state-based actors were caught off guard by the speed with which global civil society used the Web to effectively mobilize people, raise issue awareness, and lobby for particular policy responses." The landmines case illustrates NGO leadership in expanding the scope of global governance. The MAI case shows NGOs playing a key role in limiting the expansion of global governance. As Herman (1998: 21) explains, "A coalition of groups used the Internet to stop the treaty cold. Hundreds of advocacy groups, attempting to galvanize opposition to the MAI, used terms and examples that brought their message to the public." In a sense, they were using a key engine of globalization, the Internet, to inflict a blow on another part of globalization: the rapid growth of foreign direct investment and spread of MNCs (Walter 2001).

◼ Take Two: The Dark Side of Nonstate Actors

On September 11, 2001, terrorists hijacked four American airplanes, flying two into the World Trade Center towers in New York, another into the Pentagon in Washington, while the fourth crashed in western Pennsylvania. This attack on the symbols of American financial and military power was widely credited to the network of terrorist organizations known as Al-Qaeda and led by Osama bin Laden. Because nonstate actors are frequently credited with helping to set agendas for global governance and manage problems emerging from globalization, most of the literature on this phenomenon deals with the "good guys"—the human rights groups, the environmental groups, the grassroots and international NGOs involved in humanitarian relief and development assistance. Not all NGO activities, however, can be clearly defined; neither should we overlook the presence and activities of the "dark side" in shaping agendas and efforts at global governance.

Terrorist groups and networks, along with organized criminal groups such as the Mafia, drug traffickers, and paramilitary forces are not new participants in international politics. Both states and the international community have waged war on the international drug cartels based in Colombia and their suppliers in South America and Southeast Asia, the Mafia in Italy, Russia, and other venues, and paramilitary forces in Africa and Asia, just as the international community is waging war against Muslim extremists, including Al Qaeda. Our challenge is to understand the diverse character of these actors, the roles they play, the strategies they employ, and the ways in which their proliferation is reshaping international and domestic politics.

While 191 sovereign states are the major constituents of the international system, thousands of NGOs, informal associations, loose networks, coalitions, and social movements are also part of that system. They must work within the state-centric framework, but their emergent roles as part of a nascent global civil society are often crucial to the success or failure of global governance. Nonstate actors do not have the same kind of power resources as states. They are not sovereign; they cannot make laws; they do not possess the coercive power of armies or police authority. Nevertheless, we cannot understand efforts to deal with global and regional issues without examining the nature, activities, and roles of these nonstate actors.

■ The Range of Nonstate Actors

A variety of terms are used to describe different types of nonstate actors. The International Campaign to Ban Landmines, for example, was a loose, transnational network of numerous NGOs from different parts of the world that only established an address, bank account, and formal organizational identity when it was awarded the 1997 Nobel Peace Prize. (ICBL couldn't receive its share of the prize money until it had done this.) There are clear benefits to such a loose structure, as one analyst suggests: "The very flexible nature of the network and the respect for national campaigns enabled the ICBL to exercise the kind of power it did as a transnational civil society in establishing a treaty" (Mekata 2000: 172). The campaign against the Multilateral Investment Agreement was also a loose transnational network of some six hundred NGOs. Al-Qaeda is a network of terrorist (nongovernmental) organizations and a civil society network among a committed group of Muslim believers. Figure 6.1 provides summary definitions of key terms used to describe different types of nonstate actors.

▨ *Nongovernmental Organizations (NGOs)*

NGOs, as defined in Chapter 1, are voluntary organizations formed by individuals to perform a variety of functions and roles. Some are organized around a very specific issue area, while others are organized to address

---

Figure 6.1   Types of Nonstate Actors

- *NGOs/INGOs*
Voluntary organizations formed and organized by private individuals, operating at the local, national, or international level. Examples include Oxfam, Rotary.

- *Transnational Networks and Coalitions*
Informal and formal linkages among NGOs and ad hoc groups on behalf of a certain issue. Examples include Third World Network, Landmine Survivors Network.

- *Transnational Advocacy Networks*
A kind of transnational network dedicated to direct promotion of a specific cause. Examples include International Campaign to Ban Landmines, Al-Qaeda.

- *Social Movements*
Individuals working in large groups for major social change. Examples include Christian Pentecostalism; Mothers of the Plaza de Mayo.

- *Global Policy Networks*
Networks of governments, international organizations, multinational corporations, professionals linked in pursuit of a common policy. Examples include World Commission on Dams.

- *Experts, Epistemic Communities*
Experts drawn from governments, research institutes, international organizations, nongovernmental community. Examples include experts concerned with Mediterranean Sea, global climate experts.

- *Multinational Corporations*
Private actors doing business in three or more states whose goal is to make a profit. Examples include Nike, Shell Oil Company, Sony.

---

broad issues such as human rights, peace, or the environment (Amnesty International, The Nature Conservancy). Some provide services, such as humanitarian aid (Catholic Relief Services) or development assistance (Grameen Bank), while many do both. Oxfam, for example, not only provides emergency relief in food crises, but also works at long-term development, helping fishermen in Asia manage water resources and coastal environments. CARE delivers relief, as well as being involved in community building among women. Other NGOs are information gathering and disseminating bodies (Transparency International, an anticorruption organization). Millions of small local NGOs are active at the grassroots levels (Associación de Mujeres Campesinas de la Huasteca, Bangladesh Rural

Advancement Committee), while others operate locally, nationally, and internationally. Most NGOs are headquartered in Northern and Western developed countries (Amnesty International in London; Oxfam in Oxford, U.K., The Nature Conservancy in Washington, D.C.) and receive funding from private donors. Others have roots in the developing countries of the South, but get some funding for local programs or training from international groups (Development Alternatives with Women for a New Era [DAWN] or Tostan, an NGO addressing female genital mutilation in Africa). Some operate independently, while others are now linked to counterpart groups through transnational networks or federations.

Among the internationally oriented NGOs, federations, and networking are two important ways that NGOs are linked. The Vietnam Veterans of America, which was a key player in the landmine campaign, illustrates a national NGO operating only within the United States for many of its goals, but linked to a network of groups around the world to further the landmine campaign. In contrast, the Red Cross is officially the International Federation of Red Cross and Red Crescent Societies headquartered in Geneva, Switzerland—a federation of national chapters. Oxfam International has been transformed from a British NGO into a transnational federation, with member chapters in Australia, Belgium, Canada, Hong Kong, Ireland, the Netherlands, New Zealand, Spain, the United Kingdom, and the United States. These large, federated NGOs—Oxfam, World Wildlife Fund, Human Rights Watch, Save the Children—have shared overall goals, but leave most fundraising and activities to the individual country chapters. They differ in how much control they can exercise over chapters and how much they try to coordinate activities. Individual chapters, in many cases, may choose their own special interest. Save the Children Sweden, for example, focuses on child abuse and child advocacy to a greater extent than other chapters do (Weiss and Gordenker 1996: 28). Most NGOs, whether federations of national organizations or not, maintain an international office and secretariat that serve their members in different countries.

In a few unusual cases, NGOs take the place of states, either performing services that an inept or corrupt government is not doing, or stepping in for a failed state. Bangladesh hosts the largest NGO sector in the world (over 19,000 by one count), responding to what one Bangladeshi describes as "the failure of government to provide public goods and look after the poor, and the failure of the private sector to provide enough gainful employment opportunities" (quoted in Waldman 2003: A8). NGOs have taken on roles in education, health, agriculture, and microcredit, all of which originally were government functions. Some attribute the decline in Bangladesh's poverty rate since 1971 from 70 percent to 43 percent to this nonstate sector. Bangladesh may be a unique situation, but the failed state of Somalia has also witnessed an explosion of NGOs performing vital economic functions that the government is not handling.

Large numbers of NGOs are involved in humanitarian relief and development assistance. The Red Cross, Doctors Without Borders, the International Rescue Committee, and Oxfam are among the forty or so humanitarian relief organizations involved in complex emergencies such as the conflicts in Somalia, Kosovo, Bosnia, Congo, and Liberia, the genocide in Rwanda, and Hurricane Mitch's devastation of Central America. Development service providers include the Grameen Bank (that provides microcredit loans to poor women and men in countries such as Bangladesh), thousands of grassroots organizations, and several relief groups such as Oxfam, CARE, Catholic Relief Services, Save the Children, World Vision, and Christian Children's Fund. In fact, there is a general tendency now to integrate developmental components into relief work, focusing on agriculture, reforestation, primary health care, and microenterprise. Studies of aid efforts in the Somalia emergency in the early 1990s show that 50 percent of the relief grants to NGOs also included development-related efforts (Natsios 1996: 69).

The NGOs engaged in advocacy are often more visible and vocal than the humanitarian relief and development providers. Whether focused on human rights, peace, disarmament, indigenous peoples' rights, women's rights, labor rights, infant formula, a multilateral agreement on investment, landmines, acid rain, climate change, whales, elephants, fur seals, the Amazon rain forest, globalization, sweatshops, the World Trade Organization, World Bank, or IMF, advocacy groups have become an important part of world politics. Although they come in all shades, organizational formats, sizes, and approaches, they share "the centrality of values or principled ideas, the belief that individuals can make a difference, the creative use of information, and the employment . . . of sophisticated political strategies in targeting their campaigns" (Keck and Sikkink 1998: 2). Often, they seek to change the policies and behavior of *both* governments and IGOs.

Yet NGOs are unique organizational entities. They, like multinational corporations, are subject to the laws and rules of the nation-state in which they reside. Thus, in some states like Myanmar, NGOs are not allowed to exist; in the People's Republic of China, NGOs are only beginning to organize. In other countries like Japan, while technically legal, NGOs operated under major legal and financial constraints until the 1990s. In contrast, still other countries such as Bangladesh and Thailand are known for having large and vigorous NGO communities. Yet under traditional international law, NGOs, unlike states and international governmental organizations, have no independent international legal personality. Over time, they have been awarded responsibility for enforcing international rules in a few cases, however, and the right to bring cases in selected adjudicatory settings. This has led Willetts (2000: 206) to conclude, "The new language of the 1990s, with the concept of social partners, is revolutionary because it implies an equality of status between governments and NGOs. The partners are equal in the sense that each has legal personality, but not in the sense that they have the same rights and obligations."

■ *Networks and Coalitions*

NGOs seldom work alone for very long. The communications revolution of fax, Internet, and the Web, have linked NGOs together with each other—sometimes formally, more often informally—and with states to block or promote shared goals. Thus, transnational networks and coalitions create multilevel linkages between different organizations that each retain their separate organizational character and memberships, but through their linkages enhance power, information sharing, and reach. INGOs often are not in a position to work effectively with local people and groups. Grassroots groups need the help of other groups within their own country and often from transnational groups to have an impact on their own government or in addressing problems or needs. This is where coalitions or networks become valuable.

We can illustrate the differences in how coalitions organize by examining two coalitions that formed around the issue of protecting the elephant and banning trade in ivory. One coalition includes several of the major environmental and conservation INGOs such as World Wildlife Fund (WWF), the International Union for the Conservation of Nature and Natural Resources (IUCN, now known as IUCN-The World Conservation Union), and Trade Records Analysis of Flora and Fauna in Commerce (TRAFFIC). Most of the member organizations are based in the North where they raise funds, conduct research, educate the public, and work with IGOs such as the UN Environment Programme (UNEP) and the secretariat of the Conference of Parties to the Convention on International Trade in Endangered Species of Wild Fauna and Flora (CITES). This particular coalition is highly integrated, even sharing office space and staff. Because the member organizations have large, professional staffs of scientists and program specialists, they have a long-term presence in countries such as Kenya, South Africa, Zimbabwe, and Botswana with large elephant populations. They work with governments to create and manage protected areas for elephants and other wildlife, parks, and preserves, to monitor wildlife population changes, engage in research, and fund special projects. They also work with major ivory consumers such as Japan, China, and Hong Kong. Their funding comes from governments, foundations, corporations, as well as individual members. To facilitate coordination of their efforts, these and other participating organizations, including the EU and U.S. Fish and Wildlife Service, formed the African Elephant Conservation Coordinating Group in 1990 to develop an action plan.

In contrast to this coalition of highly professional NGOs, another coalition is loosely composed of preservation and animal rights organization. This includes groups such as Friends of the Animals, Greenpeace, the Humane Society, and Amnistie pour les éléphants. Like other coalitions formed to campaign for a specific species, this one is primarily geared toward raising public awareness and thereby influencing governmental decisions. Through a major media campaign in the late 1980s and early 1990s, it was instrumental in achieving a worldwide ban on ivory trade. In this type of loose coalition, funding comes almost exclusively from members and there is no organizational structure to aid in implementing long-term solutions. The loose coalition could successfully achieve a ban on ivory trade, but it was not geared to work with governments of both ivory-consuming and elephant-host countries to promote an overall conservation strategy that would address underlying causes of elephant population decline (Princen and Finger 1994; Princen 1995). How CITES is implemented through TRAFFIC is discussed in detail in Chapter 11.

One special type of network or coalition is a transnational advocacy network. Advocacy groups and networks bring new ideas into policy debates, along with new ways of framing issues to make them comprehensible and to attract support, new information, and resources. They also "promote norm implementation, by pressuring target actors to adopt new policies, and by monitoring compliance with international standards" (Keck and Sikkink 1998: 3). Particularly distinctive has been the use of campaigns to focus advocacy efforts, target resources, and win public support. Thus international campaigns by environmental and conservation organizations have tended to have a topical focus such as elephants, whales, the Amazon, or Africa's Great Lakes. Human rights campaigns have focused either on specific rights abuses such as torture, genocide, violence against women, and slavery, or on specific countries such as Argentina and South Africa. Peace groups have long focused on banning a particular type of weapon (nuclear, landmines, small armaments) and opposing wars (Vietnam, El Salvador, Iraq).

Key to the functioning of advocacy networks are the formal and informal connections among participating groups. Individuals, information, and funds move back and forth among them. Larger NGOs provide money and various kinds of services, such as help with organization building and training, to smaller NGOs. Small grassroots groups provide information about human rights violations or pending environmental disasters to INGOs. The information they provide may be factual or testimonial, that is, stories told by people whose lives have been affected such as the mother whose son was disappeared or tortured, the children who lost legs or arms to landmines, or the Yanomani people losing their ancestral land to ranchers who burned the rain forest to create farmland.

Increasingly, transnational advocacy networks have learned from each other (Clark et al. 1998). Environmentalists and women's groups have studied human rights campaigns for guidance in building international norms. Women's groups worked closely with environmental groups during the 1992 Rio conference. Close relationships between key players in women's rights and human rights groups led to the mainstreaming of women's rights into the human rights movement in the 1990s. Environmentalists seeking protection of spaces for indigenous peoples increasingly used the language of human rights.

■ Social Movements

The concept of social movements originated in the discipline of sociology and has been gradually adopted by political scientists and international relations scholars to facilitate study of phenomena that are not explicable in terms of institutional structures and processes. Specifically, the social movement concept focuses on how people work together to bring changes in the status quo. Such movements may form around major social cleavages such as class, religion, region, language, or ethnicity or around progressive goals such as the environment, human rights, and development, or around conservative goals such as opposition to abortion, family planning, and immigration.

NGOs often play key roles in national and transnational social movements, but when they do, their focus is on some type of social or political change. NGOs and others help in framing the issues to make them resonate with the public; they help to mobilize the necessary structures and resources; they seek to open up political structures to help accommodate the envisioned changes and to generate transnational consensus about global problems and their solutions.

Transnational social movements, then, are very similar—often identical except for terminology—to transnational advocacy networks and transnational civil society networks. As agents of global change, they provide the networks of social relations necessary for action, the resources, the information, and the ideas to mobilize people for movement goals, as well as the norms and values about participating in policymaking and implementation for people in different parts of the world often unaccustomed to thinking they have the power to make a difference. Constructivism emphasizes how social movements also seek to foster new identities—particularly transnationally—among women, indigenous peoples, victims of human rights violations, and the poor.

Transnational social movements work at many levels, trying to influence IGOs, INGOs, attentive publics and elites in key countries, governments, and the general public. Like advocacy networks, they mobilize support for change, widen public participation in international policy processes, focus attention on critical global problems, frame issues, and set agendas. Typically, movements seek to involve large numbers of individuals and groups that do not routinely work for their goals. They also vary enormously in the types of formal or informal structures they use to mobilize support—from activist networks to national and transnational organizations. And they vary in their effectiveness.

A group that gained prominence in the late 1970s, thanks to the international human rights network, was the Mothers of the Plaza de Mayo—literally the mothers and grandmothers of young men and women who disappeared during a period of Argentina's military dictatorship (1976–1983). Every day, wearing white handkerchiefs, they marched in circles in the central square in Buenos Aires to draw attention to their missing children. Originally a small gathering, the group gained momentum as the number of marchers escalated over time. New supporters joined the cause, fueled by international media attention. They wanted a full accounting by the government of the atrocities committed by the military junta. It evolved into a full-fledged social movement.

One contemporary social movement is a religious one, namely, Christian Pentecostalism. Having originated in California a hundred years ago, the movement now includes over 400 million people and is rapidly expanding in all parts of the world, particularly in the global South. The movement, centered on a rejection of secularism, is a "new transnational order in which political, social, and personal identities are defined chiefly by religious loyalties" (Jenkins 2002: 55). Samaritan's Purse, the relief agency headed by the Reverend Franklin Graham, has delivered medical care and relief with a liberal dose of proselytizing in Somalia, Rwanda, Bosnia, Kosovo, and southern Sudan (Cottle 2003). This social movement's antisecularism is similar to the antisecularism and antimodernism espoused by fundamentalist Islam and orthodox Judaism.

■ Global Public Policy Networks

Global public policy networks differ from advocacy networks and social movements, as well as from NGOs. These networks include government agencies, IGOs, corporations, professional groups, NGOs, and sometimes religious groups. The advantages of networking are expanded because the types of participants range across the spectrum from civil society to governmental and intergovernmental, corporate, and nonprofit entities. As one analyst notes, "A global public policy network can sort through conflicting perspectives, help hammer out a consensus, and translate that consensus into actions its members will be more inclined to support and implement" (Reincke 1999–2000: 47). The recently created World Commission on Dams (WCD) illustrates this phenomenon.

Beginning in the 1970s, the construction of big dams to provide energy and water for development became the target of a global campaign by NGOs concerned about the negative social, economic and ecological effects. This pitted them against government agencies, IGOs (including the World Bank), multinational corporations, and industrial and agricultural interests that favored dam construction. By the early 1990s, the conflict was imposing considerable costs on all parties—the NGOs who had to devote resources to sustain their campaigns, the World Bank (which was having trouble making loans because of public pressures), and the private companies who were losing dam construction contracts. A novel step was taken in 1998 by creating WCD, an independent international body composed of twelve commissioners representing affected peoples' groups, research institutes, hydropower companies, multilateral development banks, river basin authorities, and governments directly involved with dam building. The commission's two-year mandate was (a) to conduct a global review of the development effectiveness of large dams and (b) to establish internationally accepted criteria for dam construction. In the eyes of one analyst, the WCD "is the most innovative international institutional experiment in the area of democratic governance for sustainable development today" (Khagram 2000: 105). Other global policy networks include the Roll Back Malaria initiative involving the WHO, World Bank, UNICEF, NGOs and government agencies, and the Consultative Group on International Agricultural Research (CGIAR), whose members include governments, IGOs, foundations, corporations, and NGOs.

▓ *Experts and Epistemic Communities*

Global policy networks include experts on different subjects, drawn from government agencies, research institutes, private industry, or universities. In a world whose problems seem to grow steadily more complex, knowledge and, more important, the sharing of knowledge by experts through transnational networks is critical to understanding the problems themselves, framing issues for collective debates, and to proposing specific solutions. These epistemic communities are networks of knowledge-based experts—professionals with competence in a particular issue domain. Although they may come from a variety of academic disciplines and backgrounds, they share normative beliefs, understanding about the causes of particular problems, criteria for weighing conflicting evidence, and a commitment to seeking policy solutions (Haas 1992: 3).

Epistemic communities of experts are particularly important in addressing complex environmental issues, but in principle could be influential in shaping policy outcomes in any issue area where shared knowledge, ideas, and understanding are critical to developing consensus on the nature of the issue itself and on policy choices. For example, in the 1980s, despite the hostility among several states bordering the Mediterranean Sea, all eighteen governments participated in negotiating the Med Plan under UNEP auspices. Concern that the Mediterranean was dying led them to unite behind a cleanup program involving agreements to control many sources of Mediterranean pollution. Med Plan became the model for arrangements for nine other regional seas in the world and is widely regarded as a success. Critical to bringing together the otherwise hostile states and securing agreement on a plan, however, was the network of ecologists in UNEP, FAO, and several governments. They shared a common concern about the Mediterranean's health, the necessity of multilateral control of all pollutants, and the nature of the policies required. Also, they could draw on the expertise of regional marine scientists. They drafted the Barcelona Convention and Land-Based Sources Protocol to deal with land-based and marine-based sources of pollution. They pressed governments to regulate pollutants other than oil, including those transmitted by rivers. They encouraged governments to enforce policies for pollution control and to adopt more comprehensive measures. Not surprisingly, the strongest measures for pollution control were taken in countries where members of the epistemic community were entrenched in government agencies and influential (Haas 1990).

Other examples of epistemic communities can be found among the scientific experts on whaling (cetologists), stratospheric ozone, and global climate change as well as among experts on food aid—an eclectic group of economic development specialists, agricultural economists, and administrators of food aid programs. They can be found also among experts on nuclear proliferation and trade in services as well as many other issues. Several of these are discussed in subsequent chapters.

■ *For-Profit NGOs: Multinational Corporations (MNCs)*

Multinational corporations are a special type of NGO engaged in for-profit business transactions and operations across national borders. Since the 1970s, MNCs have been increasingly recognized as significant international actors, controlling resources far greater than those of many states.

MNCs are key actors, but their roles and behavior are also targets of NGO activism. The issue of MNCs and labor conditions has been part of many human rights NGOs' agendas; likewise, NGO activists have linked MNCs role in trade and the environment as part of the environmental agenda. NGOs have targeted MNCs such as Nike, Reebok, McDonalds, Starbucks, Home Depot, and the Gap. They have discovered the power of consumers who have been persuaded by NGOs to boycott the products of a given corporation. In the competitive environment of today's global markets, such a boycott is likely to lead the targeted corporation to terminate or modify the practice, as discussed in upcoming chapters.

As a result of NGO-led campaigns to end sweatshops and child labor, protect rain forests, boycott blood diamonds, and prevent the scuttling of a

North Sea oil rig, major corporations have responded by implementing codes of conduct, certifications that certain standards have been met, and monitoring mechanisms. Under increasing pressures by the NGO-led grass-roots campaigns, these codes of conduct have had to be continually strengthened, with corporations making concessions that would have been unthinkable in the past. As *The Economist* (Dec. 2, 1995: 18) has noted, "A multinational's failure to look like a good global citizen is increasingly expensive in a world where consumers and pressure groups can be quickly mobilised behind a cause." Thus, MNCs are a unique type of NGO and also a favorite target of NGO activists.

Toward a Global Civil Society?

There is a common tendency to equate NGOs with civil society, but the latter is really a broader concept, encompassing all organizations and associations that exist outside of the state and the market (i.e., government and business). It includes not just the kinds of advocacy groups discussed above, but also associations of professionals (doctors, lawyers, scientists, journalists), labor unions, chambers of commerce, religious groups, ethnic associations, cultural groups, sporting associations, and political parties. Most critically, civil society links individual citizens. In Wapner's (1996: 5) words, it is an arena in which "people engage in spontaneous, customary and nonlegalistic forms of association" to pursue common goals. As a result, individuals establish relationships and shared frames or understandings that govern future behavior.

Civil society is neither inherently good nor bad; people associate and work together to advance both worthy and nefarious ends. At one level, we speak of it as a "good." Hence, the explosion of democracy in many corners of the globe has bolstered the growth of civil societies in many countries. South Korea's military regime, for example, repressed civil society groups until the 1980s when it loosened up, and labor unions, student groups, and religious organizations rapidly emerged, successfully achieving democratization and its strengthening. Strong civil societies have been linked to a number of public "goods." Yet, it may also be associated with less desirable characteristics, including "the pursuit of private and frequently parochial and grubby ends" (quoted in Carothers 1999–2000: 21).

Have individuals and groups connected across nations to a sufficient extent to suggest that we now have a global civil society? Do individuals have an associational life beyond the state? Are the norms and values that individuals hold shared transnationally? Many scholars answer in the affirmative, talking in terms of a nascent global civil society. Although this is the subject of much theoretical speculation, the fact is that nonstate actors, including NGOs, are critical components of any type of a transnational civil society.

■   **The Growth of Nonstate Actors**

It was common in the 1990s to read about the explosive growth of NGOs and other nonstate actors and the power shift underway in global politics. There is no disputing that the number of NGOs has increased exponentially since the mid-1970s, as Figure 1.4 illustrates. Some calculations show over six thousand INGOs. Other figures, using a broader definition of NGOs, suggest that there may be over sixteen thousand, plus thousands more indigenous NGOs. The growth has been exponential particularly since World War II and in certain issue areas such as human rights and the environment. Yet NGOs are not just a late-twentieth-century phenomenon but have played roles in developing international law and organization for more than two-hundred years.

■   *A Historical Perspective on the Growth of NGO Influence*

The antislavery campaign was the earliest NGO-initiated effort to organize transnationally to ban a morally unacceptable social and economic practice. Its genesis lay in the establishment in 1787 and 1788 of societies dedicated to the abolition of slavery in Pennsylvania, England, and France. The history of this campaign, spanning much of the nineteenth century, is examined in Chapter 10.

In Europe and in the United States, peace societies also began appearing during the nineteenth century. A group of peace societies convened their first congress in 1849, developing the first plan for what later became the Permanent Court of Arbitration. Peace societies joined in supporting many of the ideas emerging from The Hague conferences at the end of the century, including the commitment to find noncoercive means for dispute resolution. By 1900, there were 425 peace societies throughout the world (Charnovitz 1997).

The nineteenth century also saw the establishment of transnational labor unions, NGOs promoting free trade, and groups dedicated to the strengthening of international law. In 1910, NGOs convened the World Congress of International Associations with 132 groups participating and from that emerged the Union of International Associations (UIA), which still today serves as *the* international organization documenting the landscape of international organizations.

NGOs were heavily involved in promoting intergovernmental cooperation and regime creation during the nineteenth century in functional areas such as intellectual property rights, transportation, narcotics traffic, workers' rights, agriculture, conservation of species, and sanitation. The Red Cross, for example, was influential in the development of international humanitarian law dealing with wounded soldiers. The International Chamber of Commerce (a federation of national chambers of commerce established in 1920) and the International Criminal Police Commission (created in 1923 and later renamed Interpol) were among the outgrowths of early-twentieth-century congresses dealing with commerce, transportation, and public health in which NGOs were prime movers. As one analyst noted, "'Sometimes, it is true, governments did take the lead, but it is no exaggeration to say that in most aspects of nineteenth century internationalism they followed reluctantly and hesitantly a trail blazed by others.' Behind many IGOs stood idealistic and active NGOs" (quoted in Charnovitz 1997: 212).

In the twentieth century, peace groups such as the League to Enforce Peace and the League of Nations Society of London developed the ideas that shaped the League of Nations and later the United Nations. Labor groups were active in the formation of the ILO. The League of Nations Covenant contained one provision dealing with NGOs, calling upon members "to encourage and promote the establishment and cooperation of duly authorized voluntary national Red Cross organizations having as purposes the improvement of health, the prevention of disease, and the mitigation of suffering throughout the world" (Article 25). Without specific constitutional authorization, however, the league secretariat published a quarterly bulletin on the activities and policy recommendations of NGOs and assigned a staff member to oversee relations with them.

The League of Nations also invited NGOs to participate in meetings other than those of the assembly and council, such as the 1920 Financial Conference in Brussels, the league's Maritime Committee, the 1927 World Economic Conference, and the 1932 Disarmament Conference. Many specific NGO proposals were incorporated into draft treaties. NGOs were actively involved in the league's work on minority rights, particularly in submitting petitions. Jeglantyne Jebb, founder of Save the Children International Union in 1920, drafted the Declaration of the Rights of the Child approved by the league assembly in 1924. Save the Children and other NGOs were represented on the league's Child Welfare Committee, as women's groups were also on the league's Committee on Traffic in Women and Children. In both cases, NGO representatives were considered full members of the committees, except for the right to vote. Many NGOs established offices in Geneva to facilitate contacts with the league (and have remained there since Geneva is the European headquarters of the UN).

Between 1930 and 1945, NGOs' influence diminished, in large part because governments were preoccupied with rising security threats and economic crisis and the league's role declined, but as planning for the postwar order proceeded after 1943, NGOs again became important sources of ideas shaping the UN Charter and other postwar steps. Indeed, there were representatives of 1,200 voluntary organizations at the San Francisco founding conference of the UN. They were largely responsible for both the wording "We the peoples of the United Nations," and the specific provisions for NGO consultative status with ECOSOC, as discussed below. In 1948, there were forty-one groups formally accredited; in 2002, there were more than 2,500. Since our purpose here is not to provide a systematic history of NGO development and roles, but rather to put the changes of the late twentieth century into perspective, we shall leap ahead to analyze the proliferation of NGOs that began in the 1970s and the intensification of their involvement in global governance.

▦ Explaining the Accelerated Growth of Nonstate Actors' Participation

What has spurred the accelerating growth of NGOs, networks, coalitions, and social movements and their influence on global governance since the 1970s? Four factors stand out: globalization and the emergence of interdependence issues such as the environment, development, population, food aid, and human rights; UN-sponsored global conferences; the communications revolution; and the end of the Cold War and the spread of democracy.

Globalization and interdependence issues.   As discussed in Chapter 1, there is a broad sense among academics and the general public that the world is more closely connected today than ever before. Heightening that sense is an awareness of a set of issues arising out of interdependence, whose solutions depend upon transnational and intergovernmental cooperation. The very nature of these issues is such that governments frequently do not control the information and other resources essential to governance. NGOs with their ability to collect and disseminate information, to mobilize key constituencies, and to target resources on particular goals have developed to fulfill these needs, giving them significant opportunities for influence. Even on security issues, traditionally the province of states alone, NGOs have introduced new issues and pushed specific agendas, as the case of banning landmines illustrates. New issues of AIDs and the Internet, as discussed in Chapter 12, have also seen major activity by NGOs.

Global conferences and nonstate actors.   UN-sponsored global conferences have increasingly involved participation by NGOs, as shown in Table 6.1. Since the early 1970s, NGOs, networks, and coalitions have sought opportunities to participate in agenda setting and negotiations.

Beginning with the 1972 Stockholm conference on the environment, NGOs organized a parallel forum with almost 250 NGOs participating, a pattern that was repeated at each subsequent conference, with steadily growing numbers. At the 1992 UN conference on the environment in Rio de Janeiro, some 1,400 NGOs were represented in the NGO forum. First,

Table 6.1   Participation at Selected Global Conferences

Global Conference	Number of States	Number of NGOs[a]
Environment (1972)	114	250
Children (1990)	159	45
Environment/Development (1992)	172	1400
Human Rights (1993)	171	800
Population/Development (1994)	179	1500
Social Summit (1995)	186	811
Women (1995)	189	2100
Human Settlements	171	2400
Sustainable Development (2002)	N/A	1000

Note: a. Figures vary considerably among different sources.

the conferences were intended to draw attention to select global issues and to mobilize the international community to take steps to address the issues. Hence, they put issues on the map that NGOs were often far more equipped to address than many governments. Second, they created opportunities throughout the conference preparatory processes and follow up for NGO influence. The final document of the Rio conference, Agenda 21, assigned a key role to NGOs in implementation of conference outcomes, calling for IGOs to utilize the expertise and views of NGOs in all phases of the policy process. Third, the parallel NGOs' forums spurred networking among participating groups by bringing them together from around the world for several days of intensive interactions. Those links enable NGOs to play an important role in monitoring follow-up activities.

It is important to note that each conference has been free to adopt its own rules for NGO participation. For example, the NGOs present in Stockholm were permitted to make formal statements to the conference with no limits. At the 1980 second women's conference in Copenhagen, NGO representatives were granted only fifteen minutes total speaking time. At the 1985 conclusion of the Vienna Convention on Ozone Depleting Substances, no NGOs were present; in 1987, NGOs were permitted to speak at the Montreal conference drafting the follow-up protocol to that same convention; and in 1989, there were ninety NGOs in active attendance at the London Conference on Saving the Ozone Layer. Thereafter, environmental NGOs were intimately involved in the preparations for the 1992 Rio Conference on the Environment and Development and in the negotiations on conventions for biodiversity and climate change. At the Habitat II conference in 1996, NGO representatives were allowed to sit with governments and to table amendments to texts. In contrast, the 1993 human rights conference excluded NGOs from the official process, in large part because many Asian and Arab states lobbied to restrict NGO access. Not all issue areas are equally populated with NGOs, and in any case the nature of NGO participation varies widely.

The communications revolution.   Although NGOs have benefited enormously from the face-to-face gatherings at global conferences, the communications revolution has made it possible to link individuals and groups without such contacts. The fax and, most important, the Internet and e-mail have made cohesion not tied to location possible.

Warkentin (2001) identifies six ways in which NGOs use the Internet: to facilitate internal communication and communications with partner organizations, shape public perception, enhance member services, disseminate information, encourage political participation, and realize innovative ideas. E-mail and fax have increased the volume and speed of interactions. Web sites enable NGOs to disseminate widely a particular picture of themselves and their work, recruit new members, communicate with existing members, make a large amount of information publicly available, solicit contributions, encourage people to participate politically in specific ways, and often provide the means to do this electronically.

We are just beginning to understand the impact of the communications revolution. Mathews (1997: 50–51) suggests its effects as having "broken governments' monopoly on the collection and management of large amounts of information and deprived governments of the deference they enjoyed because of it. In every sphere of activity, instantaneous access to information and the ability to put it to use multiples the number of players who matter and reduces the number who command great authority."

The Cold War's end and the spread of democracy.   The opening of political space occasioned by the collapse of communism and ending of superpower confrontation brought greater attention to the nonsecurity issues. Changes have been especially dramatic with respect to human rights, as we shall explore in Chapter 10. There is more room for other identities, including subnational and ethnic identities, as well as nonnational ones such as those that NGOs, social movements, and advocacy networks generate. The technological revolution facilitates these new communities communicating with one another.

Along with the demise of the Soviet Union and of communism has been the global spread of democratic political systems and norms. In democracies, civil society is enhanced and NGO formation encouraged. This has fueled the growth of grassroots groups and empowered individuals to become more active politically.

The growth of networks reflects the conscious efforts of activists in domestic and international NGOs who care deeply about specific issues to link with each other in order to achieve their goals. Networks don't just happen. Global conferences and the communications revolution have facilitated the networking process. So have cheap air travel, student exchanges, the Peace Corps and lay missionary programs that sent thousands of young people to work in the developing world, and political exiles from Latin America who taught in U.S. and European universities. The sense of being part of a global network and part of a nascent transnational civil society has been an unexpected legacy of the democratization movement. What is inescapable now are the density, size, and professionalism of these networks that have emerged as prime movers, framing issues and agendas, mobilizing constituencies in targeted campaigns, and monitoring compliance.

■ NGO Roles

The various roles that nonstate actors, and particularly NGOs, play in global governance are summarized in Figure 6.2. Our earlier examples of NGO activities illumined many of the strategies used by different groups. NGOs lobby governments, IGOs, and corporations through targeted campaigns and other tactics. These activities also involve mobilizing public opinion and political support within countries, using the media to publicize information, some of which may be embarrassing to the targeted government, IGO, or MNC, and conferring legitimacy on products, decisions, or institutions through strategies like "eco-labels" for tuna caught in dolphin-friendly fashion. The process of mobilization may also involve the creation of

---

Figure 6.2   NGO Governance Functions

- Perform functions of governance in absence of state authority
- Gather and publicize information
- Create and mobilize networks
- Frame issues for public consumption
- Promote new norms
- Advocate changes in policies and governance
- Monitor human rights and environmental norms
- Participate in global conferences:
    Raise issues
    Submit position papers
    Lobby for viewpoint
    Bring parties together
- Enhance public participation
- Distribute humanitarian aid
- Implement development projects

like-minded organizations in countries that are being targeted. This brings us back to networks and social movements again and the importance of the Internet, cheap travel, and the role of the UN-sponsored global conferences. As Keck and Sikkink (1998: x) point out, "Transnational networks multiply the voices that are heard in international and domestic politics. These voices argue, persuade, strategize, document, lobby, pressure, and complain. The multiplication of voices is imperfect and selective—for every voice that is amplified, many others are ignored—but in a world where the voices of states have predominated, networks open channels for bringing alternative visions and information into international debate."

NGOs can seek the best venues to present issues and to apply pressure. They can provide new ideas and draft texts for multilateral treaties; they can help government negotiators understand the science behind environmental issues they are trying to address. Development and relief groups often have the advantage of being "on the ground," neutral, and able to "make the impossible possible by doing what governments [and sometimes IGOs] cannot or will not" (Simmons 1998: 87). Yet, there are inevitably limits to their influence, and IGOs have mixed records to date in accommodating nonstate actors.

■ NGOs' Relationships to IGOs

In order for nonstate actors to play roles in global governance, they need access to the places where states endeavor to achieve consensus on norms and principles, hammer out the texts of treaties and conventions codifying rules, coordinate their policies, resolve their disputes, and allocate resources to implement programs and activities. As our earlier chapters have made clear, often these activities take place within the frameworks of IGOs, whether global or regional, general purpose or functionally specific. To exercise influence over governments' positions and IGO policies and programs, NGOs need access and recognition of their right to be consulted. They want the right to lobby governmental delegates, to participate in sessions, to obtain documents, to speak, to distribute issue papers, provide data and analysis, and even to vote.

Some IGOs have provisions in their charters for participation of nonstate actors; others have gradually established informal procedures for consultation or participation; some organizations have done little or nothing to accommodate demands from NGOs for greater voice. Although the early history of NGO and governmental interactions showed that established procedures were not essential, recent efforts by states to exclude participation in global conferences shows the benefits of constitutional provisions. We see five types of NGO activities in IGOs: (1) consultation in regime creation and implementation, (2) lobbying, (3) surveillance of governmental activities, (4) involvement in international program implementation, and (5) participation in decisionmaking. The pressures on the UN and other IGOs to accommodate and collaborate with NGOs come from NGOs themselves as well as from donor governments that favor grassroots participation; these pressures have increased dramatically since the mid-1980s.

■ The United Nations

Although the UN's members are states, the organization has long recognized the importance of nongovernmental organizations. Article 71 of the charter authorized ECOSOC (but not the General Assembly) to grant consultative status to NGOs. By 1948, forty-one groups had been formally accredited to ECOSOC; in 1968, 377 NGOs; and in 2002, 2,500 NGOs. Resolution 1296 adopted in 1968 formalized the arrangements for NGO accreditation by establishing three categories. (See Figure 6.3.)

NGOs' influence occurs primarily within ECOSOC's subsidiary bodies, and most especially within the Commissions on Human Rights, Status of Women, and Population. All accredited NGOs, however, have access to UN buildings, enabling them to sit in on public debates and lobby delegates in the corridors, and it has been through this more general access that NGOs have expanded their presence and influence within the UN. Following 9/11, however, security precautions at the UN are limiting all NGOs' access to the building.

One exception to the general pattern of NGO representation through ECOSOC categorization is the permanent observer status the General Assembly accorded the Palestine Liberation Organization (PLO) in 1978 and, as of 1998, status as a nonvoting member of the General Assembly. Since 1990, the International Committee of the Red Cross and the International Federation of Red Cross and Red Crescent Societies hold observer status in the General Assembly because of their long history of working with governments during armed conflict and their unique role in enforcing international humanitarian law.

NGOs have long sought formal access to the General Assembly. Through the Conference of Non-Governmental Organisations in Consultative Status with the United Nations Economic and Social Council (CONGO), NGOs have lobbied for participation rights. Since nothing in the UN Charter grants NGOs the right of access to UN conferences, CONGO has lobbied for standardized procedures for determining access. At present, the ECOSOC consultative arrangements are taken as the starting point, but each conference has established different rules for granting participation rights to NGOs that do not have consultative or roster status, particularly grassroots national NGOs. What NGOs are permitted to do at the conferences has varied widely, as discussed earlier.

Between 1993 and 1998, negotiations with member governments

**Figure 6.3   NGOs and the United Nations Economic and
Social Council**

• *Category 1: General Status*
Large, multifaceted international NGOs, engaged in many areas of
ECOSOC responsibilities; able to consult with officers from
Secretariat on matters of interest to the NGO; can propose items
for agenda through the Council Committee on NGOs; may designate authorized representatives to sit as observers at public meetings of ECOSOC and subsidiary bodies; may submit written statements of 2000 words after consultation with secretary-general;
can speak at ECOSOC and functional commission meetings.

• *Category 2: Special Status*
Internationally known NGOs who enjoy expertise in a particular
issue area; able to consult with others from secretariat on matters
of interest to the NGO; may designate representatives to sit as
observers at public meetings of ECOSOC and subsidiary bodies;
may submit written statements of 500 words after consultation
with secretary-general; may speak at ECOSOC and functional commission meetings on areas of interest that are not dealt with by
subsidiary bodies.

• *Category 3: Roster Status*
Smaller NGOs, with occasional interests in ECOSOC activities; able
to consult with secretariat on matters of interest to NGO; may
have representatives at public meetings concerned with matters
within their field of competence; may submit written statements
of 500 words on subjects of NGO competence; may speak at functional commission and subsidiary meets only.

Source: UN ECOSOC Resolution 1996/31. Modalities for the Consultation of
NGOs with the Economic and Social Council, Functional Commissions and
other Subsidiary Bodies.

---

yielded two resolutions from ECOSOC aimed at balanced and effective
NGO participation. The first resolution established procedures for broadened participation of all NGOs in ECOSOC itself, as well as in major conferences, but not a negotiating role. Time will tell how the latter is implemented since NGOs have in practice been drafting texts and winning
support for them for a long time. The second resolution called on the
General Assembly to consider the question of NGO participation in all
areas of the UN. But that initiative has stalled, as there are deep divisions
among member states, NGOs themselves, and the UN secretariat itself

because of mandates to control finances and streamline procedures (Alger 2002: 97–100).

Even the Security Council has initiated consultations with NGOs. In February 1997, for the first time, the Security Council permitted representatives from Oxfam, CARE, and Doctors Without Borders, to speak on the crisis in the Great Lakes region of Africa. In November 1998, humanitarian NGO representatives again met with the council to argue for a renewed peace effort in the Sudan. NGOs have also participated in Security Council discussions on AIDS as a security issue. As a result, an NGO Working Group on the Security Council has formed, organized by Amnesty International, Global Policy Forum, EarthAction, and the World Council of Churches, among others. The council president now meets with them periodically. The meetings are off-the-record and private, with the expectation that such informal consultation can help maintain strong ties, be an avenue of policy input, and provide another way to enhance the transparency of the Security Council (Alger 2002: 100–103).

Surprisingly, however, the NGOs themselves have not been united in this push to expand participation. Some major international groups worry about their influence being diluted by an influx of thousands of new grass-roots NGOs. The latter tend to view the older NGOs as a privileged elite. Also, many governments have mixed to negative feelings about NGOs. For example, governments in Africa, Asia, and Latin America often feel threatened by the pressures of human rights NGOs; G-8 governments are not always keen on NGO pressure for economic justice; and the Non-Aligned Movement opposes expanded NGO access to the General Assembly. "Delegations feared changes that might weaken or even eventually sweep away nation-states' monopoly of global decision-making" (Paul 1999: 2).

Although the issue of General Assembly access has bogged down, NGOs have continued to set new precedents for collaboration with the UN itself, with governments, and each other, but there still are substantial obstacles to overcome. The late 1990s language of "social partnership" implies a more equal status between governments and NGOs, but leaves unresolved the question of their legal status and ability to exercise political influence in the UN system that still revolves heavily around interstate diplomacy and only slowly is moving toward more pluralist global governance. As Donini (1996: 83) soberly admits, there is a "rapidly evolving 'NGO galaxy' and the not-so-rapidly evolving 'UN solar system.'"

■ *UN Agencies*

Some UN specialized agencies have provisions for NGO participation similar to those of ECOSOC. For example, the ILO's unique tripartite system of representation means continual labor union participation. Similarly, the charters of both UNESCO and the International Maritime Organization call for "consultation and cooperation with NGOs." UNESCO's programs for scientific, education, and cultural interchanges involve many NGOs and individuals. In fact, UNESCO helped create the International Union for the Protection of Nature in 1948 (now IUCN).

Still other organizations have gradually incorporated NGOs into discussions. UNEP, for example, has built extensive links with many national and international environmental groups to offset its own small size and resources. It created an Environmental Liaison Centre to serve as a network and informational clearinghouse for over six thousand NGOs concerned with the environment and development, and involved NGOs directly in the preparatory and negotiating phases of the Montreal Protocol on Substances that Deplete the Ozone Layer.

Most UN agencies with field programs and offices, in fact, now involve NGOs in implementing projects and, increasingly, in decisionmaking regarding field programs. For example, after the UN General Assembly in 1989, Resolution 44/211, called on UNDP to coordinate country-level development programs, UNDP developed the policy approach of "sustainable human development" and began to emphasize participatory community development. Actual results, measured by contacts with community associations and indigenous NGOs, have varied from country to country and program to program. Pakistan implemented civil society empowerment "in dramatic fashion" in part because of the Pakistani special adviser to the head of UNDP, but many directors of UNDP African offices ignored the initiative (Stiles 1998: 202–211).

In addition to UNDP, UN field programs in UNICEF, FAO, UNHCR, and UNFPA involve NGOs in decisionmaking. Frequently, the relationship among these different organizations and NGOs is best characterized as a form of subcontracting—that is, the governments agreeing that a UN agency should undertake a particular project and the agency subcontracting that project to one or more NGOs. This is particularly common with respect to development programs.

UN-NGO subcontracting also best describes the relationship in complex humanitarian crises and failed states in the 1990s. The main coalitions of humanitarian NGOs—InterAction and the International Council of Voluntary Agencies, along with the ICRC (International Committee of the Red Cross) and International Federation of the Red Cross and Red Crescent Societies—participate in the meetings of the UN's Inter-Agency Standing Committee chaired by the undersecretary-general for humanitarian affairs. The UN High Commissioner for Refugees and Office for the Coordination of Humanitarian Affairs also meet regularly in New York and Geneva with the main operational NGOs in the field (CARE, the International Rescue Committee, Save the Children Federation, World Vision, Doctors Without Borders, Oxfam, etc.) because they depend on the talent, resources, and flexibility of the major NGOs to address crises. These same organizations have become sufficiently important that they command ready access to the UN secretary-general as well.

A major tension has surfaced in these UN-NGO efforts to deal with the chaos of complex humanitarian emergencies. They bring different mandates and competencies to the relief efforts; they compete with each other for scarce donor government resources; they serve different constituencies; and they measure success in different ways. NGOs work with fewer inhibitions about state sovereignty, governmental approval, and strategic coherence than UN agencies that depend on governmental support. UN agencies, however, lack grassroots links and sufficient staff to carry out complex operations in remote areas, hence, the efforts of recent years to establish operational coordination (Natsios 1996: 74–78).

▮ The Major Economic Institutions

The World Bank has been both the target of NGO campaigns (e.g., structural adjustment and energy policies) and the initiator of cooperation in implementing bank-financed projects in fields ranging from health care to judicial reform. The bank has responded to some NGO pressures, for example, when it established the post of adviser on women in 1977 and incorporated the women-in-development agenda across its activities in the late 1980s. Likewise, in response to pressure from environmental groups, the bank began "greening" its programs by creating an Environment Department in 1987, requiring environmental impact statements, and expanding its lending for environmental projects. Environmental groups have targeted campaigns against specific bank projects such as big dams; they have cultivated formal and informal contacts with bank staff; they have honed their research and, hence, the expertise they bring to discussions of environmental issues; and they have utilized national and international networks in their efforts to achieve bank reform (O'Brien et al. 2000: 128–130).

A key problem for NGOs seeking access to and influence in World Bank policy has been physical access to documents since, unlike the UN General Assembly, ECOSOC, and Security Council, the bank does not make documents available to the public. This problem was partially solved following the 1987 creation by NGO activists of the Bank Information Center through the cultivation of relationships with individuals who were willing to help provide access to information. What had clearly started as an initiative of Northern (primarily U.S.) environmental NGOs was gradually broadened to Southern NGOs and issues of the human and environmental consequences of the bank's structural adjustment policies (Keck and Sikkink 1998: 148–149).

Since 1994, when the bank shifted emphasis to participatory development approaches, it has provided legitimacy to NGO involvement, seeing collaboration with them as a way to improve the bank's efficiency as a development agency, as described in Chapter 9. The bank categorizes its NGO interactions along lines of operational collaboration, economic and sector work, and policy dialogue, and now issues an annual report on the first of these and maintains a joint NGO-bank committee to facilitate NGO access to senior bank staff.

The shift in the World Bank's approach was part of a broader shift toward civil society empowerment among multilateral development agencies in the 1980s that NGOs helped bring about. The reason, as one observer noted, is that NGOs "are perceived to be able to do something that national governments cannot or will not do" (quoted in Stiles 1998: 201). The regional development banks described in Chapter 9 have tended to follow the World Bank's lead with respect to NGO links. One result of the banks' opening to NGO participation, however, is that they now face escalating demands for more NGO participation in policymaking since NGOs claim they better represent grassroots movements and organizations, even in countries with elected governments (Casaburi et al. 2000: 493–517).

In contrast, the IMF has been very slow to develop formal contacts with NGOs since its specialized focus on monetary policy does not lend itself easily to NGO input. Yet during the 1990s, under intense pressure, IMF expanded relations with civil society groups including business associations, academic institutes, trade unions, NGOs, and religious groups. Jubilee 2000's success in getting the IMF and other lenders to support debt reduction for the most heavily indebted developing countries is illustrative of the shift. (For more on this, see Chapter 9.)

Outside the UN system at present, but crucial to international economic governance and of intense concern to many environmental NGOs, labor unions, NGOs concerned with economic justice, and activists involved in the backlash against globalization is the World Trade Organization. Although the draft charter of the International Trade Organization that was originally envisaged after World War II, as discussed in Chapter 3, had provided for consultations with NGOs, the GATT failed to establish any formal links with NGOs and a "culture of secrecy" dominated multilateral trade negotiations. The agreement establishing the WTO, however, did empower the General Council to "make appropriate arrangements for consultation and cooperation with nongovernmental organisations concerned with matters related to those of the WTO" (Article v.2). Likewise, Article 13.2 permitted dispute settlement panels to seek information from "any relevant source" and to consult experts.

As a result of these constitutional provisions and a 1996 decision, the WTO Secretariat has primary responsibility for relations with NGOs. This has been pursued thus far in two ways: through regular secretariat briefings for NGOs and through symposia with NGO representatives. In addition,

WTO's General Council agreed to provide information on WTO policy-making and to circulate most documents as unrestricted. What WTO has not done, however, is to grant NGOs any form of consultative status and that has been one reason for the confrontational relationship described in Chapter 9.

Environmental and other NGOs have campaigned for greater WTO participation, portraying the organization as secretive and lacking in accountability. They argue that civil society organizations can help make the world trading system more transparent and legitimate, accountable to people, not governments. This argument over NGO participation in the WTO, however, resembles a similar problem for the World Bank and IMF. Many activists espouse ideas that do not conform to liberal economic theory. Hence, what they seek is not reform and participation in the established organizations, but radical changes in institutional structures, policies, and programs. With such groups, the WTO finds itself in what one group of analysts has called, "the dialogue of the deaf" (O'Brien et al 2000: 141–153). To date, the WTO has made few further changes in the way it relates to NGOs, fueling antiglobalization activists' efforts to target the WTO. (For more, see Chapter 9.)

■ Participation in Global Conferences

How NGOs participate in global conferences has expanded over time with a general pattern emerging. Before most conferences begin, NGOs undertake considerable publicity and agenda-setting activities. For example, prior to the first conference of UN Special Sessions on Disarmament held in 1978 (and subsequently in 1982 and 1988), NGOs organized meetings and activities especially through churches to engage the public in debate; they published materials to increase public awareness of disarmament issues; some groups initiated protest activities in the United States, Canada, Western Europe, and Japan to pressure governments; a Washington-based network of forty U.S. groups tried to influence U.S. policy by meeting with government officials and members of Congress, knowing how important U.S. leadership would be. NGOs promoted transnational networking by convening the International NGO Conference on Disarmament in the spring of 1978, prior to the intergovernmental conference itself, with five hundred representatives of eighty-five different international NGOs and over two hundred national NGOs from forty-six different countries (Atwood 1997). Women's NGOs followed a similar strategy leading up to each of the three global conferences. Local, subregional, national, regional, and then international meetings were convened by NGOs discussing the issues, using the occasions to pressure national delegations, and adopting a global convention strategy. Such meetings formed a critical link with grass-roots constituencies.

A variety of NGO activities also take place during the actual global conferences. For example, during the disarmament conferences, representatives from the NGO community organized sessions with official delegates; provided information in informal briefings to those who were not acquainted with the issues, particularly delegates from small and poor countries; and organized joint activities at the conference. NGOs lobbied governments and also provided a variety of parallel activities for NGOs themselves aimed at mobilizing public awareness about disarmament, establishing and strengthening NGO networks, and providing information and services to NGO participants. Sometimes, parallel NGO conferences are held simultaneously, but not always. On the issue of disarmament, there was no parallel NGO forum. But during the 1990s, parallel conferences became the norm.

The activity of NGOs in the disarmament discussions established precedents that were followed in the subsequent women's conferences and the conferences on human rights and the environment. NGO activity proved particularly significant in connection with the 1992 United Nations Conference on the Environment and Development (UNCED) in Rio, the 1994 Cairo International Conference on Population and Development (ICPD), and the various UN conferences on women. NGOs developed a number of alternative ways of participating. One noteworthy example is the inclusion of individuals from NGOs on government delegations to the conference. In some cases, this was done with the understanding that the individual's role was to advise the government, but not to conduct negotiations without government instruction; in other cases, individuals were free to represent their NGO and to conduct negotiations. For the 1994 Cairo conference on population and development, for example, governments were urged to include NGOs on their delegations. Many would argue that this growing NGO activity represents the "democratization" of international relations by promoting the involvement of ordinary people in addressing global issues and the nascence of a global civil society. The impact of NGOs on the substantive outcomes of global conferences is difficult to measure, but there is little dispute that their success is only possible when they work with states.

■ *For the Future: A Forum of Their Own?*

For several decades proposals have been floated to give civil society actors a forum of their own. The People's Millennium Assembly held in 2000 was an ad hoc version of such a forum. While the names have varied—including a UN Parliamentary Assembly, a Forum of Civil Society, a Second Assembly—the ideas are basically the same. To proponents, nonstate actors, including NGOs, religious, and civic organizations, should have a venue for consultations among themselves and should have standing within the organization. Such an assembly would give voice to heretofore unrepresented groups, add transparency to international political processes, and potentially add accountability.

▨ *Relationships with the European Union*

Because most NGOs are based in Northern countries, especially in North America and Western Europe, it is not surprising that NGO relations with regional organizations are most intensive in these geographic regions. The relationships between the EU and NGOs and other nonstate actors have grown in ways unanticipated by the EU's founders.

The EU's Economic and Social Committee is composed of representatives from various economic and social areas. To ensure that diverse interests are represented, national representatives are drawn from three relatively equal groups: employers, including commercial organizations, banks, and insurance companies; workers, usually members of trade unions; and others, including agriculture, small business, and the professions. Representatives act in a personal capacity, not as official representatives of particular organizations. Coalitions form around functional issues of common concern. These groups provide opinions on community matters such as agriculture, industry, social and cultural affairs, regional development, environment, and health. They perform many of the same roles as NGOs operating in global conferences. They provide information; they meet with delegations; they organize conferences and convene meetings; they seek contact with other EU institutions and give opinions. In short, the NGOs have an advisory role with the Economic and Social Committee. Their direct impact on EU policy and decisionmaking was clearly intended to be limited, however, as neither the council nor the commission is obligated to accept the committee's advice. By the time it is consulted, negotiations are already well along and it is difficult to change their course. Yet on a few issues such as agriculture, freedom of movement for workers, transport, social policy, and the environment, the council and the commission must consult the committee.

As the EU has evolved, economic and social interest groups have increasingly found it useful to take their positions directly to either the commission or the council in Brussels. This is different than in the past when such interest groups would have either preferred to approach their own national governments or national associations to act on their behalf. Going directly to the council or commission can involve direct lobbying in the case of larger, more powerful groups or participation in an alliance of groups. So-called Euro-groups have formed transnational links among national interest groups with similar concerns. Of the approximately twelve hundred Euro-groups surveyed in 1999, about two-thirds are business- and agriculture-related associations with the other one-third comprised of public interest groups or associations of the professions. Larger groups include the European Trade Union Confederation, the European Environmental Bureau, and the European Bureau of Consumers' Associations. Also prominent, especially during the 1980s, was the European Round Table of Industrialists, formed by CEOs of the largest MNCs, including Nestlé, Fiat, Philips, Royal Dutch Shell, and Unilever.

The agriculture lobby is the strongest Euro-group. It includes broad-based groups like the Committee of Professional Agricultural Organisations and very specialized groups representing a particular agricultural interest such as the pasta manufacturers or olive oil producers. It has a staff of over fifty individuals and is well financed, while others have fewer staff and limited resources. This strong representation of agricultural interests is not surprising, given the importance of and controversy surrounding the Common Agricultural Policy.

Public interest groups have also flourished in part due to the growth in power of the European Parliament and in part due to the perception of a democratic deficit. Well-financed and established groups like Greenpeace and Friends of the Earth are influential. Some of the other public interest groups have actually been established and funded by the commission to create demand for a constituency in the European Union. A transnational group in support of homeless people, European Federation of National Organisations Working with the Homeless, is a prominent example. But public interest groups are most influential at the agenda-setting stage, since they lack adequate financing compared to the business and agricultural groups.

The commission is the primary target for Euro-groups and it depends on them for information, specific recommendations, and enhanced legitimacy. Contacts are both formal and informal through various advisory committees, direct meetings with officials, and through oral and written communications. Compared to the NGO-UN relationship, the interactions between the EU and NGOs are a more regularized, institutionalized process.

For nonstate actors to be involved in global governance, they need to "get to the table" where international rules and principles are being established and where implementation procedures are established. That is why access to what happens within IGOs is important. In the European Union, the interactive process between the governmental institutions and the NGOs is also viewed as fundamental to the EU's legitimacy. Yet, access and participation by some does not guarantee influence and impact by all.

■ NGO Influence and Its Limits

This chapter can barely do justice to the burgeoning literature on the activities and influence of NGOs and other nonstate actors involved in global governance today. But NGOs can still be an elusive subject to study. If one adopts the realist theoretical framework, they do not generally appear on the radar screen, as international relations is a state-centric system. Yet for liberals, they have become increasingly important subjects, along with transnational networks and relations more generally. Constructivists have elaborated on the influence of ideas and norms for which NGOs and other nonstate actors may be important sources and transmitters. They have also argued that states' interests are not fixed, but may be changed by actions of nonstate actors.

Social scientists, however, face a major challenge in tracing, substantiating, and measuring these lines of influence. The sheer numbers and diversity of groups pose challenges for data gathering. There is also the normative challenge of maintaining distance from the views of NGOs themselves who often claim greater influence than may in fact be the case. This final section lays out a framework for analyzing nonstate actor influence and assessing the limits to its effectiveness.

■ Sources of Influence

Nonstate actors lack the types of power traditionally associated with influence in international politics. They do not have military or police forces like governments and they tend to have only limited economic resources, unlike governments and MNCs. Instead, they must rely on soft power. For advocacy groups, this means credible information, expertise, and moral authority that enable them to get governments, business leaders, and publics to listen, recalculate their interests, and act. For operational or service groups, this means having organizational resources such as flexibility to move staff rapidly to crisis areas and strong donor bases, or links with grassroots groups that enable them to operate effectively in often remote regions of developing countries. For all types of groups, the strength and density of the networks that link the local to the national and global are key. NGOs' influence depends a great deal on their flexibility in employing a variety of tactics and strategies.

Determinants of effectiveness.   As in the analysis of power and influence of other global governance actors, including states and IGOs, determining the effectiveness of NGOs involves identifying what is being attempted, characteristics of the targets, the strategies being used, managerial and leadership skills, and the resources applied. What makes this process particularly complex is its transnational, multilevel character. That is, data and analysis are required on both domestic and international institutional contexts, in addition to the capabilities and strategies of the NGOs themselves. In effect, this means analyzing three levels of political games.

The analysis of advocacy groups' effectiveness differs significantly from that of operational and service groups where the focus is on measurable changes in the conditions toward which aid is directed. Advocacy groups' effectiveness in targeting individual countries depends a great deal on the "characteristics of the targets and especially their vulnerability to both material and moral leverage" (Keck and Sikkink 1998: 207). For example, countries receiving large amounts of military and economic aid can be vulnerable to pressure if the donor country(s) is persuaded to use its leverage on behalf of promoting human rights. A wild card variable affecting both advocacy and operational groups, however, is nationalism and a country's determination to protect its sovereignty from external influence—whether from other governments, NGOs, or IGOs. If a country cares a great deal about its international image, it may be sensitive to external or transnational pressure. The openness of domestic institutions in countries targeted by advocacy campaigns will affect NGOs' leverage, channels for exercising influence, and potential effectiveness, as will the strength of domestic civil society. It was harder to halt the Three Gorges Dam in China where civil society is weak than the Narmada Dam in India where it is strong. Likewise, as we have seen earlier, the openness of IGOs to NGO access and participation will be a significant variable in their ability to exercise influence.

Measures of NGO influence.   One scholar has argued, "Today it is . . . NGOs which run the refugee camps, provide disaster relief, design and carry out development projects, monitor and attempt to contain the international spread of disease, and clean up an ever more polluted environment" (Murphy 2000: 795). Although this tells us something about the influence of NGOs today, measuring the full scope of their influence requires much more.

NGOs' influence can be measured in part by their very proliferation, especially in developing countries. The latter trend vastly expands the potential reach of transnational networks, the mobilization potential of advocacy campaigns, and the monitoring and implementation capabilities of NGOs.

Another measure of certain NGOs' influence is the Nobel Peace Prize. Several NGOs have received Nobel prizes over the last century, including the Institut de Droit International (1904), the Red Cross (1917, 1944, 1963), Amnesty International (1977), International Physicians for the Prevention of Nuclear War (1985), the International Campaign to Ban Landmines (1997), and Doctors Without Borders (1999). The prize brings critical attention not only to the organization but also to its cause more generally.

NGO effectiveness may also be analyzed by linking NGO demands for new norms, plans of action, or treaties to changes in agendas, in governmental positions, corporations, and international institutions. Did NGOs' actions result in a change in governmental policy? A change in IGO programs? A change in the actual behavior of states, international institutions, and corporations? Effectiveness at this level is difficult to chart, as often there may be many explanations for change in policy and behavior besides the influence of nonstate actors.

Most critically, NGOs' effectiveness must be measured by their impact on people and problems. It is not enough to get declarations approved, plans adopted, organizations formed, or treaties signed, although that can be a major accomplishment, witness the International Campaign to Ban Landmines. The ultimate measures of NGOs' effectiveness and influence lie in the difference they have been shown to make in the problems they claim to address. Was a humanitarian crisis alleviated? Did the success of the Jubilee 2000 campaign for international debt relief alleviate the poverty and suffering in indebted countries? Did the ban on ivory trade help to preserve elephant populations? Did development aid channeled through NGOs improve the well-being of individuals? These are some of the questions addressed in subsequent chapters.

◼ Limits on NGO Influence

There are significant limits on NGOs' influence. In the words of Ghai (2001: 239), "No matter how idealistic or committed, INGOs simply cannot replace the work of governments and UN agencies in the business of poverty eradication. . . . they cannot cover all areas relevant to an integrated approach to poverty eradication, nor are they organized to attain universality in their coverage of countries."

An important set of limits arises from the size and diversity of the NGO community. NGOs have no single agenda; those working within the same issue may have divergent agendas. During the 1980s, for example, the nuclear freeze movement was quite splintered. The U.S.-based Nuclear Weapon Freeze Campaign focused on stopping the U.S.-Soviet nuclear arms race, emphasizing that both sides should take action. In contrast, the European counterparts were most concerned with the planned deployment of weapons in Europe. They advocated unilateral action to prevent deployment. The failure of these groups to unite is one explanation for their limited impact during the 1980s (Cortright and Pagnucco 1997). During the women's conferences of the 1990s, NGOs pushing for women's rights met pressures from religious groups or other NGOs supporting traditional family values. Such pressures can, under certain circumstances, cancel each other out. The fact is groups can be found on almost any side of every issue, resulting in countervailing pressures.

A second set of limits arises out of the multilevel games in which NGOs must be effective to be successful. Grassroots organizations in developing countries "put pressure on local councils; national NGOs seek to influence their governments; and transnational networks lobby international organizations, governments, and, increasingly, multinational corporations" (Ottaway 2001: 273). NGOs may fail to persuade key people at any one of these levels and find their influence limited.

Money is a key resource for NGOs and fundraising is notoriously difficult. NGOs do not have the option of collecting taxes like states. If they take money from corporations or governments, they risk compromising their independence, their very identity as an organization, and their ability to "bite the hands that feed them" (Spiro 1996: 966). Yet, as governments and IGOs have channeled development and humanitarian assistance to NGOs, the latter have become much more dependent on this funding. In 1998, public sector funding accounted for 40 percent of NGO budgets versus only 1.5 percent in 1970 (Simmons 1998: 94). Not only does public funding jeopardize NGO activity, but private funding does also. Often NGOs find themselves competing for the same scarce pool of resources.

A further danger for NGOs that become more involved in service delivery through IGO or government subcontracting, or in formal participation in international institutions of various kinds, is bureaucratization. The process of granting NGOs consultative status at the UN may have negative results. As P. J. Simmons (1998: 94) notes, "Many of the schema for increasing NGO involvement may simply foster predictable and bureaucratic behavior . . . potentially dulling the passion and richness of views that can emanate from narrowly focused groups."

In addition, we have already begun to see a backlash against NGOs from states, IGOs, and MNCs. The limits posed on NGOs at the UN since 1998, the U.S.-backed decision not to hold further global conferences, the opposition of many developing countries to hearing NGO representatives in the Commission on Human Rights, and the decision to hold the WTO 2001 ministerial meeting in Qatar where NGO presence could be sharply limited demonstrate that governments retain the power to shut NGOs out of international institutional decisionmaking forums. In short, the balance of power still favors governments and corporations whose hard-power resources outweigh the soft-power resources of NGOs.

Finally, a study of two hundred years of NGO participation suggests that there may be a cyclical pattern to NGOs' influence. During the period between 1850 and 1914, the NGO role in global governance continuously increased, then fell during World War I only to rise significantly during the 1920s and to fall again in the 1930s and early 1940s. It rose again after World War II, plateaued in the 1950s, began to rise again in the 1960s, and surged in the 1990s. There is no assurance, however, that it will continue that upward trajectory. The study suggests that there are two key variables influencing the cycle: the needs of governments and the capabilities of

NGOs (Charnovitz 1997: 268–270). Is it the wishful thinking of civil society activists that argues for the inevitability of NGOs' growing influence and
participation in global governance?

Representation, accountability, and transparency.   Whom do NGOs
represent? Frequently, they claim to represent the "true" voice of broad
groups of people—the poor, women, the elderly, students, children, rural
populations, unemployed persons, peasants, immigrant workers, the
oppressed. Representativeness is something that elected governments claim
as the basis of their legitimacy. Yet how can we be sure these groups are
indeed NGOs' constituents? Often in the case of transnational networks or
large international NGOs, it is an elite group based in a large Northern city
that claims to speak on behalf of poor, disadvantaged people in another part
of the world, usually the South. This criticism is less valid than in the past
as NGOs and grassroots groups have proliferated in developing countries
and Northern NGOs have learned to treat the latter more as partners. Still,
as the multilateral development banks, for example, open up to greater participation of civil society, they have to make decisions about the rights and
responsibilities of various groups, and they will confront questions such as
the following: "Who is more representative: an NGO with global reach
opposed to the construction of a bridge because of its environmental
impact, or the inhabitants of an isolated town whose livelihood might benefit from the construction of the bridge?" (Casaburi et al. 2000: 514).

A further aspect of the representativeness issue is the reality that a
handful of large international NGOs dominate most issue areas. Eight
major NGO federations, including CARE, Oxfam, World Vision, Doctors
Without Borders, and Save the Children, control about half of the $8 billion
relief funds (Simmons 1998: 2). And, since IGOs cannot be expected to
grant consultative or participatory rights to all NGOs, how do you establish
a process for determining the worth of a given NGO? Should you choose
only the largest, most international, best-funded NGOs? What criteria, if
any, do you use for selection on the basis of orientation or agenda?
ECOSOC's revised criteria endeavor to strike a balance on some of these
issues.

A further side of the issue is, indeed, the question of democracy within
NGOs. Very few of even the large international NGOs that have individual
members have provision for members to elect officers and direct policy on
particular issues. Amnesty International and the Sierra Club are two notable
exceptions. This links to the question of NGOs' accountability. And,
because NGOs and their networks tend to serve narrow mandates and not to
have to be accountable to diverse constituencies, they do not usually face
trade-offs among issues in the same ways that governments do. This is what
gives them freedom to pursue a campaign against landmines or human

rights violations or whaling. Their leadership generally enjoys a great deal of discretion in deciding what policies to pursue and in what way. Yet, what are the safeguards on them besides their own moral integrity and the knowledge that if they get it wrong they lose some of their credibility? Major funders can ask questions; so can journalists, as happened with the issue of donations to the American Red Cross following September 11. In theory, so can other NGOs, although they rarely want to criticize each other publicly; churches and other religious groups could be a source of scrutiny.

NGOs' lack of transparency is a further problem. Very few NGOs provide information about their personnel, operations, funding sources, and expenditures, and even their sources. In fact, according to the 2003 Global Accountability Report published by One World Trust, only four of seven NGOs surveyed publish annual reports online. Only three (the Red Cross, Oxfam International, and Worldwide Fund for Nature) provide financial information. According to the report, IGOs were more transparent. Among the organizations surveyed (eighteen), the International Federation of the Red Cross and Red Crescent Societies earned top marks on both governance and information disclosure (*Foreign Policy* 2003: 16–17). Should NGOs, then, be subject to the types of pressures currently being placed on governments by the World Bank and IMF, for example, to make their economic and fiscal policies more transparent, or on corporations by governments and IGOs to be more open about their operations? Governments can, of course, require NGOs to report on funding and expenditures as part of their licensing requirements. NGOs can also regulate themselves and make themselves more transparent to increase their credibility as contributors to global governance.

Do NGOs serve the public good?   Many NGOs do contribute positively to the global public's good. The evidence lies in the success NGOs can claim in institutionalizing human rights norms, providing humanitarian relief, and promoting environmental protection and corporate good practices with respect to human rights and the environment, as well as in alleviating poverty, disease, and malnutrition. Yet we must be mindful of the dangers of broad generalization, both about the character of NGOs (not all "wear white hats") and the scope of the problems they seek to alleviate. There are clear limits to their influence and effectiveness.

■ Is State Sovereignty Diminished by Nonstate Actors' Influence?

Transnational networks clearly challenge traditional concepts of state sovereignty by presuming that it is "both legitimate and necessary for states or nonstate actors to be concerned about the treatment of the inhabitants of another state" (Keck and Sikkink 1998: 36). Although the frontier between what is domestic and what is international becomes fuzzier and fuzzier, as Keck and Sikkink (1998: 212) also note, "Sovereignty is eroded only in clearly delimited circumstances"—in particular issue areas—and states retain the ability to reassert control, albeit at a high price in some circumstances. Nonstate actors are but one of the actors in global governance. In Chapter 7, we examine the complex relationship among states and other actors.

■ Suggested Further Reading

Florini, Ann M., ed. (2000) *The Third Force: The Rise of Transnational Civil Society.* Tokyo and Washington: Japan Center for International Exchange and the Carnegie Endowment for International Peace.

Josselin, Daphne, and William Wallace, eds. (2001) *Non-State Actors in World Politics.* New York: Palgrave.

Keck, Margaret E., and Kathryn Sikkink. (1998) *Activists Beyond Borders: Advocacy Networks in International Politics.* Ithaca: Cornell University Press.

Khagram, Sanjeev, James V. Riker, and Kathryn Sikkink, eds. (2002) *Restructuring World Politics. Transnational Social Movements, Networks, and Norms.* Minneapolis: University of Minnesota Press.

O'Brien, Robert, Anne Marie Goetz, Jan Aart Scholte, and Marc Williams. (2000) *Contesting Global Governance: Multilateral Economic Institutions and Global Social Movements.* New York: Cambridge University Press.

Reincke, Wolfgang H. (1998) *Global Policy Networks: Governing Without Government?* Washington: The Brookings Institution.

■ Internet Resources

Amnesty International: www.amnesty.org
CARE: www.care.org
Catholic Relief Services: www.catholicrelief.org
Christian Children's Fund: www.christianchildrensfund.org
Consultative Group on International Agricultural Research: www.cgiar.org
Doctors Without Borders: www.msf.org
EarthAction: www.earthaction.org
European Federation of National Organisations Working with the Homeless: www.feantsa.org
Friends of the Animals: www.friendsofanimals.org
Greenpeace: www.greenpeace.org
International Campaign to Ban Landmines: www.icbl.org
International Chamber of Commerce: www.iccwbo.org
International Committee of the Red Cross: www.icrc.org
International Federation of Red Cross and Red Crescent Societies: www.ifrc.org
International Rescue Committee: www.theIRC.org
International Save the Children Alliance: www.savethechildren.net/namepage/center.html
Interpol: www.interpol.com
One World Trust: www.oneworldtrust.org
Oxfam: www.oxfaminternational.org

Roll Back Malaria Initiative (WHO): www.rbm.who.int/
Save the Children Federation: www.savethechildren.org
Transparency International: www.transparency.org
Union of International Associations: www.uia.org
IUCN-The World Conservation Union: www.iucn.org
World Commission on Dams: www.dams.org
World Trade Organization and NGOs: www.wto.org/wto/ngo/intro.htm
World Vision: www.wvi.org
World Wide Fund for Nature: www.panda.org

7

The Roles of States
in Global Governance

■ States in Action

Following the September 11, 2001, terrorist attacks on the World Trade Center and Pentagon, the United States quickly secured wide support for the "war on terrorism" and approval from the UN Security Council for a far-reaching resolution calling on states to undertake a number of actions to deal with this threat to international peace and security. Among them was a requirement to submit regular reports on steps they were taking. By March 2003, a surprising number of states had complied and also taken steps to cut off funding sources for terrorist groups, to arrest suspected terrorists, and to step up efforts to coordinate police and intelligence activities.

In November 2002, the United States won unanimous support for a Security Council resolution (S/1441) condemning Iraq's material breach of its obligations under the terms of the 1991 ceasefire ending the Gulf War and authorizing the resumption of weapons inspections in Iraq. Four months later, the Security Council was locked in one of its most divisive debates ever, and the United States failed to win support even from Chile, Mexico, Cameroon, Guinea, and Angola for a second resolution authorizing military action against Iraq. France and Russia both threatened to use their veto power if the draft resolution was brought to a vote; they along with Germany, China, and the smaller countries on the council all preferred to give inspections more time. They were not persuaded that Iraq posed sufficient immediate threat to international peace and security to justify military action and they refused to sanction a U.S.-led war. NATO and the EU were also divided.

In September 2003, a group of twenty-one developing countries, led by China, Brazil, India, and South Africa, blocked progress toward a new global trade agreement under the WTO. They argued that the United States, EU, and Japan had to dismantle their costly agricultural subsidy programs and open their markets to more developing country agricultural exports if the multilateral trade system was going to serve both rich and poor states.

These examples illustrate the continuing importance of states as central actors in global governance, for the international system remains fundamentally a system of sovereign states, albeit one in which nonstate actors have proliferated in numbers and influence. It is states that create IGOs and international norms and law to serve their needs for order and collective action. IGOs depend on states for funding and operational capabilities. International norms and rules are effective only to the degree that states comply with them. NGOs' participation in intergovernmental conferences, humanitarian relief, development assistance, and other activities is heavily dependent on states' approval.

Both realists and liberals acknowledge the primacy of states in global governance, although they differ on the roles of other actors. Neoliberal institutionalists and constructivists emphasize the importance of institutions, norms, and networks in influencing state behavior.

■ States and Other Actors: A Complex Interaction

Many factors shape the roles states play in the networks of international organizations. Clearly, states' relative power matters. In keeping with realist and neorealist theory, global and regional hegemonic powers have created IGOs to consolidate their dominance and influence. As might be expected, patterns of global governance often appear to favor the wealthy and powerful. Yet, outcomes do not always conform to the distribution of power, for multilateral diplomacy affords numerous opportunities for building coalitions and other initiatives that can put small states or middle powers in influential leadership positions. Not all states care equally about the multitude of issues on global and regional agendas, allowing further openings for states other than major powers to play key roles. The decisionmaking processes of some IGOs privilege some states more than others. Thus, the veto power of the five permanent members of the Security Council gives them particular influence over outcomes while the weighted voting systems in the World Bank and IMF have a similar effect.

States use international organizations in a variety of ways as discussed in Chapter 1. Multilateral diplomacy provides opportunities for states to form regional blocs and coalitions as well as to link specific issues together so as to enhance their bargaining power. States may use international organizations to gain a collective stamp of approval on specific actions, points of view, and principles; they may seek to create new rules, enforce existing ones, and settle disputes. The information IGOs and NGOs gather and analyze improves the quality of information available to governments. International meetings afford opportunities for gathering information on other governments' attitudes and policies. This continuing interaction in the international community also enhances the value of states maintaining a good reputation including compliance with international rules and norms. The existence of both global and regional organizations allows states to shop for the best forum in which to pursue their interests. Yet, IGO meetings also force governments to take positions on issues from the Middle East to environmental degradation, from China's human rights record to the status of women. To coordinate participation in various IGOs and ensure effective participation, many governments have developed specialized decisionmaking and implementation processes, such as interagency committees. Internationally approved norms and principles, whether on human rights, the law of the sea, or trade, force states to realign their policies if they wish to enjoy the benefits of reciprocity from other states.

Chapter 6 documented many ways in which NGOs and transnational advocacy groups seek to influence states. Many of those interactions depend on characteristics of domestic politics, such as political culture, norms, policy processes, attitudes of different social groups, and public opinion. Nondemocratic states, for example, tend to limit the presence and activities of NGOs within their territories and to oppose expanded NGO participation in global governance.

For liberals and constructivists, domestic politics plays a key role in shaping state policies, international commitments, and attitudes toward global governance. Understanding why states choose to cooperate multilaterally and their relative predisposition toward global governance may well depend more on domestic political dynamics than on the interactions between states, IGOs, and NGOs (Mingst 2003).

State sovereignty is clearly a key variable in global governance and is currently contested, as discussed in Chapters 1 and 3. The UN Charter makes clear that sovereignty cannot stand in the way of responses to aggression and threats to peace. International customary and treaty law also limit sovereignty. And increasingly, sovereignty is interpreted as carrying responsibilities, including the responsibility to protect persons, not just the integrity of states' territory and independence. Yet some states do not have the capacity to exercise effective authority over their territories and populations, and the outright failure or collapse of others further challenges traditional interpretations of sovereignty. As Kofi Annan said in his 1999 address to the UN General Assembly, "State sovereignty, in its most basic sense, is being redefined by the forces of globalization and international cooperation. The State is now widely understood to be the servant of its people, and not vice versa . . . [with] renewed consciousness of the right of every individual to control his or her own destiny" (United Nations 1999).

Yet for the networks of IGOs, NGOs, states, and individuals to create and sustain patterns of international cooperation and governance, they must influence even the largest, most powerful states in the system, as well as large numbers of small states and middle powers. These states must value global governance as a means to induce other states to change their behavior, to redefine their interests, and to accept certain constraints, albeit with adequate assurances of reciprocity. Global governance is also most likely to be strengthened if it fits the domestic profiles of the dominant countries (Cowhey 1993: 186), but they must accept it as an influence and constraint on their own behavior.

For analytical purposes, we look first at the key role the United States has played as the dominant, hegemonic power since World War II and at the factors that have shaped its mixed record as a supporter of multilateralism. We then examine some of the roles other major powers have played, the niche roles of certain middle powers such as Canada, Australia, and India, and the ways in which smaller states have used multilateral diplomacy to enhance their own influence within the networks of international organizations.

■ The Key Role of the United States

▨ *The Historical Record*

As the dominant power after World War II, the United States played a key role in shaping the international system structure, including the establishment of many IGOs, from the UN to the Bretton Woods institutions and the International Atomic Energy Agency. The provisions of the UN Charter, for example, were consistent with U.S. interests, and until the 1960s the United States could often count on the support of a majority on most major issues. This enabled the United States to use the UN and its specialized agencies as instruments of its national policies and to create institutions and rules compatible with U.S. interests. The UN and other organizations such as NATO also served domestic political purposes by creating a web of international entanglements and domestic-support constituencies that made it difficult for future administrations to return to more isolationist policies (Mingst and Karns 2000: 48). Sewell (2000) identifies this period from the end of World War II to the early 1970s as one of "lordly unilateralism."

Over time, the United States has used the UN, the specialized agencies, and the OAS for collective legitimation of its own actions, such as in Korea in 1950, Cuba in 1960, the Dominican Republic in 1965, the Iran hostage crisis in 1979, the first Gulf War in 1990–1991 and the September 11, 2001, terrorist attacks on the World Trade Center and Pentagon. NATO was similarly useful for responding to the crisis in Kosovo in 1999.

From the late 1960s to mid-1980s, however, the United States was much more ambivalent about many international institutions. It withdrew from the ILO in 1978 (rejoining it more than two years later) and from UNESCO in 1984 (rejoining it in 2003), because of politicization and bureaucratic inefficiency. Developing countries' demands in the 1970s for a New International Economic Order led Washington to oppose many UN-sponsored development programs. Washington's alienation from the UN was borne out in the steep drop in U.S. voting with the majorities in the General Assembly in 1981. (See Figure 7.1.) In the Security Council, the United States used its veto thirty-four times between 1976 and 1985. (See Table 4.1.) During the same period, North-South tensions between U.S. and Latin American states' policies led to the OAS becoming almost moribund. Congressional support for paying IGO dues weakened. Beginning in 1985, Congress imposed a series of conditions on contributions and withheld full payment as a strategy to force change (Karns and Mingst 2002).

U.S. antipathy to the United Nations moderated somewhat during the second term of the Reagan administration. Changes in Soviet policy under Mikhail Gorbachev created new opportunities for UN action in settling regional conflicts, as discussed in Chapter 8. Subsequently, the UN's success in handling new peacekeeping challenges and war against Iraq in 1991 generated widespread optimism about an expanding UN role in the post–Cold War era. In 1993, the Clinton administration articulated a foreign

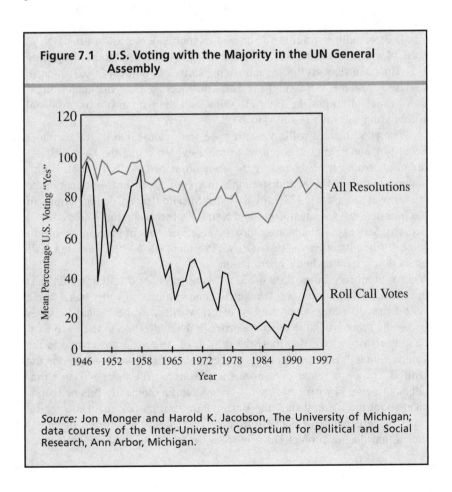

Figure 7.1   U.S. Voting with the Majority in the UN General Assembly

Source: Jon Monger and Harold K. Jacobson, The University of Michigan; data courtesy of the Inter-University Consortium for Political and Social Research, Ann Arbor, Michigan.

policy of assertive multilateralism, designed to share responsibilities for global peace with other countries by working through an invigorated UN. Likewise, in the early 1990s, the OAS enjoyed a "rebirth" as discussed in Chapter 5, APEC and NAFTA were created, and NATO's role was redefined.

The United States' post–Cold War support for multilateral institutions has, however, been more complex and fragile than the public rhetoric suggests. U.S. voting with the majority on roll call votes in the UN General Assembly reached its lowest point ever in 1990 (10 percent) and improved only slightly in subsequent years. By mid-decade, the problems in Somalia, Rwanda, and Bosnia overshadowed successes elsewhere. The United States shifted to a more unilateral strategy in a number of cases, demonstrated in the effort to deny Boutros-Ghali a second term as UN secretary-general in 1996, the Senate's rejection of the Comprehensive Test Ban Treaty in 1999, and the refusal to support the International Criminal Court (1998), the convention banning antipersonnel landmines (1997), and the Kyoto Protocol on climate change (1997).

U.S. muddling multilateralism and its ambivalence toward the UN, in particular in the 1990s, was nowhere more visible than in the deepening U.S. financial debt to the organization (Karns and Mingst 2002). Indeed, Congress became increasingly resistant to meeting U.S. financial obligations, especially after the 1994 elections, and the pattern of congressional withholding was only resolved in 2000.

The U.S.' blatant willingness to go to war against Iraq in 2003 without Security Council authorization was further evidence that the United States did not consider itself bound by the obligations of the UN Charter. It also underscored the Bush administration's sharp unilateral turn—evident in the withdrawal from the 1973 Anti-Ballistic Missile Treaty, denunciations of the International Criminal Court and Kyoto Protocol, and the 2002 National Security Strategy that advanced provocative ideas about preemptive use of force. "When it comes to our security," President Bush (2003) averred, "we really don't need anybody's permission."

As Ikenberry notes (2003: 533), "America's 'new unilateralism' has unsettled world politics. . . . At no other time in modern history has a single state loomed so large over the rest of the world. . . . the United States is becoming more crucial to other countries in the realization of their economic and security goals. . . . [but] the growth of American power makes the United States less dependent on weaker states, and so it is easier for the United States to resist or ignore these states." Ikenberry argues that although some key officials have a "deep and ideologically driven skepticism about multilateralism," the Bush administration has attacked specific types of agreements, especially in arms control and new types of agreements that do not protect U.S. freedom of action with escape clauses or veto rights. After the September 11, 2001, terrorist attacks, the United States clearly recognized the importance of waging the war on terrorism multilaterally. Likewise, the United States has actively championed the WTO. Thus, U.S. policies continue to show a mixed record on multilateralism.

■ Explaining U.S.-IGO Relationships

Over time, U.S.-IGO relationships have depended on at least four dynamic factors. First, the relationship depends on the nature of the issues. Resistance to meeting UN financial contributions, for example, has occurred most often where significant policy differences have existed between the United States and other members and, hence, when the United States has found itself isolated and in opposition to the majority. This has led to perceptions that the UN (or other institutions) is a hostile place, with the United States pulling back from multilateralism and using its financial contributions as a tool of influence. Second, the relationship depends on the dynamics of U.S. domestic politics—including presidential leadership (or the lack thereof), executive-legislative relations, lobbying by domestic groups, and public opinion. While bipartisanship and consensus on foreign policy marked executive-legislative relations during the early Cold War years, after the controversy over the Vietnam War, Congress became more assertive in international affairs generally and in defining the terms of U.S. participation in the UN, other IGOs, and treaties.

Third, the U.S.-IGO relationships can be partially explained by American political culture. Exceptionalism has a long history in the national political culture (Luck 1999). These roots are complemented and reinforced now by the United States' standing as the sole superpower and the exceptional size and strength of its military capability and economy. Fourth, from the viewpoint of many both inside and outside of the United States, the exceptional power that the United States currently enjoys explains its unilateralist tendencies. The United States does not have to act just like another state in the international system. Its structural power, its domestic politics, and political culture justify unilateralism.

The United States has more easily embraced the multilateralism of the international financial institutions in part because it has tremendous power over those organizations. It controls almost 20 percent of the votes on the executive board of the IMF and World Bank; both institutions are located in Washington D.C., and their staffs of economists, trained mainly in U.S. educational institutions, give the United States inordinate influence. The fact that officials in the IMF and World Bank actively court the U.S. executive branch and Congress indicates their close relationship. When even these economic institutions have proved too unwieldy for American tastes, the United States has turned to smaller groups such as the G-7 or the Paris

Club. Concerned about the future of the global multilateral trade system in the early 1990s, the United States embraced the formation of APEC and NAFTA, both of which were also seen as sources of leverage against the EU's single market.

There is a longstanding debate among American elites and the public regarding the conditions under which the United States should respond multilaterally versus unilaterally. Nye (2001–2002) suggests seven key tests for U.S. decisionmakers to use in evaluating the multilateral and unilateral alternatives. He reserves unilateral action for a handful of critical national security issues, arguing that the United States should show a general preference for multilateralism whenever possible, although he acknowledges that sometimes the United States has to go it alone.

The notion of global governance has not decisively entered U.S. discourse. When it has, it is generally viewed as negative, associated with world government and an unacceptable diminution of sovereignty or, with the UN, a place where U.S. money is squandered, the U.S. vote demeaned, and inefficient and bloated bureaucracy are rampant. It is also associated with the U.S. military having to take orders from an incompetent UN command and being unable to stop the war in Bosnia.

Yet in the 1996 campaign, coming just after the newly created World Trade Organization superceded the GATT, public debate for the first time centered on the polemic that U.S. trade rules should "never" be subject to review by "foreigners" or, worse yet, to regulation by an international body (Mingst 1999). This led to the outcry that America's very sovereignty was being undermined although the United States has been subject to GATT's rules and regulations, including its dispute settlement procedures, since the 1940s and led in negotiating those rules. Much of the same debate surrounded the establishment of the International Criminal Court. Opponents argued there should be no way that U.S. soldiers could be brought before that body for actions while they were performing peacekeeping functions.

But in U.S. domestic politics, nothing is that simple. There are no opinion polls that tap the full range of views about global governance. Data show that Americans do believe in internationalism, although internationalism is a duality with both a cooperative and an interventionist face. Polls have found general support for multilateralism and for strengthening the United Nations. In a poll of American and European attitudes, the Chicago Council on Foreign Relations and German Marshall Fund of the United States (2002) found 61 percent of Americans said that the United States should not act alone in responding to international crises if it did not have the support of allies. A clear majority of Americans also favored ratifying the Kyoto Protocol and the International Criminal Court. Still, as Gordenker (2003: 283) notes, "The internalization of international norms in American political life is remarkably thin." If global governance means relinquishing various degrees of national governmental controls to other groups or if it means a diminution of sovereignty, then the response by U.S. decisionmakers is apt to be a resounding "no" in most instances, with the Congress, in particular, strongly opposed (Mingst 1999).

U.S. ambivalence is the conundrum of the hegemon with a strong history and political culture embracing its own exceptionalism. Yet it was also U.S. political culture that led it to promote multilateral institutions as a device for building a more peaceful, stable democratic world, for sharing burdens, and for solving problems of cooperation. International institutions have historically mirrored U.S. institutions in their organizational structures and procedures. With power, however, comes the belief that one can "go it alone." As Sewell (2000: 4) posits, "The prerogative of leadership as unilateral choice thus becomes verbally buttressed as the systemic imperative of hegemony. Leadership so conceived induces a supposition that the rules of the system exist mainly in order to constrain others."

The United States has the power to act alone, but by acting unilaterally, the United States risks undermining the very multilateral system that it established, the system that is congruent with American interests "95 percent of the time" (Friedman 2001: A19). As Cronin (2001: 113) explains, "When a hegemon fails to act within the boundaries established by its role, the credibility of the institutions and rules it helped to establish weakens. IOs act as the chief legitimizing agents of global politics. When these organizations are undermined, the legitimacy of the international order itself is threatened. If this persists over time, the hegemonic order declines." The actions of the United States and the effectiveness of global governance are, therefore, closely intertwined.

It may be tempting to believe that the new unilateralism in U.S. foreign policy under the Bush administration is a consequence of the U.S.' overwhelming power in the world today. Ikenberry argues that this is a superficial reading of the situation. Despite the influence of neoconservatives that advocate using U.S. power to reshape Iraq and the Middle East as well as withdrawal from multilateral norms and institutions, he suggests (2003: 540), "The United States is not structurally destined to disentangle itself from the multilateral order and go it alone. . . . The sources of U.S. multilateralism stem from the functional demands of interdependence, the long-term calculations of power management, and American political tradition and identity."

■ Other Powerful States

The United States is not the only powerful state in global governance. The other permanent members of the UN Security Council (Russia, Great Britain, France, and China) are important actors, along with Japan and

Germany, whose economic weight has given them influence on many global governance issues. The roles of these other powerful states have changed over time and have varied among regional and global institutions.

During the Cold War, the former Soviet Union was a competing hegemonic power. It created two regional organizations: the Warsaw Pact defensive alliance, the Soviet bloc's response to NATO, and the Council for Mutual Economic Assistance (COMECON), the response to the Marshall Plan and the European Common Market. In both, the Soviet Union dictated major policies and programs and used economic and military coercion to maintain its dominance. It clashed frequently with the United States in the UN. The Security Council veto power was an important tool for blocking the objectives of the West and protecting its own interests. Between 1945 and 1975 the Soviet Union used its veto 114 times, many of those on membership applications. In the 1960s and 1970s, the Soviet Union often sided with the newly independent states in the General Assembly, supporting self-determination for colonial peoples, the Palestine Liberation Organization, and the New International Economic Order agenda. This strategy permitted it to vote with the majority in the General Assembly a high percentage of the time. For ideological reasons, the Soviet Union and other bloc members were not part of the Bretton Woods institutions but did participate in many other functional agencies.

With respect to the UN, the Soviet attitude changed dramatically in 1987. After years of opposition, the Soviet Union adopted a facilitative attitude toward using the UN to monitor and legitimize its troop withdrawal from Afghanistan and end the Iran-Iraq War. These changes were hastened by the speed and thoroughness of the Soviet Union's dismemberment in 1991.

Today, although Russia is clearly a diminished power with meager economic means, it still exercises influence as a major power. As one indicator of its diminished capability, Russia's assessment for the UN dropped from 8.7 percent in 1991 to less than 2.0 percent after 2000. Yet the veto power makes it imperative to have Russian support for all Security Council operations. Russia's participation in the G-8 and NATO partnership further assures that its voice will be heard on noneconomic issues.

Both Great Britain and France continue to occupy positions of global importance disproportionate to their size and economic resources. Both are key players in the World Bank and International Monetary Fund, contributing key personnel and financial resources and voting consistently with other large developed countries. Both jealously guard their permanent seats on the Security Council in debates on UN reform. Since 1990, both have played active roles in UN peacekeeping and enforcement operations, providing troops in the Gulf War and Bosnia, as well as commanders to the UN Protection Force in the former Yugoslavia (UNPROFOR). Each has also assumed responsibility for a subcontracted enforcement operation—Great Britain in Sierra Leone and France in Rwanda and Congo.

Britain and France have carved different niches in global governance, although both retain substantial influence in the third world, owing to continuing ties with their former colonies through the Commonwealth and the Organisation Internationale de la Francophonie (or Francophonie) respectively. Britain occupies key positions in the Geneva Group for review of budgets and programs, in ECOSOC, the ICJ, the ILO, and WHO. British delegates and secretariat members are frequently noted for their skill in drafting resolutions and other documents. Britain also pays a larger share of expenses than its 5 percent assessment, assuring its privileged position in many specialized agencies and programs. In addition, Britain's support of NATO and special relationship with the United States enhance its influence in Washington and in many IGOs. France places great stake in its Security Council veto power although Table 4.1 indicates the relative infrequency with which it has used that power. It also attaches critical importance to its membership on the International Monetary Fund and World Bank's executive boards (and long held the IMF director-generalship) and to UNESCO, located in Paris and traditionally dominated by francophone interests and personnel. Unlike Britain, however, French commitment to NATO has been problematic ever since it withdrew from the joint military command in 1965. Both France and Great Britain exercise great-power leadership in the European Union, but their visions of Europe differ significantly, as discussed in Chapter 5. Given the EU's qualified majority voting system, neither can fully dominate.

France and Great Britain used their positions as major powers to shape global governance efforts, sometimes in concert with the United States, at other times diverging. Both have been key supporters of such initiatives as the International Criminal Court, the Kyoto Protocol on climate change, the landmines treaty, and the Comprehensive Test Ban Treaty, all of which were rejected by the United States.

The fifth permanent member of the Security Council, China, has historically been far less active or interested in international institutions. The Republic of China (ROC) originally held China's Security Council seat, which it continued to occupy long after the Chinese revolution brought the People's Republic of China (PRC) to power in Beijing and sent the ROC government to Taiwan. In 1971, third-world votes granted the PRC the Chinese seat and Taiwan walked out of the body.

The communist regime in China was long suspicious of multilateral institutions, afraid that they might be used to constrain China's actions and, therefore, undermine its sovereignty. In 1966, it was a member of only one international organization. During its first decade of UN membership, the PRC played a very low-key role, which one analyst called the "Club of

One" (Kent 2002). Although it supported the G-77 and the nonaligned group positions on decolonization and economic development issues, it remained uninvolved in security issues. Only in 1981 did China begin to pay its share of peacekeeping assessments when threatened with the loss of voting rights under UN Charter Article 19.

In the 1990s, China's position on security issues showed its ambivalence and longstanding concern for upholding the principle of nonintervention. Although it opposed using force against Iraq in the Gulf War, sanctions against Libya, Yugoslavia, and others, and muscular peacekeeping in Bosnia and elsewhere, China did not want to be the "odd country out" by exercising its veto. Thus it abstained on key votes. Between 1990 and 1999, China abstained on forty-one Security Council votes. Morphet (2000a: 165) concludes, "It is likely that China normally abstains rather than uses its veto because of its concern to keep the UN international machinery intact and in use." As one of the P-5, China's views have to be taken into account. As a self-proclaimed leader of the third world and an opponent of hegemony, China's stance often supports the latter while accommodating the former.

Until the 1980s, China showed no interest in participating in the international economic organizations. China's move to create a market economy, however, its rapid economic growth, and increasing share of world trade made it important for China and for the functioning of the global rules-based economy to bring it into the IMF, World Bank, and GATT/WTO. The PRC assumed China's seats in the IMF and World Bank in 1980, with its own seat on their executive boards. In 2001, China was accepted into the World Trade Organization following fifteen years of negotiations over the terms of entry. (See Chapter 9.)

China's push for WTO membership is an indicator of its awareness that big-power status requires participation in the networks of international organizations. After years of relative isolation, China began in the 1990s to seek a greater role. For example, it fought hard to host the 1995 Fourth World Conference on Women, believing that a successful conference would bring prestige to China. Also in the same year, China agreed to accept selected ILO labor standards, initiating a process to modify domestic law to accommodate the changes.

As discussed in Chapter 5, Asia has generally lagged in creating regional organizations, in part because of China's communist government and in part because China preferred to deal with its regional neighbors bilaterally rather than multilaterally. The gradual shift in Chinese policy in the 1990s reflected a fear of being excluded and recognition that joining APEC and participating in dialogues with ASEAN were ways that China could build relations in Southeast Asia, support the cause of less developed countries, and promote its interests. It is a long way, however, from exercising any kind of regional hegemony.

Despite its big-power status and rising economic importance, China remains a marginal player in global governance. Sovereignty issues occupy top priority on China's agenda. China still prefers bilateral channels where it can exercise greater influence; if forced into acting multilaterally, it will, preferring consensus decisionmaking. On economic issues, China still free rides, pleading special treatment as a developing country and rhetorically supporting others so positioned. And despite having promised to alter domestic legislation in labor, human rights, and environment in compliance with international conventions, adjustment to international norms has been a slow, incomplete process. But other states give China space and leeway. China's economic prowess and expectation of future economic dominance position it firmly as a key actor in global governance.

The ranks of the world's major powers clearly include Germany and Japan, yet neither is a permanent member of the Security Council, and their historical experiences as the defeated World War II powers have had a major impact on their individual willingness and capacity to make certain types of international commitments. Because of Germany's pivotal geographic position in Cold War Europe, there was a concerted effort to bring it into the fold of international institutions in order both to constrain German power and to signal the Soviet Union that West Germany was a key member of the Western alliance. Thus, West Germany (the Federal Republic of Germany) became a member of NATO in 1955, a founding member of the European Community in 1956, but not a member of the UN until both Germanys were admitted in 1973. The Western European Union was established to facilitate rearmament of West Germany. Japan, because of the absence of Asian regional arrangements, did not become as institutionally enmeshed, although it did join the UN in 1956. In the 1980s, Japan used its strong economic position to exercise increasing leadership in the World Bank and International Development Association where it was the second largest donor.

With respect to the UN, neither Germany nor Japan actively participated until the 1980s, when their respective financial contributions were increased. Japan then lobbied successfully for some of its nationals to be appointed to top UN positions (e.g., in the WHO and UNHCR) and increased its quiet influence behind the scenes. Neither country contributed to peacekeeping operations nor took an active role on security issues. In both Germany and Japan, however, the 1991 Gulf War stimulated national debates over their international roles. Both had been asked to provide significant monetary contributions to the war, yet neither was a member of the Security Council. Both had constitutional impediments to participation in any collective enforcement or peacekeeping operation. The result was that in 1992 the Japanese Diet (Parliament) approved legislation permitting up to two thousand Japanese troops to be deployed in UN peacekeeping missions under limited conditions. The German Constitutional Court ruled in 1994 that German military forces could participate in UN peacekeeping operations and those of other international organizations such as NATO and the Western European Union (WEU).

Germany and Japan are key UN financial supporters. Japan is the second largest contributor to the UN, with an assessed contribution set at almost 20 percent, more than the combined share of France, Great Britain, China, and Russia. Germany is third, with an assessment of 9.5 percent. Japan and Germany's power in the international economic organizations, including the IMF, World Bank, WTO, and G-7, is also strong.

Germany has made multilateralism a cornerstone of its foreign policy and the strong German economy gives it substantial clout in the EU. Japan exercises substantial influence in the Asian Development Bank, where a Japanese national has always been president and where Japan and the United States each exercise the largest voting share—13 percent. Japan, along with Australia, was instrumental in the creation of APEC. Early in the 1997–1998 Asian financial crisis, Japan tested the idea of an Asian monetary fund with heavy Japanese support, but withdrew it in the face of strong U.S. opposition.

Thus, both Germany and Japan's roles in the networks of international organizations evidence their economic power, but also acceptance of continuing constraints on any major security roles. The differences between them and many of the middle powers lie in the economic resources they contribute and the influence they command as a result.

■ **Middle-Power States**

The so-called middle-power states have played and continue to play an important role in both IGOs and global governance more generally. Although there are no widely accepted definitions of middle power, generally they are "middle" in terms of relative power or size. In terms of policies, they tend to pursue multilateralism, take compromise positions in disputes, and engage in coalition building to secure reform in the international system. Canada, Australia, Norway, Sweden, Argentina, Brazil, India, Nigeria, and South Africa are among the middle powers that have played uniquely facilitative roles during and after the Cold War, when disputing parties were wary of great-power involvement.

Many middle powers have been frequent contributors to UN peacekeeping. As one commentator noted with respect to the Canadian role in peacekeeping, "while it often served U.S. interests," Canada's actions showed "a powerful aura of independence and the implicit sense it served higher interests than simply those of the United States, or even the West" (quoted in Granatstein 1992: 224–225). The Canadian niche is in the early phases of peacekeeping: helping to train peacekeepers, setting up command structures and providing communication facilities, linguistic facility, and medical expertise. As an expression of its commitment to regional security, Australia assumed leadership of the UN-sanctioned peacekeeping and nation-building activities in East Timor in 1999, providing military forces, police, and civilian personnel. Indian participation in traditional peacekeeping operations in the Middle East and in the Congo satisfied India's hope for international recognition. Indian generals commanded operations in Korea, in the Congo, Bosnia, and the Middle East. Participation in peacekeeping also helped India project its nonaligned state image and claim to leadership in the Non-Aligned Movement. Much like India, Nigeria also saw contributions to peacekeeping operations as an important strategy. Thus, Nigeria volunteered troops for service in the Congo even before its own independence was official. It participated in UN peacekeeping in Lebanon in the late 1970s as well as in Namibia in 1989–1990. In the 1990s, Nigeria orchestrated ECOWAS's intervention in Liberia and later in Sierra Leone, provided financing and three-quarters of the manpower for the operations. Similarly, Brazil and Argentina have been significant contributors to peacekeeping operations in the 1990s.

In the post–Cold War era, several middle-power states have taken key leadership roles on particular governance issues where the major powers have failed. These include Norway on Middle East peace negotiations in the early 1990s, Sweden on gender issues, Canada on landmines and human security issues, and South Africa in regional peacemaking. Canada, unlike many other middle powers, has strong roles in international economic governance in the G-7.

It is not unusual to find middle powers playing key roles in regional governance. Canada, for example, has also shown its leadership in the ASEAN Regional Forum (ARF), running workshops on peacekeeping for other members and on the practice of regional multilateralism for the Chinese. In 1989, Australia with Japan took the initiative to create APEC. Prime Ministers Bob Hawke and Paul Keating supported the endeavor, in part to support the claim that Australia was essentially a part of Asia, and in part because Australia favored trade and economic liberalization. It continues to take the lead in over one-third of APEC's economic and technical cooperation projects and also a key role in the ASEAN Regional Forum and CSCAP. In contrast, India has had little experience in regional cooperation as its own dominance and conflicts with Pakistan have effectively precluded the establishment of regional governance arrangements in South Asia. Nigeria's regional role has been largely limited to peacekeeping efforts.

Middle-power states have also been leaders of coalitions. India helped create the Non-Aligned Movement in the 1950s, and it used the movement to reinforce its activist multilateral agenda. In the first UN General Assembly session in 1946 and later in the nonaligned summits, India spoke out about racism in South Africa and led the push to end apartheid and colonialism. Australia helped established the Cairns Group of Fair Trading Nations to push reform in international agricultural trade during the GATT trade negotiations in the early 1990s. This coalition crossed both the East/West divide and the North/South divide. It provided the intellectual leadership and managed the difficult negotiations in support of a freer, open, and nondiscriminatory international trade regime in agriculture (Higgott and Cooper 1990).

Yet middle-power states' roles are not always positive ones. India, for example, has also been a multilateral spoiler in efforts to curb nuclear non-proliferation, refusing to sign both the Treaty on the Non-Proliferation of Nuclear Weapons (1970) and the Comprehensive Nuclear Test Ban Treaty (1996). Then in 1998, India stunned the world by testing a nuclear device, pushing Pakistan to do likewise and triggering an arms race on the subcontinent.

■ **Small States, Developing States**

For the large number of less developed countries and small states, IGOs, including the UN, enlarge their voice and offer opportunities to set global agendas, particularly through adroit use of coalition building and issue-linkage strategies. In fact, many small states actually pick and choose the issues of highest priority around which to focus their limited resources. For example, Malta made its mark in the late 1960s by urging adoption of the norm of the seabed and other commons areas as "the common heritage of humankind." Algeria (not Nigeria, Africa's larger power) provided leadership for the Group of 77's campaign for a New International Economic Order in the 1970s. Uganda has made HIV/AIDS its niche issue in international forums, based on the government's success in fighting the disease. The Netherlands and Costa Rica have both focused on international law, especially human rights.

Multilateral agreements are also valuable to weaker states in creating constraints on the dominant powers' autonomy. Ikenberry (2003: 535–536) adds, "The more that the powerful state can restrain itself in a credible fashion, the more that weaker states will be interested in multilateral rules and norms that accomplish this end."

By analyzing the roles of small states in the networks of international organizations, one can discover how skillful use of multilateral diplomacy can alter the power equation, leading to outcomes that serve the interests of people, groups, and states that are not necessarily considered powerful. For example, Kuwait, because it was a sovereign state and UN member, had great success in mobilizing the international community's response to Iraq's invasion in 1990. Yet the patterns vary widely across the spectrum of international institutions. Most small developing states have little opportunity to voice their positions in the international economic organizations. For example, in the WTO, where there are an estimated 1,200 formal and informal meetings annually, LDCs have neither the personnel and expertise nor resources to attend all of the meetings of interest. Thus, their only opportunity to influence outcomes is at the end of the process when all the compromises have already been made and negotiators are loath to reopen discussions. In an effort to narrow this gap, the WTO and UNCTAD jointly sponsor the International Trade Centre to provide technical assistance to developing countries.

Small states have been able to bargain with major powers for support on key issues in return for economic concessions. In the Gulf War in 1990, for example, some small states that were members of the Security Council at the time agreed to back the U.S.-supported UN response in return for favors. Both Egypt and Malaysia received financial rewards, while Ethiopia negotiated a promise by the United States to broker a peace with rebels, and Yemen, an opponent of the Gulf War, saw a withdrawal of U.S. aid for its failure to support enforcement action. In 2003, the smaller nonpermanent members of the Security Council (such as Guinea, Angola, and Cameroon) were courted extensively by both sides in the divisive debate over Iraq.

For most developing countries, the most important impact of IGOs comes from the functional programs of specialized agencies. They are the direct beneficiaries of most development assistance programs, but the competition is fierce, especially with the end of the Cold War, donor fatigue, and the proliferation of new states in Central Asia and Eastern Europe all competing for scarce resources.

For small and developing states, but really for all states, participation in the networks of international organizations not only aids in achieving foreign policy objectives directly but also increases the number of avenues that can be taken. Opportunities for employing strategies of coalition building and forum shopping are an integral part of multilateral diplomacy in these arenas. We turn then to look at these strategies.

■ State Strategies

▪ *Forum Shopping*

Following its independence in 1962, Jamaica chose to focus much of its diplomatic activity on eradicating racial discrimination. In so doing, it used its membership in the Non-Aligned Movement, the Caribbean Community, the Organization of American States, the Commonwealth, and the UN to push for action on the issue. Instead of selecting a single forum, it chose the diplomatic equivalent of a "full court press." By contrast, despite consensus that Africans should as much as possible resolve regional conflicts within the OAU (now AU), some African states have preferred to take disputes to the UN where they hoped to gain more support for their own cause. More recently, the number and severity of many African conflicts have exceeded regional resources and drawn UN involvement, as illustrated by the UN taking over peacekeeping from ECOWAS in Liberia in 2003.

For situations requiring peacekeeping or enforcement, states have little choice but to turn to the UN, as peacekeeping is still embryonic or nonexistent in all regional organizations. The OAU experimented with observer groups in Rwanda, Burundi, and the Congo. Nigeria, however, chose the umbrella of ECOWAS to legitimate its interventions in Sierra Leone and Liberia without securing Security Council approval, although that approval eventually followed. Although ASEAN might have seemed a good choice for dealing with the crisis in East Timor in 1999, that organization's strong norm of noninterference provided more protection for Indonesia than opportunity for the Timorese and their supporters. Since 1995, the United States has shown a preference for NATO over the UN for peacekeeping roles in Bosnia, Kosovo, and Afghanistan.

In short, the multiplicity of international forums means that states can often choose where to take certain issues. Although some issues logically belong only within the relevant specialized organization, the increasing interrelatedness of many issues makes the neat compartmentalization of these IGOs outdated. Thus, for example, NGOs have increasingly pressed for labor and environment issues linked to trade to be addressed in the WTO, not in the ILO or UNEP.

■ Coalition Building

We discussed in Chapter 1 how states use multilateral arenas to build coalitions to pool their power and resources to obtain better outcomes than they might by going it alone. Such coalitions have served pragmatic and organizational purposes as well. As discussed in Chapter 4, regional groups formed in the UN as a way of dealing with the UN Charter provisions for electing nonpermanent representatives to the Security Council, ECOSOC, and the ICJ. The Cold War produced a set of competing groups under the leadership of the Soviet Union and United States, plus a growing group of nonaligned countries. The formation of the UN Conference on Trade and Development in 1964 led to the coalition of Latin American, African, and Asian states under the umbrella of the Group of 77, marking the divide between North and South, developed versus developing states. (See

Chapter 4.) Since the mid-1960s, group diplomacy has been pervasive throughout much of the UN system, as well as in regional organizations (Morphet 2000b). Governance requires agreement on actions to be taken and this, in turn, requires the formation of coalitions across existing groups. Often, small states or middle powers play key roles in bridging the differences between the positions of different groups.

Groups utilize a variety of strategies and tactics. They can work together in informal political groups and use electoral power for leadership positions and representation on committees. They can try to form overarching coalitions with other like-minded groups. They can convene major conferences in other venues or even establish their own organizations in support of specific causes. The Commonwealth, the Non-Aligned Movement, and Contact Groups illustrate the way three such groupings operate and how they change over time.

The Commonwealth.   One of the oldest and most global groups is the Commonwealth, a voluntary organization of fifty-four states on every continent except Antarctica, representing 30 percent of the world's population. A successor to the British empire, the Commonwealth has not been a formal caucusing group at the United Nations since the early 1960s but operates as an intergovernmental body through periodic summit meetings, serviced by a small secretariat located in London. Members frequently consult each other regarding issues and positions discussed in numerous international forums. The Commonwealth also operates at the societal level. Over seventy professional associations are part of the Commonwealth family, including the Commonwealth Parliamentary Association with 14,000 parliamentarians at the state and local level, the Association of Commonwealth Universities with five hundred members, and the Commonwealth Foundation with Civil Society, providing links to NGOs. As Vale and Black (1994: 14) conclude, "The Commonwealth has many personalities: international organisations, global networks, diplomatic clubs, amongst others. Underpinning these, however, is an intricate and complex set of linkages."

The Commonwealth can be best characterized by its flexible and informal style, preference for minimal procedures, and small group meetings, facilitated by use of the English language and common legal systems, educational systems, and business heritage. Meetings are quite informal affairs where leaders discuss issues and arrive at a consensus; formal votes are not taken.

Current issues on the Commonwealth's agenda range from fostering democracy and promoting gender equality to the impacts of globalization, human development, and concerns of small states. The Commonwealth was a vehicle for former colonies such as India to press for speeding the decolonization process in other British colonies and for the struggle against apartheid in South Africa. African, Asian, and Latin American members pressed for both general sanctions and bans on sports and cultural activities.

Since both North and South are represented in the Commonwealth, international economic issues are of longstanding interest. The goal is to develop new ideas and approaches. For example, on the critical question of technical cooperation, the Commonwealth developed a mechanism whereby technology was transferred from one developing country to another, facilitated by the Commonwealth Fund for Technical Cooperation established in 1971. The idea of South-South assistance has subsequently diffused to other organizations such as the Francophonie.

The Commonwealth complements the work of the United Nations, the Non-Aligned Movement, and the Group of 77, and does not try to replace or supplant those other organizations or groups (Ramphal 1984). As Margaret Doxey (1992: 13) concludes, the Commonwealth has shown a "surprising capacity to respond to changing circumstances and a resilience to internal stress. . . . it provides a kind of club within which views can be expressed, ideas shared and advice sought and given on a confidential basis. And it offers a multilateral framework within which bilateral links can be readily cultivated."

The Non-Aligned Movement (NAM).   The development of the Non-Aligned Movement can be traced to shortly after the formation of the United Nations when the issue of Palestine divided the organization. Those who opposed the formation of Israel and supported a Palestinian homeland were joined by several states that were not allied with either the Soviet Union or the United States. Beginning with the Arab-Israeli issue, Yugoslavia, Egypt, and India under the dynamic leadership of Josip Broz Tito, Gamal Abdul Nasser, and Jawaharlal Nehru, respectively, sought to unite like-minded states behind a more inclusive agenda of opposition to colonialism, the right of self-determination, and support for fundamental principles of human rights, including antiracism. They sought to influence world affairs and fight for a place at the negotiating table in international bodies without affiliating with either of the two dominant Cold War blocs. The Non-Aligned Movement was born at the Bandung Conference in 1955.

The first summit conference of the twenty-five heads of state affiliated with NAM actually convened in 1961 in Belgrade. Periodic conferences have been held ever since then (e.g., Algiers 1973, Havana 1979, Harare 1986, Nicosia 1988, Jakarta 1992, Cartagena 1995). Unlike the Commonwealth, the NAM did not create formal structures, adopt a constitution, or designate a secretariat. Members prefer a nonhierarchical, rotational, and inclusive style where the chairship rotates among member states and the chairing state provides administrative support for that year. NAM operates through a panoply of working groups, contact groups, task forces, and committees. As divisive as some of the issues addressed by these various groups have been, none has proven to be fatal, because NAM is more a political movement or loose coalition.

The relationship between the Non-Aligned Movement and the Group of 77 is one of overlapping membership where the former originally concentrated on the political issues arising out of the Cold War and colonialism, while the latter embraced the economic agenda. Many Commonwealth members are also part of both NAM and the G-77. After the mid-1960s, however, the Non-Aligned Movement took up the North-South economic agenda, blurring any distinction, although the G-77 had the greater (and louder) voice.

There has long been a potential split in the NAM along ideological lines between radical and moderate states. The radicals (Cuba, Algeria) positioned themselves as natural allies of the then Soviet Union, while the moderates (Kenya, Nigeria) were committed to a more even-handed approach and feared a move to the ideological left. The latter faction essentially won that debate, confirming that one of the reasons for the longevity of the movement itself was its basically nonideological and highly pragmatic stance. As Morphet (1993: 379) concludes, "The long-standing moderate mainstream grip on the non-aligned has produced results in terms of ensuring that non-aligned or Southern concerns (such as Palestine, Namibia and South Africa) have been put on the global agenda and, by dint of pressure or persuasion, eventually dealt with by the global community including the superpowers."

With the Soviet Union's demise and the Cold War's end, the movement has refocused energies on representing the nonwestern, smaller states who often lack an institutionalized voice in established international organizations and bodies. To that end, the NAM Caucus in the UN Security Council serves to promote a common position on security issues. NAM has not been very successful, however, at acquiring a voice in the new international political environment. It played virtually no role in the 1991 Gulf War; it stood on the sidelines in Yugoslavia's breakup; it has exercised no influence in the Israeli-Palestinian conflict.

Since the Cold War's end, small ad hoc groups of states have frequently joined together to deal with particular issues such as trade or armed conflicts.

Contact Groups and friends. The use of ad hoc informal groups of states to support UN peace-related efforts dates back to the late 1970s and the efforts of the Contact Group on Namibia to work alongside the UN Security Council. That group involved high-ranking members of five UN missions (Canada, France, Germany, Great Britain, and the United States) in a decade-long series of negotiations, which eventually led to independence for a democratic Namibia. (See Chapter 8 for further discussion.)

In the 1990s, such groups proliferated. A small number of member states, usually between three and six members, organized as Friends of the Secretary-General and included at least one interested member of the P-5. The "friends" keep in close contact with the secretary-general and support his efforts to find a peaceful solution to a crisis. The group is kept small so that meetings can be quickly convened. More than one country is used to exert pressure on parties and present a common view that speaks for the international community at large. The purpose is to keep a peace process on track and coordinate the work of mediators, either prior to reaching a formal agreement or in implementing an agreement. "Friends" groups have been formed, for example, for Haiti (Canada, France, United States, Venezuela); Georgia (France, Germany, Russia, United Kingdom); and Tajikistan (Afghanistan, Iran, Turkey, United States, Uzbekistan). One study identifies fourteen Friends of the Secretary-General (Prandt and Krasno 2002). In an effort to advance peaceful settlement of the Israeli-Palestinian conflict, the UN, the United States, Russia, and the EU form the so-called Quartet—a further illustration of the value attached to collaborative approaches.

Groups and coalitions, then, provide order and give coherence to a world of 191 states with an already crowded international agenda. They put issues on the table, establish negotiating positions, and engage in bargaining. Should one forum not be useful, states search for others and even create new ones compatible with their interests. The composition of coalitions and groups changes constantly, as once-moderate states become more radical and the radicals more moderate and agendas shift. Thus, while membership in many groups may be rather constant, positions within the group are often in continuous flux. Negotiations within such groups, like negotiations between groups, can be time consuming and arduous and form part of the complexity and challenges of multilateral diplomacy.

■ The Challenges of Multilateral Diplomacy: Negotiating Across Cultures

Differing national interests, variations in negotiating styles, language, and cultural differences can all play a role in making it difficult for states to reach agreement. In Chapter 1, we looked at some of the features of multilateral diplomacy. Here, we examine two particular challenges: cultural differences and variations in national negotiating styles.

▩ *Does Culture Matter?*

Early in the international organization process, diplomacy was the province of a small elite in the foreign ministries of the predominant European countries. French was a common language (and before that, Latin). Beginning with The Hague Conferences, however, that quickly changed as Japan, China, the Ottoman Empire, Latin American countries, the United States, and many others became active participants. Cross-cultural and language differences became potentially important variables in negotiation. And while professionals in foreign ministries (or the Department of State) might be trained in other languages and cultures, the same does not necessarily hold for people from other governmental ministries who have increasingly become involved in diplomacy as the scope of issues in international relations has broadened. With officials from many different agencies ranging from defense to health, science, and agriculture now involved in negotiating roles, but not being trained as diplomats, sensitivity to cultural differences and ability to accommodate them are likely to be diminished. The same is true for private business and NGOs, elected representatives, and political appointees to international conference delegations. The potential for cultural misunderstandings getting in the way of negotiators' efforts to reach a common solution is considerable.

During the 1994 UN-sponsored International Conference on Population and Development in Cairo, Joan Dunlop, president of the International Women's Health Coalition asserted, "It is really extraordinary that in an international U.N. forum, we are talking about sexual and reproductive health and the empowerment of women. These are things that many people of different cultures can understand." Not necessarily. The Arabic translation of "family leave" describes spouses leaving each other after a birth. The Russian text suggests that the whole family is going on vacation. In Russian, "reproductive health" means health that reproduces itself again and again. The concept of female empowerment has no meaning to Chinese without knowing which kind of power is being discussed—personal, political, or physical (Mingst and Warkentin 1996: 171). The problem of cross-cultural meanings of words can be a major problem in any negotiation, but particularly so in the multiparty, multilingual settings of most multilateral diplomacy.

There is a lively debate among scholars and practitioners about whether culture matters in multilateral negotiations. It is not just a matter of language and translation, but of "mind systems" or modes of thought that differ, as well as of ideas that cannot be rendered accurately in another language (Bozeman 1971: 5). As an example, Russian language and culture contain no equivalent to the concept of mediation in dispute resolution—hence, the phenomenon of a neutral third party helping parties to a dispute find a mutually acceptable resolution is incomprehensible.

Some experts on negotiation minimize the role of cultural factors in negotiation because of the socialization that occurs in the international diplomatic culture. Yet we cannot eliminate the effect of cross-cultural differences. "Culture can affect the process of negotiation and the participants' negotiating styles as well as the outcomes of the deliberations" (Mingst and Warkentin 1996: 172). In cross-cultural negotiations, value differences matter.

Glen Fisher, a former diplomat with training in social anthropology, argues that the more pronounced the cultural differences between the negotiating parties, the greater the "potential for misunderstanding" and the more time they will lose "talking past each other" (Fisher 1980). Differences in values, mannerisms, types of verbal and nonverbal communication, and understandings of status, Fisher found, can have a negative effect on parties' trust in each other and ability to communicate even before they get to the substance of negotiation. A number of studies have now been done of differing national negotiating styles, and these are useful for understanding some of the dynamics affecting multilateral negotiations.

▪ Negotiating Styles

Different countries also have different negotiating styles, largely based on the value of social relationships, status, and face. In non-Western cultures, group interests define individual needs, producing what Cohen (1997) calls a "high context" negotiating style. "Face" or one's standing in the eyes of the group must be preserved above all else. Members of such cultures are "highly sensitive to the effect of what they say on others. Language is . . . a device for preserving and promoting social interests as much as a means for transmitting information. High-context speakers must weigh their words carefully." Personal relationships are key to any conduct of business and must be cultivated before there can be any frank discussions (Cohen 1997: 32). In negotiations, states then begin with establishing basic principles, preferring to work on the details later, once personal relationships are solidified.

In contrast, Americans, Australians, or other westerners who come from "low-context" cultures where individualism is strong value individual rights, needs, self-expression, and personal enterprise. "Indirection is much disliked. 'Straight-from-the-shoulder' talk is admired. . . . People have little time or patience for 'beating around the bush' and wish to get down to business and move on to another problem. Why waste time on social trivialities. . . . results are definitely more important than relationships." Because language is a means of conveying information, content matters. "Face" does not carry the same importance as in a high-context culture. Nonverbal gestures don't matter much (Cohen 1997: 33). Thus, most Western and especially American negotiators prefer to get right to the details, deriving principles after the fact.

The contrast in negotiating style can be dramatic. As discussed in Chapter 5, the "ASEAN Way" is a system of consensual decisionmaking through discussion and consultation in which open disagreement and controversy are avoided at all costs. A key objective is maintaining harmony among members. Prolonged consultation, mutual adjustment, synthesis when possible, and postponement when necessary tend to characterize the interactions among the ASEAN members. American negotiators, however, are "generally more anxious for agreements because 'they are always in a hurry' and basically 'problem solving oriented.' . . . Their catchphrase might be, 'Some solution is better than no solution'" (Cohen 1997: 114). While high-context negotiators may prefer informal, unwritten arrangements that allow all participants to save face and to minimize unpleasant concessions, low-context negotiators, and most especially the United States, prefer to spell out agreements and obligations, resolve ambiguities, and bind participants.

In the case of human rights negotiations, culture clearly matters, but it does not matter all the time. In the negotiations on economic issues, we would not expect culture to matter as much as differences in negotiating styles. Both could matter when issues of national security are at stake. Yet how states approach these areas of negotiations may also vary. Some from the developing world take an "axiomatic-deductive" approach, starting with general principles, preferring to leave particular details to be worked out later. The Western developed countries have tended toward a "factual-inductive approach," preferring to get down to discussion of concrete details and resolving specific issues before the broader principles are crystallized. Yet over time and with repeated negotiations the two sides may be able to reach agreement, or one or both sides may change beliefs and therefore their policy objectives, or they may never agree.

■ Getting Agreement

States have adopted several techniques to facilitate agreement and cooperation. One approach has been the use of consensus decisionmaking discussed in earlier chapters. This has been steadily increasing in the UN, where over three-quarters of the General Assembly's resolutions are approved by consensus, and in the Security Council since the early 1990s. It marks decisionmaking in many regional organizations and has been adopted for the WTO. Although coalitions, blocs, and individual states may be just as active in trying to forge consensus as in marshaling votes, the outcome tends to be less divisive because states' positions are not readily apparent. Consensus procedures, however, can obscure divisions and, hence, make implementation of measures problematic. They can also contribute to inertia if there is no agreement, as demonstrated in the breakdown of WTO talks in Cancun in 2003.

A second technique for facilitating agreement is "power steering," which involves getting agreement first among a small group of key states, then getting other states to accept their recommendation. It has been used by the five permanent members of the Security Council and by the major contributors who now "power-steer" the budgetary and programmatic agenda through what is known as the Geneva process. That approach could well be extended to include countries most directly affected by issues as a way to decrease the number of participating parties.

Third, leadership makes a significant difference in facilitating multilateral negotiation, as discussed in Chapter 1. Key individuals can mute the adverse effects of cultural and political differences through the use of a variety of negotiating and mediation techniques to construct acceptable bargains. Power matters, to be sure, and powerful states cannot be ignored, but power does not necessarily equate with leadership and diplomatic skill. Multilateralism requires both. That often comes from representatives of small states or middle powers, not necessarily from major powers. It may also come from a coalition of states or from NGOs or from an international civil servant. Leadership may determine whether the major issues of the day in peace and security, economic well-being, human rights, and the environment are effectively addressed. It is to those issues that we now turn in subsequent chapters.

■ **Suggested Further Reading**

Alger, Chadwick F., Gene M. Lyons, and John E. Trent, eds. (1995) *The United Nations System: The Policies of Member States.* Tokyo: United Nations University Press.

Bozeman, Adda B. (1971) *The Future of Law in a Multicultural World.* Princeton: Princeton University Press.

Cohen, Raymond. (1997) *Negotiating Across Cultures: International Communication in an Interdependent World.* Rev. ed. Washington, D.C.: U.S. Institute for Peace Press.

Karns, Margaret P., and Karen A. Mingst, eds. (1990) *The United States and Multilateral Institutions. Patterns of Changing Instrumentality and Influence.* Boston: Unwin Hyman.

Luck, Edward C. (1999) *Mixed Messages. American Politics and International Organization 1919–1999.* Washington, D.C.: Brookings Institution Press.

Ruggie, John Gerard, ed. (1993) *Multilateralism Matters: The Theory and Praxis of an Institutional Form.* New York: Columbia University Press.

■ **Internet Resources**

The Commonwealth: www.thecommonwealth.org
Non-Aligned Movement: www.nam.gov.za/

PART 3

The Need
for Global Governance

8

The Search for Peace and Security

■ Case Study: Somalia as a Watershed

In 1991 and 1992, civil order in Somalia totally collapsed as warring clans seized control of different parts of the country. Widespread famine and chaos accompanied the fighting, forcing hundreds of thousands of civilians to the brink of starvation. Control of food was a vital political resource for the Somali warlords and a currency to pay the mercenary gangs who formed their militias. In November 1992, with as many as one thousand Somalis dying every day and three-fourths of Somalia's children under the age of five already dead, UN Secretary-General Boutros-Ghali informed the Security Council that the situation "had deteriorated beyond the point at which it is susceptible to the peacekeeping treatment. . . . The Security Council now has no alternative but to decide to adopt more forceful measures" (UN Security Council 1992: 2).

The UN was slow to react because the Security Council assumed that it needed the consent of the Somali warlords to provide humanitarian assistance, as in traditional peacekeeping operations. A contingent of five hundred lightly armed Pakistani peacekeeping troops had been deployed in August 1992 as the UN Operation in Somalia (UNOSOM I) with a mandate to protect relief workers, but it was totally inadequate for the task at hand.

On December 3, 1992, under Resolution 794, the Security Council authorized a large U.S.-led military/humanitarian intervention including 26,000 U.S. troops, the Unified Task Force or UNITAF, known to the American public as Operation Restore Hope. Its goal was to secure ports and airfields, protect relief shipments and workers, and assist humanitarian relief efforts. At this point, there were forty INGOs operating in Somalia, almost all of them Northern-based groups, including the major relief groups. The secretary-general also wanted UNITAF to impose a ceasefire and disarm the factions, but U.S. leaders (in both the outgoing G. H. W. Bush and incoming Clinton administrations) were reluctant to enlarge the mission's objectives, preferring to commit U.S. forces only to limited humanitarian tasks. President Bush thought the Somali operation would be "an easy victory"—one that would provide excellent media coverage of

277

U.S. soldiers delivering food aid to starving Somalis, and by January 20 when he left office, the soldiers would be on their way home. This important misjudgment by American officials of the political (and military) situation in Somalia would prove fatal. Their disagreement with UN officials over objectives also produced considerable friction between the White House and the UN headquarters in New York and complicated relations between the various UN contingents in Somalia.

Despite these problems, the U.S.-led effort was largely successful in achieving its humanitarian objectives, supplying food to those in need and imposing a de facto ceasefire in areas of its deployment. Yet, the larger tasks of peacemaking in Somalia remained unfulfilled. This led to recurring problems in 1993, as UNITAF was replaced by UNOSOM II—a smaller force lacking much of the heavy equipment and airpower the U.S. had brought to Somalia. UNOSOM II, with 20,000 troops and 8,000 logistical personnel from thirty-three countries, included 5,000 U.S. soldiers (as compared to 26,000 in UNITAF). It was authorized to use force when disarming the factions, but that exposed the peacekeepers to increased risk as some of the militias—especially those led by General Mohamed Farah Aidid—resisted such efforts. When twenty-three Pakistani soldiers were killed by Aidid's soldiers in June 1993, UNSOM II gave up any pretense of impartiality and targeted General Aidid for elimination. As one observer noted (Conroy 1994: 12), this converted the UN's role from neutral peacekeeper to active belligerent, putting UNOSOM "in the worst of all possible worlds, which past peacekeepers had scrupulously avoided . . . [and] made it one of the players in the conflict."

Four months later, in October 1993, eighteen U.S. soldiers were killed by Aidid's soldiers and the body of one dragged through the streets of Mogadishu, leading to a public outcry in the United States that echoed unease in other countries over the UN's role in Somalia. Almost ten years later, it inspired the book and movie *Blackhawk Down*. Nowhere else except in the United States was the reaction as far-reaching, however, and little note was taken of the hundreds of Somali dead. President Clinton announced that the U.S. contingent would be strengthened temporarily, but that all forces would be withdrawn by March 1994. Peacekeeping operations in Haiti and Bosnia were also affected as the administration rethought its commitment to the UN, especially to operations that entailed risk of casualties. Within days, in fact, the U.S. halted the landing of American troops and advisers in Haiti where they were to participate in the UN-aided transition to a democratic government—all because demonstrators in Port-au-Prince threatened to create "another Somalia." Six months later, in April 1994, the United States blocked any meaningful response by the Security Council to the unfolding genocide in Rwanda, unwilling even to call the Hutu massacres of Tutsi "genocide" or to contemplate another international intervention in a messy African civil conflict. Eight months later, in June 1994, President Clinton released Presidential Decision Directive (PDD) 25 that sharply restricted the circumstances under which the United States would support, let alone participate in UN peacekeeping operations.

UNISOM remains a controversial undertaking (see Clarke and Herbst 1996; Agnelli and Murphy 1995). It began at the height of post–Cold War enthusiasm for UN peacekeeping and precipitated a significant retreat from such activities. Because the United States wanted to keep the operation short, and was afraid to risk the lives of American soldiers, the Somali warlords gained leverage by targeting U.S. and other UN forces. After the U.S. withdrew its troops in March 1994, it became only a matter of time before all UN forces were withdrawn. UN operations in Somalia finally ceased in March 1995, having succeeded in ending the famine but not in helping the Somalis to reestablish a national government or to end their internal strife, something they only began to do in 2001.

Somalia became a symbol of a failed UN post–Cold War peacekeeping effort and a set of lessons, rightly or wrongly, for future peacekeeping in situations of state failure, civil war, and complex humanitarian disaster. It is a critical case for understanding the dilemmas posed by the changing nature of armed conflicts in the post–Cold War world; by complex humanitarian crises and state failure in an era when human security is beginning to be seen as more important than state security; and by the international community's efforts to use more muscular military force in dealing with conflicts.

■ Wars as the Genesis for Pieces of Security Governance

War is *the* fundamental problem in international politics; it has also been a primary factor motivating the creation of IGOs from the Concert of Europe in the nineteenth century, to the League of Nations and the United Nations in the twentieth century. Underlying functionalist theory is the premise that getting states to work together in solving practical problems of international relations will build the conditions for enduring peace. International law was traditionally seen as providing the rules that would help create order in the relations among states, and international courts or arbitration procedures would provide means to settle legal disputes peacefully. Hence, despite being the most destructive century in human history, the twentieth was also the century of building pieces of governance for preventing war.

Yet the nature of wars and conflicts has changed in significant ways in the last fifty years and concepts of security have also begun to shift. Studies of war have shown a sharp decrease in the incidence of interstate war, or wars between two or more states. The number of intrastate conflicts or conflicts within states resulting from the collapse of an already weak state as in Somalia, ethnic conflict as in the former Yugoslavia and Rwanda, or civil war among rival groups as in Angola, has risen dramatically. Also on the increase are civil wars that become internationalized, that is, where groups or other states intervene, as in the Congo and Sierra Leone. Yet, the UN Charter was written to deal with interstate conflicts, as was the League of Nations Covenant preceding it. Most developing countries remain jealous of their sovereignty and wary of commitments that compromise the principle of nonintervention in states' domestic affairs.

Complicating many intrastate conflicts are humanitarian disasters resulting from the fighting, from ethnic cleansing or genocide, from the collapse of governmental authority, and from famine and disease. Yet traditionally, security in the Westphalian system meant *state* security—the security of borders, control over population, and freedom from interference in the government's sovereignty over its internal affairs. With the body of internationally recognized human rights norms steadily expanding in the second half of the twentieth century, the balance between the rights of sovereign states and the rights of people began to shift. Increasingly, one finds suggestions that *human* security should take precedence over security of governments or states. It is this shift that provides legitimacy to pressures for armed intervention to protect human beings against the violence of governments, paramilitary forces, militias, and police.

The changing nature of conflicts and complex humanitarian disasters are two challenges to peace in the twenty-first century. The others are weapons of mass destruction (chemical, biological, and nuclear) and terrorism. None are new. Efforts to deal with the first date to the earliest days of the League of Nations and the UN; efforts to deal with the latter began with the rise of international terrorism in the 1970s. Both gained new momentum after the attacks on the World Trade Center and Pentagon in 2001.

The pieces of security governance include many of the core elements of international law and organizations (see Figure 8.1). The UN provides

---

Figure 8.1   Pieces of Security Governance

- A global IGO
- Norms on the use of force
- International conventions
- Regional collective defense treaties
- Enforcement mechanisms
- Peaceful settlement mechanisms
- Peacekeeping
- Humanitarian intervention
- Peacebuilding

Figure 8.2   Global and Regional Security IGOs

United Nations

Security Council	International Atomic Energy Agency (IAEA)
General Assembly	Dept. of Peacekeeping Operations (DPKO)
Secretary-General	Office for Coordination of Humanitarian Affairs (OCHA)
International Court of Justice	High Commissioner for Refugees (UNHCR)

Regional IGO Venues for Security

Europe	Asia	Middle East	Africa	Latin America
NATO	ASEAN	Arab League	AU	OAS
WEU	ARF	GCC	ECOWAS	
OSCE				
CIS				

Figure 8.3   Security-Related INGOs

Peace Groups	Disarmament Groups
Women's International League for Peace and Freedom	Abolition 20
Stockholm International Peace Research Institute	Greenpeace
International Peace Academy	ICBL
	International Physicians for the Prevention of Nuclear War

Humanitarian Relief Groups

ICRC	Save the Children Federation
Doctors Without Borders	World Vision
CARE	Catholic Relief Services
Oxfam	Lutheran Federation

the global structures for dealing with security issues, and each of the five major geographic regions has at least one IGO dealing with security issues (see Figure 8.2). As Inis Claude (1964: 198) noted in his classic text, *Swords into Plowshares,* "Collective approaches to peace must rest upon assumptions concerning the nature and causes of war. . . . various approaches to peace through international organization have been advocated, formulated, and attempted, each of them resting upon a distinctive conception of the nature of war and therefore emphasizing a correspondingly distinctive solution for the problem of war." In addition, many NGOs have long been active in trying to promote peaceful settlement of conflicts, disarmament, and humanitarian relief (see Figure 8.3).

■ *IGO Venues for Security*

The idea of a global organization to promote security among states was born in the early years of the twentieth century and promoted by a few prominent statesmen and a number of peace groups during World War I and again during World War II. The history of these efforts is covered in Chapters 3 and 4. Regional security organizations were a product largely of the Cold War and grew out of the competing alliance systems of the two superpowers. Much of this history in covered in Chapter 5.[1]

Both the League and the UN reflected convictions that a permanent international organization made up of all peace-loving states could provide a framework for preventing future wars. The League of Nations Covenant and the UN Charter focused extensively on basic principles for preventing war, on mechanisms for peaceful settlement of disputes, and on provisions for enforcement actions. Both recognized the special prerogatives of major powers with respect to peace and security and the necessity of a small decisionmaking body with authority to take action on behalf of all members. A key difference was the league requirement for unanimity among council members in contrast to the UN Security Council requirement for a majority of the nonpermanent members, coupled with no opposition from any permanent member (the veto power).

Both the UN and the League of Nations were also based on the concept of collective security articulated by U.S. President Woodrow Wilson as an alternative to the traditional balance of power politics that had frequently led to wars. Regional security arrangements have generally been either traditional alliances—formal or informal commitments for mutual aid in case of attack—or collective defense organizations that involve more institutional development and commitments on the part of members.

How do global and regional security organizations relate to one another? Chapter VIII of the UN Charter recognizes the rights and responsibilities of regional organizations to "make every effort to achieve peaceful settlement of local disputes" before referring them to the Security Council.

When a regional organization seeks to use force, however, Security Council authorization is required. This is supposed to ensure the UN's primacy with respect to enforcement. In 1994, for example, the Security Council authorized NATO to take a series of actions in the former Yugoslavia. In another instance, however, Security Council authorization of the Economic Community of West African States (ECOWAS) operation in Liberia (ECOMOG) in late 1992 came three years after the operation began. The NATO bombing of the former Yugoslavia and Kosovo in 1999 was never authorized by the Security Council, which contributed to the intense controversy over the legitimacy of those actions, similar to the U.S.-led war in Iraq.

The UN, regional organizations, and NGOs utilize different governance approaches to peace and security problems. ASEAN, the OAU, and OAS, for example, frequently use preventive diplomacy and mediation. The UN, Arab League, ECOWAS, and European Union have employed sanctions while NATO took on enforcement and peacekeeping roles in the 1990s for the first time, as did ECOWAS. The ASEAN Regional Forum illustrates informal dialogue as an approach to security cooperation. Some NGOs focus primarily on arms control and disarmament issues. Others are very much involved in humanitarian relief. Underlying all approaches are the norms related to the use of armed force.

Norms Related to the Use of Force

Outlawing war.   Although the league's covenant required member states to respect and preserve the territorial integrity and political independence of states and to try different methods of dispute settlement, it contained no explicit prohibition on the use of force to settle disputes. In 1928, most states signed the Pact of Paris or Kellogg-Briand Pact, "to condemn recourse to war for the solution of international controversies, and renounce it as an instrument of national policy." This was the basis for incorporation into Article 2 (sections 3 and 4) of the UN Charter the obligation of all members to settle disputes by peaceful means and "to refrain in their international relations from the threat or use of force against the territorial integrity or political independence of any state." These obligations have often been honored more in the breach than in fact, leading some legal scholars to suggest that Article 2(4) is effectively dead (Arend and Beck 1993). The reality is more complicated. The use of force for territorial annexation is now widely accepted as illegitimate, witness the broad condemnation of Iraq's invasion of Kuwait in 1990 and the large number of states that contributed to the U.S.-led multilateral effort to reverse that occupation. The use of force in self-defense against armed attack is accepted, but the response must be proportional to the provocation. A large majority of states accept the legitimacy of using force to promote self-determination, to replace illegitimate regimes, and to correct past injustices. Two cases illustrate the disagreements that can arise, however, over legitimate uses of force. In the first case, although the United States contended that the government of Manuel Noriega in Panama was illegitimate and therefore the United States was justified in using force to remove it in 1989, there was near universal condemnation of the American action. In the second case, the UN Security Council refused in 2003 to authorize use of force against Iraq, leading the United States to form an ad hoc coalition for war.

Promoting humanitarian concerns.   Other important norms relating to the use of force include the humanitarian norms contained in the four 1949 Geneva Conventions, two additional Protocols concluded in 1977, and treaties dealing with poison gases, chemical and biological weapons, and landmines. These are designed to protect civilians, prisoners of war, and wounded soldiers as well as to ban particular methods of war (e.g., do not bomb hospitals) and certain weapons that cause unnecessary suffering (e.g., poisonous gases). Together these establish the legal basis for war crimes. International human rights law, including the Universal Declaration of Human Rights, the International Covenant on Political and Civil Rights, and the conventions on torture, genocide, refugees, and children, together with the fundamental principle of nondiscrimination between peoples enshrined in Article 1 of the UN Charter, establish the basis for crimes against humanity. These are all now incorporated in Article 8 of the International Criminal Court Statute. (See Figure 8.4.) Some of the laws regarding armed conflict apply only to interstate wars and not to civil wars.

What is to be done, however, when states or nonstate actors ignore

---

Figure 8.4   Crimes Against Humanity

- Attack against or any effort to exterminate a civilian population
- Enslavement
- Deportation or forcible transfer of population
- Imprisonment or other severe deprivation of physical liberty
- Torture
- Rape, sexual slavery, forced prostitution, pregnancy, and sterilization
- Persecution of any group or collectivity based upon political, racial, national, ethnic, cultural, religious, or gender grounds
- Enforced disappearance of persons

humanitarian norms and large numbers of people are at risk? Since 1990, there has been a growing debate over whether there is an emerging norm legitimizing humanitarian intervention. The Genocide Convention was the first to admit the possibility of UN action under the charter to prevent or suppress crimes against humanity. Ad hoc war crimes tribunals such as the Nuremberg and Tokyo trials after World War II or Yugoslav and Rwandan tribunals, along with the International Criminal Court, provide means to prosecute those accused of crimes. Military intervention to enforce compliance is a different story, although the Universal Declaration of Human Rights warns that people whose rights are violated may "be compelled to have recourse, as a last resort, to rebellion against tyranny and oppression." In other words, there is a moral right to resist, but is the use of armed force to rescue others a logical next step?

The evolution of human rights and humanitarian norms has placed new demands on the UN, other IGOs, and international actors to curb abuses, with the media and global networks of NGOs publicizing situations involving mass starvation, ethnic cleansing, genocide, or mutilations like those by rival groups in Sierra Leone and Liberia. This has led to debate over humanitarian intervention that invokes differing views of state sovereignty and ethical views derived from the "Just War" tradition.

Although primarily a Western and Christian doctrine dating from medieval times, Just War concepts also draw on ancient Greek philosophy and are found in the Koran. The Just War tradition sets out ethical bases for using force other than in self-defense. (See Figure 8.5.) These touch on issues of who has authority to make decisions on use of force (e.g., the Security Council); causes justifying force (e.g., massive violations of

---

Figure 8.5   The Just War Tradition and the Use of Force

- Right authority
- Just cause
- Right intentions
- Last resort
- Proportionality
- Reasonable hope of achieving the desired outcome
- Relatively rapid withdrawal of forces

human rights); when force may be justified (e.g., when all other possibilities have been exhausted); the means used and likelihood of a successful outcome.

"*Le droit d'ingérence*" (the right to interfere), first popularized by the NGO Médecins Sans Frontières (Doctors Without Borders), gives priority to humanitarian aid to victims of war over respect for state sovereignty. NGOs, civil society activists, and IGOs have gradually pushed for acceptance of national and international accountability, and for using human rights norms to judge state conduct.

Two senior UN officials (Tharoor and Daws 2001: 23) summarized the controversy over humanitarian intervention: "To its proponents, it marks the coming of age of the imperative of action in the face of human rights abuses, over the citadels of state sovereignty. To its detractors, it is an oxymoron, a pretext for military intervention often devoid of legal sanction, selectively deployed and achieving only ambiguous ends." As UN Secretary-General Kofi Annan said in his 1999 address to the General Assembly (Annan 1999b), "State sovereignty . . . is being redefined by the forces of globalization and international cooperation. The State is now widely understood to be the servant of its people, and not vice versa . . . [with] renewed consciousness of the right of every individual to control his or her own destiny. These parallel developments . . . demand of us a willingness to think anew—about how the United Nations responds to the political, human rights and humanitarian crises affecting so much of the world."

His speech triggered a major General Assembly debate on the subject of sovereignty and intervention. The UN Charter itself makes clear that sovereignty cannot stand in the way of responses to aggression and threats to peace or states' obligations to meet their commitments under the charter. International customary and treaty law limit sovereignty. And, increasingly, sovereignty is interpreted as carrying responsibilities, including the responsibility to protect persons. The large-scale crises of the 1990s showed that force may be the only means to halt genocide, ethnic cleansing, and other crimes against humanity. Again, Kofi Annan (1999b) captured the problem when he said, "If humanitarian intervention is, indeed, an unacceptable assault on sovereignty, how should we respond to a Rwanda, to a Srebrenica—to gross and systematic violations of human rights that offend every precept of our common humanity? . . . But surely no legal principle—not even sovereignty—can ever shield crimes against humanity." Who, then, is responsible? The answer is the "community of states and ultimately everyone" (Vincent 1986: 127). This leads to the debate over who can legitimately authorize humanitarian intervention, especially involving armed force.

Given their colonial experiences, many Asian and African countries are skeptical about altruistic claims by Western countries. Along with Russia and China, they have been insistent on Security Council authorization as a prerequisite for intervention. It is their protection against new forms of imperialism. Developing countries were not indifferent to the consequences of state failure, however. In supporting ECOWAS' intervention in Liberia, for example, Zimbabwe took the position that "when there is no government in being and there is just chaos in the country," domestic affairs should be qualified to mean "affairs within a peaceful environment" (quoted in Damrosch 1993: 364). In the debate over whether interventions by regional organizations such as those by ECOWAS and by NATO in Kosovo require Security Council authorization, the Non-Aligned Movement and G-77 adopted declarations in 1999 and 2000 stating, "We reject the so-called 'right of humanitarian intervention' [without Security Council authorization] which has no legal basis in the UN Charter or in the general principles of international law" (available at www.nam.gov.za).

The controversy over NATO's 1999 intervention in Kosovo led UN Secretary-General Kofi Annan to call for examination of the legal, moral, operational, and political questions relating to humanitarian intervention. In response, an independent International Commission on Intervention and State Sovereignty (ICISS) was established. Led by former Australian Foreign Minister Gareth Evans and Mohamed Sahnoun of Algeria, the ICISS proposed six criteria for military intervention for human protection: right authority, just cause, right intention, last resort, proportional means, and reasonable prospects. The "threshold" criteria include "large scale loss of life, actual or apprehended, with genocidal intent or not, which is the product either of deliberate state action, or state neglect or inability to act, or a failed state situation; or large scale 'ethnic cleansing,' actual or apprehended, whether carried out by killing, forced expulsion, acts of terror or rape" (ICISS 2001a: 32). "Our purpose," the commission's report noted, "is not to license aggression with fine words, or to provide strong states with new rationales for doubtful strategic designs, but to strengthen the order of states by providing for clear guidelines to guide concerted international action in those exceptional circumstances when violence within a state menaces all peoples" (ibid.: 35).

International law requires multiple cases to demonstrate the existence of a new customary practice. So, too, Finnemore and Sikkink (1998) argue that when new norms are raised, there is a period of conflict between advocates of the new and supporters of the old. If a large enough group of states are prepared to adopt the new, it will replace the old. Those violating the old norm can set in motion "norm cascades" that result in new norms replacing old. The debate over whether there is a norm of humanitarian intervention, therefore, is likely to persist for several years. Views on its importance as well as that of other security-related norms will be strongly influenced by different international relations theories.

▪ Linking International Relations Theories and Security Governance

International relations theorists differ sharply in their views of appropriate strategies for responding to the use of armed force and conflicts. Realists come in "hard" and "soft" varieties when dealing with threats of force, breaches of the peace, and the search for ways to settle conflicts peacefully. The "hard" variety hold firm to traditional realist views about states' likely use of force. They don't see many differences between the dynamics that give rise to interstate and intrastate conflicts. Security dilemmas affect parties to both. In realists' eyes, balance of power and force itself are key means to resolve conflicts. Hence, other states might deny arms to the stronger side of a conflict or provide them to the weaker side in an effort to create a balance of power. Should any consideration be given to intervention by a third party, for realists, only great powers, and especially the United States, have the resources to influence the parties or intervene effectively. Yet their incentives to do so are often limited.

The "soft" variety of realists comes closer to liberals in some respects as they envisage a broader range of options and actors. Diplomacy and mediation are among the options "soft" realists consider valuable for dealing with conflicts and use of force, in order to change parties' cost/benefit analyses in favor of peaceful settlement versus war. They also recognize the role of international organizations and states other than great powers as interveners.

Liberals have traditionally been the primary supporters of international law and organization as approaches to peace. Consequently, they envision a variety of roles for parties outside a conflict situation—what are termed third parties—in the search for peaceful means to settle disputes, avert war, stop fighting once it has started, secure a negotiated settlement, and build conditions for lasting peace. Both NGOs and IGOs, as well as individuals and ad hoc groups, are among the actors that may contribute to peace processes.

Most security governance is based on liberal international relations theory. Yet, it is important to draw on the work of multiple schools of thought. Constructivism, for example, is increasingly being applied to explain the evolution and role of norms. In spite of the rich literatures on both conflict and conflict resolution, there is no definitive theory setting forth clear conditions under which wars will occur or peace will be secured. The contextual factors shaping human choices—the choice for war or the choice to settle a dispute—defy tidy conclusions. In short, we know a lot about both, but not enough to lay out a formula for governance.

The broadest category of security governance "pieces" is also the oldest: mechanisms for peaceful settlement of disputes. It is to that we now turn.

■ Mechanisms for the Peaceful Settlement of Disputes

As early as the Greek city-states, there was agreement about the desirability of settling disputes peacefully. The 1899 and 1908 Hague Conferences produced Conventions for the Pacific Settlement of International Disputes, laying the foundations for mechanisms still in use today. These assume that war is a deliberate choice for settling a dispute and that it is possible to create mechanisms to influence actors' choices. For example, one assumption is that war can result from ignorance and that providing information through an independent commission of inquiry can change the choice. Another assumption is that states often get themselves into "dead-end streets" from which a third-party mediator can help them escape. The Hague Conventions established the international community's stake in preventing war. They created mechanisms for third-party roles variously labeled good offices, inquiry, mediation, conciliation, adjudication, and arbitration that were incorporated into the League of Nations Covenant and Chapter VI of the UN Charter. The latter specifies a sequence of ways the Security Council can promote peaceful settlement of disputes, from inquiry to mediation.

The involvement of the UN or any IGO, NGO, individual, state or coalition of states, or ad hoc group in efforts to find a peaceful settlement of a conflict is a third-party intervention. Some high-profile situations such as the former Yugoslavia or the Middle East generate multiple third-party efforts. Sometimes those efforts occur sequentially; sometimes they are simultaneous; but they are often messy and rife with questions of who does what, when, and where. The post–Cold War era witnessed an explosion of conflicts, of peacemaking efforts, and of systematic efforts by scholars and practitioners working together to study and draw lessons from them (Crocker, Hampson, and Aall 1999, 2001; Stedman, Rothchild, and Cousens 2002).

There is little consensus among scholars and practitioners about the requirements for successful third-party intervention, preventing or ending war, and getting parties to conflicts to implement peace agreements, although there are many conclusions about conditions that *may* contribute to success or failure. The use of peaceful settlement mechanisms, however, does not necessarily mean no use of force. Force can be critical to securing a peaceful outcome in some situations, such as Bosnia in 1995. Every situation is unique. Determining who can most effectively intervene, what means are required, and what political goals should be set are key issues. Should the parties to the conflict be separated, should the weaker side be armed to secure a balance of power, should a negotiated ceasefire be the goal, should interveners seek an agreement ending the dispute but leave implementation to the parties, or should they seek agreement and assist with implementation? Finally, what constitutes success? Is it a permanent end to a dispute (the Namibian case); a freeze on active fighting (Cyprus); a short- to medium-term end to violence (Cambodia); getting parties who previously would not speak to each other to meet face-to-face (Oslo peace process); or building the foundations for long-term peace (Kosovo, East Timor, and Afghanistan)? Many answers to the who, what, and when questions depend upon the stage of the conflict at which intervention occurs. Trying to deal with a conflict situation before the level of armed violence escalates rapidly can be very different from trying to find a peaceful solution to a conflict with high levels of violence that has been going on for many years.

■ Preventive Diplomacy

In the words of former UN Secretary-General Boutros Boutros-Ghali (1992: 45), "Preventive diplomacy is action to prevent disputes from arising between parties, to prevent existing disputes from escalating into conflicts and to limit the spread of the latter when they occur." Most often, it takes the form of diplomatic efforts, sometimes coupled with economic sanctions or arms embargoes. From late 1992 until 2001, however, the UN deployed 1,000 peacekeeping troops to prevent the spread of violence from other regions of the former Yugoslavia into Macedonia. This preventive deployment was an important innovation.

Preventive diplomacy is intended to change the calculus of parties regarding the purposes to be served by political violence and to deter them from choosing to escalate the level of conflict. This is far easier to do early in a conflict, when the level of violence is low. It becomes increasingly difficult as violence grows. Hence, successful preventive diplomacy depends upon its timeliness. But can it succeed? Realists tend to be skeptical, especially with ethnic conflicts. There is ample evidence, however, that preventive diplomacy can succeed and that "the realist argument . . . underestimates the interests at stake for the international community and overestimates the cost differential between acting early and acting late" (Jentleson 2001: 251). The costs of waiting tend to be much higher than those for preventive action. One study estimates that had the U.S. and Europeans succeeded in preventing the Bosnian war, their costs would have been $33.3 billion, as opposed to the estimated $53.7 billion they spent on intervention (up to the Dayton Accords in 1995). Similar estimates show the U.S. and others spent $7.3 billion in Somalia, compared with an estimated $1.5 billion to prevent the conflict. Preventive deployment in Macedonia cost $0.3 billion compared with an estimated $15 billion had that conflict escalated to intermediate levels (Brown and Rosecrance 1999: 225).

Preventing conflicts is rarely easy, but studies show the opportunities missed in Somalia, Bosnia, Rwanda, Kosovo, and Zaire (Sahnoun 1994; Jentleson 1999). This has provoked debate about early warning systems. Steps have been taken to increase the UN Secretariat's capacity for intelligence gathering on situations that might threaten international peace or produce humanitarian disasters (such as famine or genocide), but whether they would make a difference depends on the extent to which the secretariat and Security Council members are willing to act. In Rwanda, there were seven UN agencies, ten large NGOs, and diplomats from most nations of the world reporting developments. There were at least five summit meetings of regional leaders under OAU and other auspices in 1995 and 1996. There was ample information available about the severity of the looming crisis. Yet, in April 1994, the UN Security Council decided to withdraw its observers from Rwanda, just as the massacres of Tutsi were escalating. There were also plenty of warnings prior to the disintegration of Yugoslavia in 1991. The United States and the European Community undertook a number of diplomatic efforts, coupled with economic sanctions, but lacked clear, unambiguous goals and appropriate leverage. It was a classic case of missed opportunities and belated intervention.

Yet, preventive diplomacy has had numerous success stories. One important actor has been the OSCE High Commissioner for National Minorities, a post established in 1992 after the EU failed to prevent Yugoslavia's bloody dissolution. The commissioner is independent, impartial, and focuses on noncoercive problemsolving. As Max van der Stoel, the first commissioner, notes (1999: 69), "The two principal instruments for conflict prevention [are] early action and early warning. . . . I collect and receive information on national minority issues from a very wide variety of sources. . . . I travel to areas where the minority in question is particularly sizable, where problems may be acute, or where the local situation may be indicative of a broader problem. I meet with local authorities, minority representatives, and other relevant personalities. . . . My task is to try to prevent violent conflict." The OSCE commissioner has been active in many European states such as Ukraine, Croatia, Estonia, and Macedonia dealing with national minority issues of jobs, education, linguistic rights, and political participation.

Another example of regional preventive diplomacy involves the competing claims in the South China Sea. The disputes threatened to escalate into armed clashes among China, Vietnam, the Philippines, Indonesia, Brunei, Malaysia, and Taiwan in the late 1980s and early 1990s, when the 1982 Law of the Sea Convention's rules were to take effect. Yet, the countries had little experience of cooperation and no regional IGO to provide mechanisms for third-party settlement. A former Indonesian diplomat and a Canadian academic devised a track-two diplomatic approach of informal workshops, starting with practical issues rather than the territorial and jurisdictional issues, to build confidence among the participants. Over a decade, thirty-two meetings took place and covered issues from marine science and navigational safety to law. In July 1992, they got ASEAN members to issue a formal Declaration on the South China Sea, pledging to resolve their territorial or jurisdictional disputes by "peaceful means through dialogue and negotiation. . . . to exercise self-restraint in order not to complicate the situation" (Djalal and Townsend-Gault 1999: 109-133). In 2002, ASEAN members approved an agreement with China recognizing the need for cooperation to avoid conflict over the islands.

A specific approach often used in third-party efforts to settle conflicts peacefully, where violence has already occurred, is mediation.

▪ Mediation

Mediation is "a mode of negotiation in which a third party helps the parties find a solution which they cannot find by themselves" (Zartman and Touval 1996: 446). It is very much a political process that may involve persuading the parties to accept mediation in the first place or include multiple mediators over time, for different phases of a conflict and search for settlement. For mediation to have a chance, a conflict must be at what is called a "hurting stalemate" or "ripeness." This refers to the calculation of the costs and benefits of continuing conflict versus cooperating in some form of settlement.

Mediators can come from a single state or group of states, an IGO, or NGO; they may be individuals such as former President Jimmy Carter, or an ad hoc group. "Multiparty mediations" involving multiple mediators simultaneously or sequentially are well illustrated in the case studies of the Middle East and former Yugoslavia later in this chapter. A mediator may play a variety of roles: organizer, educator, visionary, interpreter, conciliator, provocateur, risk taker, catalyst for change, and policymaker (Crocker, Hampson, and Aall 1999: 686).

Key to a mediator's potential success, however, is adaptation to the particular situation. A mediator such as former President Jimmy Carter or the International Red Cross can be helpful in a situation of increasing violence, in the prenegotiation phase, or in postnegotiation implementation. Some situations call for "mediation with muscle" such as the U.S. could bring to the Bosnian situation or Middle East (Hampson 2001: 400) to halt fighting and provide both incentives and assurances for formal settlements.

Relationships matter, including relationships of trust with the parties to the conflict, with a sponsoring institution such as the UN, with a mediator's own government, and with other third parties. The UN ended up mediating the conflict in El Salvador because then Secretary-General Javier Pérez de Cuéllar and his special representative (Alvaro de Soto) came from the region and were committed to the negotiations (Crocker, Hampson, and Aall 1999: 683). George Mitchell led the International Body in the Irish peace process largely because he had personal ties in Ireland, was well known, and was trusted by leaders in Dublin, London, and Belfast (ibid.: 684). Staying power also matters—that is, the ability and willingness to stick with the mediation process as long as necessary. Initiating direct, secret talks between Israel and the Palestinians in the early 1990s required the quiet, long-term commitment that Norway provided (with the knowledge and support of the United States), as well as a close relationship with both parties. A humanitarian NGO may have the moral authority and track record of assistance to persuade a government to implement an agreement mediated by others. An ad hoc group of states called the Contact Group for Namibia that included the United States, Canada, the United Kingdom, France, and Germany was able to negotiate an agreement in 1978 for Namibian independence from South Africa because of the relationships the countries had with the different parties. They were unable, however, to persuade South Africa to implement the agreement until more than a decade later (Karns 1987). The contact group idea was later adopted by four Latin American countries (Colombia, Mexico, Panama, and Venezuela) that formed the Contadora Group to mediate in the Central American conflicts of the 1980s; it was also employed by France, Britain, the United States, Russia, and Germany in the Bosnian conflict beginning in 1994.

In multiparty mediations especially, coordination matters. As the title (*Herding Cats*) of one book on the subject implies, however, "Organizing the diverse third-party peacemaking entities is a lot like organizing cats. As anyone who has lived with them can tell you, cats cannot be organized. Gaining a cat's cooperation is a complicated matter . . . [to] persuade it at least to give your idea some thought" (Crocker, Hampson, and Aall 1999: 4). The mediator's challenge entering into a conflict is to make a coherent whole out of multiple initiatives of individuals, states, and organizations; to build on earlier efforts; and to move the process forward.

Mediation does not work in all situations, even if the mediator is a good fit and skillful. The readiness of a mediator may not be matched by the "ripeness" of a conflict. Likewise, preventive diplomacy may not forestall escalating violence and war. The global landscape is littered with failed attempts at both preventive diplomacy and mediation. No amount of effort by any number of well-intentioned third parties over a long period of time will necessarily bring a resolution of some seemingly intractable conflicts such as the Kashmir, Cyprus, and Israeli-Palestinian situations. Yet, there are also enough successful attempts to fuel hopes that these governance tools can be valuable in dealing with threats to peace and security. Two other peaceful settlement tools are legal in character.

■ *Adjudication and Arbitration*

Adjudication and arbitration involve referring a dispute to an impartial third-party tribunal for binding decision. These methods emphasize finding a basis for settlement in international law rather than in a political/diplomatic process or formula, but can be used only when states give their consent to submit a dispute and be bound by the outcome. Although generally reluctant to give up such control to third parties, states have found these approaches useful for certain types of disputes. The two differ in the permanence of the tribunals, the scope of their jurisdiction, and the extent to which parties can control the selection of arbitrators or judges.

Arbitration dates back at least to the early Greek city-states. It was incorporated into the Jay Treaty of 1794 and the 1814 Treaty of Ghent involving the United States and Great Britain; it was employed for settling the *Alabama* claims between the United States and Great Britain arising out of the U.S. Civil War; and it was a major focus of the Hague Peace Conference of 1899, which established the Permanent Court of Arbitration at The Hague. Despite its name, the latter is a list of names of potential international arbitrators—lawyers, judges, diplomats, academics, and former government officials. Arbitration panels can be composed of a single neutral individual such as the UN secretary-general, or a panel of three individuals (two of whom have been chosen by the parties and a neutral third member selected by agreement, or an impartial third party such as the president of the ICJ. Tribunal composition can range up to five or even as many as nine members, as in the case of the Iran-U.S. Claims Tribunal that has been in operation since 1981 dealing with several thousand claims arising out of the seizure of U.S. hostages by Iran in 1979. The agreement between parties to resort to arbitration defines the issues to be decided, the method for selecting arbitrators, the machinery and procedures to be used, and how the expenses will be paid.

About 450 international arbitrations have been conducted between 1800 and 1990 (Bilder 1997: 160). More recent cases include the 1977 Beagle Channel arbitration conducted by the Vatican between Argentina and Chile, the 1988 Taba arbitration between Israel and Egypt, and the 2002 arbitration by the Permanent Court of Arbitration of the border dispute between Ethiopia and Eritrea. The Organization of African Unity (now African Union) also established its own Commission of Mediation, Conciliation, and Arbitration.

As for adjudication, we noted in Chapters 3 and 4 the relatively limited use of the ICJ for dispute settlement. The ICJ and other international courts have one primary advantage over arbitral tribunals: they are already in existence and the international community pays the expenses of the proceeding. Distinguishing between legal or justiciable disputes and political or nonjusticiable disputes is a difficult task, however, and countries that wish to avoid adjudication will frequently protest that certain disputes are inherently inappropriate for adjudication. Iran made this argument in the case concerning U.S. diplomatic and consular staff in Tehran (*United States v. Iran*, referred to hereafter as the Tehran hostages case [ICJ 1980]) as did the United States in the Nicaragua case (*Nicaragua v. United States* [ICJ 1984a]). There can also be significant questions regarding the ICJ's jurisdiction to hear a case. Where parties to a dispute have agreed to submit it to the court, there would rarely be a question; where one state endeavors to bring another before the court on the basis of a clause in a particular treaty or where they have both accepted the ICJ's optional clause, the respondent state may challenge the court's jurisdiction, however, arguing that it had not consented in advance to the court's jurisdiction over a particular type of dispute. In such cases, the court holds initial hearings to determine whether both states have consented, in fact, and whether it does have jurisdiction. Sometimes, unwilling respondent states will refuse to appear before the court at all—as did France in the nuclear tests cases (*New Zealand v. France* [ICJ 1974]) brought against its nuclear testing by Australia and New Zealand; Iran in the Tehran hostages case; and the United States in the Nicaragua case.

The Nicaragua case is instructive for the limitations on adjudication as a means of dealing with a peace and security issue. Officially titled The Case concerning Military and Paramilitary Activities in and Against Nicaragua (ICJ 1984a) arose out of the 1979 victory of the left-wing Sandinistas over long-time Nicaraguan dictator General Somosa, and U.S. concerns about ties between the Sandinistas, Cuba, and the Soviet Union. In 1984, Nicaragua brought suit in the ICJ, charging that the United States was illegally using military force against it and intervening in its internal affairs through mining of harbors, attacks on ports, a naval base, and oil installations, support of the Contras (a paramilitary force of some 10,000), and efforts to damage the economy and undermine the political system. Because it involved one of the two superpowers, the case was closely watched by many less developed countries.

The United States strongly opposed Nicaragua's claims, arguing that the ICJ had no jurisdiction over the case. When the court determined it did have jurisdiction, the United States announced it would not participate in the proceedings and withdrew its acceptance of the court's jurisdiction for any Central American case. In 1985, the United States took the further step of terminating its general acceptance of the court's compulsory jurisdiction.

The ICJ's 1986 ruling represented a stunning defeat for the United States and a moral victory for Nicaragua. The court found the mining of

Nicaragua's harbors, attacks on port installations, and support for the Contras infringed the prohibition of the use of force. The justices rejected the U.S. claim of collective self-defense on behalf of El Salvador. The court also found no basis in international law for a general right of intervention in support of an opposition to the government of another state, however just its cause might appear.

Following the ruling, Nicaragua tried unsuccessfully to get the Security Council to enforce the decision. The case had little impact on the conflicts in Central America, but did lead to a significant increase in the ICJ's stock among developing countries. Thereafter, many accepted the ICJ's jurisdiction, withdrew previous reservations to court jurisdiction, and brought cases before the court.

The Nicaragua case had a distinctly negative effect on the United States, reinforcing suspicions about international institutions. The United States, nonetheless, brought new cases to the court and participated in others such as those brought by Iran after a U.S. naval ship accidentally shot down an Iranian airliner and by Libya after the U.S. tried to extradite two Libyan intelligence agents who were suspects in the bombing of Pan American Flight 103 over Lockerbie, Scotland.

States have used both adjudication and arbitration to resolve territorial and maritime boundary disputes, questions of river usage, and fishing zones. In the 1980s, the United States and Canada asked the ICJ to determine the lines of their respective jurisdiction in the Gulf of Maine. These two historically friendly countries were not likely to use force, but they needed a neutral third party to resolve the legal issues surrounding the drawing of boundaries. In contrast, Chad and Libya did fight over their boundary, subsequently submitting their claims to the ICJ for resolution. In 2004, five boundary disputes were on the ICJ's docket: Qatar-Bahrain, Benin-Niger, Malaysia-Singapore, Nicaragua-Colombia, and Nicaragua-Honduras. In addition, the ICJ ruled on the boundary dispute between Cameroon and Nigeria, determining the border between the two countries, including sovereignty over the potentially oil-rich Bakassi Peninsula and the maritime boundary.

What leads states to use arbitration or adjudication? In some cases, bilateral treaties specify one or the other to resolve disputes. For example, because bilateral treaties between the United States and Iran stipulated submitting disputes to the ICJ, the United States based its Tehran hostages appeal on those treaties, as well as on the Vienna Conventions on Diplomatic Relations. Past success or failure in either armed conflict or peaceful settlement attempts is likely to influence states' future choice of methods (Hensel 2001: 106). Despite agreeing to be bound by the outcome, however, one or another party to arbitration or adjudication may decide not to implement a settlement, giving rise to compliance and enforcement issues. They may seek Security Council help in enforcing a judgment, as Nicaragua did, or use other "self-help" measures to secure compliance of the recalcitrant party. Therefore, it is to collective security, enforcement, and sanctions that we now turn.

■ Collective Security, Enforcement, and Sanctions

Collective security is based on the conviction that peace is indivisible and that all states have a collective interest in countering aggression whenever and wherever it may appear. It assumes that potential aggressors will be deterred by the united threat of counterforce mobilized through an international organization like the league or the UN. If enforcement is required, however, then a wide range of economic and diplomatic sanctions as well as armed force may be utilized.

The League of Nations, as noted in Chapter 3, failed entirely to respond to the Japanese invasion of Manchuria in 1931, and in the case of the Italian invasion of Ethiopia in 1935, only responded belatedly with voluntary sanctions. Chapter VII of the UN Charter provides the legal foundation for the UN's collective security role and specifically for enforcement decisions that bind all UN members. It specifies actions the UN can take with respect to threats to the peace, breaches of the peace, and acts of aggression. Because the P-5's veto power in the Security Council assures that no collective measures can ever be instituted against any of them, the UN is a limited collective security organization. The Cold War made concurrence among the council's members almost impossible to achieve and Chapter VII was invoked on only two occasions. It dealt primarily with regional conflicts, utilizing various forms of peacekeeping and mechanisms for peaceful settlement of disputes. The situation changed dramatically in the late 1980s with the Cold War's end, unprecedented cooperation among the P-5, and the success of the Gulf War. Since 1989, Chapter VII has been invoked on many occasions to authorize the use of force or various types of sanctions. In Bosnia, Haiti, Northern Iraq, East Timor, and Sierra Leone, the Security Council authorized the use of force either by a regional organization such as NATO (Bosnia) or by a "coalition of the willing" led by a country willing to commit military forces to the effort such as the United States (Haiti), Australia (East Timor), France (Rwanda), and Great Britain (Sierra Leone).

Regional organizations are specifically recognized in the UN Charter (Chapter VIII). Their security roles are supposed to complement the UN, providing alternate avenues for peaceful settlement of local disputes or for enforcement action. A critical provision of Article 53, however, states, "No enforcement action shall be taken under regional arrangements or by regional agencies without the authorization of the Security Council."

In examining collective security and enforcement efforts, we shall look briefly at the UN's experience in Korea in the 1950s and the Gulf War in 1991, the decade-long effort to get Iraq to comply with the conditions imposed on it at the end of the Gulf War, the lessons of the now extensive experience with sanctions, and how regional collective enforcement efforts mesh with those of the UN.

■ Collective Security Efforts Involving Armed Force

Korea.   When North Korean forces invaded South Korea in June 1950, the sanctioning of U.S.-led UN forces to counter the invasion of South Korea was made possible by the temporary absence of the Soviet Union from the Security Council in protest against the UN's refusal to seat the newly established communist government of the People's Republic of China. The "Uniting for Peace Resolution" was used by the General Assembly to authorize continuance of those forces once the Soviet Union returned to the Security Council and exercised its veto. The UN provided the framework for legitimizing U.S. efforts to defend the Republic of Korea and mobilizing other states' assistance. A U.S. general was designated as the UN commander, but took orders directly from Washington. Some fifteen states contributed troops during the three-year war. Since the 1953 ceasefire, the United States has maintained a strong military presence in South Korea; the UN has maintained a token presence.

The Gulf War.   Iraq's invasion of Kuwait in the summer of 1990 triggered unprecedented actions by the UN Security Council in response to this act of aggression against a UN member state. Unity among all five permanent members of the Security Council, including the Soviet Union (despite its longstanding relationship with Iraq), facilitated the passage of twelve successive resolutions over a four-month period, activating Chapter VII of the charter. These included, most importantly, Resolution 678 of November 29, 1990, authorizing member states "to use all necessary means" to reverse the occupation of Kuwait and "restore peace and security in the region."

The military operation launched under the umbrella of Resolution 678 and Article 42 of the charter was a U.S.-led multinational effort resembling a subcontract on behalf of the organization. U.S. commanders did not regularly report to the UN secretary-general nor did senior UN personnel participate in military decisionmaking. UN flags and symbols were not used by coalition forces. After the fighting ceased in late February 1991, a traditional, lightly armed peacekeeping force (UN Iraq-Kuwait Observer Mission [UNIKOM]) was organized to monitor the demilitarized zone between Iraq and Kuwait.

The U.S.-led military action in the Gulf was widely regarded as exemplifying a stronger post–Cold War UN, but also came under critical scrutiny. Germany and Japan contributed substantial monetary resources, but were excluded from key decisions on the Security Council since they were not members—a fact that spurred their interest in securing permanent membership on the council. Many developing countries, while supporting the action, were also troubled by the autonomy of the U.S.-led operation. The Gulf War marked only the beginning, however, of efforts to deal with Iraq's threats to regional peace. We examine below the continuing challenge of getting it to comply with the arms control regime imposed under the ceasefire and the effects of the ongoing sanctions.

▓ Enforcement and Sanctions

Sanctions have long been a favorite tool in states' efforts to get others to do what they wanted them to do. Unilaterally imposed sanctions, however, have always been problematic because they do not close off alternative markets and sources of supply for the target state(s). Organizing multilateral sanctions without a multilateral forum or organization through which to reduce the diplomatic transaction costs of securing other states' cooperation is a difficult undertaking. Hence, beginning with the League of Nations, the potential for using sanctions as an instrument of security governance was significantly enhanced. The number of examples of multilateral sanctions was relatively limited, however, prior to the Cold War's end. The league applied voluntary sanctions once (Italy). The UN imposed mandatory sanctions under Chapter VII only twice (Southern Rhodesia and South Africa) before 1990. The Arab League imposed sanctions on Israel in 1948, and the OAS imposed them on Cuba between 1964 and 1975. The United States organized multilateral sanctions involving sensitive technologies against the Soviet Union and other communist countries through an ad hoc group known as CoCom. The Commonwealth imposed a sports ban and other sanctions on South Africa. Beginning with the economic sanctions imposed on Iraq in 1990, the UN Security Council utilized different forms of sanctions in fourteen situations over the next eleven years. Eleven of the cases involved intrastate conflicts; three related to terrorism. Regional organizations also applied sanctions in a number of the same situations in the 1990s. In addition, there are innumerable examples of states (especially the United States) imposing unilateral arms embargoes, as well as trade restrictions and other measures (Hufbauer 2000). This has led one study to dub the 1990s the "sanctions decade" (Cortright and Lopez 2000).

The governance problem for which sanctions are employed is the challenge of getting a state that threatens international peace and security to change its behavior. Sanctions are typically viewed as a cheaper and easier tool than armed force. Particularly when comprehensive trade sanctions are used and fully enforced, thus choking off the target economy, they are expected to have a political effect by imposing the costs of economic and other forms of deprivation on the offending state's government and people. They are a means of coercion and punishment. By implication, the pain of sanctions will be lifted once there is a change of behavior, which may also mean a change of government. An alternative approach to sanctions is a bargaining model (carrot-and-stick approach) in which specific types of sanctions are integrated with inducements to effect a step-by-step change process. The target state is offered rewards for taking successive steps in the desired direction, rather than having to do everything that was expected in order to see any lifting of sanctions.

The most extensive enforcement undertaking to date is the effort since 1991 to get Iraq to comply with the complex terms of the April 1991 ceasefire agreement, particularly the arms inspections regime, designed to force Iraq to dismantle its production of nuclear, chemical, and biological weapons. Let us look briefly at this experience.

The challenges of getting Iraq to comply.   When Iraq invaded Kuwait in August 1990, the Security Council immediately invoked Chapter VII to condemn the invasion and demand withdrawal. Subsequent resolutions imposed mandatory economic and transport sanctions against Iraq and established a sanctions committee to monitor implementation. Following the Gulf War, on April 3, 1991, the Security Council passed Resolution 687, enumerating terms of the ceasefire agreement and a far-reaching plan for dismantling Iraq's weapons of mass destruction. The resolution stated that Iraq must accept the destruction, under international supervision, of all of its chemical and biological weapons and ballistic missiles; it must agree not to acquire or develop any nuclear weapons and place all nuclear-usable material (such as for power plants) under international control. The resolution also required Iraq to compensate victims for losses or damages using money from the sale of oil, and it created a Compensation Commission to administer the fund and resolve claims against Iraq. The earlier sanctions were to continue until all the provisions were carried out to the Security Council's satisfaction. The only exception was oil sales authorized under the 1995 Oil for Food Program to pay for food and medical supplies.

The disarmament sanctions regime involved the most intrusive international inspections ever established. The UN Special Commission for the Disarmament of Iraq (UNSCOM) was created to oversee the destruction of Iraq's chemical and biological weapons and their production and storage facilities, and to monitor its long-term compliance. The International Atomic Energy Agency (IAEA), a UN agency established in the 1950s, was responsible for inspecting and destroying Iraq's nuclear weapons program.

Between 1991 and 1998, inspectors moved all over Iraq, carrying out surprise inspections of suspected storage and production facilities, destroying stocks of materials, and checking documents. Iraq continually thwarted UNSCOM and IAEA inspectors, removing equipment, claiming to have destroyed material without adequate verification, arguing that some sites were off limits, and complaining about the makeup of the commission. It severed all cooperation in November 1998 and inspectors were withdrawn. Although the successor to UNSCOM, the UN Monitoring, Verification, and Inspection Commission (UNMOVIC) was allowed to begin inspections anew in November 2002, its work was cut short by U.S. military action against Iraq in March 2003.

The problems that the IAEA and UNSCOM encountered mirror the broader problems with international enforcement. Although the IAEA succeeded in destroying Iraq's existing nuclear weapons materials and production facilities, UNSCOM was unable to certify that it knew the full extent of Iraq's chemical and biological weapons production facilities since those materials are easily concealed. Furthermore, destroying weapons stocks and production facilities did not destroy the knowledge base that Iraq had developed or its access to technologies especially for biological and chemical weapons. This would require a long-term program of monitoring and the political will to maintain it.

By the late 1990s, the Iraq sanctions had become increasingly controversial. Malnutrition, contaminated water supplies, increased infectious disease, and higher infant and child mortality rates had produced a humanitarian crisis that generated widespread sympathy and calls for ending sanctions, although the suffering was not entirely attributable to sanctions (Hoskins 1997: 91–147; Garfield 1999). The Iraqi government also exacerbated the crisis for political purposes and rejected international proposals to alleviate it. Only reluctantly after some time, for example, did it decide to cooperate with the Oil for Food Program. Nonetheless, sanctions fatigue among neighboring and other nations that relied on trade with Iraq grew and compliance eroded as unauthorized trade and transport links multiplied (Cortright and Lopez 2002: 1). The United States and Great Britain, however, insisted on complete compliance before the sanctions could be lifted and rejected proposals by Russia, France, and other countries to reward Iraq's cooperation and encourage further progress by partially lifting sanctions. The result was a stalemate.

In 2001 and 2002, NGOs, human rights groups, and independent research centers initiated proposals for ending the stalemate with Iraq. These focused on the idea of "smart sanctions" intended to keep the pressure on Iraq to comply with the disarmament provisions by hitting the government's leaders where it would hurt, but to lift most restrictions on civilian imports. No action was taken.

Lessons from the Iraq experience and sanctions decade.   The Iraq experience demonstrates three types of problems with comprehensive sanctions. The first involved the large-scale negative humanitarian effects, especially of general trade sanctions such as imposed on Iraq, Haiti, and the former Yugoslavia. This changed many people's perception of the pain/gain trade-offs in sanctions. The second problem was that strangling a target state's economy did not necessarily impose any economic pain on government leaders—and prospects for compliance were low unless sanctions affected them specifically. Slobodan Milosevic in Yugoslavia, Saddam Hussein in Iraq, and the Taliban in Afghanistan were unlikely to change their behavior unless personal sources of wealth and the resources used to support their policies were targeted. Third, in intrastate conflicts and failed states, generalized sanctions were largely ineffective against the leaders of armed factions or in an environment absent normal governmental controls over taxation, documentation of imports and exports, or borders. In short, a major lesson of the sanctions decade is that sanctions must be tailored to the specific situation if they are to be effective. Ultimately, measuring the political effectiveness of sanctions is a tricky business. It is useful, therefore, to look at other situations in which the UN applied sanctions during the 1990s and how sanctions strategies were varied to achieve different goals.

From 1994 on, no new general trade sanctions were initiated by either the Security Council or regional organizations. Instead, targeted sanctions were used, including arms embargoes, financial sanctions (notably freezing assets of governments and/or individuals), travel bans and aviation sanctions, and commodities sanctions (specifically, oil, timber, and diamonds). (See Table 8.1.) Targeting has involved not just "what" but also "who," as the international community endeavored to affect specific individuals and rebel groups, reduce ambiguity and loopholes, and avoid the high humanitarian costs of general sanctions.

The purposes for which sanctions were employed also broadened. During the 1990s, sanctions were used to counter aggression (Iraq), to restore a democratically elected government (Haiti), to respond to human rights violations (Yugoslavia, Rwanda, and Somalia), to end wars (Angola, Sierra Leone, Ethiopia, and Eritrea), and to bring suspected terrorists to justice (Libya, Sudan, and Afghanistan). In 2001, the Security Council took the unprecedented step of imposing sanctions on Liberia for its violations of sanctions imposed on Sierra Leone and the rebel group RUF (Revolutionary United Front) that had helped prolong the terrible violence in Sierra Leone. Following September 11, 2001, with Resolution 1373, the council established a broad set of financial and other sanctions designed to control terrorism.

In addition, the Security Council recognized in the late 1990s that monitoring was crucial to getting states and other actors to comply with sanc-

Table 8.1 Selected IGO Sanctions

Type of Sanction	IGO	Target Country	Years
Arms Embargo	UN	South Africa	1978–1993
		Iraq	1990–
		Yugoslavia	1991–1996, 1998–2001
		Haiti	1993
		Angola and UNITA	1993–2002
		Libya	1992–
		Somalia	1992–
		Liberia	1992–
		Rwanda	1992–1995
		Afghanistan	1990–2000
		Sierra Leone	1997
		Sierra Leone (rebels only)	1998–
		Eritrea	2000
		Ethiopia	2000
Export or Import Limits	CoCom	Soviet Bloc (technology)	1952–1991
(ban exports of selected	UN	Cambodia (logs, oil)	1992–1994
technologies, diamonds,	UN	Haiti (oil)	1993–1994
timber, etc., or place	UN	Angola (diamonds)	1993, 1998–2002
embargo on imports	UN	Sierra Leone (oil, diamonds)	1997–1998, 2000–2003
of oil, etc.)	UN	Liberia (diamonds)	2001
Asset Freeze	UN	Iraq	1990–2003
		Libya	1993–1999
		Yugoslavia	1992–1995, 1998–2000
		Haiti (junta only)	1994 1993–1994
		Angola (UNITA only)	1998–2002
		Afghanistan	1999–2001
		Liberia	2001
Withdrawal of	UN	Sudan	1996–
Diplomatic Relations	UN	Angola (UNITA only)	1997–2002
Denial of Visas	UN	Libya	1992–1999
(travel bans)	UN	Haiti	1994
	UN	Angola (UNITA only)	1997–2002
	UN	Sudan	1996–
	UN	Sierra Leone (rebels only)	1998–
	UN	Iraq	1999–2003
	EU	Yugoslavia	1999
	UN	Afghanistan	1999–2001
	UN	Liberia	2001–
Cancellation of Air Links	UN	Iraq	1990–
		Yugoslavia	1992–1995
		Libya	1992–1999
		Haiti	1994
		Sudan	1996
		Angola (UNITA)	1997–2002
		Afghanistan	1999–2001
Comprehensive Sanctions	Arab League	Israel	1948–
	OAS	Cuba	1964–1975
	UN	Southern Rhodesia	1965–1980
	UN	Iraq	1990–2003
	UN and EU	Yugoslavia	1992–1995
	OAS	Haiti	1990
	UN	Haiti	1993–1994
	UN	Bosnian Serbs	1994
	ECOWAS	Sierra Leone	1997–

tions. In most cases, little if anything had been done to implement, monitor, and enforce sanctions. The council established independent expert panels to gather data on sanctions violators, supply routes, networks, and transactions; named and shamed violators by publicly identifying them; and strengthened the UN's own capacity to administer various types of sanctions. In 2000, with the arms embargo against Ethiopia and Eritrea, the council began to set time limits (generally twelve months) for sanctions, thereby leaving open whether they would be renewed or not. The United States and United Kingdom oppose time limits on the grounds that they weaken the coercive impact, giving targets an incentive not to comply in the hope sanctions will not be renewed. Other countries argue that time limits force the council to look at each sanctions case periodically to determine whether or not to renew and to respond to adverse humanitarian impacts.

Also, NGOs now play significant roles in the implementation, monitoring, and evaluation of sanctions. For example, several NGOs documented the extent of the illegal trade in so-called conflict diamonds. Others organized a consumer awareness campaign to target the diamond industry while more than one hundred U.S. groups led by Physicians for Human Rights created the Campaign to Eliminate Conflict Diamonds to press for legislation regulating diamond imports to the United States. Independent research groups and institutes such as Global Witness, the International Peace Academy, the Kroc Institute at Notre Dame University, and Partnership Africa Canada have done much of the research on the impact and utility of sanctions and on reform proposals. Private industries, such as banks and financial institutions, or corporations such as De Beers (the international diamond company), have played major roles in the implementation of financial and commodities sanctions. So, too, have entities such as the Financial Action Task Force (FATF) created by the G-7 in 1989 to deal with money laundering, the Offshore Group of Banking Supervisors that helps to monitor offshore banking, and the newly created World Diamond Council formed to implement a global certification system for diamonds. For enforcing financial sanctions, no government or international association can match the capacity and importance of the U.S. Treasury Department's Office of Foreign Assets Control.

In short, a number of lessons have been learned in the last decade about how to target and monitor sanctions to strengthen their impact and respond more effectively to various threats to international peace and security. The case of Angola illustrates the changes and the continuing dilemmas posed by efforts to use sanctions for enforcement.

Angola: Learning from experience?   The government of Angola and the National Union for the Total Independence of Angola (UNITA) have been at war since 1974 when Angola gained its independence from Portugal. The war has gained notoriety for the large number of amputees resulting from thousands of landmines sowed by both sides, for horrific human rights abuses, for the Cuban troops sent to aid the Marxist-oriented government, and for the use of the country's rich resources to sustain the fighting. The government relied on oil exports; UNITA benefited from the sale of diamonds. The UN attempted in a variety of ways to end the fighting during the 1990s using peacekeepers, negotiations, and sanctions. Our concern here is strictly with the sanctions efforts.

The Security Council first imposed an arms embargo and oil sanctions on UNITA in 1993. UNITA's repeated violations of a 1994 ceasefire agreement led to tightening the sanctions in 1997 with a travel ban for senior UNITA officials, aviation ban for flights to UNITA territory, and diplomatic sanctions that closed UNITA offices in other countries. In 1998, a diamond embargo and targeted financial sanctions were added. In taking these steps, the Security Council gave up trying to mediate between the Angolan government and UNITA and sought to isolate the rebels, restrict their resources for arms and fuel, and to help the government gain the upper hand.

Next to the Iraq sanctions, the Angolan sanctions by 2002 were the longest in effect, but until 1999 had had little impact on UNITA's military capabilities because there had effectively been almost no monitoring to ensure compliance. That changed when an independent panel of experts was created to investigate sanctions violations and recommend ways to enhance compliance. It focused on UNITA's finances, especially on the role of the diamond trade and on sources of UNITA's weapons and mercenaries. The panel identified governments (Bulgaria, Ukraine, and Russia), companies, and individuals (the presidents of Togo and Burkina Faso) who were violating sanctions in various ways. By mid-2001, the monitoring group reported that the sanctions were producing results: arms deliveries were "drastically reduced"; countries were no longer providing safe havens to UNITA officials; and diamond export revenues had dropped significantly. Complementing the Security Council's more assertive role in enforcing the sanctions against UNITA, the Southern African Development Community (SADC) undertook in 2001 to block exports of UNITA diamonds and to monitor air traffic in the region—a key step for blocking arms or fuel.

Long considered a failure, the Angola story is now "one of the most important developments in sanctions policy in recent years" (Cortright and Lopez 2002: 71). The keys to success lay in tightening and targeting the sanctions against UNITA, keeping the pressure on both UNITA and sanctions violators through the investigative and monitoring processes, and using a combination of public exposure (naming and shaming) and quiet diplomacy with affected governments. The lessons learned in dealing with Angola were applied to the conflict in Sierra Leone and also to counterterrorism efforts, which are discussed below.

Yet, the sanctions decade has shown the limited role of IGOs other than the UN in the use of this tool for enforcement. This puts the UN's legitimacy and reputation at stake when sanctions are used. Targeted sanctions appear likely to become the norm along with more careful monitoring of compliance. Sanctions that would exacerbate an existing humanitarian crisis are not likely to win much support. Finally, as a result of the long stalemate with Iraq, time limits will probably be placed on sanctions to forestall difficulties in terminating them in the future.

A security governance approach initiated during the Cold War when neither sanctions nor other enforcement tools were easily used, at least by the UN, namely peacekeeping, has come under considerable critical scrutiny as a result of its post–Cold War record of mixed success and significant failure. It is to that we now turn.

■ Peacekeeping

Peacekeeping was the major innovative approach to promoting peace and security during the Cold War that enabled the UN to play a positive role in dealing with regional conflicts at a time when hostility between East and West prevented the use of the charter provisions for collective security and enforcement. It has taken different forms and evolved dramatically since the Cold War's end removed superpower involvement in many regional and civil conflicts and opened a political space for expanding peacekeeping operations. The UN defines peacekeeping as "an operation involving military personnel, but without enforcement powers, undertaken by the United Nations to help maintain or restore international peace and security in areas of conflict" (UN 1996c: 4). Since there is no charter provision for peacekeeping, it lies in a "grey zone" between the peaceful settlement provisions of Chapter VI and the military enforcement provisions of Chapter VII, and is sometimes referred to as "Chapter VI and a half." Some operations in the 1990s crossed that "grey zone" and more closely resembled enforcement, creating controversy and operational problems that we address below. It has become common, therefore, to talk about three generations of operations: traditional or first-generation peacekeeping; second-generation, complex peacekeeping and peacebuilding operations designed to implement a peace agreement and build conditions for stable, long-term peace; and third-generation operations involving greater use of force and an absence of parties' consent, combining efforts to enforce an end to violence and rebuild a viable state.

Peacekeepers' tasks have varied significantly over time and with different types of operations. Post–Cold War operations have frequently involved both military and civilian personnel with mandates that called for more than securing a ceasefire and hoping that a peaceful settlement of the conflict might follow. New mandates reflected convictions that the international community could help create conditions for long-term stability and peace, as well as respond to complex humanitarian emergencies of many post–Cold War conflicts. Figure 8.6 shows the different types of tasks associated with first-, second-, and third-generation peacekeeping that are discussed below.

Figure 8.6 Types of Peacekeeping Tasks	First Generation	Second Generation	Third Generation
Observation and Monitoring			
Ceasefires and withdrawal of forces	X		
Democratic elections		X	
Human rights		X	
Arms control		X	
Separation of Combatant Forces			
Establish buffer zones	X		
Deter onset or spread of war	X		
Limited Use of Force			
Maintain or restore civil law and order	X	X	X
Restore peace			X
Deliver aid		X	X
Humanitarian Assistance/ Intervention			
Open food & medical supply lines; guard supplies		X	X
Protect aid workers		X	X
Protect refugees		X	X
Create safe havens			X
Peacebuilding (Nation/State Building)			
Rebuild and train police		X	
Repatriate refugees		X	
Provide interim civil administration		X	
Oversee transition to indigenous authority		X	

■ *Distinguishing Between Enforcement and Peacekeeping*

The key distinction between enforcement and peacekeeping lies in the use of force and consent of the parties to the conflict. Traditionally, peacekeepers used military force only as a last resort and in self-defense and were deployed with states' consent, but even limited use of force is fraught with political and legal controversy: How much is limited force? Are such forces really used defensively? In particular, can forces under UN command, as opposed to those led by a single state, use military force effectively? These questions have been widely debated as a result of the UN's experience in Somalia and Bosnia where the Security Council's mandates blurred the line between enforcement and peacekeeping. As Thakur and Schnabel (2001: 16) note, "Turning a peacekeeping mission into a fighting force creates two problems. First it calls for a long commitment. Foreign armies, including those fighting under the UN blue flag, cannot impose peace on civil wars without also imposing foreign rule: this was the logic of colonialism. Second, they cannot join the fray without taking sides in the civil war. But to take sides is to become aligned to one and therefore the enemy of the other."

In post–Cold War intrastate conflicts there was no peace to keep, no ceasefire to monitor, and no consent to a peacekeeping mission from the local parties who were either not states or included a failed state, such as Somalia. The consequence is that peacekeepers have been harassed, kidnapped, and attacked by warring parties.

In principle, peacekeeping has numerous advantages over collective security and enforcement. Where an operation does have the approval of parties to a conflict, there is at least nominal consent to cooperate with peacekeeping forces. Also, most operations have required relatively small numbers of troops from contributing states. Only in a few instances has the UN required large military units, precisely because the line between enforcement and peacekeeping was blurred and the tasks required an ability to mount military operations. An added advantage of traditional peacekeeping is that no aggressor need be identified, so no one party to the conflict is singled out for blame—making it easier for most states, and the parties themselves, to approve an operation.

Since the permanent UN military forces envisioned by the charter (Articles 43–45) were never created, peacekeeping operations have relied on ad hoc military, civilian, or police units volunteered by member states. During the Cold War, these were drawn almost exclusively from the armed forces of states other than the permanent members of the Security Council (often small, neutral, and nonaligned members) to keep the superpowers out of regional conflicts or, in the case of postcolonial problems, to keep former colonial powers from returning. A given for UN operations is their multinational composition. Among the countries that have been frequent contributors are Canada, Sweden, Norway, Australia, Brazil, Argentina, Bangladesh, Jordan, Nigeria, Kenya, Ghana, India, Pakistan, Fiji, and Nepal.

The size of peacekeeping forces has varied widely from small missions numbering less than one hundred to major operations in the Congo in the 1960s, and Cambodia, Somalia, and Bosnia in the early 1990s, requiring over 20,000 troops. When a new mission is approved or a mission mandate expanded, the UN's Department of Peacekeeping Operations (DPKO) is responsible for determining the exact force requirements, for seeking the necessary contingents and logistical support, and for appointing a UN force commander from the top officer corps of a member country. Since the end of the Cold War and with larger operations, the United States has contributed forces for UN-authorized peacekeeping for the first time, but only in Somalia, Bosnia, Haiti, and Kosovo, and then only under U.S. or NATO command. It has provided logistical support, particularly air- and sealift for troops and equipment, for almost all peacekeeping operations since 1956.

It is not always easy to get states to contribute military forces (or other types of personnel) for UN peacekeeping missions. With post–Cold War operations often entailing higher risk of casualties, some member states have been unwilling to allow their troops to participate. Some countries' units have proven more effective than others, making some more desirable than others. The UN's financial difficulties in recent years meant reimbursement has been slow, making it difficult for many developing countries to afford the cost of contributing forces. Yet, for many countries, there are important goals to be served by peacekeeping participation. The difference between poorer countries' military salary levels and those paid by the UN makes the added income attractive. For Canada and the Scandinavian countries, for example, it underscores their commitment to multilateralism in addressing world problems. For Argentina, which became an active contributor to peacekeeping operations in the 1990s, this was a way of showing support for U.S. foreign policy and for international peace. It also provided new roles for the military during the country's transition to democracy. Brazil's contributions, by contrast, reflected political interests, particularly its desire to secure a permanent seat on the Security Council (Velazquez 2002). (The same motivation was true for Germany and Japan.) In addition, most of Brazil's deployments were to Portuguese-speaking countries (Angola, Mozambique, and East Timor), showing solidarity with other former Portuguese colonies.

Still, the problem of recruiting forces persists and has led to periodic proposals for a permanent or standby UN peacekeeping force. Absent this more efficient approach, a few countries, notably Canada and the Scandinavian countries, have earmarked portions of their military forces specifically for peacekeeping assignments and trained them accordingly.

In a few cases where states have not come forward with offers of peacekeeping contingents, private solutions have been adopted, with combatant states hiring companies such as Executive Outcomes, Sandline International, or Combat Force to contain internal violence. By this means weak governments in Sierra Leone, Papua New Guinea, Angola, and Bosnia have tried to fill the peacekeeping vacuum (Brayton 2002).

Peacekeeping operations have not been limited to the UN. Regional organizations have undertaken them in a few cases, such as the OAU in Chad in 1981, ECOWAS in Liberia and Sierra Leone, and NATO in Bosnia, Kosovo, and Afghanistan. Russia and the Commonwealth of Independent States (CIS) took on peacekeeping roles in three civil conflicts arising from the collapse of the USSR, specifically in Moldova, Georgia, and Tajikistan. Instances of unilateral and ad hoc multilateral peacekeeping include the Multinational Force and Observers (MFO) Group in the Sinai, deployed in 1979 after the Camp David Accord between Egypt and Israel and still in place; the Commonwealth operation in Zimbabwe; the U.S.-led Multinational Force (MNF) in Beirut; and the Indian Peacekeeping Force (IPKF) in Sri Lanka, all in the 1980s. The International Security Assistance Force (ISAF) deployed in Afghanistan in December 2001 is a further example of ad hoc multilateral peacekeeping, although it became a NATO operation in 2003.

Some, but not all, of these non-UN missions were authorized by UN Security Council resolutions. In all cases, there has been an expectation that they will conform to UN peacekeeping norms. Such "subcontracting" offers the advantages of reducing burdens on the UN and of potentially more effective intervention given knowledge of the players in local conflicts. Regional actors' interests can be a complicating factor, however; states may have taken sides in the conflict or see it in relationship to a regional competition for power. In fact, regional peacekeeping efforts have generally not resulted from a UN initiative, but "out of the (often self-interested) policy agendas of regional actors" (MacFarlane 2001: 79). Regional organizations other than NATO generally lack administrative, financial, military, and logistical capacities for peacekeeping. This is particularly true in Africa and among the non-Russian members of the CIS. In some instances, small UN or OSCE observer missions have been deployed to enhance transparency and socialize regional military forces. Another strategy has been capacity building and logistical support, something that the United States, Britain, and France pushed in the late 1990s in hopes that African states could take greater responsibility for interventions in African conflicts.

Before turning to an assessment of peacekeeping's successes and failures, let us examine more closely the three generations and the situations in which peacekeeping has been used.

■   *Traditional or First-Generation Peacekeeping*

First-generation peacekeeping was used primarily during the Cold War in the Middle East and in conflicts arising out of the decolonization process in Africa and Asia when the interests of the United States and the Soviet Union were not directly at stake. (See Table 8.2.) In the late 1980s, it facilitated the withdrawal of Soviet troops from Afghanistan and supervision of the ceasefire between Iran and Iraq. It has also been used to maintain the ceasefire along the Iraq-Kuwait border since the Gulf War and to end the conflict between Ethiopia and Eritrea in 2001. All of these conflicts were interstate, with the exception of the Congo in the 1960s, and the operation's purpose was to contain or stabilize the fighting until negotiations produced a lasting peace agreement. The peacekeepers were either unarmed or lightly armed, often stationed between hostile forces to monitor truces, troop withdrawals, or provide a buffer zone, and authorized to use force only in self-defense. They provided impartial assurance to the parties desiring a settlement (or at least a ceasefire) and, during the Cold War, a guarantee that the United States and Soviet Union would not directly intervene.

Cold War conflict between the superpowers meant that many important issues of peace and security, including the Vietnam conflict, never made it to the UN agenda. Nevertheless, the innovation of peacekeeping provided a valuable means to limit superpower involvement in regional conflicts (with

Table 8.2   First-Generation Peacekeeping Operations (Representative Cases)

Operation	Title	Location	Duration	Maximum Strength
UNEF I	First UN Emergency Fund	Suez Canal, Sinai Peninsula	Nov. 1956– June 1967	3,378 Troops
UNFICYP	UN Peacekeeping Force in Cyprus	Cyprus	March 1964– present	6,411 Military Observers
UNEF II	Second UN Emergency Force	Suez Canal, Sinai Peninsula	Oct. 1973– July 1979	6,973 Troops
UNDOF	UN Disengagement Observer Force	Syrian Golan Heights	June 1974– present	1,450 Military Observers
UNIFIL	UN Interim Force in Lebanon	Southern Lebanon	March 1978– present	7,000 Military Observers
UNIMOG	UN Iran-Iraq Military Observer Group	Iran-Iraq border	August 1988– February 1991	399 Military Observers
UNMEE	UN Mission in Ethiopia and Eritrea	Ethiopia/Eritrea border	Sept. 2000– present	4,200 Troops, 400 Civilians

regional consent) and for coping with threats to peace and security posed by the emergence of new states, border conflicts among those states, and the intractable conflicts in the Middle East. In the process, the UN and international community developed a body of experience and practice in peacekeeping that was to prove even more valuable in the late 1980s and the 1990s, when the Cold War's end created political conditions conducive to expanding the tasks given to peacekeepers (and new types of threats demanding creative responses). The success of UN peacekeeping activities in the late 1980s led to the Nobel Peace Prize in 1988 and many new missions.

■ *Second-Generation Peacekeeping and Peacebuilding*

In the 1990s, second- and third-generation peacekeeping evolved out of the international community's efforts to terminate persistent civil conflicts in Central America, Southern Africa, and Southeast Asia, and to address collapsing state institutions, violent civil conflicts, and complex humanitarian emergencies in the former Yugoslavia, Angola, Mozambique, Somalia, Sierra Leone, and East Timor. (See Table 8.3.) The two generations differ in the "muscularity" of response (i.e., use of force) and consent of parties. The governance challenge in developing second-generation peacekeeping was not only how to end violent conflicts, especially civil wars, but also how to prevent renewed hostilities and rebuild stable polities. The UN and regional IGOs have taken on these challenges with occasional successes and some striking failures (Doyle and Sambanis 2000: 779).

In second-generation peacekeeping, "the peacekeeping mission was an integral component of the peace agreement and was meant to complete the peace settlement by providing third-party international military reinforcement for the peace process" (Thakur and Schnabel 2001: 11) as well as a significant civilian role in laying the foundations for long-term stability. Consent of the parties signing the peace agreement was initially assured, but might not persist throughout a lengthy implementation process, especially if paramilitary forces or militias renewed violence. Second-generation peacekeeping operations are frequently described as "complex peacekeeping" because their mandates involve both civilian and military activities and multidimensional tasks. (See Figure 8.6.) While troop contingents may provide observer activities characteristic of traditional first-generation operations, other military personnel and civilians, along with NGOs, UN agencies such as UNHCR, UNICEF, and UNDP, and regional institutions such as OSCE are involved in the various peacebuilding activities such as human rights education, monitoring, and enforcement; clearing landmines; organizing and supervising democratic elections; repatriating and resettling refugees; organizing interim civil administration; and rebuilding the police and judiciary. For example, the UN Observer Mission in El Salvador (ONUSAL) broke new ground for second-generation peacekeeping with a mandate to monitor and verify

Table 8.3   Second- and Third-Generation Peacekeeping Operations (Representative Cases)

Operation	Title	Location	Duration	Maximum Strength
ONUC	UN Operation in the Congo	Congo	June 1960–June 1964	19,828 Troops
UNTAG	UN Transition Assistance Group	Namibia, Angola	April 1989–March 1990	70 Military Observers
ONUCA	UN Observer Group in Central America	Costa Rica, El Salvador, Guatamala, Honduras, Nicaragua	Nov. 1989–July 1992	1,098 Military Observers
UNPROFOR	UN Protection Force	Former Yugoslavia (Croatia, Bosnia, Macedonia)	March 1992–Dec. 1995	30,500 Troops and Civilians
UNTAC	UN Transition Authority in Cambodia	Cambodia	March 1992–Dec. 1995	15,900 Troops, 3,600 Police, 2,400 Civilians
UNOSOM I, II	UN Operation in Somalia	Somalia	Aug. 1992–March 1995	28,000 Troops, 2,800 Civilians
UNIMIH	UN Mission in Haiti	Haiti	Oct. 1993–March 1996	2,548 Troops, 5,000 Authorized
MONUC	UN Mission in Democ. Rep. of Congo	Congo	1999–Present	4,300 Military, 500 Observers
UNMISET	UN Mission in Support of East Timor	East Timor	2002–Present	3,500 Troops, 651 Civil. Police, 1,200 Civilians
UNMIK	UN Interim Administ.	Kosovo	1999–Present	3,478 Civil Police 3,591 Civilians 38 Military

human rights violations and make recommendations for their future elimination. Its unique human rights mandate gave it broad powers to visit any place, receive communications from individuals or groups, hold meetings and interviews, make recommendations, support judicial authorities, create educational and informational campaigns, and use the media. As "the most extensive human rights verification operation ever undertaken" (UN 1996c: 429), it helped bring a measure of political stability and human rights protection to El Salvador.

These peacebuilding activities signify the recognition that in societies rent by civil strife, failure to address root causes of conflict may lead to a new cycle of violence. Thus, "prevention and rebuilding are inextricably linked . . . leading to the conclusion that formal agreement ending a civil war is meaningless unless coupled with long-term programs to heal the wounded society" (Weinberger 2002: 248; see also Leatherman et al. 1999). Often, this has involved transferring a Western model of domestic governance norms, new democratic political institutions, and policy preferences to the affected state, supporting the constructivist argument about the relationship between international norms and the identity of states. Realism, however, better explains why these norms reflect the domestic norms of the major Western states. Also, "instead of allowing 'failed states' to evolve new forms of domestic governance or disappear into the dustbin of history, peacebuilders work toward reconstructing these states as effective sovereign entities" (Paris 2000: 43). To explore second-generation peacekeeping, we will look particularly at different roles peacekeepers have played in two post-conflict situations: Namibia and Cambodia.

Namibia: The first experiment in peacebuilding.   Namibia, formerly known as Southwest Africa, was a former German colony administered by South Africa after the end of World War I under a League of Nations mandate, but never turned over to the UN as a trust territory, unlike most other mandates. Its status was the subject of two advisory opinions and extended discussions in the UN Security Council and General Assembly over many years because of South Africa's continued occupation and extension of its policies of racial separation (apartheid) to the territory. In 1966, the General Assembly declared South Africa's rule illegal and in 1971, the ICJ ruled against South Africa as well. In the late 1970s, five major Western powers working in cooperation with the UN persuaded South Africa and the main Namibian liberation group, the Southwest Africa People's Organization (SWAPO) to establish terms for Namibian independence (Karns 1987). Implementation stalled, however, as South Africa cited the presence of Soviet-backed Cuban troops in neighboring Angola as a threat to its security. In August 1988, agreement was finally reached on the withdrawal of Cuban and South African troops in Angola that opened the way to Namibian independence, and the UN moved to initiate a major peacekeeping operation in Namibia and a smaller one in Angola.

The UN Transition Assistance Group in Namibia (UNTAG), deployed in April 1989, was the most ambitious UN undertaking up to that point and the first second-generation operation. Its mandate included: supervision of the ceasefire between South African and SWAPO forces, monitoring the withdrawal of South African forces and the confinement of SWAPO forces to bases, supervising the civil police force, securing repeal of discriminary legislation, arranging for the release of political prisoners and return of exiles, assisting in drafting a new constitution, and creating conditions for free and fair elections. With military and civilian personnel from 109 countries, UNTAG managed the process by which Namibia moved step-by-step from war to a ceasefire, full independence, and ongoing political stability. It is widely regarded as one of the UN's greatest peacekeeping success stories. This led the UN and the international community to undertake other complex missions, not all of which enjoyed the same success.

Cambodia: Experimenting with interim administration.   In October 1991, the Agreements on a Comprehensive Political Settlement of the Cambodia Conflict were signed in Paris with strong UN support. ASEAN also played a key role by spearheading an international campaign to isolate Vietnam for its 1978 invasion and occupation of Cambodia and leading the search for a diplomatic settlement. U.S. and Soviet cooperation led China and Vietnam to support a ceasefire among the rival forces of the Vietnamese-backed Han Sen government, the Khmer Rouge, and former Prince Norodim Sihanouk, along with the demobilization of armies, repatriation of refugees, and organization of elections. The agreements ending the twenty-year war in Cambodia "charged the UN—for the first time in its history—with the political and economic restructuring of a member state as part of the building of peace under which the parties were to institutionalize their reconciliation" (Doyle 1995: 26).

A small advance mission (UN Advance Mission in Cambodia [UNAMIC]) helped the four Cambodian parties implement the ceasefire. In March 1992, the UN Transition Authority in Cambodia (UNTAC) was deployed. The military component of UNTAC was charged with supervising the ceasefire and disarming and demobilizing forces; the civilian personnel assumed full responsibility for administering the country during the eighteen-month transition period, including control over Cambodia's foreign affairs, defense, finance, and public security. UN personnel also monitored the police, promoted respect for human rights, assisted in the return of 370,000 Cambodian refugees from camps in Thailand, organized the 1993 elections that returned civil authority to Cambodians, and rehabilitated basic infrastructure and public utilities. Up to 22,000 military and civilian personnel were assigned to UNTAC at its peak, leading Secretary-General Boutros Boutros-Ghali to observe, "Nothing the UN has ever done can match this operation" (*UN Chronicle* 1993: 26).

UNTAC's presence helped end the civil war and bring peace of sorts to most of the country. UNTAC was unable, however, to achieve a complete ceasefire, demobilization of forces (with the Khmer Rouge, in particular, retaining a significant military capability), or its full civil mission. Cambodia, therefore, illustrates the difficulty of carrying out all aspects of a complex peacekeeping and peacebuilding mission. General John Sanderson, the Australian commander of UNTAC from 1992 to 1993 has observed (2001: 159), "UNTAC was a peacekeeping mission which achieved its objectives but failed to leave the country in the progressive democratic state intended by those who set up the peace process." The reasons, he states, included the long delay in the UN's arrival after the Paris agreements, insufficient attention to building an effective rule of law and justice system, and the UN's limited role in the constitutional process. UNTAC, which cost the UN $1.8 billion, was abruptly terminated after Cambodia's successful 1993 elections, but the military seized power in July 1997, erasing many of its gains. Sanderson questions whether the UN is any better equipped a decade later to undertake the tasks of occupying, governing, and building institutions for long-term political stability.

The UN built on its experience in Namibia and Cambodia in both Kosovo and East Timor, undertaking even more extensive administrative responsibilities. In neither case, however, was there a prior peace agreement; both also involved more muscle and less consent, making them better examples of third-generation peacekeeping. In a number of other situations, the UN's role was more limited and the results widely regarded as successful. For example, in Mozambique between 1992 and 1994, with little international publicity, the UN peacekeeping mission helped move this African nation from a fifteen-year civil war with over a million casualties and five million refugees, complicated by severe drought, to stable peace, a 10 percent economic growth rate, and rising human development levels. Likewise, in the Eastern Slavonia region of Croatia in 1996–1997, the UN learned from some of UNPROFOR's failures in Bosnia to facilitate extensive institutional reforms and the reintegration of the Croatian Serbs.

Second-generation peacekeeping has provided the international community with tools for a second chance at preventive action. Yet, the conflicts in Somalia, Rwanda, Angola, Congo, Bosnia, Sierra Leone, Kosovo, and East Timor demanded more than peacekeeping and peacebuilding. The challenges included not only civil wars, but also collapsed state structures, humanitarian emergencies caused by starvation, disease, or genocide; and widespread human rights abuses.

▪ Third-Generation Peacekeeping: Blurring the Line with Enforcement

The key feature of third-generation peacekeeping operations is the absence of consent from all parties and the need for greater use of force to protect refugees and civilians from attack or genocide, to impose a ceasefire, and perhaps to compel parties to seek a peaceful solution. Thus, they cost more and have a greater probability of casualties for peacekeepers. They have often required the "muscle" of major military powers (e.g., the United

States, Britain, and France) with their logistical capability, personnel, heavy equipment, and even air power. They tend to be controversial because they blur the line between peacekeeping and enforcement actions under Chapter VII. Yet, frequently, the force size and configuration did not equip the peacekeepers to carry out an enforcement mission; in some instances, force commanders and/or UN officials were reluctant to use force with results that were often catastrophic to the very people the UN was supposed to protect. Third-generation operations have provoked heated discussions within the UN and among independent analysts about if and when the UN can effectively use military force. Somalia and Yugoslavia were both third-generation operations. (See Table 8.3.) Having examined Somalia in the chapter's introduction, let us look briefly at the UN's experience with peacekeeping in the former Yugoslavia and especially Bosnia.

Former Yugoslavia and Bosnia.   Yugoslavia played a unique role in the Cold War competition between East and West and was a country where fault lines of ethnic, religious, and political differences were buried for half a century. Its unraveling unleashed conflicts, the ferocity of which shocked those who imagined that Europe in the 1990s was immune from such horrors. It also raised issues central to international order and international law, such as self-determination, individual and group rights, and the use of force to serve humanitarian ends. Between 1991 and 1996, the Security Council devoted a record number of meetings to debate over whether to intervene, to what end, and with what means. UN peacekeepers, when finally sent to the region in 1992, encountered massive and systematic violations of human rights, a situation demanding more vigorous military action, and very little interest by the parties in making peace. Yugoslavia came to represent a microcosm of problems with peacekeeping, Chapter VII enforcement actions, efforts to address human rights abuses, and members' failure to provide adequate resources to carry out the Security Council's mandates.

The efforts of Serbian leader Slobodan Milosevic in the late 1980s to push Serbian nationalism yet maintain Yugoslavia's unity provoked strong separatist movements in Slovenia, Croatia, and Bosnia-Herzegovina and, ultimately, war. Slovenia and Croatia declared their independence in June 1991, followed by Bosnia-Herzegovina and Macedonia in 1992. The problem of Kosovo simmered untended until 1998–1999. Because Slovenia was fairly homogeneous, independence proceeded relatively calmly there; but Croatia and Bosnia-Herzegovina were not. The large Serb populations were determined not to be a part of these new states. Bosnia's heterogeneous Muslim, Croat, and Serb population made it the scene of the fiercest fighting. Nationalist leaders of each group fueled ancient suspicions and hostilities; each group's military and paramilitary forces attempted to enlarge and

Map 8.1   Former Yugoslavia

ethnically cleanse its territorial holdings. The resulting war killed over two hundred thousand people, produced millions of refugees, and subjected thousands to concentration camps, rape, torture, and genocide.

Initially in 1991, the United Nations largely deferred to EU diplomatic efforts, consistent with Chapter VIII of the charter. Despite their commitments to an EU Common Foreign and Security Policy, the Europeans could not agree on what their role should be, whether sanctions should be applied, how much force (if any) should be employed, or whether to grant diplomatic recognition to the newly declared states. The many ceasefires that were negotiated rapidly broke down as the fighting escalated.

In September 1991, the Security Council appointed former U.S. Secretary of State Cyrus Vance as the secretary-general's personal envoy to secure agreement from all the Yugoslav parties on a UN peacekeeping operation. The UN Protection Force for Yugoslavia (UNPROFOR) was authorized in February 1992 and initially deployed in the heavily Serbian areas of Croatia, and subsequently in three UN protected areas of Croatia to maintain a ceasefire, disband and demilitarize armed forces (both regular and irregular), ensure protection of basic human rights, and assist humanitarian agencies in returning refugees to their homes.

Meanwhile, however, fighting broke out in Bosnia-Herzegovina. The Bosnian Serbs, aided militarily by the rump Yugoslavia (composed of Serbia and Montenegro), attacked Muslim villages, shelled the city of Sarajevo (closing its airport), and drove hundreds of thousands from their homes. In June 1992, the Security Council authorized the dispatch of peacekeepers to Sarajevo to reopen the airport and support humanitarian relief efforts, but not, however, to stop the ethnic cleansing by Bosnian Serb forces in the Muslim-populated areas they had occupied. Later in 1992, the Security Council invoked Chapter VII calling on member states to "take all necessary measures" nationally or through regional organizations to facilitate delivery of humanitarian aid (Resolution 770). It authorized the creation of UN "safe areas" in six Bosnian cities and enforcement of a "no-fly zone" over Bosnia, removal of heavy weapons from urban centers, economic sanctions on Serbia and Montenegro, and air strikes against Bosnian Serb forces attacking the "safe areas." In the first experiment in cooperation between UN peacekeepers and a regional military alliance, U.S. and European forces under NATO auspices monitored compliance with the economic sanctions, implemented the no-fly zone over Bosnia, and eventually, in August 1995, conducted air strikes against Bosnian Serb positions.

All sides interfered with relief efforts and targeted UN peacekeepers and international aid personnel. The UN safe areas were anything but safe for the civilians who had taken refuge in them. Srebenica, in particular, became a humiliating defeat when UN peacekeepers failed to prevent the massacre of more than 7,000 Bosnian Muslim men and boys by Bosnia Serbs in July 1995 (United Nations 1999a). Under constant pressure for further action, the Security Council met almost continuously and passed resolution after resolution, progressively enlarging UNPROFOR's mandate. The International Criminal Tribunal for the Former Yugoslavia was established in 1993. But resolutions did not produce the manpower, logistical, financial, or military resources needed to fulfill the enlarged mandate. UN members lacked the political will for a full-scale enforcement action against the Bosnian Serbs and their Serbian backers in a situation where their national interests did not seem directly at stake and the outcome could not be assured.

The UN's peacekeeping role in Bosnia and Croatia ended with the U.S.-brokered Dayton Peace Accord of November 1995. In Bosnia and Croatia, UNPROFOR was replaced by the NATO Implementation Force (IFOR) of 60,000 combat-ready troops, including 20,000 Americans and units from almost twenty non-NATO countries (including Russia). IFOR was NATO's first effort to do what UN peacekeepers have done in the past: separate forces, supervise withdrawals, interpose themselves between parties, and provide a safe environment in which peace may take root. In late 1996, IFOR was replaced by a smaller NATO Stabilization Force (SFOR), which has an indefinite mandate, acknowledging the scale of the peacekeeping and peacebuilding tasks.

Alongside NATO, there are a large number of other organizations involved in implementing different parts of the Dayton accords and dealing with Bosnia's extensive needs. The UN itself was charged with monitoring and reforming Bosnia's police forces—a difficult task because of the shortage of police personnel and high levels of distrust among the Bosnian groups. The OSCE was to build the foundations for representative government and democracy. It has overseen elections and promoted human rights and civil society groups. The ad hoc International Conference on the Former Yugoslavia, made up of representatives from the EU, the United States, and other major interested parties, was responsible for appointing a civilian High Representative to monitor the implementation process, promote compliance by the parties, mobilize and coordinate the international civilian presence (i.e., UN and other IGOs as well as NGO humanitarian groups). A key design flaw, however, was the High Representative's lack of authority over these various entities and lack of resources.

NATO's presence effectively put Bosnia under military occupation in the name of the international community, although NATO troops were reluctant to behave as occupiers and refused to arrest prominent war criminals. The very large number of NGOs and IGOs active in Bosnia presented a host of coordination problems. Most UN agencies operate in largely autonomous fashion, pursuing their respective mandates, such as aiding children (UNICEF) or promoting development projects (UNDP and the World Bank). NGOs, too, are reluctant to lose their individual identity by cooperating too closely with each other or IGOs.

The Bosnian experience demonstrates the dangers of third-generation peacekeeping. Nine years after the Dayton Peace Accords, Bosnia remains a kind of international protectorate under quasi-colonial authority. The country is dependent on aid. Its economy is criminalized and stagnant. There is no unified police force trusted by all three communities (Muslim, Serb, and Croat) and little civil society development to provide the basis for long-term democratization. Only in 1999 was UNHCR with SFOR's presence successful in encouraging refugees to return to minority areas. With the persistence of the Serb Republika Srpska, the country remains effectively partitioned. In short, "The goal of a viable, unified, self-governing state remained distant. . . . the conflict was frozen still. . . . How long," asked one observer (Allin 2002: 45–46), "was NATO prepared to stay"?

The UN's problems in Bosnia, as well as those in Somalia, Kosovo, and elsewhere, led to efforts in the late 1990s inside and outside the UN to evaluate conditions for success and failure in peacekeeping.

■ Evaluating Success and Failure in Peacekeeping

The evolution of peacekeeping has expanded the international community's security governance tools. At the peak of enthusiasm for the UN's ability to maintain peace and security in the post–Cold War world, the Security Council convened an unprecedented summit meeting in January 1992. The heads of state and government of the council's fifteen members asked Secretary-General Boutros Boutros-Ghali to prepare an analysis of the possibilities for strengthening the UN's role. The outcome was *An Agenda for Peace*, a blueprint for the enhanced UN role, published in July 1992. When the *Supplement to the Agenda for Peace* was published in January 1995, a much more cautious approach prevailed. The difficulties of Somalia, Rwanda, and Bosnia had illuminated the obstacles the UN faced in meeting the demands placed upon it and the complexities of dealing with intrastate conflicts.

Yet what defines success? An end to fighting? A political solution in the form of a peace agreement? A period of years (two, five, ten?) without renewed violence? Some suggest that different types of missions should be evaluated with different criteria. Traditional, first-generation missions, for example, might be assessed in terms of their ability to abate the fighting (Diehl 2000). The first UN Emergency Force (UNEF I) averted war between the Arab states and Israel for eleven years. Peacekeepers in the UN Disengagement Observer Force (UNDOF) can take credit, at least in part, for the tranquility of the Golan Heights since 1974. The Congo force (UN Operation in the Congo [ONUC]) succeeded in preventing the secession of

Katanga province and helped restore a modicum of order. The UN Force in Cyprus (UNFICYP) has averted overt hostilities between the Greek and Turkish communities on Cyprus, although it could not prevent the 1974 invasion by Turkish forces. There has been no renewal of hostilities either between Iraq and Iran or Iraq and Kuwait. Yet fifty years of experience demonstrate that having international monitors for a truce does not give parties any incentives to resolve their conflict, witness the UN's continuing presence in Kashmir, the Middle East, and Cyprus.

Second-generation missions involving arms control verification and election supervision tend to be more successful because they are most similar to traditional peacekeeping. Thus, peacekeepers have compiled an excellent record in facilitating elections in Namibia, Cambodia, Mozambique, El Salvador, Eastern Slavonia, East Timor, and elsewhere.

Those missions that differ most from traditional operations tend to have the greatest difficulties, often because the forces are not well designed to carry out the mandate given them. Many of the peacebuilding tasks would fit this. As Diehl (2000: 352) notes in this regard, "Although peacekeeping may provide one of the necessary conditions in the nation-building process (e.g., peace), peacekeepers are not necessarily suitable for developing government infrastructure. Highly coercive missions may also be incompatible with peacekeeping philosophy, functions, and design. In those cases, operations may be better conducted by standard military forces, which have the training, equipment, size, and rules of engagement suitable for coercive missions." In fact, since Somalia, the UN and regional IGOs have relied on "coalitions of the willing" led by countries such as France, Nigeria, Australia, or Great Britain for missions that involved both pacification and nation-building.

Also, because second- and third-generation operations combine a number of different tasks, the overall assessment of such operations may be mixed. In Somalia, for example, the UN and U.S. forces were successful in achieving the humanitarian task of providing food to starving Somalis. Where they failed was in the pacification and nation-building tasks. More than ten years after its completion, the Namibian operation is widely perceived as a success. It had the consent of the warring parties; strong Security Council support; and personnel in the field who adapted the mission to the needs of the situation (Howard 2002). Namibia has conducted subsequent elections and has a developing economy. Cambodia is now regarded as a short-run success with longer-term mixed reviews. Comparisons are frequently made between the repeated failures of UN peacekeeping efforts in Angola during the 1990s and the success in Mozambique. They highlight some of the other factors that can facilitate success in second-generation peacekeeping such as parties' desire for peace; the resources made available by the international community; wide deployment of police monitors; extensive training of election monitors; the energy, skill, and improvisation of the secretary-general's special representative in the country; and even-handed treatment of the parties. As Satish Nambiar (2001: 173), the Indian general who commanded UNPROFOR from 1992 to 1993, has commented, "A vital requirement for any UN operation to be successful is that of continuous political support."

The mixed picture of success and failure in second- and third-generation peacekeeping operations has underscored the reality that each conflict situation is unique, and each effort to end that conflict and secure a stable peace must be tailored to the particular situation. A growing body of studies has produced findings related to questions of success and failure. One study (Howard 2001) concludes that learning and adaptation by personnel in the field during the course of an operation can make a critical difference to an operation's success. Similarly, she found that application of lessons from one operation to another by UN Secretariat personnel in New York could also make a difference but did not always occur. Another study looked at cases where peacekeeping operations were linked to a peace accord such as in Namibia, Central America, and post–Dayton Bosnia, finding, for example, with respect to peacebuilding, the "transformation of warring parties into political parties" through demobilization of soldiers, demilitarization, and disarmament was critical (Stedman 2001: 738). Without this, they note, other goals such as economic development, democratization, and protecting human rights have little chance of success. Similarly important are police and judicial reform to enhance civilian security, given the role police play with respect to law and order as the most visible arms of a state in society (Mani 1999: 4).

A study by Doyle and Sambanis (2000) also found that a formal peace agreement is strongly correlated with peacebuilding success, and under such circumstances, UN involvement in the peacebuilding process is also important. Other keys to peacebuilding success include ending the support of regional neighbors and other international actors for parties in intrastate conflicts, and higher levels of economic development at the beginning of the conflict. Wars with an ethnic or religious component and a large number of factions are less likely to be resolved and less susceptible to peacebuilding efforts. Likewise, the greater the degree of human misery produced by the conflict, the less likely peacebuilding will be successful. Where parties, such as in Angola and Sierra Leone, depend on exports of primary products such as diamonds and oil for buying arms and personal enrichment, peacebuilding is less likely to be successful because there is too much temptation to renew war to loot resources (Doyle and Sambanis 2000).

The UN itself undertook a number of steps in response both to increased demand for peacekeeping in the 1990s and the difficulties and failures encountered. In 1992 and 1993, there were major reforms of the Department of Peacekeeping Operations (DPKO), including the addition of military staff from member states and experts in de-mining, training, and civilian police. In 2000, Secretary-General Kofi Annan established an expert panel to review UN peace and security activities. The Brahimi Report (UN General Assembly and Security Council 2000), named for its chair, a former foreign minister of Algeria, addressed its recommendations both to member states and to the secretariat. They called for strengthening the planning and management of complex peace operations, the secretariat's information gathering and analysis capacity in order to improve conflict prevention, and the staffing of DPKO to increase its size and competence. The report also signaled doctrinal changes, namely, the need to prepare for more robust peacekeeping.

Because all instances of third-generation peacekeeping involved major humanitarian emergencies, decisions to intervene triggered debates about an emerging norm of humanitarian intervention, based on the evolution of both humanitarian and human rights norms and on emerging concepts of "human security."

■ *Humanitarian Intervention*

Horrific as earlier twentieth-century conflicts had been, post–Cold War conflicts were marked by the humanitarian disasters they produced: displaced populations, refugees, starvation, deliberate targeting of civilians, rape, widespread abuses of human rights, ethnic cleansing, and genocide. The UN High Commissioner for Refugees and humanitarian NGOs have been challenged as never before to cope with human tragedy on a massive scale. In 1999, the U.S. National Intelligence Council (1999: 25A) estimated that 35 million people—a number nearly equal to the population of Argentina—faced humanitarian crises in the last decade of the twentieth century. "Civilians have increasingly become the key targets for combatants in many conflicts," the report noted. "War has become as much about displacing people as moving borders." (See Figure 8.7.) The inability of some "quasi-states" (Jackson 1990) to exercise effective authority over their territories and populations and the outright collapse of others have resulted in anarchy, chronic disorder, massive flight of refugees, and deadly civil wars waged without regard for laws of armed conflict (Zartman 1995; Rotberg 2003).

Beginning with the creation of safe havens and no-fly zones in Northern and Southern Iraq in April 1991 to protect Iraqi Kurds and Shiites, the international community took the first of several coercive actions, without the consent of authorities in the respective states, to halt

Figure 8.7   Humanitarian Crises

Time	Country	People at Risk
1981–1993	Central America	1.8 million refugees
1991	N. Iraq	2.5 million refugees
1992–1993	Somalia	300,000 deaths 1 million refugees 95% population malnourished
1955–present	Sudan	2 million deaths
1991–1995	Bosnia	250,000 deaths 2.7 million displaced 1.4 million refugees
1994	Rwanda	850,000 deaths 1.1 million refugees
1995–1996	Burundi	150,000 deaths 1 million displaced
1999	Kosovo	800,000 refugees
1998–present	Congo	2.3 million refugees

widespread suffering or death. These were the first steps toward endorsing a norm of humanitarian intervention. Other interventions motivated in part by humanitarian crises included Somalia, Bosnia, Rwanda, Sierra Leone, East Timor, and Kosovo.

Although it was not the only armed intervention without prior authorization from the UN Security Council, the 1999 NATO action in Kosovo was by far the most controversial and a watershed in the debate over humanitarian intervention. It was triggered not by state failure but by Yugoslav (Serbian) rejection of a political settlement for Kosovo and growing evidence of ethnic cleansing. Kofi Annan captured the dilemma Kosovo posed when he stated on March 24, 1999, as NATO bombing began, "It is indeed tragic that diplomacy has failed, but there are times when the use of force may be legitimate in the pursuit of peace. . . . [but] the Council should be involved in any decision to resort to the use of force" (UN 1999c). Although Russia, China, and other countries loudly protested the illegality of NATO intervention, the UK argued, "force can also be justified on the grounds of overwhelming humanitarian necessity without a UNSCR" (Roberts 1999: 106). The rejection of Russia's own Security Council resolution condemning the NATO action by a vote of 12 to 3 is cited by proponents of legality as evidence of emerging customary law. Yet the debate over Kosovo also questioned whether NATO's military action worsened the humanitarian crisis by prompting the large refugee outflow, civilian casualties of bombing, and destruction of infrastructure such as power plants and bridges on the Danube.

Selectivity has clearly been a problem. The UN intervened in Somalia but ignored the civil wars in Sudan and Liberia that continued to produce large-scale loss of life to deliberate starvation, forced migrations, and massive human rights abuses, including enslavement of children. The UN and NATO focused on the former Yugoslavia but ignored the war in Chechnya and the continuing civil war in Afghanistan (until September 11, 2001). Selective media and NGO attention played a role, but varying national interests and political will did also.

Furthermore, international action was often too little or too late to save thousands of human lives in Somalia, Srebrenica, Rwanda, and Sierra Leone. UN Secretary-General Kofi Annan authorized independent examinations of what went wrong in Rwanda, Srebrenica, and Kosovo. The Independent Inquiry on Rwanda reported, "The responsibility for the failings of the United Nations to prevent and stop the genocide in Rwanda lies with a number of different actors, in particular the Secretary-General [then Boutros Boutros-Ghali], the Secretariat [in which Annan was Head of the Department of Peacekeeping Operations at the time], the Security Council, UNAMIR [UN Assistance Mission in Rwanda] and the broader membership of the United Nations" (UN 1999b). Acknowledging the failures, Annan stated, "Of all my aims as Secretary-General, there is none to which I feel more deeply committed than that of enabling the United Nations never again to fail in protecting a civilian population from genocide or mass slaughter" (UN 1999d).

Regardless of selectivity, egregious errors, and controversy, the very fact that debate is taking place and that the Security Council during the 1990s repeatedly referred to humanitarian crises as threats to international peace and security under Chapter VII marks a change. Not once during the Cold War had any council resolution referred to humanitarian intervention. And the reality is that the 1990s were, in the words of the International Commission, "a revolutionary decade for humanitarian action. . . . The Security Council authorized more than a dozen Chapter VII operations in response to conscience-shocking human catastrophes; regional organizations were seized with these issues and responded; militaries and humanitarian agencies adopted new policies and practices. . . . the lives of literally hundreds of thousands were saved" (ICISS 2001b: 220). If a new norm of humanitarian intervention emerges from the current debate, then there is all the more need for early warning, for preventive actions where such crises can be anticipated, and for peacebuilding once interventions have taken place. For the former, states, IGOs, and NGOs will need to collaborate in expanding their collective intelligence gathering and analytic capabilities.

In the future, however, IGOs, including the UN, are less likely to be the interveners than are coalitions of willing states. The reasons have to do with the absence of standby UN forces, the weakness of most regional IGOs, and the reality that "it is only states [and only a handful] that have the capabilities to fly thousands of troops halfway round the world to prevent or stop genocide or mass murder" (Wheeler 2000: 310).

Humanitarian concerns have long motivated advocates of arms control and disarmament who have seen particular weapons as inhumane or who want to eliminate wars entirely by eliminating the weapons of war.

■ Arms Control and Disarmament

The concept of disarmament, which includes limiting, controlling, and reducing the weapons for waging war, has long had a prominent place in proposals to promote peace. Thucydides reported that Sparta sought to get Athens to abstain from building fortifications. In the twelfth century, the Catholic Church proposed banning crossbows. Immanuel Kant called for eliminating standing armies in his "Preliminary Articles of Perpetual Peace Between States," and Jeremy Bentham in 1789 published a set of arms control proposals as a prelude to peace. The United States and Great Britain agreed in the 1817 Rush-Bagot Treaty to demilitarize the Canadian-American frontier, thereby bringing the idea of disarmament into the realm of diplomacy. Numerous proposals were put forward in the nineteenth century, some by heads of state, many others by newly formed peace groups, but only in the twentieth century would they begin to bear fruit. Even then, the history of disarmament and arms control efforts is a mixed one. The movement has been highly successful in getting the subject established permanently on IGO agendas. Yet, as Claude notes (1964: 267), "It is important to avoid confusing long hours of international debate, vast piles of printed documents, and elaborate charts of institutional structure with meaningful accomplishment." Still, there have been a number of notable achievements since the early 1960s, particularly with regard to controlling chemical, biological, and nuclear weapons of mass destruction (WMD).

▓ *Putting Arms Control on the Agenda*

The effort to create international rules and agreements limiting armaments began with the first Hague Conference in 1899 with a vague resolution urging states to reduce their military budgets. Peace groups unsuccessfully pushed for more and pioneered a number of strategies used by NGOs much later in the twentieth century, such as petitions, lobbying delegates, and publishing a daily chronicle. Women's peace groups, such as the Women's International League for Peace and Freedom, pushed for arms control at the Paris Peace Conference, and the resulting Versailles Treaty ending World

War I imposed severe restrictions on German military forces and armaments and established on-site, on-demand inspections. Article 8 of the League of Nations Covenant dealt specifically with disarmament, charging the League Council with responsibility for drafting agreements. Generally, league efforts confronted sharp national differences, however, over the relationship of disarmament to security guarantees and relative power positions. The major arms control agreements of the interwar period were largely negotiated outside the league. These included the 1922 Washington Naval Conference in which the United States, Great Britain, Japan, France, and Italy agreed to limit the number of capital ships (battleships at that time) and not to build any new ones for ten years. The building moratorium was extended in the London Naval Treaty of 1930 and limits also set on the size of destroyers and submarines. Perhaps the most enduring arms control agreement was the 1925 Geneva Protocol for the Prohibition of the Use in War of Asphyxiating, Poisonous or Other Gases, and of Bacteriological Methods of Warfare. This entered into force in 1928 and remains in effect today.

The UN Charter did not envision a major role for the UN with respect to arms control and disarmament, although Article 26 did give the Security Council responsibility for formulating plans for regulation of armaments. Disarmament as an approach to peace had been discredited during the interwar era because it had failed to avert the outbreak of World War II. The charter had just been signed, however, when the use of two atomic bombs on Japan on August 6 and 10, 1945, unveiled a scientific and technological revolution in warfare. The advent of nuclear weapons immediately put disarmament and arms control on the UN's agenda, with the General Assembly's very first resolution calling for the creation of the Atomic Energy Commission to propose how to ensure that atomic energy was only used for peaceful purposes. Hence, the nuclear threat not only transformed world politics itself, but also made the UN the key place where statespersons sought to persuade each other that disarmament and arms control were imperative.

Although nuclear weapons were the high-profile issue, arms control and disarmament efforts were also directed at chemical and later biological weapons, conventional weapons, missile technology, and most recently, antipersonnel landmines. The primary goal has been the negotiation of international conventions limiting or banning various categories of weapons, reducing arms expenditures or arms transfers and sales.

Over time, the UN General Assembly created special bodies for discussion of arms control and disarmament issues, including the Disarmament Commission, which in 1952 replaced the Atomic Energy Commission and the Commission for Conventional Armaments. Over the next three decades, there were successive reorganizations with accompanying name changes.

Much of this organizational reshuffling reflected an ongoing debate about which countries should participate in disarmament negotiations. In reality, the most fruitful negotiations on most issues have taken place outside the UN, usually among the relevant major powers. Regional IGOs have gotten involved in arms control issues largely through efforts to create regional nuclear weapon-free zones.

■ Limiting Proliferation of Nuclear Weapon Capability

Preliminary agreements between the United States and Soviet Union were crucial to efforts to create an international regime for nuclear nonproliferation. Following President Eisenhower's Atoms for Peace proposal in 1954, the two superpowers had (surprisingly) collaborated in creating the International Atomic Energy Agency in 1957 to spread information about peaceful uses of atomic energy and provide a system of safeguards to prevent diversion of fissionable material. The Cuban Missile Crisis in 1963 provided impetus for the two to sign the Partial Test Ban Treaty (PTBT). They then participated in UN-organized negotiations for a treaty banning the spread of nuclear weapons. In 1967, the two superpowers signed the resulting Treaty on the Non-Proliferation of Nuclear Weapons (NPT), which was then opened to other nations to sign and entered into force in 1970.

The essence of the NPT is a bargain that in return for non-nuclear weapons states' pledge not to develop weapons, they will be aided in gaining access to peaceful nuclear technologies. In return, the declared nuclear weapons states promised to give up their weapons at some future time. NPT effectively created a two-class system of five declared nuclear weapons states (United States, Soviet Union/Russia, Britain, France, and China) and everyone else. Although accepted by most states, this two-class system has always been offensive to others, most notably India (which conducted a peaceful nuclear test in 1974 and five weapons tests in 1998). All but four states (India, Pakistan, Cuba, and Israel) are now parties to the NPT. Three states that previously had nuclear weapons programs—South Africa, Brazil, and Argentina—became parties in the 1990s along with three states—Belarus, Kazakhstan, and Ukraine—that gave up nuclear weapons left on their territory after the dissolution of the Soviet Union. In 1995, the UN-sponsored NPT Review Conference agreed to an indefinite extension of the treaty, conditioned on renewed efforts toward disarmament and a pledge by the nuclear weapons states to conclude a Comprehensive Test Ban Treaty.

Critical to the nuclear nonproliferation regime is the IAEA-managed safeguard system of inspections. The foundations of this system were laid by the Federation of American Scientists in studies begun in 1946 and after 1957 in international scientific meetings at Pugwash (Canada). Although the system appeared operational and reliable for many years, the discovery of a secret Iraqi nuclear weapons program in 1991—in direct violation of Iraq's safeguard agreements with the IAEA and its obligations under the NPT—brought the entire system under scrutiny. The IAEA Board of Governors agreed to strengthen nuclear safeguards through increased access to information, facilities, and sites. Further doubts about the system, however, were fueled by North Korea's refusal in 1993 to admit inspectors to suspect sites. These grew in December 2002, after North Korea abrogated the 1994 agreement that renewed inspections and expelled the IAEA's inspectors, subsequently claiming in March 2003 to have already developed nuclear weapons. Concerns about the security of controls on nuclear materials and scientists in the former Soviet Union pointed up the difficulties of trying to prevent proliferation to so-called rogue states or terrorist groups. Although Libya gave up its nuclear program in late 2003, Iran remains a concern. How the international community deals with North Korea's noncompliance with the NPT inspections system and with suspected Russian assistance to Iran's nuclear program will have a major impact on the future of the NPT-based regime. Similarly, following discovery in early 2004 that Pakistan's chief nuclear scientist was part of a secret network of nuclear suppliers, it became clear that new strategies would be needed to prevent proliferation.

Another important part of the nuclear nonproliferation regime is getting those states that already have nuclear weapons to accept a ban on testing. The first step took place in 1963, shortly after the Cuban Missile Crisis when the United States, Soviet Union, and Great Britain agreed to the Partial Test Ban Treaty. In the 1990s, France and China, under pressure from Asia-Pacific countries, agreed to stop testing, and in 1996, the Comprehensive Test Ban Treaty (CTBT) was concluded under UN auspices. India and Pakistan's 1998 tests set back efforts to bring the CTBT into force, but the most important blow was the failure of the U.S. Senate to ratify the treaty in 1999. The CTBT is intended to serve two key roles: to prevent the declared nuclear weapons states and other parties to the treaty from developing new weapon designs and to reconfirm the strong international norm against nuclear proliferation. CTBT strengthens the NPT regime through an extensive International Monitoring System using seismic and other sensors to detect prohibited detonations; authority for challenge inspections in cases of suspected cheating; and a new Comprehensive Test Ban Treaty Organization, based in Vienna, to implement the verification procedures. CTBT can only enter into force, however, after ratification by the forty-four nations that as of 1996 had research or nuclear power reactors. This group includes all the states known or suspected to have weapons and the aspiring states such as Iraq, North Korea, and Iran. In addition to the United States, China, India, Pakistan, and Israel have yet to ratify the treaty. There is, however, a global moratorium on testing that has been effectively in place since 1998.

The final piece of the nonproliferation regime is the regional nuclear weapon-free zones. Four zones now exist covering well over one hundred states in Latin America, Southeast Asia, the South Pacific, and Africa. (See Figure 8.8.) Treaties for all but the African zone are now in effect. They preclude nuclear weapons states from placing nuclear weapons on the territory of states within the zone and prohibit the acquisition, testing, manufacture, or use of such weapons. Protocols attached to each of the treaties and signed by the nuclear weapons states bind the latter to respect denuclearization and not to use or threaten to use nuclear force against any of the parties. These zones indicate the widespread support for nuclear disar-

---

Figure 8.8   Nonproliferation Regimes for Weapons of Mass Destruction

Date	Title
1957	International Atomic Energy Agency
1963	Partial Test Ban Treaty
1967	Outer Space Treaty (1967)[a]
1967	Treaty of Tlatelolco (Latin American Nuclear Free Zone Treaty) (1968)
1968	Nuclear Non-Proliferation Treaty (1970)
1971	Seabed Treaty (1972)
1972	Biological Weapons Convention (1974)
1979	SALT Treaty (United States-Soviet Union)
1985	Treaty of Rarotonga (South Pacific Nuclear Free Zone Treaty) (1986)
1991	START I Treaty (United States-Russia)
1993	START II Treaty (United States, Russia, and three other former Soviet Republics) (2000)
1993	Chemical Weapons Convention (1997)
1995	Bangkok Treaty (Southeast Asia Nuclear Weapon Free Zone Treaty) (2002)
1996	Pelindaba Treaty (Africa Nuclear Weapon Free Zone Treaty)

a. The parenthetical date listed is the year of entry into force as determined by the minimum number of ratifications needed.

mament outside the relatively small group of states that already have or seek to acquire nuclear weapons.

Although nuclear proliferation and disarmament remain high-priority issues, concerns about other weapons of mass destruction have steadily risen as the ease of developing or acquiring chemical and biological weapons has become more apparent. Fears that terrorist groups that cannot be bound by international treaties might use such weapons, as the Japanese group Aum Shinrikyo did in the Tokyo subway system in 1994, fuel those concerns.

▪ *Chemical and Biological Weapon Prohibition*

Since 1969, the issue of chemical and biological weapons (CBW) has appeared regularly on the agenda of the UN General Assembly. Pressures for controls on these weapons of mass destruction stemmed from the fact that large stockpiles of various CBW were known to exist in a number of countries and CBW had been used in several conflicts, for example, by the United States in Vietnam and by Iraq in the Iran-Iraq War. Also, although the destructive power of nuclear weapons is well known, that of chemical and biological weapons is less so. Chemical weapons, if effectively used, have the potential to kill tens of thousands of people; the potential toll from biological weapons could number in the hundreds of thousands. Both could also be used against livestock or agriculture, magnifying the potential economic or environmental damage. Since one of the major principles behind arms control efforts is to reduce the destructiveness of armed conflicts, major efforts for more than a century have been directed at suppressing chemical and biological weapons as instruments of warfare. These efforts have been given added impetus with the threat that terrorist groups could acquire and use CBW.

During the Cold War period, the United States and United Kingdom refused to agree to a prohibition of chemical weapons, while the Soviet Union pushed for a ban on both chemical and biological weapons. The United States, in fact, had never become a party to the 1925 Geneva Protocol, although in 1969 President Nixon announced that the United States would never use chemical weapons except in response to their use by others, and he called for ratification of the Geneva Protocol, which was accomplished in 1975. Simultaneously, the United States unilaterally renounced the use or production of biological weapons, and in 1971 the major powers agreed to a Convention on the Prohibition of the Development, Production and Stockpiling of Bacteriological (Biological) and Toxin Weapons and on Their Destruction.

The Biological Weapons Convention (BWC) came into force in 1975 and now has 146 parties. Although the treaty calls for destruction of existing stocks and restriction of materials to research purposes, there is no provision for inspection. Several states, most notably Iraq, Iran, Libya, Egypt, and Syria, as well as Russia, are suspected to possess such weapons. Every treaty review conference has called for steps to address the weaknesses, and in 1994 the state parties to the treaty authorized an ad hoc group to draft proposals for a protocol to strengthen the effectiveness and implementation of the BWC. In 2001, the United States rejected the draft text and the approach taken by the ad hoc group, insisting a traditional arms control approach would not work with biological weapons and that the proposals to strengthen the BWC would compromise U.S. national security and confidential business information of the bio-tech industry. The United States pushed a different approach involving an initiative by the G-8 in 2002 to create a Global Partnership Against the Spread of Weapons and Materials of Mass Destruction, to which the Bush administration pledged $10 billion. In addition, the World Health Organization acted in 2002 to strengthen its surveillance system in the event of biological weapons attack; the informal Australia Group of thirty-three states and the EU Commission in 2002 tightened export control measures to keep CBW out of the hands of terrorist groups; and NATO took initiatives also to deal with biological weapons attacks. Still, many European and developing countries were deeply troubled by the U.S. rejection of the treaty revision process, and it will likely be many years before negotiations to tighten controls on biological weapons bear fruit.

Although stalled during the Cold War, efforts to eliminate chemical weapons moved much farther during the 1990s. The United States and Russia agreed to reduce their chemical weapon stocks in 1990, opening the way for the Conference on Disarmament to draft a long-awaited Chemical Weapons Convention (CWC). In 1993, the Chemical Weapons Convention was signed banning the production, acquisition, stockpiling, retention, or usage of such weapons. The CWC, unlike the biological weapons convention, includes on-site verification provisions and the threat of sanctions against violators, including those who have not signed the treaty. It came into effect in 1997 and now has 147 parties. Notably absent are Iraq, Libya, Syria, Egypt, North Korea, and Israel. The UN-related Organization for the Prohibition of Chemical Weapons (OPCW) that is charged with implementing the inspections began operations in early 1997. The OPCW has conducted hundreds of inspections at military and industrial facilities; as of 2001, half of the declared chemical weapon production capacity in eleven countries had been destroyed or converted to peaceful purposes and three of the four states known to possess chemical weapons had met the first deadline for destroying stockpiles (www.opcw.org).

The key difference between the chemical and biological weapons conventions and the NPT is the acceptance by all parties of a total ban on possession, development, and use of these weapons of mass destruction. In other words, there is no two-class system; total disarmament is the core regime norm. Both CBW treaties require parties to enact domestic legislation to permit criminal prosecution of individuals and companies that violate treaty provisions. All three treaties have in common an agreement between the two superpowers. In the case of the Biological Weapons Convention, Britain's support was also important. For the Comprehensive Test Ban, commitments of France and China were key. Only by having these major powers "on board" could the UN proceed with drafting the treaties. Yet, the experiences of the CTBT and BWC demonstrate the damage done when U.S. support for multilateral arms control treaties is lost.

The CBW regimes have incorporated other control efforts. The Australia Group mentioned above was formed after information about how Western trade with Iraq had aided that country's chemical weapons program in the 1980s (Chevrier 2002: 146). The group coordinates information and export policies on CBW to prevent trade in chemicals, biological agents, and equipment to make CBW. In South America, the Mendoza Accord of 1991 commits seven countries (Argentina, Brazil, Chile, Bolivia, Ecuador, Paraguay, and Uruguay) to a complete CBW prohibition. The UN Special Commission on Iraq (UNSCOM) and its successor, UNMOVIC, were responsible for overseeing efforts to eliminate Iraq's CBW between 1991 and 1998 and in 2002–2003. Their experience, however, also demonstrates the difficulties of getting violators to comply with international agreements and norms and of sustaining support for intrusive counterproliferation efforts against a violator. Russia is another concern, as it has not met deadlines for destroying stockpiles of chemical weapons. Some attribute this to lack of funding, others to political instability or disagreements between federal and regional authorities. Continued Russian noncompliance could provide other states with an excuse to delay or ignore their obligations. In addition, there is a close relationship between implementation of the two CBW treaties: "problems with the implementation of the CWC . . . have had a negative impact in the negotiations to strengthen the BWC" (Chevrier 2002: 152).

A very different path to arms control, however, was followed in a recent initiative involving a very conventional, but widely used and deadly weapon—landmines.

■ Banning Landmines

Just as nuclear arms were the symbol of the Cold War, antipersonnel landmines have become the symbol of the post–Cold War era. These weapons were increasingly used in the 1990s by irregular military forces in Angola, Afghanistan, Cambodia, and Bosnia. Landmines cause an unprecedented number of civilian injuries as unsuspecting people go into mined areas.

Worldwide as many as 110 million mines remain activated. Although land-mines cost as little as $3 each, de-mining costs can run $300 to $500 per mine. These weapons captured the attention and concern of the NGO community in a way not seen in other arms control issues, in part because they are a human security issue.

The International Campaign to Ban Landmines (ICBL) was launched in 1992 through coordinated efforts of nine organizations, including Vietnam Veterans of America and the International Red Cross. The campaign, uniting over one thousand different NGOs in fifty-five countries, benefited enormously from the growth of the Internet. Its objectives were to ban the use, production, stockpiling, and sale, transfer, or export of antipersonnel landmines; to conclude, implement, and monitor a landmine treaty; and to provide resources for de-mining, mine awareness programs, and victim rehabilitation and assistance.

The campaign organized a media effort aimed at raising public awareness of the human toll of landmines and selling the problem as a humanitarian rather than an arms control issue (Thakur and Maley 1999). Bolstered by the death of one of its supporters, Princess Diana, the campaign pushed for conclusion of the Convention on the Prohibition of the Use, Stockpiling, Production and Transfer of Anti-personnel Mines and on their Destruction in the record time of fourteen months between October 1996 and December 1997. Under the strong leadership of the Canadian Foreign Minister Lloyd Axworthy, countries supporting a treaty banning landmines participated in an ad hoc negotiating process that bypassed the UN Conference on Disarmament. Over one hundred countries signed the convention, but among the states refusing to sign was the United States, which argued that landmines were essential to national defense in Korea. Within a short time, more than forty countries had ratified the treaty, ushering it into international law in 1999. In acknowledgment of the ICBL's success, its coordinator Jody Williams was awarded the Nobel Peace Prize in 1997.

Among the convention's unusual features are the detailed role outlined for the NGOs, particularly the ICRC, in assessing the scope of the problem and providing financial and technical resources for implementation. NGO monitors report through the secretary-general to meetings of state parties that are attended by relevant governmental and nongovernmental organizations. UN Mine Action Centers in Cambodia, Afghanistan, Bosnia, and Angola train local people in de-mining techniques. Local UN support groups such as UNA/USA have initiated "Adopt a Minefield" programs to pay for de-mining activities.

The ICBL has concluded that the treaty is proving effective. One hundred and twenty-five countries have ratified it; another eighteen have signed but not yet ratified it; mine use has ceased in several countries where it had been prevalent; there have been large reductions in mine stockpiles (more than 34 million mines destroyed by sixty-one states); and casualties from landmines have declined. In addition, production and trade have dropped, although Myanmar, China, India, North and South Korea, Pakistan, Russia, Egypt, and the United States are among the countries still producing mines. Iraq is the only country that has not formally stated it is no longer exporting them. With respect to aid to victims and mine-clearing efforts, more than $1.4 billion has been contributed.

The issue of prohibiting and dismantling landmines is unique in the annals of arms control because of NGOs' key roles in pushing the issue to the top of the international agenda and in the treaty's enforcement. It is one of the few security issues that cannot be linked, however, to the Middle East conflict, a case study of which we now turn to as a way of illustrating many of the pieces of security governance.

■ Putting Together the Pieces of Security Governance

For more than a century, the Middle East has been the setting for one of the most dangerous, seemingly intractable conflicts in the world: the struggle between two peoples—Jews and Palestinian Arabs—claiming the same homeland. The competition between these two sets of national aspirations is complicated by the fact that the land they claim is holy for Jews, Christians, and Muslims; by Arab nationalism; and by the presence of a large percentage of the world's oil reserves in the region. Since the end of World War II, there have been four interstate wars and two uprisings by the Palestinian population within the territory occupied by Israel. Terrorism has been a tool of all sides. The search for a peaceful settlement has been frustrated by violence, hostile propaganda, refusal by one or both parties to compromise on basic principles, and deep-seated mistrust. Other security threats in the region, such as the eight-year war between Iran and Iraq in the 1980s, Iraq's invasion of Kuwait, and Iraq's efforts to develop weapons of mass destruction, cannot be disentangled from the Israeli-Palestinian-Arab state conflict. Almost every approach to security governance has been tried at some time or another to resolve these threats peacefully or, at least, to halt violence.

▪ *The Arab-Israeli Conflict*

IGOs, NGOs, and states have all played significant roles in efforts to deal with the Arab-Israeli conflict. There have been innumerable official and nonofficial mediations, preventive diplomacy, and peacemaking efforts by the UN, the United States, the European Union, NGOs, and others.

The roles of IGOs and NGOs.   Under the League of Nations' mandates system, Britain administered Palestine, Transjordan, and Iraq, while France assumed the same role for Syria and Lebanon, and the new organization endorsed the British government's 1917 Balfour Declaration promising a Jewish homeland in Palestine. Between World Wars I and II, large numbers of Jews emigrated to Palestine, triggering strong protests from Arab inhabitants, including a general strike from 1936 to 1939. The Holocaust fueled Zionism and sympathy for a Jewish homeland. With Jewish immigration surging after World War II, Arab fears rising, and clashes escalating, Britain relinquished its mandate and turned the problem over to the new United Nations. This was the first instance of countries using the UN as the world's "trauma center."

Before Israel was created on May 14, 1948, the UN first appointed a special commission to find a peacemaking formula (a partition plan) and mediators (Swedish Count Bernadotte and American Ralph Bunche) to bring the two sides closer together. When the Arab states attacked Israel, the UN sought a ceasefire with the help of UN mediator, Ralph Bunche, who then devised a way to help the parties maintain it (the UN Truce Supervision Organization or UNTSO—a forerunner of other peacekeeping operations that is still in existence). Then, the UN established what was expected to be a temporary agency to aid the 600,000 Palestinian refugees, the UN Relief and Works Agency (UNRWA).

The UN General Assembly has been a primary forum for debate on the Arab-Israeli conflict. For Israel and the Palestinians, it was also a critical legitimizer, first with the 1947 partition plan that proposed creating two states, then in Israel's UN membership (1949), the PLO's acceptance as legitimate representative of the Palestinian people (1974), and recognition of Palestinian rights to self-determination and statehood (1970 and 1974). The UN was also of great value to the Arab states and Palestinians between 1949 and 1974 for preventing solution on terms acceptable only to Israel and for publicizing the Palestinian cause.

Because of differences among the P-5 on Middle East issues, the Security Council was often less central. Still, it established the framework for a just solution in Resolution 242 after the Six-Day War in 1967, when Israel more than doubled its territory by occupying the West Bank, Gaza, and Golan Heights. Resolution 242 affirmed the principle of exchanging land for peace: in return for Israeli withdrawal from territories occupied in 1967, all states in the region would acknowledge the sovereignty, territorial integrity, and independence of every other state and the right to live in peace. The resolution also recognized the need to guarantee freedom of navigation in international waterways, to find a just solution to the refugee problem, and to establish guarantees of independence and boundaries. Later, the council delegitimized the creation of Israeli settlements in the Occupied Territories (1979) and changes in the status of Jerusalem (1969 and 1980). With Resolution 1397 (2002), it affirmed "a vision of a region

Map 8.2   Middle East

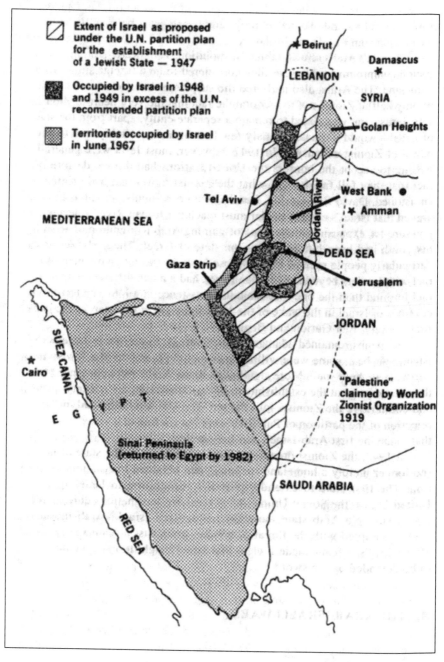

where two states, Israel and Palestine, live side by side within secure and recognized borders."

In addition to UNTSO, the UN has organized four peacekeeping operations in the Arab-Israeli conflict since 1948. Two of these remain along the Syrian and Lebanese borders with Israel, although the UN Interim Force in Lebanon (UNIFIL) is among the UN's least-effective peacekeeping efforts. Its contingents have been shot at, overrun by Israeli forces, and taken hostage. Still, the Security Council and parties to the conflict prefer having peacekeepers present to abandoning their mission. The United Nations Emergency Force (UNEF I), created during the 1956 Suez Crisis, initiated first-generation peacekeeping. It was withdrawn just prior to the 1967 Six-Day War at the request of Egypt's President Nasser. UNEF II was established following the 1973 Yom Kippur War to implement the disengagement agreement between Israel and Egypt and terminated in 1979 following the Camp David accords, when an ad hoc multilateral force was recruited to patrol the Sinai.

Peacekeeping operations have been a key way to contain the conflict between Israel and its neighboring Arab states, as well as to forestall direct superpower intervention during the Cold War. They have done little to steer Israel and the Arab states toward a peaceful settlement, however. During U.S.-brokered negotiations in July 2000, the Palestinians unsuccessfully proposed an international monitoring operation to oversee Palestinian statehood and Israeli withdrawal.

Every UN secretary-general has endeavored to use his position and diplomatic skills directly or indirectly through a special representative to mitigate immediate threats or acts of violence and to continue the search for peaceful settlement of the Arab-Israeli conflict. Experience has shown, however, that the secretary-general can only be effective in a mediating role when he has strong backing from the P-5. Even then, his and the UN's leverage are limited because they cannot provide either side with sufficient incentives and guarantees to conclude and enforce peace. Only major powers can provide the latter. Furthermore, Israel has not seen the UN as an impartial actor since the 1960s, when the Arab states gained the support of the Non-Aligned Movement, and has often pushed measures that led the United States to exercise its veto in the Security Council in Israel's defense, a pattern that continues today. The UN retains its humanitarian role with regard to Palestinian refugees, its peacekeeping role, and its forum role, but has had to collaborate with others in pursuing the mediating and peacemaking roles.

Three other IGOs have played roles with respect to the conflict: the Arab League, the Non-Aligned Movement, and the Organization of the Islamic Conference (OIC). The Arab League has derived much of its energy from the conflict with Israel. It imposed an embargo on trade with Israel. At its first summit in 1964, it pushed the Palestinians to create the PLO by calling for establishment of the Palestinian National Council, then pushed the idea of Palestinian rights first within the Non-Aligned Movement and subsequently in the UN. The Arab states had not foreseen, however, how the PLO would become an independent voice for the Palestinians (independent, that is, of the Arab governments). Beginning in the late 1960s, what had been a conflict between Arab states acting on behalf of the Palestinians and Israel was gradually transformed into a triangular conflict with the Palestinians as an independent third party. Differences among Arab states after the 1967 war weakened the Arab League as an effective player. It reentered the scene in March 2002 by endorsing a proposal by Saudi Arabia to normalize relations with Israel in return for withdrawal from the Occupied Territories, establishment of a Palestinian state in the West Bank and Gaza Strip, and a "just solution" of the refugee problem.

Between 1961 and 1975, the NAM was the first forum in which the Arab states sought broad support for the Palestinian cause. Ideas endorsed at Non-Aligned summits subsequently were incorporated into UN General Assembly resolutions. At its first summit in 1961, the NAM declared its support for "full restoration of all the rights of the Arab People of Palestine"; it endorsed the struggle for liberation in 1964; it accepted the PLO as the legitimate representative of the Palestinians in 1973 and as a full member in 1975; and in 1979, it affirmed the need for a Palestinian state. Radical Arab states never got the NAM, however, to support efforts to challenge Israel's membership in the UN. In fact, the NAM affirmed Israel's right to exist at the 1970 summit. With most developing countries among its members, the NAM made an excellent forum in which to build a united third world on this as well as other issues (Morphet 1983: 8–12).

The Organization of the Islamic Conference was formed in 1969 by conservative Muslim states concerned about the issue of Jerusalem after the 1967 war. When the OIC's charter was approved in 1972, one of the organization's key objectives was "to co-ordinate efforts for the safeguarding of the Holy Places and support of the struggle of the people of Palestine, and help them to regain their rights and liberate their land." Many of the OIC's actions, however, duplicated those of the NAM.

Numerous NGOs are active in the Middle East, including major international humanitarian groups such as the Red Cross/Red Crescent Societies, Doctors Without Borders, and Save the Children that aid Palestinian refugees throughout the region, not just in the Occupied Territories. Indigenous groups are increasing in countries where they are permitted to organize. In addition, peace groups such as the American Friends Service Committee have endeavored to play a role in fostering dialogue and trust among the peoples of the region. Because many NGOs have funding from outside the region, however, their motives have often been suspect.

Key states. States have aided and blocked efforts to manage the Arab-Israeli conflict. To ascertain the degree of support in Israel for peace at any given time, however, one must delve into Israel's fractious democratic politics. In the Arab states, with single leaders and largely authoritarian regimes, such domestic politics matter less. Still, one frequently hears Arab leaders refer to the "Arab street"—a general reference to their increasingly aware and potentially volatile people. The PLO may be the legitimate representative of the Palestinians, but it is by no means the only Palestinian organization, and Yasser Arafat has had competitors for leadership for most of the last thirty years. While he himself is authoritarian by instincts, pressure for greater democracy has been growing and few think Arafat can control all Palestinian groups. Hamas, for example, is an important supporter of suicide bombings in the Occupied Territories and also provides many social services. Clearly, the willingness of Israel, the various Arab states—moderate, radical, peacemaking, or rejectionist—and the Palestinian groups, especially the PLO, to meet, to compromise, and to make peace are key to any governance efforts.

The Arab states, Israel, and the Palestinians all expect that they need a "mediator-umpire" to help them resolve their differences. From the Arab and Palestinian perspective, only the United States has leverage to get Israel to make concessions because Israel currently receives about $3 billion a year from the United States, making it the single largest recipient of U.S. aid. From the Israeli point of view, only the United States can provide incentives for the Arab states and Palestinians (Stein and Lewis 1996: 463).

Every U.S. president since Lyndon Johnson has been drawn into the Middle East conflict, often more than he wanted to be. Former National Security Adviser and Secretary of State Henry Kissinger initiated shuttle diplomacy to secure disengagement agreements between Egypt and Israel and Syria and Israel, after the 1973 war, since they would not talk directly with each other. Kissinger also perceived, however, that the stalemated outcome of that war had created conditions in which it might be possible to go further. From this was born the idea of a step-by-step peace process that contrasted sharply with earlier efforts to convene a peace conference and formulate a comprehensive peace plan acceptable to all parties. That peace process has persisted since the mid-1970s, sometimes stalled and little more than a cover for parties' unwillingness to move forward, at other times productive of new steps such as the 1979 Camp David Accord, the U.S.-PLO dialogue begun in 1988 after Arafat renounced terrorism, the Oslo agreement (1993), and the Israeli-Jordanian agreement (1994). The second Palestinian uprising or Intifada that began in September 2000, however, and the increased violence between Israelis and Palestinians, unraveled much of the trust and progress achieved over many years.

American policy has remained highly consistent over the years based on its interests in ensuring the security of Israel, achieving an Arab-Israeli peace settlement, maintaining access to Middle East oil, combating terrorism, preventing the spread of nuclear and chemical weapons, and promoting the stability and democratization of Arab states. Prior to 1989, blocking Soviet influence in the region was also a major interest. The United States has consistently insisted that Israel not be required to give up any land occupied in 1967 without gaining recognition and security guarantees from the Arab states. It regards East Jerusalem as occupied territory and whatever the final solution to the problem of Jerusalem, it opposes division of the city. The United States was slow to accept the concept of Palestinian rights, and only with the 1993 Oslo agreement did it endorse a Palestinian entity. It has helped maintain Israel's military superiority and tacitly accepted its nuclear weapons program (Quandt 2001: 5–6). In 2002, President George W. Bush called for the creation of an independent Palestinian state within three years and proposed a "new roadmap to peace." Continuous violence among the parties, however, suggests the process is derailed, if not dead, leaving the conflict as intractable as ever.

Western European countries share many American interests, but have not always agreed with the United States on how to achieve them. They have also sought to enhance the common foreign policy of the European Community/Union by playing a mediating role in the Middle East. The first joint EC statement on the Middle East was issued shortly after the 1973 war. In 1977, long before the United States would talk directly with the PLO, the EC undertook efforts to promote this, and in 1980 declared that the PLO would have to be a participant in negotiations for a peace settlement. It joined the UN, United States, and Soviet Union in sponsoring the 1991 Madrid Conference, which marked the first time all parties sat around the same table. Since then, EU officials have periodically traveled to the region in an effort to sustain the peace process or halt the violence of the second Intifada.

One European country, in particular, however, assumed a special role—namely, Norway. From January to August 1993, this small, northern European state facilitated the first secret talks between Israel and the PLO. These produced a Declaration of Principles that became the Oslo Accord signed by Yasser Arafat and Yitzhak Rabin in September 1993. The accord changed the landscape of the Middle East for the rest of the 1990s. Why Norway? As a member of the Norwegian foreign ministry team noted, "Other countries had closer contact with the PLO than did Norway, and others had an even more unstrained relationship with Israel, but few had our trusted relationship with both. . . . We were able to provide the perfect camouflage for such a channel" (Egeland 1999: 531–532).

The Norwegian-facilitated talks did not attempt to solve all problems at once, but concentrated on building the confidence of Israeli and Palestinian participants in their ability to deal with each other. The Oslo Accord outlined a step-by-step process to Palestinian self-rule in selected West Bank areas and Gaza, democratic elections, and international economic assistance for areas under Palestinian rule. Yet Israel's failure to carry out key parts of the agreement and the PLO's failure to stop terrorism ultimately derailed what had looked so promising. The breakdown of the Oslo process and failure of subsequent U.S.-led mediation efforts highlight a number of lessons for security governance.

Lessons about peace processes.   First, direct talks do not ensure progress, nor do large, general peace conferences intended to resolve all major issues. While face-to-face negotiations symbolize mutual recognition and legitimacy, when there is deep mistrust among the parties, such talks are rarely successful without the presence of a mediator.

Second, predicting when the Arab-Israeli situation may be ripe for further steps toward peaceful resolution is very difficult. Norway seized an historic window when its quiet contacts revealed the possibilities for informal, secret negotiations. Yet, in September 2000, the Israeli-Palestinian peace process collapsed. Some might suggest that peace in the Middle East is simply impossible. Others might suggest that the parties were not yet sufficiently convinced that violence would not allow them to prevail, hence not ready to make the necessary painful concessions.

Third, only the United States has the resources to provide incentives, assurances, and guarantees when the time is ripe for progress, and sustained, personal involvement of the U.S. president is essential to progress. Presidents Carter, Bush (both father and son), and Clinton have all discovered this. In the Arab cultures where individual leaders dominate, only the U.S. president can convey the necessary messages (Stein and Lewis 1996: 469). Still, no diplomatic effort will succeed when the parties themselves are not prepared to take the difficult steps required to resolve outstanding major issues.

Fourth and finally, there is still a role for the UN, Arab League, NGOs, the EU, and individual states like Norway. The forum and legitimating functions of IGOs have proven immensely useful in the past and will likely again in the future. Peacekeeping, refugee assistance, and political and economic development aid for a Palestinian state are all areas where UN agencies, the EU, and many NGOs have experience and resources for peace-building.

The Arab-Israeli conflict is often linked with terrorism. Arab states,

Israelis, and Palestinians alike have used terrorism at one time or another. Beginning in the early 1970s, it was a primary means by which Palestinian groups sought to increase international awareness of their cause. Many observers would label Israel's heavy use of military force in the Occupied Territories as state terrorism, while Jewish settlers have carried out acts of terrorism as well. Libya, Syria, and Iraq have supported or sponsored terrorism. The governance approaches for dealing with terrorism, however, differ significantly from those applied to the Arab-Israeli and other Middle East conflicts, and since the problem is not exclusively a Middle East problem, those approaches are much broader in scope and will be addressed shortly.

Other Middle East Threats to International Peace

Persistent and pervasive as the impact of the Arab-Israeli conflict has been on the Middle East and international security, we single out two other threats to international peace to illustrate briefly other applications of pieces of governance. These involve the long Iran-Iraq War in the 1980s and Iraq's WMD programs.

In the case of the Iran-Iraq War, patient, quiet diplomacy by then UN Secretary-General Javier Peréz de Cuéllar is widely credited for securing a peaceful solution. With more than one million casualties on both sides and the use of chemical weapons by Iraq, this conflict had threatened oil supplies and Persian Gulf security for most of the 1980s. The UN deployed a small (399-man) military observer group (UNIIMOG) from August 1988 to February 1991 to supervise the ceasefire.

The Middle East is the only region of the world without any regional arms control agreements. The multiple, overlapping conflicts and domestic instability in many countries have precluded such cooperative security steps. Israel's undeclared nuclear capability and its superior conventional forces have spurred other states, particularly Iran, Libya, and Iraq, to seek their own nuclear, chemical, or biological weapons capability to counter Israel's (and each other's). Egypt, for example, refused to sign the chemical weapons convention unless Israel signed and ratified the NPT. Conventional arms sales to the region have long been high. Some states are parties to the NPT, CTBT, CWC, and BWC, but as the case of Iraq has amply demonstrated, such commitments may be meaningless. The newest worries are that terrorist groups will gain access to WMD and increase the already serious new security threats terrorism poses. The question is whether security governance approaches can be adapted to cope with these new threats.

New Threats to Security: Coping with Terrorism

Terrorism is an old threat to individual, state, and regional security that has taken on a number of new guises, making it a much greater threat to international peace and security. Terrorist acts occurred in Greek and Roman times, often as individual acts of violence against a ruler. In the Middle Ages, such acts were perpetrated against groups, while during the French Revolution, acts of terrorism were sponsored by the state itself. Organized state terrorism reached its zenith in Nazi Germany and in the Soviet Union under Josef Stalin. The Middle East conflict spawned a cycle of terror following the 1967 Arab-Israeli war and Israeli occupation of the West Bank, Gaza, and the Golan Heights. Various Palestinian and other Arab groups began using terrorism to draw attention to their cause of establishing a homeland (or destroying Israel). Terrorism has also been a tool of various European anarchist and Marxist groups, the Irish Republican Army (IRA), Basque separatists in Spain, Colombian and other drug traffickers, the Tamil Tigers in Sri Lanka, Chechen rebels in Russia, Islamic fundamentalists, Hindu nationalists, and many other groups in different parts of the world.

Terrorism is a quintessentially political act. The political purposes may be more or less explicit, depending on the nature of the perpetrating group. It has typically been viewed as a weapon of the weak who cannot achieve their political aims through normal political processes. Contemporary terrorism differs in some respects from that of the past. Terrorist acts are directed not only at heads of state but against innocent civilians. The goals are not limited to overthrowing a government or leader, or gaining an independent Tamil, Palestinian, or Basque homeland, but include eliminating Western, and especially American, presence in Islamic holy lands. The ease of international travel and telecommunications have made transnational terrorism less confined to a particular geographic place and enabled terrorist groups to form global networks and to move money, weapons, and people easily from one area to another. An implicit link has come also from groups copying each other's tactics—the so-called demonstration effect. The possibility that terrorists might acquire biological, nuclear, chemical, or miniaturized weapons has raised the dangers of terrorist attacks and also made detection more problematic.

Terrorism involves four major elements: (1) premeditation, where the perpetrator has decided to commit a terrorist act to instill terror or fear in others; (2) political, religious, or ideological motivation—a cause; (3) targets that are generally noncombatants and often appear to be chosen at random, ranging from innocent bystanders, tourists, soldiers, and bureaucrats to those holding prominent positions; and (4) secretiveness, where terrorists belong to clandestine groups or are sponsored by states (Pillar 2001).

Terrorist acts have taken a variety of forms, making them difficult to deter or prevent. During the 1970s, airline hijackings were a popular method for projecting a message. For example, in 1976, an Air France plane with mostly Israeli passengers was hijacked by two German Baader

Meinhoff members and two members of the Popular Front for the Liberation of Palestine (PFLP) and flown to Uganda. Israeli commandos subsequently seized the airfield and liberated the passengers. Among the numerous other cases, Arab terrorists hijacked a Lufthansa flight in 1977; members of the Lebanese Party of God seized a TWA flight to Beirut in 1985, while Abu Nidal's Arab Revolutionary Command hijacked an Egypt Air flight to Malta in the same year. Hostage taking has been another tactic used by terrorist groups. Two notable incidents include the seizure of fifty-two American diplomats at the U.S. Embassy in Iran in 1979 by Iranian students, and the 1985 seizure of the Italian cruise ship *Achille Lauro*, taking all of its passengers hostage.

The most common terrorist incidents involve the use of bombs on airplanes, trucks, cars, ships, or suicide bombers. Prominent examples include Pan American Flight 103 that blew up over Lockerbee, Scotland, in 1988; the bombing of the U.S. Marine barracks in Lebanon in 1983 that killed 241 marines; the bombing of a West Berlin disco in 1986 that was ultimately linked to Libya; the 1993 World Trade Center bombing; the 1995 and 1996 bombings in Saudi Arabia against U.S. military installations; the simultaneous attacks on the U.S. embassies in Nairobi, Kenya, and Dar es Salaam, Tanzania, in 1998; and the boat-delivered bombing of the USS *Cole* in 2000 in Yemen. In addition, although the four planes involved in the September 11, 2001, attacks were initially hijacked, they were turned into lethal weapons of mass destruction in a new twist on the old car-bomb strategy. Suicide bombings were pioneered by young members of the Tamil Tigers in Sri Lanka, and then adopted by young Palestinians during the second Intifada, and by the September 11 hijackers. Public buses, markets, and restaurants in the Occupied Territories and Israel itself have been popular targets for Palestinian suicide bombers.

A different set of concerns surrounds the possibility of terrorist groups gaining control of weapons of mass destruction or the materials to produce them. The sarin attack on the Tokyo subway in 1995 by Aum Shinrikyo was a warning of the pandemonium and casualties (twelve deaths, 5,000 hospitalized) that a chemical attack could produce. The ease with which chemical weapons especially can be fabricated and used makes this a major concern. There are more problems with terrorists acquiring and delivering biological and nuclear weapons. Nonetheless, these concerns magnify the importance of controlling weapons of mass destruction.

After a lull in the 1980s, terrorist activity escalated in the 1990s with both the perpetrators and targets becoming more diverse. Just as earlier, much of it arose out of the Middle East, from the Palestinians' quest for self-determination, their own internal conflicts over strategy, rivalries among various Islamic groups, and the rise of Islamic fundamentalism. The number of religious-based groups as a proportion of active terrorist groups has increased significantly since 1980. Many individuals and groups were trained in Afghanistan during the *mujahideens'* war against the Soviet Union and went on to commit many terrorist acts in the 1990s. Of particular importance was the development of Al-Qaeda—a shadowy network of Islamic fundamentalist groups in many countries—led by Osama bin Laden and disaffected individuals from Saudi Arabia, Egypt, and Yemen that has drawn recruits from around the world. The groups are linked by hatred of the United States and Israel and desire to destroy freedom and the rule of law. Al-Qaeda has become known for bombing large, symbolic American targets.

■ International Responses to Terrorism

Legal instruments have been a primary means by which the international community has responded to terrorism. Twelve conventions now form the core body of international law dealing with terrorism (see Table 8.4). Hijackings, for example, led to three treaties on airline and airport safety that declared terrorist acts against civil aviation illegal and sought to ensure the safety of the flying public. These measures, including the Convention for the Suppression of Unlawful Seizure of Aircraft (1970) that required

Table 8.4 International Terrorism Conventions

Year	Convention
1963	Convention on Offences and Certain Acts Committed on Board Aircraft. Requires states to take custody of offenders.
1970	Convention for the Suppression of Unlawful Seizure of Aircraft. Requires parties to punish hijackers with severe penalties.
1971	Convention for the Suppression of Unlawful Acts against the Safety of Civil Aviation. Provisions for protections of airports.
1973	Convention on the Prevention and Punishment of Crimes against Internationally Protected Persons, including Diplomatic Agents. Punish those harming diplomats.
1979	Convention against the Taking of Hostages. Seizure of hostages punishable.
1980	Convention on the Physical Protection of Nuclear Material. Protect material during transport on land, sea, air.
1988	Convention for the Suppression of Unlawful Acts against the Safety of Maritime Navigation. Obliges parties to prosecute offenders who commit unlawful acts against ships.
1988	Protocol for the Suppression of Unlawful Acts against the Safety of Fixed Platforms located on the Continental Shelf. Safety for fixed platforms.
1988	Protocol on the Suppression of Unlawful Acts of Violence at Airports Serving International Civil Aviation
1991	Convention on the Marking of Plastic Explosives for the Purposes of Detection. Curbs use of unmarked and undetectable plastic explosives.
2001	International Convention for the Suppression of Terrorist Bombings. Denies safe havens to persons wanted for terrorist bombings.
2002	International Convention for the Suppression of the Financing of Terrorism. Obligates states to prosecute or extradite persons accused of funding terrorist activities. Requires banks to enact measures to identify suspicious transactions.

parties to punish hijackers with severe penalties, along with increased airport security, dramatically reduced incidents of airline hijacking. Concern about similar problems at sea led to the conclusion in the late 1980s of several conventions that guarantee safety of maritime navigation and fixed platforms on the continental shelf (i.e., drilling rigs). New international rules were established in an effort to curb hostage taking, while the Convention on the Physical Protection of Nuclear Material concluded in 1980 was designed to protect nuclear material during its transport and to complement other parts of the WMD legal regimes. The two most recent conventions aim at the problems of bombings and terrorist financing.

Legal prohibitions are neither definitive nor sufficient in themselves, however. Complicating all international efforts to deal with terrorism is the absence of a broadly accepted definition of terrorism. The UN General Assembly, even in the aftermath of September 11, still struggles over this problem. Two issues dominate the discussion: whether official acts of a state's armed forces should or should not be included in the definition of terrorism and whether violent acts conducted in a struggle against foreign occupation should be considered terrorism. In the first case, the United States and its allies want acts of official armed forces excluded from any definition of terrorism. In the second case, the Organization of the Islamic Conference contends that national liberation groups should be exempted on the grounds that "one person's terrorist is another person's freedom fighter." No agreement is likely soon (Burns 2002: 7–8).

There are other more pragmatic reasons why legal prohibitions are unlikely to be effective in combating terrorism. Terrorists almost always have networks of supporters in a resident population, making them very difficult to capture. Protecting populations from random and unexpected acts of violence is a virtually impossible task, given the availability of guns and bombmaking materials in the international marketplace, and the necessity, at least in Western democratic states, of balancing civil and human rights with antiterrorist efforts. Committed individuals or groups of terrorists are not only difficult to deter, but also to capture and punish.

Beyond creating a framework of international rules dealing with terrorism lie individual and collective state efforts to increase security, counterintelligence activities, interventions, and cooperation among national and international law enforcement agencies (Interpol and Europol) in tracking and apprehending terrorists. There is a shared interest among all targeted countries in the public good of destroying global terrorist networks, but the United States has the greatest stake in this effort, having become the primary target of transnational terrorism in the 1980s and 1990s. Many countries will likely free-ride on U.S. efforts (Enders and Sandler 2002: 162–163).

Sanctions have been another approach to dealing with states supporting terrorism, specifically Libya, Sudan, and Afghanistan. Well before September 11, 2001, the UN Security Council applied sanctions against three countries—Libya, Sudan, and Afghanistan—for their roles in support-ing terrorism. Also, the United States used the State Department's List of States Sponsoring Terrorism as a basis for sanctions ranging from a ban on economic aid and dual-use technologies to voting against World Bank loans to Iran, Iraq, Syria, Libya, Cuba, North Korea, and Sudan.

Key to counterterrorism efforts is cutting the sources of funds for ter-rorist activities and getting countries that harbor, aid, and support terrorists to stop such activities. Targeted sanctions provide a number of means for this, but there are also some significant governance challenges to surmount in order to make sanctions effective. Financial sanctions can only be effec-tive if bank secrecy is ended (including Swiss banks) and offshore financial havens in Caribbean and Pacific island nations such as the Barbados, Antigua, Nauru, and Vanuatu are closed down to terrorists and money laun-derers. Countries have to develop the legal and technical capabilities to monitor financial transactions, interdict accounts of particular individuals, and act quickly in order to deny terrorists time to move funds. A bigger challenge is developing means to regulate informal money transmissions systems such as *hawala,* an ancient system that allows money transfers without actual money movement or wire transfers. Also, the major financial powers (mostly OECD countries) have to be willing to cooperate. Diplomatic and aviation sanctions can be used to pressure countries harbor-ing and aiding terrorists to end their support. Measures to cut trafficking in arms, drugs, illicit diamonds, and other commodities are other governance tools.

The UN used various approaches to deal with Libya, Sudan, and Afghanistan's roles in international terrorism. To pressure Libya into giving up the two men indicted for the bombings of Pan American Flight 103 and France's UTA 772 (1989), the Security Council in 1992 and 1993 imposed travel sanctions, flight bans, diplomatic sanctions, an embargo on aircraft parts, and a ban on payments for flight insurance. In 1999, after Libya delivered the two suspects for trial in the Netherlands, UN (but not U.S.) sanctions were suspended.

Sudan was first put on the U.S. State Department list in 1993 for aiding groups including Al-Qaeda, Hamas, and Islamic Jihad. Osama bin Laden was then living in Sudan and there were a number of terrorist training camps in the country. After Sudan was implicated in an assassination attempt against Egyptian President Hosni Mubarek in 1995, the Security Council imposed diplomatic sanctions and a ban on international flights. The first led Sudan very quickly to expel Osama bin Laden; the second was never implemented because of the already severe humanitarian situation caused by Sudan's long civil war and because Egypt refused to support the flight ban. Even before September 11, Sudan had taken a number of other measures to counter terrorism, including signing several of the UN conventions; after September 11, when the United States certified that Sudan was providing intelligence information on Al-Qaeda and other networks, the Security Council lifted the diplomatic sanctions.

Sanctions against Afghanistan were ineffective until after the September 11 attacks when they became an incentive for change. UN members concluded in 1999 that a neutral UN role was impossible and only the Taliban's removal would end its support for terrorism (harboring Osama bin Laden after he fled Sudan), its continuing civil war, its role in the heroin trade, and its harsh treatment of women. Accordingly, the Security Council imposed an arms embargo, aviation and financial sanctions, a ban on sale of acetic anhydride used in processing opium into heroin, diplomatic restrictions, and a travel ban on Afghanistan. It took the unprecedented step of setting up an office for sanctions monitoring along with a panel of experts, because the six neighboring countries had such weak border control capabilities there was no hope of making sanctions effective without assistance. Even so, sanctioning a country that had been at war for decades, was overflowing with arms, and whose economy was "almost entirely illegal" was easy to declare but difficult to enforce (Cortright and Lopez 2002: 57). The diplomatic isolation, however, was effective: only three countries recognized the Taliban as the legitimate government of Afghanistan. They were also deprived of resources for economic development and of international air transport. The sanctions did not get the Taliban to end their support for terrorism, but following their overthrow in December 2001, lifting sanctions became an incentive for the new government. Financial sanctions, travel, transit, and arms embargoes remained in place on Taliban and Al-Qaeda leaders. September 11 made the fight against terrorism global and sanctions one tool among many.

■ *International Responses to September 11, 2001*

The September 11, 2001, attacks on the World Trade Center and the Pentagon were the most devastating terrorist acts to date. They elicited immediate and general condemnation by the international community. A day after the attacks, the UN Security Council passed Resolution 1368 condemning the heinous acts of terrorism and calling for international cooperation to punish those responsible. Most important, the resolution affirmed that the attacks were a breach of international peace under Chapter VII, thus giving the council authority to take action and legitimizing U.S. responses as self-defense. Never before had Chapter VII been invoked in connection with terrorist attacks. In addition, the North Atlantic Council invoked Article 5 of the NATO Treaty for the first time ever, declaring the attack on the United States an attack against all members and calling forth an automatic and unconditional commitment to assist in the war on terrorism.

Two weeks later, on September 28, 2001, the Security Council adopted Resolution 1373, obliging all states to clamp down on the financing, training, and movement of terrorists and to cooperate in a campaign against them, even with force if necessary. The resolution called on states to take a number of measures, including suppressing the financing of terrorist groups, freezing their assets, blocking the recruitment of terrorists, and denying them safe haven. The resolution also established the Counter Terrorism Committee (CTC) comprised of the fifteen members of the Security Council and designed to monitor states' capability to deny funding and/or haven to terrorists. The CTC analyzes reports from states concerning their capacity to deny terrorists needed resources. As of December 2003, it had received a total of 537 reports from member states, some of them second and third reports. The Security Council relies on a group of six independent experts to monitor states' efforts and correspond with them about implementation.

The European Union's responses to September 11 include steps to improve cooperation among its members in the fight against terrorism. Its borders, while designed to facilitate trade and free movement of peoples, have enabled terrorists and would-be terrorists to move easily across the continent. Different laws, different definitions of offenses, differences in sentencing, and differences in requirements for extradition hamper EU-wide law enforcement. Cooperation in general is more ad hoc, dependent on individual contacts and personalities. The commission has stepped up efforts begun prior to 9/11 to adopt a uniform definition of terrorism and require states to collect and exchange intelligence data about terrorists with counterparts in other EU countries. Since law enforcement remains generally a prerogative of EU member states, whether these measures will provide an effective regional governance structure is unclear. As September 11 brought to the fore, however, neither a national nor regional governance structure nor state nor regional norms are sufficient in themselves to address the problem of international terrorism effectively. The threat of terrorism is global, just as the networks of terrorist groups are global in scope.

One of the major responses to the September 11 attacks was the U.S.-led action in Afghanistan to root out the terrorist training camps, the Taliban government that had sanctioned Al-Qaeda and other terrorist groups, and the Al-Qaeda leadership. In December 2001, with the Taliban removed, the International Security Assistance Force (ISAF) became operational in Afghanistan. Operating with the UN Chapter VII authorization but as an ad hoc multilateral force, ISAF was charged with creating the security conditions essential for delivering humanitarian aid and protecting the capital, Kabul. It was also to assist the Afghan Interim Authority and train

Afghan armed forces and police. ISAF was not a conventional postconflict peacebuilding operation, however, since there was no peace agreement with the Taliban, no termination of the conflict, no reconciliation of contending parties, and a continuing presence of U.S. troops carrying out antiterrorism activities (Weinberger 2002). In August 2003, NATO assumed responsibility for ISAF in its first-ever operation outside Europe.

Addressing the problem of financing for terrorism is one of the thorniest problems, as most states have inadequate money-laundering legislation and ability to monitor financial transactions or the informal banking networks that are widely used by many terrorist organizations to transfer funds. The Al-Qaeda network raises money from a variety of sources and moves it in many different ways, for example, hawala as well as through mosques and charitable groups. Some of Al-Qaeda's funds have been traced to Sierra Leone and Liberia's role in the diamond trade, giving new importance to sanctions targeting conflict diamonds. The Convention for the Suppression of Financing for Terrorism is but one small part of an effort that includes the U.S. Treasury Department, finance ministries, and law enforcement agencies around the world, major banks, the IMF, the Financial Action Task Force (FATF) created by the G-7 in 1989, the Caribbean Financial Action Task Force, EU initiatives, and many others. There is no international organization with the mandate and expertise to direct and coordinate global efforts to deal with the problem of terrorist financing.

Terrorism, especially in its newer forms, has been described as the "privatization of war" in the twenty-first century (Nye 2002: 24). As such, it presents new threats to security and new governance challenges. Many pieces of security governance—such as preventive diplomacy, adjudication, mediation, peacekeeping, and arms control—are irrelevant when dealing with terrorism. Although there is wide agreement about the threat, the lack of an agreed definition makes effective legal or enforcement actions problematic in many situations. The weakness of most states' banking regulations and the ease of moving large amounts of money rapidly around the globe pose major problems for efforts to block terrorists' funding. This requires new modes of enforcement ranging from controls on money laundering and transparency of banking transactions to targeted sanctions such as those on conflict diamonds and leaders of states that support terrorism. It requires delegitimizing the appeal of suicide bombings among young people in groups such as Hamas, Islamic Jihad, and the Tamil Tigers. In cases where grievances are known, such as the Palestinian cause, renewed efforts to find peaceful and just solutions are needed. In cases such as Al-Qaeda where there are no specific political objectives, but rather broad anti-American sentiments, fundamentalist Islamic or other religious concerns, or deep alienation from static societies such as Saudi Arabia and Egypt, identifying appropriate governance responses is a far more elusive task.

■ The Challenges of Human Security

We began this chapter with a case study of the civil conflict in Somalia that was emblematic of many post–Cold War security problems of the 1990s. We end the chapter with the terrorist attacks of September 11, 2001, and the new security threats that terrorism poses. In the nine years between the two events, there were an extraordinary variety of threats to international peace and security and a corresponding variety of new governance approaches introduced. Neither negates the continuing value of older governance approaches.

Traditionally, international peace and security have meant states' security and the defense of states' territorial integrity from external threats or attack. As suggested by our discussions of an emerging norm of humanitarian intervention and a responsibility to protect, the concept of human security—the security of human beings in the face of many different kinds of threats—is beginning to take hold. It has become the foundation of some middle powers' foreign policy, such as Canada. These concerns for human security are reflected in discussions in succeeding chapters about the need to eradicate poverty and reduce the inequalities exacerbated by globalization, to promote environmentally sustainable development and greater respect for human rights norms, as well as to address the growing security threat posed by the HIV/AIDS pandemic. The concept of human security has arisen from greater understanding of how socioeconomic deprivation and exclusion, human rights abuses, and epidemiological threats have "a direct impact on peace and stability within and between states" (Newman 2001: 241). It also grows out of the increased involvement of actors other than states, and especially of civil society. In short, threats to peace and security are being defined not only in terms of state security but also in terms of human security. Existing security governance structures are ill equipped to deal with many new issues. Hence, the challenge is to enhance the effectiveness of existing pieces of governance for dealing with ongoing problems and to find innovative approaches for new ones.

■ Notes

1. Portions of this chapter are drawn from Karen A. Mingst and Margaret P. Karns. (2000) *The United Nations in the Post–Cold War Era,* 2nd ed. Boulder: Westview Press. Reprinted with permission of Westview Press.

■ Suggested Further Reading

Cortright, David, and George A. Lopez. (2002) *Sanctions and the Search for Security.* Boulder: Lynne Rienner Publishers.

Crocker, Chester A., Fen Osler Hampson, and Pamela Aall, eds. (2001) *Turbulent Peace: The Challenges of Managing International Conflict.* Washington, D.C.: United States Institute for Peace Press.

International Commission on Intervention and State Sovereignty. (2001) *The Responsibility to Protect: Report of the International Commission on Intervention and State Sovereignty.* Ottawa: International Development Research Centre for ICISS. The report is also available at http://www.iciss-cisse.gc.ca.

Jentleson, Bruce W. (1999) *Opportunities Missed, Opportunities Seized: Preventive Diplomacy in the Post–Cold War World.* Lanham, MD: Rowman and Littlefield.

Larsen, Jeffrey A., ed. (2002) *Arms Control: Cooperative Security in a Changing Environment.* Boulder: Lynne Rienner Publishers.

Stedman, Stephen John, Donald Rothchild, and Elizabeth M. Cousens. (2002) *Ending Civil Wars: The Implementation of Peace Agreements.* Boulder: Lynne Rienner Publishers.

Thakur, Ramesh, and Albrecht Schnabel, eds. (2001) *United Nations Peacekeeping Operations: Ad Hoc Missions, Permanent Engagement.* Tokyo: United Nations University Press.

■ Internet Resources

Campaign to Eliminate Conflict Diamonds: www.endconflictdiamonds.org/
Center for Nonproliferation Studies: www.cns.miis.edu
Human Security Bulletin: www.humansecurity.info
International Atomic Energy Agency: www.iaea.org
International Campaign to Ban Landmines: www.icbl.org
International Commission on Intervention and State Sovereignty:
    www.dfait-maeci.gc.ca/iciss-ciise/
International Crisis Group: www.intl-crisis-group.org
North Atlantic Treaty Organization: www.nato.int/
Organization for the Prohibition of Chemical Weapons: www.opcw.org
Organization for Security and Cooperation in Europe: www.osce.org
Stockholm International Peace Research Institute: www.sipri.org
UN Department of Peacekeeping Operations: www.un.org/Depts/dpko/home.htm

9

Promoting Human Development and Economic Well-Being

■ Case Study: Debt Relief

In August 1982, Mexico announced that it could pay neither the interest nor the principle due on its foreign debt. The idea of a country going bankrupt was unheard of, but Mexico was not alone. For example, in 1980, the debt of all developing countries was $567 billion; by 1992, it had reached $1.6 trillion and by 2000, $2.2 trillion. More than forty countries are caught in the so-called debt trap. They include a significant number of the world's poorest countries, especially in Africa, as well as middle-income countries in Latin America and Asia. Despite paying back over three times the $567 billion, debtors still owed 250 percent more than in 1980 (Ambrogi 1999: 3; data from www.johannesburgsummit.org). In 2001, Argentina defaulted on its debt and with that economic collapse the population living below the poverty line rose to 50 percent (Pettifor 2003: 4). Shortly thereafter, both Brazil and Turkey experienced crises as well. In the wake of the Iraq war, that country's debts, estimated at $120–130 billion, have become a factor in discussions of its reconstruction.

There are many reasons for the debt crisis. During the Cold War, loans for political reasons by governments such as the United States paid little attention to countries' creditworthiness. In the early 1980s, commercial banks were eager lenders, flush with OPEC petrodollars. The World Bank and IMF added to the debt burden with loans for structural adjustment programs and tough conditions that often triggered adverse economic consequences. Falling prices of commodities such as copper in the 1980s, combined with severe drought in many African countries and a steep rise in interest rates, made it impossible to service or refinance debts and meet basic human needs. In a number of cases, elites used the money for unprofitable projects, and in other cases, corrupt leaders siphoned funds destined for development needs. Thus, both debtors and creditors share blame for the debt crisis (Collins, Gariyo, and Burdon 2001: 137).

Overall, during the 1980s and early 1990s, there were significant changes in financial flows to developing countries, including a shift from official development assistance provided by governments and multilateral institutions to private capital flows, as well as a shift from syndicated bank lending to bond lending. The latter has given developing countries more choices and access to credit but with a higher risk of overindebtedness (Palley 2003).

The consequences of high debt levels and financial crises have been significant for many developing countries. Least-developed countries in Africa, for example, have spent four times more for debt servicing than on social services or education. Repayment crowds out opportunities for investment in the economy; infrastructure suffers; health care and education spending is cut; and poverty increases. As one commentator concludes, "Ordinary people did not benefit from many of the loans that gave rise to this debt, but under the rules of the global economic game, they bear the principal burden of repayment, keeping both them and future generations unjustly chained in dehumanizing poverty" (Ambrogi 1999: 3). Financial crises and debt have deepened the dependence of developing countries on foreign creditors and international institutions such as the IMF, limiting their citizens' ability to control their own policies and institutions.

In the mid-1990s, increasing public recognition of the debt problem and the suffering caused by IMF-mandated conditions led to a popular movement known as Jubilee 2000: a coalition of development-oriented NGOs, church, and labor groups that launched its campaign in Great Britain and drew its name from a biblical text (Leviticus 25) calling for remission of obligations every fifty years. Jubilee 2000 advocates debt cancellation to overcome injustice and poverty, rather than rescheduling, reduction, or mandated policy reforms, believing that such conditions adversely affect the poor who unfairly bear the greatest economic burden caused by debt. "Breaking the Chains of Debt" became a loud rallying cry. Jubilee also called attention to so-called odious debt—debts incurred by corrupt regimes and dictatorships on which, they argued, creditors should not have a claim. The group gained a broad international following with over sixty national Jubilee campaigns. By June 1999, petitions circulated in over one hundred countries had garnered more than seventeen million signatures (Collins, Gariyo, and Burdon 2001: 135).

The Jubilee campaign was especially adroit at simplifying a complex issue, placing it within a moral framework, and pressing creditors for debt adjustment. Although there are major issues of sound economic policy and "moral hazard" at stake, issues of fairness and global economic justice also mark this debate. Fairness is at issue in what countries get rescued from economic crisis, on what terms, as well as who bears the burden of adjustment. Justice rejects solutions that allow the IMF to protect its own claims and demands protection of the human rights of citizens in debtor nations.

In 1996, the IMF and World Bank undertook a major policy shift called the Heavily Indebted Poor Countries Initiative (HIPC). Bringing together various creditors, including the multilateral development banks, the Paris Club (official creditors), and other bilateral and commercial lenders, the plan proposed to provide forty-one most indebted poor countries with a means of achieving sustainable levels of debt. Never before had countries' debt been canceled or substantially rescheduled. Given the highly restrictive criteria, however, plans had been approved by 1999 for only four countries: Uganda, Bolivia, Guyana, and Mozambique.

Jubilee 2000 mobilized demonstrations to put pressure on international leaders. With fifty thousand supporters lining roads, bridges, and riverbanks around Cologne during the G-7/8 meeting in June 1999, leaders agreed to double their commitment to debt cancellation and to forgive the debts of at least twenty nations by 2000. Government pronouncements were full of references to "faster, deeper, and broader debt relief." Jubilee kept up its campaign at the September 2000 IMF-World Bank meeting in Prague, at numerous forums including the UN Economic Commission for Africa and the Commonwealth Secretariat, and in developing countries where they pressed countries to channel debt savings to poverty-reduction programs such as increasing primary-school enrollment. In 2003, twenty-six countries had debt relief packages in operation, average debt service was about 30 percent less, and social spending about 45 percent higher than in 1999 (Coate 2003: 190).

Although the debts of the poorest countries pose dilemmas of global economic justice, financial crises in middle-income countries such as Argentina, Brazil, Mexico, Turkey, and Indonesia pose severe threats to the stability of the global economy itself. The 1997–1998 financial crisis that began in Thailand, then spread throughout Asia to Brazil and Russia, demonstrated the consequences of globalization and, specifically, the liberalization of capital markets.

The debate over how to deal with the debts of larger countries (and the negative economic and social consequences of defaults) has major implications for the future structure of economic governance, especially the role of the IMF. The IMF itself has proposed a Sovereign Debt Restructuring Mechanism aimed at "market-access" countries whose debt is unsustainable. It is an effort to provide something currently missing, namely a process for orderly negotiation with creditors that is transparent, predictable, and productive of settlements consistent with countries' ability to pay, i.e., sustainable. It also calls for a dispute resolution forum independent of the IMF to verify parties' claims. Jubilee has put forward a framework comparable to the U.S. legal code on bankruptcy, including an independent court wherein all creditors and debtor nations' citizens would have their interests treated equally (Raffer 1990: 301–313). It recognizes a role for the IMF in lending to debtor countries during negotiations and in analyzing debt sustainability, but would include all debts and allow for citizen input. The alternative proposals differ sharply. The IMF is interested in improving capital market efficiency and, thereby, stimulating economic development. It explicitly excludes debts owed to the IMF and other multilateral institutions; it provides for no citizen input on the legitimacy of debts incurred by corrupt or nondemocratic regimes. The NGOs are interested in canceling corruptly accumulated debt and relieving developing countries of the burden of large interest payments to rich countries, the IMF, and other financial institutions. Calling the IMF's proposal unbalanced, they want citizen input during the debt verification stage so that citizens could request the invalidation of odious debts and a fully transparent negotiation process (Pettifor 2003).

Debt relief illustrates how issues of economic governance and promoting economic growth and well-being touch highly political questions of "who gets what" as well as questions of fairness and justice. Some argue that the international financial system since World War II has facilitated the period of greatest economic growth in history; others argue that this system "has been largely imposed by a small group of powerful financial agents . . . [and] has led to instability and recurrent financial crises that have severely harmed the interests of poor countries and their people" (Pettifor 2003: 2).

■ An Evolving Global Economy

The visibility of the Jubilee movement and of economic issues today makes it hard to remember that international economic relations in 2004 are vastly different than they were at the end of World War II in 1945, let alone in 1900. In 1945, there were roughly fifty sovereign states; economies were largely national; there was limited interdependence; policies were elite led. There were also four competing sets of ideas and economic systems in the world. The Soviet Union had established a model of socialist, command economies, dominated by central planning and state ownership of all land and industry. There were a handful of liberal market systems led by the United States. The imperial preference systems of the major European colonial powers maintained privileged relationships between their economies and colonies. Finally, a majority of countries pursued mercantilist, statist economic policies. Tariff and other barriers impeded the growth of trade, movement of capital, and the convertibility of currencies. There was no precedent for and no international institutions providing assistance to countries experiencing economic difficulties, or for development, let alone debt relief. Functional IGOs such as the Universal Postal Union and the International Telegraph Union had been established during the nineteenth century to help states coordinate their use of new technologies and to manage rising economic interdependence, but the scope of their activity was limited, as discussed in Chapter 3.

Today, there are 191 sovereign states; almost all national economies are open to some degree and linked in patterns of complex interdependence that include globalized production in some industries, global financial markets, and vastly expanded world trade—elements of a single global economy. Multinational corporations and markets are important actors alongside states, and NGOs are making their voices heard. One idea dominates: liberal (or neoliberal) market capitalism, with socialist and statist economic policies largely discredited because of their failure to produce sustained economic growth. Yet along with globalization comes a need for expanded governance. A large number of formal and informal international institutions, both global and regional, have been established to help countries manage international economic relations, and to promote development and growth. These are important pieces of economic governance. As the debt relief case highlights, the fairness of these pieces, especially to poor, less developed countries, is disputed.

Much of this chapter, then, is the story of how ideas concerning both national economic systems and the global economy have addressed economic growth and human development. It is also the story of how various pieces of governance, global and regional, formal and informal, have been created and what roles they now play in international economic relations.[1] Economic globalization in recent years has accentuated the need for coordination of countries' economic policies; for rules to manage currency exchange and to reduce trade barriers; for mechanisms to resolve trade disputes and deal with financial and debt crises; and to address linkages between trade, labor issues, and the environment. These changing needs have been met through reforms of already existing institutions as well as the creation of new ones. Let us look at the evolution of the key ideas of global economic governance.

■ The Globalization of Liberal Economic Norms

Liberal economic norms have a long genesis dating from the eighteenth-century British economist Adam Smith down to contemporary thinkers. Underpinning these norms is the belief that human beings act in rational ways to maximize their self-interest. As a result, markets develop to produce, distribute, and consume goods, enabling individuals to improve their own welfare. Competition within markets ensures that prices will be as low as possible. Thus, in stimulating individual (and therefore collective) economic growth, markets epitomize economic efficiency. Government institutions play a role, providing basic order in society, facilitating free flow of trade, and maximizing economic intercourse. At the international level, if national governments and international institutions encourage the free flow of commerce and do not interfere in the efficient allocation of resources provided by markets, then increasing interdependence among economies will lead to greater economic development for all states.

Yet all states are not at the same level of economic development. Less developed states are unable to provide basic infrastructure, the foundation of development. Their governments and people are unable to save for investment, resulting in a financing gap. This gap must be narrowed for development to occur. If the state cannot provide sufficient financing, then grants and loans from other countries, international organizations, and private investors may be used to jump-start the economic development process on a temporary basis.

■ The Bretton Woods Institutions and the Washington Consensus

The Bretton Woods institutions have been integral to the growth of a liberal economic order. As discussed in Chapter 3, the World Bank was to rehabilitate war-damaged economies and provide development capital to narrow the financing gap. The International Monetary Fund was to provide short-term aid to compensate for balance-of-payments shortfalls and ensure a stable monetary system. The General Agreement on Tariffs and Trade (GATT) was to facilitate economic growth through reduced barriers to international trade in lieu of the proposed International Trade Organization. All three institutions have experienced changes in orientation as described below, but they remain the cornerstones of the liberal economic order that now encompasses almost all countries. And by the beginning of the 1990s, there emerged a version of liberal economic ideology called the Washington Consensus. This held that only by following the "correct" economic policies, as espoused by the Bretton Woods institutions and the U.S. government, could states achieve economic development. The Washington Consensus became the dominant approach to economic prosperity undergirding almost all international development lending and IMF aid to countries experiencing financial and debt crises. Ingredients of the consensus include using public expenditures in a pro-growth, pro-poor way for basic health care, education, and infrastructure; fiscal discipline; privatization of industry; liberalization of trade and foreign direct investment; government deregulation in favor of open competition; and tax reform. Today, there is less agreement between the U.S. government and international financial institutions, so "any Washington consensus has simply ceased to exist" (Williamson 2003: 12).

■ The Role of Multinational Corporations

MNCs are the vanguard of the liberal order. They are "the embodiment par excellence of the liberal ideal of an independent world economy. [They have] taken the integration of national economies beyond trade and money to the internationalization of production. For the first time in history, production, marketing, and investment are being organized on a global scale rather than in terms of isolated national economies" (Gilpin 1975: 39). For liberals, MNCs represent the most efficient mechanism for economic development and improved well-being. MNCs invest capital worldwide, they open new markets, they introduce new technologies, provide jobs, and finance projects that industrialize and improve agricultural output. They are the transmission belt for capital, ideas, and economic growth and an important piece of economic governance.

Early forerunners of today's MNCs include the Greek, Phoenician, and Mesopotamian traders, the British East India Co., the Hudson Bay Co., Levant Co., and the Dutch East India Co. in the seventeenth and eighteenth centuries. The prominence of MNCs has increased dramatically, however, since the 1960s, facilitated in part by the formation of the European common market and by liberalization of trade generally. Although there are over 45,000 MNCs, with more than 280,000 foreign affiliates, MNCs are actually very concentrated. Just one percent of the MNCs own half the total of existing foreign assets. The overwhelming majority are based in the Western industrialized countries with just a handful in Asian and Latin American states. Exploitative practices by many MNCs in developing countries and concerns about their political influence have made them targets of criticism, just as critics are concerned with the failure of many developing countries to challenge liberal economic ideas more generally.

■ The Critics of Liberal Economic Norms

The Economic Commission for Latin America (ECLA) was among the first to question the applicability of liberal economic thinking to developing states. It argued in the 1950s that if the developing countries adopted liberal economic strategies, they would become forever mired in dependency (Furtado 1964). ECLA's critique and its prescription for extricating countries from dependency became the basis for the establishment of the UN Conference on Trade and Development (UNCTAD) in the 1960s and for the proposed New International Economic Order (NIEO) in the 1970s.

When the UNCTAD was founded in 1964, many newly independent states from Africa and Asia, along with the Latin American countries, formed the Group of 77 (G-77). A primary concern was the GATT, which they viewed as serving the interests of the developed world. In their view, the inherently unequal international liberal trading system could not be made more equal without major changes. The UNCTAD secretariat played a key role in shaping the work of the G-77 because of the limited expertise of many governments on these issues. UNCTAD's dynamics were characterized by group bargaining because of the G-77's unity and by challenges to the predominant liberal thinking about economic development. Working in two successive special sessions of the UN General Assembly, in global conferences on food, population, and women, as well as in UNCTAD, the

G-77 secured adoption of the Declaration on the Establishment of a New International Economic Order in May 1974 and the Charter of Economic Rights and Duties of States in the same year. The September 1975 Seventh Special Session of the UN General Assembly marked the peak of confrontation between North and South that dominated not only UNCTAD but much of the UN system, including specialized agencies as discussed in Chapter 4.

The G-77 sought changes in six major areas of international economic relations in the proposed NIEO. Each was designed to alter the relationship of dependency between the developed and developing countries. First, the South sought changes in international trade, including adjustment in the terms of trade in order to stabilize the prices of such commodities as coffee, cocoa, bauxite, tin, and sugar and link those prices with the price of finished products imported from developed countries. The G-77 also demanded greater authority over natural resources and foreign investment in developing countries, particularly through regulation of MNCs. They wanted improved means of technology transfer to make it cheaper and more appropriate for the local population. To propel development, the South also demanded increased foreign aid and improved terms and conditions. Although the G-77 won adoption of the Generalized System of Preferences (GSP) by GATT in 1971, waiving the nondiscrimination rule, GSP schemes were applied unilaterally by the European Community, the United States, and others. They could be withdrawn at any time. Still, it was a step toward establishing the principle of preferential treatment for developing country exports. The G-77 also won more favorable terms for commodity price stabilization, but on most other issues the North refused to negotiate. No common fund was established to stabilize commodity prices. No regulations on MNCs were concluded.

Two other issues pushed by the G-77 remain on the agenda today— debt relief, as discussed above, and restructuring of the international financial institutions. In the latter case, advocates of the NIEO sought changes, specifically in the weighted voting structures of the World Bank and International Monetary Fund and in the developed-country bias within the WTO. They sought, in short, to alter basic power relationships in international economic affairs. Since no major changes have been made at the bank or fund, the issue persists. Consensus voting in the WTO has increased the influence of developing countries over new trade negotiations.

Because most NIEO proposals were defeated and the G-77 gradually splintered with the wide acceptance (some say triumph) of economic liberalism and the diverging interests of many members, UNCTAD has become a less active organization. While in 1992, 690 meetings were held among the various working groups, five years later that number had decreased to

225 meetings. But the founding of UNCTAD and subsequent actions by the G-77 within the UN system provided the first fundamental and sustained challenge to the dominant liberal economic ideology.

The other major challenge to economic liberalism came from statist mercantilism that emphasizes the role of the state and the subordination of all economic activities to the goal of state building. Where liberals see the mutual benefits of international trade, mercantilists see states as competing with each other to improve their own economic potential. Statist policies stress national self-sufficiency rather than interdependence, limited imports of foreign goods through substitution of domestic products and high tariffs, and restricted foreign direct investment. The "tigers" of East Asia, including South Korea, Singapore, and Taiwan, successfully used this approach to economic development during the 1980s and early 1990s.

Despite these challenges, economic liberalism has triumphed. The issue is how to soften its impact on those adversely affected. UNDP introduced the human development index (HDI) in the early 1990s to underscore that development is about improving the quality of life for human beings, not just promoting economic growth. The index is based on a composite of indicators, including infant mortality, life expectancy, and literacy. UNICEF calls for "adjustment with a human face." The IMF, World Bank, UN, and OECD endorsed "A Better World for All" in 2000, setting quantitative objectives for reducing poverty. The norms of economic liberalism are firmly embedded, but some of the most egregious inequities are being discussed and addressed. Indeed, the norms seem to be shifting from an emphasis on economic security of the state to economic security and well-being for the individual. The pieces of global economic governance address both types of economic security.

■ Pieces of Global Economic Governance

Promoting human development and economic well-being has become a central activity of the Bretton Woods institutions along with various UN agencies, regional IGOs, and NGOs. The World Bank and IMF continue to provide core pieces of economic governance dealing with development and finance. The WTO is the heart of the multilateral trade system, while institutionalized macroeconomic coordination takes place in the G-7. Functional regimes, multinational corporations, and regional arrangements provide other key pieces of global economic governance.

▨ *Development and Finance:*
The World Bank, IMF, UN System, and NGOs

The world continues to be divided between the North and South, between rich and poor, both between states and within states. Whether that gap is successfully being bridged or not depends on one's perspective. Proponents of economic liberalism point to average per capita incomes in developing countries that have doubled over a fifty-year period, with the GNPs (gross national product) of some economies growing more than five times and third-world countries enjoying an ever-increasing share of world exports. Their detractors contend that the gap between rich and poor is increasing. The richest 20 percent control 86 percent, while the share of the poorest 20 percent declined to 1.1 percent. Yet both acknowledge that the challenge of economic governance is to narrow the gap between rich and poor by stimulating economic growth and development.

The World Bank and International Monetary Fund.   Both the World Bank and the International Monetary Fund are based on the liberal notion that economic stability and development are best achieved when trade and financial flows occur with as few restrictions as possible. Yet their missions differ, the bank emphasizing development and the fund finance.

World Bank.   The World Bank's initial task was to facilitate reconstruction in post–World War II Europe. In fact, because the task proved so great, the United States financed the bulk of it bilaterally through the European Recovery Program (or Marshall Plan) rather than multilaterally through the bank. During the 1950s, however, the bank shifted from reconstruction to development. Its purpose is to loan funds, with interest, to states proposing major economic development projects. These funds are generated from member-state contributions and from international financial markets. The loans are designed to complement private capital by funding projects that private banks would not support, such as infrastructure (dams, bridges, highways), social services (education, healthcare), and government restructuring. Unlike private banks, the World Bank attaches economic and, increasingly, political conditions to its loans in the form of policy changes it would like to see states make to promote economic development and alleviate poverty.

To aid the bank in meeting the needs of developing countries, the International Finance Corporation (IFC) was created in 1956, the first of four subsidiary members of the World Bank "family." IFC provides loans to promote the growth of private enterprises in developing countries. Its 174 members have committed a portfolio of $21.7 billion, with annual disbursements of $2.5 billion. Today, this figure is dwarfed by foreign direct investment in developing countries (over $190 billion). Another bank family member, the Multilateral Investment Guarantee Agency (MIGA), established in 1988, was meant to further augment private capital's contribution to less developed countries by insuring investments against losses. Such losses may include expropriation, governmental currency restrictions, and losses stemming from civil war or ethnic conflict. In 1960, the establishment of the International Development Association (IDA) provided no-interest "soft" or concessional loans to the poorest countries with repayment schedules of fifty years. With $120 billion cumulative lending, or about $4.5 billion annually, IDA has to be continually replenished or added to by major donor countries. If poor countries attain a certain level of GNP per capita, they graduate and are no longer eligible for concessional lending.

Loan approval and monitoring is an interactive process between governments and bank officials, other bilateral donors, and groups. Often, other UN agencies, the regional development banks, and NGOs participate in both project design and implementation. The World Bank's 181 members have lent more than $350 billion over the life of the organization, with annual lending at slightly over $10 billion and almost one hundred new projects annually. Until the 1990s, loans were granted exclusively to governments and often combined with loans from the principal bilateral donors (United States, Japan, Germany, United Kingdom) and other international organizations to complete projects. This restriction now has been relaxed and private groups can also be loan recipients.

Since the 1950s, there have been major shifts in development strategies. At times, the bank, the fund, and the UN itself have been at the forefront of articulating new strategies and, at other times, they have responded to changes initiated by the bilateral donor community during the 1990s by NGOs .

During the 1950s and 1960s, the World Bank emphasized large infrastructure projects (dams, electric facilities, telecommunications). In the 1970s, under the leadership of Robert McNamara, the bank shifted to a basic needs orientation, funding projects in health, education, and housing geared to improve the economic needs of the masses. During the 1980s, the mantra became private sector involvement and the idea that economic development must be sustainable, that is, able to meet present needs of alleviating poverty, supporting marginalized populations, and promoting environmentally sound projects without compromising the ability of future generations to do the same. Sustainable development depends on good governance, which the bank began promoting in the late 1990s along with poverty alleviation. The bank's history, then, is described by Pincus and Winters (2002: 1) as "institutional stretching, incremental change, goal proliferation, and wider consultation."

Of these various changes, the reorientation toward support of the private sector has been the most profound. While the founding Articles of Agreement supported private investment, the bank was prohibited from making loans without government guarantees until the IFC was established. The bank now strongly supports private sector involvement and privatization of government-owned industries in the expectation that growth will trickle down and everyone will eventually benefit (Miller-Adams 1999). Likewise, when areas of the economy are privatized, taking government out of direct management of economic production, the government's fiscal burden is reduced and state spending can increase in the social sector for education and health. These changes were first elucidated in the 1991 *World Development Report*. Thirty to 40 percent of the bank's lending is now to those areas where the private sector is most involved. The 1997 *World Development Report* signaled the bank's concern with a more effective state role in the economy. Some regions have experienced economic growth as a result of policy changes. Yet, in states that have undergone privatization, government savings have not always been channeled to social expenditures; instead they have been cut, placing already marginalized populations in economic jeopardy. Some privatization funds have provided for corporate welfare, for firms such as Coca-Cola and Marriott, but done little to alleviate poverty. Adverse environmental consequences of some bank projects, rising poverty levels, and concerns about bank policies generally have led some critics to charge "Fifty years is enough" and call for radical change (Danaher 1994).

International Monetary Fund.   Originally, the IMF's purpose was to lend money to countries to meet short-term fluctuations in currency exchange rates, thus enabling members to establish free convertibility among their currencies and maintain stable exchange rates. Funds to meet "temporary" balance-of-payments difficulties were allocated by quotas. Members contributed to the fund according to quotas negotiated every five years. The quota was paid in both gold and in local currency (later so-called special drawing rights [SDRs] provided added liquidity). Members could withdraw funds according to the amount contributed, with a one-time service charge of 3/4 percent on each transaction plus length of time the money was borrowed. These arrangements were typically for twelve to eighteen months. While quota restrictions have been relaxed, one IMF facility, the Stand-by Arrangements, still meets this need within the IMF framework. Facilities have also been established for other groups of countries, notably the very poor. For example, the Poverty Reduction and Growth Facility established in 1987 and the Heavily Indebted Poor Countries Initiative adopted in 1996 were designed to assist those eligible (about forty-one countries) in reducing their external debt burdens to sustainable levels, while not compromising growth potential. The Compensatory Financing Facility aids countries with shortfalls or excesses in cereal import costs.

Although the IMF was not designed to be an aid agency, its role in development has grown, insofar as stable currency values and currency convertibility are necessary for trade and development. While some states' balance-of-payments shortfalls are temporary and can be accommodated through Stand-By Arrangements, other states experience long-term structural economic problems and, following the 1982 Mexican debt crisis, the IMF became increasingly involved in dictating policy changes as conditions of lending.

The IMF's role, too, has changed, expanding beyond currency convertibility to helping countries with chronic balance-of-payments difficulties and heavy debt. Beginning with the 1982 Mexican debt crisis, it took on the role of intermediary in negotiations between creditor and debtor countries, then became involved in bailouts and structural adjustment lending. The latter requires recipients to institute economic policy reforms or achieve certain conditions (referred to as conditionality), in return for financial assistance. It is aimed at overcoming structural bottlenecks in countries' domestic economies and governmental policies, as well as stimulating trade liberalization and private sector involvement. Figure 9.1 shows the diverse range of suggested policies, all compatible with a liberal economic view.

The IMF has also introduced a surveillance process, involving annual consultations with member governments to appraise exchange rate policies within the framework of general economic and policy strategies. The purpose is to anticipate problems before crises break out. The IMF offers technical assistance to members whereby state officials are trained at the IMF Institute and in regional training centers in data collection, management of central banks, and fiscal and monetary policy.

The IMF played a key role in the transitions of Russia and other former communist countries to market economies during the 1990s. It provided financial resources to make external adjustment more orderly, including credits of $27 billion to enable states to avoid external arrears and ease debt servicing. Russia alone received $11.2 billion during the 1998 financial crisis. The most advanced economies in Central Europe and the Baltic states achieved rapid success, using the funds to liberalize foreign trade and reduce inflation. The less advanced states, including Russia, were not as successful, especially in the short term. By 2000, however, Russia's economy was seeing the benefits of liberalization, privatization, and financial stabilization in the resumption of economic growth. The IMF, and indeed the international financial community, had never before embarked on such a giant undertaking.

The IMF's response to the Asian financial crisis tells a different story. Beginning in Thailand in 1997 and spreading to other countries in Asia, including Indonesia and South Korea in early 1998, exchange rates plummeted, stock markets fell, and real GDP dropped. Individuals lost their jobs as companies went bankrupt or were forced to restructure. Millions of people (an estimated 40 million in Indonesia alone) who had achieved middle-class status in Southeast Asia's economic boom of the late 1980s and

Figure 9.1   IMF Structural Adjustment Programs

PROFILE	GOALS
Profile of a Country in Need of Structural Adjustment	*Typical Goals of Structural Adjustment Programs*
Large balance-of-payments deficit	Restructure and diversify productive base of economy
Large external debt	Achieve balance-of-payments and fiscal equilibrium
Overvalued currency	Create a basis for noninflationary growth
Large public spending and fiscal deficit	Improve public sector efficiency
	Stimulate growth potential of the private sector

TYPICAL STRUCTURAL ADJUSTMENT POLICIES

Economic Reforms	*Trade Liberation Reforms*
Limit money and credit growth	Remove high tariffs and import quotas
Devalue the currency	Rehabilitate export infrastructure
Reform the financial sector	Increase producers' prices
Introduce revenue-generating measures	
Introduce user fees	*Government Reforms*
Introduce tax code reforms	Cut bloated government payroll
Eliminate subsidies, especially for food	Eliminate redundant and inefficient agencies
Introduce compensatory employment programs	Privatize public enterprises
Create affordable services for the poor	Reform public administration and institutions
	Private Sector Policies
	Liberalize price controls
	End government monopolies

1990s, were forced back into poverty. The huge inflows of private invest-ment capital that had fueled rapid development stopped, creating a crisis of confidence in the Asian economies. The spreading contagion hit Russia and Brazil by the summer of 1998, but also affected American industries that exported to Asia and retirees whose pensions were invested in stocks and real estate in Asia. The crisis revealed the weakness of many Asian coun-tries' banking systems, their heavy levels of short-term debt and current account deficits, along with the corruption of "crony capitalism" that closely tied business and government. The crisis triggered social and political upheaval, especially in Indonesia, leading to the resignation of long-time President Suharto in May 1998.

The IMF responded with large controversial bailout packages to three of the affected countries (Thailand, $17 billion; Indonesia, $36 billion; and South Korea, $58 billion), each accompanied by lengthy sets of conditions that the country was supposed to follow and by monitoring devices to ensure compliance. Governments had to agree to carry out extensive structural reforms that would transform their economies from semimercantilist to more market-oriented economies. In South Korea, for example, the newly elected government of President Kim Dae Jung pledged to lift restrictions on capital movements and foreign ownership, permit companies to lay off workers, and undertake measures to make economic transactions more transparent, including revamping financial reports and restructuring financial institutions. The reforms were largely successful from an economic perspective, although the government is still a dominant player in the economy. Politically, the reforms led to public campaigns to boycott foreign products and publicize how foreigners benefited at the expense of Koreans (Moon and Mo 2000).

Overall assessments of the IMF response to the Asian financial crisis are mixed. The IMF approach was similar to that in previous crises in Latin America, calling for higher interest rates and taxes, reduced public spending, breaking up monopolies, restructuring banking systems, and greater financial transparency. Yet the fund misdiagnosed the problem and its prescription proved inappropriate, especially in the Indonesian case. In the words of one analyst, "All the IMF did was make East Asia's recessions deeper, longer and harder" (Stiglitz 2000: 60). Also, the breadth of conditions meant that countries accepting IMF aid were forced to give up much of their economic sovereignty.

The affected countries did not recover as rapidly as expected; economic and financial problems deepened; high interest rates pushed more indebted companies into bankruptcy; budget cuts eliminated social services and pushed more families below the poverty line, leading to backlash against governments and the IMF; and internationally, the deflationary pressures spread to other countries. These negative outcomes shook faith in the IMF and liberal economic solutions. Some critics focus on the so-called moral hazard problem of IMF rescue packages that encouraged international investors to engage in still more reckless behavior because they counted on the fund's safety net. Whose interests was the fund serving? Others feel that more money and fewer conditions would have helped pull the countries out of crisis faster. Still others advocate limiting the fund's attention to balance-of-payments issues and managing crises, not development or economies in transition. And some critics focus on the secrecy of negotiations between the fund and member countries, arguing for greater transparency in IMF decisionmaking.

Globalization makes it difficult to stop a financial crisis once it has started, given the speed of short-term capital movements. The problem is that the IMF has tended to serve the interests of creditors (including itself) and the developed countries, rather than developing countries. There is a recognized need for closer monitoring of the financial sector, domestic financial systems, and private capital flows. The IMF has streamlined its procedures so that it can act more rapidly in a financial crisis, recognized the mistakes in its fiscal policy advice, and increased resources for emergency lending through its New Arrangements to Borrow (Cooper 2002). Still, the IMF and its policies remain highly controversial, perpetuating calls for reform, especially to increase openness.

Collaboration with NGOs.   The bank and fund from their inception were elite-run institutions that dealt with borrowing governments, central banks, finance ministries, and international private lenders. For the first four decades neither had direct relationships with civil society or NGOs. Since the mid-1990s, both have been pressured to be more open and accountable.

During much of the life of the World Bank, NGOs played few formal or even informal roles, given the bank's top-down organizational culture. For example, between 1973 and 1988, NGOs were involved in only 6 percent of the bank's projects. After the 1988 World Bank and IMF annual meeting, however, the relationship began to change in response to pressure from NGOs and internal bank efforts to work more directly with beneficiaries, many of them allied with NGOs who were critical of the environmental and social consequences of bank lending. This change coincided with both worldwide democratization, which facilitated the growth of NGOs, and a change in policy in many bilateral development agencies that channeled increasing funds through the NGOs, as discussed in Chapter 6. By 1990, NGOs were involved in 22 percent of projects and, by the end of 1998–1999, fully 54 percent of projects involved NGOs, 70 percent of which were local community-based groups (Streeten 1999).

NGOs gradually have been given a voice in the design and execution of programs and begun to participate in broader policy dialogues, becoming instruments of accountability. In response to NGO pressures, the bank established a Gender Unit to address the needs of women in development projects, an Environmental Department to conduct environmental assessments, and an Inspection Panel to investigate charges by community organizations about bank projects (O'Brien, Goetz, Scholte, and Williams 2000). Each involves extensive participation by NGOs. Thus, although governments are still formally charged with implementation of World Bank projects, the bank has built NGO participation into projects and programs, providing greater local-level participation.

The IMF, in contrast, has always been a much more closed institution. In the late 1990s, bowing to NGO pressure, the fund initiated more contacts with NGOs, but these remained informal and noninstitutionalized. Officials were skeptical of the value of participation by members of civil society in financial issues.

The Critics of the Bank and Fund.   Critics of both the bank and fund have addressed issues of governance and process as well as decisions and policy. By convention, the IMF managing director is always a European and the World Bank president, an American. In both institutions, a limited-member executive board decides everyday policies. The executive boards operate under weighted voting systems that guarantee the voting power of the major donors commensurate with their contributions. (See Figure 9.2.)

In the IMF, for example, the United States, Germany, Japan, France, and the United Kingdom command more than 40 percent of the votes. Because of this weighted voting system, these institutions have often been viewed as tools of the great powers, a view reinforced by decisions about which countries are funded. Although both the bank and fund were originally designed to be economic, not political institutions, politics do intervene in the process of who gets financing and when. In the past, Cold War politics denied funding to Vietnam, Cuba, Afghanistan, Nicaragua, Grenada, Chile under President Allende, Laos, Cambodia, Angola, and Mozambique. In all cases, the United States opposed funding on political grounds because it disapproved of the regime in power. More recently, Argentina was denied aid during its 2001 economic collapse, where generous funding was available for Brazil and Turkey.

Domination by the few opens both institutions to trenchant criticism from developing countries that have little power within the respective institutions. Western dominance is reinforced within the bank and fund bureaucracies (2,700 and 7,000 employees respectively) that have heavy influence on funding decisions. Predominantly economists trained in Western countries in the same liberal economic tradition as U.S. decisionmakers, the bureaucrats also have strong organizational cultures of their own. Especially in the IMF, an organizational mindset has been locked into the Washington Consensus policies, irrespective of their consequences or flaws. It is not "a learning organization" (Stiglitz 2002: 231).

Since the 1980s, the most stringent criticisms have focused on structural adjustment programs, where the two institutions reinforce each other through informal cross-conditionality. States must meet the conditions stipulated by the fund before bank lending is granted, and lending by bilateral

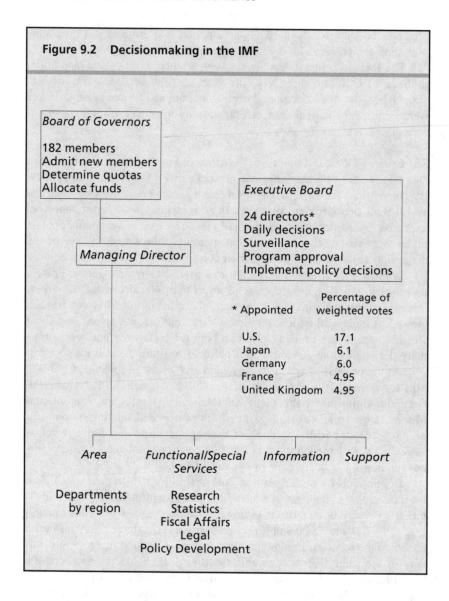

Figure 9.2   Decisionmaking in the IMF

Board of Governors

182 members
Admit new members
Determine quotas
Allocate funds

Executive Board

24 directors*
Daily decisions
Surveillance
Program approval
Implement policy decisions

Managing Director

	Percentage of weighted votes
* Appointed	
U.S.	17.1
Japan	6.1
Germany	6.0
France	4.95
United Kingdom	4.95

Area	*Functional/Special Services*	*Information*	*Support*
Departments by region	Research Statistics Fiscal Affairs Legal Policy Development		

agencies is forthcoming only after fund approval. Thus, the IMF's "stamp of international approval" serves as a prerequisite for other donors to make their own loans, giving the fund unparalleled power.

As noted earlier, some critics charge that structural adjustment reforms result in disproportionate suffering by the marginalized and already disadvantaged sectors of the population, namely the unskilled, women, and the poor. Such programs are blamed for contributing to urban riots (Nepal in 1992, Nigeria in 1988, and Ivory Coast in 1990) and for leading to the downfall of several governments (Indonesia in 1998). Public demonstrations at the annual meetings of the IMF and the World Bank attest to the increasing level of public sentiment against specific policies.

Finally, at a more general level, despite the weighted voting system, Northern opponents claim that both the fund and bank are actually being run by faceless bureaucrats who are not directly accountable to donors, while Southern opponents argue that state sovereignty is directly challenged by conditionality. Not only do measures affect areas that are traditionally the prerogative of sovereign governments, but the South also has few real alternatives to accepting the dictates of the Bretton Woods institutions.

For the first time, critics from outside the bank and fund have now been joined by officials within the organizations. The question is whether the international financial institutions have been offering the right advice. Officials have criticized IMF policies in East Asia, suggesting that they brought the world to the verge of a global meltdown. On the one hand, the IMF has promoted a culture of bailouts to countries making unwise economic decisions and, on the other, through the Washington Consensus it has pushed countries to open their economies to the risks in volatile international financial flows (Stiglitz 2002; Easterly 2001). Some critics would prefer to see the UN take on more responsibility for development, in particular, on the grounds that it is more responsive to developing countries' needs.

The UN's approach to economic development.   The UN's approach to economic development differs in some key ways from that of the Bretton Woods institutions and also has evolved over time. The UN Charter says very little about how the institution should fulfill its mandate to promote economic and social well-being. With the Bretton Woods institutions having the main responsibility, the central institutions of the UN were left with two general functions—normative and operational. With respect to the normative function, the General Assembly has historically provided general direction and supervision for economic activities through its Second Committee. The very idea of development, though not mentioned in the UN Charter, has been discussed, debated, and subsequently modified under UN General Assembly auspices.

An example of the UN's normative role in development can be seen in the evolution of the idea of sustainable development. In 1980, the General Assembly adopted the World Conservation Strategy, advocating the new but poorly defined concept of sustainable development. For those of a liberal persuasion it meant sustained growth or sustained change. For others, particularly environmentalists, it originated in the context of the renewable resources necessary to support present and future human life. Sustainability implies that economic growth should not prevent future generations from meeting their needs and operations. In 1983, the General Assembly established the World Commission on Environment and Development (WCED) headed by Prime Minister Gro Harlem Brundtland of Norway and composed of eminent persons. Its task was to formulate a new development approach around the concept of sustainable development. The 1987 Brundtland Commission Report (World Commission 1987 [*Our Common Future*]) called for development for the present without compromising the needs of future generations. That approach subsequently was adopted by a number of international organizations, NGOs, and national development agencies in Canada, Sweden, and the United States. It was the underlying theme for the 1992 UN Conference on the Environment and Development discussed in Chapter 11.

On the operational side, the UN took two approaches: creating a series of regional commissions to decentralize planning and programs, and making a commitment to technical assistance—the provision of training programs and expert advice—as its primary contribution to promoting development. ECOSOC is charged with coordinating the many different agencies and programs but has historically had difficulty doing so, because of their number and diversity and its lack of authority over the specialized agencies in particular.

The five regional commissions discussed in Chapter 4 were intended to stimulate regional approaches to development. All the regional commissions have produced high-quality economic surveys of their respective regions as well as country plans used by national governments and other multilateral institutions. Some of the commissions, however, most notably the Commission for Western Asia that encompasses the Middle Eastern countries and the Commission for Africa, have been hampered by disputes among members and lack of resources and expertise. As noted earlier, the Economic Commission of Latin America (ECLA) challenged the applicability of liberal economic thinking to developing states and provided the theoretical basis for the NIEO proposals of the 1970s. ECLA also helped establish the Central American Common Market (CACM) and the Inter-American Development Bank (IDB), as discussed in Chapter 5.

Providing technical assistance for development has been a central function of the UN system. The World Bank institutions mobilize capital and help with infrastructure, while the UN's own programs supply people skills and new technologies. This approach grew out of a December 1948 General Assembly mandate that was institutionalized in the 1950 Expanded Programme of Technical Assistance (EPTA). The UN awards fellowships for advanced training, supplies equipment for training purposes, and provides experts. Many such projects are jointly funded by the UN and specialized agencies, such as WHO, FAO, and UNESCO, or by one of the regional economic commissions. Regular budget funds for these programs are frequently augmented by voluntary contributions from member states. This UN development assistance is grant aid, not loans; hence, it does not create future burdens for recipient countries.

In 1965, the General Assembly established the UN Development Program (UNDP) as the lead organization in the provision of technical assistance. UNDP resident representatives are expected to assess local needs and priorities, coordinate programs, function as country representatives for some of the specialized agencies, and serve as the focal point between the UN and recipient government. Although the resident representative positions have grown in significance, the resources at their disposal are dwarfed by those of the bank and major bilateral aid donors. This limits their power to coordinate country-based activities, as does the autonomy of the specialized agencies. Although UNDP is primarily an operational agency, it has also played an important norm-development role since the early 1990s with its annual *Human Development Reports* and the HDI.

Despite the UN's array of development activities, in relative terms its allocations remain modest. Total UN technical cooperation assistance is more than $5 billion annually, but compared to the $500 billion in World Bank loans since its founding and the OECD's annual $55 billion contribution to development cooperation, the UN budget is nominal. And since the early 1990s, the UN system's total contribution to development has continued to decline. Fomerand (2000: 53) offers a sober (and realistic) assessment: "Under the circumstances, expectations about the development contributions of the United Nations—past, present, or future—cannot give rise to romantic flights of fancy. Hyperbolic statements about the 'unique,' 'central,' 'critical,' and 'leadership' role of the organization in international cooperation for development abound. The bare facts point to more prosaic realities." Yet while its economic contribution to the development gap may be marginal, the UN system has played a key role in elaborating a countervision of international inequality: that inequality has increased with economic globalization and that only a policy of sustainable development, aimed at alleviating individual economic insecurity, can begin to close the gap. Under Kofi Annan's leadership, the UN has also sought to increase partnerships with other actors and develop a coherent set of goals for mobilizing the international community to fight poverty and promote sustainable human development.

Partnerships and the Millennium Development Goals (MDGs). Although the World Bank began partnering in the 1980s, this approach became more commonplace in the 1990s. For example, in 1996, UNDP and

World Bank, along with the Inter-American Foundation launched a partnership program in Latin America and the Caribbean called Partnerships for Poverty Reduction that include both private and public sectors, supported by local groups. Four hundred partnerships emerged from the exercise. The UN Global Compact, discussed later in this chapter, is also an example of such a partnership, as is the International Partnership against AIDS in Africa discussed in Chapter 12. Such partnerships are predicated on an emerging normative consensus: poverty and underdevelopment are bad for business, just as they are socially and politically undesirable. Thus, the private sector is beginning to see that it is in its economic interest to join in the fight against poverty and underdevelopment, and the United Nations system has recognized that development needs to be people not state centered, incorporating civil society and private sector stakeholders.

The Millennium Declaration adopted at the UN-sponsored Millennium Summit in September 2001 incorporated a set of eight goals, known as the Millennium Development Goals (MDG). These represent a conceptual convergence—what the *Human Development Report 2003* calls a "compact among nations"—about reducing poverty and promoting sustainable human development in response to globalization. As Ruggie (2003: 305) notes, "It is unprecedented for the UN and its agencies, let alone also the Bretton Woods institutions, to align their operational activities behind a unifying substantive framework." The mutually reinforcing and intertwined MDGs include halving world poverty and hunger by 2015, reducing infant mortality by two-thirds, and achieving universal primary education. The eighth goal deals with partnerships among UN agencies, governments, civil society organizations, and the private sector as a means to achieving the other seven goals. (See Figure 9.3 for the complete list.) The goals are disaggregated into eighteen specific targets, specific time frames, and forty-eight performance indicators, with an elaborate implementation plan involving ten global task forces, MDG report cards for each developing country, regular monitoring, and a public information campaign to keep pressure on governments and international agencies.

To a large degree, the MDGs are a product of the global conferences that highlighted the interrelated nature of many development issues such as population, children, food, women, the environment, and human settlements. Consensus on the need for new forms of cooperation and partnerships does not guarantee success of the effort. One test, however, is whether new resources are forthcoming to support the MDG initiative.

At the March 2002 International Conference on Financing for Development in Monterrey, Mexico, the United States announced a "new compact for development" to increase core assistance to less developed countries over a three-year period by 50 percent, a $5 billion annual increase in U.S. bilateral aid. The EU pledged to add $7–8 billion in aid.

Figure 9.3   The Millennium Development Goals

Goal 1: Eradicate extreme poverty and hunger

Goal 2: Achieve universal primary education

Goal 3: Promote gender equality and empower women

Goal 4: Reduce child mortality

Goal 5: Improve maternal health

Goal 6: Combat HIV/AIDS, malaria, and other diseases

Goal 7: Ensure environmental sustainability

Goal 8: Develop a global partnership for development

Funds are to be placed in the new Millennium Challenge Account and used to stimulate economic growth and reduce poverty in selected states that adopt "sound policies." The latter include good governance (stopping corruption, supporting human rights and rule of law); health and education of the citizenry; economic policies promoting private enterprise, free trade, and entrepreneurship. Countries will compete for the grants (not loans), according to how well they meet the above criteria. Winners will be able to join in partnerships for development involving private sector firms, foundations, international and local NGOs, as well as states and local jurisdictions. The underlying idea behind the initiative is that since only countries with good governance will be able to attract private investors and thus will likely be successful, those countries should be rewarded.

Many questions have arisen about this initiative, such as what criteria will be used to measure governance performance? How much does corruption have to be curbed before a state qualifies, and to what extent will other assistance money be tied to the same criteria? Despite these nagging questions, the Monterrey conference represents a response to Millennium Development Goals.

Bilateral aid: Official development assistance.   Government-to-government bilateral aid, known as official development assistance (ODA), is another source of capital for developing countries. Over one-half trillion dollars has been transferred since World War II, with 95 percent of that coming from the twenty-two members of the Development Assistance Committee of the OECD (DAC). But that amount must be weighed against other considerations that reduce ODA's effectiveness in bridging the finance gap for developing countries. Bilateral aid is heavily tied to political considerations; for example, 40 percent of U.S. aid goes to just two countries, Israel and Egypt, while Africa has received only 10 percent; 25 percent of U.S. aid goes for military assistance. Aid often funds prestige projects such as airports and big hotels, with little impact on sustainable development for the poor. Not all states have met their DAC goals. Five of the twenty-two DAC countries have reached the goal of 0.7 percent of GNP for economic assistance, including Denmark at the highest (1.01 percent). The United States is dead last, at 0.11 percent of its GNP; the overall DAC average is only 0.22 percent of GNP.

Despite these limitations, ODA is important. In the early 1990s, DAC donors, like the bank and fund, agreed to promote private sector development, privatization, business training, microenterprise development, and an improved institutional environment for business. Thus, there has been consistency in approaches between bilateral aid agencies and the multilateral development institutions.

Private international finance.   Private international finance has played an increasing role in international development, gradually replacing multilateral and bilateral lenders. Since the mid-1980s, capital flows to developing countries have increased dramatically from foreign direct investment and other private sources, while official flows have declined as a percentage of capital flows, as shown in Figure 9.4. This is but another example of the private sector's growing importance in economic governance. Private international capital was essential to the success of the Asian tigers, although private capital alone was not responsible for their success. Statist policies by governments were able to harness private capital and make it productive.

Yet for less developed countries, private capital is risky and may be limiting. While less developed countries received about 27 percent of this capital, most of this investment goes to just a few countries. In 2000, for example, almost 39 percent went to China and Brazil, while Argentina, Chile, South Korea, Mexico, Singapore, and Thailand divided the rest. Africa, the most capital-poor, received only 4.3 percent. In addition, private capital flows are highly volatile. For example, in 1997, less developed countries had a net inflow of private bank lending of $4.5 billion, but in the following year, 1998, there was a net outflow of $3.4 billion, and in 2001 total foreign direct investment dropped in half from previous years' investment. Thus, while private capital flows are certainly greater than the official government or multilateral channels, and at times have been key for

Figure 9.4 Net Capital Flows to Developing Countries (1985–2000)

Billions of U.S. dollars

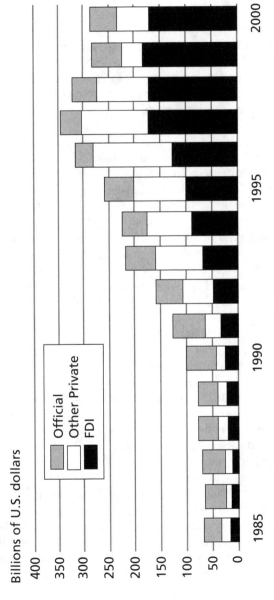

Legend:
- Official
- Other Private
- FDI

Source: World Bank Data and Staff Estimates

certain developing countries, for others they have provided little to bridge the financing gap and their very volatility make them problematic partners in sustained developed plans.

Development and finance, however, cannot be uncoupled from trade. Indeed, in the Monterrey conference, as in the global conferences, trade liberalization was viewed as a key element in sustainable development. We turn to an examination of trade.

■ Trade: From GATT to the WTO

Globalization has occurred in large part because of the expansion of trade. Indeed, a central argument in liberal economic theory is that trade is the engine of economic growth. Reversing a period of two decades when trade protection grew after World War II, international trade has grown at an average annual rate of 9 percent, thanks in part to the major actors in trade governance.

The third part of the liberal economic order was the stillborn International Trade Organization, as explained in Chapter 3. The General Agreement on Tariffs and Trade took its place; its members (called contracting parties) were initially the largest developed countries, excluding the Eastern bloc and the Soviet Union. Only gradually in the 1980s and 1990s did developing countries join the GATT, and only in 1995 did a true global trade organization, the World Trade Organization, finally come into being. Although GATT had a loose link to the UN, the WTO has none, although WTO's director-general participates in the recently created Chief Executives Board of UN agencies, chaired by the secretary-general.

GATT principles.   GATT and now the WTO are based on a number of important principles integral to the international trade regime: support of trade liberalization, since trade is the engine for economic growth and development; nondiscrimination in trade or most-favored-nation treatment (MFN), by which states agree to give the same treatment to all other members as they give to their best (most-favored) trading partner; reciprocity or granting others the same concessions they grant you; and exclusive use of tariffs as devices for protecting home markets.

At the heart of the GATT-based trading system were eight rounds of multilateral negotiations to reduce trade barriers. Negotiations in the 1960s were concerned with adapting the GATT system to the European Community and providing preferential access to Northern markets for the LDCs to stimulate economic development. The Tokyo Round, which concluded in 1979, resulted in still better treatment for the LDCs and agreements on the elimination of subsidies and rules governing such nontariff trade barriers as government procurement and technical barriers and standards. Although these enhanced the GATT-based trade system and made it fairer from the perspective of the LDCs, they did not significantly reduce growing protectionism.

The eighth or Uruguay Round concluded in December 1993 after seven years of negotiations. There were many more participants (105), making agreement more difficult. Negotiations were also affected by slower economic growth in the 1980s and 1990s, the complexity of many issues, and increased support for protectionism, especially in the United States. The Uruguay Round covered new items such as services (insurance), intellectual property rights (copyrights, patents, trade markets), and, for the first time, agriculture and textiles. Previously, agriculture was seen as too contentious an issue, complicated by both U.S. agricultural subsidies and the European Union's protectionist Common Agriculture Policy.

The 400-page document was the most comprehensive trade agreement ever, covering everything from paper clips to computer chips. Tariffs on manufactured goods were cut by an average of 37 percent. Agreement was reached to phase out agricultural subsidies and rules were expanded in the area of services. Analysts predicted that global wealth would increase by more than $200 billion per year by 2005. Yet developing countries, according to one analyst, did not get a proportionate share of the gains (Stiglitz 2002: 61).

As a result of the eight rounds of negotiations, the GATT encompassed over 45,000 binding tariff concessions, covering about $10 billion in trade among the participating countries. Still, it was not a formal organization and, because it was seen as temporary, voting and formal decisions were not normal features. Most actual decisions were taken bilaterally, then multilateralized. While it did have dispute settlement procedures, there were few ways to enforce decisions. The small bureaucracy (200) was insulated and did not consult with businesses or NGOs, or review members' trade policies.

WTO innovations.   In 1995, the World Trade Organization replaced GATT as the arbiter of trade rules, providing a formal organization for trade for the first time. The WTO incorporated the general areas of GATT's jurisdiction, as well as expanded jurisdiction in services and intellectual property through the General Agreement on Trade in Services (GATS) and the Agreement on Trade-Related Aspects of Intellectual Property Rights (TRIPS). Several new procedures were also introduced. First, the main governing body is the General Council, open to all members. There is nothing in WTO comparable to the IMF's or World Bank's executive boards. These meetings, along with regular ministerial meetings, give WTO a political prominence that GATT lacked, as WTO members conduct over 90 percent of the world's trade. Second, the WTO is a one-state, one-vote organization unlike the bank or fund but, like the GATT, actual votes have never been taken. Decisionmaking is generally by consensus. That means in all meetings, each member has the right to attend, intervene, make a motion, take initiatives, introduce and withdraw proposals, and block consensus. Relative market size is the primary source of bargaining power, and weaker states are coerced by the powerful into agreeing with the consensus. Should the powerful not get their way, they threaten to move the issue to another forum or threaten to create a new organization, and the proposals by the weak are often ignored (Steinberg 2002). With the Doha (2001) and Cancun (2003) meetings, however, a group of developing countries flexed their muscle, accusing the United States, EU, and Japan of "failing to offer sufficient compromises on agriculture and other issues" (Becker 2003: A1, 4). By shutting down the 2003 talks, the group of twenty-one developing countries (including China, Brazil, and India) raised the question of whether this "marks the end of the WTO as an effective negotiating forum" (*Economist*, Sept. 20, 2003: 26).

The most important changes from the GATT to the WTO are the establishment of the Trade Policy Review Mechanism (TPRM) and the Dispute Settlement Unit (DSU). The former conducts periodic surveillance of members' trade practices based on states' periodic reports. In this forum states can question each other about trade practices and learn how to draft trade regulations. The Dispute Settlement Unit has two distinct bodies. The first is the Dispute Settlement Body (DSB), composed of representatives from all WTO members. The DSB tries to find diplomatic options to resolving disputes; when those options are exhausted, an ad hoc panel composed of three experts chosen by the parties is convened. These panels are thus comparable to arbitral tribunals. The second component of the DSU is the Appellate Body, a standing organ that decides appeals against the decisions of ad hoc panels. Composed of seven persons, the Appellate Body has judicial characteristics, although its decisions are only binding when adopted by consensus in the DSB. After this two-step procedure, the parties are obligated to implement the recommendations. Although "compensatory measures" retaliations are permitted, only the country harmed may institute such measures and they must have the same trade effect as the violation. Because of provisions for rapid resolution and enforcement, implementation follows in sixty to ninety days. The DSU is hearing about thirty cases annually, compared to GATT's average of five. As Jackson (1998: 175) concludes, "Dispute settlement has now moved to the center stage of international economic diplomacy . . . This is a welcome step toward a more rule-oriented system that will hopefully allow better adjustment of frictions between nation-states, as well as greater predictability and reliability for entrepreneurs."

WTO cases have led to a number of ongoing controversies. One major issue concerns the product and process distinction. WTO policy prohibits countries from banning a product because of the process by which it is produced. Thus, when the EU banned the sale of hormone-treated beef in 1989 for health reasons, the United States objected. A subsequent WTO panel ruled in favor of the United States, holding that there was not enough scientific evidence about the connection between beef hormones and human health. When the EU refused to lift the ban, WTO authorized the United States to retaliate by imposing duties on EU agricultural products.

Increasingly, losers of disputes have refused to abide by panel decisions, forcing the WTO and the prevailing party to invoke drastic trade sanctions. For example, the EU is authorized to impose $4 billion in sanctions against the United States for its foreign sales corporation exporter tax that was ruled illegal by the WTO in 2002. The EU has given the United States time to change its laws and is not anxious to impose retaliatory tariffs, but the penalty is the largest ever handed down by the WTO and the verdict is important for its political repercussions.

WTO dispute settlement decisions, like the above decision, provide ammunition to critics who see the organization as a threat to national sovereignty. Others believe that such decisions force countries into taking drastic actions without trying diplomatic alternatives. They contend that the timetable imposed by WTO hinders rather than facilitates successful negotiations.

WTO's secretariat has increased in size from the GATT days, but is still small (five hundred individuals) compared to the bank, fund, and other international economic institutions. It also has quite limited powers: the director-general cannot set the agenda for WTO meetings and cannot initiate a dispute settlement case. The secretariat cannot interpret GATT rules and is generally not permitted to chair committees. Thus, the director-general is more a broker who through personal and political skills tries to build a consensus for free trade. Since trade policy is highly politicized at the national level, there is fear of giving more power to the secretariat. Despite these limitations, the secretariat does have influence through its legal, economic, and policy advice to individual delegations, supporting staff in capitals, and interactions with delegations in developing approaches on particular issues (Blackhurst 1998).

One way to understand the character of the WTO is to look at the complex negotiation process involved in bringing countries into the WTO. China offers an excellent example.

China and the WTO.   China's formal accession to the WTO in 2001 after fifteen years of negotiations was complicated by the large size of its economy and its ongoing transition from a planned to an open market economy. A 900-page accession document sets the terms of China's membership. The Chinese cabinet or state council had to revise laws to permit foreign ventures in areas previously off limits, including telecommunications, tourism, and banking. This change has led to a significant inflow of foreign investment. The agreement calls for a continuous dismantling of barriers to trade in stages. For example, in 2002, China eliminated restrictions on where foreign law firms could operate; by 2004, foreign companies will be permitted to provide health and group insurance to the Chinese; by 2006, China has promised to reduce its auto tariffs to 25 percent from its current 80–100 percent. To monitor and enforce its WTO membership, China has created a new WTO Department, inquiry centers in major cities to serve as clearinghouses for trade-related information, a Fair Trade Bureau for Imports and Exports to deal with complaints of protectionism and coordinate responses to antidumping suits, and special courts where judges will have the expertise to hear WTO-related disputes. Teams of Chinese trade officials will be sent to local areas to enforce compliance with WTO rules.

The difficulties, however, are enormous. Laws governing foreign investment and particularly joint ventures are rudimentary; the Chinese security markets are not prepared for liberalization. WTO rules must be incorporated into domestic legislation and current laws inconsistent with WTO rules clarified. It is estimated that the legislature needs to amend 570 laws, in addition to over one thousand central government rules and regulations. Among the major areas already tackled are the laws needed to enhance protection of intellectual property rights and the harmonization of local and state laws with WTO standards. Chamber of commerce committees, foreign government agencies, as well as Chinese agencies have been established to monitor the monumental task of China's compliance with WTO standards (Wonacott 2001a; Wonacott 2001b).

WTO's critics.   With a wide range of goods and services under its jurisdiction and strengthened dispute settlement mechanisms, the WTO has become a lightning rod for groups from many countries who see the organization as the epitome of the negative consequences of economic globalization, usurping state sovereignty, domestic interests, and individuals themselves, and favoring the interests of major developed countries over poor countries.

Antiglobalization NGOs are major opponents of WTO activity, charging that WTO's power to make regulations that have consequences and settle disputes with authoritative measures is an intrusion on national sovereignty. They are also critical of the lack of transparency in WTO procedures. In addition, there is a widely held perception that the organization is captive to the demands of rich governments and big multinational corporations. The fact that WTO has established consultative procedures between governments and businesses, but very few connections with the NGO community, adds to a climate of suspicion.

To other NGOs, WTO's clear adherence to the interests of free trade undermines the application of labor and environmental standards, as discussed in Chapters 10 and 11. Thus, labor movements and environmental groups have joined the opposition, believing that the WTO privileges economic liberalization over social values. The environmental groups argue that the trade rules need to be more environmentally friendly and urge the examination of environmental implications before WTO accords are passed. In 1996, WTO rejected negotiations with labor groups, referring the promotion of labor standards to the ILO instead. This was in keeping with the position of the developing states that prefer labor issues be addressed in the ILO where compliance procedures are generally loosely enforced. In contrast, labor groups from the developed world have lobbied for the WTO to take up the labor-friendly agenda, since the WTO has power to institute trade sanctions for labor violations. (For historical perspective, see Aaronson 2001; Wallach and Sforza 1999).

Whereas GATT negotiations never drew mass protests, WTO meetings have been punctuated by such demonstrations, beginning with the 1999 Seattle ministerial meetings that were largely shut down by NGO demonstrators. To quell criticism, the WTO held meetings in Dohar, Qatar, in November 2001, where only three hundred antiglobalization groups were given visas, allegedly because of lack of accommodations, adding fuel to the charges of lack of transparency. NGOs have increasingly shaped the WTO's agenda. Labor standards, food safety, environmental issues, and other aspects of the social compact are legitimately subjects of trade negotiations, although not without controversy. While in the GATT's 1994 Marrakesh meetings, NGOs had to disguise themselves as reporters, in 1996, the WTO admitted NGOs as observers, and by 1998, the WTO had staff designated to working with NGOs. In sharp contrast to the World Bank, nevertheless, NGO participation is still informal, restricted to occasional consultations for dispute settlements and participation in workshops that bring WTO officials and NGOs together, and states themselves decide whether NGOs are represented on official delegations.

Other WTO critics include the developing countries. The developed countries also acknowledged at Doha that the developing countries were at a disadvantage on trade issues, and hence needed special treatment. A new trade round (the Doha Round) aimed to improve developing countries' market access, achieve reductions in developed countries' agricultural subsidies, and renegotiate some issues from the Uruguay Round that proved impossible to implement. A door was opened for negotiations on the environment, but not on labor issues. Ironically, these demands by the South were met, in large part for noneconomic reasons; namely, both the United States and EU were committed to keeping the antiterrorist coalition together following the September 11 terrorist bombings of New York's World

Trade Center and the Pentagon. Still, as noted earlier, that consensus fell apart at the 2003 Cancun meeting, leaving the new trade round in doubt.

Despite the setbacks, Gilpin (2001: 232) concludes, "The trade regime was one of the most important achievements of the latter half of the twentieth century." The WTO, along with the World Bank and IMF, is a cornerstone of the liberal economic order and hence a key piece of global economic governance. Reductions in trade barriers have fueled growth of the world economy and globalization itself. The key unanswered question is whether future trade expansion will result in poverty reduction and sustainable global human development.

■ *Macroeconomic Policy Coordination: The Role of the G-7*

The power and dominance of the North and liberalism in the governance of international economic relations are evident not only in the prominent roles played by the Bretton Woods institutions and the WTO, but also in the influence of the Group of Seven or G-7. This is truly the "club of the rich," an informal institution with no charter, limited bureaucratic structure to aid in preparing its annual summit meetings, and no permanent secretariat. Its members, the United States, UK, France, Germany, Italy, Canada, and Japan (with the president of the European Commission present also) function as the self-appointed leaders of international economic governance. Some would suggest that when Russia joins the group for political discussions (and it becomes the G-8), it becomes the center of global governance more generally (Hajnal 1999; Bayne 2000).

The practice of convening annual summit meetings of heads of state and government of these seven leading industrial countries began in 1975, with an invitation from then French President Valéry Giscard d'Estaing at a time of financial crisis. The initial sessions were informal meetings of the leaders alone and there was no vision of permanence. Gradually, the leaders appointed "sherpas" (named after the Himalayan guides) to handle summit preparations. Today, there are more signs of institutionalization and more formality, with the meetings more scripted than informal discussions.

What roles does the G-7 play in international economic governance? Those who follow it closely emphasize the value of high-level consultations for dealing with problems that have defied solution by lower-level government officials, the ability to manage crises, to address new issues at an early stage, and to prod other institutions such as the IMF and World Bank to take action. It has also proven valuable for establishing personal relationships among leaders and opportunities to learn from each other's experiences.

Among the ongoing issues the G-7 has addressed are employment levels, the consequences of globalization, job loss, cross-border crimes, financial panic, and world poverty. Global environmental issues dominated the agenda in the years from 1989–1991, as did terrorism and drug smuggling.

Dealing with Russia and how to aid its economic transition was a major topic also in the early 1990s. Debt and financial instability were prominent issues after the 1997–1998 financial crises. As Nicholas Bayne (1999: 22) put it, "One abiding vision . . . is that the summits should make their unique contribution each year by providing leadership and agreed decisions, and then hand on their recommendations to be pursued by their cabinet colleagues or, more often, the competent international institutions. With this model the leaders only intervene at the point where they are needed."

Several steps have contributed to the gradual institutionalization of the G-7/8. Among them were the 1977 decision to make the summits annual, and the decision to use personal representatives to lay the necessary groundwork for discussions, and the expansion beyond the leaders to foreign, finance, and trade ministers meeting regularly. (For example, G-8 foreign ministers meet prior to the UN General Assembly sessions and finance ministers gather before the IMF and World Bank annual meeting.) In addition, the G-7/8 has appointed several expert groups to deal with problems such as terrorism and drugs that have no IGO "homes."

When the summits were initiated in the mid-1970s, international economic relations were in turmoil, the Bretton Woods system as originally conceived was defunct, and the United States was in a period of relative weakness, following its withdrawal from Vietnam, the resignation of President Nixon, the devaluation of the dollar, and the oil crisis. There was a strongly felt need on both sides of the Atlantic as well as the Pacific for sharing burdens. Now, in the early years of a new century, the G-7 members no longer dominate the world economy. There are new players including China, Brazil, and Mexico that need to be incorporated into the framework for governance. Summit meetings, once extremely rare, have become commonplace among members of NATO, the UN, OAS, APEC, and ASEAN, among others. The G-7 has expanded participation to deal with new economic issues. For example, in 2002, leaders of several African nations were invited to discuss the New Partnership for African Development (NEPAD), an African-developed initiative for sustainable economic growth discussed below. The deputies' meetings involve finance ministers and governors of central banks, as well as representatives from the Bretton Woods institutions and the regional development banks. Individuals from multinational corporations, banks, credit rating agencies, and think tanks are also part of the informal consultation process. The G-7 network represents, therefore, ongoing transgovernmental activities with links to the private sector.

▪ Functional Regimes: Lubricating the Liberal Economic Order

International trade and development and the international monetary system are lubricated by a network of international functional regimes. Trade cannot occur without a physical means to transport goods—hence ocean shipping and air transport were developments necessary for the expansion of international trade. Trade and financial transactions depend on the ability to communicate internationally, both through reliable postal services and electronic means. Thus, international postal services and telecommunications are critical lubricators for international trade and development and economic globalization.

In each of these areas, regimes developed to facilitate the flow of goods, people, messages, and services. Norms evolved over time that provided standards for allocating jurisdictional rights and for addressing problem areas. Such norms and technical procedures did not depend on the presence of a powerful state imposing such standards. Rather the norms and standards developed because such policy coordination worked to the benefit of all states, although technologically dominant states had key roles to play.

Ocean shipping and air transport.   Ocean shipping and air transport are two areas that have had a direct impact on expanding economic relations and contributed to the globalization of the economy. Thanks to technological improvements, both means of transport have become faster, more efficient, and cheaper. About 95 percent of international trade by weight goes by ocean shipping, or about two-thirds of all international trade by value.

The most important norms concerning shipping date back to the nineteenth century—namely, the norms of the freedom of the high seas and innocent passage through territorial waters, the right of the state to control entry of foreign ships, and flag-state jurisdiction over ships operating on the high seas. The myriad of other norms, rules, and regulations have been the product of both public and private international organizations.

Three organizations are among the most prominent. The International Maritime Organization (IMO) is the UN specialized agency designed to facilitate technical cooperation in shipping through its various committees that approve technical standards and regulations on such issues as accidents, pollution, and compensation. The Comité Maritime International (CMI) is a private organization established to promote the unification of private maritime law, harmonizing national maritime laws, liability, compensation, and salvage. UNCTAD is also concerned with shipping and represents the interests of third-world states in promoting their own shipping industries.

In the twentieth century, comparable norms evolved for air transport, as states recognized freedom of air transport above the oceans, while requiring state consent for passage over sovereign territory. In both issue areas, states have accepted norms governing damage control problems, accident prevention, and crimes such as piracy and hijacking, as well as norms to prevent pollution and environmental harm. Most of the airline and air transport norms were established through the International Civil Aviation Organization (ICAO), a specialized agency of the UN created in 1944, and the International Association of Transport Airlines (IATA) created by the airlines in 1945. At the outset, it was intended that IATA provide technical information to ICAO and that the two would work closely together. The dominance of the U.S. airline industry as supplier of aircraft, however, has meant that the United States plays a more hegemonic role in setting safety standards and norms. IATA is most concerned with facilitating flow of travelers, luggage, exchange of tickets, and fare setting. As Zacher (1996: 125–126) concludes, "The efforts of ICAO and IATA in standardizing safety, navigation, and transit regulations have had a major impact in removing barriers to the international movement of aircraft and promoting economic efficiency in air and ground operations."

Postal services and telecommunications.   The development of international postal services dates back to the creation of the Universal Postal Union in 1874. The norms governing postal services and the commitment to deliver mail across jurisdictions have not changed much over time; neither has the commitment that states of origin collect and keep the entire postal charge, with fees for services of transit states. These norms have served to promote free flow of information and commerce and ensured more exchange.

In contrast, telecommunication services have changed dramatically from the invention of the telegraph and telephone in the nineteenth century, to the radio, computers, satellites, and Internet in the twentieth century. The telecommunications revolution, the digitalization of communication, the transmission of data, e-mail, and fax have brought about fundamental changes in how the global economy operates and is connected. Information may be compressed and hence the volume of data sent much greater. By one estimate, since the founding of the International Telegraph Union (ITU) in 1865, the rate of transmission has increased over 500 million-fold (Zacher 1996: 129). At the same time, it is estimated that the cost of telecommunication services has fallen about 8 percent annually since the late 1960s.

Yet in contrast to the legal arrangements of the Universal Postal Union and air space, the telecommunications regime has been governed by informal understandings rather than formal legal edicts. These understandings parallel the principles elucidated above for the shipping and transport regime: namely, open access to space and the radio spectrum of airspace and the principle of prior use. States must respect use of specific frequencies and not transmit on them, but states also have a right to exclude foreign firms from their telecommunications industries, establishing the basis of a legal monopoly. Most telecommunications regime norms must be deduced from various agreements, statements, and the behavior of state and industry officials.

The ITU is only one among many bodies focusing on these matters. It devotes significant attention to ensuring technical standards so that states and entities are indeed connected through diverse technologies and to preventing interference in radio transmissions. Although the ITU's main purpose is to promote interconnection, it works along with the International Standards Organization, the International Electrotechnical Commission, and a group of regional bodies under the Global Standards Cooperation Group. Setting the technical standards is a key activity, thus blurring the distinction between international and national telecommunication systems.

As Zacher (1996: 225) explains, "Without multilateral regime norms and rules relating to jurisdictions the world of international commerce would probably be chaotic and a lot less active than it is at the present." These norms are integral to global economic governance. The same is increasingly true for intellectual property rights.

■ Intellectual Property Rights

One of the issues of greatest concern for multinational corporations is protection of intellectual property such as patents, trademarks, creative material (books, CDs, videos), and software. The World Intellectual Property Organization (WIPO) became a specialized UN agency in 1974, although its predecessor dates from 1883 and the Paris Convention for the Protection of Industrial Property. WIPO administers twenty-one international treaties covering the field of industrial property and copyright and related rights, providing protection for the international business community. Three registration systems are of particular import for patents, trademarks, and industrial design, which are the focus of 85 percent of WIPO's budget. Because states like the United States took until 2002 to join the Madrid Protocol for trademark protection, however, WIPO has not been as effective as it needs to be. It lacks binding and effective dispute settlement. Many national judicial settings, where enforcement actually occurs, also lack the capacity to enforce the rules.

It is for this reason that MNCs and the United States have supported using the WTO framework to force recalcitrant countries to pass laws strengthening protection of intellectual property and to enforce compliance. WTO requires members to take provisional measures, award damages, and prevent entry of counterfeit goods. While the developed countries had one year to implement the new standards, less developed countries have until 2006, and until 2011 for pharmaceuticals. To protect profits and market shares, MNCs have fought not only for harmonization of international intellectual property standards, but also for raising those protections as well. Hence, the interesting irony here is that while many see MNCs as pieces of global governance at work, providing structure and order to the globalized economy, they must use IGOs to protect intellectual property rights. Still, within individual companies and industry groups, private governance is predominant.

■ *Private Governance*

Individual firms and business associations provide a form of governance among themselves, agreeing to cooperate informally and formally, and thus providing a framework for economic activity. Some commentators refer to this process as private governance, wherein private businesses take the initiative in establishing industry-wide standards or norms of appropriate behavior or cooperating with each other to control markets as discussed in Chapter 3. With privatization and deregulation of industries in many countries, market, private, and self-regulating mechanisms have become more common. Private governance takes a number of different forms (Cutler, Haufler, and Porter 1999: 9–14), three of which are discussed.

One form of private governance involves coordination among firms through codes of conduct. Bond rating agencies such as Moody's Investors Service and Standard and Poor's illustrate a type of private governance developed by interfirm cooperation. One scholar labels such institutions "embedded knowledge networks . . . private institutions that possess a specific form of social authority because of their publicly acknowledged track records for solving problems, often acting as disinterested experts in assessing high-value transactions and in validating institutional norms and practices" (Sinclair 2001: 441). These assure investors' transparency, provide information to the markets, and establish rules for reporting, all essential governance functions. Their ratings (AAA, AA, B) are a transnational surveillance system for private market investors as well as state authorities.

Production alliances or producer cartels are another form of private governance. One of the more successful of these cartels is the diamond cartel, controlling around 80 percent of the world's diamond trade. The cartel, largely De Beers Corporation with the cooperation of the Soviet Union (now to a lesser extent Russia), makes a conscious effort to sustain the illusion that diamonds are scarce, therefore justifying high prices. The cartel works principally through the Central Selling Organisation to control the number of diamonds on the international market, the classification of diamonds, and advertising. This unprecedented level of cooperation, not achieved in any other commodity market, is attributed to De Beers' hegemony as a private corporation enjoying immunity from shareholders or government interference (Spar 1994).

A third form of private governance occurs when businesses or trade associations unite, sometimes cross-nationally, to develop industry-wide standards or enforce particular practices. The Organization for Economic Cooperation and Development has analyzed 233 such corporate codes of conduct. Some are codes applicable only to a specific firm; others are in force among firms, committing competitors to certain standards of conduct.

Self-regulation is largely a response to informal and formal pressures from shareholders (under the rubric of socially responsible investing), from NGOs, and even from governments threatening stronger regulatory action. Such pressures have led corporations to impose self-restrictions governing purchasing agreements, labor conditions and environmental standards. For example, in 2000, Starbucks Corporation agreed to buy coffee from importers who pay higher than market prices to small farmers. In the same year, McDonald's Corporation informed its egg producers that they must enforce guidelines for humane treatment of the birds or risk loss of McDonald's business. When activists found unacceptable labor conditions in El Salvadoran factories producing clothing for The Gap, the company agreed to voluntary codes, just as Levi Strauss and Nike did when confronted by similar findings in Asia, as detailed in Chapter 10.

For firms to adopt such standards and still be competitive, however, it behooves them to cooperate with others for a joint industry standard (Haufler 2002). Such has been the experience of the certification movement to protect tropical forests or the Rugmark label for carpeting. Definitive determination of whether this type of self-regulation works is still out; yet self-regulation has been increasing; certification and monitoring programs over firms have escalated, with NGOs putting pressure on companies using sophisticated mass marketing techniques.

There are advantages and disadvantages to private governance over state and IGO governance. On the positive side, firms develop relationships with each other over time and are often able to respond to changing conditions faster than a government or international bureaucracy. Yet those norms are apt to be narrowly construed. Should problems arise in implementation, firms have recourse only to state or international adjudicatory authorities (Cutler, Haufler, and Porter 1999: 340).

■ The Regionalization of Economic Governance

The Bretton Woods institutions, G-7, the WTO, and MNCs represent global responses to resolving the problems of promoting human development and economic well-being in the liberal economic framework. Regional approaches, too, have acquired new vitality with the success of the European Union discussed in Chapter 5. Indeed, regional trade blocs proliferated in the 1990s, predicated on the belief that members would experience economic benefits by taking advantage of economies of scale, spreading costs over larger regional markets, and increasing political cooperation.

There is a lively debate among economists, however, on whether regional trade blocs actually improve the economic welfare of their members through trade creation or whether trade is actually diverted and thus trade blocs reduce economic welfare (Shiells 1995).

■ *European Union's Single Market*

The European Union has undergone distinct phases in economic integration. In the first phase from 1958 to 1968, members worked to eliminate internal tariffs, dismantle quantitative import restrictions among the six original members, and establish a common external tariff and the Common Agricultural Policy. In the second phase during the 1970s and early 1980s, membership was enlarged in two waves and key institutional changes undertaken, but deeper integration stalled. In the third stage, members implemented the Single European Act to stimulate new economic growth by completing their single market and the common currency (euro) to achieve monetary union.

Breaking down the trade barriers.   The Single European Act of 1987 (SEA) provided the foundation for major economic changes and a deepening of the integration process. European economic growth had been sluggish since the mid-1970s and Japan and the United States were increasingly competitive. Completing the single market would provide the needed boost. So in 1985, the commission issued the white paper *Completing the Internal Market* (http://europa.eu.int/comm/off/white/index_eu.htm). When approved, the SEA became part of the EEC Treaty.

Under the SEA, the goal was to achieve a complete single market by December 1992, including the strengthening of community institutions to support the goal. In the internal market, free movement of goods, persons, and capital would be ensured (see Nugent 1999; Hix 1999). The process was a complicated one, involving removal of all physical, fiscal, and technical barriers to trade and harmonization of national standards through over three hundred community directives. Eliminating physical barriers involved eliminating restrictions on movement of goods and persons. This meant that customs duties, quantitative restrictions, and measures having equivalent effect needed to be eliminated. While customs barriers were abolished at the end of 1992 according to the timetable, the movement of persons proved more difficult. Since 1993, any resident of an EU member state has had the right to live and work in any other state. Most countries eliminated passport controls and adopted common visa regulations, but Britain, Ireland, and Denmark refused. States have gradually begun to recognize each other's educational and professional qualifications, necessary for the free movement of labor.

Abolishing technical barriers to trade has proven more difficult.

Although the European Court of Justice ruled in 1979 that products meeting the standards of one member could be legally sold in another (ECJ 1979 [Cassis de Dijon case], see Chapter 5), states continue to assert health and safety standards as legitimate restrictions on trade. Since harmonization of technical standards had proven difficult, the SEA adopted the less rigid approach of mutual recognition, acknowledging that states could have different standards and requirements, as long as they approximated each other.

Competition policy has also proved to be a significant technical barrier to trade. The EU Treaty prohibits giving preferences to home companies in government contracts, even though certain areas of economic activity, such as road transport, water, and financial services, were often under the control or management of state enterprises. Breaking longstanding state monopolies and prohibiting state aids to specific sectors is politically difficult, although most recognize that such practices do distort trade. The EU Commission is now more actively examining malfeasance and initiating actions against states providing uncompetitive (and therefore unfair) state aid. In addition, the council more carefully examines mergers for anticompetitive implications. In one notable instance, the EU blocked the merger of General Electric and Honeywell—two American companies with European subsidiaries that provided the basis for jurisdiction over the case. Antitrust regulations have been expanded to eliminate monopolistic sales agreements, discrimination by nationality, or predatory pricing.

The conundrum of agriculture.   Of the EU's economic policies none is more complicated or controversial than the Common Agricultural Policy (CAP). Agriculture is the most integrated of the economic sectors; it receives up to one-half of the EU's total annual expenditure; national and local governments, farmer groups, and NGOs are more heavily involved than in any other area of economic policy; and the branch of the commission handling agriculture, DGVI, is the second largest of the directorates. Agricultural policy also occupies more agenda time than any other policy area.

From the earliest days of the European Community, agriculture was seen as special or different for two reasons. The first concerns the particular characteristics of agriculture. Agriculture and foodstuffs are vital for national security, and no country wants to be dependent on other states for essentials. Yet, agriculture prices can fluctuate dramatically if left solely to market forces, and there are strong incentives to moderate those fluctuations. Hence, in most developed countries, agriculture is subsidized. The second reason for the special role of agriculture is that farmers enjoy political power disproportionate to their numbers and are well organized for lobbying both at the state and community levels.

The CAP, in contrast to the liberal trade norms discussed above, is not based on a free trade system. The intervention price determines the price at which the commission buys the crop, therefore taking it off the market. Since most crops are now produced in excess of market requirements and prices have been above world prices, the produce cannot be profitably exported. The EU purchases the surplus at the high, guaranteed prices to farmers and either stores it hoping for higher prices, donates it to food aid programs, or otherwise absorbs the loss.

CAP pays out about $41.2 billion annually to subsidize farmers who comprise 5 percent of the European work force. French farmers, in particular, benefit, receiving about 24 percent of the subsidies, but farmers in all countries have become skilled at benefiting from the system and, therefore, producing surpluses. As long as the EU maintains barriers to entry of external agricultural products, this system of subsidization will continue. CAP, because it occupies such a lion's share of the budget, is the most controversial EU policy, crowding out other expenditures while distorting international agricultural markets. It has been an issue in GATT/WTO negotiations since the late 1960s.

CAP has also proved an impediment to negotiations with new member states. The ten new members, including Poland and other former members of the Soviet bloc, increase the number of farmers in the EU by 120 percent and augment the area under cultivation by 42 percent. Should the same policy be followed, CAP could bankrupt the EU. Hence, negotiations for agricultural reform are contentious. France has agreed to modest cuts in subsidies and the new members initially receive only 25 percent of what they would be entitled to, gradually increasing to 100 percent over the next decade. Real reform of the CAP, however, has yet to take place. Division persists between those who pay for CAP and those who benefit. With the expansion estimated to cost $42 billion over the next three years, the debate will continue.

Moving to monetary integration.   The other policy area that has proven difficult to implement is monetary policy. As early as the 1960s, members of the European Economic Community declared their interest not only in economic union, but also in a monetary union. Yet not much progress on the latter was made. In 1979, the formation of the European Monetary System created some structure for coordinating financial policy; the European Currency Unit (ECU) served as a means of settling accounts; and the Exchange Rate Mechanism provided fixed, though adjustable, bands of currency exchange. But these were weak instruments. In the late 1980s, during the discussions of the single market, provisions were made for greater cooperation in monetary policy.

The Maastricht Treaty of 1992 delineated the features and timetable for movement toward the European Monetary Union (EMU). EMU meant several changes: the establishment of a single currency, the euro, and common monetary policies in which individual member states would no longer make individual decisions on monetary policy—significant steps toward integration. Not only does the single monetary unit serve as a powerful symbol of community unity (and loss of state sovereignty over currency), but member states have also agreed to relinquish their right to use exchange rates and interest rates as instruments of economic policy. As Nugent (1999: 332) explains, "The rationale is that, by creating a more stable economic and monetary environment and thus providing greater predictability for investments and markets, the single currency will promote growth and prosperity." In other words, trade would conceivably expand and economic growth accelerate—the goals of regional trade units. In this case, the euro also has political implications, for the EU can now exert a single voice in global economic affairs and the move can serve as a major step toward political integration (Hix 1999: 281).

■ *North American Free Trade Agreement (NAFTA)*
The North American Free Trade Agreement negotiated by the United States, Canada, and Mexico in 1994 differs substantially from the European Union and other regional economic schemes (Abbott 2000). As discussed in Chapter 5, NAFTA compromises one dominant economy and two dependent ones: Mexico and Canada's combined economic strength is one-tenth that of the United States. The driving force in NAFTA is not political elites but MNCs that seek larger market shares than their Japanese and European counterparts. The agreement phases out many restrictions on foreign investment and most tariff and nontariff barriers. This has allowed MNCs to shift production to low-wage labor centers in Mexico, and to gain economically by creating bigger companies through mergers and acquisitions and bigger markets.

The social, political, and security dimensions present in the European Union are absent from NAFTA, and there are neither ambitions to create an integrated community nor much in the way of institutions, as discussed in Chapter 5. Indeed, both Mexico and Canada had a long history of trying to separate themselves from the United States. Cooperation in trade and investment is not intended to lead to free movement of labor, as championed by the European Union. Quite the opposite: the United States expects that Mexican labor will not seek employment in the United States since economic development in Mexico will provide ample employment opportunities. Economic cooperation also does not mean political integration. With NAFTA, economic integration is to remain confined to specific economic sectors. Thus, there was no need to establish any kind of regional bureaucracy.

NAFTA supports the phased elimination over ten years of tariff and nontariff barriers. Specifically, tariffs on over nine thousand categories of goods produced in North America are to be eliminated by 2008. At the same time, NAFTA protects property rights of those companies making investments in the three countries. Some domestic producers are given special protection, notably the Mexican oil and gas industry and the U.S. shipping industry. The agreement, a five-volume, fifteen-pound document, is detailed and complex. It contains specific obligations on trade in goods, services, financial services, investment, intellectual property rights, technical barriers to trade, sanitary and phytosanitary measures, safeguards, and dispute settlement. It is so detailed because no secondary legislation was envisioned.

NAFTA has been generally implemented in accord with the terms of the agreement. Tariffs and quotas have been eliminated. Even during the 1994–1995 Mexican economic crisis, actions taken were careful not to be inconsistent with the NAFTA accord. By the year 2003, trade among the three countries had doubled from $306 billion to $621 billion.

Yet the debate generated by NAFTA persists. American labor groups estimate that between 150,000 to 500,000 jobs have been lost to Mexico and that over one-third of those affected never receive comparable wages again. American environmental groups fear free trade with Mexico comes at the expense of the environment. U.S. firms relocate to Mexico to skirt domestic environmental regulations. They point to the degraded environment of the border regions between the two countries as evidence.

Mexican economists are divided over the NAFTA's effects. Supporters point to the fact that Mexican exports have nearly doubled those of all Latin America put together. Since 1994, foreign investment in Mexico has reached $13 billion annually, a three-fold increase. Yet opponents, while they acknowledge a 50-percent increase in labor productivity, also report an 11-percent slide in real manufacturing wages between 1994 and 2001, as lower-skill jobs moved to China. They assert that NAFTA has had a devastating effect on Mexican small farmers because of cheap U.S. corn imports. Also, in Mexico, one of the earliest local rebellions against globalization occurred in 1994, shortly after the formation of NAFTA. An army of peasant guerrillas seized towns in the southern Mexican state of Chiapas to protest the economic and political system seen as biased against them. Feeling that economic decisions were beyond their control, individuals protested against the structures of the international and regional market, the state, and globalization. NAFTA was viewed as an example of American expansionism and exploitation of the Mexican workforce.

Similarly, NAFTA opponents in Canada, namely labor groups, have argued that manufacturing in that country is fast becoming a lost art, with increasing dependence on exports of natural resources. Because manufacturing jobs have been lost, income inequality has widened in the country. Others fear that Canadian sovereignty is threatened and national identity compromised, as foreigners from across the border make key economic decisions. These criticisms have energized NGOs and interest groups in each of the member countries.

Among the most controversial provisions of NAFTA is Chapter 11, the investor-to-state, third-party dispute resolution procedure. Because it relates to regional environmental governance as well as trade, it is explored in more detail in Chapter 11.

The EU and NAFTA, then, are very different types of regional trade blocs. Asia provides yet another contrasting experience in regional economic governance.

■ ASEAN Free Trade Area (AFTA)

The AFTA agreement is relatively brief (especially compared to NAFTA) and contains no binding commitments. It called for countries to reduce tariffs on all intra-ASEAN trade in manufactures and processed agricultural products to a zero- to 5-percent range by 2003. It does not address nontariff barriers or services, nor does it reform the ASEAN secretariat to help implement the agreement. Its primary purpose was not so much to increase intraregional trade but to attract more foreign investment to the region to take advantage of economies of scale (Narine 1999: 366). The derisory play on the acronym AFTA, "Agree First, Talk After," might well be an apt description of the agreement's lack of specificity (Kahler 2000: 554). In the aftermath of the 1997–1998 financial crisis, ASEAN recommitted itself to AFTA and accelerated the timetable for lowering barriers. Slow recovery, however, and continuing instability in Indonesia, plus reluctance to implement tariff reductions in some cases, have led to considerable flexibility in the implementation of the agreement—a characteristic consistent with the ASEAN Way discussed in Chapter 5.

Regional economic governance also includes the set of six regional development banks whose voting structures, at least in theory, give developing countries more say.

■ Regional Multilateral Development Banks

Dissatisfaction with World Bank lending and scarcity of development funds for regional projects led developing countries in Asia, Latin America, Africa, the Middle East, and the Caribbean to create regional development banks. The European Bank for Reconstruction and Development was established only in 1991, with the fall of communism and the need to aid former Soviet-bloc countries in transition to market economies. These banks are designed to promote regional programs and be more sensitive to regional needs and concerns. We look at four of them.

Inter-American Development Bank.   The oldest and among the most active of the regional development banks is the Inter-American Development Bank (IDB), with forty-six members from Latin America, the Caribbean, and North America. Founded in 1959, IDB became a leader in social sector lending (health and education) and lending to smaller poor countries during the 1960s and 1970s. In the 1980s, the IDB aligned itself more with the World Bank's economic liberalization agenda. In the 1990s, it adopted a broader approach, addressing all areas of the modern state and working to strengthen different domestic institutions including civil society. Among its targets are small-project lending to finance microentrepreneurs and small-scale farmers as part of a concerted effort to benefit low-income populations.

Like the World Bank, the IDB group currently consists of several separate agencies, which emphasize different aspects of lending. The Inter-American Investment Corporation finances small- and medium-scale private interests; the Multilateral Investment Fund promotes reforms in investment practices to stimulate private sector involvement; the Fund for Special Operations lends to the least-developed countries on concessional terms. Through these various mechanisms, the IDB annual lending has risen from $294 million in 1961 to $7.9 billion in 2001.

IDB has assumed a leadership position in the region not only because of its lending activities, but also because it chairs and convenes donor meetings. For example, the IDB convened the 1994 Summit of the Americas, hosting UNDP, regional NGOs, and governments in an effort to consolidate democracy and reconstruct the state (Tussie 1995; Nelson 2000). It has drawn NGOs into the consultation process, working, for example, with the Latin American Association of Popular Organizations (ALOP), a regional network of development NGOs.

The IDB's special advantage has always been its close relationship with states and its knowledge of the region. It maintains resident representatives in each of its borrowing countries, resulting in a steady flow of information concerning needs and problems. As one government official put it, "The IDB is the Bank that respects our creativity" (www.idb.org). Yet the institution's close relationships with governments may also be a liability. Its president (always a Latin) is closely scrutinized by the United States and international banking community, as the United States still holds one-third of the total voting power, thereby limiting IDB's autonomy.

The Asian Development Bank.   The Asian Development Bank (ADB) has also assumed a major leadership position in its respective region. Established in 1966 with headquarters in Manila, the bank currently has sixty-one member states. Its two thousand employees work in twenty-two offices around the world, including financial centers in Frankfurt and Tokyo, in Washington D.C., and special offices in Afghanistan and East Timor. With strong economic backing by Japan, the bank has long supported projects having regional impact. Recognizing that many Asian economies are small and have few economic transactions across national borders, the bank encourages subregional cooperative efforts. One example is a project for Central Asian Regional Economic Cooperation, a geographic area dominated by landlocked states, limited internal markets, and a need to rationally allocate natural resources such as energy and water. ADB funding supports projects focusing on energy, trade, and transportation in the subregion. In the aftermath of September 11, the bank accelerated its program in this highly volatile region. Two other subregional projects are the Greater Mekong subregional project that funds transportation corridors in Southeast Asia, and another focusing on the special needs of Bangladesh, Bhutan, India, and Nepal in energy, investment, transport, and water resource management. As early as 1985, ADB provided direct lending to the private sector without government guarantees. In 1989, a separate arm, the Asian Finance and Development Corporation, was established for this purpose.

Japanese financial institutions are the major underwriters of ADB's operations, and the Japanese government is the major contributor to the special concessionary funds. In 2000, the Japan Fund for Poverty Reduction was created as ADB's grant facility. This signaled to the international community that the ADB was now refocusing work on the goal of eliminating poverty and was willing to work with civil society to accomplish these objectives. The Japan Fund for Poverty Reduction may fund community-level water supply and sanitation or local-product market facilities, NGO-supported campaigns on the nutritional value of iodized salt and fortified wheat, NGO participation in habitat planning, and NGO-run counseling programs for abused girls. This emphasis represents a significant departure from traditional multilateral development bank funding for state-supported large infrastructure projects. Having a wealthy donor country within the region provides a distinct advantage. Such is not the case in Africa.

African Development Bank.   The African Development Bank (AfDB) was founded in 1966 by African states, but less than twenty years later agreed to admit nonregional members in order to augment its economic resources. The African member states remain very concerned with maintaining the bank's Africanicity for symbolic reasons. Not only are the president and its more than one thousand employees always African, but the organization has also tried to bring a uniquely African perspective to development problems.

Originally defining itself as an economic development institution, the

AfDB established only economic conditions for its loans, believing that the imposition of political criteria was unwarranted interference in the internal affairs of member states. AfDB officials, however, have increasingly moved in the direction of conditionality, albeit timidly, suggesting, for example, that if a government does not undertake measures leading toward the eventual use of the market pricing system, it will have difficulty obtaining future loans. Lending has become less project based, with more program lending and sector loans.

The arrears problem has been especially acute for the AfDB, as members that have difficulties repaying their debts choose to repay the World Bank or other international lending institutions before the AfDB. This is a significant financial constraint on the institution that on the one hand identifies with the plight of African governments and yet, on the other, must also maintain international financial viability (Mingst 1990).

The AfDB Group Vision Statement adopted in 1998 targets new areas of AfDB activity, similar to those pursued by the other regional development banks. As a result, improving environmental protection, poverty reduction, gender mainstreaming, and ensuring sustainable economic growth are part of the new language of the bank. Such initiatives may involve the private sector, either as co-financiers or as joint ventures, or in the encouragement of microenterprise. Finally, like the IDB, the bank has assumed a leadership position in the discussions on debt relief for its members.

European Bank for Reconstruction and Development.   The newest regional development bank is the European Bank for Reconstruction and Development (EBRD) founded in 1991 to aid transitions to market economies in Central and Eastern Europe and the former Soviet Union. The EBRD monitors and analyzes these countries' progress in price and trade liberalization, competition policy, enterprise restructuring, and establishing a new legal framework. Its mandate, however, requires that 60 percent of loans be to private enterprises without government guarantees. As the largest single investor in the region of Central Europe and Central Asia, its sixty members have loaned 20 to 800 billion euros to private and state sector projects.

Several features distinguish the EBRD from its sister institutions. First, it is the only regional development bank that imposes political criteria, namely that borrowing countries must be applying principles of multiparty democracy and pluralism. Thus, the bank explicitly promotes both capitalist economic development and democratization. Second, the EBRD is the first regional development bank to include in its mandate the promotion of "environmentally sound and sustainable development." Third, the bank is quite transparent. Its easily navigated website provides unprecedented access to documents, and its Compliance Hotline permits individuals or groups to report irregularities in the use of the bank's funds.

Regional economic governance structures enjoy a close relationship with their constituencies. With fewer members and more comparable needs, governance can be more closely tailored to national and local needs. Yet, these regional approaches are all firmly embedded in the liberal economic paradigm. To illustrate both global and regional approaches to economic governance, we examine the problematic case of Africa, which lags far behind much of the developing world.

■ Economic Globalization and Africa: A Problematic Case

Economic globalization is a fact of life for most states and people; for some, globalization has led to the reduction of poverty. For example, Asia's poverty rate declined from 54 percent in 1980 to 5 percent in 2000. Yet the world is only partially globalized and the benefits of globalization are not equally distributed. Forty-six percent of Africa's population lives on less than $1 a day and only 0.1 percent of the population has access to the Internet. Since 1965, GNP per capita has declined annually by .22 percent so that many people are worse off today than they were at the time of independence. Several key economic indicators suggest that sub-Saharan Africa is falling back, as other geographic areas may be moving forward. Figure 9.5 shows international development aid and foreign direct investment inflows to Africa have dropped over the last decade. Debt service ratios are the highest in the world, with over one-half of African countries falling into the highly indebted category. Even with the GATT's GSP and the EU Lome Convention's preferential access to markets, African agricultural producers could not compete in these markets against higher quality Latin American and Asian products. Trade concessions proved too little, too late, and always subject to the whims of developed countries' domestic constituencies. Globalization has brought the promise of medicines and medical technology, yet the continent suffers from the highest death rates and infant mortality on earth, as well as devastating AIDS mortality rates. The prospects for economic growth and human development remain dim.

Since Africa has not attracted private investment, development aid from the global and regional institutions, as well as NGOs, is more critical. Hence, Africa has been the testing ground for many theories of economic development. For example, in the 1960s, World Bank projects in Africa, like elsewhere, involved dams, airports, and electricity grids. Most were financed by IDA concessional loans. Few of these infrastructure projects, unfortunately, resulted in sustainable development; once built, governments could not support maintenance. Some were flawed from the outset, such as bridges built for low traffic flows.

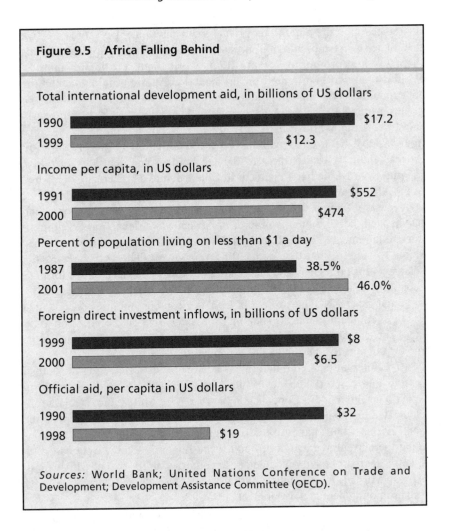

Figure 9.5   Africa Falling Behind

Total international development aid, in billions of US dollars

1990	$17.2
1999	$12.3

Income per capita, in US dollars

1991	$552
2000	$474

Percent of population living on less than $1 a day

1987	38.5%
2001	46.0%

Foreign direct investment inflows, in billions of US dollars

1999	$8
2000	$6.5

Official aid, per capita in US dollars

1990	$32
1998	$19

Sources: World Bank; United Nations Conference on Trade and Development; Development Assistance Committee (OECD).

In the 1990s, privatization became the preferred development strategy. In some states, the strategy has been surprisingly successful. Even war-torn Liberia, Sierra Leone, and Rwanda instituted some privatization policies. Small and medium firms privatized, aided by microfinance loans and NGO's teaching entrepreneurial skills. Since 1996, larger state-owned enterprises have been privatized, including airlines, banking, shipping, public utilities, and telecommunication, much to the dismay of the labor sector as governmental assets have generally been sold to multinational corporations. African private companies do not have access to sufficient capital. This has led some critics to suggest that what is occurring is a recolonialization of Africa, not by states but by MNCs. Privatization policy is predicated on the notion that private sector investment is more effective than state ownership, although no data has been collected to evaluate this theory. While promoting privatization, World Bank President James D. Wolfensohn also highlighted governmental corruption and convened the first training workshop on eliminating corruption in 1997. Yet, rooting out governmental and private sector corruption is proving to be a daunting task.

Just as the World Bank's privatization policy and good governance agenda have been controversial, so too has the IMF's involvement in Africa. The debt trap is most evident in burdensome debt service ratios, ranging from Burundi's 43 percent to Côte d'Ivoire's 30 percent, compared to the African average of about 19 percent. IMF conditionality, as described above, was infamous on the continent, well known to even the poorest and uneducated. Yet, despite the failures of African countries to meet conditionality requirements, the IMF and others continued to loan to many African states to satisfy creditors demanding repayment. The IMF became the scapegoat for both governmental leaders seeking to displace blame for poor economic performance and for the NGOs criticizing the IMF's insensitivity to human needs. NGOs working in local African communities documented how governments' reduced spending on social services, clinics, pharmacies, and education further impoverished the marginalized populations, fueling support for the Jubilee 2000 campaign.

The international community has been better at articulating goals than putting into place policies to achieve gains. The 1995 World Summit on Social Development in Copenhagen (and later the Millennium Declaration) elucidated the goal of reducing poverty by half by 2015. To accomplish the goal, Africa would have to attain 7 percent average annual growth, doubling the current average, a difficult if not impossible task. Debt cancellation for the most heavily indebted poor countries, thirty-two of which are in Africa, will help but is only a partial answer to reducing Africa's poverty and promoting human development.

The Economic Commission for Africa concluded in a 1999 report that institutional elements and capacity building have been woefully neglected in African development. A World Bank report shows that only 30 percent of African projects are likely to have a sustained impact. Policies supporting macroeconomic stabilization have undercut investment. That basic position has been expanded in the 2000 report, "Can Africa Claim the 21st Century?" a joint product of the World Bank, African Development Bank, Economic Commission for Africa, the Global Coalition for Africa, and the Africa Economic Research Consortium. The report recognizes the limits of narrow market-domain approaches, as well as the need to focus on state institutions and capacity to reduce poverty (The World Bank Group 2000b). Similarly, the UN Millennium Summit in 2000 offered international support to strengthen African governmental capacity to address poverty reduction and to respond to the AIDS crisis. The U.S. Congress, too, approved the African Growth and Opportunity Act in May 2000, which reinstates the generalized system of trade preferences and reauthorizes trade assistance programs (U.S. Congress 2000). Supporters, namely a coalition of U.S.-based multinational corporations, see the bill as positively supporting African development, while NGOs in both Africa and the United States view the bill as a tool to promote U.S. corporate interests in the economies of African states.

These initiatives paved the way for the New Partnership for African Development (NEPAD) unveiled at the G-7/8 meeting in July 2001 in Genoa, Italy, the first African-generated self-help plan. NEPAD focuses on five priority areas: institutional capacity building for peace and security; economic and corporate governance; infrastructure and information and communication technologies; central bank and financial standards; and agriculture and market access. The plan called for a major inflow of capital in exchange for better governance. At the 2002 G-7/8 Summit, President Thabo Mbeki of South Africa led the coalition of African leaders who agreed to police themselves and other African leaders, promoting good governance in return for investment capital destined for the priority areas. The transformation of the OAU to AU, discussed in Chapter 5, is intended to reinforce the commitment to good governance.

The terrorist attacks of 9/11 led some major Western donors to conclude that major efforts must be made to prevent Africa from becoming the next cradle of terrorism. Thus, at the WTO meetings in Doha in November 2001, the G-7/8 meetings in June in Alberta, and the UN General Assembly in November 2002, the developed countries were ready not only to support NEPAD, but also to begin a new round of trade negotiations with an agenda sensitive to African agricultural interests. The failure of the 2003 Cancun meeting, however, showed how difficult the latter will be.

In Africa, NEPAD has generated substantial interest. In meetings of legislators, lawyers, civil servants, judges, and other groups across the continent, discussion is focused on its potentialities, although some NGOs fear that there is too much attention to integration in the world market and not enough to the social agenda. These meetings, however, suggest that there is growing recognition that capital mobilization must be domestic and external aid should serve as a complement to Africa's own efforts.

Given the poor record of promoting economic development and human well-being in Africa in the past, are these initiatives adequate? The legacy of colonialism and the particularly harsh geographic conditions found on the continent have not changed. Indigenous regional IGOs lack the will and funds to support policy initiatives, the NEPAD aside. Nevertheless, the World Bank's Vice President for Africa, Callisto Madavo, claims, "We are working with Africa very differently from the way we have worked in the past. We are listening more. We are leaving the space to Africans to lead their own efforts" (quoted in Beattie et al. 2001). Africa's problematic record, the debt crisis, and adverse effects of globalization have not quelled criticisms of globalization itself and of the liberal economic system.

■ From Critiques of the Liberal Economic System to the Antiglobalization Movement

Historically, the developing countries have expressed their dissatisfaction with the international liberal economic system through the United Nations system and in particular in UNCTAD, as discussed earlier. Along with a few developed states, many have criticized the central pieces of economic governance, sought to regulate multinational corporations, and formed alternative forms of governance, most successfully in OPEC and a few other resource cartels. Some NGOs, too—both large, Northern-based groups and smaller grassroots groups—have challenged the liberal economic paradigm. Many criticisms are rooted in concerns for equity, fairness, and social justice. Some opponents of the liberal economic paradigm have formed mass-based antiglobalization groups.

■ *Critiques of the Central Pieces of Economic Governance*

Many critics of global economic governance would agree that "the current global rules and economic governance institutions are in need of repair, updating, and relegitimization" (Helleiner 2001: 260). Yet the nature of those reforms is in dispute. At one extreme are the laissez-faire advocates who prefer to see the abolition of the IMF and World Bank, leaving governance to the markets. Similar views are held by antiglobalizers who want to reduce international trade and investment, thus reducing the need for global institutions. More moderate are those who envision a new international financial architecture, often involving more regulation of global finance, early interventions to prevent crises, more transparency, and more representation in international financial institutions. Some critics want the World Bank to work on getting the incentives right—emphasizing project quality over volume of lending and choosing more carefully countries to be "rewarded" with economic assistance. Others call for an overhaul of IMF conditionality, emphasizing minimized interventions and more flexibility (Bird and Joyce 2001: 87).

Weighted voting in both the bank and fund is not likely to change, but reformers want more opportunity for input by the developing countries and NGOs. Reformers also want more social clauses in trade agreements to prohibit child or prison labor or to promote environmental protection. Reformers believe that the major international economic institutions can be fine-tuned, enabling them to become more effective and more transparent.

Still, as one analyst notes, "The serious multilateral discussions on financial architecture all have taken place in committees set up and dominated by one or more members of the G-7" (Armijo 2001: 391).

■ From Controlling MNCs to Partnering with MNCs

Critics of the liberal economic model have long been dissatisfied with the role the multinational corporations play in economic affairs, as discussed earlier, believing that they occupy a position of preeminence without being subject to international or state controls. Their goal has been mechanisms to regulate the MNCs. Yet what is to be regulated, even defining MNCs, and the scope of regulations have always been problematic.

The UN Commission on Transnational Corporations spearheaded the first effort beginning in 1974, by developing information systems about MNCs to help countries negotiate restrictions and creating an international code of conduct to govern their behavior. Yet by the mid-1980s, economic liberalism had triumphed and privatization and deregulation were prominent on the international agenda. So discussions of regulating MNCs were quietly abandoned. The search for an international code of conduct officially met its demise in 1994 when the work of the commission was integrated into UNCTAD. The mandate changed dramatically: to provide governments interested in attracting foreign investment with the support to do so.

The OECD has the clearest model for regulation of MNCs in the developed world. Its thirty members, all industrialized states with liberalized economies, have agreed to *voluntary* guidelines for MNCs. The OECD model is a simple one: MNCs are to be given the same treatment as domestic corporations. Thus, host country policies on employment and labor practices, environment, and combating bribery apply to both domestic and foreign corporations. Although the text of the guidelines never defines what a multinational corporation is, the principles and standards for conduct of business are designed to encourage multinational corporation activity. Should disputes arise between host countries and MNCs, they are encouraged to utilize appropriate international dispute settlement mechanisms such as the World Bank's Centre for the Settlement of Investment Disputes (CSID).

In 1997, the member governments of the OECD took a further step to regulate multinational corporations by signing the Convention on Combating Bribery of Foreign Public Officials in International Business Transactions. The treaty calls on countries to enact legislation to criminalize foreign bribery. The OECD monitors state compliance, requiring governments to report on enforcement measures, and threatening sanctions for corporations found paying bribes. Although somewhat vague, this represents an important step in curbing corporate bribery at the international level. The draft of a Multilateral Agreement on Investment (MAI) was withdrawn in 1999 under heavy pressure from NGOs, as discussed in Chapter 6.

Some NGOs have assumed the task of monitoring MNC behavior, empowered by technologies that enhance their organizational and communication abilities. Transparency International (TI) is the only NGO devoted to combating corruption worldwide, especially in business transactions. TI's annual Corruption Perceptions Index is widely used by the public and private sectors. Key to TI's success is its network or coalition approach with business, governments, the OECD, and international financial institutions. Infact is a grassroots organization, which since 1977 has been educating the public about the abuses of power by giant corporations and organizing for change. The organization enjoyed notoriety and success in the infant formula campaign between 1977 and 1986, discussed in Chapter 3. Since 1993, the Tobacco Industry Campaign has been underway, part of which has included a boycott that led to the breakup of R.J. Reynolds Tobacco and Nabisco Foods, an effort to secure WHO recognition of the health impact of smoking, and a ban on tobacco ads. Where in the 1970s there were protracted debates in the UN and elsewhere on draft codes of MNC conduct, now certification programs, as discussed earlier, have established private, voluntary governance mechanisms for MNC behavior.

In a different approach, UN Secretary-General Kofi Annan proposed a global compact at the World Economic Forum in Davos, Switzerland, in 1999. He hoped to join the UN, relevant UN agencies, research centers, corporations, and NGOs, including environmental, human rights, and labor groups represented by the International Confederation of Free Trade Unions, into a partnership committed to providing the social foundations of a sustainable global economy, encouraging private sector investment in LDCs and promoting good corporate practices.

The compact revolves around nine principles that participating companies have agreed to uphold. These include adherence to international human rights law, rejection of child and forced labor, abolition of discrimination in employment, and promotion of greater environmental responsibility. More than seven hundred companies had signed the compact by February 2003, including Petro-Canada, Nokia, Lufthansa, Bayer, Volkswagen, Nike, and Dupont. Ruggie (2001; 2003) describes this approach as the creation of nested networks in which participants learn how other companies have addressed the principles, learn which practices work and which fail, and increase corporate social responsibility. The Global Compact, he says (2003: 313) "is also an experiment in devising fundamentally new forms of global governance."

Critics, including a U.S.-based NGO Alliance for a Corporate-Free UN (Corpwatch), point to the lack of mechanisms for compliance in the Global Compact. Companies can pick and choose which provisions apply. They can enhance their public images without fundamentally changing corporate practice (Utting 2002; Bruno and Karliner 2003).

■ *Organizing Differently: Intergovernmental Resource Cartels*
Challengers to the liberal economic order and to the occupiers of the seats of hegemonic power received a significant boost with the success of a group of countries that organized a particularly critical area of economic activity—petroleum exports—in the 1970s.

Founded in 1960 by Iran, Iraq, Kuwait, Saudi Arabia, and Venezuela, the Organization of Petroleum Exporting Countries (OPEC) was a response to the international oil companies that formed an oil oligopoly controlling production and sale of most of the world's traded oil in return for fixed royalties to the host governments. In 1959, these companies had cut prices unilaterally and without consultation, provoking action against them by producer governments. OPEC was designed to pressure the oil companies to reverse their pricing decision. Emboldened by the success of Muammar Qaddafi's nationalization of the Libyan oil industry in 1973 and the subsequent dramatic increases of petroleum prices that followed, other oil exporters moved to increase their control over production and pricing. In 1974, the Arab members of OPEC used an embargo to withhold oil from states supporting Israel, causing both a significant increase in oil prices (and hence revenues), but also economic disruption in the United States and the Netherlands. OPEC members had changed the terms of trade by cooperating to control the price of oil and production.

The success of OPEC energized other less developed countries to push for not just price stability, but price increases. This demand was incorporated into the proposed New International Economic Order, which OPEC members backed, thus posing a significant challenge to the liberal economic order.

Southern producers of other commodities formed cartels in copper, tin, cocoa, coffee, and bananas, but met with little success. Demand for their exports was price elastic, unlike oil, which is an essential commodity with no close substitutes. Supply for most commodities was also not price inelastic, as new producers were able to begin producing the product should prices become advantageous. Their commodities were not as homogeneous as oil, thus changing between different types of the commodity was a realistic alternative should prices increase. Finally, unlike oil where a small group of suppliers dominated and could coordinate the market, these producers were often confronted with many sellers, each ready and eager to undercut each other (Finlayson and Zacher 1988). Thus, the buoyant attitude of the commodity cartels riding on OPEC's success was short-lived. However, third-world producer demands for commodity market regulation remained a longstanding approach for those opposed to the liberal economic order.

◼ *NGOs as Critics and Challengers*

With respect to economic development, NGOs serve in a number of important capacities, as our discussion has shown. Disillusioned with past approaches, for example, NGOs working with the World Commission on Environment and Development in the 1980s helped to articulate the concept of sustainable development, changing the terms of discourse and setting new agendas.

NGOs are alternative channels for assistance serving their own missions and increasingly working in tandem with the World Bank, UNDP, and other IGOs, as well as subcontractors for donor governments. One particularly effective approach developed by grassroots NGOs is microcredit. Created in 1983 by an academic turned banker, Muhammad Yunus, the Grameen Bank in Bangladesh provides small amounts of capital to people who cannot qualify for regular bank loans. Loans average $100, although some may be as little as $10 to $20. Grameen has been a tremendous economic success, providing loans to 1.6 million borrowers who are predominantly women in 34,000 villages, lending about $30 million per month, with a loan recovery rate of 97 percent. The ability of microcredits to empower poor people, stimulate small private enterprises, and generate economic and social ripple effects has led to the creation of other such banks all over the world.

As Chapter 6 detailed, the large number of NGOs active today varies widely. Not all NGOs support greater equity over economic growth or support marginalized peoples over those economically advantaged. Not all are concerned with economic issues. Most NGOs do want policy changes; they seek a greater role for democratic governance and recognize the need for political sustainability. The impact of NGOs needs to be measured by the extent to which they can accomplish these objectives. As noted earlier in this chapter, NGOs have pressed for greater transparency in the World Bank, WTO, and IMF, as well as greater civil society participation. They have successfully championed the role of women in development and the importance of paying heed to environmental consequences of development. Some NGOs have also been leaders in the antiglobalization movement.

◼ *The Antiglobalization Movement*

To still other critics, reforming the liberal economic system, controlling MNCs, or relying on cartels or NGOs for alternative governance approaches are all inadequate. For antiglobalizers, the only alternative is to roll back aspects of economic globalization. These opponents have formed a coalition of workers, environmentalists, farmers, religious activists, women, and human rights advocates. Many of these groups found common cause in the streets of Seattle, Prague, Washington, and Calgary in demonstrating their dissatisfaction with economic globalization by staging mass protests in conjunction with meetings of the international financial institutions. Although each group has its own agenda, they are united in denouncing globalization. They want to return to governance at the local (or national) level. To many, goals of economic efficiency, of being able to buy the cheapest goods, should be replaced by support for local economies, providing local employment not exporting jobs, and by fair and environmentally friendly conditions for workers. Economic justice is a major goal. Although economic localization may not maximize economic welfare, some see it as preferable to globalization over which people have little control (Broad 2002). The antiglobalization movement, disparate as it is, represents a fundamental critique to liberal economic norms based on the belief that economic globalization is neither inevitable nor desirable. But while street demonstrations send a powerful message to other actors, antiglobalizers will have to do more if they want to alter the current system.

The antiglobalization movement is not alone in charging that economic globalization has not closed the gap between the rich and the poor. Those in the developed world, with 20 percent of the world's population, enjoy 80 percent of its wealth. Between 1970 and 2000, the gap between rich and poor expanded by 65 percent. In the 1970s, the average earnings in the North were fourteen times that of the South; by 2000, the gap had expanded to twenty-three times earnings. In terms of human development, this means that in developing countries, the population is twenty-four times more likely to be illiterate, sixteen times more likely to die by five years of age, and twenty-seven times more likely not to have basic sanitation than their counterparts in the developed world. Even within many states, the gap has widened, not only in the United States but also in developing countries like Peru, Colombia, and Mexico, where wage differentials between the rich and poor have increased. Thus, the need for economic governance has never been greater, driven in large part by the same concerns for fairness and economic justice that lie behind the campaign for debt relief. There is an unprecedented degree of consensus on core concepts and approaches now, with poverty alleviation and sustainability at the core, along with good governance, empowering women, and raising levels of human well-being. This consensus and the networks to implement it are embodied in the Millennium Development Goals. Nevertheless, major challenges lie ahead if economic development is to ultimately result in increased well-being for a greater portion of the world's people.

■ **Note**

1. Portions of this chapter are drawn from Karen A. Mingst and Margaret P. Karns. (2000) *The United Nations in the Post–Cold War Era,* 2nd ed. Boulder: Westview Press. Reprinted with permission of Westview Press.

■ Suggested Further Reading

Broad, Robin, ed. (2002) *Global Backlash. Citizen Initiatives for a Just World Economy.* Lanham, MD: Rowman and Littlefield.
Gilpin, Robert. (2001) *Global Political Economy: Understanding the International Economic Order.* Princeton: Princeton University Press.
Schott, Jeffrey J., ed. (2000) *The WTO After Seattle.* Washington, D.C.: Institute of International Economics.
Stiglitz, Joseph E. (2002) *Globalization and Its Discontents.* New York: W.W. Norton and Co. .
Zacher, Mark W., with Brent Sutton. (1996) *Governing Global Networks: International Regimes for Transportation and Communications.* Cambridge, UK: University of Cambridge.

■ Internet Resources

African Development Bank: www.afdb.org
Alliance for Corporate-Free UN: www.corpwatch.org
Asian Development Bank: www.adb.org
Asia-Pacific Economic Cooperation: www.apecsec.org
European Bank for Reconstruction and Development: www.ebrd.com
Group of Seven: www.g7.utoronto.ca
Group of 77: www.G-77.org
Human Development Reports: www.undp.org/reports/
Infact: www.infact.org
Inter-American Development Bank: www.iadb.org
International Civil Aviation Organization: www.icao.org
International Conference on Finance for Development: www.un.org/esa/ffd
International Maritime Organization: www.imo.org
International Monetary Fund: www.imf.org
International Telecommunications Union: www.itu.org
Jubilee 2000: www.jubilee2000uk.org
Millennium Development Goals: www.un.org/millenniumgoals/
North American Free Trade Agreement: www.nafta-sec-alena.org
Organisation for Economic Cooperation and Development: www.oecd.org
Organization of Petroleum Exporting Countries: www.opec.org
Transparency International: www.transparency.org
United Nations Conference on Trade and Development: www.unctad.org
United Nations Development Program: www.undp.org
United Nations Global Compact: www.unglobalcompact.org
Women's Environment and Development Organization: www.wedo.org
World Bank: www.worldbank.org
World Summit on Sustainable Development: www.johannesburgsummit.org
World Intellectual Property Organization: www.unorg/partners/business/wipo.htm
World Trade Organization: www.wto.org

10

Protecting Human Rights

■ Case Study: Child Soldiers

Armed conflicts have increasingly involved children, with an estimated 300,000 children currently participating in military activities in over fifty countries from Sri Lanka to Sudan, Congo, Côte d'Ivoire, Liberia, Nepal, and Guatemala. In Colombia, children as young as eight years old have fought for paramilitary forces. In Sierra Leone, ten thousand children fought in that country's civil war, while Myanmar has over fifty thousand young soldiers, the largest number in the world. Child soldiers carry guns, serve as human mine detectors, participate in suicide missions, carry supplies, act as spies and messengers, and provide sexual services. Dissident groups, ethnic separatist groups, paramilitary forces, and guerrilla fighters, as well as states, find children to be excellent soldiers. They follow orders and are willing to undertake dangerous missions. In the words of one Sierra Leonean recruit, "We beat and killed people" (quoted in Masland 2002: 243). Life in uniform offers children protection from the vicissitudes of daily struggle for shelter and food, and a security and structure often absent from civilian life.

So how can the human rights of this vulnerable group be protected? Their parents are often absent or unable to care for them. The community or state often forces or recruits them into service, rather than protecting them. The story of how child soldiers became a prominent human rights issue in the 1990s helps to illustrate the politics and processes of global governance for human rights issues more generally.

Both IGOs and NGOs, as well as key individuals in both, brought the issue of child soldiers to the public arena. In 1994, then Secretary-General Boutros Boutros-Ghali, answering the demands of the 1993 World Conference on Human Rights, appointed Graça Machel to investigate the various dimensions of children in conflict. A well-known figure, former minister for education of Mozambique, former first lady of Mozambique and of South Africa as Nelson Mandela's wife, she provided the impetus and energy for the task. Her 1996 report, the first comprehensive assessment of the ways children suffer during war, called for immediate action by the international community. According to Ms. Machel, it "exposed a moral vacuum in which all taboos had been eroded and discarded" (UN Press Release 1996b).

In 1997, Secretary-General Kofi Annan appointed Olara Otunnu Special Representative for Children and Armed Conflict. He proved to be a very effective spokesperson, drawing media attention to the issue, especially the abuses in Africa, and persuading regional organizations to put the issue on their agendas. Most critically, his work with UN agencies, including the Department of Peacekeeping Operations and the UN High Commissioner for Human Rights, gained acceptance of the issue as one of international peace and security. The Security Council itself has passed four resolutions and now integrates child protection into the mandates of all peacekeeping missions and training of personnel, in addition to appointing child protection advisors for the missions to Sierra Leone, Democratic Republic of the Congo, and Côte d'Ivoire.

In May 1998, a large group of NGOs formed the Coalition to Stop the Use of Child Soldiers to prevent recruitment, force demobilization, and provide rehabilitation and reintegration services. The coalition, which includes Amnesty International and Human Rights Watch, advocated the "Straight 18 principle" to ban compulsory and voluntary recruitment of children under eighteen years old and was highly effective in publicizing abuses and in urging states to prohibit the use of child soldiers in combat.

In 2000, the UN General Assembly approved the Optional Protocol to the Convention on the Rights of the Child on the Involvement of Children in Armed Conflict. Signed by 111 countries and ratified by sixty-three, it prohibits governments and nongovernmental armed groups from using children under eighteen years of age in combat. Much to the chagrin of the NGOs, however, it permits voluntary enlistment at sixteen, although proof of age and consent are required. The United States initially opposed the eighteen-year minimum age for combat, having previously sent seventeen-year-old combatants into the Gulf War, Somalia, and Bosnia, but it ratified the protocol in December 2002. ILO Convention No. 182, approved in 1999 and ratified by 143 states, makes child soldiering one of the worst forms of child labor and bans recruitment of children under eighteen. The African Charter on the Rights and Welfare of the Child, ratified by thirty-one states, is the first regional treaty to accept the same ban.

Human Rights Watch (HRW) has been particularly active in the campaign to halt the recruitment of child soldiers and to demobilize and rehabilitate those who have served. Their website relates the "stories" of child soldiers to show the human dimension. It provides information about how to write national authorities to push for ratification of the Optional Protocol and recruits individuals to become involved in national campaigns. HRW and other NGOs are involved in programs with UNICEF and its Child Protection Network to train former child soldiers in specific skills, such as carpentry, masonry, fishing, and tailoring. The real challenge for NGOs as well as IGOs and states is to enforce these standards in conflicts involving nonstate armies, guerrilla groups, or paramilitary groups. The transnational advocacy network for child soldiers helped to introduce new norms, but other pieces of global governance are very rudimentary.

The problem of child soldiers is one part of the larger issue of children's rights. In January 1990, the Convention on the Rights of the Child (CRC) was signed by ninety-one states; by 2004, 194 states had ratified it, with only the United States and Somalia failing to ratify. Implementation, however, has been fraught with contradictions and dilemmas. The answer to this paradox is not difficult to find. On the one hand, the CRC legally abolishes the concept that children are possessions of their guardians and recognizes them as human beings of equal value. Thus, children have the right to survival and development; their best interests are of primary consideration; they have the right to express views freely; and they have the right to enjoy benefits without discrimination. On the other hand are conflicting rights of the parents, community, family, or state to subordinate the rights of an individual child to the right of the family to subsistence or to the state to use its citizens on behalf of the safety and welfare of the collectivity (Gerschutz and Karns forthcoming).

Monitoring state compliance with the CRC and Optional Protocol on Child Soldiers occurs through a state-based reporting system with an independent body of experts analyzing reports. The process was designed as an interactive one both to elicit more information from states and establish priorities for implementation, and to aid states in setting measures for meeting international standards of practice. UNICEF, with field offices in 131 states, plays a key role in the process, working closely with the Committee on the Rights of the Child. UNICEF presses governments to submit reports, supports workshops with civil society, provides follow-up at the field level, translates recommendations into local languages, and distributes information locally. Implementation and enforcement rest with state authorities.

Child soldiers are not new. During the Middle Ages children were sent from Europe to the Middle East in the Children's Crusade, but the issues of children's rights are largely a recent phenomenon. They are part of the general increased attention to human rights issues since World War II, and particularly since the 1970s, that has spurred the development of international human rights norms.[1]

■ The Roots of Human Rights Norms

The Holocaust—Nazi Germany's campaign of genocide against Jews, Gypsies, and other "undesirables" that took the lives of six million innocent men, women, and children during World War II—was a powerful impetus to the development of a human rights movement. South Africa's egregious policy of apartheid—systematic repression and violence against the majority of the country's population solely on the basis of race—had a similar mobilizing effect. The dissolution of the Soviet Union and the downfall of communist regimes there and in Eastern Europe liberated international efforts to promote human rights from the ideological conflict and propaganda campaigns of the Cold War.

In the 1990s, events in Bosnia and Rwanda prompted pressure for prosecution of those responsible for war crimes and genocide, and television pictures of starving children in Somalia provoked public demands that something be done. In each case, the revolution in communications technologies magnified the horror of the events by broadcasting pictures worldwide of genocide, ethnic violence, and the use of child soldiers in remote regions of the world. Instantaneous news broadcasts report the abuses of governmental regimes against their own people. Suppressed groups or their supporters can use the Internet to mobilize help and develop broad coalitions. Technology has helped create the idea of international human rights and led to pressure by states and individuals for pieces of global governance. The fact that eighty-five of the 191 member states of the UN are now liberal democracies magnifies the pressure for human rights governance. The forces of liberalization and globalization have also contributed to the erosion of absolute state sovereignty and the gradual acceptance of international accountability for how states treat their citizens. The roots of international human rights norms can be found in all major religions and in widely divergent philosophical traditions.

■ Religious Traditions

Hinduism, Judaism, Christianity, Buddhism, Islam, and Confucianism all assert both the dignity of individuals and people's responsibility to their fellow humans. Hindus prohibit infliction of physical or mental pain on others. Jews support the sacredness of individuals, as well as the responsibility of the individual to help those in need. Buddhism's Eight-Fold Path includes right thought and action toward all beings. Islam teaches equality of races and racial toleration, as well as respect for all human beings. While the relative importance of these values may vary, Paul Gordon Lauren (1998: 11) notes, "Early ideas about general human rights thus did not originate exclusively in one location like the West or even with any particular form of government like liberal democracy, but were shared throughout the ages by visionaries from many cultures in many lands who expressed themselves in different ways."

■ The Philosophers and Political Theorists

Like the world's religious thinkers, philosophers and political theorists have conceptualized human rights, although they differ on many specific issues and ideas. Human rights philosophers from the liberal persuasion traditionally have emphasized individual rights that the state can neither usurp nor undermine. John Locke (1632–1704), among others, asserted that individuals are equal and autonomous beings whose natural rights predate both national and international law. Public authority is designed to secure these rights. Key historic documents detail these rights, beginning with the English Magna Carta in 1215, the French Declaration of the Rights of Man in 1789, and the U.S. Bill of Rights in 1791. For example, no individual should be "deprived of life, liberty, or property, without due process of law." Political and civil rights, including free speech, free assembly, free press, and freedom of religion, deserve utmost protection according to liberal theories. To some theorists and many U.S. pundits, these are the only recognized human rights.

[margin note: pol & legal rights]

[margin note: vs.]

Theorists influenced by Karl Marx and other socialist thinkers concentrate on those rights that the state is responsible for providing. Emerging from Marx's concern for the welfare of industrialized labor, the duty of states is to advance the well-being of their citizens; the right of the citizens is to benefit from these socioeconomic advances. This view emphasizes minimum material rights that the state must provide to individuals. Individuals have the right to education, healthcare, social security, and housing, although the amount guaranteed is unspecified. Without those guarantees, socialist theorists believe political and civil rights are meaningless. The socialist states of the former Soviet bloc, as well as many European social welfare states, ranked economic and social rights as highly or more highly than political and civil rights.

[margin note: ecc-soc rights]

Some contemporary writers have focused on human rights for specific groups such as children, as discussed above. Indigenous peoples have also been singled out for special consideration, as have women and refugees. Some scholars suggest that democratic governance is also a basic human right.

■ The Debate: Universal Human Rights or Cultural Relativism

Are human rights truly universal, that is, applicable to all peoples, in all states, religions, cultures, and protected groups? In recent years the debate over universal rights versus cultural relativism was reopened by a group of developing states, including China, Colombia, Cuba, Indonesia, Iran, Iraq, Libya, Malaysia, Mexico, Myanmar, Singapore, Syria, Vietnam, and Yemen. The strongest advocates for cultural relativism were Asian states whose ancient cultures had been least affected by colonialism and whose recent, rapid economic growth and large populations had renewed national confidence. They argued that the principles in the Universal Declaration and other human rights documents represented Western values that were being imposed on them and that the West was interfering in their internal affairs with its own definition of human rights. Asian states have completed few ratifications of the human rights treaties, with the exception of the Convention on the Rights of the Child. The region also has the lowest rates of participation in the individual complaint proceedings of any other regional group (Bayefsky 2001).

Are there Asian values that are distinct from those of the West? Amartya Sen, Indian essayist and winner of the 1998 Nobel Prize in Economics, is among those who have explored this question. His survey of the diverse Asian cultural and religious traditions from Confucianism to Buddhism found "conscious theorizing about tolerance and freedom in substantial and important parts of the Asian tradition." Since there is no "grand dichotomy," Sen argues, the case for universal human rights is stronger (Sen 1997: 27, 30). As the legal scholar and activist Abdullahi An-Na'im notes, "Detailed and credible knowledge of local culture is essential for the effective promotion and protection of human rights in any society" (An-Na'im 1999: 147). In his view, however, there has evolved a universal meaning of human rights, which includes but is not confined to the Western tradition.

Others disagree, suggesting that the so-called Asian version of human rights, placing the family and community over the individual, is not just an Asian construct. They point to challenges from the Islamic world, as well as from the West itself. Saudi Arabia, for example, at the time the Universal Declaration on Human Rights was being drafted, questioned the Western bias of Article 16 on marital choice and Article 18 on freedom of religion. Since the 1970s, the Islamic challenge to the notion of universal human rights has been even stronger. The Iranian revolution opposed the separation of religious and secular authority and challenged women's rights over family choice. Even some Western scholars have argued that human rights is a Western construct embedded in liberal individualism and that the notion of universal human rights is yet another manifestation of Western hegemonic domination (Ignatieff 2001).

The debate was joined in the preparatory and plenary sessions of the 1993 World Conference on Human Rights in Vienna. Much of the debate is clearly political, taking place between authoritarian states and Western democratic states eager to promote political change. The debate over universality versus cultural relativism also engages particularly sensitive issues with respect to religion, culture, women's status, protection of children, family planning, and practices such as female circumcision. The debate also calls into question key principles, namely sovereignty and noninterference in the domestic affairs of states. Acceptance of the universalist position with respect to human rights justifies interference in the affairs of others and threatens national sovereignty, while regionalization or particularization of human rights norms provides an umbrella of protection. This is one of the reasons why enforcement of human rights standards remains so problematic.

The Final Declaration and Programme of Action of the 1993 World Conference on Human Rights affirmed, "All human rights are universal, indivisible and interdependent and interrelated." Regional human rights standards "should reinforce universal human rights standards." This statement clearly implies a subordination of sovereignty and noninterference to global human rights norms. This view was affirmed by Secretary-General Kofi Annan, in defense of the UN's support of human rights and democracy, after Osama Bin Laden criticized the UN for representing Western interests. Annan said, "Bin Laden is wrong. . . . when Bin Laden affirms that democracy and human rights are just Western products, I find that insulting for the people of the Third World whom he claims to defend. When a father learns that his son has been tortured, when a woman learns that her husband has been thrown in prison for no reason, their reaction is the same wherever they are. In the West or in the Third World, they shout out the same anger, they cry the same tears" (Annan 2001b [quoted in *Le Figaro*]).

Yet even the final document at the Vienna conference included the qualification that "the significance of national and regional particularities and various historical, cultural and religious backgrounds must be borne in mind." The debate is not over.

■ Human Rights Institutions and Mechanisms

IGOs, in particular the United Nations, and NGOs have played key roles in the process of globalizing human rights. They have been central to establishing the norms, institutions, mechanisms, and activities for giving effect to this powerful idea that certain rights are universal. States have seldom been prime movers in this process, although their acceptance of and support for human rights is clearly critical. The international human rights movement—a dense network of human rights-oriented NGOs—and a number of dedicated individuals have been responsible for drafting much of the language of human rights conventions and for mounting transnational campaigns to promote human rights norms. The role of these groups and individuals and the processes by which they have persuaded policymakers in powerful states to adopt human rights policies demonstrate the power of ideas to reshape definitions of national interests.

■ Nongovernmental Organizations and the Human Rights Movement

NGOs have long been active in human rights activities. Anti-slavery groups were among the first and most active of the early human rights movements. In the late eighteenth century, abolitionists in the United States (Society for the Relief of Free Negroes Unlawfully Held in Bondage), Great Britain

(Society for Effecting the Abolition of the Slave Trade in Britain), and France (Société des amis des noirs) organized to promote ending the slave trade. Although by themselves not powerful enough to effect immediate international change, the group was strong enough in Great Britain to force Parliament in 1807 to ban the slave trade for British citizens. Less than a decade later, the Final Act of the Congress of Vienna in 1815 included an Eight Power Declaration that the slave trade was "repugnant to the principles of humanity and universal morality" (Lauren 1996: 27). Willingness to sign a statement of principles, however, did not mean states were ready to take specific measures to abolish the practice.

In the 1860s, individuals concerned about protecting those wounded during war established the International Committee of the Red Cross (ICRC). Under the leadership of Swiss national Henry Dunant, who was motivated by his observation of war, several conferences were organized to elucidate principles governing care of wounded individuals, rights of prisoners of war, and neutrality of medical personnel. The ICRC and its national affiliates became the neutral intermediaries for protecting wounded individuals during war, and the Geneva Convention of 1864 for the Amelioration of the Condition of the Wounded in Armies in the Field laid the foundation for international humanitarian law.

Many human rights NGOs were established in the late 1970s after the two international covenants went into effect and after the 1975 Helsinki Accords were signed. The latter recognized human rights principles and gave a basis for governments and NGOs to monitor human rights in Eastern Europe and the Soviet Union. This spurred the establishment of new groups, as did the growing number of disappearances and other human rights abuses in Latin America. One study has counted 325 international human rights NGOs and found that about seventy-five of them were formed after 1979. Twenty percent were established after the end of the Cold War. Over 60 percent are located in either Western Europe or North America. Significant variations can be found among the organizations in terms of size, budget, number of paid staff, and volunteers (Smith and Pagnucco with Lopez 1998).

Despite the diversity, NGOs perform a variety of functions and roles, both independently and in conjunction with IGOs, in the international human rights regime. These include providing information and expertise in drafting human rights conventions, monitoring violations, implementing human rights norms, and mobilizing public support and publicity campaigns within countries for changes in national policies. They may also undertake operational tasks, providing relief aid for victims of human rights abuses. In addition, NGOs provided much of the momentum for the 1993 World Conference on Human Rights in Vienna, the 1995 Fourth World Conference on Women in Beijing; and the 2001 World Conference against Racism, Racial Discrimination, Xenophobia and Related Intolerance.

As discussed in Chapter 6, a major strategy used by NGOs generally involves organizing transnational campaigns on specific issues. In the human rights field, there have been a variety of such campaigns dating back to the beginning of the nineteenth century, including those against slavery, child labor, apartheid, sweatshops, violence against women, torture, and disappearances, as well as on behalf of colonial peoples, persecuted minorities, India's "untouchables," children, and women. Many of these campaigns have involved both local groups and transnational coalitions. They take advantage of new communication technologies and link issues in ways that resonate with larger constituencies. As constructivists might argue, these campaigns shape discourse and ideas leading to learning across multiple constituencies and norm creation.

Given the variety of NGO activities, how do human rights groups evaluate their relative importance? When surveyed, 37 percent judged that their most important activity is educational; 31 percent gave primacy to reporting human rights violations; and 20 percent saw work in lobbying governments as most critical. When asked to judge organizational success, 33 percent of the NGOs ranked publicity activities as most successful; 25 percent mentioned contacting governments and IGO officials, while only 11 percent reported success in actually changing policy or legislation (Smith and Pagnucco with Lopez 1998).

As strong and vocal as the NGOs are on the issue of international human rights, they do not always get their way. At the Vienna Conference on Human Rights, a number of key NGO demands were not included in the final document, including rights of groups such as the disabled, victims of AIDS, and indigenous peoples. NGOs were restricted from participating in actual drafting of documents. NGOs in the human rights movement have amassed considerable power in international forums, but they are still not equal partners with states. Much of their success, however, has been due to opportunities presented by the League of Nations and UN.

■ League of Nations

The League of Nations Covenant made little mention of human rights, despite persistent efforts by some delegates to include principles of racial equality and religious freedom. In one of the fascinating stories of the deliberations, the Japanese government and its representatives, Marquis Kimmochi Saionji and Baron Nobuaki Makino, sought to convince the principals, including the U.S. President Woodrow Wilson, to adopt a statement on human rights and racial equality. As a victorious and economically advanced power, the Japanese felt they had a credible claim. They earnestly believed that such basic rights would not be rejected. Yet the initiative was blocked, the U.S. representatives immediately recognizing that such a provision would doom Senate passage of the peace treaty (Lauren 1996: 82–93). The league's covenant did, however, include specific provision for protection of minorities and some dependent peoples.

The league was able to address the issue of dependent peoples in part because the legitimacy of maintaining colonies was already being questioned. Thus, the idea developed that the colonies held by the defeated powers of World War I, namely Turkey and Germany, would be placed under the mandate system laid out in Article 22 of the covenant. Until they were ready for independence, a designated victor nation would administer the mandate. The league, in turn, would supervise the system through a Permanent Mandates Commission.

The Mandates Commission, though it had no real power, including having no right of inspections, acquired a reputation of being thorough and neutral in its administration. Britain became the administering power for Palestine, Transjordan, Iraq, and Tanganyika, while France assumed the same role for Syria and Lebanon, and the league endorsed the Balfour Declaration on a Jewish homeland in Palestine. Britain and France divided responsibility for Cameroons and Togoland, Belgium got the mandate for Rwanda-Urundi, while South Africa was named mandatory for South West Africa and Japan administered several Pacific islands. Between 1932 and 1947, pressure from the Mandates Commission led to independence for the Arab mandates of Lebanon, Syria, Iraq, and Transjordan, with Palestine a glaring exception. Most of the mandates held in Africa, namely Cameroons, Togoland, Rwanda-Urundi, and smaller islands in the Pacific were transferred to the United Nations trusteeship system in 1946. South West Africa was the sole exception. South Africa continued to administer the territory as its own, claiming that the demise of the league relieved South Africa from any obligations to the league's successor organization. An advisory opinion issued by the International Court of Justice in 1950 at the request of the UN General Assembly stated that South Africa was acting illegally and could not unilaterally change the legal status of the territory. But South Africa ignored the opinion and South West Africa (or Namibia) did not attain independence until 1989.

The idea of the mandate system was a triumph, giving those under its supervision a greater degree of protection from abuses than they would have enjoyed in its absence. The system reflected the growing sentiment that territories were not to be annexed following wars, that the international community had responsibilities over dependent peoples, and the eventual goal was self-determination.

The 1919 Paris Peace Conference was as much a gathering of states as a gathering of peoples and groups. The powerful promise of a right to self-determination brought groups from all over the world, not just from areas formerly part of the defeated Austro-Hungarian, German, Russian, and Ottoman empires. As a result, the rights of minorities and its corollary, the responsibilities of states, was a major topic. What emerged from the negotiations was a set of five agreements known as the Minority Treaties that required beneficiaries of the peace settlement such as Poland, Czechoslovakia, Yugoslavia, Romania, and Greece "to assure full and complete protection" to all their inhabitants "without distinction of birth, nationality, language, race, or religion." They also provided for civil and political rights and a number of guarantees. Similar obligations were imposed on the defeated states. These stipulations constituted "obligations of international concern" that would be guaranteed by the League of Nations. Later, the league made admission of new members contingent on a pledge to protect minority rights and created special mechanisms to help monitor and implement this minority rights regime. Minority rights were a major agenda item for the league council, assembly, and committees and the league's various activities created "significant precedents for increased international protection of human rights" (Lauren 1998: 117).

In other human rights activities, the league made a study of slavery after intensive lobbying by the British Anti-Slavery and Aborigines Protection Society, establishing a Temporary Slavery Commission whose report led to the International Convention on the Abolition of Slavery and the Slave Trade of 1926. Although the latter did not list specific practices, discussions within the commission covered slavery in all forms, serfdom, forced marriage, child labor, debt bondage, and native labor. The treaty was pathbreaking in setting the standard, but weak in terms of enforcement. The league had no way of monitoring whether its provisions were or were not followed.

The league also established the first principles on assisting refugees and the Refugee Organization. Appointed in 1920, the first commissioner was mandated by the league to aid Russian refugees only, to spend league funds only for administration and not on actual relief, and to provide only temporary assistance. As limited as the mandate was, this step by the league was the first recognition that the international community has responsibility for protecting this group of people. Because of budgetary restrictions and lack of cooperation, these measures were insufficient to address the major humanitarian crisis of the twentieth century, the refugees fleeing the Holocaust (Loescher 1993: 37).

Pressed by NGOs, the league also devoted attention to issues of women's and children's rights, as well as the right to a minimum level of health, and in 1924 approved the Declaration on the Rights of the Child. In the 1930s, the assembly discussed the possibility of an international human rights document, but no action was ever taken.

Rights of workers were an integral part of the International Labour Organization's agenda, as discussed in Chapter 3. The ILO's mandate to work for the improvement of workers' living conditions, health, safety, and livelihood was clearly consistent with concepts of economic and social rights. Between 1919 and 1939, the ILO approved sixty-seven conventions, covering such issues as hours of work, maternity protection, minimum age, and old-age insurance, and in 1926, it was the first organization to introduce a procedure for supervising the standards established. Because it did not die with the league, but became a UN specialized agency, ILO's work provided a foundation for other human rights activity in the UN system.

■ United Nations

A very different climate from that of the Paris Peace Conference shaped the drafting of the UN Charter. President Franklin Roosevelt's famous Four Freedoms speech in 1941 called for "a world founded upon four essential freedoms," and his vision of "the moral order" formed a normative base for the Allies in their fight against Germany and Japan (Roosevelt 1941). The liberation of Nazi concentration camps in the closing weeks of World War II revealed the full extent of the Holocaust and drew attention to human rights as an international issue that required more than talk. Peace itself seemed to rest ultimately on respect for individual rights. Thus, not surprisingly, the UN Charter took a major step beyond the League of Nations Covenant with respect to human rights. At the founding conference in San Francisco, a broad spectrum of groups from churches to peace societies, along with delegates from a number of small states, pushed for the inclusion of human rights language. The preamble reaffirmed "faith in fundamental human rights, in the dignity and worth of the human person, in the equal rights of men and women and of nations large and small." Although more weakly worded than advocates had hoped, human rights was referred to seven times in the UN Charter, placing the promotion of human rights among the central purposes of the new organization.

The UN Charter adopted a broad view of human rights, going beyond the right of self-determination espoused by the League of Nations. Included in Article 1 is the statement that the organization would be responsible for organizing cooperation in solving various international problems, including those of a "humanitarian character," and "in promoting and encouraging respect for human rights and for fundamental freedoms for all without distinction as to race, sex, language, or religion." Articles 55(c) and 56 amplify the UN's responsibility to promote "universal respect for, and observance of, human rights and fundamental freedoms for all" and the obligation of member states to "take joint and separate action in cooperation with the Organization for the achievement of the purposes set forth in Article 55."

These provisions did not define what was meant by "human rights and fundamental freedoms," but they established that human rights were a matter of international concern and that states had assumed some as yet undefined international obligation relating to them. Despite the inherent tension between establishing international standards and Article 2(7)'s principle of noninterference in a state's domestic affairs, these provided the UN with the legal authority to undertake the definition and codification of human rights. The first step in this direction was laid by the General Assembly's passage on December 10, 1948, of the Universal Declaration of Human Rights to "serve as a common standard of achievement for all peoples of all nations." Taken together, the UN Charter and the Universal Declaration of Human Rights represented a watershed in the revolution that has placed human rights at the center of world politics.

In 1946 and 1947, the UN's Economic and Social Council established the Commission on Human Rights, the Commission on the Status of Women, and the Sub-Commission on the Prevention of Discrimination and Protection of Minorities (now known as the Sub-Commission on the Protection and Promotion of Human Rights). Other entities, including the High Commissioner for Human Rights and various treaty-review committees, have been created since the 1970s and are discussed below. (See Figure 10.1.) The hub of the UN system's human rights activity is the Commission on Human Rights. It has borne primary responsibility for drafting and negotiating the major documents that elaborate and define human rights norms, including the Universal Declaration on Human Rights and the international covenants. Along with other commissions, it also conducts studies and issues reports. Although the UN received thousands of complaints of human rights violations, ECOSOC denied the Commission on Human Rights the authority to review these complaints until 1970 and then only confidentially. The fifty-three member states of the commission meet annually to hear state complaints and individual petitions, as well as address major human rights themes such as racism and the politically controversial violations of human rights in Israeli-occupied Arab territories.

The Human Rights Commission drew public attention in May 2001 when the United States was voted off the commission for the first time since the panel's founding. Those who voted against the United States, including some of its allies, did so because of perceived U.S. lack of support for the UN, its continued support of Israel, and its efforts to single out China and Cuba for their human rights abuses. The commission again drew strong adverse publicity in 2002 when Libya was elected chair, a step that made the body's credibility questionable.

The General Assembly's attention to human rights has reflected the majority at any given time. In the General Assembly's first session in 1946, India and other countries introduced the issue of South Africa's treatment of its Indian population, beginning debate over what would become the UN's longest-running human rights issue: apartheid in South Africa. Colonialism was another prominent human rights issue during the UN's

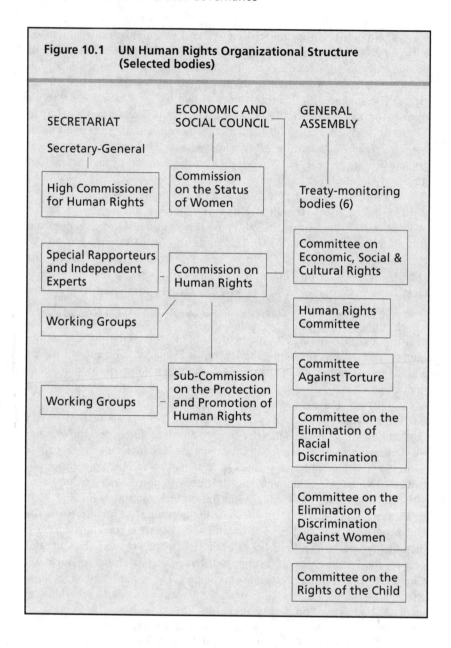

Figure 10.1 UN Human Rights Organizational Structure (Selected bodies)

first twenty years, and debates over various colonial issues occupied an increasing share of General Assembly agendas in the 1950s and 1960s. Yet the General Assembly's role was circumscribed because its members were seen as exercising a blatantly double standard. In the 1970s, for example, many third-world states criticized white racism, Zionism, and neocolonialism, while at the same time ignoring issues of black racism, sexism in Muslim countries, and violations of human rights in the Soviet Union and Eastern European countries. That politicization of human rights undermined the General Assembly's legitimacy and its effectiveness as a forum for human rights issues.

The UN Trusteeship System replaced the league's mandate system and covered the remaining mandates as well as territories that had belonged to the defeated powers of World War II and the U.S.-administered Strategic Trust Territory of the Pacific Islands. The Permanent Mandates Commission was replaced by the Trusteeship Council (with the exception of the Trust Territory of the Pacific Islands, which was handled by the Security Council), and general supervision of the trusteeship system moved to the General Assembly. The administering powers pledged to advance the eleven trust territories toward self-government and to promote educational, economic, and human rights goals. Similar to the mandate system, the Trusteeship Council received state reports and conducted investigations seeking further information. But the council also was empowered to receive individual petitions reporting abuses and to conduct on-site missions every three years. In fact, so many petitions were submitted that special procedures had to be developed to cope with the volume.

Neither the Security Council nor the ICJ has had significant human rights responsibilities. In the case of the former, several human rights-related issues have been deemed threats to international peace, including apartheid, the unilateral declaration of independence by a white minority regime in Southern Rhodesia (now Zimbabwe), and ethnic cleansing and genocide in Bosnia and Rwanda. The growing overlap between these two areas was discussed in Chapter 8. The ICJ's role has been minimal. For example, it confirmed the principle of self-determination in the *Western Sahara* case (ICJ Case 1975), noting that "self-determination requires a free and genuine expression of the will of the peoples concerned." It noted in the *Namibia* advisory opinion (ICJ Opinion 1971) that South Africa had violated its obligations toward South West Africa (Namibia) under the Universal Declaration of Human Rights.

As the legal scholar Louis Henkin (1998: 512) admits, "The purpose of international concern with human rights is to make national rights effective under national laws and through national institutions." If that is true, then the task of international organizations like the UN is particularly problematic because it poses the possibility of interfering in the domestic affairs of states, one of the hallmarks of state sovereignty. Yet, the UN and regional organizations have undertaken a variety of functions and roles, as described below. With the UN as the centerpiece, the international human rights regime has come to encompass a variety of responsibilities and actors helping to establish the standards for as well as monitor, promote, and enforce human rights.

■ The Processes of Human Rights Governance

In just over fifty years, an international human rights regime has emerged that has articulated norms and standards in human rights and codified these standards in treaties, legal decisions, and practices. IGOs and NGOs, at both the global and regional level, have engaged in monitoring the human rights records of states, receiving reports of abuses and compliance. Both have worked to promote the norms of the regime, educate countries about how to modify their legal systems, and enforce compliance when states have committed gross violations of human rights norms. Both have also been concerned with publicizing human rights abuses and records and with human rights education.

■ *Setting Human Rights Standards and Norms*

The prominent role of NGOs in pushing for domestic laws and international treaties that set human rights standards has already been discussed. We can best illustrate that role here with a critical case.

NGOs and the anti-slavery movement.   The nineteenth-century anti-slavery movement was not only one of the first examples of NGO activity, but as discussed above, it also helped create the norm prohibiting slavery. Supported by a diverse constituency in Great Britain, including religious groups (Quakers, Methodists, and Baptists), textile workers, rural housewives, and wealthy businessmen, the movement caught the attention of like-minded individuals in France and the Americas, forming what may be called the first transnational advocacy network. They worked tirelessly to abolish slavery, using a variety of tactics, including letter writing, petitions, popular theater, and public speeches. They networked with others across the Atlantic, sending freed slaves on public speaking tours, exchanging strategies and information. Later, the Anti-Slavery and Aborigines' Protection Society played a key role in lobbying the League of Nations and in writing the 1926 International Convention on the Abolition of Slavery, as well as the 1956 Supplementary Convention on the Abolition of Slavery, Slave Trade and Institutions and Practices Similar to Slavery. In the intervening quarter of a century, the group had expanded its agenda to include practices such as child labor, trafficking in human beings, and forced labor. In 1990, with a broadened orientation, the group changed its name to Anti-Slavery International. It and other NGOs continue to play key roles in setting human rights standards in many areas.

The key role of the United Nations and treatymaking.   The UN's core role in the international human rights regime is its activity in defining and elaborating what constitutes internationally protected rights. Its two initial actions were the Universal Declaration of Human Rights and the

Convention on the Prevention and Punishment of the Crime of Genocide. Under the leadership of Eleanor Roosevelt, then chair of the Commission on Human Rights, these documents articulated a far-reaching rights agenda for the UN. In particular, the Universal Declaration elucidated thirty principles, including rights critical for the exercise of political freedom and for the preservation of civil society, as well as social and economic rights. Since the declaration was only a General Assembly resolution, the expectation was these rights would be set forth in treaties that would bind states to respect them.

Although other human rights conventions were approved in the 1950s, it took until 1966 for the General Assembly to approve the International Covenant on Economic, Social, and Cultural Rights and the International Covenant on Civil and Political Rights. Both became operative in 1976 following the necessary number of ratifications. Together with the Universal Declaration, they are known as the "international bill of rights." That it took almost thirty years to define these legal standards suggests the difficulty of the task in a world where states jealously guard national sovereignty. Indeed, not all states have ratified the covenants. The United States, for example, did not ratify the Covenant on Civil and Political Rights until 1992 and has yet to ratify the Covenant on Economic, Social, and Cultural Rights. China has now ratified the latter but not the former. Other states have ratified the covenants but attached reservations, declarations, or interpretative statements that in some cases undercut the whole intent. The same pattern is found with other human rights treaties. For example, states have attached 204 such qualifications to the 1990 Convention on the Rights of the Child, and registered 132 qualifications to the Convention on the Elimination of Discrimination Against Women (Bayefsky 2001). The price of ratification has often been highly qualified, weaker conventions.

The covenants and the other human rights treaties exemplify the standard-setting character of the UN's role in human rights. Subjects include women, slavery and forced labor, torture, refugees, apartheid, and various kinds of discrimination. (See Table 10.1.) These same standards are also found in national constitutions, legal documents, and court cases, often referencing directly the major UN standard-setting documents.

Regional human rights standards. Regional human rights bodies are also involved in the standard-setting process, though to varying degrees. Most have adopted similar standards, although the relative importance attached to different kinds of rights has varied. The European system is viewed as the most successful system of human rights protection in terms of the broad consensus attained and the strength of the procedures established, and the 1961 European Social Charter incorporates economic and social rights, including protections against poverty and sexual harassment.

Table 10.1   Selected UN Human Rights Conventions

Convention (grouped by subject)	Year Opened for Ratification	Year Entered Into Force	Number of Ratifications, Accessions, Acceptances (2002)
General Human Rights			
International Covenant on Civil and Political Rights	1966	1976	144
International Covenant on Economic, Social, and Cultural Rights	1966	1976	145
Racial Discrimination			
International Convention on the Elimination of All Forms of Racial Discrimination	1966	1969	153
International Convention on the Suppression and Punishment of the Crime of Apartheid	1973	1976	100
Rights of Women			
Convention on the Political Rights of Women	1953	1954	111
Convention on the Elimination of All Forms of Discrimination Against Women	1979	1981	170
Slavery and Slave-Like Practices			
International Convention on the Abolition of Slavery and the Slave Trade (1926), as amended in 1953	1953	1955	92
Supplementary Convention on the Abolition of Slavery, the Slave Trade, and Institutions and Practices Similar to Slavery	1956	1957	117
Convention for the Suppression of the Traffic in Persons and Exploitation of the Prostitution of Others	1950	1951	71
Refugees and Stateless Persons			
Convention Relating to the Status of Refugees	1951	1954	141
Protocol Relating to the Status of Refugees	1967	1967	139
Children			
Convention on the Rights of the Child	1989	1990	191
Convention Concerning the Prohibition and Immediate Action for the Elimination of the Worst Forms of Child Labour	1999	2000	129
Optional Protocol to the Convention on the Rights of the Child on the Involvement of Children in Armed Conflicts	2000	2002	
Optional Protocol to the Convention on the Rights of the Child on the Sale of Children, Child Prostitution and Child Pornography	2000	Not yet in force	
Other			
Convention on the Prevention and Punishment of the Crime of Genocide	1948	1951	129
Convention Against Torture and Other Cruel, Inhuman or Degrading Treatment or Punishment	1984	1987	130
Convention Concerning Indigenous and Tribal Peoples in Independent Countries	1989	1991	17

Source: University of Minnesota Human Rights Library Website. *Human Development Report,* 1999 (United Nations).

The 1953 European Convention on Human Rights and Fundamental Freedoms covers political and civil rights. The charter was revised in 1996 and about three-quarters of the forty-five states have ratified it.

The inter-American human rights regime, embedded in the Organization of American States and Inter-American Convention on Human Rights, highlights political and civil rights. Widespread abuses in the 1970s and 1980s, including state-sanctioned torture and disappearances in several countries, undermined the regime. In the 1980s, Latin America experienced what has been called a "norms cascade," a rapid shift toward recognizing the legitimacy of human rights norms elucidated in the regional convention, as well as the international conventions (Lutz and Sikkink 2000: 638). With the emergence of democratic regimes throughout the region, a return to the standards explicit in the regime is occurring, as discussed in Chapter 5.

The African Charter on Human and Peoples' Rights, passed in 1981 and entered into force in 1986, is of special interest for two reasons. First, specific attention is given to collective rights compatible with African traditions (Buergenthal 1995). The preamble notes "the virtues of [African] historical tradition and the values of African civilization, which should inspire and characterize their reflection on the concept of human and peoples' rights." Among the peoples' rights are the rights to development, to self-determination, and to full sovereignty over natural resources. The family is singled out as "the natural unit and basis of society," which the state has the duty to assist. This emphasis is controversial, as some believe it reinforces oppressive family structures and marginalizes women (Mutua 1999: 359). Second, the African Charter is unique because of the ubiquitous presence of "clawback clauses." These are qualifications or limitations for a specific standard. For example, fundamental civil and political liberties are guaranteed except for reasons previously laid down, or subject to law or order, or for protection of national security. In other words, these clauses permit states to suspend fundamental rights with little protection and undermine the standards articulated in the African Charter (Mutua 1999: 358).

Conspicuously absent from the regional picture are Asian and Middle Eastern norms, standards, and institutions. In the Asian case, this is consistent with the general predisposition to informal arrangements over defined agreements and to manage disputes without recourse to quasi-judicial or judicial bodies. It is also consistent with the fact that Asian countries often operate domestically with several different legal cultures, and the region shares few common characteristics. As noted in Chapter 5, ASEAN has only recently begun to include human rights issues on its agendas.

Three generations of human rights standards. Because human rights standards have evolved from diverse traditions and over time, it is customary to refer to three generations of human rights. So-called first-generation human rights are those associated with political and civil rights. These are clearly linked to Western liberalism. Second-generation rights build upon the socialist view of economic and social rights. Third-generation human rights center on the idea that certain groups, including indigenous peoples, colonial peoples, women, and children, have collective rights such as self-determination and economic and social development. Recently, some theorists have added the right to a safe environment, the right to peace and human security, and the right to live in a democracy.

The contemporary debate revolves around the relative priority attached to these different generations of human rights. In Western liberal thinking, political and civil rights are clearly given higher status, while in many other parts of the world, priority goes to collective rights such as the right to development that was endorsed by the 1993 Vienna conference. Disagreement is one of the reasons for the lack of political will for international human rights enforcement and implementation. Just as the West has dominated economic relations, it has tried to dominate human rights standard setting. Thus, the strongest part of both international and regional human rights governance mechanisms protects civil and political rights, while the other two generations of human rights have received less attention. It is also far more difficult to establish standards of compliance for economic and social rights.

The attitude of some NGOs may be changing, however. Amnesty International's major policy committee, the Standing Committee on the Mandate, spent several years discussing whether economic and social rights should be incorporated into the AI mandate. In August 2001, that organization committed itself to developing capacity in both first- and second-generation rights, focusing on "grave violations" in each category. The change reflected the realization that all political and civil rights could be wiped out by economic and social deprivation. Yet, there is also a realization that focusing on these rights may dilute AI's effectiveness because the definitions and standards are less clear.

Do human rights standards and treaties change state behavior? Some studies suggest that states ratify treaties because of external pressures or rewards but have little intention of changing their behavior. Other studies point to significant cases where ratifying treaties has led to changes in state behavior. Turkey's efforts to comply with European human rights conventions and the efforts by states in Eastern Europe to comply with regional European norms are each powerful examples of the pull of compliance. Yet as Weissbrodt (2003: 89) aptly put it, "Getting countries to toe the mark is only possible when there is a mark to toe." Setting standards is not enough to ensure the observance of human rights. Those rights have to be effective in national settings, where states are both creators of human rights norms and the primary violators. The UN and some regional bodies have moved incrementally from articulating norms to monitoring states' behavior.

■ Monitoring Human Rights

Monitoring the implementation of human rights standards requires procedures for receiving complaints of violations from affected individuals or interested groups and reports of state practice. It may also be accompanied by the power to comment on reports, make recommendations to states, appoint working groups or special rapporteurs, and vote on resolutions of condemnation. Publicity and public shaming are key tools.

The ILO was the first international organization to establish procedures for monitoring human rights within states—in this case, workers' rights. In 1926, it instituted the system of annual meetings of the Committee of Experts to examine state reports on treaty implementation. This system still operates. When problems are found, the committee may seek further explanation or call for a change in state policies. The tripartite structure of state representation in the ILO facilitates this monitoring because delegations are composed of representatives from government, labor, and management. It is also easier for the ILO to criticize state (i.e., governmental) practices.

UN approach.   With only states represented in the UN and on the Commission on Human Rights, however, monitoring is much more problematic than standard-setting but steps have been taken to strengthen the monitoring tasks. In 1967, for example, the fifty-three member Commission on Human Rights was empowered for the first time to examine gross violations in South Africa and Southern Rhodesia. Further investigations against specific states followed, setting a new precedent for monitoring. In 1970, ECOSOC Resolution 1503 authorized the commission to undertake confidential investigations of individual complaints that suggest "a consistent pattern of gross and reliably attested violations." This procedure, however, has proved weak: the examination occurs in private and terminates with only a report to the commission. Nonetheless, the commission significantly expanded its activities during the 1970s, creating working groups to study specific civil rights problems such as forced disappearances, torture, religious discrimination, and the situation in Chile after the 1972 coup. In its first report in 1981, for example, the Working Group on Disappearances reported information about 11,000–13,000 cases of disappearances from fifteen countries, ten of them in Latin America. By 1996, however, the same working group reported the virtual end of disappearances in the Western Hemisphere (Lutz and Sikkink 2000: 637). The Commission on Human Rights also appointed thematic and country rapporteurs as well as independent experts. Their record may be mixed, but at least they have some power of initiative as independent individuals.

The Subcommission on the Prevention of Discrimination and Protection of Minorities also was reactivated in the 1970s. It has the advantage of being composed of independent experts (now twenty-six in number) and plays a key role in screening petitions from individuals and NGOs prior to consideration by the commission. In this connection, it has been an important forum for NGO activities. In 1999, its name was changed to the Sub-Commission on the Promotion and Protection of Human Rights, reflecting its broader agenda.

Further initiatives in UN monitoring activities accompanied the entry into force of specific treaties, many of which required states to submit reports of their progress toward implementation. The General Assembly has established six committees of independent experts elected by the parties to each treaty to review the reports. One of the most thorough is the Human Rights Committee designed to process state reports under the Covenant on Civil and Political Rights. It conducts open meetings, thus exposing states' human rights practices and its own actions to publicity by the media. The committee cannot take a binding decision against a persistently offending state. Also, only forty-five out of 135 states that are party to the covenant have accepted the optional provision that allows individual petitions, and out of the one thousand complaints filed with the secretary-general each year, no more than fifty are considered by the committee. In 1992, the Human Rights Committee decided to publish its general conclusions after review of states' reports, thus removing the veil of secrecy. It has also appointed rapporteurs and special missions to deal with massive human rights violations in countries such as Rwanda, Georgia, Colombia, the former Yugoslavia, and Democratic Republic of the Congo.

In the 1990s, for the first time, the UN Security Council became involved in human rights monitoring in conjunction with the end of El Salvador's civil war and election-monitoring activities in more than twenty countries, as discussed in Chapter 8.

Do UN monitoring and resolutions make a difference? One argument contends that over time repeated condemnations can change attitudes, as was true, in part, in the case of South Africa. But that case is not so clear since the repeated condemnations were subsequently coupled with sanctions designed to bar participation in international sporting events, interrupt travel routes, and impose an arms embargo and economic costs, as discussed below. We cannot be sure whether it was the repeated condemnations that led to the change in behavior or the monitoring or enforcement actions. Another point of view holds that public condemnations can antagonize states and harden their positions, leading to precisely the opposite of the intended effect. Since 1970, the General Assembly has repeatedly condemned Israel for its policies in the Occupied Territories, even establishing the Special Committee on Israeli Practices in the Occupied Territories to report to the General Assembly on Israeli abuses. Yet Israel (supported by the United States) remains defiant. At the 2001 World Conference Against Racism, Israel and the United States exited the proceedings. Attitudes were not changed; rather, retrenchment may have occurred.

Still another reaction to UN monitoring is illustrated by the case of China in the 1990s. In August 1989, following the Tiananmen Square massacre, the subcommission approved a resolution criticizing human rights in China—the first direct action against a permanent member of the Security Council. Thereafter, China was a regular target of the subcommission's attention, NGO interventions, and Western nations' pressure. Yet China fought back, challenging the more aggressive monitoring actions by the subcommission and drawing strong support from many developing countries. Together they challenged the extent of NGO involvement, the independence of the subcommission members, the open proceedings, and the secret voting. In 1993, when China succeeded in blocking a vote on any resolution dealing with its human rights situation, the limits of UN monitoring of ongoing, systematic abuse of human rights by a powerful state became clear. China has continued its success in blocking discussions of its human rights record.

European and other regional experience with monitoring.   Of the regional human rights regimes, the Europeans have developed the most effective machinery for human rights monitoring. The European Convention on Human Rights established two institutions relevant for monitoring: the European Commission of Human Rights and the European Court of Human Rights. Until 1998, the commission heard complaints both from member states regarding other states' records and from individuals or groups of individuals. Only about 10 to 15 percent of cases were deemed admissible. If admissible, then the commission undertook an investigation. If still no agreement was reached, then the case went to the court for the adjudicative process. In 1998, however, the procedure was streamlined. The European Commission of Human Rights was eliminated and the court reorganized with several chambers. Individuals themselves could be parties to cases and the court's jurisdiction was compulsory. Currently, the court receives over one hundred phone calls and about eight hundred letters daily. It decides between fifty and one hundred cases annually. The European Court of Human Rights has become, for most purposes, the primary court for civil and political rights in Europe. As Janis and Kay (1990: vii) conclude, "Remarkably, sovereign states have respected the adverse judgments of the Court . . . [and] have reformed or abandoned police procedures, penal institutions, child welfare practices, administrative agencies, court rules, labor relations, moral legislation, and many other important public matters."

By contrast, in Latin America, while the Inter-American Commission on Human Rights and the Inter-American Court of Human Rights have the authority to monitor human rights records, they are not very active. In one representative year (1997), the Inter-American Court of Human Rights issued six decisions and fourteen advisory opinions. The low number of cases in the Latin American system is especially surprising, since anyone can bring suit on behalf of groups or individuals whose rights are being violated and authorities have a broad and permissive interpretation of exhausting domestic remedies. Essentially, states (and individuals) have not availed themselves of this instrument. States fear violations of sovereignty and interference in activities that typically have been subject to state jurisdiction. The Inter-American Commission, however, has been active in issuing reports outlining human rights abuses. For example, the commission issued several reports on torture and arbitrary detention in Uruguay during the mid-1970s. Later in the 1970s and 1980s, the commission reported on abuses in Paraguay and conducted an on-site investigation in Argentina (Lutz and Sikkink 2000). A special commission was established in 1978 to carry out observations in Nicaragua, where it visited cities, hospitals, and jails and conducted interviews with political prisoners. Although the commission concluded that solution to the problems remained within domestic jurisdiction, it represented a breakthrough. The commission was able to use its power of conducting on-site visits to monitor an abusive regime and publicly condemn it.

Likewise in Africa, while the Commission on Human and People's Rights may hear complaints and make recommendations to governments, they are highly ineffective. The commission has the authority to examine state reports and issue communications about potential violations as part of their monitoring function, but the commission's reports are hamstrung by specific conditions: information cannot be based on media reports, often one of the major alternative sources of information; reports may not be written in language insulting to the government; and reports must be issued in a timely fashion. The commission is also hindered by the poor quality of the state reports submitted. Some state reports are insanely short—three pages—while others are filled with abstract platitudes, yielding very little information necessary for effective monitoring (Mutua 1999: 348–349). Thus, while the commission has the authority to monitor behavior, in practice the states submit little relevant information and states themselves cannot be criticized.

So the regional picture is a murky one. The region where the human rights record is the best (Europe) is the same region that has the most active regional body involved in monitoring. Where abuses are greater, the monitoring system is weaker (Latin America) or effectively nonexistent (Africa). While these two regional bodies have been increasingly active in issuing general reports of systematic abuses, the system for individual petitions remains weak. In Asia and the Middle East, the lack of regional organizations with any human rights mandate means that human rights monitoring is left either to international institutions like the UN or to NGOs.

NGO monitoring: Amnesty International and Human Rights Watch. With regional monitoring capacities relatively weak, particularly in the developing world, NGOs have stepped in to fill the gap. These include Amnesty International, Human Rights Watch, the International Commission of Jurists, and the Lawyers Committee for Human Rights, as well as a plethora of groups concerned with specific human rights issues.

Amnesty International (AI), founded in 1961, has become perhaps the most effective human rights NGO for a number of reasons (Clark 2001; Welch 2001a). Replying on accurate research and modest member contributions, utilizing publicity and associated threats, AI has been able to capitalize on its reputation as an impartial, highly professional, politically neutral organization. Its centralization in the London-based secretariat, as well as strong national chapters, enhance its effectiveness. Focusing initially on individuals whose political or civil rights were being violated, so-called prisoners of conscience in every type of political regime, AI was able to forge direct links between individuals whose rights were being violated and their supporters. AI members lobbied for better prison conditions, publicized abuses in the respective judicial system, and they kept issues in the international public eye. High-profile cases maintained the momentum of the organization. AI was particularly involved in the cause of human rights in Uruguay and Paraguay, issuing reports of abuses, sending observers to trials, and lobbying governments. It was also instrumental in bringing international attention to the Argentinean military regime's policy of massive abductions and disappearances in the early 1980s.

Over the years, AI has broadened its approach, moving beyond riveting individual cases to situations where there have been patterns of human rights abuses. Reports of systematic patterns of abuses are reinforced by specific cases. Most attention has been paid to several areas: prisoners of conscience, concern for fair and prompt trials, abolition of the death penalty, torture and inhumane treatment of prisoners, and disappearances. In each, AI has mounted campaigns in countries in which there is a reasonable likelihood of success. In these areas, AI is particularly adroit at monitoring, focusing on offending states and making these states accountable to the UN or other international bodies. AI has generally won high praise (and a 1977 Nobel Peace Prize) for providing information to IGOs. In fact, the UN has little capacity to gather its own information pertinent to its monitoring mandate and by one estimate receives between 80 and 90 percent of its information from NGOs, with AI being the major source. Thus, an increasing percentage of AI's expenditures has been allocated to research. Compared to many other human rights NGOs, AI has been able to work extremely effectively within IGOs, and especially the UN (Schulz 2001).

Human Rights Watch (HRW) was founded in 1978 following the Final Act of the Conference on Security and Cooperation in Europe (the Helsinki Accords). Like AI, HRW is said to be a highly effective organization, but its strategy has been different. It evolved out of the need to address Basket III of the Accords, "Respect for Human Rights and Fundamental Freedoms, Including Freedom of Thought, Conscience, Religion, or Belief." Although the document did not represent new standards, it took place in the context of the movement to liberalize Eastern Europe. Human rights groups were formed in several central European states to monitor progress and to review compliance over time. Helsinki Watch was formed to monitor implementation, and its two American founders were particularly committed to mobilizing the U.S. government to take a more active stand on these issues. The timing was auspicious. U.S. President Jimmy Carter was a vocal supporter of human rights, rights abuses in some parts of the Western Hemisphere received considerable publicity, and foundation money flowed in support of the Helsinki process. Thus, what began as Helsinki Watch was transformed into Human Rights Watch with a more global reach and its initial emphasis on political and civil rights expanded (Thomas 2001). For example, Human Rights Watch recently began issuing reports on caste violence and child labor in India in cooperation with Indian NGOs. Each issue affects millions of people—in the first case, the 160 million Indian "untouchables" or *Dalits,* and in the second case, the estimated 60 to 115 million working Indian children. The issue appeared on the agenda of the 2001 World Conference Against Racism in Durban thanks to HRW's efforts, but in deference to Indian sensitivities it was kept out of the final documents.

HRW relies on the financial support of large and powerful foundations, in contrast to the membership-based AI. The organization is quite centralized in the United States (both New York and Washington), compared to AI's strong (more than 4,200) local chapters with representatives in 140 countries and territories and over one million members. Most of HRW's personnel focus on communication, compared to AI's attention on research, although research remains in HRW's purview. HRW's emphasis has remained on civil and political rights, while second-generation rights are generally not seen as appropriate to HRW's mandate, despite the movement after the Vienna Conference on Human Rights that declared the different generations of human rights are, in fact, inseparable. And while AI has focused on the UN system, HRW has concentrated on the U.S. government.

Both organizations, as well as most other human rights organizations, are legitimized by their accurate documentation of abuses. On-site investigations are key, as are reports of abuses that have been thoroughly checked and rechecked. Armed with this information, they have acquired sufficient legitimacy to pressure governments and international organizations and to develop networks with like-minded NGOs.

Grassroots and international NGOs, as well as IGOs, have taken full advantage of new communications technologies. The breakthrough came in 1996 when the UN Office of the High Commissioner for Human Rights launched its website. For the first time, NGOs could have access to both official documents and to government reports to the treaty bodies. As access to official information became easier, the NGOs became adept at using the technology to communicate with their own constituencies, gathering signatures, creating list serves, and mobilizing action networks in far-flung parts of the world. They could collaborate with their colleagues electronically in writing statements. They could publish quickly and communicate to an ever-growing audience evidence of human rights abuses, as the Zapatistas in Chiapas, Mexico, did so effectively.

Whether in southern Mexico, Liberia, Rwanda, or East Timor, local NGOs have been able to get their messages out to a receptive audience around the world, and in doing so, force the traditional media and governments to pay attention to issues and situations. At the same time, increasing IGO sophistication in the use of the new technology has led to individuals being able to file a petition directly with the European Court of Human Rights in their own national language. In short, the change in communications has propelled human rights to the forefront of the international agenda in a way never before envisioned.

NGOs have become empowered and legitimated by the fact that they seldom act alone, but cooperate with other like-minded groups and individuals, as discussed in Chapter 6. They establish networks, some very loose, coming together only occasionally, and others very tight, coordinating joint actions often and across issues. It is through such networks that NGOs are able to articulate a moral consciousness, empower domestic opposition, and pressure governments themselves (Risse, Ropp, and Sikkink 1999).

The UN treaty bodies depend heavily on information compiled by NGOs in preparing for dialogue with states. Many state reports are self-serving, rarely disclosing treaty violations. So the NGOs, with their unique local information base, have undertaken the task of critically evaluating such reports, gathering information, pushing states for compliance, and publicizing abuses. Yet the relationships between NGOs and the treaty bodies vary. For example, the Committee on the Rights of the Child enjoys the closest working relationship with NGOs, which regularly review state reports, maintain dialogue with local NGOs, and help to disseminate information. In other cases, like the Committee Against Torture, concerned NGOs are called upon on only an ad hoc basis, while the Committee on the Elimination of Discrimination Against Women does not formally solicit information from the NGOs. So while NGOs may enjoy a unique capacity to engage in monitoring, their ability to carry out this function depends on the political space provided by each separate treaty body.

Monitoring, both through IGOs and NGOs, has developed unanticipated capacities, but its measurable impact is still limited. Changes in attitudes and behavior also require proactive efforts to educate people, including government officials and ordinary citizens, about international human rights norms, and to promote new ways of thinking and acting.

■ *Promoting Human Rights*

Translating norms and rhetoric into actions that go beyond stopping violations to changing long-term attitudes and behavior is the challenge of promoting human rights. These efforts have been scattered throughout the UN system and include recent activities in support of democratization as well as many economic and social programs.

UN role.   The UN has played a far more active role in human rights promotion since the Cold War's end, owing to the conceptual links forged between norms of human rights and the operational activities of many parts of the system. For example, the UN has promoted democratization and associated political rights through its electoral assistance programs, such as in Namibia, Nicaragua, Cambodia, and Mozambique. These programs have provided aid to more than twenty countries in organizing and holding free and fair elections.

UN development activities and other operational programs of the specialized agencies have linked the language of human rights with development activities. The right to development was endorsed by the 1993 Vienna conference on human rights. The World Bank's promotion of good governance includes political and civil rights. UNDP's annual *Human Development Reports* have increasingly focused on rights-related issues, including democratization in the 2002 report. The Millennium Development Goals discussed in Chapter 9 represent an amalgam of all three generations of rights.

In 1993, the UN took the key step of creating the Office of the High Commissioner for Human Rights (UNHCHR) to centralize responsibilities and provide a visible international spokesperson for human rights in the same way that the UN High Commissioner for Refugees focuses international attention on that problem. The individual is appointed by the secretary-general with the approval of the General Assembly. The second holder of that office, former Irish President Mary Robinson, was a visible and sometimes controversial spokesperson for the UN's role in promoting human rights, demonstrating the difficulty in balancing advocacy with quiet diplomacy.

The office is the focal point for the promotion of human rights; it provides advisory services to states that request them, including setting up field presences to monitor situations; it seeks to coordinate the UN system-wide human rights activities and tries to rationalize and strengthen the UN machinery in the field of human rights. It supports human rights education programs.

NGO role.   NGOs have become increasingly important in the promotion of human rights. They have been active in providing education on human rights in Cambodia, Central America, Kosovo, and more recently in Afghanistan. The Unrepresented Nations and Peoples Organization (UNPO), with fifty members representing 100 million persons, has played a unique promotional role. It assists and empowers unrepresented nations and peoples such as Australia's Aborigines to represent themselves more effectively. It provides training in international and human rights law, so that the groups can represent themselves diplomatically. Another NGO, Cultural Survival, has an extensive education and outreach program, working directly with teachers and students to raise awareness about indigenous peoples, ethnic minorities, and human rights. Through its publications, it has helped to shape the debate on the third-generation rights affecting indigenous peoples. And Amnesty International-USA has sponsored the development of human rights educational curricula, lobbying state educational boards for its inclusion, and mobilizing local groups to push for the changes.

Regional organizations.   Virtually all of the regional organizations undertake promotional activities with respect to human rights, in part because educational activities are relatively noncontroversial. The approaches of the various organizations are quite similar. For newly created states, or states wishing to join an organization, seminars are given regarding human rights and how to incorporate provisions for their protection into constitutions. For special groups, like women, educational programs are held detailing specific rights. There are training programs for judges, police, and other officials and public relations campaigns elucidating fundamental rights. Teachers are given special training, especially if rights and responsibilities are changed. Promotional activities are by their nature long-term solutions to the human rights problem. They do not mitigate current abuses.

Enforcing Human Rights

Of the various governance tasks in human rights, enforcement is the most problematic largely because states' compliance is key and international institutions have limited capacity to compel compliance.

States and enforcement.   States have always been the major enforcers of human rights norms and remain so, even though the international community has increasingly undertaken various enforcement activities and states are the primary human rights violators. States generally use two approaches to enforcement: legal means and coercive measures.

National courts.   National courts are one means for dealing with human rights violations. Two cases illustrate the ways judicial action may operate. The first is a 1980 U.S. case, *Filartiga v. Pena-Irala* (*Filartiga* 1980). Under the U.S. Alien Tort Claims Act of 1789, federal courts have jurisdiction in civil cases filed by aliens for an action committed in violation of the law of nations or a U.S. treaty. Using this statute, the Filartiga family filed suit against Mr. Pena-Irala, a former police inspector in Paraguay, but residing in the United States. The Filartigas accused Pena-Irala of kidnaping and torturing their son to death while both were residing in Paraguay. Drawing on the UN Charter, the Universal Declaration, the UN Declaration against Torture, and other documents and practices that constituted customary international law of human rights, the court took the case and subsequently ruled against Pena-Irala, labeling him "an enemy of all mankind" and awarding the Filartiga family compensation and punitive damages intended to serve a deterrent effect. Pena-Irala had already been deported to Paraguay and there was no way to enforce the judgment in that country, but following this case, other U.S. federal courts heard numerous cases involving specific human rights abuses in other countries, including three cases against an Argentinean general for disappearances of individuals, one case against the Chilean military, and another against a Guatemalan general for torture. The Alien Tort Statute is also being invoked in *Doe v. UNOCAL*, where an American oil company (UNOCAL) is accused of using forced labor provided by the Burmese government in construction of a facility in that country (http://oz.uc.edu/thro). National courts in Spain and Italy have likewise indicted individuals responsible for human rights violations in Latin America, claiming jurisdiction on the basis of protection of nationals or the principle of universality. The second illustrative case is the well-publicized one involving the former Chilean dictator Augusto Pinochet. Under a warrant issued by a Spanish judge seeking extradition, Pinochet was detained in Great Britain in 1998 for crimes allegedly committed while head of state. With the help of human rights NGOs, the Spanish judge found evidence that some of those crimes were committed against Spanish nationals living in Chile, hence the legitimacy of Spain's legal standing. But Spain also claimed jurisdiction on the basis of crimes against humanity, which any state could legitimately claim. The case went to the British House of Lords, which examined both the legal and political implications of the case, given Pinochet's position as former head of state and his position as a senator for life in Chile. Ultimately, its Judicial Committee, Britain's highest court, upheld Pinochet's arrest on the basis of international prohibitions against torture and murder and argued that these activities were outside the official duties of a head of state. Thus, they rejected Pinochet's claim of sovereign immunity. Pinochet's ill health, however, was used as justification for turning him over to Chilean authorities and hence avoiding political repercussions (Sondrol 2000). Although Chile stripped him of immunity from prosecution and ill health enabled him to evade prosecution, the case set the potential precedent that individual leaders could be held accountable in other jurisdictions for human rights violations committed against their own people. The Westphalian hold on sovereignty was thereby loosened.

Coercive measures.   Where national courts are used by individual plaintiffs or activist judges, governments themselves may undertake unilateral coercive measures against other states for egregious human rights abuses. South Africa provides an example where the international community, namely the UN General Assembly, recommended international sanctions against that country for its apartheid policy, but little happened until the 1980s when key states changed their policies. In the United States, attitudes began to change when leading civil rights activists, politicians, and movie industry figures engaged in a campaign of civil disobedience to draw attention to apartheid. Responding to public pressure, Congress called for a review of U.S. policy and for sanctions and, in 1986, approved the Comprehensive Anti-Apartheid Act over a presidential veto. Other powerful states followed suit, including Great Britain. The imposition of sanctions provided a morale boost to opponents of apartheid and a means to inflict pain on the South African business community and, through them, on the government. By the early 1990s, apartheid officially ended and a majority democratic government was installed in 1994. Sanctions by key states were partly responsible for the changes in South Africa, along with the persistent campaign by the international community.

A second example is that of China after the Tiananmen Square suppression of the student-led pro-democracy movement in June 1989. The United States immediately instituted an arms embargo and canceled new foreign aid and high-level talks. It was joined by other states, including Japan and members of the European Union. By one estimate, China may have lost $11 billion in bilateral aid over a four-year period. By 1990, however, Japan ended its sanctions, arguing that economic engagement was necessary for regional stability. The United States continued its sanctions in the name of human rights, although gradually cracks appeared. Opponents of sanctions argued that positive changes were occurring in China and trade sanctions might be counterproductive. Thus in 1994, China was granted most-favored-nation status without human rights conditions attached (Donnelly 1998: 120–124). In this case, coercive actions on behalf of human rights were undermined by economic interests. As discussed in Chapter 8, enforcement is difficult in most situations and generally requires multilateral action.

UN enforcement.   The UN's enforcement authority, as discussed in Chapters 4 and 8, is found in Chapter VII of the UN Charter. Under that provision, if the Security Council determines that human rights violations threaten or breach international peace, it has the authority to take enforcement actions. The two Cold War cases of enforcement both involved gross violations of the rights of black majorities by white minority governments, one in the breakaway British colony of Southern Rhodesia and the other in South Africa. In the first case, the Security Council imposed economic sanctions, seeking to isolate the white minority regime and cause a change in behavior. In the second, the Security Council imposed an arms embargo. In neither of these cases, however, did the council make an explicit linkage between human rights violations and security threats. The sanctions weakened the minority regimes, but did not directly change their policies nor force either government from power. As discussed in Chapter 8, sanctions can be a blunt instrument causing significant harm to ordinary citizens unless the measures are targeted in specific ways. During the 1990s, the Security Council and OAS imposed sanctions on Haiti to force a restoration of a democratically elected government. Ethnic conflict and massive human rights violations in the former Yugoslavia, Rwanda, and Somalia also led to UN sanctions (EU sanctions also, in the case of Yugoslavia), as did the horrifying use of mutilation by rebel and government forces in Sierra Leone.

Enforcement action may also involve the use of military force. The post–Cold War era witnessed a series of unprecedented enforcement actions authorized under Chapter VII to deal with ethnic conflicts that produced some of the worst human rights violations and toughest policy dilemmas for states, IGOs, and NGOs. Ethnic cleansing in Bosnia, genocide in Rwanda, famine in Somalia, the flight of thousands of Kurds from Iraqi repression, the persecution of Albanians in Kosovo, and the treatment of the East Timorese by the Indonesians provoked media attention and public demands that leaders "do something." Humanitarian interventions have involved the use of UN or regional peacekeeping forces to protect relief workers, guard medical and food supplies, run convoys, shield civilians from further violence, shelter displaced people, and provide safe havens. By their very presence, they exert pressure on offending governments, hoping that certain activities cease until peace can be restored. As discussed in Chapter 8, humanitarian intervention is an emerging, but still contested norm.

Material and economic aid to victims would normally not be considered enforcement, but is definitely undertaken to alleviate suffering. The UN High Commissioner for Refugees, established in 1950 to deal with the plight of European refugees, has generally coordinated these activities, working alongside the World Health Organization, World Food Programme, UNICEF, and NGOs such as the International Committee of the Red Cross, Doctors Without Borders, Save the Children, CARE, and Oxfam. Most of the estimated 20 million refugees are now located in the developing world, where state services are lacking or nonexistent. UNHCR funds are also limited, as the agency depends solely on voluntary contributions from states and is forced to raise money for each new humanitarian crisis that appears.

Humanitarian intervention has been applied only selectively and not always successfully. The international community paid little attention to the brutal civil wars in the Sudan, Liberia, and Sierra Leone, despite blatant human rights violations. Yet, it did choose to act in other situations, reflecting the increased importance of human rights norms in world politics. Many governments are suspicious of strengthening the UN, or any IGO's power to intervene in what many still regard as their domestic jurisdiction. Yet the UN has set some important precedents for enforcement in the human rights field since the Cold War's end.

Regional enforcement.   Only the European human rights regime has been concerned with enforcement although, more recently, Latin America has also. In the European Convention on Human Rights, forty-four out of sixty-six articles deal with enforcement. The caseload of the European Court of Human Rights (ECHR), which was established by the Council of Europe in 1958, has increased gradually, to well over one hundred cases annually. And because its role is to protect individual rights, it may hear cases that would not be heard in an individual's home state. For example, Great Britain has no bill of rights but under the European Convention its citizens may file claims against their own government in the ECHR. The court's judgments are directly enforced in the national courts of states that are parties to the European Convention. States are obligated to inform the Council of Europe of actions taken to comply with the court's judgment. Sometimes that means paying compensation, which is relatively easy to enforce. Other times, the court may declare that national laws or practices are in conflict with the convention and thus new legislation needs to be enacted, making it more difficult to assure enforcement. Bulgaria, for example, had to change its laws after a 1998 decision found that country's legal procedures inadequate for investigating charges of wrongdoing by police and other officials. The police also had inadequate guidelines for detentions. Occasionally, states choose not to enforce the court's decisions.

Great Britain reacted to the court's ruling that its detention period for suspected terrorists in Northern Ireland was too long by withdrawing from those specific parts of the convention. Still, the European system exhibits the only case of states yielding sovereignty to an international human rights court to enforce its judgments.

The changes in the OAS with respect to enforcing norms of democracy, as discussed in Chapter 5, represent important steps toward greater enforcement of human rights, especially the right to democracy. Actions taken when democratically elected governments were threatened in Haiti, Peru, and Venezuela suggest that this region is charting a new course in human rights enforcement.

In Africa, the African Commission can make rulings but its decisions are nonbinding and formulaic. There is little reference to international jurisprudence. For example, the commission in *Constitutional Rights Project v. Nigeria* challenged Nigeria's administration of the death penalty but merely declared Nigeria to be in violation of the African Charter and recommended that the country free the petitioners (Mutua 1999: 349). The decision was ignored. The newly formed African Human Rights Court, designed to compensate for some of the deficiencies of the commission, grants only discretionary access to individuals and NGOs. While the court's findings are binding on states, it must rely on shaming techniques for actual enforcement. Neither the charter nor the commission has enforceable remedies or mechanisms for monitoring whether states have complied with human rights standards.

Ad hoc international criminal tribunals and the International Criminal Court. The ad hoc international criminal tribunals and the newly established International Criminal Court discussed in Chapter 3 are the international mechanisms for enforcement in cases of war crimes and crimes against humanity. Both rely on states to turn over indicted individuals, or on individuals to turn themselves over, to the appropriate tribunal for trial. For cases tried in these courts, judgments involve individuals charged with massive abuses of human rights. Sentences would be carried out either in the home state or a third-party state.

NGO enforcement efforts. Strictly speaking, NGOs lack capacity to compel compliance with human rights norms through coercive measures such as sanctions or military force. Nor, as we have seen, do most IGOs. Yet NGOs have used a number of strategies to get states to alter their behavior, with some success. One of the oldest NGOs has undoubtedly the greatest legitimacy and the best record in getting states to comply with international human rights standards, namely the International Committee of the Red Cross. It owes its unique role to the Geneva Conventions on humanitarian law, wherein it is designated special responsibilities, among them to hold states accountable for violations, to protect and assist military and civilian victims of conflict, and to serve as an intermediary between warring parties.

Other NGOs have debated whether to promote sanctions and boycotts as a means to changing state behavior, but feared that such actions might jeopardize their neutrality. The World Council of Churches (WCC) confronted this dilemma head-on in its Program to Combat Racism (PCR) beginning in the late 1960s. The WCC is a confederation of 340 regional and national Christian churches with a membership of over 400 million people, funded over 80 percent from European sources. The PCR focused on institutionalized white racism in southern Africa and adopted two enforcement approaches. First, a Special Fund disbursed over $4 million in the 1970s to liberation groups in southern Africa to support their struggle against white minority regimes. Second, in the late 1970s, the WCC joined a global campaign for change by pressuring MNCs to adopt a set of key principles in their southern African operations or, alternatively, pressure for withdrawal of all investment in the region. These were sensitive strategies for churches in central Europe that relied on state tax support and close relations with the banking community (Welch 2001b). Nonetheless, this strategy resonated with the membership and was one part of the global campaign to end white rule in southern Africa, including apartheid in South Africa itself.

■ Global Human Rights Governance in Action

▦ Genocide and Ethnic Cleansing

Regrettably, genocide is an international fact of life. During the twentieth century millions were victims of genocide. World War II was a key event in number of victims and in the recognition that genocide was a crime against humanity. Hitler's Aryan supremacy policy led directly to the Holocaust and the systematic extermination of six million Jews, Gypsies, and so-called undesirable peoples by the Nazi regime. The postwar trials held at Nuremberg made the world aware of the deliberate acts committed in the name of racial superiority. Yet trials organized by the victors against the vanquished made it painfully obvious that there was no international law prohibiting genocide. In fact, prior to 1944, the term *genocide* did not exist. It was coined by a Polish lawyer, Raphael Lemkin, who along with Chilean and Greek jurists, was largely responsible for drafting the genocide convention. The process was a laborious one, however. An ECOSOC committee, the Ad Hoc Committee on Genocide, spent two years writing the convention. Some countries believed that such a convention was worthless since it could never be enforced. In 1948, however, the General Assembly unanimously adopted the Convention on the Prevention and Punishment of Genocide. The treaty defines the crime of genocide and lists acts that are prohibited. It calls for persons committing genocide to be punished, for states to enact legislation, and for persons charged to be tried either in the state where the crimes were committed or by an international tribunal. (See Figure 10.2 for key provisions.)

The Genocide Convention was rapidly signed and ratified and widely recognized as a major advance in international human rights law. Yet others worried about how the treaty would be interpreted and enforced. For exam-

---

Figure 10.2   The Genocide Convention

Article I   Genocide, whether committed in time of peace or in time of war, is a crime under international law which they undertake to prevent and punish.

Article II   Genocide means any of the following acts committed with intent to destroy, in whole or in part, a national, ethnical, racial or religious group, as such:
(a) Killing members of the group;
(b) Causing serious bodily or mental harm to members of the group;
(c) Deliberately inflicting on the group conditions of life calculated to bring about its physical destruction in whole or in part;
(d) Imposing measures intended to prevent births within the group;
(e) Forcibly transferring children of the group to another group.

Article III The following acts shall be punishable:
(a) Genocide;
(b) Conspiracy to commit genocide;
(c) Direct and public incitement to commit genocide;
(d) Attempt to commit genocide;
(e) Complicity in genocide.

Article IV   Persons committing genocide or any of the other acts enumerated in Article III shall be punished, whether they are constitutionally responsible rulers, public officials or private individuals.

Article V   The Contracting Parties undertake to enact...the necessary legislation to give effect to the provisions of the present Convention and to provide effective penalties for persons guilty of genocide or any of the other acts enumerated in Article III.

ple, it does not specify how many people have to be killed for it to be considered genocide, but only addresses the intention on the part of the perpetrators to destroy a group of people "in whole or in part." In contrast to later human rights treaties, the convention created no permanent treaty bodies to monitor situations or provide early warnings of impending or actual genocide. And for many years it seemed to have little effect. In former East Pakistan (now Bangladesh), Cambodia, Sudan, and China millions of people were killed or forced to flee their homelands. The international community paid little attention.

Two post–Cold War cases, the former Yugoslavia and Rwanda, illustrate the dilemmas associated with application of the Genocide Convention. Were these cases genocide? In other words, was there a systematic attempt by one group to exterminate another group in whole or in part? Or were these brutal civil wars, where atrocities were committed by both sides? If genocide was being committed, the parties to the convention were obligated to respond under Article I, but proving genocide is problematic. Few perpetrators leave behind the kind of extensive documentation compiled by the Nazis detailing their intentions and actions. In the cases of Yugoslavia and Rwanda, the UN and member states failed to act decisively to stop the killing.

During the Yugoslav civil war, the term *ethnic cleansing* was coined to refer to systematic efforts by Croatia and the Bosnian Serbs to remove peoples of another group from their territory, but not necessarily to wipe out the entire group or part of it as specified in the Genocide Convention. In Bosnia, Muslim civilians were forced by Serb troops to flee towns for Muslim areas within Bosnia or for neighboring countries. Some were deported to neighboring Macedonia, others placed in concentration camps. Sixty thousand Bosnian women were raped by Serb forces.

The UN Commission on Human Rights appointed envoys to investigate the situation. Initially, in 1992, they reported "massive and grave violations of human rights." Several months later, another report concluded "the Muslim population are the principal victims and are virtually threatened with extermination." In December 1992, the General Assembly passed a resolution describing Serbia's ethnic cleansing of Bosnia's Muslims as a form of genocide and condemned its actions. In April 1993, the International Court of Justice issued a unanimous order to Serbia to follow the Genocide Convention. And in June 1993, the World Conference on Human Rights appealed to the Security Council to take measures to end the genocide in Bosnia. The council created a Commission of Experts that heard hundreds of hours of taped testimony and sifted through intelligence information. Its final report issued in 1995 concluded that while all sides were committing war crimes, only the Serbs were conducting a systematic campaign of genocide. Even before the report was issued, however, the

Security Council created the International Criminal Tribunal for the Former Yugoslavia, then instituted an arms embargo on all parties, and later imposed trade sanctions on Serbia, condemning it for human rights violations. In December 1995, when the Dayton peace agreement was signed, the war had resulted in 200,000 deaths, 30,000 people missing, and 2.7 million homeless, approximately 60 percent of whom were internally displaced.

Why didn't the Security Council undertake more direct action? Was ethnic cleansing in Bosnia equivalent to genocide? The UN Commission of Experts, the International Court of Justice, and the UN Human Rights Commissions all said yes. Only Serbia had a conscious policy of systematic genocide. Doctors Without Borders disagreed. Still other groups maintained that all sides were guilty. The fact was Security Council members lacked the political will to stop the killing.

In 1998, international attention turned to the Yugoslav province of Kosovo, where the population was divided between Serbs (10 percent) and Albanian Kosovars (90 percent). Serbia had begun a campaign years earlier to strip Kosovars of their political autonomy and expelled ethnic Albanians from positions in government and business. In 1998, Serbian leader Slobodan Milosevic used the Serbian military to terrorize the Albanians, destroying their villages in the process. Reports of massacres of Albanians by Serbs surfaced, as large numbers of Albanians left their homes in a well-publicized mass exodus to bordering countries. The NGO community, most notably the Physicians for Human Rights, provided evidence that the refugees were being systematically targeted.

The United Nations never formally determined that genocide was committed in Kosovo, but the humanitarian crisis prompted the NATO intervention discussed in Chapter 8. The ultimate irony may be that ethnic cleansing worsened in Kosovo when NATO military action commenced. By launching an air war rather than sending in ground troops, NATO was unable to control movements on the ground and either halt the ethnic cleansing or protect the civilian population.

The evidence in support of genocide in Rwanda is much more definitive. In April 1994, following the death of the Rwandan and Burundian presidents in an air crash, Hutu extremists in the Rwandan military and police began systematically slaughtering the minority Tutsis as well as moderate Hutus, in a campaign of violence orchestrated by Radio Libres des Milles Collines. In a ten-week period, some 800,000 were killed out of a total Rwandan population of seven million.

Even before the plane crash, reports from NGOs and UN peacekeepers warned that there were plans to target the Tutsi population. In January 1994, General Romeo Dallaire's warnings of an impending genocide went unheeded at UN headquarters, which was embroiled in Somalia's problem.

Immediately after the plane crash, the former U.S. ambassador to Rwanda wrote a memo predicting widespread violence. General Dallaire requested additional UN troops to augment his small, 2500-member peacekeeping force in order to quell the violence. He also requested U.S. action to block the radio broadcasts (Gourevitch 1998). Instead, he was forced to withdraw for the safety of his troops and confine activities to evacuating foreigners.

Why did the international community fail to respond? Power (2002) traces the reasons for the U.S. failure to take any action to self-serving caution and the belief at first that the killings were merely "random tribal slaughter." When evidence mounted to the contrary, it was ignored and officials avoided using the term *genocide,* knowing full well that if invoked, they would be forced to take action under the terms of the Genocide Convention. Gourevitch (1998) and Barnett (2002) place harshest blame on the UN, which should not have withdawn when it did. Virtually all the key Security Council members preferred taking no military action, and the secretariat ignored the problem. Other scholars have suggested that the genocide occurred so fast, beginning in outlying areas with undependable communication lines to the outside world, that the world could not have reliably known enough or had the time to prevent the genocide (Kuperman 2001).

Whatever the reasons, the Rwandan case demonstrates failure to enforce the international norm prohibiting genocide despite the evidence that genocide was occurring. The fact that it occurred outside centers of power, in a continent already rife with ethnic and racial strife, provides some explanation, but the case points to the practical limitations to enforcing massive human rights violations. The UN's independent inquiries discussed in Chapter 8 and the international tribunals for both Yugoslavia (including Kosovo) and Rwanda are institutionalized responses to this failure of global governance.

■ Violence Against Women

Violence against women has been a problem for centuries, but until recently it has been hidden in the private sphere of family and communal life where local authorities and national governments did not intervene and the international community turned a blind eye. Forced marriages at a young age, physical abuse by spouses, including disfigurement and rape, crippling dowry payments, female genital mutilation, and honor killings occur within the home and family. A gendered division of labor forces women into sweatshop labor, prostitution, and trafficking in their bodies; and in civil and international wars, women are raped, tortured, and forced into providing sexual services for troops. An estimated 300,000 Chinese women in Nanjing were raped during World War II by Japanese forces as were 200,000 to 400,000 East Pakistani (Bangladeshi) women in that country's war of independence in 1970, 60,000 Bosnian women by Serb forces in

1993, and 250,000 women in Burundi's and Rwanda's ethnic conflicts in 1993–1994. Yet only recently have these abuses against women come to be viewed as human rights issues. Even though there was a "mountain of evidence of systematic rape" during World War II, it was not brought up as a war crime in the Nuremberg and Tokyo war trials (Tetreault 1997). The first prosecution of war criminals for using rape as a systematic instrument of ethnic cleansing came in the ICTY's proceedings.

Although the United Nations and its specialized agencies took up women's issues beginning in 1946, discussion was not framed in terms of women's rights as human rights until the 1980s and 1990s. Only as women's rights were increasingly viewed as part of universal human rights did violence against women become a subject of international discussion. Violence against women, thus, illustrates the evolution of gender-based issues, as well as the interaction between the IGO and NGO communities in developing standards, promoting norms, and enforcing them.

NGO work on this issue dates from 1976 when a group of Northern women organized the International Tribunal on Crimes Against Women, including two thousand women activists from forty different countries. The conference was, ironically, a reaction to the 1975 UN Women's Conference in Mexico City, which did not address the issue of violence against women. The tribunal, by contrast, heard testimonials of women who had suffered from domestic (dowry-death) or community violence (rape and sexual slavery). It provided a major impetus to publicizing gender violence and to networking and alliance building. It opened up an issue that had heretofore been regarded as private, protected from outside interference. It contributed also to the adoption of the Convention on the Elimination of All Forms of Discrimination Against Women (CEDAW) in 1979.

During the 1980s, small groups of experts, based in the UN system, convened intergovernmental meetings with participants from multiple agencies, including the Division for the Advancement of Women and the Crime Prevention and Criminal Justice Division of the UN Department of International Economic and Social Affairs. Among those working in the UN system, violence against women became a criminalized activity with far-reaching implications for the family and the community. The first UN survey on violence against women was published in 1989. Yet the organization itself still separated women's rights and human rights conceptually and bureaucratically, with the Human Rights Commission in Geneva and the Commission on the Status of Women in New York. Women's rights and human rights did not become conceptually joined until the 1990 publication of both an article written by activist Charlotte Bunch, entitled "Women's Rights are Human Rights" (Bunch 1990), and of vivid examples of gender violence. The 1993 World Conference on Human Rights endorsed this concept and put the issue of violence against women on the agenda.

The success of the Vienna conference in marrying human rights and women's rights can be attributed to the ninety or so human rights and women's NGOs that organized the Global Campaign for Women's Human Rights. A key element in that campaign was the focus on gender-based violence. At the NGO forum, the Global Campaign organized the Global Tribunal on Violations of Women's Human Rights, presided over by four international judges. It heard testimony of women from twenty-five countries who had suffered a variety of abuses and put a human face on domestic violence, torture, political persecution, and other problems. The joint efforts of women's and human rights groups produced Article 18 of the Vienna Declaration and Programme of Action that declared: "The human rights of women and of the girl-child are an inalienable, integral and indivisible part of universal human rights." Violence against women and other abuses in situations of war, peace, and domestic family life, including sexual harassment, were identified as breaches of both human rights and humanitarian norms. Subsequently, the Declaration on the Elimination of Violence Against Women was adopted by the UN General Assembly in 1993, calling for a special rapporteur on violence against women, and for states to take steps to combat violence in accordance with provisions of that declaration. Dr. Radhika Coomeraswamy of Sri Lanka was appointed as the first Special Rapporteur on Violence Against Women in 1994.

The UN system was not the only locus of activity. Members of the European Union also undertook to combat gender violence as a result of the interest of key states that had strong domestic feminist lobbies. These included Germany, Sweden, Finland, and Austria. Both the Maastricht Treaty (1993) and the Amsterdam Treaty (1997) established important mechanisms. The former expanded EU competence to include justice and home affairs, while the latter explicitly highlighted respect for human rights and the rule of law. In 1996, the widely publicized Belgian case of sexual abuse of young girls drew attention to the fact that gender violence was occurring not just "out there in the developing world" but right at home. The European Women's Lobby with its 2,700 affiliates brought the issue to the public agenda through its Policy Action Center on Violence Against Women, established in 1997. This precipitated a response from the European Parliament's activist Women's Rights Committee. With enlargement to the East opening borders of the East European states to the West and the Schengen Convention opening EU's internal borders, trafficking in women and violence emerging from that practice became a broader European issue. Two outcomes include the DAPHNE Initiative that gives financial support to public institutions and NGOs compiling data and developing good practices concerning violence against women and the STOP-Program that assists victims of trafficking (Joachim 2002).

To press states to take steps to deal with violence against women, both

Amnesty International and Human Rights Watch established Women's Human Rights programs to investigate reports of violations of women's rights by state agents. For example, one HRW report issued in 2000 found that in five states, notably Pakistan, Peru, Russia, South Africa, and the United States, violence against women was still being met with indifference. With respect to female genital mutilation, NGOs have been instrumental in framing that issue as one of human rights, an example of violence against women, and also a health issue. In Senegal, a group called Tostan has educated villagers about the health dangers, trained them to use the oathing system that condemns genital mutilation, and moved from village to village to discourage the practice. It was aided by UNICEF and UNESCO, both of which helped to provide educational material and financial support, as well as publicity for the project. As with many issues connected with women and violence against women, the practice is a deeply rooted one. Trying to effect change and enforce a new practice cannot be easily accomplished through government edict or judicial authority, much less international organizations based in faraway countries. The lesson learned is that a coalition of local leaders and women facilitators can use peer pressure to change attitudes (Mackie 2000). Locally based NGOs can utilize the resources provided by the international organizations.

■ The U.S. Role

The United States plays a key role in the international human rights regime, promoting the standards of the regime, while hindering and sometimes even blocking their implementation. Historically, it was a leader supporting international mechanisms for accountability in war, the prohibition of genocide, the Geneva Conventions on war crimes and humanitarian law, the Nuremberg and Tokyo war trials, and the ad hoc tribunals for Yugoslavia and Rwanda. After all, the United States was founded on liberal principles guaranteeing the political and civil rights of individuals and was a beacon for others. Former first lady Eleanor Roosevelt chaired the Commission on Human Rights when it completed the Universal Declaration and Genocide Convention in 1948. Jimmy Carter won the 2002 Nobel Peace Prize for his human rights and peacemaking activities both as president in the late 1970s and as private citizen.

Yet the U.S. record is a mixed one. The United States signed but has never ratified many key human rights documents, including the Convention Relating to the Status of Refugees, the International Covenant on Economic, Social, and Cultural Rights, the Convention on the Elimination of Discrimination Against Women, the Convention on the Rights of the Child, and the Rome Treaty establishing the International Criminal Court. In fact, the Senate ratified no treaties in the 1950s, and only one each in the 1960s, 1970s, and 1980s. It took forty years to ratify the Genocide

Convention that the United States helped draft. The reasons for this record vary: some human rights conventions are seen as employing a double standard, punishing some states and not others; there was fear that treatment of African Americans and Native Americans might come under international scrutiny, as well as concern that the U.S. military might be constrained by treaty commitments. When the United States eventually ratified the Genocide Convention, for example, it attached reservations that diluted the treaty's intent. The United States has often attached reservations to treaties for any provisions that may be contrary to the U.S. Constitution. On these grounds, the United States added a reservation to the Covenant on Civil and Political Rights relating to the death penalty for persons under the age of eighteen years. Sometimes understandings are attached that constitute unilateral statements regarding interpretation of a treaty. Such an understanding was attached to the Convention on the Elimination of All Forms of Racial Discrimination, saying that the provisions would be implemented by the federal government to the extent that it has jurisdiction in such matters. In virtually every case, the United States also adds the declaration that the particular treaty is not self-executing, that is, it does not create rights that are directly enforceable (Buergenthal 1995: 290–298).

The United States may also work to thwart treaties already in force. In the case of the Convention against Torture, the United States opposes strengthening the treaty by incorporating a system of regular inspections of prisons and detention centers in every country to look for potential abuses. These cases of U.S. nonratification, ratification with reservations, understandings, and declarations, and sometimes outright obstructionism have led Ignatieff (1999: 61) to conclude that the United States is "a nation with a great rights tradition that leads the world in denouncing human rights violations but which behaves like a rogue state in relation to international legal conventions."

Why is the United States ambivalent about committing itself to the international human rights regime? Why does the United States have an aversion to domestic application of international treaties? Why does the United States seem to act as a rogue state? Patrick (2002) and Moravcsik (2002) each explain this ambivalence by referring to several factors. American exceptionalism, discussed in Chapter 7, has led the United States to see its role as helping to establish basic human rights standards, but to be cautious about applying such standards to itself. Similarly, a superpower or hegemon does not have to bow to the demands of others; neither does it intend to be circumscribed by the actions of others. The United States is very sensitive to the specter of losing its authority to an unelected and unaccountable global bureaucracy. Its decentralized political system, including the separation of powers at the national level and federal structure, is another factor. Treaty ratification requires two-thirds consent by the Senate, and implementation of measures may entail financial obligations authorized by both houses of the U.S. Congress and compliance by federal, state, and local authorities. When the subject matter is controversial, the tendency has been for U.S. presidents not to send the treaty to the Senate, therefore avoiding any confrontation.

Has U.S. ambivalence toward the international human rights regime made a difference? At one level, the answer is "of course." When international institutions clash with a sole superpower that controls essential financial resources, it makes a difference. Yet, at another level, adherence to human rights norms is firmly established in a strong network of NGOs and democratic states, supported by public opinion. The norms are firmly implanted where U.S. ambivalence has no impact, such as in the European Convention on Human Rights. This has led Moravcsik (2002: 365) to conclude, "The consequences of U.S. nonadherence to global norms, while signaling a weakening in theory, is probably of little import in practice." The verdict may still be out. Indeed, the International Criminal Court, so strongly promoted by human rights advocates and many states, but so firmly opposed by the United States, may offer a key test.

■ Expanding Human Rights in the Age of Globalization

There has been remarkable progress in human rights global governance since World War II. The normative basis of international human rights has been established. Monitoring instruments are in place, but some of those mechanisms are in danger of being politicized, with self-serving state reporting and the legitimacy of committees questionable. Promotional activities include an expanding conception of what is considered human rights, including activities protecting women, children, refugees, and indigenous peoples, even though such activities may conflict with other societal and cultural values.

When peer pressure, shaming, NGO campaigns, and other strategies fail to get states to improve their human rights records, enforcement remains an option, although perhaps a weak one, as it butts squarely against state sovereignty and may be in conflict with other interests. The international community's failure to prevent genocide in Bosnia and Rwanda illustrates these tensions.

Globalization has been both an impediment to the development of international human rights and a stimulus. Economic globalization has created more opportunities for MNCs to exploit cheap labor in developing countries. It has harnessed livelihoods in communities everywhere to global markets, creating new vulnerabilities. Just as there has been a backlash against economic and cultural globalization, so too there may be a backlash against political globalization implicit in human rights governance and a renewed debate over universality. Yet economic globalization has also brought more attention to the vast economic disparities both in and between societies, disparities that undermine human rights. Globalization of communication has meant that human rights abuses and atrocities are given widespread publicity, generating significant and often rapid responses. It has given NGOs and individuals a powerful new medium to broadcast their concerns, to create networks, and to take actions. It has created an international audience that is sensitized and ready to act on human rights issues. Protecting human rights has, indeed, become a global enterprise.

■ Note

1. Portions of this chapter are drawn from Karen A. Mingst and Margaret P. Karns. (2000) *The United Nations in the Post–Cold War Era*, 2nd ed. Boulder: Westview Press. Reprinted with permission of Westview Press.

■ Suggested Further Reading

Barnett, Michael. (2002) *Eyewitness to a Genocide. The United Nations and Rwanda*. Ithaca: Cornell University Press.

Clark, Ann Marie. (2001) *Diplomacy of Conscience: Amnesty International and Changing Human Rights Norms*. Princeton: Princeton University Press.

Forsythe, David P. (2000) *Human Rights in International Relations*. Cambridge, UK: Cambridge University Press.

Lauren, Paul Gordon. (2003) *The Evolution of International Human Rights. Visions Seen*, 2nd ed. Philadelphia: University of Pennsylvania Press.

Risse, Thomas, Stephen C. Ropp, and Kathryn Sikkink. (1999) *The Power of Human Rights. International Norms and Domestic Change*. Cambridge, UK: Cambridge University Press.

■ Internet Resources

African Charter on Human and People's Rights: available at www.umn.edu/humanrts/
Amnesty International: www.amnesty.org
Anti-Slavery International: www.antislavery.org
Coalition to Stop the Use of Child Soldiers: www.child-soldiers.org
Cultural Survival: www.cs.org
Doe v. UNOCAL: http://oz.uc.edu/thro
European Court of Human Rights: www.echr.coe.int/
Feminist Majority Foundation: www.feminist.org/afghan
Gendercide Watch: www.gendercide.org
Human Rights Watch: www.hrw.org
Inter-American Court of Human Rights; Inter-American Convention on Human Rights: Both available at www.umn.edu/humanrts/
International Committee of the Red Cross: www.icrc.org
Tostan: www.tostan.org
United Nations Children's Fund: www.unicef.org
United Nations High Commissioner for Human Rights: www.unhchr.ch
University of Minnesota Human Rights Library: www.umn.edu/humanrts/
Unrepresented Nations and Peoples Organization: www.unpo.org
World Council of Churches: www.wcc-coe.org

11

Protecting the Environment

■ **Case Study: Tropical Forests in the Brazilian Amazon**

The Amazon River basin is as large as the whole of the United States or Western Europe. Not only are more than one-half of the world's tropical forests found in the region, but also over 60,000 species of plants, 1,000 species of birds, 300 different kinds of mammals, and 2,000 species of fish and aquatic mammals, making it one of the world's great centers of biodiversity. Nine countries in the region share this rich biodiversity that many claim to be part of the common heritage of mankind.

Yet the Amazon is under severe environmental stress from accelerating deforestation. In the three years following the 1992 Rio Conference on sustainable development, the rate of deforestation doubled. Timber is cut both legally and illegally for wood and lumber for domestic and international markets. Forests are cleared for roads, farming, and ranching. With forest cut, soil erosion clogs the rivers, streams silt, and fragile soils are exposed to the elements. Endangered species such as the jaguar and rare plants no longer have suitable habitat, and genetic materials for agriculture and medicines are lost. Deforestation also leads to increased carbon emissions—with Brazil now among the world's significant polluters.

Deforestation is also rampant in Southeast Asia, particularly in Indonesia. Illegal logging operations, estimated at 80 percent of total logging, have deforested much of the landscape. Every year, an area the size of Connecticut is stripped of trees, threatening soil productivity and endangering orangutans and Sumatran tigers. Much of the wood is shipped to Malaysia and Singapore, which then manufacture wood products for large consumer markets in Taiwan and China. These are the same countries that imposed strict conditions on logging activities on their own territory and have protected parks and reserves.

Among the most affected species are mahogany trees—highly valued "green gold." Most of the mahogany is cut illegally, then shipped out of Brazil and other countries with fraudulent documents to four major companies in the North that manufacture pieces for consumer markets in the United States, Europe, and Asia.

459

Greenpeace has launched a campaign to protect Brazil's ancient forests from illegal logging. In October 2001, it published a devastating analysis, linking the illegal mahogany trade to Brazilian operators, corrupt governments, and private individuals, as well as MNCs. Brazil unilaterally canceled all mahogany operations in response to the Greenpeace initiative, admitting widespread illegal operations, and the study became the centerpiece of the 2002 Ancient Forest Summit.

The protection of tropical forests has long been on the international agenda. In the 1970s, UNCTAD's Integrated Programme for Commodities, in collaboration with FAO, studied tropical timber, hoping to guarantee both fair prices and product sustainability. In 1982, the International Tropical Timber Organization (ITTO) was established, designed to deal with production and resource management for producers and trade for consumers. During the 1990s, the ITTO and its Successor Agreement established the goal of having all tropical timber entering international trade come from sustainably managed sources.

The 1992 Convention on Biological Diversity (CBD) reiterates the principle of national sovereignty over domestic resources, but it also obligates states to conserve biological diversity. States committed themselves to developing national plans and wealthy states pledged to provide funding for states unable to pay. Biotechnology and pharmaceutical interests are obliged to share profits with local entities, a controversial provision. In addition to the CBD, a number of other specific treaties address various parts of the wildlife and plant protection problem. The Convention on International Trade in Endangered Species of Wild Fauna and Flora (CITES) negotiated in 1973 has 160 members and provides protection in international commerce for threatened species. Appendix I prohibits all international trade in specific species, while Appendix II provides a lower level of protection. In 2002, after ten years of work by the NGOs and CITES, members voted to extend international protection to big-leaf mahogany.

How can biodiversity be preserved by focusing on the loss of tropical forests? It is clear that, broad statements of international commitment aside, the main responsibility rests with states. Brazil, for example, has turned over 12 percent of protected land to indigenous peoples. Specific jurisdictions like Mato Grosso have extensive and effective aerial monitoring of forest areas. Alternative crops are subsidized and medicines from indigenous plants protected. Such projects are jointly funded, often by the Inter-American Development Bank and NGOs like Environmental Defense Fund and World Wide Fund for Nature. National parks have been set aside in Brazil and Malaysia and national environmental agencies have been established. In 1989, Brazil listed mahogany under Appendix III of CITES, which permits individual countries to propose regulation of trade in a specific species. Many criticize this procedure because it does not require consultation. Greenpeace found the measure was not working; neither were other measures that Brazil tried. Until Brazil's corrupt system is cleaned up, other alternatives must be used to protect tropical forests and mahogany.

In 1993, the World Wide Fund for Nature (and its U.S. affiliate World Wildlife Fund) and Greenpeace brought together a group of three hundred individuals to form the Forest Stewardship Council (FSC), based in Oaxaca, Mexico. The FSC, an independent organization operating in some fifty countries, offers certification that wood moving in the $50 billion international market comes from sustainable forests, i.e., there is attention to tenure rights, indigenous peoples, and community rights with minimal environmental impact. FSC requires highly detailed technical information on both forest management practices and a "chain of custody" as wood moves from forest to consumer. Major stakeholders meet in chambers to discuss issues and monitor compliance. Only wood receiving certifications carries the FSC logo. While 5 percent of the world's forests are currently certified under the FSC standards, demand for FSC products has accelerated. Currently, over seven hundred companies are certified to sell the approved products. FSC is having results. As Conroy (2002: 215) concludes, "There is evidence that financial markets are paying increasing attention to these dimensions of corporate practice, rewarding firms that become leaders, and punishing those that lag behind."

The World Bank and International Monetary Fund have occasionally used their conditionality to address the problem of tropical forests. In 1997, for example, the IMF suspended lending to Cambodia because of its illegal logging practices, but reversed the decision two years later after assurances by authorities of better monitoring. NGOs, however, report that the tracking system has completely broken down and pressure for reinstating the loans was strong because of Cambodia's dependence on loans to meet its budget.

The international financial institutions have worked for innovative solutions in partnerships with others. For example, the International Finance Corporation, using funds from the Global Environmental Facility, has actively supported a private nonprofit Costa Rican organization that seeks to protect that country's tropical forests. The NGO, FUNDECORE, works with private landowners, providing incentives for them to start new forest plantations on deforested land and to practice sustainable forestry.

Solutions to deforestation are controversial. The Ancient Forest Summit with the parties of the Convention on Biological Diversity ended in failure in 2002. France, Germany, and Russia supported strong and immediate actions, while major timber exporting countries (Brazil, Canada, and Malaysia) opposed a strong action plan. Neither did the Johannesburg Summit in the same year come to a positive conclusion. Timber-rich countries in the South, for whom deforestation is only part of the larger picture of poverty and indebtedness, need financial resources to achieve sustainable forest management, and such resources have not been forthcoming from the North.

Environmental issues, like the protection of tropical forests, have drawn the attention of the international community to the need for global environmental governance; states cannot act alone. The issues of population pressures, natural resource exploitation, and pollution are not only uniquely interdependent, they are collective goods problems. States left to their own devices in a globalized world may suffer joint losses or fail to realize gains; both individuals and the international system in general suffer. Under such conditions, multilevel governance becomes imperative.

■ Relating Environmental Problems to Security, Economics, and Human Rights

A contemporary ecosystem perspective confirms that various environmental issues are integrally related to each other and have critical economic repercussions. For example, accelerating population growth rates have implications for environmental policies. First, the population increase is not uniformly distributed, with 98 percent of the growth in the LDCs. Second, higher levels of economic development in the North mean increased demands for natural resources and energy. Poverty in the South adversely affects the environment, too. The quality of the commons diminishes as individuals try to meet their needs and degrade spaces through both agricultural and industrial practices. The practices that individuals engage in to survive may no longer be sustainable, damaging the environment, causing pollution, and using up precious resources. The desire for economic growth at any cost may also lead to unsound decisions, which adversely affect the quality of the environment.

Environmental issues not only have a connection to economics, but also to human rights (Schulz 2001: 115–117). Leading environmentalists have met stiff opposition, harassment, and violent ends. Environmental activist Chico Mendes, the leader of the Brazilian rubber tappers, was murdered in 1988 by individuals from the timber and logging community. The leader of the Greenbelt movement in Kenya, a female activist Wangari Maathai, has been imprisoned for her activities and harassed for leading demonstrations both against the selling of public land in Nairobi to developers and for the protection of open spaces. Ken Saro-Wiwa, environmental activist of the Movement for the Survival of Ogoni People, led the fight against environmental and economic exploitation by the Nigerian government and Royal Dutch Shell oil company, before he was murdered by his political opponents. It is Mr. Saro-Wiwa who claimed that the environment is man's first right.

Finally, lack of critical resources poses a threat to a state's security and unsustainable environmental practices pose a threat to human security, potentially leading to resource-motivated violence and intrastate and interstate wars. The search to guarantee supply of nonrenewable natural resources such as petroleum motivated Japan's aggression in China and Southeast Asia and the German invasion of the southern Russian oil fields during World War II. The same search fuels conflicts in the Caspian Sea basin and the South China Sea. The need for usable water for agricultural productivity and human needs has led to violence between Egypt, Sudan, and Ethiopia, neighboring upper riparian states in the Nile basin, as well as to major disputes in the Middle East over access to the Jordan, Tigris-Euphrates, and Indus river waters. Peasants living on depleted land create political and economic instability, moving into urban areas or regions inhabited by others, changing the ethnic balance, and causing social unrest and violence. Sometimes those movements advocate the overthrow of established governments in an attempt to get their fair share of usable land and resources. Mass migrations, triggered by soil erosion, deforestation, flooding, and hunger burden neighboring states with refugees and in some cases threaten regional peace and stability, as conditions in Haiti and Southeast Asia confirm (Homer-Dixon 1999; Klare 2001).

In short, issues once perceived as "merely environmental" have far-reaching economic, human rights, and security implications. Having emerged only since the 1960s for the most part, these issues are likely to be at the forefront of the global agenda in the twenty-first century.

■ The Emergence of the Environment as an Issue Area

International environmental issues are of relatively recent vintage. At the intergovernmental level, international commissions for the Rhine and Danube Rivers were established during the nineteenth century to foster cooperation among users, and the International Joint Commission between the U.S. and Canada was formed in 1909 to address boundary problems, including environmental issues linked to shared waters. At the nongovernmental level, among the first environmental organizations were the Society for the Protection of Birds (1889) and the Sierra Club (1892). The Society for the Preservation of the Wild Fauna of the Empire (1903) became the first international environmental NGO, to be followed in 1913 by the Commission for the International Protection of Nature (subsequently renamed in 1956, the International Union for the Conservation of Nature). While these organizations accomplished important objectives, their activities were not supported by national or international governmental activity (McCormick 1999).

During the 1960s, a broader interest in the environment resulted in a variety of responses. Rachel Carson's *Silent Spring* and Jacques Yves

Cousteau's *The Living Sea* opened the doors to the modern environmental movement. Each galvanized environmental activists and helped to cement in the public consciousness the notion of the interdependence of all living things. Individual events, such as the Torrey Canyon oil spill and the photographs of the Earth from space taken by astronauts in 1969 also proved to be catalysts for a view of the planet as a single ecosystem. Over the course of the next thirty years, interest in environmental issues broadened in scope to include both the protection of the natural environment and the curbing of the destructive effects of industrialization.

Biologist Garrett Hardin's article, "The Tragedy of the Commons," published in 1968, set the stage for the theoretical and practical collective goods dilemmas posed by many environmental issues, as discussed in Chapter 2. Hardin suggested some simplistic strategies to overcome this tragedy of the commons. Yet, thirty-five years after Hardin's suggestions were published, the struggle for multilevel environmental governance continues.

■ The Pieces of Global Environmental Governance

International conferences have played a key role in the evolution of global environmental governance, as have NGOs and epistemic communities. They have put environmental issues on the international agenda and provided frameworks for negotiations and subsequent institutionalization. Since the UN Charter itself contains no mention of environmental protection, UN-sponsored conferences filled a critical gap in the evolution of environmental governance.[1]

International Ad Hoc Conferences and the Articulation of Norms: From Stockholm to Johannesburg

The Stockholm Conference.   In the late 1960s, Sweden and other Nordic states proposed an international conference on the environment. The first international conference on the biosphere was held in 1968 under UNESCO's auspices. It was followed in 1972 by the UN Conference on the Human Environment (UNCHE) or the Stockholm Conference. The latter effectively put environmental issues on the agenda of the UN and many governments, initiating the piecemeal construction of international environmental institutions, expansion of the environmental agenda, increasing acceptance of international environmental standards and monitoring regimes, and extensive involvement of NGOs, scientific, and technical groups in policymaking efforts. Perhaps most important, it thrust into the popular consciousness the notion of "Spaceship Earth." The slogan "Think Globally, Act Locally" became an important symbol of the movement.

During the preparatory meetings for the 1972 conference, UNCHE Secretary-General Maurice Strong, a Canadian businessman, provided the leadership to bridge the divergent interests of North and South by forging the conceptual links between development and environment. The North emphasized issues such as preservation of species and the need to curb environmental and transborder pollution. The South, however, feared that environmental regulation could hamper economic growth and divert resources from economic development. Many LDCs were reluctant even to attend the conference and had to be persuaded that environmental problems were neither a concern of the rich only nor a plot to keep them underdeveloped.

The Stockholm Declaration, a soft-law statement of twenty-six principles, called on states and international organizations to coordinate activities. It endorsed states' obligation to protect the environment and responsibility not to damage the environment of other states. It also recognized the principle that environmental policies should enhance developing countries' economic potential and not hamper the attainment of better living conditions. The Stockholm participants agreed not to use environmental concerns as justification for discriminatory trade practices or as a way to decrease access to markets. Conferees called for creation of a new UN body to coordinate environmental activities and promote governmental cooperation—the United Nations Environment Programme (UNEP). The Stockholm Conference also inaugurated the practice of a parallel NGO forum, run simultaneously with the official conference, as discussed in Chapter 6. Almost 250 NGOs participated, setting an important precedent.

Moving to sustainable development.   The consensus forged at Stockholm on integrating the environment and development was later challenged by the LDCs. The South argued that environmental concerns diverted attention from the need for changes in the international power structure, while Northern environmentalists questioned the continuing emphasis on economic growth in the face of diminishing global resources. That tension led the UN General Assembly in 1983 to establish the World Commission on Environment and Development (WCED or Brundtland Commission), discussed in Chapter 9, to develop the concept of sustainable development. Its report, *Our Common Future,* called for "development that meets the needs of the present without compromising the ability of future generations to meet their own needs" (World Commission 1987: 8). It sought to balance ecological concerns with the economic growth necessary to reduce poverty. The report underscored that the South cannot develop in the same way the industrialized countries did because humanity could not survive a similarly radical transformation in the environment.

The Brundtland Commission's approach was adopted in 1987 by UNEP and later by the World Bank, NGOs, and many national development agencies. It became the rallying cry of the environmental movement and a concept articulated by academics, state officials, and leading scientists. It acknowledged that poverty is a critical source of environmental degradation; it required that people begin to think about critical links between agriculture, trade, transportation, energy, and the environment; and it called attention to the long-term view (Esty 2001). The commission also called for a second global conference on the environment twenty years after Stockholm.

The Rio Conference.   The 1992 UN Conference on the Environment and Development (UNCED), held in Rio de Janeiro, was convened in the aftermath of a series of key scientific findings during the 1980s that suggested mounting international environmental problems, namely, the discovery of the ozone hole over Antarctica, the growing evidence of global warming or climate change, and the accumulating data on loss of biodiversity and depletion of fisheries. These developments shaped the Rio Conference agenda and were crucial steps in the struggle to get North and South to work together.

The Rio Earth Summit was the largest of the UN-sponsored global conferences both in the number of participants and in the scope of the agenda. As with other conferences, a series of preparatory meetings were used to articulate positions, hammer out basic issues, and negotiate the text for all conference documents. NGOs played key roles in the preparatory process and the conference. Although the environmental movement began in the North and continued to be dominated by Northern NGOs, by the 1980s it had spread in the South. UNCED provided even further impetus through opportunities for networking with the unprecedented number of participating NGOs. The 1400 accredited environmental organizations included not only traditional, large, well-financed NGOs, such as the World Wide Fund for Nature and the International Union for the Conservation of Nature, but also many new grassroots groups that typically were poorly financed and had few previous transnational linkages. Although NGOs were excluded from negotiations over the most important final documents, their persistence paid off as they were given the capability of participating at all levels, from policy- and decisionmaking to implementation.

The major outcome of UNCED was Agenda 21, an 800-page blueprint that articulated key principles and provisions for managing various environmental sectors. Key principles included the right of sovereign states to exploit their resources, the right of states to develop, priority to the needs of the developing countries, and more financial assistance to the poorer countries, all favoring the South. At the same time, both the North and

South accepted that deforestation, degradation of water supplies, atmospheric pollution, and desertification were threats to global security and that states were responsible for exercising control over their own environmentally damaging activities. The North acknowledged that the major responsibility for global environmental problems rested with the developed countries, and it agreed to increase foreign assistance for specific environmental institutions. Yet Agenda 21 included no mandatory rules. Follow-up was voluntary. Thus, while it provided a useful catalogue of problems, implementation of solutions was woefully inadequate. This has led one pessimistic analyst (Urquidi 2002: 1) to conclude, "Agenda 21 remained on the bookshelves, gathering dust." He attributes the failure to the unwillingness of states to take action.

What did the Rio Earth Summit accomplish? On the institutional side, it led to the creation of the Commission on Sustainable Development and restructuring of the Global Environmental Facility. The conference is credited with integrating environmental and development policies worldwide, empowering the environmental movement, linking business profitability to support for the environment, and providing the impetus for bringing into force the conventions on climate change, biodiversity, desertification, and law of the sea, two of which were approved at the conference (climate change and biodiversity). Rio led indirectly to the linkage of trade and the environment in the WTO and to the "greening" of the World Bank's programs. It also led to recognition that the goal of sustainable development depends not only on governments, businesses, IGOs, and NGOs, but also on ordinary people.

Many of the initiatives depended on state implementation, however, and that record is disappointing. For example, it took five years to draft the Kyoto Protocol to the Rio-approved Framework Convention on Climate Change and ten years to get state commitments. Then the United States refused to participate.

Conferences following the Earth Summit, including the 1995 Social Summit in Copenhagen, the 1995 Fourth Women's Conference in Beijing, and the 1996 Habitat II Conference in Istanbul; each reinforced the discourse of sustainable development. For example, the 1993 Cairo conference on population built on the Rio foundations emphasizing the need to slow population growth rates. Recognizing that low birth rates were essential to implementing sustainable development, the conferees in Cairo agreed to a twenty-year plan, focusing on birth control, economic development, and the empowerment of women. By consensus, the states agreed that these objectives could not conflict with national laws, religious beliefs, or cultural norms. In addition, international conventions were signed following Rio, including the UN Convention on Biological Diversity, the UN Convention to Combat Desertification, and the UN Fish Stocks Agreement, among others. And at a more local level, over six thousand cities and towns around the globe created their own local "Agenda 21" for the purposes of long-term planning.

Rio Plus 10; Johannesburg Summit (2002).   The purpose of the UN World Summit on Sustainable Development, Rio Plus 10, was to build on the ambitious, yet poorly executed agenda of Rio. Those gathered, including one hundred presidents and prime ministers, 10,000 delegates, and almost one thousand NGOs (8,000 members from civil society), hoped to stem the rising toll of poverty and curb pollution and deforestation, which had only accelerated during the 1990s. The South wanted more aid for economic growth. The Europeans wanted targets and timetables, while the United States found targets unnecessary. The divisions were profound. To add to the discontent, NGOs were still not permitted to be full participants. By the time the Johannesburg Summit convened, there was also increasing disillusionment with the notion of sustainable development. The term was perceived as a "buzzword largely devoid of content," and some officials, especially in the developing world, had begun to argue that "sustainable" refers to continuity of economic growth without even acknowledging the term's environmental dimension (Esty 2001: 74).

Thus, while the environmental NGOs tried to hold on to what they had previously gained, states did little preparatory groundwork for the 2002 summit in contrast to Rio. Only the European Union held preparatory meetings. States also avoided clear, postsummit obligations such as fundamental assessments of energy resources, forests, soil, and water management practices.

The major outcome of the summit, the Plan of Implementation, included some targets to be achieved: access to clean water and proper sanitation, and restoration of fisheries by 2015, reduction of biodiversity loss by 2010, and better use of chemicals by 2020, as well as more use of renewable energy, but with no target or plan specified. These goals with long time horizons were to be achieved through partnerships between governments, citizen groups, and business (called action coalitions), many of which had already been forged before Johannesburg.

The 2002 summit is generally seen as disappointing compared to previous gatherings. Some have suggested that the summit signaled the diminishing returns from the mega-conference approach. Yet the ad hoc conference process over the course of three decades had put the issue on the international agenda, forced states to adopt national agendas, socialized states to accept new norms of behavior, and brought together the scientific community and environmental NGOs who learned from each other. As constructivists argue, this process led to significant shifts in perceptions and behavior that are the foundations of global environmental governance (Haas 2002).

■ NGO Roles in Environmental Governance

NGOs have played an important role in environmental issues since the nineteenth century. But since the 1960s, with the burgeoning environmental movement and especially following the 1972 Stockholm Conference, the number and scope of both internationally based NGOs and small, locally based environmental NGOs in the LDCs have expanded. The World Directory of Environmental Organizations lists 22,600 environmental organizations—the larger umbrella organizations. The European Environmental Bureau, the liaison office between the EU organs and NGOs, lists 132 European NGO members, representing 14,000 member organizations. Bangladesh, alone, claims 10,000 environmentally oriented NGOs. Numbers, of course, do not indicate influence. Neither are these groups united in approach or ideological orientation; some prefer to work within the status quo, others desire radical change. NGOs have given individual citizens a voice in environmental governance and their names have become well known in many countries, for example, Earthwatch, Environmental Defense, The Nature Conservancy, Sierra Club, World Wide Fund for Nature, Conservation International, Rainforest Action Network, and Earth Island Institute.

Environmental NGOs perform a number of key functions in environmental affairs. First, they serve as generalized international critics. Because they are not attached to nation-states and do not depend on states for funds, they are able to take critical positions, using the media to publicize their dissatisfaction. For example, Greenpeace publishes Greenpeace Waste Trade Update, pointing out the inadequacies of the 1989 Basel Convention on the Control of Transboundary Movements of Hazardous Wastes and Their Disposal. Rainforest Action Network launched an initiative against Amazon deforestation precipitated by cattle ranching, by targeting Burger King for buying beef from the region. And it was Greenpeace's indictment of Brazil's mahogany practices that led that country to stop all shipments. Second, NGOs function as part of epistemic communities. Individual experts from NGOs, along with their counterparts in IGOs and state agencies, may well form part of an epistemic community dedicated to pushing an environmental agenda. And sometimes the epistemic communities try to change the way people think about issues in the interest of environmental preservation. The World Wide Fund for Nature (WWF), for example, is talking to consumers and medical practitioners in Asia to try to alter behavior in using endangered species like bears and rhinos for medicinal purposes. Third, NGOs may function through IGOs, try to alter the structure of the IGOs, offer mechanisms for dispute settlement, and work in tandem with IGOs. For example, NGOs interested in limiting whaling sought to change the structure of the International Whaling Commission through expanded membership and enhanced NGO participation, thereby strengthening the regulation and resulting in stricter enforcement mechanisms. Fourth, NGOs can perform on-site inspection functions, just as TRAFFIC does with respect to the CITES convention, as discussed below.

Finally, and perhaps most important, NGOs attempt to influence states' environmental policy directly. They provide information about policy options. Some NGOs like the World Resource Institute have extensive research staffs and provide valuable information for policymakers. Some may initiate formal legal proceedings against states for failing to comply. The Earth Island Institute used this approach in the tuna/dolphin controversy, appealing to U.S. courts to enforce the Marine Mammal Protection Act. They may work through states' legislative or bureaucratic processes to pressure authorities to impose sanctions against other parties.

NGOs may work directly with states to package issues in ways that enhance the possibility of compliance with sets of obligations stemming from treaties or other sources. Debt-for-nature swaps, the acquisition of debt usually by a conservation NGO and its redemption in local currency to be used for conservation purposes, is one such example. Beginning in 1987, NGOs such as Conservation International, the World Wide Fund for Nature, and the Nature Conservancy arranged such swaps in Bolivia, Costa Rica, Ecuador, Zambia, Madagascar, and the Philippines, with local NGOs getting title to the preserved land. In 2002, the same three NGOs joined with the United States and Peru for a debt swap that generates funds for local conservation groups to protect ten tropical rain forest areas. The NGOs contributed $1.1 million and the U.S. government allocated $5.5 million to cancel part of Peru's debt to the United States. As a result, Peru can save $14 million in debt payments and will provide local currency equivalence toward conservation projects. Projects in states are widely recognized as NGO funding opportunities, for it is in states that environmental policy is made and implemented. For example, WWF has funded Zambia's national game preserves with USAID help, training locals in antipoaching strategies and using funds received from the tourist trade for reinvestment into local development projects. Although much more is needed, NGOs achieve environmental objectives by promoting economic development and local participation.

Although it is widely recognized that NGOs function in an increasing number of diverse arenas, their impact is still a matter of dispute (Wapner 1996; Haas 2001). They have had major impacts on monitoring of environmental quality and national compliance, with Greenpeace keeping track of national compliance for many treaties and the World Conservation Union tracking compliance for species conservation treaties. Monitoring helps governance actors and gives NGOs information for publicizing abuses and engaging in actions. NGOs have played a major role in activating environmental constituencies around the world, availing themselves of the Internet to provide information and mobilize action groups. For example, the

Biodiversity Action Network (BIONET), established in 1993, serves as an information clearinghouse with its broad-based list-serve passing on information about biodiversity practices and abuses worldwide. Thus, practices in faraway places can be publicized and international pressure brought to bear on the problem.

Despite the increased roles for NGOs, it is still states that have primary responsibility for governance. States have a much greater ability to engage in bargaining and compromise, whereas environmental NGOs, particularly those with a committed core constituency, are less able to participate in the give and take of governance. Thus, the very strength of NGOs—their level of commitment and focus—may also be their greatest weakness.

■ The Role of Epistemic Communities

Epistemic communities perform a vital role in the global environmental governance process. In the early years of the 1970s, the dominant epistemic community concerned with the international environment was resource managers and liberal economists. Gradually, as environmental issues gained attention, the community expanded to include ecologists and other environmental scientists. Scientists have become the linchpin of the epistemic community, forming networks of professionals who develop the vital data to expose problems and consult with governments and international agencies about the best way to proceed. On many environmental issues, there may be several epistemic communities, each sharing a belief in what science has revealed, but possibly differing from other epistemic communities. When there is agreement among scientific elites, then international action will be more forthcoming. When epistemic communities disagree, as they have over several major issues such as climate change, then they, too, become a key part of the political process.

UNEP's Mediterranean Action Plan was developed with the help of epistemic communities, as discussed in Chapter 6. After 1972, individual experts participated in meetings in a professional but unofficial capacity; UNEP administrators relied on the epistemic community for getting the data to establish the monitoring program and to modify it in accord with the data received. These individuals were also active in the domestic bargaining processes, fostering learning among governmental elites. As Haas (1990: 188) concludes, "The transnational alliance between the ecological epistemic community and national marine scientists led governments to define their interests, so that they accepted a collective program that was increasingly comprehensive and complied with such arrangements domestically."

To be successful, epistemic communities have to be continually nurtured, new research opportunities presented, and new networks developed. For an epistemic community to be legitimate, members have to come from both developing and developed countries, a difficult task when such scientific specialists may not be available from the South. Regardless, they still remain elite-driven governance mechanisms (Haas 2001).

The international ad hoc conferences have been vital contributors in the evolution of global environmental governance, stimulating NGO and epistemic community activity. Each is vital to environmental regimes and institutions.

■ Global Environmental Regimes and Institutions

The result of the ad hoc conference process was not only the formation of epistemic communities and the revitalization of NGOs, but also concrete results and key principles. In many cases, those principles were translated into specific standards incorporated into environmental treaties and specific global institutions.

■ *Principles of an Environmental Regime*

The principles and norms governing the environment have evolved over a long time and certain core principles are generally recognized as customary law. The first is the no significant harm principle. This came from the 1941 *Trail Smelter Arbitration* between the United States and Canada and from Principle 21 of the Stockholm Declaration. States have the responsibility to ensure that activities within their jurisdiction not cause environmental damage to others. The second principle is the good neighbor principle of cooperation. According to Stockholm Principle 27, states agree to cooperate should environmental problems arise. There are also emerging principles that are not yet recognized as binding international law. Many of these were incorporated in the Rio Declaration on Environment and Development, including the polluter pays principle, the precautionary principle (take action on the basis of scientific warning), and the preventive action principle (take action within one's own state). There is also the nondiscrimination principle that obligates states to treat domestic and international environmental concerns in the same way and, finally, the principles of sustainable development and intergenerational equity.

Because most of these are emerging principles, environmental law is mostly soft law. Although nonbinding, soft law is critical because it foreshadows rules for future treaties, describes acceptable norms of behavior, and codifies developing rules of customary practice.

■ *Global Environmental Agreements*

The principles of environmental regimes have also developed and been refined in more than 140 multilateral environmental agreements, over half of which have been negotiated since the early 1970s. These agreements articulate both the normative content of a specific issue and spell out implementation and compliance. With the growing number of such treaties, there have been changes in subject and scope. Before the 1970s, most of the agreements were very specific, applying to one species or a local or regional problem. Since the 1970s, the agreements have broadened to deal with the negative effects of wide-ranging economic activities and global problems. Figure 11.1 lists specific examples of both global and regional arrangements. Some of these are linked to specific organizations while others are freestanding, autonomous arrangements. Most call for a conference or meeting of the parties that have decisionmaking powers, a small secretariat, and one or more specialized subsidiary bodies, often convened on an ad hoc basis (Churchill and Ulfstein 2000).

The Convention on International Trade in Endangered Species (CITES) is an example of such a flexible agreement involving three levels of protection or lists. Species that are threatened with extinction receive the greatest degree of protection, and trade is not permitted under any circumstances. For those species needing intermediate levels of protection, such as polar bears and grizzly bears, trade is permitted but highly regulated. Parties meet every two years to review the species on the three lists and determine whether to add, delete, or transfer species from one list to another. Such alterations between first- and second-level protection requires approval of two-thirds of the parties. Although the positions of some species—notably elephants and rhinos—have been hotly contested, provisions for virtually continuous reassessment give the agreement flexibility. State and regional variations in levels of protection enhance that flexibility.

CITES implementation mechanisms are also unique. TRAFFIC verifies compliance with CITES rulings, working directly with governments to provide monitoring information, training, and education programs for wildlife-trade enforcement officers. In 2000, in the Cayman Islands, for example, TRAFFIC personnel stopped the export of over one thousand live lizards, frogs, orchids, and other plants and animals. If TRAFFIC is not directly enforcing provisions or training state officials to enforce, they are publicizing abuses to pressure governments to augment their enforcement.

■ *International Environmental Institutions*

The creation and subsequent strengthening of international environmental institutions has been a permanent legacy of the ad hoc conferences. These institutions play a key role in the process of global governance. They have helped to set standards and participated in the negotiation of the treaties listed in Figure 11.1. They monitor state behavior. They aid state members, NGOs, and other IGOs in the promotion of environmental standards. And, occasionally, these institutions enforce environmental norms. Five institutions stand out, three of which were created specifically to address environmental problems and two of which, while originally tasked with development and trade, have been pressured to respond to environmental issues.

**Figure 11.1   Global and Regional Environmental Agreements
(selected)**

Year   Global Environmental Agreements

1946   International Convention for the Regulation of Whaling
1971   Convention on the Conservation of Wetlands of
       International Importance Especially as Waterfowl Habitat
1972   Convention for the Protection of the World Cultural and
       Natural Heritage
1972   Convention on the Prevention of Marine Pollution by
       Dumping of Wastes and Other Matter
1973   Convention on International Trade in Endangered Species of
       Wild Fauna and Flora (CITES)
1974   Convention for the Prevention of Marine Pollution from
       Land-Based Sources
1977   Environmental Modification Convention
1979   Convention on the Conservation of Migratory Species of
       Wild Animals
1979   Convention on Long-Range Transboundary Air Pollution
       Concerning the Control of Emissions of Nitrogen Oxides
       or Their Transboundary Fluxes
1980   Convention on the Conservation of Antarctica Marine Living
       Resources
1982   UN Convention on the Law of the Sea
1983   International Tropical Timber Agreement
1985   Vienna Convention for the Protection of the Ozone Layer
1987   Montreal Protocol on Substances that Deplete the Ozone
       Layer
1989   Convention on the Control of Transboundary Movements of
       Hazardous Wastes and Their Disposal
1991   Protocol on Environmental Protection to the Antarctic
       Treaty
1992   Convention on the Protection and Use of Transboundary
       Watercourses and International Lakes
1992   UN Convention on Biological Diversity
1992   UN Framework Convention on Climate Change
1994   UN Convention to Combat Desertification in Those
       Countries Experiencing Serious Drought and/or
       Desertification, Particularly in Africa
1997   Kyoto Protocol to UN Framework Convention on Climate
       Change
1998   Convention on the Prior Informed Consent Procedure for
       Certain Hazardous Chemicals and Pesticides in
       International Trade
2000   Convention on the Conservation and Management of the
       Highly Migratory Fish Stocks of the Western and Central
       Pacific
2001   Convention on Persistent Organic Pollutants

(continues)

Figure 11.1 (continued)

Year	Regional Environmental Agreements
1976	Convention for the Protection of the Marine Environment and the Coastal Region of the Mediterranean
1979	Convention on Long-Range Transboundary Air Pollution in Europe
1979	Convention on the Conservation of European Wildlife and Natural Habitats
1991	Agreement Between the Government of Canada and the Government of the USA on Air Quality
1991	Convention on the Ban of the Import into Africa and the Control of Transboundary Movement and Management of Hazardous Wastes Within Africa
1993	North American Agreement on Environmental Cooperation Between the Government of Canada, the Government of the United Mexican States, and the Government of the United States of America
1994	Convention on the Conservation and Management of Pollock Resources in the Central Bering Sea
1994	Convention for the Protection of the Black Sea Against Pollution
1996	Inter-American Convention for the Protection and Conservation of Sea Turtles
1996	Agreement on the Conservation of Cetaceans of the Black Sea, Mediterranean Sea and Contiguous Atlantic Area

Note: For additional information, see data in Ronald B. Mitchell 2003. International Environmental Agreements Website. Available at www.uoregon.edu/itchell/iea/.

United Nations Environment Programme (UNEP). UNEP was the chief product of the Stockholm Conference and was established by the General Assembly in 1972. With Maurice Strong as its first executive director, UNEP became the champion of the new environmental agenda, and by establishing its headquarters in Nairobi, Kenya, the first UN agency based in a developing country. With a relatively small professional staff and an annual budget of about $200 million, its mandate is to promote international cooperation in the field of the environment, serve as an early warning system to alert the international community to environmental dangers, provide guidance for the direction of environmental programs in the UN system, and review implementation of these programs.

UNEP functions through a Governing Council, which sets general policy and reports to the General Assembly through ECOSOC. The Committee of Permanent Representatives, composed of all member states, provides leadership on a continual basis. One of UNEP's most important units, the Scientific and Technical Advisory Panel, provides scientific advice to the Global Environment Facility. The panel of twelve individuals offers strategic advice and maintains a roster of experts for consultation.

Although it has no direct programmatic responsibilities, UNEP has an active agenda. It cosponsored the negotiations for the Basel Convention on Hazardous Waste (1989) and provides secretariat support for that convention, as well as for the Montreal Protocol on Substances that Deplete the Ozone Layer (1987) and the UN Convention on Biological Diversity (1992). It has operational responsibilities, overseeing implementation and coordination of the International Registry of Toxic Chemicals, the Global Environmental Monitoring System, and the Regional Seas Program.

UNEP has also worked closely with other IGOs. Monitoring atmospheric quality has been the responsibility of UNEP and the World Meteorological Organization, while monitoring ocean quality falls to UNEP and the International Oceanographic Council. UNEP, FAO, and WHO conduct studies of freshwater quality.

During its early years, UNEP was strengthened by the dynamic leadership of its first executive directors Maurice Strong and Mustapha Tolba. Yet UNEP has always been handicapped by its limited leverage over the specialized agencies and national governments, its small budget, and its location outside other UN centers. UNEP has been a venue for North/South confrontation, which came to a head in 1997 when the United States, United Kingdom, and Spain threatened to withhold funds until reforms were taken. Fearing the UNEP bureaucracy had been captured by LDC interests, the North wanted to strengthen the role of national environmental ministers in determining UNEP policies.

Global Environmental Facility (GEF).   In 1991, the Global Environmental Facility was created at the suggestion of France and Germany. Under the World Bank's auspices, its purpose is to fund environmental projects with global benefits in low- and middle-income countries. The four priorities are ozone, international waters, biodiversity, and climate change. For example, with respect to biodiversity, between 1991 and 1999, GEF allocated $991 million in grants and mobilized an additional $1.5 billion in cofinancing for biological diversity projects. The GEF's project for industrial water pollution control in the Gulf of Guinea in the amount of $6 million enables the donor organizations to ensure the health of the ecosystem by creating local institutions to monitor pollution levels and to train scientists and technicians. In general, GEF funds are designed to induce the developing countries to take environmental actions, covering the cost differential between a project initiated with environmental objectives and an alternative project undertaken without attention to global environmental concerns. In addition, through a series of small grants ($50,000–$250,000), it subsidizes grass-roots groups. For example, a grant to the Royal Society for the Conservation of Nature, a local NGO in Jordan, which was responsible for the Azraq Oasis, enabled it to begin environmentally sound rehabilitation activities in that arid region. During the first decade of its activity, GEF allocated $4.2 billion to environmental projects and attracted $11 billion in cofinancing.

While the World Bank is the dominant partner in administering this facility and in organizing the application process, other agencies are also involved. UNEP provides scientific oversight and helps in selecting priorities. UNDP coordinates with other bilateral donors and GEF involves NGOs in both the planning and execution. As a result, the GEF has emerged as a useful complement to other sources of financial assistance for environmental projects in less developed countries. It has enabled the World Bank to call itself a green institution and augmented the amount of funding for environmental activities.

GEF, like UNEP, has encountered political problems. To many countries in the South, GEF, because of its association with the World Bank, came to overrepresent the interests of the industrialized North, while failing to address more localized problems such as soil erosion and urban air pollution in the South. In the mid-1990s, GEF was restructured to better accommodate the contending interests. Every three years, the GEF Assembly meets with all countries to review general policies. Day-to-day oversight is the prerogative of the 32-seat Governing Council, with fourteen members from the North, two from the transitional countries, and sixteen from the South. Decisions in that body require double majorities—one from the funder states, and another from 60 percent of the developing member states. Despite organizational changes, problems still continue in the amount of funding available, but commitments in excess of $2.75 billion have been made.

Commission on Sustainable Development (CSD).   The Commission on Sustainable Development was created following the Rio Conference as a body to encourage and monitor implementation of Agenda 21, review reports from states, and coordinate sustainable development activities within the UN system, overlapping in part with UNEP. Since it first convened in 1993, an important task for the CSD has been strengthening the participation of major societal groups, including NGOs, indigenous peoples, local governments, workers, businesses, women, and the young, in decisionmaking and pioneering innovative arrangements for civil society participation. Located in New York, the commission is the venue for discussion of issues related to sustainable development. Yet the CSD lacks both the power to make binding decisions and to command its own financial resources. It is the economic institutions like the World Bank and the WTO that exercise that power.

The World Bank: A rocky road to becoming green.   The World Bank is the largest multilateral donor for economic development and, as such, it has been under the most pressure to make its economic development policies compatible with environmental sustainability. Its record has been a mixed one. On the one hand, by the end of the 1980s, bank officials began to acknowledge environmental problems and responded by establishing regional environmental bureaus to evaluate environmental impact. The 1991 establishment of the GEF was another bank response. The bank now funds environmental projects, including conservation programs in the Baltic Sea wetlands area, expanded sewage treatment plants for Mumbai (India), and programs to reduce industrial pollution in the Liaoning province of China, among others. Bank reports reflect "the green discourse," including sustainable development and environmentally friendly language, and the organization works much more closely with environmental NGOs, as discussed in Chapter 9.

Yet, the bank's commitment to environmental sustainability is continually questioned. For example, in a 1991 memo, which inadvertently became public, then bank chief economist Lawrence Summers justified transferring pollution from the developed to the developing world. In his view, the economic costs of pollution could be reduced by exporting it to LDCs, where pollution was relatively low and wages were low. As he rationalized, the poor cannot possibly worry about environmental problems. In addition, major projects funded by the bank continue to bear the brunt of criticism. Brazil's Amazon basin development project, Indonesia's population relocation from Java to neighboring islands, and several dam projects have come under intense scrutiny. Such projects have forced people to move to environmentally fragile areas and sometimes put them in competition with indigenous people. (See Rich 1994; Fox and Brown 1998.)

Many of these project-specific criticisms come from NGOs. Opposition to dam construction was led by the International Rivers Network, which beginning in the mid-1980s targeted campaigns against China's Three Gorges, Malaysia's Bakun, and India's Sardar Sarovar projects, among others (Khagram 2000). In 2001, a coalition of 150 NGOs from thirty-nine countries wrote the bank urging that it not only stop funding the dam on the Kunene River in Namibia, but that it also consider a moratorium on funding new dams until environmental guidelines were met (Ezzell 2001).

In response to NGO pressure, in 1993, the World Bank established the

Inspection Panel composed of three independent experts unaffiliated with the bank to examine cases brought by citizens of developing countries. These citizens must show that they are being adversely affected by the bank's projects, that the bank is not following policies, and that bank officials have failed to respond to citizens' concerns. Seventeen claims have been heard, most revolving around environmental or human rights issues. The panel has recommended seven investigations, but the bank has upheld only two—the Arun III Hydroelectric Dam Project in Nepal and the Western Poverty Reduction Project in China (also a dam project). In two other cases, one in Argentina and one in Paraguay, the bank approved a more limited review. In only one case, Nepal's Arun III Dam project, was the project subsequently canceled after seven years of contentious activity. The Inspection Panel found that the bank and the Nepalese government had not provided adequate land and resettlement compensation to the affected indigenous people and that they had not undertaken a thorough environmental assessment consistent with their own guidelines. While the procedures worked in this case, they are cumbersome. Clearly, the most important avenue of influence over the bank and its environmental policies is through states. Ironically, major states affected by the inspection panel system, namely Brazil and India, have led the movement to limit the scope of the panel's jurisdiction, preferring economic development projects, even if there is an environmental cost (Fox 2001).

Although the bank has acknowledged many of its practices as environmentally unsound and its Inspection Panel now solicits suggestions from NGOs, dams and other such projects will continue to be funded by the bank. The real debate is over whether the bank has fundamentally altered its attitude toward development. The same question is also salient in the area of trade.

From the GATT to WTO: The greening of trade.   Neither the multilateral development banks with their economic development mandate nor the international trade organizations whose goal is promotion of international trade were initially supportive of environmental initiatives. In fact, when members of GATT were invited to work on the preparatory conference for the Stockholm environmental conference, they attended, fearing that world market competitiveness would decline should antipollution standards be passed. The Trade and Environment Working Group established within GATT sought to avoid situations where pollution control systems would interfere with international trade. As Damian and Graz (2001: 600) remind us, "The guiding principle at GATT was above all to prevent distortions and hindrances to trade, and to keep the environment on the margins of trade."

Yet GATT, like other trade organizations, had to adjust to a new reality.

Many of the multilateral environmental agreements listed in Figure 11.1 include environmentally friendly provisions that could restrict trade. The mantra of sustainable development carried with it recognition that restrictions on trade may serve environmental objectives. Thus, GATT was forced to address the conflict between trade, development, and the environment. Highly publicized GATT legal disputes arose over precisely this issue. The U.S. Marine Mammal Protection Act prohibited the importation of Mexican tuna because tuna were caught with nets that entangled threatened (but not endangered) dolphins. GATT ruled in favor of Mexico, favoring trade over environmental protection. Despite the cries of the environmental community, the decision was never formally approved by GATT's governing body and thus set no precedent. GATT provisions in force at the time required states to treat all like products equally, without paying attention to process or how a product was made. Such issues continue to be highly contested.

The provisions of WTO, like GATT, are not at first reading friendly to environmental concerns. Article XX requires that states treat all like products as national equivalents. The only exceptions include measures to protect human, animal, and plant life or health, or are related to the conservation of exhaustible natural resources. If those conditions arise, then countries can ban the products, so long as they do not just protect their own industries and do not unfairly discriminate. The organization did establish a Committee on Trade and Environment (CTE) under pressure from the EU and the United States. Meeting in closed sessions, its main concerns since 2000 have been twofold: to clarify the status of the relationship between the multilateral environmental agreements and the WTO; and to address the legality of eco-labeling, bringing the practice under WTO rules. Its Dispute Settlement Body has made several decisions in favor of environmental interests as well as opening itself up to public participation with "friends of the court" briefs.

Two dispute settlement cases suggest movement toward an environmental opening. In the first case, the WTO trade panel ruled that the United States could not block Venezuelan and Brazilian petroleum imports under the guise of clean-air legislation. That decision and its affirmation by the Appellate Body incited the ire of the environmental community. Yet the body reasoned that the U.S. clean-air law could be upheld, but that the same standard must be applied to both foreign and domestic suppliers. Once the United States administered the environmentally friendly act without bias to domestic or foreign suppliers, then it was acceptable.

In the second case, a WTO trade panel in 1998 initially ruled that the United States had illegally blocked the importation of shrimp from countries not safeguarding sea turtles, which were caught at the same time. The Appellate Body sustained the decision. Similar to the first case, it affirmed that the U.S. law was legitimate and did not contravene WTO restraint of trade principles. The body asserted, however, that the United States had neither followed proper procedures nor entered into meaningful negotiations with the offending governments. In short, the WTO panel opened the door to an environmental justification for banning trade in a product when the purpose is to safeguard an endangered species, assuming that proper procedures are followed (Weinstein and Charnovitz 2001: 151–152).

The WTO is far from a green institution. It still has no organizational commitment to environmental protection, nor has it accepted the precautionary principle as grounds for restricting trade, the major principle that guides EU environmental policy. Unlike the EU, WTO has not mandated environmental labeling that gives full information to consumers. Instead, WTO has given greater weight to scientific proof over the precautionary principle, often solidified in sessions held behind closed doors with little opportunity for public participation. Its legal decisions, while moving in the direction of accepting trade restrictions for the purposes of environmental protection, are very narrowly constructed. Yet, in the view of some, "The WTO is light years ahead of where it was years ago in protecting the environment" (Weinstein and Charnovitz 2001: 151). In the view of many others, it still has a long way to go.

■ Global Governance in Action

Ozone depletion and global warming present unique challenges for global governance. Both problems are difficult to assess from a scientific viewpoint, requiring sophisticated and often controversial procedures. Both problems affect future generations, with the immediate effects indeterminate, making it more difficult to mobilize an affected constituency. Both involve practices and products that are synonymous with modern standards of living. Both involve the necessity of imposing economic costs to protect the environment against unsubstantiated future dangers. Yet while the two issues share similarities, they have been handled in different ways. The case of ozone depletion shows the promise of global governance, while the global warming case illustrates the pitfalls.

■ Ozone Depletion: Anatomy of Success

Ozone depletion was thrust onto the international agenda in 1975, following a report submitted by two American scientists attributing depletion of the ozone layer to use of chlorofluorocarbons (CFCs). A widely used chemical in refrigeration systems, the correlation between use of CFCs and ozone depletion was a contested one for several years among scientists. But in a little less than a decade, following publication of new data confirming a widening ozone hole over Antarctica, most states and scientific experts acknowledged the problem. The United States and European states were both the major producers of CFCs and the major consumers, although usage in the new industrializing countries such as India, China, Brazil, and Mexico, was rising at about 10 percent annually.

The success of the international approach to governance of ozone can be attributed to several factors. Most important may have been the critical role of key nations who provided leadership on the issue, including the United States, Canada, and Norway. The support of those countries rested on a mobilized public that articulated the issue and on supportive NGOs. In particular, the U.S. government became active due to several catalytic events. Multilateral institutions were also critical, particularly UNEP whose executive director Mustafa Tolba played a key role in mobilizing an international constituency and initiating consultations with key governments, private interest groups, and international organizations. He argued for flexibility, applied pressure, and floated his own proposals as a stimulus to participants (Benedick 1998). Scientists provided convincing data on the extent of the problem and monitoring the problem, giving the process scientific validation. MNCs that produced CFC's, including Dow Chemical and Dupont, found suitable substitutes for most uses. Since only a small percentage of their business depended on this one product, they were able to accept a compromise with little effect on their profitability. The conditions proved ripe for a negotiated approach.

Furthermore, the negotiating process and procedures were handled expeditiously. The process was subdivided into smaller problems and the treaty was a flexible instrument that could be made stricter should the scientific evidence warrant change, or loosened had the ozone hole problem been shown to be less severe. The parties agreed to compliance mechanisms that were independent of any formal dispute settlement procedures. An Ad Hoc Working Group of Legal Experts on Non-Compliance was established. It was to offer conciliatory measures to encourage full compliance, in a cooperative, nonjudicial, and nonconfrontational way. Finally, the secretariat of UNEP is at the center of the implementation process.

Beginning in 1985, states promised to cooperate on research and data acquisition in the first phase agreed to in the 1985 Vienna Convention. The second phase was the 1987 Montreal Protocol on Substances that Deplete the Ozone Layer and the 1990 London agreement that further tightened states' agreement to phase out ozone-depleting chemicals. While the negotiations were not easy, at the end of the process, states agreed to permanent, quantitative emission limits on CFCs for all countries, although some international trading in emission entitlements was permitted. The industrialized countries agreed to pay for the incremental costs of compliance for developing countries and the GEF offered financial assistance to transition economies. Hence, the Multilateral Fund for the Implementation of the Montreal Protocol assists the less developed countries in complying with controlling ozone-depleting substances. Over $12 billion in funds have been allocated to 3,300 projects in 121 countries. And noncompliant countries are brought to an implementation committee.

In addition, there is a procedure for states to ask the Ozone Secretariat (after consultation with a technical committee) for relief should specific industries be adversely affected by the chemical restrictions. In 2003, the U.S. Environmental Protection Agency made such a request on behalf of California and Florida tomato and strawberry growers. The growers claim they needed to use methyl bromide, a chemical for which there is no suitable alternative. The request was a controversial one, with environmental groups fearing any dilution of the treaty. The United States already consumes 25 percent of the world's supply. As one U.S. official put it, there is concern that "the isolation of the United States on other international issues, including the Kyoto climate treaty and . . . Iraq could result in the exemption being rejected even if justified" (Revkin 2003: A20).

Although the final verdict on whether ozone depletion has been permanently curbed is still out, preliminary evidence suggests the ozone hole is closing. Global production of CFCs has declined, although production in the developing world has grown slightly. Consumption has declined 75 percent since implementation. While there is a continued demand for products using CFC-like compounds, research for substitutes has been promising. States have instituted measures with the treaty's provisions, but whether this will result in a visible change in the ozone is not yet known (Litfin 1994; Chasek 2001).

▓ *Global Warming: The Pitfalls of Global Governance*

The issue of global climate change or global warming has proven more complicated. There are scientific facts that are indisputable. The preponderance of greenhouse-gas emissions comes from the burning of fossil fuels in the industrializing Northern countries for power generation and from automobile emissions, but deforestation of the tropics is also a cause. Yet the models of climate change are rudimentary. There is dispute about whether global temperatures have actually risen and by how much. While most agree that the globe's temperature appears to be between .3 to .6 degrees centigrade higher than in 1990, scientists disagree about projected increases in the future and what impacts that will have. Global warming may positively affect some, while negatively impacting others. Small island states, coastal regions, and some agricultural crops have the most to lose. There is also disagreement about the appropriate scientific strategies to be taken— voluntary restraints versus authoritative regulations. Adding to the complexity is the fact that burning of fossil fuels for energy is viewed as a necessity, both for industrialized countries to continue high rates of economic growth and for the developing countries to become industrialized. Under these exigencies, negotiating an international agreement on greenhouse-gas emissions has proven to be a highly contested political process (Chasek 2001).

With scientific uncertainty and differing political interests, the negotiations have resulted in a series of confrontations over timetables and targets. A relatively weak UN Framework Convention on Climate Change was signed in 1992 in Rio de Janeiro and became effective in 1994. That document, however, did not include legally binding obligations to reduce carbon dioxide emissions to an agreed level.

The Kyoto Protocol of 1997 amended the 1992 UN convention. It provided for stabilizing concentration of greenhouse gases and delineated international goals for reducing emissions by 2010. Developed countries, including the United States, the European Union, and Japan, were required to reduce their overall greenhouse-gas emissions by at least 5 percent below 1990 levels over the next decade; Japan committed to 6 percent, the United States to 7 percent, and the European Union to 8 percent. In neither the Kyoto Protocol nor the earlier agreement, unlike in the Montreal Protocol, were developing countries included in the emission limitation requirement.

The protocol provides for flexible mechanisms designed to make the emission targets more cost-efficient, although not all the details have been specified. Trading of international emission shares is permitted, allowing countries that achieve deeper reductions to trade those credits. Credits can also be earned from carbon sinks such as forests that absorb the carbon dioxide from the air as they grow and help slow the buildup of gas in the atmosphere. Debate focuses on whether sinks can be used to meet all of the emission reductions or only part. Joint implementation permits countries to participate in projects for emission reductions and allows each to receive part of the credit. Each mechanism represents a highly complex scientific technique designed to reduce emissions, yet each comes with economic costs.

In contrast to the Montreal Protocol where the United States played a leading role in support of the treaty, the United States has raised major objections to the Kyoto Protocol and refused to participate. Whereas in the Montreal Protocol, all countries were given quantitative emission limits, in the Kyoto Protocol, the developing countries are excluded, giving particularly China and India an unfair economic advantage since they would not be restricted in the emission of greenhouse gases. The U.S. position was not shared by the Europeans or the Japanese—both of the latter signed the protocol and have already made significant efforts to reduce emissions. The EU as a whole agreed to cut emissions 8 percent below those of 1990, some states agreeing to cut 21 percent while permitting others to be exempted. The United States wants to be able to use its vast carbon sinks to offset the preponderance of its required emission reductions, and again, the Europeans disagree. Like in the Montreal Protocol, international trading in emission entitlements is permitted. Countries that are subject to emission ceilings can engage in joint implementation and carry out joint projects in countries not subject to ceilings.

Compared to the ozone agreement, regulation of CO_2 emissions to control global warming touches not only more countries directly, but affects a much greater part of the economy. This is particularly true for the United States where the average per capita CO_2 emissions are over two times those of the European countries and over eight times those of countries in Asia and South America. Concern about the economic impact of the emissions reductions and what they meant for the energy-intensive American lifestyle led the U.S. government to delay signing the protocol, then to sign only as President Clinton was leaving office. His successor, President George W. Bush, however, withdrew the signature and has made it clear that the United States will not support the current agreement.

Industry-wide opposition in the United States was very strong from the outset. An industry-supported group, the Global Climate Coalition, with $15 million in campaign contributions from the oil industry alone during the 1996 elections, opposed all mandatory limitations on greenhouse-gas emissions and has sponsored public relations campaigns, lobbying, and supporting political candidates favorable to their position. This group has emphasized the scientific uncertainties and the high economic costs of compliance. It portrays the treaty as the product of antibusiness environmental extremists. The coalition has been extremely successful in influencing the United States, but much less successful in influencing other states or international groups (Levy and Egan 2000). While industry offered key support to the Montreal Protocol, its concerted opposition to the Kyoto Protocol has had a determining effect on the U.S governmental position. Yet some splits in the oil industry position are evident: BP and Shell have begun to accept the validity of global warming and favor action, while Exxon remains opposed.

The agreement has two triggers for ratification. The first required ratification by fifty-five countries, a requirement that was easily met. The second requires ratifications by developed countries representing 55 percent of that group's 1990 carbon dioxide emissions. Japan, the EU, Canada, and several smaller industrialized countries have ratified. Before the agreement becomes operational, however, Russia (with 17 percent of emissions) must join, since the United States and Australia have each said they will not join.

Meanwhile, U.S. emissions have continued to increase. In 2000, they were 13 percent higher than in 1990. Although the United States is not party to the treaty, the Chicago Climate Exchange opened in 2003 with a market-based system of emission trading. U.S. companies are participating in the climate exchange in anticipation of eventual mandatory requirements.

Governance by entities outside of the state is apt to be most contested when major economic interests are at stake and when the interests of the most powerful state are threatened. When economic interests are less critical or can be the subject of bargaining and when interests of those other than the hegemon are jeopardized, then there may be more space for negotiation. That is one of the critical lessons learned from the ozone and global greening comparison.

■ Regional Environmental Governance

Understanding global environmental governance requires looking beyond global issues and responses. Regional actions represent another stratum of multilevel environmental governance. The EU, NAFTA, ASEAN, and regional environmental agreements have each responded to the environmental agenda, although with differing results.

■ *European Union*

Among the regions, the European Union has the strongest and most innovative environmental policies, as well as serving as spokesperson for the environmental movement worldwide. But it did not start out that way. There was no mention of the environment in the original EC Rome Treaty. It was not until the Single European Act of 1987 called for accelerated integration of a single economic market that the environment was mentioned for the first time. Balanced growth meant integrating environmental policies. Ten years later, in the Treaty of Amsterdam, signatories agreed that "environmental protection requirements must be integrated into the definition and implementation of Community policies and activities . . . in particular with a view to promoting sustainable development." The rationale for these measures is an economic one. Harmonizing environmental standards within the EU levels the economic playing field (Axelrod and Vig 1999). EU environmental principles were based on the precautionary principle, on the principles that preventive action should be taken and that the polluter should pay. Unlike the WTO, the EU has set environmental standards at all stages of the process, from production (emission standards) to distribution (eco-labeling) and consumption.

The EU has approved over two hundred pieces of environmental regulation, covering such issues as air, water, soil, and waste disposal. For example, in the area of air pollution, the EU has adopted increasingly strict directives on air pollution by vehicles, large plants, and power stations, the phasing out of CFCs, prohibitions against various forms of noise pollution, and an energy tax on carbon dioxide emissions. On water pollution, the EU has common standards for surface and underground water, drinking water, and toxic substances. Environmental impact assessments have been mandatory since 1985 for all public and private projects above a certain size, and consultation with the public is required.

Most of the legislation was passed in the 1970s and 1980s. Since then, the pace of community environmental legislation has slowed. First, there has been a movement toward passage of directives over regulations. Most environmental legislation has come in the form of directives; that is, the EU sets out the framework directive with comprehensive long-term objectives, but it is left to the member states to decide the specific methods to be employed and to pass the appropriate legislation. For example, the EU passed the Integrated Pollution Prevention and Control Directive in 1996, a directive aimed at instituting permit requirements for large industrial users to take specific measures to minimize air, water, and land pollution. States themselves have discretion for establishing specific standards in keeping with technical requirements and local environmental circumstances. Similarly, in 1996, the EU passed the Ambient Air Quality and Auto Emissions Standards. While the directive does not establish specific standards for all parameters, some are established for thirteen of the major pollutants, tightening standards for sulfur dioxide, nitrogen dioxide, and lead, among others. This approach to governance gives space for local and national variation, but establishes overall community standards that help to level the economic playing field. The EU's work is facilitated by the fact that most member states have very effective environmental agencies.

Two major innovations occurred during the 1990s. In 1992, the EU Council initiated rules for granting EU eco-labels for environmentally friendly products, enabling the consumer to choose those types of goods. Labeling of products from production to consumption phases is a prominent EU approach. And in 1994, the European Environment Agency was established to collect data and provide information for new environmental legislation. The LIFE (Financial Instrument for the Environment) fund is designed to support states' compliance with environmental guidelines by funding projects that enable a state to comply with environmental regulations.

As environmentally sensitive and technically advanced as the EU is in terms of environmental issues, political differences and implementation problems are still prevalent. Denmark, the Netherlands, Germany, Austria, Finland, and Sweden are very strong supporters of environmental protection. Having adopted higher national standards, these countries have pushed for stronger community-wide regulations. The relatively less developed states such as Greece, Portugal, and Spain have more lax standards and have been laggards in meeting the framework directives.

Yet the EU's approach—and the probable explanation for its success— is to combine both management and enforcement strategies in order to achieve a binding common policy. The EU takes a problem-solving approach, aiding governments to meet environmental guidelines. Funds from LIFE might jump-start a project. States may be given extra time to comply, in order to improve domestic government capacity; national administrators from one jurisdiction may be sent to another to aid their government officials. The commission may interpret guidelines when uncertainty exists. The commission monitors implementation and issues summary reports on violations, although it may not make on-site inspections nor may it investigate direct violations. Annual violations of specific laws range between two hundred and three hundred cases and sanctions may be imposed. Most revealing, it is estimated that about 95 percent of EU environmental laws have also been implemented as national laws (Commission of the European Communities 1998). "This twinning of cooperative and coercive instruments in a 'management-enforcement ladder' makes the EU exceedingly effective in combating detected violations, thereby reducing noncompliance to a temporal phenomenon" (Talberg 2002: 610). The European Court of Justice is also not afraid to act and has made some unfriendly decisions. In April 1998, for example, the ECJ rejected the standing of Greenpeace and local NGOs to sue the European Commission. This may have a chilling effect on environmental activism (Stevis and Mumme 2000). Yet, more often, the court has upheld EU law.

Despite the relative success of the EU environmental approach, environmental NGOs have not always found it easy to gain access into EU governance. They have responded by forming EU-wide umbrella organizations and establishing offices in Brussels. But while their domestic counterparts have exercised considerable power at the national level, the EU-wide groups lack economic resources compared to their rivals, are heterogeneous, and have been less able to mobilize mass constituencies.

With the 2004 EU expansion, the environmental agenda will become contested once again, as these new members are at a lower level of economic development and have only weak environmental regulations. Many of the 80,000 EU rules they must implement deal with the environment. The multilevel governance approach should be able to accommodate national variation in the transition period. Yet within the core EU states, it is clear that there has been a profound transformation. As the mayor of one Ruhr town put it, "Twenty years ago, this city didn't have anybody who dealt with environmental issues. Today, we have a whole department and they get involved in everything—construction, industrial development, noise abatement. . . . But what has changed even more intensively is the attitudes of the people. They want something done for environmental protection, and they know environmental protection doesn't stop at the border" (quoted in Andrews 2001: A3).

■ *North American Free Trade Agreement*

The North American Free Trade Agreement signed in 1995 approached environmental protection from two different angles. First, NAFTA addressed sanitary and phytosanitary measures (animal and plant health). Each country is entitled to establish its own level of protection in these areas and prohibit the importation of products that do not meet these sanitary or health standards. Second, NAFTA developed an explicit linkage between trade and the environment. The debate over inclusion of this linkage pitted trade economists against environmentalists. The former argued that if Mexican prosperity resulted from the trade agreement, then environmental regulations would follow. There was little need to directly incorporate environmental provisions. Environmentalists, on the other hand, using sustainable development language, argued for enforcement of environmental laws and regulations (Fox 1995).

In the final agreement, provisions to both promote sustainable development as well as strengthen and enforce environmental laws and regulations were included. Each party is able to maintain its own level of environmental protection and ban imports produced in violation of those standards. The conditions for such a ban were carefully specified: there could be no discrimination between domestic and foreign suppliers, nor could such bans create unnecessary obstacles to trade. Only legitimate objectives could be served by the environmental restrictions. Environmental measures could not be "applied in an arbitrary or unjustifiable manner" or "constitute a disguised restriction on international trade or investment." When disputes arise over the application of the standard, the burden is to prove that it is contrary to NAFTA. Expert environmental advice is sought in such cases.

Although NAFTA is the first international trade agreement to incorporate strong environmental actions and provide for NGO consultations, multinational corporations are also guaranteed clear and transparent rules to protect investor rights. They have the right to sue host governments under NAFTA's Chapter 11. The World Bank's International Centre for Settlement of Investment Disputes handles these claims. Two cases illustrate the complexity, uniqueness, and shortcomings of Chapter 11.

Ethyl Corporation, a U.S. company, brought suit against Canada. Canada had banned MMT, an Ethyl product added at the refinery to enhance octane in unleaded gasoline. Canada justified the ban based on environmental criteria, claiming that the product was a harmful air pollutant and caused air pollution control devices in cars to malfunction. Ethyl claimed Canada's action was a violation of national treatment and violated protection given to foreign investors under Chapter 11. It sought $251 million in damages. The case became embroiled in jurisdictional and administrative procedural issues. Ethyl was finally awarded $13 million, though in most experts' opinion, the whole case could have been avoided had procedures been followed (Swan 2000).

A second case involved Methanex Corporation, a Canadian corporation, in a suit against the United States for a California decision to ban its additive MTBE from gasoline. The additive was used to reduce auto air pollution, but California argued that it was contaminating drinking water supplies. Methanex argued that the ban was not based on scientific evidence and that water pollution issues could be solved by fixing leaking underground storage tanks at gas stations. The NAFTA Panel ruled in August 2001 against Methanex. It left the case unsettled, however, suggesting Methanex would have to prove that California intentionally banned MTBE to hurt foreign producers. That proof was not given (Strohm 2001).

Chapter 11 is controversial for several reasons. First, the arbitration itself is conducted in secret. The decisions have been ambiguous, weighed down in jurisdictional and procedural issues, with no method for clarification. Second, Chapter 11 decisions have tended to support the interests of the MNCs against state environmental regulation, much to the chagrin and anger of some states and the NGO community. Third, the United States and Canada, both of which had favored the article for their multinational corporations, have been surprised that it has been used against their state interests. Fourth, it is still unclear how the decisions can be enforced.

While to a few observers, NAFTA represents the greenest-ever trade agreement, the verdict is still out. MNCs and companies seem to be winning many disputes, but the increasing number of such cases and the publicity suggest that change may be occurring. NAFTA expanded the environmental agenda by agreeing to the North American Agreement on Environmental Cooperation. Unlike the EU approach, the agreement does not call for common standards, but encourages compliance with domestic law, facilitates capacity building in member states, and promotes cooperation. Thus, it is a more consultative approach, consistent with NAFTA (Stevis and Mumme 2000).

ASEAN

Not all of the regions have successfully dealt with specific environmental governance issues. ASEAN provides an example of a regional organization whose agenda has broadened to include environmental issues and who has increasingly incorporated NGOs into its activity. Yet when confronted with an environmental crisis, its members were unable to act multilaterally.

The haze problem in Southeast Asia has been a persistent one since the mid-1980s (Cotton 1999). Caused by poor forestry and land practices in Indonesia, it is estimated that over 15 percent of the land has been burned. This includes land cleared for new settlers from the island of Java to outlying islands where they have encountered opposition from indigenous peoples. The damage from the haze is estimated to have caused $4.5 billion in detrimental health effects and stoppages in aviation in the region. The problem worsened in 1987, again in 1994, and was its most extreme in 1997–1998. The haze in the air could also not hide the disturbances on the ground. Excessive grazing, overuse of chemical fertilizers, and urban pollution are making the region one of the most environmentally damaged.

ASEAN countries began cooperating on environmental policy in 1977; by 1989, annual meetings of governmental environmental specialists were being held; and in 1994, NGOs and indigenous peoples were given a role in multilateral consultations. Yet environmental cooperation was never high on the agenda. The rhetoric found in the ASEAN Strategic Plan of Action on the Environment of the 1990s was not followed by actions. Nothing different occurred during the haze crisis. Domestic private enterprise concerns prevailed and the Asian financial crisis intervened. Neither was the Indonesia government interested in responding. Its environmental minister had insufficient powers. Local governments were under a political patronage system linked to the then ruling Suharto family and had strong economic ties to the private enterprises engaged in the destructive practices. When actions were taken, the concern was that environmental protection could hurt economic competitiveness.

The haze crisis stimulated the activity, however, of both local and international NGOs. Two Indonesian-based umbrella NGOs—the Indonesian Network for Forest Conservation and the Indonesian Environmental Network—challenged government policy by publicizing abuses and instituting legal action against the government. They enlisted the support of international NGOs like the World Wide Fund for Nature, which was already involved in Indonesia's national parks and biodiversity initiatives. Their activities became even more visible with the decision of the Centre for Remote Imaging, Sensing and Process at National University of Singapore to publish satellite imagery of the extent of the haze problem on the Internet. These activities were direct departures from the ASEAN policy of not intervening in the internal affairs of states. NGOs have taken center stage, proposing consultation procedures that involve NGOs and local stakeholders.

Elliott (2003) offers two explanations for ASEAN's failure to develop appropriate responses, normative and material. Normatively, ASEAN members do not see themselves as a region sharing an ecological identity. A common identity is also compromised by the regional commitment to liberal economic development, by the ASEAN Way and the slow process of consensus politics, and by the principle of noninterference in domestic affairs. Materially, states in the region lack the capacity for monitoring and implementation and are hindered by poor coordination between jurisdictions (both interstate and intrastate). Although NGOs have been revitalized, no environmental NGOs are accredited to ASEAN.

■ Regional Environmental Agreements

Some environmental agreements are focused on a specific issue in a specific region. In many parts of the world, states have grappled with problems of river basin development and environmental issues, including the Nile River affecting Egypt, Ethiopia, and Sudan; the Jordan River shared by Israel, Jordan, Lebanon, and Syria; the Indus River shared by Afghanistan, India, and Pakistan; and the Colorado River and Rio Grande shared between the United States and Mexico. Many of these groups of countries have signed agreements for the allocation of available water supplies and for protecting water quality, but some have left out key participants; others have refused to follow through with treaty obligations; and still others have not yet begun to address the extant environmental dimension.

One of the most persistent of these river basin issues is the Danube River basin. The issues are multiple: polluting agents like phosphates, pesticides, sodium hydroxide, along with fragments of munitions, asbestos, and other chemicals entering the Danube and its feeder rivers, the Sava and Drava Rivers. The presence of some of these agents accelerated with the war in the Balkan region. The subsequent decline of the fishing industry as a result of these pollutants is another problem. While several regional treaties have tried to address the issues in an integrated way, most have been negotiated around one issue.

The Danube River has been dammed at several locations for hydroelectric power. Among the most internationally contentious dams is the Gabcikovo-Nagymaros hydroelectric project. The project, originally begun in 1977 under a treaty signed by Czechoslovakia and Hungary, incorporated the Szigetkoz ecosystem, home to four hundred unique species of fauna and flora. In the 1980s, opposition by NGOs mounted. In 1992, Slovakia, following the dissolution of Czechoslovakia, blocked the Danube and diverted the river into a canal, creating both an open sewer with untreated wastewater from Bratislava and polluting water tables in the Szigetkoz. In 1993, the issue went before the International Court of Justice, the first time that a lawsuit in that venue would consider the interests of governments. Hungary argued that the treaty was no longer valid; Slovakia contended that as a state successor to Czechoslovakia the treaty was valid and that upriver nations had the right to reroute border rivers. The broader environmental community advocated preserving the Szigetkoz ecosystem, as represented in position papers from an international coalition of NGOs (Greenpeace, Sierra Club) (Bekker 1998).

The ICJ judgment (Case Concerning the Gabcikovo-Nagymaros Project) came down in 1997. The court held that both Hungary and Slovakia had breached their obligations under the original treaty. Hungary's unilateral suspension and abandonment of the project was unlawful, as was Slovakia's unilateral diversion of the Danube. The court concluded that the treaty created an integrated joint project, a joint investment program, and a legal regime designed to increase hydroelectric power, improve navigation, and insure flood control. It recognized that negotiations on these issues needed to continue using current environmental standards to protect water quality and nature. Although the case is not primarily an environmental case, it did offer recommendations on the way that new environmental standards could be reinterpreted during negotiations (ICJ Case 1997).

The International Court of Justice has not been a major governance institution on environmental issues. In another case (ICJ 1993, Case Concerning Certain Phosphate Lands in Nauru [Nauru v. Australia]), Australia agreed to settle out of court, which meant restoring the environment of Nauru. Although specific international arbitration or international court cases will not be the primary platform for environmental issues in this millennium, these bodies are becoming more sensitive to specific environmental concerns when state interests conflict.

Regimes and institutions at the global, regional, and local level all contribute to environmental governance. They provide the principles and rules that have become embedded in the organizations. These are used to establish the agenda and contribute to more-comprehensive policies. They help to develop state and international capacities Thus, it is these institutions that determine whether national policy responses are forthcoming (Keohane, Haas, and Levy 1993). Global and regional governance will not overshadow state actions, but in the new millennium, state actions take place in a much more dense network of governance institutions.

■ The Challenges of Implementation, Compliance, and Effectiveness

A lively debate among academics and policymakers found in the pages of the journals *Global Environmental Politics, Environment,* and *Global Governance* explores whether environmental governance institutions need substantial restructuring. On one side are those who argue for greater centralization of environmental institutions through a world or global environmental organization since UNEP has a weak mandate, insufficient powers, and inadequate resources to address problems, and other arrangements are decentralized and only address certain issues. They believe problems in global environmental governance such as lack of resources and poor coordination can be resolved by creating a new architecture. On the other side are those who suggest that restructuring or creating a new architecture will divert attention from the major institutional and policy issues such as confusion over the norm of sustainable development and the challenge of integrating nonstate actors and civil society into the governance process. As Najam (2003: 373) asserts, "It is not only that new organizational maneuvering is likely to be insufficient to revive the spirit of the Rio compact or to integrate with civil society networks; it is also that any new organizational arrangement is likely to remain as stymied as the current arrangement until these other issues of global environmental governance are tackled first."

The only suitable approach to environmental governance is multilevel. There will continue to be various pieces—global, regional, national and local, public and private. Given the variety of issues to be addressed and varying levels of national interests at stake, these pieces are apt to remain just that—pieces of multilevel governance.

Still, there are critical questions to be addressed. Do the various pieces actually contribute to solving specific problems? That question can only be answered sequentially by examining implementation, compliance, and effectiveness separately. Have the parties (or states) taken measures in their own domestic jurisdiction to give effect to the international accords (implementation)? Have the parties not only established a framework, but also have they adhered to the provisions of the accord? Have they complied by following through with the steps necessary to implement the international accord (compliance)? These questions require state actions. One study of fourteen cases finds that most states do comply with their binding international environmental commitments, although they are very conservative in making those commitments in the first place (Victor, Raustiala, and Skolnikoff 1998). For many states, especially developing countries, failure to implement and comply is a failure of state capacity. Thus, enhancing state capacities is a crucial requirement for environmental implementation and compliance.

How effective are environmental agreements (Jacobson and Weiss 1995)? Although compliance may be high, that does not tell us much about effectiveness—whether the environmental problem is managed or made less severe. That assessment requires yet another level of analysis. Young (1999: 277) in his study of three environmental regimes poses the question and answer a bit differently: "Do international regimes or, more broadly, institutional arrangements in international society matter in that their operation accounts for a significant proportion of the variance in collective outcomes?" Our research has convinced us that the answer to this question is a clear-cut "yes." Future research will provide further answers to these questions.

■ Note

1. Portions of this chapter are drawn from Karen A. Mingst and Margaret P. Karns. (2000) *The United Nations in the Post–Cold War Era,* 2nd ed. Boulder: Westview Press. Reprinted with permission of Westview Press.

■ Suggested Further Reading

Benedick, Richard Elliot. (1998) *Ozone Diplomacy. New Directions in Safeguarding the Planet.* Enlarged ed. Cambridge, MA: Harvard University Press.

Elliott, Lorraine. (2003) *The Global Politics of the Environment.* 2nd ed. London: Macmillan.

Homer-Dixon, Thomas F. (1999) *Environment, Scarcity, and Violence.* Princeton: Princeton University Press.

Lipschutz, Ronnie D. (2004) *Global Environmental Politics: Power, Perspectives, and Practice.* Washington, DC: CQ Press.

Weiss, Edith Brown, and Harold K. Jacobson. (1998) *Engaging Countries. Strengthening Compliance with International Environmental Accords.* Cambridge: MIT Press.

Young, Oran R., ed. (1999) *The Effectiveness of International Environmental Regimes. Causal Connections and Behavioral Mechanisms.* Cambridge: MIT Press.

■ Internet Resources

Commission on Sustainable Development: www.un.org/esa/sustdev/csd.htm
Convention on Biological Diversity: www.biodiv.org
Convention on International Trade in Endangered Species: www.cites.org
Forest Stewardship Council: www.fscoax.org
Friends of the Earth International (Netherlands): www.foei.org
Global Environmental Facility: www.gefweb.org
International Court of Justice: www.icj-cij.org
International Tropical Timber Organization: www.itto.or.jp
Montreal Protocol: www.unep.org/ozone/montreal.html
NAFTA: www.sice.oas.org/trade/nafta/naftatce.asp
The Nature Conservancy: www.nature.org
Rainforest Action Network: www.ran.org
TRAFFIC: www.traffic.org
UN Environment Programme: www.unep.org
UN Framework Convention on Climate Change; Kyoto Protocol: www.unfccc.int
UN Johannesburg Summit 2002: www.johannesburgsummit.org
U.S. affiliate World Wildlife Fund: www.worldwildlife.org
World Wide Fund for Nature: www.panda.org

PART 4

The Dilemmas
of Global Governance

12

Dilemmas of Global Governance in the Twenty-First Century

In the preceding chapters, we have explored a variety of old and new issues and pieces of governance within four traditional issue categories: peace and security, economic development and well-being, human rights, and environmental protection. What makes global governance distinctive, however, from traditional international organization approaches is the way in which issues often defy neat categorization and, hence, require innovative governance approaches. In this concluding chapter, we explore two more recent, crosscutting issues—AIDS and the Internet—to illustrate how the issues, actors, and approaches differ. We then return to the broad challenges of global governance introduced in Chapter 1, namely, legitimacy, accountability, and effectiveness.

■ New Issues, Diverse Approaches

▦ HIV/AIDS: A New Threat to Human Security

Public health and disease are hardly new issues, but globalization has had a dramatic effect on the transmission, incidence, and vulnerability of individuals and communities to disease through migration, air transport, trade, and troop movements. Intensified human mobility poses major problems for containing outbreaks of cholera, influenza, HIV/AIDS, tuberculosis, West Nile Virus, SARS, and other diseases that can be carried in a matter of hours from one part of the globe to another, long before symptoms may appear. The greatest challenge for global governance, however, is the HIV/AIDS epidemic. Not just a health or humanitarian problem, it threatens economic and social development in the world's poorest regions and is a major threat to human security.

In the twenty years since HIV/AIDS was first recognized, more than 22 million people have died, 5 million in 2002 alone, and over 42 million individuals are currently living with the disease. By far the worst affected region is Africa where 70 percent of the adults and 80 percent of the children currently affected live and where the rate of infection is still rising rapidly. In four southern African countries, national adult prevalence exceeds 30 percent; in Botswana, for example, it has reached 38.8 percent. More than half of those infected are women and the number of AIDS orphans in Africa is estimated at over 13 million. Africa's tragedy is exacting a terrible human cost, but has thus far not significantly affected other parts of the world because of the continent's marginal status in global economics and politics. That will change in the years ahead. Infection rates are rising rapidly in many Asian countries, especially India and China, in Russia and other successor states of the Soviet Union. One analyst has predicted that "the coming Eurasian pandemic threatens to derail the economic prospects of billions and alter the global military balance" (Eberstadt 2002: 22). At current rates, more than 100 million people worldwide are projected to be infected by 2005. Only a few countries such as Thailand, Uganda, Senegal, and Brazil have succeeded in slowing or reversing the rate of infection.

Since 2000, concern about HIV/AIDS has reached the highest levels of most governments and international organizations. Speaking at a special session of the UN Security Council held in January 2000, World Bank President James Wolfensohn stated, "Many of us used to think of AIDS as a health issue. We were wrong . . . nothing we have seen is a greater challenge to the peace and stability of African societies than the epidemic of AIDS." Prior to a special session of the UN General Assembly in June 2001, the International Crisis Group's report "HIV/AIDS as a Security Issue" noted, "Where it reaches epidemic proportions, HIV/AIDS can be so pervasive that it destroys the very fibre of what constitutes a nation: individuals, families and communities; economic and political institutions; military and police forces. It is likely then to have broader security consequences."

What makes HIV/AIDS such a formidable challenge to global governance? First, there is no cure. Second, the disease is highly mutable and some of the mutations are resistant to drugs used to treat the disease. "No state is an island when it comes to AIDS, and there are no national firewalls" (Booker and Minter 2002: 77). Third, it is disproportionately affecting those in the primary productive years of fifteen to forty-five, including teachers, workers, parents, civil servants, managers, healthcare workers, and soldiers. It thus has enormous economic and social impact, including impoverishment, weakening of family bonds, disruption of education, and, in some situations, famine. The World Bank now considers AIDS the single greatest threat to economic development in sub-Saharan Africa (P. W. Singer 2002: 149). Fourth, studies show unique links between AIDS and the military with higher infection rates among soldiers than in the regular civilian population all around the world. Estimates of the infection rates in African armies run as high as 50 percent in the Congo and 80 percent in Zimbabwe (UNAIDS 1998). Not only will AIDS "hollow-out" the mili-

Figure 12.1   Adults and Children Living with HIV/AIDS (estimated as of end of 2002)

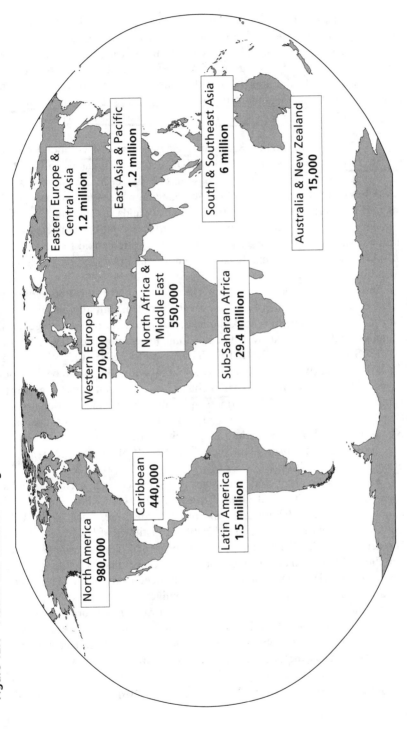

Eastern Europe &
Central Asia
1.2 million

East Asia & Pacific
1.2 million

South & Southeast Asia
6 million

Australia & New Zealand
15,000

Western Europe
570,000

North Africa &
Middle East
550,000

Sub-Saharan Africa
29.4 million

North America
980,000

Caribbean
440,000

Latin America
1.5 million

Total: 42 million

Source: UNAIDS and WHO, 2002

502   The Dilemmas of Global Governance

taries of many countries, but it also challenges the future of peacekeeping. Deploying military forces from around the world in conflict zones puts peacekeepers not yet infected at risk where the sex industry is one of the few businesses still operating and risks the spread of disease from those already infected to the areas where they are deployed and to their home states. In short, "peacekeeping forces are . . . among the primary mechanisms of spreading the disease at a mass level to new areas" (P. W. Singer 2002: 152).

As discussed in Chapter 8, failed states pose one of the major security threats in the world today. The HIV/AIDS epidemic threatens to increase the threat of state failure. While disease has always been a weapon of war, AIDS has created complex new links to genocide where rape has been used for political purposes in Bosnia, Congo, and Rwanda. In addition, children orphaned by AIDS create new pools of disaffected and disconnected children at risk of being exploited as child soldiers, which could fuel conflicts. In short, the governance challenges are enormous in addressing the spread and effects of AIDS.

International responses to the AIDS epidemic have mirrored evolving awareness of the multifaceted nature of the problem. Initially, in 1986, the World Health Organization took the lead, but gradually other UN agencies became involved so that by 1996, the Joint Programme on HIV/AIDS or UNAIDS was created by UNICEF, UNDP, UNFPA, UNESCO, WHO, and the World Bank (with UNDCP and ILO subsequently joining) to be the lead agency for global action. UNAIDS illustrates the importance of network approaches in its mission of partnerships with UN agencies, national governments, corporations, religious organizations, grassroots groups, and NGOs to "catalyze, strengthen and orchestrate the unique expertise, resources, and networks of influence that each of these organizations offers" (www.unaids.org).

The many actors include the pharmaceutical companies, foundations such as Wellcome Trust of Great Britain and the Gates Foundation, and major public health laboratories and research institutes such as the U.S. Centers for Disease Control and the National Institutes of Health. States are key actors as well. The earliest WHO actions, for example, were to stimulate the creation of national AIDS programs. Governments' willingness to acknowledge HIV/AIDS as a major issue has been a critical first step. Their commitment to enlarging public health budgets is a second one. Where leaders have made AIDS a top priority, as in Brazil under former President Fernando Henrique Cardoso and in Uganda under President Yoweri Museveni, they have mobilized national resources and reduced infection rates. Key NGOs include Doctors Without Borders and CARE, both of which report and treat victims, distribute AIDS-related drugs, and train healthcare workers, as well as GNP+ (Global Network of People Living with HIV/AIDS) and International Association of Physicians in AIDS Care. Local NGOs are also critical helpers, along with individual AIDS activists such as China's Dr. Wan Yanhai and Zackie Achmat, chair of South Africa's Treatment Action Campaign.

The UN has convened global AIDS conferences every two years to raise awareness and mobilize responses. Three UN Security Council sessions in 2000 and 2001, along with reports by the International Crisis Group and others, increased global awareness of AIDS as a security threat. The 2001 Special Session of the General Assembly resulted in unanimous adoption of a Declaration of Commitment and a Global HIV/AIDS and Health Fund with a target of $7–10 billion in annual expenditure by 2005 in the most affected poor- and middle-income countries.

Preventive measures have involved relatively little controversy, except where countries denied that an AIDS problem exists. The same is not true for treatment measures, which have raised economic and ethical questions. In the mid-1990s, the development of antiretroviral, multidrug "cocktails" led many in developed countries, especially in the United States, to think that AIDS was no longer a threat. Until 2000, few questioned why the drugs were rarely available to millions of infected persons in Africa and Asia. Then AIDS activists and health professionals began to raise the difficult economic and ethical issues these drug therapies pose. In the United States, the drug cocktails cost $10,000 to $15,000 per person a year. The high price reflects research costs, high profit rates, and patents that give producers a monopoly on pricing. Drug companies and governments, particularly the U.S. government, have blocked the use of generic drugs (see Figure 12.2).

Beginning in 1998, however, Brazilian drug companies began to produce and distribute generic antiretroviral drugs for about $3,000 a year. In February 2001, the Indian drug company Cipla announced that it would sell generic cocktails to the African anti-AIDS campaign of Doctors Without Borders for $350 per patient per year (McNeil 2001a: A1). From the standpoint of the WTO-based international trade regime and the major pharmaceutical companies, protection of intellectual property rights and patents was crucial. Yet many developing countries, including India, were exempt from WTO rules on intellectual property under agreements that granted them lengthened timetables to comply with patent rules. From the point of view of caregivers, AIDS activists, and ethicists, making generic and low-cost drug therapies available as widely as possible would meet urgent public health needs and eliminate discrimination between treatment for the rich and poor. From a practical standpoint, in countries such as Brazil that have made generic antiretroviral drugs available for free to everyone who needs them, the programs have paid for themselves by cutting the death rate, new hospitalizations, transmission rates, and improving overall public health (Tina Rosenberg 2001: 28–29).

Figure 12.2 Twenty Years of HIV/AIDS

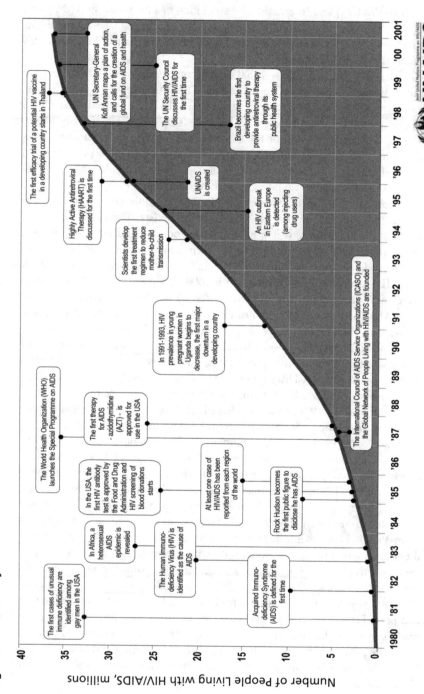

May 2001

The pharmaceutical companies face a dilemma: they want to be seen as helping to fight AIDS, yet they feel compelled to protect their patents and high prices to provide revenues for research and development of new drugs. They adopted two strategies: one of creating partnerships with individual countries for exclusive distribution at reduced prices and another involving lawsuits against states that wanted to make cheaper substitutes. The first approach, adopted by five companies working with WHO, reached far fewer people than anticipated and prices were still too high for most Africans. The second approach gained public attention in South Africa, where a 1997 law allowed the government discretion to limit patent rights in manufacturing and importing medicines, and became a public relations nightmare for the companies, fueling an international campaign against their stand on generic AIDS drugs.

NGOs such as Oxfam, ACT UP, and Africa Action created the transnational Treatment Action Campaign to exert pressure on the pharmaceutical companies to reduce prices of antiretrovirals for developing countries and for African states in particular. Student activist groups became involved. ACT UP (AIDS Coalition to Unleash Power) New York and Health Group Coalition mounted public campaigns and organized demonstrations with banners proclaiming "Essential Drugs for All Nations." The notion of profiteering pharmaceutical companies and the immorality of the high cost of drugs resonated with many people. As UN Secretary-General Kofi Annan (2001a: 5) told African leaders in the African Summit on HIV/AIDS and Other Related Infectious Diseases in April 2001, "There has been a worldwide revolt of public opinion. People no longer accept that the sick and dying, simply because they are poor, should be denied drugs which have transformed the lives of others who are better off."

Quiet diplomacy, mounting global activist pressures, and increasing competition from generics have forced the pharmaceutical manufacturers to alter pricing strategies in poor countries and stop their efforts to thwart the sale of generics. The drugs have gotten a lot cheaper—in some cases, as cheap as a dollar a day. Illustrative of the variety of partnerships that AIDS-related initiatives require, the Global Alliance for Vaccines and Immunization (GAVI) that is supporting efforts to develop an AIDS vaccine, receives funding from the Bill and Melinda Gates Children's Vaccine Program, the Rockefeller Foundation, the International Federation of Pharmaceutical Manufacturers Associations, as well as UNICEF, WHO, and the World Bank. The UN's Annan undertook to spur other partnerships. In April 2001, by meeting with the senior executives of the six largest pharmaceutical companies, plus Dr. Gro Harlem Brundtland (director-general of WHO) and Peter Piot (executive director of UNAIDS), Annan was able to gain agreement "to combine incentives for research with access to medication for the poor . . . "(quoted in UN Chronicle 2001 ["Combine

Incentives"]: 7). In addition, the Global Business Coalition on HIV/AIDS, which is composed of about 100 member firms, was given the mandate by Annan to convince MNCs operating in Africa to participate in AIDS prevention by offering counseling, condoms, and treatment, including the antiretroviral cocktail, for affected employees. Coca-Cola and Daimler Chrysler, for example, are participating, along with Anglo American, AngloGold, and De Beers mining companies in southern Africa (McNeil 2001b; Schoofs 2001). Richard Holbrooke, president of the coalition on HIV/AIDS, has said, "If Anglo American and De Beers take leadership, it will pressure other companies to take similar steps. . . . Up to now, business has been doing less than 10 per cent of what they should have done" (Lamont 2002).

The governance challenges posed by the AIDS epidemic remain enormous, requiring strong partnerships and large commitments of public and private funds for treatment, prevention, and research. Thanks to globalization, "Although new technologies and breakthroughs may allow us to cure once devastating diseases, new contagions and long-dormant ones will pose new threats" (Gomez-Dantes 2001: 417), making health issues major governance challenges in the twenty-first century. Another set of challenges is posed by the growth of the Internet.

■ The Internet: Empowerment and Domain of Private Governance

The exponential growth of the Internet in the 1990s is the latest development in the communications revolution that over the last thirty years has transformed international politics and business, made the ideas of an international community, global village, or global civil society feasible, and created new concepts of space and reality—cyberspace and virtual reality. As the historian William McNeill (1990: 168) notes, this revolution is "the central disturber of our age." The Internet has played a major role in globalization and the diffusion of ideas, culture, and technology; it has provided the electronic infrastructure for linking NGOs and advocacy groups in different parts of the world. That same infrastructure has created global financial markets and facilitated rapid transfers of funds in the drug trade, international crime syndicates, and terrorist networks, and it has created new forms of commerce. The Internet has also raised a host of new governance issues, and the need for new sets of rules and new types of authorities to enforce those rules. What makes it a striking case study in global governance is the predominance of private authorities and modes of governance and the limited roles of national governments and IGOs. By giving rise to new and unique patterns of international cooperation, one analyst argues, the Internet has transformed the global communications order (Drake 2001: 26).

The Internet began as a communications network under the auspices of the U.S. Department of Defense with four host computers in 1969. The goal was to facilitate secure exchanges of military and scientific information among a small group of university researchers, government scientists, and computer engineers. In 1990, it was opened to commercial users and service providers and, as a result, gradually privatized and transformed, especially by its mass popularization. When the U.S. National Science Foundation turned over the core infrastructure to higher speed, privately owned "backbones" in 1995, the Internet included 44,000 networks covering 160 countries and 26,000 commercial entities (Spar 1999: 34). In 2003, it was estimated that there were over 70 million network nodes or hosts and over 200 million users of this network of networks.

There are four sets of governance issues relating to the Internet. First, who establishes and manages the infrastructure, including the physical connections and interoperability of different systems so that information can move across national borders and be usable? Also, who sets the technical standards for the Internet so that various networks are able to communicate? A related issue involves the allocation and management of such scarce resources as domain names and Internet Protocol (IP) numbers. Second, what rules govern Internet usage, including the economic issues of service provision, compensation, and means of commercial exchanges across borders? The late 1990s witnessed a technological race to develop the means of electronic exchanges and the corresponding need to set rules. Third, who sets the rules governing the substantive content of communications and commerce on the Internet, including intellectual property rights for software, publishing, music, and financial services? Finally, who provides security and enforcement for financial and commercial transactions and for the integrity of information and messages being exchanged?

These questions of how to govern the Internet are particularly challenging because the rules governing the "real" world and global communications prior to the explosion of Internet usage are outmoded or irrelevant in the "virtual" world. The concepts of private ownership of ideas, intellectual property rights, contract law, local enforcement, and government regulation are all directly challenged by the Net. The highly decentralized though interconnected nature of the Internet makes any universal regulatory framework counterproductive and marginalizes the role of governments. Not surprisingly, then, it is generating conflicts of interest between private business, governments, and traditional Net users. Many governments have an interest in controlling the substantive content of Internet communications, blocking the flow of pornography, for example, or information deemed damaging to the state. Traditional users have a strong interest in wanting to keep cyberspace as open as possible. Private businesses need rules of property, currency, and enforcement to advance their commercial interests.

During the Internet's early years of operation, the rules were really the product of a small epistemic community of technologically sophisticated users. There were clear norms of behavior, a working language, and codes of conduct. At one level, this persists in the rules governing domain names and IP numbers. With respect to technical standards, a suborganization of the Internet Society (ISOC), the Internet Engineering Task Force, is responsible for the Transmission Control Protocol/Internet Protocol. This subgroup is open to all users. Decisions are based on discussions in several forums and on a system of qualified majority voting. New technical standards are tested for a period of time to ensure effectiveness and then relayed to the public via e-mail lists. Thus, this aspect of Internet governance takes place outside established governmental or international standardization bodies and, ultimately, through adoption globally by millions of users.

With respect to governance of domain names, the key actor since 1998 has been the Internet Corporation for Assigned Names and Numbers (ICANN), a California-based, not-for-profit group that manages the Internet's address system under contract with the U.S. Department of Commerce. ICANN allocates domain names, establishes rules for reallocation of names, and sets regulations for selling domain names. It represents a new "hybrid form of international organization" (Drake 2001: 42). Despite its apparently clear procedures, ICANN's decisions in reality "often have been taken in a loose and nontransparent manner" (Drake 2001: 42). This raises the issue, Stellin notes (2002: B4), of "how a small private-sector organization based in the United States could address policy questions related to the Internet's address system in a way that took into account often divergent public, private, and global interests."

There are few rules yet on substantive content because the technology of the "virtual" undermines authorities and rules developed for the "real" world. For example, the U.S. government tried unsuccessfully both through congressional legislation and through the World Intellectual Property Organization (WIPO) to establish copyright protection for material on the Internet in the same way printed matter is covered. Thus, a definition of "fair use" for material on the Internet remains in dispute between those wanting free flow of information and those wanting restrictions either for property rights or content. In the absence of public governance, then, private firms such as IBM, Infringatek, the Business Software Alliance, and the Copyright Clearance Center have experimented with technologies and licensing rules to control dissemination of on-line property.

Rules of usage and substantive content also apply to commercial transactions via the Internet. There are numerous possibilities for fraud and corruption as well as threats to the security of funds and identity. As the Internet has grown, so, too, have these problems. As one observer wrote,

"Enforcing a local smut ordinance on the unbounded Internet . . . is akin to ordering dandelions to quit floating their spore. How do you control a decentralized network of more than 50,000 interconnected networks? How do you censor information when it flows down infinite paths among 30 million computers?" (Quitter 1995). Internet security and enforcement issues have larger ramifications for global governance, however, with respect to illegal transfers of funds by drug traffickers, crime syndicates, and terrorist networks. Electronic fund transfers have made possible global financial markets and a global banking network and, in turn, been a boon to money laundering. This international public policy problem amounts by some estimates to between $300 billion and $1 trillion annually. Much of the effort to regulate and control this activity has been concentrated within and among the developed countries, although a number of developing countries, including small island states such as the Bahamas, Cayman Islands, Marshall Islands, and Nauru are major offshore banking centers. The Financial Action Task Force (FATF) recommended in 1996, in a broad effort to address money laundering, that restrictions be placed on the use of new technologies for remote, anonymous financial transactions conducted outside traditional financial institutions. Also, secure Internet connections are being used by the informal network of Financial Intelligence Units (drawn largely from developed-country finance ministries) and the U.S. Treasury to share information (Williams 2001: 124).

Much of the governance challenge of enforcement and security for the Internet is a technological one. Private companies like RSA Data Security, Verisign, and Microsoft have developed firewalls and encryption to protect on-line transmissions from hackers and others. The major international credit card companies, Visa and MasterCard, have joined forces to develop a structure for easy and secure transactions on the Internet under their Secure Electronic Transaction protocol.

Despite the Internet's global reach, these initiatives have come largely from within developed countries. In the short term, Drake (2001: 52) argues, "given the very asymmetric participation in Internet communications and commerce, formal and informal deals struck among groups of like-minded industrialized countries could provide enough international order on issues such as the balance between freedom of expression and pornography, hate speech, cybercrime, privacy protection, encryption, digital signatures and electronic contracting." He adds, however, that "as Internet usage deepens around the world, truly global responses to some of these issues might be needed." Yet as Spar (1999: 47) reminds us, "On the Internet, some degree of anarchy is acceptable, even desirable. In fact, many users came to cyberspace precisely because of its anarchy, its anonymity, its secretiveness, and lack of rules. Yet as the Internet becomes increasingly a mass media, anarchy can no longer suffice." Certainly, the potential criminal uses of the Internet and its value for drug traffickers and terrorist networks create powerful security interests in stronger governance.

Yet the Internet is not just a means of communication. The global technology gap is already widening the global poverty gap. For anyone with access, the Net is a leveler, enabling the free flow of information and the formation of virtual communities, a nascent civil society. Yet those without access are excluded from cyberspace and isolated by the digital divide. That is why a small group within the UN Secretariat is dedicated to getting new countries online, recently helping three countries (Afghanistan, Bhutan, and East Timor) acquire domain names and develop the technical setups in country, including alternative electrical power sources (Spindle 2003). In 2003, the UN used a global summit approach of bringing together all key stakeholders in a broad range of Internet-related issues in the World Summit on the Information Society. Another is planned in 2005. So, Internet governance entails not only establishing rules and modalities for security and enforcement, but also ensuring that other values of participation and equity are met as well.

We have focused here on the challenges of governing the Internet itself. The Net, however, is having significant effects on existing pieces of global governance more broadly, by empowering individuals and groups, thereby creating virtual communities and networks with global reach; by undermining the importance of traditional sources of state power such as military capability and governments themselves; and by increasing the need for diverse coalitions of major powers, middle powers, small states, NGOs, IGOs, private corporations, and key individuals. As Nye (2002: 25) notes, "The information revolution, technological change and globalisation will not replace the nation-state but will continue to complicate the actors and issues in world politics. . . . [Even] the largest power since Rome cannot achieve its objectives unilaterally in a global information age."

■ What Makes Global Governance Different?

Three distinct characteristics emerge from the discussion of HIV/AIDS, governing the Internet, and the variety of issues covered in previous chapters that illustrate how what we call global governance today is different from what we used to refer to simply as international organizations or international regimes. First, the policy problems cut across several distinct issue areas and, hence, cannot be neatly categorized as economic, political, or social problems to be dealt with by the appropriate international or national institutions. Second, states and intergovernmental institutions such as IGOs are no longer the only important actors in dealing with these international problems. Civil society in the form of NGOs, transnational advocacy networks, and social movements demand inclusion in governance efforts across a range of different issues. Expert groups and epistemic communities are essential for the knowledge and expertise they can provide on environmental and other issues. Private corporations have become increasingly important partners and suppliers of resources that governments are less able or willing to provide. As the discussion of HIV/AIDS shows, partnerships, coalitions, and networks are an integral feature of newer governance efforts. These require new types of leadership skills; they may also generate tensions among various actors; and they put an added premium on coordination. Third, there is no single model of global governance to fit all issues and policy problems, just as there is no single structure of global governance but a multitude of pieces that do not fit together in a complete puzzle. Such is the nature of global governance.

No Neat Categories, No Easy Fit

Contemporary governance issues often do not fit traditional boxes. AIDS may be a health issue at its core, but it has economic, political, and even security dimensions. Trafficking in women and children, like the older problems of piracy and slavery, may be economically motivated, but it violates core human rights norms. The Internet impacts how the economy operates, how politics are conducted, and creates new communities—local, national, international, real, and virtual. The issue of child soldiers is an issue of children's human rights, but the problem is closely linked to the dynamics of failed states and ethnic conflicts, deepening poverty, and even the AIDS epidemic. Global warming and rain-forest biodiversity are fundamentally environmental issues, yet any action or inaction has critical economic and political ramifications.

The old strategy of creating a new IGO to address new problems, just as governments created new national bureaucracies, is no longer sufficient. No single intergovernmental organization could deal with the various dimensions of many contemporary issues. The UN system had to create a joint program, UNAIDS, to coordinate its own efforts, but those alone are insufficient. A variety of other partners from civil society, the corporate sector, regional IGOs, governments both national and local, and the health research community are essential to addressing the prevention, treatment, and research requirements of the battle against AIDS. So, too, did various actors join with WHO in addressing the SARS epidemic in 2003. As Kalb (2003: 36) describes, [SARS research] "has moved at a lightning pace, fueled by dramatic advances in technology, unprecedented scientific cooperation and a pressing sense of international crisis."

Proliferating Actors: The Need for Networks and Partnerships

The proliferation of new actors has generated a good deal of controversy over whether states are being replaced as the primary actors in global politics; indeed, liberal and realist theorists differ in the importance each accord to nonstate actors. A major question for global governance efforts is how to provide for representation or input from civil society in policymaking institutions, a question we shall return to shortly. Essential to the roles and influence of nonstate actors are the networks, coalitions, partnerships, joint ventures, and other relationships they form with each other, with states and governmental agencies, and with IGOs. Among the characteristics of global governance are the blurred boundaries between public and private actors and between domestic and international actors and domains as well. The AIDS case study and the plethora of partnerships emerging from the Millennium Development Goals illustrate well the approach. Given the dynamic nature of many contemporary issues, however, coalitions, partnerships, and networks are likely to be subject to frequent change. They also vary from issue to issue. This is what makes the study of global governance complex and challenging.

Unquestionably, the proliferation of nonstate actors has diminished the power of states to shape international policy outcomes. Unquestionably also, "Sovereignty's status and relevance are contested increasingly within international organizations and forums" (Weiss 2000: 796). Although some states have failed, still, the sovereign, territorially based state remains a cornerstone of the international system and will continue to do so. The puzzle for students of global governance is how much importance to accord to states versus nonstate actors and how much importance to impute to state sovereignty. With respect to threats to peace and security, states have always assumed a prominent position and continue to do so. Yet, even in security issues, the meaning of sovereignty is being challenged. As we noted in Chapter 8, emerging norms of human security and humanitarian intervention, if confirmed, make responsibility to protect people a new aspect of sovereignty. Likewise, the concepts of sustainable development and human rights challenge sovereignty and the principle of nonintervention.

Still, major powers like the United States may not be willing to have their power and sovereignty undermined. The exceptionalist and sovereigntist impulses in American foreign policy have led the United States to refuse to participate in multilateral action on global warming, banning landmines and nuclear testing, and creating an international criminal court. The interesting story for global governance is that on the one hand, coalitions of states and NGOs proceeded without the United States, and on the other, there is an as-yet-unanswered question about how the U.S. refusal to participate will affect implementation. China has worked hard to keep its human rights record from examination by the UN Commission on Human Rights, as Russia has worked to keep outside groups from interfering with its handling of Chechnya. State power could be seen, however, as just one end of a continuum of states' roles in global governance. At the opposite end of that continuum would be failed states and states lacking capacity to implement international trade or environmental rules, for example. In between lie failures of states' political will to provide resources for collective action and, also, their commitment to action (Chayes and Chayes 1995). As Nye warns with respect to the United States, "Even the unilateralists and sovereigntists will find that international institutions are necessary because many of the issues raised by globalization are inherently multilateral" (Nye 2002).

■ Organized Chaos Among the Pieces

The pieces of global governance do not fit together in one coherent puzzle. They are complex and dynamic, varying from issue to issue. Core pieces of the puzzle depend on the problem area, although as noted earlier, many contemporary issues do not fit neatly within traditional issue areas. In peace and security, states are strong and IGOs prominent only to a limited degree. NGOs and other nonstate actors have had relatively limited impact at the margins in providing humanitarian relief, lobbying for arms control and disarmament measures, or mediating disputes. With respect to war crimes and crimes against humanity, there are well-established international law and norms, yet the last decade witnessed horrific episodes of genocide and ethnic cleansing and slow processes for prosecuting the war criminals of Rwanda and Bosnia. For economic development, there are multiple and strong development institutions at both the international and regional level that provide the major pieces, but those pieces depend on state cooperation and increasingly delegate delivery of development aid to NGOs. In international finance, financial markets and networks make private actors central to governance, limiting the authority and control of states and even the IMF. NGO coalitions have shown their potential power in the success of Jubilee 2000/Plus with respect to restructuring debts of the poorest states, and in efforts to block the Multilateral Agreement on Investment in 1997 and to disrupt the Seattle WTO meeting in 1999.

These pieces, however, are neater than many parts of global governance. If Rosenau (1995: 13) is right that global governance is "systems of rule at all levels of human activity—from the family to the international organization—in which the pursuit of goals through exercise of control has transnational repercussions," then we need to be prepared for much more complex, multilayered, and crosscutting processes and interactions. As we have noted at different points throughout the book, some of this is attributable to globalization and its profound consequences for the authority, policymaking, and policy-implementing capacity of states, as well as for the empowerment of other actors. Some of the messiness is a direct consequence of the proliferation of actors and the absence of models for dealing with new policy issues such as governing the Internet. Transnational and transgovernmental policy and advocacy networks, both institutionalized and ad hoc, intersect each other and also domestic processes, creating interaction effects that alter the ways in which policy is made as well as the outcomes. These characteristics enable new political forces to influence global policymaking and generate combinations of old and new pressures. Neither traditional realist, nor to a large extent, liberal approaches can readily explain these complex political processes of conflict, competition, coalition building, and cooperation.

Much as the Commission on Global Governance (1995: 4) concluded, global governance is a "broad, dynamic, complex process of interactive decisionmaking that is constantly evolving and responding to changing circumstances." Supranational authority is not a reality now, any more than it was in 1945 when the UN was founded (with the exception of the EU). Yet, this fuzzy, messy, dynamic, complex phenomenon faces a number of key challenges—challenges that are endemic to governance in general.

■ Challenges for the Future

We return now to three issues that were briefly discussed in Chapter 1: legitimacy, accountability, and effectiveness. These are central to governance at any level, but for global governance, absent any single structure or set of structures, there can be no single set of prescriptions for enhancing democratic representation of civil society in international institutions and policymaking processes, no single standard for measuring effectiveness, and no single standard for legitimacy or accountability. These challenges arise at two levels: individual actors in global governance need to be legitimate, accountable, and effective, and global governance generally must be legitimate, accountable, and effective, having positive impact on people's lives and meeting standards of equity, fairness, and justice. While there are a number of proposals for reform of particular institutions, many of which were discussed in earlier chapters, there is much less discussion of these challenges for global governance more broadly, with the exception of the economic area where the late 1990s witnessed considerable discussion of reforming the global financial architecture.

▨ *The Challenge of Legitimacy*

To be accepted as legitimate by the international community, various structures and processes of global governance must accommodate the participation of civil society in some fashion, since one of the distinctive characteristics of global governance is the inclusion of both state and civil society participants. The challenge of democratizing global governance structures is not just one of formal procedures or legal safeguards, important as those can be. If it is true, as Dallmayr (2002: 154–155) argues, that "to gain legitimacy, public policies require the endorsement (or at least consultation) of all affected, then global policymaking needs to rely on the broadest possible participation on a global scale." Widening or globalizing political participation, he continues, also contributes to "fostering of a genuine sense of global or cosmopolitan justice. . . . [And] 'democratic process is the best means for changing conditions of injustice and promoting justice.'" Hence, legitimacy depends in large part on the diversity and breadth of support for pieces of global governance.

Participation gives people a sense of ownership and a stake in outcomes of policymaking. An important part of the story of this book is how nongovernmental organizations and other civil society actors have broadened participation in particular institutions. In the World Bank, for example, a majority of projects now involve NGO direct participation. Some security-related NGOs now engage in regular consultations with the UN Security Council. Human rights NGOs provide data about human rights abuses to the UN network that states themselves are reluctant to report. Environmental agreements like CITES employ NGOs as monitors of cross-border traffic in endangered species. Multilayered governance provides multiple venues for participation by transnational actors.

An additional aspect of the legitimacy challenge, however, is that individual actors must be democratized. This is a particular challenge because globalization has undermined some aspects of liberal democracy in states. As Murphy (2001: 350) notes, "In our globalized' world of weakened states, many—perhaps most—substantive collective decisions have been delegated to the market. . . . In a world in which we let the market do much of our collective business, increasingly unequal market power means increasingly less democracy." States that are not currently democratic will face continuing pressure for political change, as will IGOs and NGOs that are perceived to suffer from "democratic deficits." The antiglobalization demonstrators in Seattle, Genoa, Washington, and Cancun signaled their concerns about the impact of globalization and the undemocratic character of the World Bank, IMF, WTO, and G-7/8. NGOs themselves may only represent self-selected elites, as discussed in Chapter 6. Thus, merely giving access to select NGOs may tend to give an ever-larger agenda-setting role to elite groups, because they are the ones that are apt to be transnationally linked.

To be considered legitimate, global governance cannot be considered an American, Western, or a liberal economic project that is only compatible with the power and preferences of the U.S., large Western-based multinational corporations, Northern NGOs, and Western-trained experts. Nor can it be considered an activity that the U.S. can control. International institutions, be they the United Nations, the International Monetary Fund, the Global Environmental Facility, or Human Rights Watch cannot be controlled by the preferences of a dominant state if they are going to remain legitimate in a globalized world. Participation by developing countries cannot be marginalized by de facto decisionmaking in the hands of a small number of developed countries (as with the Quadrilateral Group in the WTO) if legitimacy is to persist, nor can the UN Security Council maintain its legitimacy indefinitely if there is no revision of its membership. As Woods (1999: 43) reminds us, "A symmetry of power must exist within the institution because it is unlikely to endure over time if powerful states or groups of states can simply flout the rules." In addition, global governance must represent wider liberal, social, and political values such as the concepts of human security, human development, poverty alleviation, and sustainable development embody.

The challenge is a difficult one, particularly because any sense of global political identity or international community is embryonic and contested. Some see the international community, for example, as the major developed countries led by the United States that create the rules and institutions. Others see the UN General Assembly as the embodiment of the international community. Still others see it as international opinion generated by media images and global communications, or as a moral concept rooted in the conviction of common humanity, or as a virtual community that is brought to life by policymakers, activists, and the media seeking to pursue the common good ("What is the International Community?": 30–46).

Finally, global governance will not be widely regarded as legitimate unless its pieces combat the gross inequalities of power, wealth, and knowledge of today's world. These inequalities have profound implications for promoting justice in the international community. Democratization requires accountability. Legitimacy and justice also require effectiveness. Let us turn to these other global governance challenges.

▓ The Challenge of Accountability

Who watches the governors? In a perfectly functioning democracy, the people through electoral processes provide a semblance of accountability. But that will never be possible at the international level. Thus, accountability must be built into global governance in different ways. One of those is by enhancing the transparency of decisionmaking within institutions such as the IMF and WTO. States' own accountability and transparency has been significantly enhanced through requirements for reporting the status of human rights or trade law implementation, and on-site weapons inspections, as well as by the vigilance of NGO monitoring. While IGOs must inform members of activities and decisions, as well as the grounds on which decisions are taken, closed IMF or Security Council meetings and consensus decisionmaking often limit accountability because there is no published record of activity and position. P-5, the WTO's Quadrilateral Group, G-7, and other exclusive group consultations leave out large numbers of other interested actors. Unanimous voting, while probably the best way to assure accountability, proved that it was not practical as a decision-making procedure for international collective action in the League of Nations. Yet, as Woods (1999: 45) warns, "Accountability needs to reflect [*sic*] not just in formal representation but equally in decisionmaking procedures and rules and also in the implementation of decisions."

Improving accountability in international actors has been difficult, but steps have been taken in the right direction. The UN itself has developed many forms of budgetary control to improve that institution's accountability to the major donors. The World Bank's Inspection Panel investigates allegations by NGOs, states, and private actors who assert that the bank is not following its own procedures. The Structural Adjustment Participatory Review Initiative involves the NGOs in discussions about appropriate economic adjustment policies, providing a form of accountability to the international financial institutions.

Ensuring NGO accountability is also important since their numbers and reach can be extensive and their organizational structure often obscure. Often it is assumed that NGOs are more accountable to people in general, since they may claim to represent broad constituencies. Yet they rarely, in fact, have internal democratic mechanisms for selection of officers, and many might better be seen as elite groups rather than representative groups. In few cases are there mechanisms to guarantee the transparency of their actions, especially to those most affected by their work or on whose behalf they make claims. One mechanism of NGO accountability is money. Since NGOs depend on private contributions, if they are perceived as not answerable to their donors, contributions will likely diminish and they will be unable to function.

MNCs and international business coalitions are difficult to make accountable. The G-7's Financial Action Task Force and the OECD's regulations on bribery of foreign officials are two effective governmental examples. NGOs like INFACT and Transparency International provide accountability for the private business sector, using publicity and public pressure to ensure accountability for a broader constituency.

Lack of transparency in some situations is an essential ingredient for ensuring that participants in decisionmaking can reach agreements and decisions without the outside political pressures that openness would make impossible. The dual challenge for making global governance accountable is one of balancing the needs for transparency and openness with the need for efficacy.

■ The Challenge of Effectiveness

Good global governance needs to be effective, actually addressing and sometimes resolving global governance problems, including human insecurity and inequality. Programs need to accomplish their objectives; individual actors themselves must be effective; there must be bridges between the mechanisms developed and the operations implemented; specific institutions must be able to enforce the agreed-upon behaviors or even to improve compliance (Coglianese 2000).

There are myriad examples of IGO reforms designed to improve effectiveness of the organizations themselves and the programs they administer. UN reforms have cut the number of employees, streamlined operations, based personnel decisions on merit and performance rather than national origin, and created a Department of Humanitarian Affairs to improve performance. Shifting the World Bank's focus to the world's poorest countries and providing loans on a selective basis to countries within that group that met standards of good governance, for example, is an attempt to sharpen the bank's mission and make it more effective in what it does, instead of trying to do everything. The fact that most development assistance is now delivered by NGOs reflects an assessment that they are more effective in working with grassroots groups and in delivery than IGO staffs or bilateral donors. Getting a summit of heads of state and government to endorse the Millennium Development Goals was an important source of political leverage over member states and UN agencies. Concrete, measurable policy objectives was a second step followed by the creation of global task forces, annual reporting requirements, and a public information campaign to increase pressure on governments and international agencies. As Ruggie warns (2003: 306–307), "The fact that the MDG effort is without precedent, . . . does not, of course, guarantee its success. . . . At the same time, the very existence of the MDGs has shifted the ground somewhat." In striving to make governance efforts effective, the key is what works, what makes a positive difference.

At the heart of the challenge of effectiveness for global governance is the need to increase human security and diminish inequality. As Amartya Sen (2001) describes, "The central issue, directly, or indirectly, is inequality: between peoples as well as between nations. The relevant inequalities include disparities in affluence, but also gross asymmetries in political, social, and economic power. A crucial question concerns the sharing of potential gains from globalization between rich and poor countries, and between different groups within countries." These disparities have critical ramifications, as a UN panel warned several months before the September 11 attacks: "In the global village, someone else's poverty very soon becomes one's own problem: of lack of markets for one's products, illegal immigration, pollution, contagious disease, insecurity, fanaticism, terrorism" (UN 2001a [Report of the High-Level Panel]). Thus, HIV/AIDS, cholera, drug-resistant tuberculosis, and other health problems that disproportionately affect the world's poor today can quickly move to every continent and penetrate the enclaves of the rich. In a global economy driven by information technology, the fact that the richest 20 percent of the world's population account for over 93 percent of the Internet users while the poorest 20 percent account for only 0.2 percent of the users increases the concentration of wealth and resources. Addressing inequality effectively becomes imperative not only for reasons of global security, but also for reasons of equity, fairness, and justice.

Yet, finding the approaches that will make global governance efforts more effective will not be easy. As Weiss (2000: 807) posits, "Globalisation is neither uniform nor homogeneous. . . . Its present manifestation is fundamentally different in scale, intensity and form from what preceded. . . . Students and professors, policy analysts and practitioners should not feel uncomfortable about admitting their uneasiness and ignorance about . . . the best way to address a bewildering array of global problems." In fact, globalization fundamentally affects the nature of collective action at both domestic and international levels. States become less effective as property rights are difficult to maintain and legal rules easily evaded. IGOs cannot regulate the globalized market place, leaving the hegemony of financial markets, businesses as well as criminal groups, untamed. And private regimes are several steps away from providing democratic accountability. This leads Cerny (1995: 620–621) to conclude, "Institutions, of course, overlap and interact in complex ways but no longer sufficiently coincide on a single optimal scale in such a way that they could be efficiently integrated into a multitask hierarchy like the nation-state. Some are essentially private market structures and regimes; some are still public intergovernmental structures, and some are mixed public-private." Since there will be no single model or structure providing equity, justice, and greater participation, accountability and effectiveness will entail a struggle (Dallmayr 2002: 156).

One approach to improving effectiveness is through learning, whether by organizations or individuals, as the constructivists suggest. Lessons learned from one actor may be valuable not only for that same actor, but also utilized by other actors. States have learned from the success of the NGOs in framing issues for public consumption and using the Internet to create networks, mobilize support, create advocacy campaigns, and get issues such as landmines, child soldiers, violence against women, or species loss on the international agenda. States have learned the value of intensive on-site inspections for arms control as well as human rights and leaned on international institutions to undertake such activities.

International development institutions have learned from NGO experiences that reaching out to people in local communities, to those affected, and involving them in the planning and execution of projects will lead to greater project success. Some IGOs have learned that decisions are better if they are taken at the lowest possible level, based on the EU's experience with subsidiarity. A number of UN peacekeeping operations and the UN Department for Peacekeeping Operations benefited from both first- and second-level learning. The chaos and confusion of having many different organizations involved in humanitarian relief operations in Somalia, Bosnia, and Kosovo led the UN both to create a Department of Humanitarian Affairs and to make UNHCR the position of lead agency in humanitarian disasters. Another example of IGO learning, combined with successful outside pressures, resulted in the creation of the World Commission on Dams to review proposed dam projects.

To be viewed as fair and just, global governance needs not only to be effective in addressing problems, but also to reduce inequalities, be responsible to people, protect the innocent, and allow economic and social human needs to be fulfilled, resulting in what one author has called a "Global New Deal" (Felice 2003). The pieces of global governance now in place represent an evolution whose foundations can be traced back over the last two centuries. The challenges of legitimacy, accountability, and effectiveness, with their corollary demands for equality, fairness, and justice, require an ongoing struggle among evolving sets of participants over time.

■ Suggested Further Reading

Cutler, A. Claire, Virginia Haufler, and Tony Porter, eds. (1999) *Private Authority and International Affairs*. Albany: State University of New York Press.

Felice, William F. (2003) *The Global New Deal. Economic and Social Human Rights in World Politics*. Lanham, MD: Rowman and Littlefield.

Hall, Rodney Bruce, and Thomas J. Biersteker, eds. (2002) *The Emergence of Private Authority in Global Governance*. New York: Cambridge University Press.

Singer, Peter. (2002) *One World. The Ethics of Globalization*. New Haven: Yale University Press.

Woods, Ngaire. (1999) "Good Governance in International Organization," *Global Governance* 5:1 (January–March), 39–61.

■ Internet Resources

Global Business Coalition on HIV/AIDS: www.businessfightsaids.org
GNP+: www.gnpplus.net
Health Gap: www.healthgap.org
International Association of Physicians in AIDS Care: www.iapac.org
International Council of AIDS Service Organizations: www.icaso.org
International Crisis Group: www.intl-crisis-group.org
Internet Engineering Task Force: www.ietf.org
Internet Society: www.isoc.org
UNAIDS: www.unaids.org
UNICEF: www.unicef.org
World Summit on Information Society: www.itu.int/wsis/

Acronyms

ACP	African, Caribbean, and Pacific countries (EU Lomé Convention)
ACT UP	AIDS Coalition to Unleash Power
ADB	Asian Development Bank
AfDB	African Development Bank
AFL-CIO	American Federation of Labor/Congress of Industrial Organizations
AFTA	ASEAN Free Trade Area
AI	Amnesty International
AIDS	Acquired Immune Deficiency Syndrome
ALOP	Latin American Association of Popular Organizations
APEC	Asia-Pacific Economic Cooperation
ARF	ASEAN Regional Forum
ASEAN	Association of Southeast Asian Nations
ASEAN-ISIS	ASEAN Institutes for Strategic and International Studies
AU	African Union
BIONET	Biodiversity Action Network
BWC	Biological Weapons Convention
CACM	Central American Common Market
CAP	Common Agricultural Policy (EU)
CARICOM	Caribbean Community
CARIFTA	Caribbean Free Trade Association
CBD	Convention on Biological Diversity
CBW	chemical and biological weapons
CEDAW	Convention on the Elimination of All Forms of Discrimination Against Women
CENTO	Central Treaty Organization
CEPAL	See ECLA
CFCs	chlorofluorocarbons
CFSP	Common Foreign and Security Policy (EU)
CGIAR	Consultative Group on International Agricultural Research
CICC	Coalition for the International Criminal Court

CIS	Commonwealth of Independent States
CITES	Convention on International Trade in Endangered Species of Wild Fauna and Flora
CMI	Comité Maritime International
CoCom	Coordinating Committee for Multilateral Export Controls
COMECON	Council of Mutual Economic Assistance
COMESA	Common Market for Eastern and Southern Africa
CONGO	Conference of Non-Governmental Organisations in Consultative Status with the UN Economic and Social Council (ECOSOC)
COPA	Committee of Professional Agricultural Organisations
CPC	Committee for Programme and Coordination (UN)
CRC	Convention on the Rights of the Child
CSCAP	Council for Security Cooperation in the Asia Pacific
CSCE	Conference on Security and Cooperation in Europe (now OSCE)
CSD	Commission on Sustainable Development
CSW	Commission on the Status of Women
CTBT	Comprehensive Test Ban Treaty
CTC	Counter Terrorism Committee
CTE	Committee on Trade and Environment (WTO)
CWC	Chemical Weapons Convention
DAC	Development Assistance Committee (OECD)
DAWN	Development Alternatives with Women for a New Era
DPKO	Department of Peacekeeping Operations (UN)
DSB	Dispute Settlement Body (WTO)
DSU	Dispute Settlement Unit (WTO)
EBRD	European Bank for Reconstruction and Development
EC	European Community (also known as European Economic Community, or EEC)
ECHR	European Court of Human Rights
ECJ	European Court of Justice (also known as the Court of Justice of the European Communities and the Court of Justice of the European Union)
ECLA	Economic Commission for Latin America (CEPAL in Spanish)
ECOMOG	ECOWAS Cease-fire Monitoring Group
ECOSOC	United Nations Economic and Social Council
ECOWAS	Economic Community of West African States
ECSC	European Coal and Steel Community
ECU	European Currency Unit
EEB	European Environmental Bureau
EEC	See EC

EFTA	European Free Trade Association
EMU	European Monetary Union
EP	European Parliament
EPC	European Political Cooperation
EPTA	Expanded Programme of Technical Assistance
ESC	Economic Security Council
ETUC	European Trade Union Confederation
EU	European Union (previously referred to as EC or EEC)
Euratom	European Atomic Energy Community
FAO	Food and Agriculture Organization
FATF	Financial Action Task Force
FEANTSA	European Federation of National Organisations Working with the Homeless
FSC	Forest Stewardship Council
FTAA	Free Trade Area of the Americas
G-7	Group of Seven
G-8	Group of Eight
G-77	Group of 77
GATS	General Agreement on Trade in Services
GATT	General Agreement on Tariffs and Trade
GAVI	Global Alliance for Vaccines and Immunizations
GCC	Gulf Cooperation Council
GEF	Global Environmental Facility
GNP	gross national product
GNP+	Global Network of People Living with HIV/AIDS
GONGO	government-organized nongovernmental group
GSP	Generalized System of Preferences
HDI	Human Development Index
HIPC	Heavily Indebted Poor Countries (Initiative)
HIV	Human Immunodeficiency Syndrome
HRW	Human Rights Watch
IAEA	International Atomic Energy Agency
IATA	International Association of Transport Airlines
IBRD	International Bank for Reconstruction and Development (also known as World Bank)
ICANN	Internet Corporation for Assigned Names and Numbers
ICAO	International Civil Aviation Organization
ICBL	International Campaign to Ban Landmines
ICC	International Criminal Court
ICISS	International Commission on Intervention and State Sovereignty
ICJ	International Court of Justice
ICPD	International Conference on Population and Development

ICRC	International Committee of the Red Cross
ICSID	International Centre for the Settlement of Investment Disputes
ICTR	International Criminal Tribunal for Rwanda
ICTFY	International Criminal Tribunal for the Former Yugoslavia
ICUN	International Union for the Conservation of Nature
IDA	International Development Association
IDB	Inter-American Development Bank
IFAD	International Fund for Agricultural Development
IFC	International Finance Corporation
IFOR	Implementation Force (NATO Force in former Yugoslavia)
IGO	intergovernmental organization
ILO	International Labour Organization
IMF	International Monetary Fund
IMO	International Maritime Organization
INGO	international nongovernmental organization
INSTRAW	International Research and Training Institute for the Advancement of Women
Interpol	International Criminal Police Organization
IO	international organization
IPKF	Indian Peacekeeping Force in Sri Lanka
IPPNW	International Physicians for the Prevention of Nuclear War
IRA	Irish Republican Army
ISAF	International Security Assistance Force
ISOC	Internet Society
ITO	International Trade Organization (stillborn precursor of GATT/WTO)
ITTO	International Tropical Timber Organization
ITU	International Telecommunications Union (formerly International Telegraph Union)
IUCN	International Union for the Conservation of Nature and Natural Resources (now known as "IUCN-The World Conservation Union")
LAFTA	Latin American Free Trade Association
LDC	less developed country (also referred to as the South)
LIFE	Financial Instrument for the Environment (EU)
LOS	Law of the Sea
MAI	Multilateral Agreement on Investment
MDGs	Millennium Development Goals
MEP	Members of European Parliament
Mercosur	Common Market of the South; Southern Cone Common Market; Mercado Commun del Sur; Southern Common Market
MFN	most-favored-nation principle

MFO	Multinational Force and Observers Group in the Sinai
MIGA	Multilateral Investment Guarantee Agency
MNC	multinational corporation
MNF	Multinational Force
NAFTA	North American Free Trade Agreement
NAM	Non-Aligned Movement
NATO	North Atlantic Treaty Organization
NEPAD	New Partnership for Africa's Development
NGO	nongovernmental organization
NIC	newly industrializing country
NIEO	New International Economic Order
NPT	Nuclear Nonproliferation Treaty
OAS	Organization of American States
OAU	Organization of African Unity
OCHA	Office for Coordination of Humanitarian Affairs (UN)
ODA	official development assistance
OECD	Organisation for Economic Co-operation and Development
OEEC	Organization for European Economic Cooperation
OIC	Organization of the Islamic Conference
OIHP	Office of International d'Hygiène Publique
ONUC	United Nations Operation in the Congo
ONUCA	United Nations Observer Group in Central America
ONUSAL	United Nations Observer Mission in El Salvador
ONUVEN	UN Civilian Observer Mission in Central America
OPCW	Organization for the Prohibition of Chemical Weapons
OPEC	Organization of Petroleum Exporting Countries
OSCE	Organization for Security and Cooperation in Europe (formerly CSCE)
P-5	Permanent Members of the UN Security Council
PAFTAD	Pacific Trade and Development Conference
PCIJ	Permanent Court of International Justice
PCR	Program to Combat Racism (World Council of Churches)
PD	Prisoner's Dilemma
PDD	Presidential Decision Directive
PECC	Pacific Economic Cooperation Council
PFLP	Popular Front for the Liberation of Palestine
PFP	Partnership for Peace
PLO	Palestine Liberation Organization
PRC	People's Republic of China
PTBT	Partial Test Ban Treaty
QMV	Qualified Majority Voting
ROC	Republic of China
RPF	Rwandan Patriotic Front
RUF	Revolutionary United Front (Sierra Leone)

SACEUR	Supreme Allied Commander Europe
SADC	Southern African Development Community
SARS	Severe Acute Respiratory Syndrome
SDR	Special Drawing Rights (IMF)
SEA	Single European Act
SEATO	Southeast Asian Treaty Organization
SELA	Latin American Economic System
SFOR	Stabilization Force (NATO)
SHAPE	Supreme Headquarters Allied Powers Europe
SIPRI	Stockholm International Peace Research Institute
SWAPO	South West Africa People's Organization
TI	Transparency International
TNC	transnational corporation
TPRM	Trade Policy Review Mechanism (WTO)
TRAFFIC	Trade Records Analysis of Flora and Fauna in Commerce
TRIPS	Trade-Related Aspects of Intellectual Property Rights
UIA	Union of International Associations
UK	United Kingdom
UN	United Nations
UNAIDS	United Nations Joint Programme on HIV/AIDS
UNAMIC	United Nations Advance Mission in Cambodia
UNAMIR	United Nations Assistance Mission in Rwanda
UNAVEM I, II	United Nations Angola Verification Mission
UNCED	United Nations Conference on the Environment and Development
UNCHE	United Nations Conference on the Human Environment (also, Stockholm Conference)
UNCLOS	United Nations Conference on the Law of the Sea
UNCTAD	United Nations Conference on Trade and Development
UNDCP	United Nations Drug Control Programme
UNDOF	United Nations Disengagement Observer Force
UNDP	United Nations Development Program
UNDPKO	United Nations Department for Peacekeeping Operations
UNDRO	United Nations Disaster Relief Organization
UNEF I, II	United Nations Emergency Force
UNEP	United Nations Environment Programme
UNESCO	United Nations Educational, Scientific, and Cultural Organization
UNFICYP	United Nations Force in Cyprus
UNFPA	United Nations Fund for Population Activities
UNGOMAP	United Nations Good Offices Missions in Afghanistan and Pakistan
UNHCHR	United Nations High Commissioner for Human Rights
UNHCR	United Nations High Commissioner for Refugees

UNICEF	United Nations Children's Fund
UNIDO	United Nations Industrial Development Organization
UNIFEM	Voluntary Fund for the United Nations Decade for Women
UNIFIL	United Nations Interim Force in Lebanon
UNIIMOG	United Nations Iran-Iraq Military Observer Group
UNIKOM	United Nations Iraq-Kuwait Observer Mission
UNITA	National Union for the Total Independence of Angola
UNITAF	Unified Task Force on Somalia (also known as Operation Restore Hope)
UNMIH	United Nations Mission in Haiti
UNMOVIC	United Nations Monitoring, Verification, and Inspection Commission
UNOSAL	United Nations Observer Mission in El Salvador
UNOSOM I, II	United Nations Operation in Somalia
UNPO	Unrepresented Nations and People's Organization
UNPROFOR	United Nations Protection Force (in the former Yugoslavia)
UNRWA	United Nations Relief and Works Agency for Palestine Refugees in the Near East
UNSCOM	United Nations Special Commission for the Disarmament of Iraq
UNSCR	United Nations Security Council resolution
UNTAC	United Nations Transitional Authority in Cambodia
UNTAG	United Nations Transition Assistance Group
UNTSO	United Nations Truce Supervision Organization
UPU	Universal Postal Union
USAID	United States Agency for International Development
VAT	value added tax
WCC	World Council of Churches
WCD	World Commission on Dams
WCED	World Commission on Environment and Development (also known as the Brundtland Commission)
WEDO	Women's Environmental and Development Organization
WEU	Western European Union
WFP	World Food Programme
WHA	World Health Assembly
WHO	World Health Organization
WID	women in development
WIPO	World Intellectual Property Organization
WMD	weapons of mass destruction
WMO	World Meteorological Organization
WTO	World Trade Organization
WWF	World Wide Fund for Nature (originally the World Wildlife Fund); U.S. affiliate uses the old name (WWF)

References

Aaronson, Susan Ariel. (2001) *Taking Trade to the Streets. The Lost History of Public Efforts to Shape Globalization.* Ann Arbor: The University of Michigan Press.

Abbott, Frederick M. (2000) "NAFTA and the Legalization of World Politics: A Case Study." *International Organization* 54:3 (Summer): 519–547.

Abbott, Kenneth W., and Duncan Snidal. (1998) "Why States Act Through Formal International Organizations." *Journal of Conflict Resolution* 42:1 (February): 3–32.

Abdulla, Abdul Kahleq. (1999) "Gulf Cooperation Council: Major Origin and Process," in *Middle East Dilemma,* edited by Michael Hudson. Washington: Taurus and Co. Accessed at www.ciaonet.org/book/hudson/hudson07.html.

Acharya, Amitav. (1997) "Ideas, Identity, and Institution-building: From the 'ASEAN Way' to the 'Asia-Pacific Way?'" *The Pacific Review* 10:3: 319–346.

———. (2001) *Constructing a Security Community in Southeast Asia: ASEAN and the Problem of Regional Order.* New York: Routledge.

———. (2003) "The Evolution of Norms: The Social Construction of Non-Interference in Asian Regionalism." Paper presented at the Annual Meeting of the International Studies Association, February 25–March 1, Portland, OR.

Adler, Emanuel, and Michael Barnett, eds. (1998) *Security Communities.* Cambridge, UK: Cambridge University Press.

Aggarwal, Vinod K. (1998) "Analyzing Institutional Transformation in the Asia-Pacific." In *Asia-Pacific Crossroads: Regime Creation and the Future of APEC,* edited by Vinod K. Aggarwal and Charles E. Morrison. New York: St. Martin's Press, pp. 23–64.

Agnelli, E., and Craig Murphy. (1995) "Lessons of Somalia for Future Multilateral Humanitarian Assistance Operations." *Global Governance* 1:3 (Sept.–Dec.): 339–366.

Alagappa, Muthiah. (1994) "Regionalism and Security: A Conceptual Investigation." In *Pacific Cooperation: Building Economic and Security Regimes in the Asia-Pacific Region,* edited by Andrew Mack and John Ravenhill. Boulder: Westview Press, pp. 152–179.

Aldrich, George H., and Christine M. Chinkin. (2000) "A Century of Achievement and Unfinished Work." *American Journal of International Law* 94:1 (Jan.): 90–98.

Alger, Chadwick F. (2002) "The Emerging Roles of NGOs in the UN System: From Article 71 to a People's Millennium Assembly." *Global Governance* 8:1 (Jan.–Mar.): 93–117.

Alger, Chadwick F., Gene M. Lyons, and John E. Trent, eds. (1995) *The United*

Nations System: The Policies of Member States. Tokyo: United Nations University Press.

Allin, Dana H. (2002) *Nato's Balkan Interventions.* Adelphi Paper 347. London: Oxford University Press.

Alter, Karen J. (1998) "Who are the 'Masters of the Treaty'?: European Governments and the European Court of Justice." *International Organization* 52:1 (Winter): 121–147.

———. (2000) "The European Union's Legal System and Domestic Policy: Spillover or Backlash?" *International Organization* 54:3 (Summer): 489–518.

Altman, Lawrence K. (2003) "No Cases of SARS Have Been Transmitted on Airlines Since March, W.H.O. Report." *New York Times* (May 20): A6.

Ambrogi, Thomas E. (1999) "Goal for 2000: Unchaining Slaves of National Debt." *National Catholic Reporter* (March 26): 3–6.

Andrews, Edmund L. (2001) "Frustrated Europeans Set to Battle U.S. on Climate." *New York Times* (July 16): A3.

An-Na'im, Abdullahi A. (1999) "The Cultural Mediation of Human Rights: The Ar-Arqum Case in Malaysia." In *The East Asian Challenge for Human Rights*, edited by Joanne R. Bauer and Daniel A. Bell. Cambridge, UK: Cambridge University Press, pp. 147–168.

Annan, Kofi. (1999a) "Two Concepts of Sovereignty." *The Economist* 352 (September 18): 49–50.

———. (1999b). *Annual Report of the Secretary-General to the General Assembly.* SG/SM/7136 GA/9596 (20 September).

———. (2000) "We The Peoples: The Role of the United Nations in the 21st Century." Available at http://www.un.org/millennium/sg/report/full.htm.

———. (2001a) "From the Secretary-General: Facing It Head-On. We Can. We Must." *UN Chronicle* 38:1 (March): 4–6.

———. (2001b) "Interview conducted by *Le Figaro.*" Reported in *Global Development Briefing.* Accessed 8 November at www.developmentex.com/contact_us/briefing.asp.

Antonenko, Oksana. (1999–2000) "Russia, NATO and European Security After Kosovo." *Survival* 41:4 (Winter): 124–144.

Arend, Anthony Clark, and Robert J. Beck. (1993) *International Law and the Use of Force: Beyond the UN Charter Paradigm.* London: Routledge.

Argyris, Chris, and Donald A. Schon. (1978) *Organizational Learning: A Theory of Action Perspective.* Reading, MA: Addison-Wesley.

Armijo, Leslie Elliott. (2001) "The Political Geography of World Financial Reform: Who Wants What and Why?" *Global Governance* 7:4 (Oct.–Dec.): 379–396.

Ascher, William. (1983) "New Development Approaches and the Adaptability of International Agencies: The Case of the World Bank." *International Organization* 37:3 (Summer): 415–439.

Atwood, David C. (1997) "Mobilizing Around the United Nations Special Sessions on Disarmament." In *Transnational Social Movements and Global Politics. Solidarity Beyond the State,* edited by Jackie Smith, Charles Chatfield, and Ron Pagnucco. Syracuse: Syracuse University Press, pp. 141–158.

Axelrod, Regina S., and Norman J. Vig. (1999) "The European Union as an Environmental Governance System." In *The Global Environment. Institutions, Law and Policy,* edited by Norman J. Vig and Regina S. Axelrod. Washington, DC: Congressional Quarterly Press, pp. 72–97.

Axelrod, Robert, and Robert O. Keohane. (1986) "Achieving Cooperation under Anarchy: Strategies and Institutions," in *Cooperation under Anarchy,* edited by Kenneth Oye. Princeton: Princeton University Press, pp. 226–254.

Babarinde, Olufemi. (2003) "The African Union Debuts: Following in the Footsteps of the EU?" *EUSA Review* (Summer): 11–12.

Baehr, Peter R., and Leon Gordenker. (1992) *The United Nations in the 1990s.* New York: St. Martin's Press.

Baldwin, David A. (1993) "Neoliberalism, Neorealism, and World Politics." In *Neorealism and Neoliberalism. The Contemporary Debate,* edited by David A. Baldwin. New York: Columbia University Press, pp. 3–28.

Barnett, Michael. (1995) "Partners in Peace? The UN, Regional Organizations, and Peace-keeping." *Review of International Studies* 21:4: 411–434.

———. (2002) *Eyewitness to a Genocide. The United Nations and Rwanda.* Ithaca, NY: Cornell University Press.

Barnett, Michael, and Martha Finnemore. (1999) "The Politics, Power, and Pathologies of International Organizations." *International Organization* 53:4 (Autumn): 699–732.

Bayefsky, Anne F. (2001) *The UN Human Rights Treaty System: Universality at the Crossroads.* Ardsley, NY: Transnational Publishers. Available on-line at www.yorku.ca/hrights/.

Bayne, Nicholas. (1999) "Continuity and Leadership in an Age of Globalisation." In *The G8's Role in the New Millennium,* edited by Michael R. Hodges, John J. Kirton, and Joseph P. Daniels. Burlington, VT: Ashgate, pp. 21–43.

———. (2000) *Hanging in There: The G7 and G8 Summit in Maturity and Renewal.* Burlington, VT: Ashgate.

Beattie, Alan et al. (2001) "IMF and World Bank to Learn from Africa." *Financial Times* (February 16).

Becker, Elizabeth. (2003) "Delegates of Poorer Nations Walk Out of World Trade Talks." *New York Times* (September 15): A1, A4.

Beigbeder, Yves. (2000) "The United Nations Secretariat: Reform in Progress." In *The United Nations at the Millennium: The Principal Organs,* edited by Paul Taylor and A. J. R. Groom. New York: Continuum, pp. 196–223.

Bekker, Peter H. F. (1998) "Gabcikovo-Nagymaros Project (Hungary/Slovakia) Judgment (ICJ, September 25, 1997)." *American Journal of International Law* 92:2 (April): 273–278. The text of the judgment may be found at the ICJ website.

Benedick, Richard Elliot. (1998) *Ozone Diplomacy. New Directions in Safeguarding the Planet,* enlarged ed. Cambridge, MA: Harvard University Press.

Bergsten, C. Fred. (1997) "APEC in 1997: Prospects and Possible Strategies." In *Whither APEC? The Progress to Date and Agenda for the Future,* edited by C. Fred Bergsten. Washington: Institute for International Economics, pp. 3–17.

Bernier, Ivan, and Martin Roy. (1999) "NAFTA and Mercosur: Two Competing Models?" In *The Americas in Transition: The Contours of Regionalism,* edited by Gordon Mace, Louis Belanger, and contributors. Boulder, CO: Lynne Rienner Publishers, pp. 69–91.

Bertrand, Maurice. (1985) *Some Reflections on Reform of the United Nations.* UN Joint Inspection Unit JIU/REP/85. Geneva: United Nations.

Bilder, Richard B. (1997). "Adjudication: International Arbitral Tribunals and Courts." In *Peacemaking in International Conflict: Methods and Techniques,"* edited by I. William Zartman and J. Lewis Rasmussen. Washington: United States Institute for Peace Press, pp. 155–190.

Bird, Graham, and Joseph P. Joyce. (2001) "Remodeling the Multilateral Financial Institutions." *Global Governance* 7:1 (Jan.–Mar.): 75–93.

Blackhurst, Richard. (1998) "The Capacity of the WTO to Fulfill Its Mandate." In

The WTO as an International Organization, edited by Anne O. Krueger. Chicago: The University of Chicago Press, pp. 31–58.

Bloomfield, Richard T. (1994) "Making the Western Hemisphere Safe for Democracy? The OAS Defense-of-Democracy Regime." In *Collective Responses to Regional Problems: The Case of Latin America and the Caribbean,* edited by Carl Kaysen, Robert A. Pastor, and Laura W. Reed. Cambridge: American Academy of Arts and Sciences, pp. 15–28.

Bodin, Jean. (1967) *Six Books on the Commonwealth.* Oxford, UK: Basil Blackwell.

Bolton, John. (2002) "U.S. Position on the BWC: Combating the Biological Weapons Threat." Remarks in Tokyo, August 26, 2002. Available at www.state.gov/t/us/rm/13090.htm.

Booker, Salih, and William Minter. (2002) "AIDS in Africa: Is the World Concerned Enough?" *Great Decisions 2002.* New York: Foreign Policy Association, pp. 71–80.

Boswell, Terry, and Dimitris Stevis. (1997) "Globalization and International Labor Organizing: A World-System Perspective." *Work and Occupations* 24:3 (August): 288–308.

Boutros-Ghali, Boutros. (1992) *An Agenda for Peace: Preventive Diplomacy, Peacemaking, and Peacekeeping.* New York: United Nations.

———. (1995a). *An Agenda for Peace,* 2nd ed. New York: United Nations.

———. (1995b) *Supplement to An Agenda for Peace.* New York: United Nations.

Bozeman, Adda B. (1971) *The Future of Law in a Multicultural World.* Princeton: Princeton University Press.

Brayton, Steven. (2002) "Outsourcing War: Mercenaries and the Privatization of Peacekeeping." *Journal of International Affairs* 55:2 (Spring): 303–329.

Broad, Robin, ed. (2002) *Global Backlash. Citizen Initiatives for a Just World Economy.* Lanham, MD: Rowman and Littlefield.

Brown, Bartram S. (2002) "Unilateralism, Multilateralism and the International Criminal Court." In *Multilateralism and U.S. Foreign Policy. Ambivalent Engagement,* edited by Stewart Patrick and Shepard Forman. Boulder, CO: Lynne Rienner Publishers, pp. 323–344.

Brown, Michael E., and Richard N. Rosecrance. (1999) *The Costs of Conflict: Prevention and Cure in the Global Arena.* Lanham, MD: Rowman and Littlefield.

Bruno, Kenny, and Joshua Karliner. (2003) *Earthsummit.biz. The Corporate Takeover of Sustainable Development.* Oakland, CA: Food First Books.

Bueno de Mesquita, Bruce. (2000) "Popes, Kings, and Endogenous Institutions: The Concordat of Worms and the Origins of Sovereignty." *International Studies Review* 2:2 (Summer): 93–118.

Buergenthal, Thomas. (1995) *International Human Rights in a Nutshell,* 2nd ed. St. Paul, MN: West Publishing.

Bull, Hedley. (1977) *The Anarchical Society: A Study of Order in World Politics.* New York: Columbia University Press.

Bulwer-Thomas, Victor, ed. (2001) *Regional Integration in Latin America and the Caribbean: The Political Economy of Open Regionalism.* London: Institute of Latin American Studies.

Bunch, Charlotte. (1990) "Women's Rights Are Human Rights: Toward a Re-Vision of Human Rights." *Human Rights Quarterly* 12:4: 486–500.

Burns, Regina. (2002) "Combating Terrorism Continues as Global Priority." *The Interdependent* 28:1 (Spring): 7–8.

Bush, George W. (2003) "We Don't Need Permission." Transcript of presidential news conference, March 7. Accessed at www.newsmax.com/archives/articles/ 2003/3/7/95754.shtml.

Caballero-Anthony, Mely. (1998) "Mechanisms of Dispute Settlement: The ASEAN Experience." *Contemporary Southeast Asia* 20:1 (April): 38–66.

Cammett, Melani. (1999) "Defensive Integration and Late Developers: The Gulf Cooperation Council and the Arab Maghreb Union." *Global Governance* 5:3 (July–Sept.): 379–402.

Caporaso, James A. (1993) "International Relations Theory and Multilateralism: The Search for Foundations." In *Multilateralism Matters: The Theory and Praxis of an Institutional Form*, edited by John Gerard Ruggie. New York: Columbia University Press, pp. 51–90.

Carothers, Thomas. (1999–2000) "Civil Society: Think Again." *Foreign Policy* 117 (Winter): 18–29.

Carson, Rachel. (1962) *Silent Spring*. Cambridge, MA: Houghton Mifflin.

Casaburi, Gabriel, Maria Pia Riggirozzi, Maria Fernanda Tuozzo, and Diana Tussie. (2000) "Multilateral Development Banks, Governments, and Civil Society: Chiaroscuros in a Triangular Relationship." *Global Governance* 4:4 (Oct.–Dec.): 493–517.

Cerny, Philip G. (1995) "Globalization and the Changing Logic of Collective Action." *International Organization* 49:4 (Autumn): 595–626.

———. (1996) "The Paradox of the Competition State: Structure, Agency, and the Logic of Globalization." Paper presented at the Joint Meeting of the Japan Association of International Relations and the International Studies Association. Makuhari, Japan.

Charnovitz, Steve. (1997) "Two Centuries of Participation: NGOs and International Governance." *Michigan Journal of International Law* 18:183 (Winter): 184–286.

Chasek, Pamela S. (2001) *Earth Negotiations. Analyzing Thirty Years of Environmental Diplomacy*. Tokyo: United Nations University Press.

Chayes, Abram, and Antonia Handler Chayes. (1993) "On Compliance." *International Organization* 47:2 (Spring): 175–206.

———. (1995) *The New Sovereignty: Compliance with International Regulatory Agreements*. Cambridge: Harvard University Press.

Chazan, Naomi, Peter Lewis, Robert A. Mortimer, Donald Rothchild, and Stephen John Stedman. (1999) *Politics and Society in Contemporary Africa*, 3rd ed. Boulder, CO: Lynne Rienner Publishers.

Chevrier, Marie Isabelle. (2002) "Chemical and Biological Weapons." In *Arms Control: Cooperative Security in a Changing Environment*, edited by Jeffrey A. Larsen. Boulder, CO: Lynne Rienner Publishers, pp. 143–161.

Chicago Council on Foreign Relations and German Marshall Fund of the United States. (2002) *A World Transformed: Foreign Policy Attitudes of the U.S. Public after September 11*. Available at www.worldviews.org/docs/U.S.9-11v2.pdf.

Churchill, Robert R., and Geir Ulfstein. (2000) "Autonomous Institutional Arrangements in Multilateral Environmental Agreements: A Little-Noticed Phenomenon in International Law." *American Journal of International Law* 94:4 (October): 623–659.

Clark, Ann Marie. (2001) *Diplomacy of Conscience: Amnesty International and Changing Human Rights Norms*. Princeton: Princeton University Press.

Clark, Ann Marie, Elisabeth J. Friedman, and Kathryn Hochstetler. (1998) "The Sovereign Limits of Global Civil Society: A Comparison of NGO Participation in UN World Conferences on the Environment, Human Rights, and Women." *World Politics* 51:1 (October): 1–35.

Clarke, Walter, and Jeffrey Herbst. (1996) "Somalia and the Future of Humanitarian Intervention." *Foreign Affairs* 75:2 (March–April): 70–85.

Claude, Inis L., Jr. (1964) *Swords into Plowshares: The Problems and Progress of International Organization,* 3rd ed. New York: Random House.

———. (1965) *The Changing United Nations.* New York: Random House.

Coate, Roger. (2003) "Introduction to the Millennium Development Goals." In *Global Agenda: Issues Before the 58th General Assembly of the United Nations,* edited by Angela Drakulich. New York: United Nations Association of the United States of America, pp. 164–200.

Coglianese, Gary. (2000) "Globalization and the Design of International Institutions." In *Governance in a Globalizing World,* edited by Joseph S. Nye, Jr. and John D. Donahue. Washington: The Brookings Institution Press, pp. 297–318.

Cohen, Raymond. (1997) *Negotiating Across Cultures: International Communication in an Interdependent World,* rev. ed. Washington, DC: U.S. Institute for Peace Press.

Collins, Carole J. L., Zie Gariyo, and Tony Burdon. (2001) "Jubilee 2000: Citizen Action Across the North-South Divide." In *Global Citizen Action,* edited by Michael Edwards and John Gaventa. Boulder, CO: Lynne Rienner Publishers, pp. 135–148.

Commission of the European Communities. (1998) *Fifteenth Annual Report on Monitoring the Application of Community Law.* COM (1998) 317 Final (Brussels, May 19).

Commission on Global Governance. (1995) *Our Global Neighbourhood: Report of the Commission on Global Governance.* Oxford, UK: Oxford University Press.

Congressional Quarterly. (2000) *The Middle East,* 9th ed. Washington: CQ Press.

Conroy, Michael E. (2002) "Can Advocacy-Led Certification Systems Transform Global Corporate Practices?" In *Global Backlash. Citizen Initiatives for a Just World Economy,* edited by Robin Broad. Lanham, MD: Rowman and Littlefield, pp. 210–215.

Conroy, Richard. (1994) "Peacekeeping and Peace Enforcement in Somalia." Paper presented at the Annual Meeting of the International Studies Association, Washington, DC (March 30–April 2).

Cooper, Andrew F., John English, and Ramesh Thakur, eds. (2002) *Enhancing Global Governance. Towards a New Diplomacy.* Tokyo: United Nations University, pp. 162–186.

Cooper, Richard N. (2002) "Chapter 11 for Countries?" *Foreign Affairs* 81:4 (July/August): 90–103.

Cortright, David, and George A. Lopez. (2000) *The Sanctions Decade: Assessing UN Strategies in the 1990s.* Boulder, CO: Lynne Rienner Publishers.

———. (2002) *Sanctions and the Search for Security.* Boulder, CO: Lynne Rienner Publishers.

Cortright, David, and Ron Pagnucco. (1997) "Limits to Transnationalism: The 1980s Freeze Campaign." In *Transnational Social Movements and Global Politics: Solidarity Beyond the State,* edited by Jackie Smith, Charles Chatfield, and Ron Pagnucco. Syracuse, NY: Syracuse University Press, pp. 159–174.

Cottle, Michelle. (2003) "Bible Brigade." *The Atlantic Monthly* (April 21–28): 16–18.

Cotton, James. (1999) "ASEAN and the Southeast Asian Haze: Challenging the

Prevailing Modes of Regional Engagement." Australia National University, Dept. of International Relations, Working Paper No. 1999/3. (Canberra: June).

Council of Europe Statute. Available at www.coe.fr/index.asp.

Cousteau, Jacques Yves, with James Dugan. (1963) *The Living Sea*. New York: Harper and Row.

Cowhey, Peter F. (1993) "Elect Locally–Order Globally: Domestic Politics and Multilateral Cooperation." In *Multilateralism Matters. The Theory and Praxis of an Institutional Form*, edited by John Gerard Ruggie. New York: Columbia University Press, pp. 157–200.

Cox, Robert W. (1969) "The Executive Head: An Essay on Leadership in International Organization." *International Organization* 23:12 (Spring): 205–230.

———. (1986) "Social Forces, States and World Orders: Beyond International Relations Theory." In *Neorealism and Its Critics*, edited by Robert O. Keohane. New York: Columbia University Press, pp. 204–254.

———. (1992a) "Globalization, Multilateralism and Democracy." The John W. Holmes Memorial Lecture. *ACUNS Reports and Papers* (2).

———. (1992b) "Toward a Post-hegemonic Conceptualization of World Order: Reflections on the Relevancy of Ibn Khaldun." In *Governance Without Government: Order and Change in World Politics*, edited by James N. Rosenau and Ernst-Otto Czempiel. New York: Cambridge University Press, pp. 132–159.

Cox, Robert W., and Harold K. Jacobson. (1973) *The Anatomy of Influence. Decision Making in International Organization*. New Haven: Yale University Press.

Crawford, Neta C. (2002) *Argument and Change in World Politics: Ethics, Decolonization, and Humanitarian Intervention*. New York: Cambridge University Press.

Crocker, Chester A., Fen Osler Hampson, and Pamela Aall, eds. (1996). *Managing Global Chaos: Sources of and Responses in International Conflict*. Washington: United States Institute for Peace Press.

———. (1999) *Herding Cats: Multiparty Mediation in a Complex World*. Washington: U.S. Institute for Peace Press.

———. (2001) *Turbulent Peace: The Challenges of Managing International Conflict*. Washington: United States Institute for Peace Press.

Cronin, Bruce. (2001) "The Paradox of Hegemony: America's Ambiguous Relationship with the United Nations." *European Journal of International Relations* 7: 1: 103–130.

Crossette, Barbara. (1999) "Kofi Annan Unsettles People, as He Believes U.N. Should Do." *New York Times* (December 31): A1, 8.

———. (2000) "A Gigantic Gathering of World Leaders." *New York Times* (September 10): Sect. IV2.

Cupitt, Richard, Rodney Whitlock, and Lynn Williams Whitlock. 1997) "The (Im)mortality of International Governmental Organizations." In *The Politics of Global Governance: International Organizations in an Interdependent World*, edited by Paul F. Diehl. Boulder, CO: Lynne Rienner Publishers, pp. 7–23.

Cutler, A. Claire, Virginia Haufler, and Tony Porter. (1999a) "Private Authority and International Affairs." In *Private Authority and International Affairs*, edited by A. Claire Cutler, Virginia Haufler, and Tony Porter. Albany: State University of New York Press, pp. 3–28.

———. (1999b) "The Contours and Significance of Private Authority in

International Affairs." In *Private Authority and International Affairs*, edited by A. Claire Cutler, Virginia Haufler, and Tony Porter. Albany: State University of New York Press, pp. 333–376.

Daalder, Ivo H., and James M. Goldgeier. (2001) "Putting Europe First." *Survival* 43:1 (Spring): 71–91.

Dallmayr, Fred R. (2002) "Globalization and Inequality: A Plea for Global Justice." *International Studies Review* 4:2 (Summer): 137–156.

Damian, Michel, and Jean-Christophe Graz. (2001) "The World Trade Organization, the Environment, and the Ecological Critique." *International Social Science Journal* 170 (Dec.): 597–610.

Damrosch, Lori Fisler, ed. (1993). *Enforcing Restraint: Collective Intervention in International Conflicts*. New York: Council on Foreign Relations.

Danaher, Kevin, ed. (1994) *50 Years Is Enough: The Case Against the World Bank and the International Monetary Fund*. Boston: South End Press.

Deng, Francis M. et al. (1996) *Sovereignty as Responsibility: Conflict Management in Africa*. Washington, DC: The Brookings Institution.

Deutsch, Karl, Sidney A. Burrell, and Robert A. Kann. (1957) *Political Community and the North Atlantic Area*. Princeton, NJ: Princeton University Press.

Diehl, Paul F. (1993) *International Peacekeeping*. Baltimore: Johns Hopkins University Press.

———. (2000) "Forks in the Road: Theoretical and Policy Concerns for 21st Century Peacekeeping." *Global Society* 14:3: 337–360.

Dinan, Desmond. (1999) *Ever Closer Union: An Introduction to European Integration*, 2nd ed. Boulder, CO: Lynne Rienner Publishers.

Djalal, Hasjim, and Ian Townsend-Gault. (1999) "Managing Potential Conflicts in the South China Sea: Informal Diplomacy for Conflict Prevention." In *Herding Cats: Multiparty Mediation in a Complex World*, edited by Chester A. Crocker, Fen Osler Hampson, and Pamela Aall. Washington: United States Institute for Peace Press, pp. 107–134.

Doe V. UNOCAL. (2002) 963 I Supp. 880 (CD Cal. 1997); 9th Circuit. Nos. 00-56603, 00-57197. September 18.

Donini, Antonio. (1996) "The Bureaucracy and the Free Spirits: Stagnation and Innovation in the Relationship Between the UN and NGOs." In *NGOs, the UN, and Global Governance*, edited by Thomas G. Weiss and Leon Gordenker. Boulder, CO: Lynne Rienner Publishers, pp. 83–102.

Donnelly, Jack. (1998) *International Human Rights*, 2nd ed. Boulder, CO: Westview Press.

Doxey, Margaret. (1992) "The Commonwealth in a Changing World, Behind the Headlines." *Canadian Institute of International Affairs* (Summer): 13.

Doyle, Michael W. (1995) *UN Peacekeeping in Cambodia: UNTAC's Civil Mandate*. Boulder, CO: Lynne Rienner Publishers.

Doyle, Michael W., and Nicholas Sambanis (2000) "International Peacebuilding: A Theoretical and Quantitative Analysis." *American Political Science Review* 94:4 (December): 779–801.

Drake, William J. (2001) "Communications." In *Managing Global Issues. Lessons Learned*, edited by P. J. Simmons and Chantal de Jonge Oudraat. Washington DC: Carnegie Endowment for International Peace, pp. 25–74.

Easterly, William. (2001) *The Elusive Quest for Growth. Economists' Adventures and Misadventures in the Tropics*. Cambridge: MIT Press.

Eberstadt, Nicholas. (2002) "The Future of AIDS." *Foreign Affairs* 81:6 (Nov./Dec.): 22–45.

Economist, The. (1995) "Multinationals and Their Morals." (Dec. 2): 18–19.

————. (2002) "Doubts Inside the Barricades." (Sept. 28): 63–65.

————. (2003) "The WTO under Fire." (Sept. 20): 26–28.

Egeland, Jan. (1999) "The Oslo Accord: Multiparty Facilitation Through the Norwegian Channel." In *Herding Cats: Multiparty Mediation in a Complex World,* edited by Chester A. Crocker, Fen Osler Hampson, and Pamela Aall. Washington: United States Institute for Peace, pp. 529–546.

Elliott, Kimberly Ann. (2000) "Getting Beyond No . . . ! Promoting Worker Rights *and* Trade." In *The WTO After Seattle,* edited by Jeffrey J. Schott. Washington: Institute for International Economics, pp. 187–204.

Elliott, Lorraine. (1998) *The Global Politics of the Environment.* London: Macmillan.

————. (2003) "ASEAN and Environmental Cooperation: Norms, Interests, and Identity." *The Pacific Review* 16:1: 29–52.

Enders, Walter, and Todd Sandler. (2002) "Patterns of Transnational Terrorism, 1970–1999: Alternative Time-Series Estimates." *International Studies Quarterly* 46:2 (June): 145–165.

Enia, Jason S., and Margaret P. Karns. (1999) "Testing the Strength of Regional Cooperation: The Asian Financial Crisis as Threat or Opportunity." Paper presented at the Annual Meeting of the American Political Science Association, September 2–5, Atlanta, GA.

Esty, Daniel C. (2001) "A Term's Limits." *Foreign Policy* 126 (Sept.–Oct.): 74–75.

European Court of Justice. (1964) *Flaminio Costa v. Enel.* Case 6/64 in the Court of Justice of the European Communities, *Reports of Cases Before the Court.*

————. (1979) Cassis de Dijon Case, officially, *Rewe-Zentral AG v. Bundesmonopolverwaltung fur Branntwein.* Case 120/78 in the Court of Justice of the European Communities, *Reports of Cases Before the Court.*

————. (1995) Union Royale belge des sociétés de football association, *ASBL v. Bosman* in the Court of Justice of the European Union, *Reports of Cases Before the Court.*

Ezzell, Carol. (2001) "The Himba and the Dam." *Scientific American* (June): 80–89.

Fawcett, Louise, and Andrew Hurrell, eds. (1995) *Regionalism in World Politics: Regional Organization and International Order.* New York: Oxford University Press.

Felice, William F. (2003) *The Global New Deal. Economic and Social Human Rights in World Politics.* Lanham, MD: Rowman and Littlefield.

Filartiga v. Pena-Irala 630 F.2d 876 (2d Cir. 1980); *Filartiga v. Pena-Irala* 577 Supp. 860 (SD. N.Y. 1984).

Finkelstein, Lawrence S., ed. (1988) *Politics in the United Nations System.* Durham, NC: Duke University Press.

Finlayson, Jock A., and Mark W. Zacher. (1988) *Managing International Markets. Developing Countries and the Commodity Trade Regime.* New York: Columbia University Press.

Finnemore, Martha. (1996) *National Interests in International Society.* Ithaca, NY: Cornell University Press.

Finnemore, Martha, and Kathryn Sikkink. (1998) "International Norm Dynamics and Political Change." *International Organization* 52:4 (Autumn): 295–305.

————. (2001) "Taking Stock: The Constructivist Research Program in International Relations and Comparative Politics." *Annual Review of Political Science* 4: 391–416.

Fisher, Glen. (1980) *International Negotiation. A Cross-Cultural Perspective.* Chicago: Intercultural Press, Inc.

Fleshman, Michael. (2001) "Drug Price Plunge Energizes AIDS Fight." *African Recovery* 15:1–2 (June): 1, 9–10.

Florini, Ann M., ed. (2000) *The Third Force: The Rise of Transnational Civil Society.* Tokyo and Washington: Japan Center for International Exchange and the Carnegie Endowment for International Peace.

Fomerand, Jacques. (1990) "Strengthening the UN's Economic and Social Programs: A Documentary Essay." *ACUNS Report* 2.

———. (1996) "UN Conferences: Media Events or Genuine Diplomacy?" *Global Governance* 2:3 (Sept.–Dec.): 361–375.

———. (2000) "International Approaches to Development: The United Nations and Its Limits." *Seton Hall Journal of Diplomacy and International Relations* I:1 (Summer/Fall): 51–59.

———. (2002) "Recent UN Textbooks: Suggestions from an Old-fashioned Practitioner." *Global Governance* 8:3 (July–Sept.): 383–403.

Foreign Policy. (2002a) "What Is the International Community?" 132 (Sept./Oct.): 30–46.

———. (2002b) "Debate: Happily Ever NAFTA." 132 (Sept./Oct.): 58–65.

———. (2003) "NGO, Heal Thyself!" (Mar./Apr.): 16–17.

Forsythe, David P. (1991) *The Internationalization of Human Rights.* Lexington, MA: D. C. Heath.

———. (2000) *Human Rights in International Relations.* Cambridge, UK: Cambridge University Press.

Fox, Annette Baker. (1995) "Environment and Trade: The NAFTA Case." *Political Science Quarterly* 110:1 (Spring): 49–68.

Fox, Jonathan. (2001) "The World Bank Inspection Panel: Lessons from the First Five Years." *Global Governance* 6:3 (July–Sept.): 279–318.

Fox, Jonathan, and David Brown, eds. (1998) *The Struggle for Accountability: The World Bank, NGOs and Grassroots Movements.* Cambridge, MA: MIT Press.

Franck, Thomas M. (1990) *The Power of Legitimacy Among Nations.* New York: Oxford University Press.

Franck, Thomas M., and Georg Nolte. (1993) "The Good Offices Function of the UN Secretary-General." In *United Nations, Divided World: The UN's Role in International Relations*, 2nd ed., edited by Adam Roberts and Benedict Kingsbury. Oxford, UK: Clarendon Press, pp.143–182.

Friedman, Thomas L. (1999) *The Lexus and the Olive Tree: Understanding Globalization.* New York: Anchor Books.

———. (2001) "95 to 5." *New York Times* (May 29): A19.

Fukuyama, Francis. (1989) "The End of History?" *National Interest* (Summer): 3–35.

Furtado, Celso. (1964) *Development and Underdevelopment: A Structural View of the Problems of Developed and Underdeveloped Countries.* Berkeley and Los Angeles: University of California Press.

Garfield, Richard. (1999) *Morbidity and Mortality Among Iraqi Children from 1990–1998: Assessing the Impact of Economic Sanctions.* Kroc Institute for International Peace Studies, University of Notre Dame, and the Fourth Freedom Forum, Occasional Paper Series 16:OP:3. Available at www.fourthfreedom.org/php/t-si-index.php?hinc+garf.hinc.

Garfinkel, Simon. (2003) "The Net's Faltering Democracy." *Technology Review* (March): 30.

Garnaut, Ross. (1996) *Open Regionalism and Trade Liberalization: An Asia-Pacific Contribution to the World Trade System.* Singapore: Institute of Southeast Asian Studies.

Garrett, Geoffrey, R. Daniel Kelemen, and Heiner Schulz. (1998) "The European Court of Justice, National Governments, and Legal Integration in the European Union." *International Organization* 52:1 (Winter): 149–176.

Gerschutz, Jill M., and Margaret P. Karns. (Forthcoming) "Transforming Visions into Reality: Actors and Strategies in the Implementation of the Convention on the Rights of the Child." In *Children's Human Rights—Progress and Challenges,* edited by Mark Ensalaco and Linda Majka. Lanham, MD: Rowman and Littlefield.

Ghai, Dharam. (2001) "Human Solidarity and World Poverty." *Global Governance* 7:3 (July–Sept.): 237–241.

Gill, Stephen. (1994) "Structural Change and Global Political Economy: Globalizing Elites and the Emerging World Order." In *Global Transformation: Challenges to the State System,* edited by Yoshikazu Sakamoto. Tokyo: United Nations University Press.

Gilpin, Robert. (1975) "Three Models of the Future." *International Organization* 29:1 (Winter): 37–60.

———. (1987) *The Political Economy of International Relations.* Princeton: Princeton University Press.

———. (2001) *Global Political Economy. Understanding the International Economic Order.* Princeton: Princeton University Press.

Ginsberg, Roy H. (1989) *Foreign Policy Actions of the European Community: The Politics of Scale.* Boulder, CO: Lynne Rienner Publishers.

Glendon, Mary Ann. (2001) *A World Made New: Eleanor Roosevelt and the Universal Declaration of Human Rights.* New York: Random House.

Glennon, Michael J. (2003) "Why the Security Council Failed." *Foreign Affairs* 82:3 (May/June): 16–35.

Gomez-Dantes, Octavio. (2001) "Health." In *Managing Global Issues: Lessons Learned,* edited by P. J. Simmons and Chantal de Jonge Oudraat. Washington DC: Carnegie Endowment for International Peace, pp. 392–423.

Gordenker, Leon. (1967) *The UN Secretary-General and the Maintenance of Peace.* New York: Columbia University Press.

———. (2003) "What UN Principles? A U.S. Debate on Iraq." *Global Governance* 9:3 (July–Sept.): 283–289.

Gore, Albert. (1994) "The OAS and the Summit of the Americas." Speech given by the Vice President of the United States. U.S. Department of State Dispatch 5, 48 (November).

Gourevitch, Philip. (1998) *We Wish to Inform You That Tomorrow We Will Be Killed with Our Families. Stories from Rwanda.* New York: Farrar Straus and Giroux.

———. (2003) "The Optimist: Kofi Annan's U.N. has never been more important and more imperiled." *The New Yorker* (March 3): 50–73.

Granatstein, J. L. (1992) "Peacekeeping: Did Canada Make a Difference? And What Difference Did Peacekeeping Make to Canada?" In *Making a Difference? Canada's Foreign Policy in a Changing World Order,* edited by John English and Norman Hillmer. Toronto: Lester Publishing, pp. 222–236.

Gregg, Robert W. (1993) *About Face? The United States and the United Nations.* Boulder, CO: Lynne Rienner Publishers.

Grieco, Joseph M. (1993) "Anarchy and the Limits of Cooperation: A Realist Critique of the Newest Liberal Institutionalism." In *Neorealism and*

Neoliberalism: The Contemporary Debate, edited by David A. Baldwin. New York: Columbia University Press, pp. 116–140.

Groom, A. J. R. (2000) "The Trusteeship Council: A Successful Demise." In *The United Nations at the Millennium: The Principal Organs,* edited by Paul Taylor and A. J. R. Groom. New York: Continuum, pp. 142–176.

Gruber, Lloyd. (2000) *Ruling the World. Power Politics and the Rise of Supranational Institutions.* Princeton, NJ: Princeton University Press.

Haacke, Jurgen. (1999) "The Concept of Flexible Engagement and the Practice of Enhanced Interaction: Intramural Challenges to the ASEAN Way." *The Pacific Review* 12:4: 581–611.

Haas, Ernst B. (1964) *Beyond the Nation-State: Functionalism and International Organization.* Stanford: Stanford University Press.

———. (1990) *When Knowledge Is Power. Three Models of Change in International Organizations.* Berkeley: University of California Press.

Haas, Peter M. (1990) *Saving the Mediterranean. The Politics of International Environmental Cooperation.* New York: Columbia University Press.

———. (1992) "Introduction: Epistemic Communities and International Policy Coordination." *International Organization* 46:1 (Winter): 1–35.

———. (2001) "International Environmental Governance: Lessons for Pollution Control Since UNCHE." In *Managing a Globalizing World,* edited by Jonge Oudraat and P. J. Simmons. Washington: The Carnegie Foundation, pp. 310–353.

———. (2002) "UN Conferences and Constructivist Governance of the Environment." *Global Governance* 8:1 (Jan.–Mar.): 73–91.

Hajnal, Peter I., ed. (1999) *The G7/G8 System: Evolution, Role and Documentation.* Burlington, VT: Ashgate.

Hall, Brian. (1994) "Blue Helmets." *New York Times Magazine* (January 2): 22.

Hall, Rodney Bruce, and Thomas J. Biersteker, eds. (2002) *The Emergence of Private Authority in Global Governance.* New York: Cambridge University Press.

Hampson, Fen Osler. (2001) "Parent, Midwife, or Accidental Executioner? The Role of Third Parties in Ending Violent Conflict." In *Turbulent Peace: The Challenges of Managing International Conflict,* edited by Chester A. Crocker, Fen Osler Hampson, and Pamela Aall. Washington: United States Institute for Peace, pp. 387–406.

Hampson, Fen Osler, with Michael Hart. (1995) *Multilateral Negotiations: Lessons from Arms Control, Trade, and the Environment.* Baltimore: The Johns Hopkins University Press.

Hardin, Garrett. (1968) "The Tragedy of the Commons." *Science* 162 (December 13): 1243–1248.

Hardin, Russell. (1982) *Collective Action.* Baltimore: Johns Hopkins University Press.

Harris, Stuart. (1994) "Policy Networks and Economic Cooperation: Policy Coordination in the Asia-Pacific Region." *The Pacific Review* 7:4: 381–395.

———. (2000) "Asian Multilateral Institutions and Their Response to the Asian Economic Crisis: The Regional and Global Implications." *The Pacific Review* 13:3: 495–516.

Hasenclever, Andreas, Peter Mayer, and Volker Rittberger. (2000) "Integrating Theories of International Regimes." *Review of International Studies* 26: 3–33.

Haufler, Virginia. (2002) "Industry Regulation and Self-Regulation: The Case of Labour Standards." In *Enhancing Global Governance. Towards a New*

Diplomacy, edited by Andrew F. Cooper, John English, and Ramesh Thakur. Tokyo: United Nations University Press, pp. 162–186.

Hawkins, Peter. (1997) "Organizational Culture: Sailing Between Evangelism and Complexity." *Human Relations* 50:4: 417–440.

Held, David. (1997) "Democracy and Globalization." *Global Governance* 3:3 (Sept.–Dec.): 251–267.

Held, David, and Anthony McGrew, eds. (2002) *Governing Globalization. Power, Authority, and Global Governance.* Cambridge, UK: Polity Press.

Helleiner, Gerald K. (2001) "Markets, Politics, and Globalization: Can the Global Economy Be Civilized?" *Global Governance* 7:3 (July–Sept.): 243–263.

Helman, Gerald B., and Stephen R. Ratner. (1992/93) "Saving Failed States," *Foreign Policy* 89 (Winter): 3–20.

Hemmer, Christopher, and Peter J. Katzenstein. (2002) "Why Is There No NATO in Asia? Collective Identity, Regionalism and the Origins of Multilateralism." *International Organization* 56:3 (Summer): 575–607.

Henderson, Jeannie. (1999) *Reassessing ASEAN.* IISS Adelphi Paper 328. New York: Oxford University Press.

Henkin, Louis. (1979) *How Nations Behave: Law and Foreign Policy*, 2nd ed. New York: Columbia University Press.

———. (1998) "The Universal Declaration and the U.S. Constitution." *PS: Political Science and Politics* 31:3 (September): 512.

Hensel, Paul R. (2001) "Contentious Issues and World Politics: The Management of Territorial Claims in the Americas, 1816–1992." *International Studies Quarterly* 45:1 (March): 81–109.

Hensley, Scott. (2001) "AIDS Epidemic Traps Drug Firms in a Vise: Treatment vs. Profits." *Wall Street Journal* (March 2): A1, A6.

Herman, Lawrence. (1998) "Internet Flex Muscles in MAI Negotiations." *Financial Post* (April 30): 21.

Higgott, Richard. (1994) "Ideas, Identity and Policy Coordination in the Asia Pacific." *The Pacific Review* 7:4: 367–378.

———. (1998) "The Pacific and Beyond: APEC, ASEM and Regional Economic Management." In *Economic Dynamism in the Asia-Pacific: The Growth of Integration and Competitiveness,* edited by Grahame Thompson. London: Routledge, 1998, pp. 335–355.

Higgott, Richard A., and Andrew Fenton Cooper. (1990) "Middle Power Leadership and Coalition Building: Australia, The Cairns Group, and the Uruguay Round of Trade Negotiations." *International Organization* 44:4 (Autumn): 589–632.

Hirst, Monica. (1999) "Mercosur's Complex Political Agenda." In *Mercosur: Regional Integration, World Markets,* edited by Riordan Roett. Boulder, CO: Lynne Rienner Publishers, pp. 35–48.

Hix, Simon. (1999) *The Political System of the European Union.* London: Macmillan.

Hocking, Brian, and Dominic Kelly. (2002) "Doing the Business? The International Chamber of Commerce, the United Nations, and the Global Compact." In *Enhancing Global Governance: Towards a New Diplomacy?,* edited by Andrew F. Cooper, John English, and Ramesh Thakur. Tokyo: United Nations University Press, pp. 203–228.

Hoffmann, Stanley. (2001) "The Debate About Intervention." In *Turbulent Peace: The Challenges of Managing International Conflict,* edited by Chester A. Crocker, Fen Osler Hampson, and Pamela Aall. Washington: United States Institute for Peace, pp. 273–284.

Holbrooke, Richard. (1998) *To End a War*, rev. ed. New York: The Modern Library.

Homer-Dixon, Thomas F. (1999) *Environment, Scarcity, and Violence.* Princeton: Princeton University Press.

Hopkins, Raymond F. (1990) "International Food Organizations and the United States: Drifting Leadership and Diverging Interests." In *The United States and Multilateral Institutions: Patterns of Changing Instrumentality and Influence*, edited by Margaret P. Karns and Karen A. Mingst. Boston: Unwin Hyman, pp. 177–204.

Hopmann, P. Terrence. (2000) "The Organization for Security and Cooperation in Europe: Its Contribution to Conflict Prevention and Resolution." In *International Conflict Resolution After the Cold War,* edited by Paul C. Stern and Daniel Druckman. Washington: National Academy Press, pp. 569–615.

Hoskins, Erik. (1997) "The Humanitarian Impacts of Economic Sanctions and War in Iraq." In *Political Gain and Civilian Pain: Humanitarian Impacts of Economic Sanctions,* edited by Thomas G. Weiss et al. Lanham, MD: Rowman and Littlefield, pp. 91–148.

Howard, Lise Morjé. (2001) "Learning to Keep the Peace? United Nations Multidimensional Peacekeeping in Civil Wars." Unpublished doctoral dissertation. University of California, Berkeley.

———. (2002) "UN Peace Implementation in Namibia: The Causes of Success." *International Peacekeeping* 9:1 (Spring): 99–132.

Hufbauer, Gary C. (2000). *Economic Sanctions Reconsidered*, 3rd ed. Washington: Institute for International Economics.

Huntington, Samuel. (1993) "The Clash of Civilizations." *Foreign Affairs* 72:3 (Summer): 22–49.

Hurd, Ian. (2002) "Legitimacy, Power, and the Symbolic Life of the UN Security Council." *Global Governance* 8:1 (Jan.–Mar.): 35–51.

———. (2003) "Stayin' Alive/Too Legit to Quit: A Response to Michael J. Glennon." *Foreign Affairs* 82:4 (July/Aug.): 204–205.

Hurrell, Andrew. (1995a) "Regionalism in the Americas." In *Regionalism in World Politics: Regional Organization and International Order,* edited by Louise Fawcett and Andrew Hurrell. New York: Oxford University Press, pp. 250–282.

———. (1995b) "Explaining the Resurgence of Regionalism in World Politics," *Review of International Studies* 21: 331–358.

Ignatieff, Michael. (1999) "Human Rights: The Midlife Crisis," *New York Review of Books* (May 20): 58–62.

———. (2001) "The Attack on Human Rights." *Foreign Affairs* 80:6 (Nov./Dec.): 102–116.

Ikenberry, G. John. (2003) "Is American Multilateralism in Decline?" *Perspectives on Politics* 1:3 (September): 533–550.

Independent International Commission on Kosovo. (2000) *The Kosovo Report: Conflict, International Response, Lessons Learned.* Oxford, UK: Oxford University Press.

International Commission on Intervention and State Sovereignty. (2001a) *The Responsibility to Protect: Report of the International Commission on Intervention and State Sovereignty.* Ottawa: International Development Research Centre for ICISS.

———. (2001b) *The Responsibility to Protect: Research, Bibliography, Background. Supplementary Volume to the Report.* Ottawa: International Development Research Centre for ICISS. The report is also available at www.iciss-cisse.gc.ca.

International Court of Justice, Advisory Opinion. (1949) *Reparation for Injuries Suffered in the Service of the United Nations. ICJ Reports,* 174.

———. (1951) *Reservations to the Convention on the Prevention and Punishment of the Crime of Genocide. ICJ Reports,* 15.

———. (1962) *Certain Expenses of the United Nations, ICJ Reports,* 168.

———. (1971) *Legal Consequences for States of the Continued Presence of South Africa in Namibia. ICJ Reports,* 144.

———. (1975) *Western Sahara (Spain v. Morocco), ICJ Reports,* 12.

International Court of Justice, Contentions Case. (1949) Corfu Channel Case (*Great Britain v. Albania). ICJ Reports,* 18.

———. (1962) Case Concerning the Temple of Preah Vihear (*Cambodia v. Thailand). ICJ Reports,* 6.

———. (1969) North Sea Continental Shelf Cases (*Federal Republic of Germany v. Denmark; Federal Republic of Germany v. Netherlands). ICJ Reports,* 3.

———. (1973) Fisheries Jurisdiction Case (*United Kingdom v. Iceland). ICJ Reports,* 49.

———. (1974) Nuclear Tests Cases (*New Zealand v. France). ICJ Reports,* 253.

———. (1980) Case Concerning United States Diplomatic and Consular Staff in Tehran (*United States of America v. Iran). ICJ Reports,* 3.

———. (1984a) Case Concerning Military and Paramilitary Activities in and Against Nicaragua (*Nicaragua v. United States). ICJ Reports,* 292.

———. (1984b) Gulf of Maine Area case (*Canada v. United States of America). ICJ Reports,* 246.

———. (1992) Questions of Interpretation and Application of the 1971 Montreal Convention Arising from the Aerial Incident at Lockerbie (*Libyan Arab Jamahiriya v. United Kingdom). ICJ Reports,* 3.

———. (1993) Case Concerning Certain Phosphate Lands in Nauru (*Nauru v. Australia). ICJ Reports,* 322.

———. (1997) Case Concerning the Gabcikovo-Nagymaros Project (*Hungary v. Slovakia). ICJ Reports,* 1.

———. (2002) Case Concerning the Land and Maritime Boundary Between Cameroon and Nigeria (*Cameroon v. Nigeria). ICJ Reports,* n.a.

International Crisis Group. (2001) "HIV/AIDS as a Security Issue." Available at www.intl-crisis-group.org.

International Monetary Fund. (2002) "The Design of the Sovereign Debt Restructuring Mechanism—Further Considerations." (November), available at www.imf.org/external/np/pdr/sdrm/2002/112702/pdf.

Jackson, John H. (1998) "Designing and Implementing Effective Dispute Settlement Procedures: WTO Dispute Settlement, Appraisal and Prospects." In *The WTO as an International Organization,* edited by Anne O. Krueger. Chicago: University of Chicago Press, pp. 161–180.

Jackson, Robert H. (1990) *Quasi-States: Sovereignty, International Relations and the Third World.* Cambridge, UK: Cambridge University Press.

Jacobson, Harold K. (1984) *Networks of Interdependence: International Organizations and the Global Political System,* 2nd ed. New York: Alfred A. Knopf.

Jacobson, Harold K., William M. Reisinger, and Todd Mathers. (1986) "National Entanglements in International Governmental Organizations." *American Political Science Review* 80:1 (March): 141–160.

Jacobson, Harold K., and Edith Brown Weiss. (1995) "Strengthening Compliance with International Environmental Accords: Preliminary Observations from a Collaborative Project." *Global Governance* 1:2 (May–August): 119–148.

Janis, M., and R. Kay. (1990) *European Human Rights Law*. Hartford: University of Connecticut Law School Foundation Press.

Jayasuriya, Kanishka. (1994) "Singapore: The Politics of Regional Definition." *The Pacific Review* 7:4: 411–420.

Jenkins, Philip. (2002) "The Next Christianity," *Atlantic Monthly* 290:3 (October): 53–65.

Jentleson, Bruce W. (1999) *Opportunities Missed, Opportunities Seized: Preventive Diplomacy in the Post–Cold War World*. Lanham, MD: Rowman and Littlefield.

———. (2001) "Preventive Statecraft: A Realist Strategy for the Post–Cold War Era." In *Turbulent Peace: The Challenges of Managing International Conflict*, edited by Chester A. Crocker, Fen Osler Hampson, and Pamela Aall. Washington: United States Institute for Peace Press, pp. 249–264.

Jetly, Rajshree. (2003) "Conflict Management Strategies in ASEAN: Perspectives for SSARC." *The Pacific Review* 16:1: 53–76.

Joachim, Jutta. (2002) "Comparing the Influence of NGOs in Transnational Institutions: The UN, the EU and the Case of Gender Violence." Unpublished paper presented at the Annual Convention of the International Studies Association, New Orleans, March 24–27.

Job, Brian L. (2000) "Alliances and Regional Security Developments: The Role of Regional Arrangements in the United Nations' Promotion of Peace and Stability." In *New Millennium, New Perspectives: The United Nations, Security, and Governance*, edited by Ramesh Thakur and Edward Newman. Tokyo: United Nations University Press, pp. 108–130.

———. (2004) "The UN, Regional Organizations, and Regional Conflict: Is There a Viable Role for the UN?" In *The UN and Global Security*, edited by Richard Price and Mark Zacher. London: Palgrave Macmillan, pp. 227–243.

Johnston, Alastair Iain. (1999) "The Myth of the ASEAN Way? Explaining the Evolution of the ASEAN Regional Forum." In *Imperfect Unions. Security Institutions Over Time and Space*, edited by Helga Haftendorn, Robert O. Keohane, and Celeste A. Wallander. Oxford, UK: Oxford University Press, pp. 286–324.

Jönsson, Christer. (1986) "Interorganization Theory and International Organization." *International Studies Quarterly* 30:1: 39–57.

Jordan, Michael J. (2000) "Who's In, Who's Out: UN Security Council Mulls Reform." *Christian Science Monitor* (October 16).

Josselin, Daphne, and William Wallace, eds. (2001) *Non-State Actors in World Politics*. New York: Palgrave.

Kahler, Miles. (1992) "Multilateralism with Small and Large Numbers." *International Organization* 46:3 (Summer): 681–708.

———. (2000) "Legalization as Strategy: The Asia-Pacific Case." *International Organization* 54:3 (Summer): 549–572.

Kalb, Claudia. (2003) "Tracing SARS." *Newsweek* (April 28): 36–37.

Karns, Margaret P. (1987). "Ad Hoc Multilateral Diplomacy: The United States, The Contact Group, and Namibia." *International Organization* 41:1 (Winter): 93–123.

Karns, Margaret P., and Karen A. Mingst. (2002) "The United States as 'Deadbeat'? U.S. Policy and the UN Financial Crisis." In *Multilateralism and U.S. Foreign*

Policy. Ambivalent Engagement, edited by Stewart Patrick and Shepard Forman. Boulder, CO: Lynne Rienner Publishers, pp. 267–294.

Karns, Margaret P., and Karen A. Mingst, eds. (1990) *The United States and Multilateral Institutions. Patterns of Changing Instrumentality and Influence.* Boston: Unwin Hyman.

Katsouris, Christina. (1999) "Creditors Making 'Major Changes' in Debt Relief for Poor Countries." *Africa Recovery* 13:2–3 (Sept.): 1, 12–15.

Katzenstein, Peter J., ed. (1996) *The Culture of National Security: Norms and Identity in World Politics.* New York: Columbia University Press.

Kaul, Inge. (2000) "Governing Global Public Goods in a Multi-actor World: The Role of the United Nations." In *New Millennium, New Perspectives: The United Nations, Security, and Governance,* edited by Ramesh Thakur and Edward Newman. Tokyo: United Nations University Press, pp. 296–315.

Kearney, A. T. (2003) "Measuring Globalization: Who's Up, Who's Down?" *Foreign Policy* 134 (Jan.–Feb.): 60–72.

Keck, Margaret E., and Kathryn Sikkink. (1998) *Activists Beyond Borders: Advocacy Networks in International Politics.* Ithaca, NY: Cornell University Press.

Kent, Ann. (2002) "China's International Socialization: The Role of International Organizations." *Global Governance* 8:3 (July–Sept.): 343–364.

Keohane, Robert O. (1980) "The Theory of Hegemonic Stability and Change in International Economic Regimes 1967–1977." In *Change in the International System,* edited by Ole Holsti, R. M. Siverson, and A. L. George. Boulder, CO: Westview, pp. 131–162.

———. (1984) *After Hegemony: Cooperation and Discord in the World Political Economy.* Princeton: Princeton University Press.

———. (1993) "Institutional Theory and the Realist Challenge After the Cold War." In *Neorealism and Neoliberalism: The Contemporary Debate,* edited by David A. Baldwin. New York: Columbia University Press, pp. 269–300.

Keohane, Robert O., and Lisa L. Martin. (1995) "The Promise of Institutionalist Theory." *International Security* 20: 1 (Summer): 39–51.

Keohane, Robert O., and Joseph S. Nye, Jr. (1971) *Transnational Relations and World Politics.* Cambridge: Harvard University Press.

———. (1977) *Power and Interdependence: World Politics in Transition.* Boston: Little Brown.

———. (2000) "Introduction." In *Governance in a Globalizing World,* edited by Joseph S. Nye, Jr. and John D. Donahue. Washington: Brookings Institution Press, pp. 1–41.

Keohane, Robert O., and Stanley Hoffmann, eds. (1991) *The New European Community: Decision-Making and Institutional Change.* Boulder, CO: Westview Press.

Keohane, Robert O., Peter M. Haas, and Marc A. Levy. (1993) "The Effectiveness of International Environmental Institutions." In *Institutions for the Earth. Sources of Effective International Environmental Protection,* edited by Peter M. Haas, Robert O. Keohane, and Marc A. Levy. Cambridge: MIT Press, pp. 3–26.

Khagram, Sanjeev. (2000) "Toward Democratic Governance for Sustainable Development: Transnational Civil Society Organizing Around Big Dams." In *The Third Force: The Rise of Transnational Civil Society,* edited by Ann M. Florini. Tokyo and Washington: Japan Center for International Exchange and the Carnegie Endowment for International Peace, pp. 83–114.

Khagram, Sanjeev, James V. Riker, and Kathryn Sikkink, eds. (2002) *Restructuring World Politics. Transnational Social Movements, Networks, and Norms.* Minneapolis: University of Minnesota Press.

Kim, Soo Yeon, and Bruce Russett. (1997) "The New Politics of Voting Alignments in the General Assembly." In *The Once and Future Security Council,* edited by Bruce Russett. New York: St. Martin's Press, pp. 29–57.

Kindleberger, Charles P. (1973) *The World in Depression, 1929–39.* Berkeley: University of California Press.

———. (1986) "International Public Goods Without International Government." *American Economic Review* 76 (March): 1–13.

Klare, Michael T. (2001) *Resource Wars. The New Landscape of Global Conflict.* New York: Henry Holt and Co.

Klotz, Audie. (1995) *Norms in International Relations: The Struggle Against Apartheid.* Ithaca, NY: Cornell University Press.

Knight, W. Andy. (2002) "The Future of the UN Security Council: Questions of Legitimacy and Representation in Multilateral Governance." In *Enhancing Global Governance: Towards a New Diplomacy,* edited by Andrew F. Cooper, John English, and Ramesh Thakur. Tokyo: United Nations University Press, pp. 19–37.

Knight, W. Andy, and Randolph B. Persaud. (2001) "Subsidiarity, Regional Governance, and Caribbean Security." *Latin American Politics and Society* 43:1 (Spring): 29–56.

Kobrin, Stephen J. (1998) "The MAI and the Clash of Globalizations." *Foreign Policy* 112 (Fall): 97–109.

Koremenos, Barbara, Charles Lipson, and Duncan Snidal. (2001) "The Rational Design of International Institutions." *International Organization* 55:4 (Autumn): 761–799.

Kostakos, Georgios. (1998) "Division of Labor Among International Organizations: The Bosnian Experience." *Global Governance* 4:4 (Oct.–Dec.): 461–484.

Krasner, Stephen D. (1976) "State Power and the Structure of International Trade." *World Politics* 28:3 (April): 317–347.

———. (1982) "Structural Causes and Regime Consequences: Regimes as Intervening Variables." In *International Regimes,* edited by Stephen D. Krasner. Ithaca, NY: Cornell University Press, pp. 1–21.

———. (1993) "Westphalia and All That." In *Ideas and Foreign Policy,* edited by Judith Goldstein and Robert O. Keohane. Ithaca, NY: Cornell University Press, pp. 235–264.

———. (1999) *Sovereignty: Organized Hypocrisy.* Princeton: Princeton University Press.

Kraus, Keith, David Dewitt, and W. Andy Knight. (1995) "Canada, the United Nations, and the Reform of International Institutions." In *The United Nations System and the Politics of Member States,* edited by Chadwick F. Alger, Gene M. Lyons, and John E. Trent. Tokyo: United Nations University Press, pp. 132–185.

Ku, Charlotte. (2001) *Global Governance and the Changing Face of International Law.* The John W. Holmes Memorial Lecture. ACUNS Reports and Papers No. 2.

Kuperman, Alan J. (2001) *The Limits of Humanitarian Intervention. Genocide in Rwanda.* Washington, DC: Brookings Institution Press.

Lamont, James. (2002) "UN Looks to Businesses for Help in Fight Against AIDS." *Financial Times,* August 30.

Langille, Brian. (2001) "Labor Rights." In *Managing Global Issues. Lessons*

Learned, edited by P. J. Simmons and Chantal de Jonge Oudraat. Washington DC: Carnegie Endowment for International Peace, pp. 469–507.

Larsen, Jeffrey A., ed. (2002) *Arms Control: Cooperative Security in a Changing Environment*. Boulder, CO: Lynne Rienner Publishers.

Lauren, Paul Gordon. (1996) *Power and Prejudice. The Politics and Diplomacy of Racial Discrimination*, 2nd ed. Boulder, CO: Westview.

———. (1998) *The Evolution of International Human Rights: Visions Seen*. Philadelphia: University of Pennsylvania Press.

Lauterpacht, Hersch. (1968) "The Grotian Tradition in International Law." In *The British Year Book of International Law*. London: Oxford University Press, pp. 1–56.

Leatherman, Janie et al. (1999) *Breaking Cycles of Violence: Conflict Prevention in Intrastate Crises*. West Hartford, CT: Kumarian Press.

Lee, Kelley, and Richard Dodgson. (2000) "Globalization and Cholera: Implications for Global Governance." *Global Governance* 6:2 (April–June): 213–236.

Legro, Jeffrey W. (1996) "Culture and Preferences in the International Cooperation Two-Step." *American Political Science Review* 90:1 (March): 118–137.

Leifer, Michael. (1996) *The ASEAN Regional Forum*. IISS Adelphi Paper No. 302. London: Institute for Strategic Studies.

Levy, David L., and Daniel Egan. (2000) "National and Transnational Strategies in Climate Change Negotiations." In *Non-State Actors and Authority in the Global System*, edited by Richard A. Higgott, Geoffrey R. D. Underhill, and Andreas Bieler. London: Routledge, pp. 138–153.

Lipschutz, Ronnie D. (1992) "Reconstructing World Politics: The Emergence of Global Civil Society." *Millennium* 21:3: 389–420.

———. (1997) "From Place to Planet: Local Knowledge and Global Environmental Governance." *Global Governance* 3:1(Jan.–April): 83–102.

Lipson, Charles. (1984) "International Cooperation in Economic and Security Affairs." *World Politics* 37 (October): 1–23.

Litfin, Karen T. (1994) *Ozone Discourses. Science and Politics in Global Environmental Cooperation*. New York: Columbia University Press.

Loescher, Gil. (1993) *Beyond Charity. International Cooperation and the Global Refugee Crisis*. New York: Oxford University Press.

Lowe, V., and M. Fitzmaurice, eds. (1996) *Fifty Years of the International Court of Justice*. Cambridge: Cambridge University Press.

Lowenthal, Abraham F. (1990) *Partners in Conflict: The United States and Latin America in the 1990s*, rev. ed. Baltimore: Johns Hopkins University Press.

Luck, Edward C. (1999) *Mixed Messages. American Politics and International Organization 1919–1999*. Washington DC: Brookings Institution Press.

Luck, Edward C. (2003) "Stayin' Alive/The End of an Illusion: A Response to Michael J. Glennon" *Foreign Affairs* 82:4 (July/Aug.): 201–202.

Lutz, Ellen L., and Kathryn Sikkink. (2000) "International Human Rights Law and Practice in Latin America." *International Organization* 54:3 (Summer): 633–659.

Mace, Gordon, Louis Belanger, and contributers. (1999) *The Americas in Transition: The Contours of Regionalism*. Boulder, CO: Lynne Rienner Publishers.

MacFarlane, S. Neil. (2001) "Regional Peacekeeping in the CIS." In *United Nations Peacekeeping Operations: Ad Hoc Missions, Permanent Engagement*, edited by Albrecht Schnabel and Ramesh Thakur. Tokyo: United Nations University Press, pp. 77–99.

Mack, Andrew, and John Ravenhill, eds. (1994) *Pacific Cooperation: Building Economic and Security Regimes in the Asia-Pacific Region*. Boulder, CO: Westview Press.

Mackie, Gerry. (2000) "Female Genital Cutting: The Beginning of the End." In *Female Circumcision in Africa: Culture, Controversy, and Change*, edited by Bettina Shell-Duncan and Ylva Hernlund. Boulder, CO: Lynne Rienner Publishers.

Mani, Rama. (1999) "Contextualizing Police Reform: Security, the Rule of Law and Post-Conflict Peacebuilding." *International Peacekeeping* 6:4 (Winter): 9–26.

March, James G., and Johan P. Olsen. (1989) *Rediscovering Institutions: The Organizational Basis of Politics*. New York: The Free Press.

Marin-Bosch, Miguel. (1998) *Votes in the UN General Assembly*. The Hague: Kluwer Law International.

Marquis, Christopher. (2003) "The U.N. Begins Choosing the Judges for New Court." *New York Times* (February 6): A3.

Masland, Tom. (2002) "Voices of the Children: We Beat and Killed People." *Newsweek* (May 13): 24–30.

Mathews, Jessica T. (1997) "Power Shift." *Foreign Affairs* 76:1 (Jan.–Feb.): 50–66.

Mattli, Walter. (2001) "Private Justice in a Global Economy: From Litigation to Arbitration." *International Organization* 55:4 (Autumn): 819–847.

Mattli, Walter, and Anne-Marie Slaughter. (1998) "Revisiting the European Court of Justice." *International Organization* 52:1 (Winter): 177–209.

Mayer-Schonberger, Viktor, and Deborah Hurley. (2000) "Globalization of Communication." In *Governance in a Globalizing World*, edited by Joseph S. Nye, Jr. and John D. Donahue. Washington DC: Brookings Institution Press, pp.135–151.

McCormick, John. (1999a) "The Role of Environmental NGOs in International Regimes." In *The Global Environment. Institutions, Law, and Policy*, edited by Norman J. Vig and Regina S. Axelrod. Washington, DC: Congressional Quarterly Press, pp. 72–98.

———. (1999b) *The European Union: Politics and Policies*, 2nd ed. Boulder, CO: Westview Press.

McDonald, John W. (1993) "International Conference Diplomacy: Four Principles." Excerpted from *Conflict Resolution Theory and Practice: Integration and Application*, edited by J. D. Sandole and Hugo van der Werwe. New York: Manchester University Press, pp. 248–259.

McNeil, Donald G., Jr. (2001a) "Indian Company Offers to Supply AIDS Drugs at Low Cost in Africa." *New York Times* (February 7): A1.

———. (2001b) "Coca-Cola Joins AIDS Fight in Africa." *New York Times* (June 22).

McNeil, William H. (1990) "Winds of Change." *Foreign Affairs* 69:1 (Fall): 152–175.

Mearsheimer, John J. (1990) "Back to the Future: Instability in Europe After the Cold War." *International Security* 15 (Summer): 5–56.

———. (1994/95) "The False Promise of International Institutions." *International Security* 19:3 (Winter): 5–49.

Mekata, Motoko. (2000) "Building Partnerships Toward a Common Goal: Experiences of the International Campaign to Ban Landmines." In *The Third Force: The Rise of Transnational Civil Society*, edited by Ann M. Florini. Tokyo and Washington: Japan Center for International Exchange and the Carnegie Endowment for International Peace, pp. 143–176.

Mikdashi, Zuhayr. (1972) *The Community of Oil Exporting Countries. A Study in Governmental Cooperation*. Ithaca, NY: Cornell University Press.

Miller-Adams, Michelle. (1999) *The World Bank. New Agendas in a Changing World*. London: Routledge.

Milner, Helen. (1991) "The Assumption of Anarchy in International Relations Theory." *Review of International Studies* 17 (January): 67–85.

Minear, Larry. (1994) "Humanitarian Action in the Former Yugoslavia: The U.N.'s Role, 1991–1993." Occasional Paper No. 18. Providence, RI: Thomas J. Watson Institute for International Studies.

Mingst, Karen A. (1987) "Inter-Organizational Politics: The World Bank and the African Development Bank." *Review of International Studies* 13: 281–293.

———. (1990) *Politics and the African Development Bank*. Lexington, KY: The University Press of Kentucky.

———. (1999) "Global Governance: The American Perspective." In *Globalization and Global Governance*, edited by Raimo Vayrynen. Lanham, MD: Rowman and Littlefield, pp. 87–102.

———. (2003) "Domestic Political Factors and Decisions to Use Military Force." In *Democratic Accountability and the Use of Force in International Law*, edited by Charlotte Ku and Harold Jacobson. Cambridge, UK: Cambridge University Press, pp. 61–80.

Mingst, Karen A., and Margaret P. Karns. (2000) *The United Nations in the Post–Cold War Era*, 2nd ed. Boulder, CO: Westview Press.

Mingst, Karen A., and Craig P. Warkentin. (1996) "What Difference Does Culture Make in Multilateral Negotiations?" *Global Governance* 2:2 (May–August): 169–188.

Miskel, James F., and Richard J. Norton. (1998) "Humanitarian Early-Warning Systems." *Global Governance* 4:3 (July–Sept.): 317–330.

Mitrany, David. (1946) *A Working Peace System*. London: Royal Institute of International Affairs.

Mittelman, James H. (1996) "The Dynamics of Globalization." In *Globalization. Critical Reflections*, edited by James H. Mittelman. Boulder, CO: Lynne Rienner Publishers, pp. 1–19.

Moon, Bruce E. (1998) "Regionalism Is Back! Now What?" *Mershon International Studies Review* 42, Supplement 1 (May): 338–342.

Moon, Chung-In, and Jongryn Mo. (2000) *Economic Crisis and Structural Reforms in South Korea: Assessments and Implications*. Washington: The Economic Strategy Institution.

Moravcsik, Andrew. (1997) "Taking Preferences Seriously: A Liberal Theory of International Politics." *International Organization* 51:4 (Autumn): 513–553.

———. (1998) *The Choice for Europe: Social Purpose and State Power from Messina to Maastricht*. Ithaca, NY: Cornell University Press.

———. (2002) "Why Is U.S. Human Rights Policy So Unilateralist?" In *Multilateralism and U.S. Foreign Policy. Ambivalent Engagement*, edited by Stewart Patrick and Shepard Forman. Boulder, CO: Lynne Rienner Publishers, pp. 345–376.

Morgenthau, Hans. (1967) *Politics Among Nations*, 4th ed. New York: Knopf.

Morphet, Sally. (1983) "The United Nations: Does the Rhetoric Matter? A Case History of Palestine 1947–1983." Document no. 223, International and Commonwealth Section, Research Department, Foreign and Commonwealth Office, United Kingdom.

———. (1986) "The Palestinians and Their Right to Self-Determination." In

Foreign Policy and Human Rights Issues and Responses, edited by R. J. Vincent. Cambridge, UK: Cambridge University Press, pp. 85–103.

———. (1993) "The Non-Aligned in 'The New World Order,' The Jakarta Summit, September 1992." *International Relations* 11: 4 (April): 359–380.

———. (2000a), "China as a Permanent Member of the Security Council." *Security Dialogue* 31:2 (June): 151–166.

———. (2000b) "States Groups at the United Nations and Growth of Member States at the United Nations." In *The United Nations at the Millennium,* edited by Paul Taylor and A. J. R. Groom. London: Continuum, pp. 224–270.

Munoz, Heraldo. (1998) "The Right to Democracy in the Americas." *Journal of Inter-American Studies and World Affairs* 40:1 (Spring): 1–18.

Murphy, Craig. (1984) *The Emergence of the NIEO Ideology.* Boulder, CO: Westview Press.

———. (1994) *International Organization and Industrial Change.* New York: Oxford University Press.

———. (2000) "Global Governance: Poorly Done and Poorly Understood." *International Affairs* 75:4: 789–803.

———. (2001) "Political Consequences of the New Inequality." *International Studies Quarterly* 45:3 (September): 347–356.

Murphy, Sean D. (1999) "Progress and Jurisprudence of the International Criminal Tribunal for the Former Yugoslavia." *American Journal of International Law* 93:1 (Jan.): 57–97.

Mutua, Makau. (1999) "The African Human Rights Court: A Two-Legged Stool?" *Human Rights Quarterly* 21:2: 342–363.

Najam, Adil. (2003) "The Case Against a New International Environmental Organization." *Global Governance* 9:3 (July–Sept.): 367–384.

Nambiar, Satish. (2001) "UN Peacekeeping Operations in the Former Yugoslavia— from UNPROFOR to Kosovo." In *United Nations Peacekeeping Operations: Ad Hoc Missions, Permanent Engagement,* edited by Albrecht Schnabel and Ramesh Thakur. Tokyo: United Nations University Press, pp. 167–181.

Narine, Shaun. (1999) "ASEAN into the Twenty-first Century: Problems and Prospects." *The Pacific Review* 12:3: 357–380.

———. (2002) "ASEAN in the Aftermath: The Consequences of the East Asian Economic Crisis." *Global Governance* 8:2 (Apr.–June): 179–194.

Natsios, Andrew S. (1996) "NGOs and the UN System in Complex Emergencies: Conflict or Cooperation?" In *NGOs, the UN, and Global Governance,* edited by Thomas G. Weiss and Leon Gordenker. Boulder, CO: Lynne Rienner Publishers, pp. 67–82.

Nelson, Paul. (2000) "Whose Civil Society? Whose Governance? Decisionmaking and Practice in the New Agenda of the Inter-American Development Bank and the World Bank." *Global Governance* 6:4 (Oct.–Dec.): 405–432.

Ness, Gayl D., and Steven R. Brechin. (1988) "Bridging the Gap: International Organizations as Organizations." *International Organization* 42:2 (Spring): 245–273.

Newman, Edward. (1998) *The UN Secretary-General from the Cold War to the New Era: A Global Peace and Security Mandate?* New York: St. Martin's Press.

———. (2001) "Human Security and Constructivism." *International Studies Perspectives* 2:3 (August): 239–251.

Nordic UN Project. (1991) *The United Nations in Development: Reform Issues in Economic and Social Fields.* Stockholm: Almqvist and Wiksell International.

Northledge, F. S. (1986) *The League of Nations: Its Life and Times. 1920–1946.* New York: Holmes and Meier.

Nugent, Neill. (1999) *The Government and Politics of the European Union*, 4th ed. London: The Macmillan Press.

Nye, Joseph S. (2001/02) "Seven Tests: Between Concert and Unilateralism." *The National Interest* (Winter): 5–13.

———. (2002) "The New Rome Meets the New Barbarians." *The Economist* (March 23): 23–25. (On-line edition)

O'Brien, Robert, Anne Marie Goetz, Jan Aart Scholte, and Marc Williams. (2000) *Contesting Global Governance. Multilateral Economic Institutions and Global Social Movements.* Cambridge, UK: Cambridge University Press.

Olson, Mancur. (1968) *The Logic of Collective Action.* New York: Schocken.

Ostrom, Elinor. (1990) *Governing the Commons. The Evolution of Institutions for Collective Action.* Cambridge: Cambridge University Press.

Ottaway, Marina. (2001) "Corporatism Goes Global: International Organizations, Nongovernmental Organization Networks, and Transnational Business." *Global Governance* 7:3 (July–Sept.): 265–292.

Packenham, Robert A. (1992) *The Dependency Movement: Scholarship and Politics in Dependency Studies.* Cambridge: Harvard University Press.

Packer, Corinne A. A., and Donald Rukare. (2002) "The New African Union and Its Constitutive Act." *American Journal of International Law* 96:2 (April): 365–379.

Padelford, Norman J. (1945) Unpublished letter to family and friends, June 26.

Palley, Thomas I. (2003) "Sovereign Debt Restructuring Proposals: A Comparative Look." *Ethics & International Affairs* 17:2: 26–33.

Paris, Roland. (2000) "Broadening the Study of Peace Operations." *International Studies Review* 2:3 (Fall): 27–44.

Pastor, Robert. (2001) *Toward a North American Community: Lessons from the Old World for the New.* Washington: Institute for International Economics.

Patrick, Stewart. (2002) "Multilateralism and Its Discontents: The Causes and Consequences of U.S. Ambivalence." In *Multilateralism and U.S. Foreign Policy: Ambivalent Engagement*, edited by Stewart Patrick and Shepard Forman. Boulder, CO: Lynne Rienner Publishers, pp. 1–44.

Patrick, Stewart, and Shepard Forman, eds. (2002) *Multilateralism and U.S. Foreign Policy: Ambivalent Engagement.* Boulder, CO: Lynne Rienner Publishers.

Paul, James A. (1995) "Security Council Reform: Arguments About the Future of the United Nations System." Available at http://www.globalpolicy.org/security/pubs/secref.htm.

———. (1997) "UN Reform: An Analysis." Available at http://www.globalpolicy.org/reform/analysis.htm.

———. (1999) "NGO Access at the UN." Available at http://www.globalpolicy.org/ngos/analysis/jap-accs.htm.

Payer, Cheryl. (1982) *The World Bank. A Critical Analysis.* New York: Monthly Review Press.

Pease, Kelly-Kate S. (2000) *International Organizations. Perspectives on Governance in the Twenty-First Century.* Upper Saddle River, NJ: Prentice Hall.

Peceny, Mark. (1994) "The Inter-American System as a Liberal 'Pacific Union.'" *Latin American Research Review* 29:3: 188–201.

Peck, Connie, and R. S. Lee, eds. (1997) *Increasing the Effectiveness of the International Court of Justice: Proceedings of the ICJ/UNITAR Colloquium to Celebrate the 50th Anniversary of the Court.* Geneva: UN Publications.

Pena, Felix. (1999) "Broadening and Deepening: Striking the Right Balance." In

Mercosur: Regional Integration, World Markets, edited by Riordan Roett. Boulder, CO: Lynne Rienner Publishers, pp. 49–62.

Pérez de Cuéllar, Javier. (1993) "The Role of the UN Secretary-General." In *United Nations, Divided World: The UN's Role in International Relations,* edited by Adam Roberts and Benedict Kingsbury, rev. ed. Oxford, UK: Clarendon Press, pp. 125–142.

Perrow, Charles. (1970) *Organizational Analysis: A Sociological View.* Belmont, CA: Brooks/Cole Publishing Co.

Peters, Ingo. (1999) "The OSCE and German Policy: A Study in How Institutions Matter." In *Imperfect Unions. Security Institutions Over Time and Space,* edited by Helga Haftendorn, Robert O. Keohane, and Celeste A. Wallander. Oxford, UK: Oxford University Press, pp. 195–220.

Petersen, Niels Helveg. (1997) "Towards a European Security Model for the 21st Century." *NATO Review* 45:6 (November–December): 4–7.

Peterson, M. J. (1986) *The General Assembly in World Politics.* Boston: Unwin Hyman.

Pettifor, Ann. (2003) "Resolving International Debt Crises Fairly." *Ethics and International Affairs* 17:2: 2–9.

Pillar, Paul R. (2001). *Terrorism and U.S. Foreign Policy.* Washington: Brookings Institution Press.

Pincus, Jonathan, and Jeffrey A. Winters. (2002) "Reinventing the World Bank." In *Reinventing the World Bank,* edited by Jonathan R. Pincus and Jeffrey A. Winters. Ithaca, NY: Cornell University Press, pp. 1–25.

Pogany, Isvan. (1987) *The Arab League and Peacekeeping in Lebanon.* Hong Kong: Avbury Publishers.

Poitras, Guy. (2001) *Inventing North America: Canada, Mexico, and the United States.* Boulder, CO: Lynne Rienner Publishers.

Porter, Gareth, Janet Welsh Brown, and Pamela S. Chasek. (2000) *Global Environmental Politics,* 3rd ed. Boulder, CO: Westview Press.

Power, Samantha. (2002) *"A Problem from Hell": America and the Age of Genocide.* New York: Basic Books.

———. (2003) "Rwanda: The Two Faces of Justice." *New York Review of Books* 50:1 (Jan. 16): 47–50.

Prandt, Jochen, and Jean Krasno. (2002) *Informal Ad Hoc Groupings of States and the Workings of the United Nations.* New Haven: International Relations Studies and the United Nations Occasional Papers, no. 3, ACUNS.

Preston, Julia. (1994) "Boutros-Ghali Rushes in . . . in a Violent World: The U.N. Secretary-General Has an Activist's Agenda." *Washington Post National Weekly Edition* (January 10–16): 10–11.

Price, Richard, and Nina Tannenwald. (1996) "Norms and Deterrence: The Nuclear and Chemical Weapons Taboo." In *The Culture of National Security: Norms and Identity in World Politics,* edited by Peter J. Katzenstein. New York: Columbia University Press, pp. 114–152.

Princen, Thomas. (1995) "Ivory, Conservation, and Environmental Transnational Coalitions." In *Bringing Transnational Relations Back In: Non-State Actors, Domestic Structures and International Institutions,* edited by Thomas Risse-Kappen. New York: Cambridge University Press, pp. 227–256.

Princen, Thomas, and Matthias Finger. (1994) *Environmental NGOs in World Politics: Linking the Local and Global.* London: Routledge.

Puchala, Donald J., and Roger A. Coate. (1989) *The Challenge of Relevance: The United Nations in a Changing World Environment.* ACUNS Reports and Papers No. 5.

Pundak, Ron. (2001) "From Oslo to Taba: What Went Wrong?" *Survival* 43:3 (Autumn): 31–45.

Putnam, Robert D., and Nicholas Bayne. (1984) *Hanging Together: the Seven-Power Summits.* Cambridge: Harvard University Press.

Quandt, William B. (2001). *Peace Process: American Diplomacy and the Arab-Israeli Conflict Since 1967*, rev. ed. Washington: The Brookings Institution.

Quitter, Joshua. (1995) "Vice Raid on the Net." *Time* (April 3).

Raffer, Kunibert. (1990) "Applying Chapter 9 Insolvency to International Debts: An Economically Efficient Solution with a Human Face." *World Development* 18:2: 301–313.

Rakove, Jack. (2003) "Europe's Founding Fathers." *Foreign Policy* 138 (Sept./Oct.): 28–38.

Ramcharan, B. G. (2000) "The International Court of Justice." In *The United Nations at the Millennium: The Principal Organs,* edited by Paul Taylor and A. J. R. Groom. New York: Continuum, pp. 177–195.

Ramphal, Shridath. (1984) "'Our and the World's Advantage': The Constructive Commonwealth." *International Affairs* 60:3 (Summer): 371–389.

Ravenhill, John. (2001) *APEC and the Construction of Pacific Rim Regionalism.* Cambridge: Cambridge University Press.

Reincke, Wolfgang H. (1998) *Global Public Policy. Governing Without Government?* Washington, DC: Brookings Institution Press.

———. (1999–2000) "The Other World Wide Web: Global Public Policy Networks." *Foreign Policy* 117 (Winter): 44–57.

Reus-Smit, Christian. (1997) "The Constitutional Structure of International Society and the Nature of Fundamental Institutions." *International Organization* 51: 4 (Autumn): 555–589.

———. (1999) *The Moral Purpose of the State: Culture, Social Identity, and Institutional Rationality in International Relations.* Princeton: Princeton University Press.

Revkin, Andrew C. (2003) "Bush Administration to Seek Exemptions to 2005 Ban of a Pesticide." *New York Times* (Jan. 30): A20.

Rich, Bruce. (1994) *Mortgaging the Earth: The World Bank, Environmental Impoverishment, and the Crisis of Development.* Boston: Beacon Press.

Risse-Kappen, Thomas, ed. (1995) *Bringing Transnational Relations Back In: Non-State Actors, Domestic Structures and International Institutions.* New York: Cambridge University Press.

Risse, Thomas, Stephen C. Ropp, and Kathryn Sikkink, eds. (1999) *The Power of Human Rights: International Norms and Domestic Change.* New York: Cambridge University Press.

Rittberger, Volker, ed., with Peter Mayer. (1993) *Regime Theory and International Relations.* Oxford, UK: Clarendon Press.

Roberts, Adam. (1999) "NATO's 'Humanitarian War' over Kosovo." *Survival* 41:2 (Spring): 102–123.

Roett, Riordan, ed. (1999) *Mercosur: Regional Integration and World Markets.* Boulder, CO: Lynne Rienner Publishers.

Rollick, Roman. (2002) "Botswana's High-Stake Assault on AIDS." *Africa Recovery* 16:2–3 (Sept.): 4–6.

Romano, Cesare P. R. (1999) "The Proliferation of International Judicial Bodies: The Pieces of the Puzzle." *International Law and Politics* 31: 709–751.

Roosevelt, Franklin. (1941) "Address by the President." 87th Congress. *Congressional Record* 44, pp. 46–47.

Rosenau, James N. (1992) "Governance, Order and Change in World Politics." In *Governance Without Government: Order and Change in World Politics,* edited by James N. Rosenau and E. O. Czempiel. Cambridge: Cambridge University Press, pp. 1–29.

———. (1995) "Governance in the Twenty-first Century." *Global Governance* 1:1 (Winter): 13–43.

———. (1997) *Along the Domestic-Foreign Frontier: Exploring Governance in a Turbulent World.* Cambridge: Cambridge University Press.

Rosenberg, Robin L. (2001) "The OAS and the Summit of the Americas: Coexistence or Integration of Forces for Multilateralism?" *Latin American Politics and Society* 43:1 (Spring): 79–101.

Rosenberg, Tina. (2001) "Look at Brazil." *New York Times Magazine* (January 28): 26–31, 52, 61–63.

Rotberg, Robert I., ed. (2003) *State Failure and State Weakness in a Time of Terror.* Washington: The Brookings Institution.

Rucht, Dieter. (1997) "Limits to Mobilization: Environmental Policy for the European Union." In *Transnational Social Movements and Global Politics. Solidarity Beyond the State,* edited by Jackie Smith, Charles Chatfield, and Ron Pagnucco. Syracuse: Syracuse University Press, pp. 195–213.

Ruggie, John Gerard. (1982) "International Regimes, Transactions and Change: Embedded Liberalism in the Postwar Economic Order." *International Organization* 36:2 (Spring): 379–415.

———. (1993) "Multilateralism: The Anatomy of an Institution." In *Multilateralism Matters: The Theory and Praxis of an Institutional Form,* edited by John Gerard Ruggie. New York: Columbia University Press, pp. 3–47.

———. (2001) "global_governance.net: The Global Compact as Learning Network." *Global Governance* 7:4 (Oct.–Dec.): 371–378.

———. (2003) "The United Nations and Globalization: Patterns and Limits of Institutional Adaptation." *Global Governance* 9:3 (July–Sept.): 301–321.

Russett, Bruce, Barry O'Neill, and James Sutterlin. (1996) "Breaking the Security Council Restructuring Logjam." *Global Governance* 2:1 (Jan.–Apr.): 65–80.

Rustow, Dankwart A., and John F. Mugno. (1976) *OPEC. Success and Prospects.* New York: New York University Press.

Sachs, Susan. (2003) "Internal Rift Dooms Arab League Plans to Help Avert a War by Pressing Iraq." *New York Times* (March 14): A11.

Sahnoun, Mohamed. (1994) *Somalia: The Missed Opportunities.* Washington: United States Institute for Peace.

Sakwa, Richard, and Mark Webber. (1999) "The Commonwealth of Independent States: Stagnation and Survival." *Europe-Asia Studies* 51:3: 1–29.

Sanderson, John. (2001) "Cambodia." In *United Nations Peacekeeping Operations: Ad Hoc Missions, Permanent Engagement,* edited by Albrecht Schnabel and Ramesh Thakur. Tokyo: United Nations University Press, pp. 155–166.

Schechter, Michael. (2001) "Making Meaningful UN-Sponsored World Conferences of the 1990s: NGOs to the Rescue?" In *United Nations-Sponsored World Conferences. Focus on Impact and Follow-up,* edited by Michael G. Schechter. Tokyo: UNU Press, pp. 184–217.

Scholte, Jan Aart. (1996) "Beyond the Buzzword: Towards a Critical Theory of Globalizaton." In *Globalization: Theory and Practice,* edited by Eleonore Kofman and Gillian Young. New York: Pinter, pp. 43–57.

———. (2000) *Globalization. A Critical Introduction.* New York: St. Martin's.

Schoofs, Mark. (2001) "Enlisting Multinationals in Battle." *Wall Street Journal* (Nov. 30): B1, B4.

Schott, Jeffrey J. (2000) "The WTO After Seattle." In *The WTO After Seattle*, edited by Jeffrey J. Schott. Washington, DC: Institute of International Economics, pp. 3–40.

Schraeder, Peter J. (2004) *African Politics and Society. A Mosaic in Transformation*, 2nd ed. Belmont, CA: Wadsworth/Thomson Learning.

Schulz, William F. (2001) *In Our Own Best Interest. How Defending Human Rights Benefits Us All.* Boston: Beacon Press.

Sen, Amartya. (1997) "Human Rights and Asian Values." Sixteenth Morgenthau Memorial Lecture on Ethics and Foreign Policy, Carnegie Council on Ethics and International Affairs. Summary found at http://www.cceia.org/sen.htm.

———. (2001) "A World of Extremes: Ten Theses on Globalization." *Los Angeles Times* (July 17).

Sewell, James P. (2000) "Congenital Unilateralism in a Multilateralizing World: American Scholarship on International Organization." In *Multilateralism in Multinational Perspective. Viewpoints from Different Languages and Literatures*, edited by James P. Sewell. New York: St. Martin's Press, pp. 1–42.

Shiells, Clinton. (1995) "Regional Trade Blocs: Trade Creating or Diverting?" *Finance and Development* (March): 30–32.

Sikkink, Kathryn. (1986) "Codes of Conduct for Transnational Corporations: The Case of the WHO/UNICEF Code." *International Organization* 40:4 (Autumn): 815–840.

Simmons, P. J. (1998) "Learning to Live with NGOs." *Foreign Policy* 112 (Fall): 82–96.

Simmons, P. J., and Chantal de Jonge Oudraat. (2001) "Managing Global Issues: An Introduction." In *Managing Global Issues: Lessons Learned*, edited by P. J. Simmons and Chantal de Jonge Oudraat. Washington: Carnegie Endowment for International Peace, pp. 3–24.

Simon, Sheldon. (1998) "Security Prospects in Southeast Asia: Collaborative Efforts and the ASEAN Regional Forum." *The Pacific Review* 11:2: 195–212.

Simons, Marlise. (2003) "World Court for Crimes of War Opens in The Hague." *New York Times* (March 12): A9.

Sinclair, Timothy J. (2001) "The Infrastructure of Global Governance: Quasi-Regulatory Mechanisms and the New Global Finance." *Global Governance* 7:4 (Oct.–Dec.): 441–451.

Singer, P. W. (2002) "AIDS and International Security." *Survival* 44:1 (Spring): 145–158.

Singer, Peter. (2002) *One World. The Ethics of Globalization.* New Haven: Yale University Press.

Slaughter, Anne-Marie. (1997) "The Real New World Order." *Foreign Affairs* 76:5 (Sept./Oct.): 183–197.

———. "Stayin' Alive/Misreading the Record: A Response to Michael J. Glennon" *Foreign Affairs* 82:4 (July/Aug.): 202–204.

Smith, Courtney B. (1999) "The Politics of Global Consensus Building: A Comparative Analysis." *Global Governance* 5:2 (Apr.-June): 173–201.

Smith, Graham. (1999) *The Post-Soviet States: Mapping the Politics of Transition.* New York: Oxford University Press.

Smith, Jackie, and Hank Johnston, eds. (2002) *Globalization and Resistance, Transnational Dimensions of Social Movements.* Lanham, MD: Rowman and Littlefield.

Smith, Jackie, and Ron Pagnucco, with George A. Lopez. (1998) "Globalizing

Human Rights. The World of the Transnational NGOs in the 1990s." *Human Rights Quarterly* 20: 2: 379–412.

Smith, Peter H. (2000) *Talons of the Eagle: Dynamics of U.S.–Latin American Relations,* 2nd ed. New York: Oxford University Press.

Smith, Thomas W. (2002) "Moral Hazard and Humanitarian Law: The International Criminal Court and the Limits of Legalism." *International Politics* 39 (June): 175–192.

Soesastro, Hadi. (1995) "ASEAN and APEC: Do Concentric Circles Work?" *The Pacific Review* 8:3: 475–493.

———. (1998) "Open Regionalism." In *Europe and the Asia Pacific,* edited by Hanns Maull, Gerald Segal, and Jusef Winandi. London: Routledge, pp. 84–92.

Soesastro, Hadi, and Charles E. Morrison. (2001) "Rethinking the ASEAN Formula: The Way Forward for Southeast Asia." In *East Asia and the International System: Report of a Special Study Group,* edited by Charles E. Morrison. New York: The Trilateral Commission, pp. 57–75.

Solingen, Etel. (1998) *Regional Orders at Century's Dawn: Global and Domestic Influences on Grand Strategy.* Princeton: Princeton University Press.

Sondrol, Paul. (2000) "The 'English' Patient: General Augusto Pinochet and International Law." Washington, DC: Institute for the Study of Diplomacy, Georgetown University.

Spar, Debora L. (1994) *The Cooperative Edge. The Internal Politics of International Cartels.* Ithaca, NY: Cornell University Press.

———. (1999) "Lost in (Cyber) Space: The Private Rules of Online Commerce." In *Private Authority and International Affairs,* edited by A. Claire Cutler, Virginia Haufler, and Tony Porter. Albany: State University of New York Press, pp. 31–51.

Spindle, Bill. (2003)"A Home on the Web: The Afghan Struggle for Internet Domain." *Wall Street Journal* (March 10): A1, 14.

Spiro, Peter J. (1995) "New Global Communities: Nongovernmental Organizations in International Decision-Making Institutions." *The Washington Quarterly* (Winter): 45–56.

———. (1996) "New Global Potentates: Nongovernmental Organizations and the 'Unregulated' Marketplace." *Cardozo Law Review* 18 (December): 957–969.

Stanley, William, and David Holiday. (1997) "Peace Mission Strategy and Domestic Actors: UN Mediation, Verification, and Institution-Building in El Salvador." *International Peacekeeping* 4:2 (Summer): 22–49.

Stedman, Stephen John. (2001) "International Implementation of Peace Agreements in Civil Wars: Findings from a Study of Sixteen Cases." In *Turbulent Peace: The Challenges of Managing International Conflict,* edited by Chester A. Crocker, Fen Osler Hampson, and Pamela Aall. Washington: United States Institute for Peace, pp. 737–752.

Stedman, Stephen John, Donald Rothchild, and Elizabeth M. Cousens. (2002) *Ending Civil Wars: The Implementation of Peace Agreements.* Boulder, CO: Lynne Rienner Publishers.

Stein, Arthur A. (1982) "Coordination and Collaboration: Regimes in an Anarchic World." *International Organization* 36:2 (Spring): 299–324.

Stein, Kenneth W., and Samuel W. Lewis. (1996) "Mediation in the Middle East." In *Managing Global Chaos: Sources of and Responses to International Conflict,* edited by Chester A. Crocker and Fen Osler Hampson, with Pamela Aall. Washington: United States Institute for Peace Press, pp. 463–486.

Steinberg, Richard H. (2002) "In the Shadow of Law or Power? Consensus-Based

Bargaining and Outcomes in the GATT/WTO." *International Organization* 56:2 (Spring): 339–374.

Stellin, Susan. (2002) "Internet Address Group Approves Overhaul." *New York Times* (June 29): B4.

Stevis, Dimitris, and Stephen Mumme. (2000) "Rules and Politics in International Integration: Environmental Regulation in NAFTA and the EU." *Environmental Politics* 9:4 (Winter): 20–42.

Stiglitz, Joseph E. (2000) "The Insider: What I Learned at the World Economic Crisis." *The New Republic* (April 17–24): 56–59.

———. (2002) *Globalization and Its Discontents*. New York: W. W. Norton and Co.

Stiles, Kendall W. (1998) "Civil Society Empowerment and Multilateral Donors: International Institutions and New International Norms." *Global Governance* 4:2 (April–June): 199–216.

Stoetzer, O. Carlos. (1993) *The Organization of American States*, 2nd ed. New York: Praeger.

Strange, Susan. (1996) *The Retreat of the State: The Diffusion of Power in the World Economy*. Cambridge: Cambridge University Press.

Streeten, Paul. (1999) "Components of a Future Development Strategy: The Importance of Human Development." *Finance and Development* (Dec.): 30–33.

Strohm, Laura. (2001) "Trade and Environment: A Teaching Case, MTBE and NAFTA." Unpublished case. Monterey Institute of International Studies.

Strom, Stephanie. (2003)"Grant Will Support Development of Topical H.I.V. Medications." *New York Times* (April 1): A14.

Swan, Alan C. (2000) "*Ethyl Corporation v. Canada*, Award on Jurisdiction (under NAFTA/UNCITRAL)." *American Journal of International Law* 84:1 (Jan.): 159–166.

Swarns, Rachel L. (2002) "African Leaders Drop Old Group for One That Has Power." *New York Times* (July 9): A3.

Synge, Richard. (1997) *Mozambique: UN Peacekeeping in Action 1992–99*. Washington: United States Institute for Peace.

Talberg, Jonas. (2002) "Paths to Compliance: Enforcement, Management, and the European Union." *International Organization* 56:3 (Summer): 609–643.

Taylor, Paul. (1993) *International Organization in the Modern World. The Regional and Global Process*. London: Pinter.

———. (2000) "Managing the Economic and Social Activities of the United Nations System: Developing the Role of ECOSOC." In *The United Nations at the Millennium: The Principal Organs*, edited by Paul Taylor and A. J. R. Groom. New York: Continuum, pp. 100–141.

Tetreault, Mary Ann. (1997) "Justice for All: Wartime Rape and Women's Human Rights." *Global Governance* 3:2 (May–Aug.): 197–212.

Thacker, Strom C. (1999) "The High Politics of IMF Lending." *World Politics* 52 (Oct.): 38–85.

Thakur, Ramesh. (2002) "Intervention: Sovereignty and the Responsibility to Protect: Experiences from the ICISS." *Security Dialogue* 33:3 (Fall): 323–340.

Thakur, Ramesh, and William Maley. (1999) "The Ottawa Convention on Landmines: A Landmark Humanitarian Treaty in Arms Control." *Global Governance* 5:3 (July–Sept.): 273–302.

Thakur, Ramesh, and Edward Newman, eds. (2000) *New Millennium, New Perspectives: The United Nations, Security, and Governance*. Tokyo: United Nations University Press.

Thakur, Ramesh, and Albrecht Schnabel. (2001) "Cascading Generations of Peacekeeping: Across the Mogadishu Line to Kosovo and Timor." In *United Nations Peacekeeping Operations,* edited by Ramesh Thakur and Albrecht Schnabel. Tokyo: United Nations University Press, pp. 3–19.

———, eds. (2000). *Kosovo and the Challenge of Humanitarian Intervention: Selective Indignation, Collective Action, and International Citizenship.* Tokyo: United Nations University Press.

Tharoor, Shashi, and Sam Daws. (2001) "Humanitarian Intervention: Getting Past the Reefs." *World Policy Journal* 18:2 (Summer): 21–30.

Thérien, Jean-Philippe, Michel Fortmann, and Guy Gosselin. (1996) "The Organization of American States: Restructuring Inter-American Multilateralism." *Global Governance* 2:2 (May-Aug.): 215–240.

Thomas, Daniel C. (2001) *The Helsinki Effect: International Norms, Human Rights, and the Demise of Communism.* Princeton: Princeton University Press.

Thomas, Kenneth P., and Mary Ann Tetreault, eds. (1999) *Racing to Regionalize: Democracy, Capitalism, and Regional Political Economy.* Boulder, CO: Lynne Rienner Publishers.

Touval, Saadia. (1996) "Case Study: Lessons of Preventive Diplomacy in Yugoslavia." In *Managing Global Chaos: Sources of and Responses to International Conflict,* edited by Chester A. Crocker and Fen Osler Hampson, with Pamela Aall. Washington: United States Institute for Peace, pp. 403–418.

Trail Smelter Arbitration (*U.S. v. Canada*) (1949) 3 *UN Reports of International Arbitration* 1938.

Tsebelis, George, and Geoffrey Garrett. (2001) "The Institutional Foundations of Intergovernmentalism and Supranationalism in the European Union." *International Organization* 55:2 (Spring): 357–390.

Tulchin, Joseph S. (1997) "Hemispheric Relations in the 21st Century." *Journal of Inter-American Studies and World Affairs* 39:1 (Spring): 33–44.

Tussie, Diana. (1995) *The Inter-American Development Bank.* Boulder, CO: Lynne Rienner Publishers.

Union of International Associations. *Yearbook of International Organizations.* Brussels, various years.

UNAIDS. (1998) "AIDS and the Military," May, available at www.unaids.org.

———. (2002) "AIDS Epidemic Update: December 2002," available at www.unaids.org.

United Nations, *Chronicle.* (1993). "The 'Second Generation': Cambodia Elections 'Free and Fair,' but Challenges Remain." 30:5 (November–December): 26.

———. (1997) "The Financing Problem." 2: 21.

———. (2001) "Combine Incentives for Research with Access to Medication for the Poor." 38:1 (March): 7.

———. (2001–2002a) "After the Prize, No Resting on Laurels." 39:4 (Dec.–Feb.): 39, 42.

———. (2001–2002b) "Citation." 38:4 (Dec.–Feb.): 4.

United Nations Development Program. (1969) *A Study of the Capacity of the United Nations Development System.* Geneva: UNDP.

———. (1999) *Human Development Report 1999. Globalization with a Human Face.* New York: United Nations.

———. (2003) *Human Development Report 2003. Millennium Development Goals: A Compact Among Nations to End Human Poverty.* New York: United Nations.

United Nations. (1991) *The World's Women: Trends and Statistics 1970–1990.* New York: United Nations.

———. (1992) Security Council. "Letter Dated 29 November 1992 from the

Secretary-General Addressed to the President of the Security Council." S/24868.

———. (1995) Fourth World Conference of Women. Platform for Action. A/Conf. 177/20.

———. (1996a) Report of the Expert of the Secretary-General, Ms. Graça Machel: *Promotion and Protection of the Rights of Children: Impact of Armed Conflict on Children.* A/51/306. Available at http://www.unicef.org/graca/a51-306_en.pdf.

———. (1996b) *Report on Impact of Armed Conflict Exposes Moral Vacuum, Secretary-General's Expert Tells Third Committee.* Press Release A/SHC/3382, 8 November.

———. (1996c) *The Blue Helmets: A Review of United Nations Peace-Keeping,* 3rd ed. New York: UN Department of Public Information (UNDPI).

———. (1999) General Assembly. *Address of the Secretary-General to the UN General Assembly, 20 September* (GA/9596).

———. (1999a) *Report of the Secretary-General Pursuant to General Assembly Resolution 53/35: The Fall of Srebrenica.* UN Doc.No.A/54/549, 15 November. Available online at http://www.un.org/peace/srebrenica.pdf.

———. (1999b) *Report of the Independent Inquiry into the Actions of the United Nations during the 1994 Genocide in Rwanda.* S/1999/1257, 15 December.

———. (1999c) Press Release, SG/SM/6938, 24 March, at http://www.un.org/Docs/SG/sgsm.htm

———. (1999d) Press Release, SG/SM/7263, AFR/196, 16 December. Available at http://www.un.org/Docs/SG/sgsm.htm.

———. (2000). General Assembly and Security Council. *Report of the Panel on United Nations Peace Operations.* A/55/305-S/2000/809, 21 August.

———. (2000) *Millennium Declaration.* Millennium Summit 2000: A/54/959.

———. (2001a) General Assembly. *Report of the High-Level Panel on Financing for Development Appointed by the United Nations Secretary-General,* Fifth-fifth Session, Agenda item 101, 26 June. A/55/1000. P. 3. www.un.org/esa/ffd/a55-1000.pdf.

———. (2001b) Report of the Secretary-General. *Road Map Towards the Implementation of the United Nations Millennium Declaration.* UN General Assembly 56th Session. A/56/326, 6 September.

U.S. Congress. (2000) *Africa Trade and Development Bill. Bridges Weekly News Digest* 4:18 (9 May). Available at http://thomas.loc.gov.

U.S. Department of State. (2001) "Test: Under-Secretary of State Dobriansky on US Role in Global AIDS Struggle." (June 22) Available at http://usinfo.state.gov.

U.S. Institute of Peace. (2001) "AIDS and Violent Conflict in Africa." Report issued October 15, 2001. Washington: US Institute of Peace.

U.S. National Intelligence Council Report (1999). Quoted in the *Dayton Daily News* (September 19): 25A.

———. (2000) *The Global Infectious Disease Threat and Its Implications for the United States.* NIE99-17D (January). Available at http://www.cia.gov/cia/publications/nic/report/nic99-17d.html.

Urquhart, Brian. (1991) *A Life in Peace and War.* New York: W. W. Norton.

Urquidi, Victor L. (2002) "From Rio to Johannesburg in Perspective: Will Strategies of Sustainable and Equitable Development Arise in Practice?" (Abridged version).

Utting, Peter. (2000) "UN-Business Partnerships." *UNRISD News* (The United Nations Research Institute for Social Development Bulletin), no. 23 (Autumn/Winter): 1–4.

————. (2002) "The Global Compact and Civil Society: Averting a Collision Course." *UNRISD News* (The United Nations Research Institute for Social Development Bulletin) no. 25 (Autumn/Winter): 30–33.

Vaky, Viron P., and Heraldo Munoz, eds. (1993) *The Future of the Organization of American States.* New York: The Twentieth Century Fund Press.

Vale, Peter. (1995) "Engaging the World's Marginalized and Promoting Global Change: Challenges for the United Nations at 50." *Harvard International Law Journal* 36:2: 283–294.

Vale, Peter, and David R. Black. (1994) "Seizing the Future: Post-Apartheid South Africa and the 'Post-Modern' Commonwealth." *Behind the Headlines* 5:4 (Summer): 1–16.

Van der Stoel, Max. (1999) "The Role of the OSCE High Commissioner in Conflict Prevention." In *Herding Cats: Multiparty Mediation in a Complex World*, edited by Chester A. Crocker, Fen Osler Hampson, and Pamela Aall. Washington: United States Institute for Peace, pp. 65–84.

Van Oudenaren, John. (2000) *Uniting Europe: European Integration and the Post–Cold War World.* Lanham, MD: Rowman and Littlefield.

Velazquez, Arturo C. Sotomayor. (2002) "Diversionary Peace in the Southern Cone: From Praetorianism to Peacekeeping?" Paper presented at the Annual Meeting of the American Political Science Association, Boston, August 29–September 1.

Victor, David G., Kal Raustiala, and Eugene B. Skolnikoff, eds. (1998) *The Implementation and Effectiveness of International Environmental Commitments. Theory and Practice.* Cambridge, MA: MIT Press.

Vincent, R. J. (1986). *Human Rights in International Relations.* Cambridge, UK: Cambridge University Press.

Wah, Chin Kin. (1997) "ASEAN in the New Millennium." In *ASEAN in the New Asia,* edited by Chia Siow Yue and Marcello Pacini. Singapore: ISEAS.

Waldman, Amy. (2003) "Helping Hand for Bangladesh's Poor." *New York Times* (March 25): A8.

Wallace, Helen, and William Wallace, eds. (1996) *Policy-Making in the European Union*, 3rd ed. Oxford, UK: Oxford University Press.

Wallach, Lori, and Michelle Sforza. (1999) *Whose Trade Organization? Corporate Globalization and the Erosion of Democracy. An Assessment of the World Trade Organization.* Washington, DC: Public Citizen.

Wallander, Celeste A. (1999) *Mortal Friends, Best Enemies. German-Russian Cooperation After the Cold War.* Ithaca, NY: Cornell University Press.

————. (2000) "Institutional Assets and Adaptability: NATO After the Cold War." *International Organization* 54:4 (Autumn): 705–735.

Wallensteen, Peter. (1994) "Representing the World: A Security Council for the 21st Century." *Security Dialogue* 25:1: 63–75.

Wallerstein, Immanuel. (1980) *The Modern World-System. Mercantilism and the Consolidation of the European World-Economy, 1600–1750.* New York: Academic Press.

Walter, Andrew. (2001) "NGOs, Business, and International Investment: The Multilateral Agreement on Investment, Seattle, and Beyond." *Global Governance* 7 (Jan.–Mar.): 51–73.

Walters, F. O. (1952) *A History of the League of Nations.* New York: Oxford University Press.

Waltz, Kenneth N. (1979) *Theory of International Politics.* Reading, MA: Addison-Wesley.

Wapner, Paul. (1996) *Environmental Activism and World Civil Politics.* Albany, NY: State University of New York Press.

Warkentin, Craig. (2001) *Reshaping World Politics: NGOs, the Internet, and Global Civil Society.* Lanham, MD: Rowman and Littlefield.

Warkentin, Craig, and Karen Mingst. (2000) "International Institutions, the State, and Global Civil Society in the Age of the World Wide Web." *Global Governance* 6:2 (April–June): 237–257.

Webber, Douglas. (2001) "Two Funerals and a Wedding? The Ups and Downs of Regionalism in East Asia and the Asia-Pacific After the Asian Crisis." *The Pacific Review* 14:3: 339–372.

Weinberger, Naomi. (2002) "Civil-Military Coordination in Peacebuilding: The Challenge in Afghanistan." *Journal of International Affairs* 55:2 (Spring): 245–274.

Weinstein, Michael M., and Steve Charnovitz. (2001) "The Greening of the WTO." *Foreign Affairs* 80:6 (Nov./Dec.): 147–156.

Weiss, Thomas G. (2000) "Governance, Good Governance and Global Governance: Conceptual and Actual Challenges." *Third World Quarterly* 21:5: 795–814.

Weiss, Thomas G., ed. (1998) *Beyond UN Subcontracting: Task-sharing with Regional Security Arrangements and Service-Providing NGOs.* New York: St. Martin's Press.

Weiss, Thomas G., and Leon Gordenker, eds. (1996) *NGOs, the UN, and Global Governance.* Boulder, CO: Lynne Rienner Publishers.

Weiss, Thomas G., and Amir Pasic. (1997) "Reinventing UNHCR: Enterprising Humanitarians in the Former Yugoslavia, 1991–1995." *Global Governance* 3:1 (Jan.–Apr.): 41–57.

Weiss, Thomas G., David P. Forsythe, and Roger A. Coate. (2003) *The United Nations and Changing World Politics,* 4th ed. Boulder, CO: Westview Press.

Weissbrodt, David. (2003) "Do Human Rights Treaties Make Things Worse?" *Foreign Policy* 134 (Jan./Feb.): 88–89.

Welch, Claude E., Jr. (2001a) "Amnesty International and Human Rights Watch. A Comparison." In *NGOs and Human Rights. Promise and Performance,* edited by Claude E. Welch, Jr. Philadelphia: University of Pennsylvania Press, pp. 85–118.

———. (2001b) "Mobilizing Morality: The World Council of Churches and Its Program to Combat Racism: 1969–1994." *Human Rights Quarterly* 23: 863–2001.

Wendt, Alexander. (1994) "Collective Identity Formation and the International State." *American Political Science Review* 88 (Summer): 384–396.

———. (1995) "Constructing International Politics." *International Security* 20: 1 (Summer): 71–81.

Wheeler, Nicholas J. (2000) *Saving Strangers: Humanitarian Intervention in International Society.* Oxford, UK: Oxford University Press.

White, Brian. (2001) *Understanding European Foreign Policy.* New York: Palgrave.

White, Julie. (2000) "U.N. Hosts Historic Millennium Summit." *The Interdependent* 26:3 (Fall): 5–7.

Wilkins, Rorden, and Steve Hughes. (2000) "Labor Standards and Global Governance: Examining the Dimensions of Institutional Engagement." *Global Governance* 6:2 (April–June): 259–277.

Willetts, Peter. (2000) "From 'Consultative Arrangements' to 'Partnership': The Changing Status of NGOs in Diplomacy at the UN." *Global Governance* 6:2 (April–June): 191–212.

Williams, Marc. (1991) *Third World Cooperation: The Group of 77 in UNCTAD.* New York: St. Martin's Press.

Williams, Phil. (2001) "Crime, Illicit Markets, and Money Laundering." In *Managing Global Issues. Lessons Learned*, edited by P. J. Simmons and Chantal de Jonge Oudraat. Washington: Carnegie Endowment for International Peace, pp. 106–150.

Williamson, John. (2003) "From Reform Agenda: A Short History of the Washington Consensus and Suggestions for What to Do Next." *Finance and Development* (September): 10–13.

Winham, Gilbert R., and Heather A. Grant. (1995) "NAFTA: An Overview." In *Toward a North American Community? Canada, the United States, and Mexico,* edited by Donald Barry, Mark O. Dickerson, and James D. Gainsford. Boulder, CO: Westview Press, pp. 15–31.

Wonacott, Peter. (2001a) "As WTO Entry Looms, China Rushes to Adjust Legal System." *Wall Street Journal* (Nov. 9): A13.

———. (2001b) "China Begins Career as a WTO Member." *Wall Street Journal* (Dec. 11): A14.

Woods, Lawrence T. (1993) *Asia-Pacific Diplomacy: Nongovernmental Organizations and International Relations.* Vancouver: University of British Columbia Press.

Woods, Ngaire. (1999) "Good Governance in International Organizations." *Global Governance* 5:1 (January–March): 39–61.

World Bank. (2000a) *Annual Report 2000.* Washington: The World Bank.

———. (2000b) "Can Africa Claim the 21st Century?" Report 20469 (2000/04/30). Available at www.worldbank.org.

World Commission on Environment and Development. (1987) *Our Common Future* (Brundtland Commission Report). Oxford, UK: Oxford University Press.

Wren, Christopher S. (2000) "Annan Says All Nations Must Cooperate." *New York Times* (September 6).

Young, Oran R. (1967) *The Intermediaries: Third Parties in International Crises.* Princeton: Princeton University Press.

———. (1989) *International Cooperation: Building Regimes for Natural Resources and the Environment.* Ithaca, NY: Cornell University Press.

———. (1999) *Governance in World Affairs.* Ithaca, NY: Cornell University Press.

———, ed. (1999) *The Effectiveness of International Environmental Regimes. Causal Connections and Behavioral Mechanisms.* Cambridge: MIT Press.

Yung, Fiona. (2001) "Far More than a Health Issue." *UN Chronicle* 38:1: 10–11.

Zacher, Mark W., with Brent A. Sutton. (1996) *Governing Global Networks: International Regimes for Transportation and Communications.* New York: Cambridge University Press.

Zacher, Mark W. (2001) "The Territorial Integrity Norm: International Boundaries and the Use of Force." *International Organization* 55:2 (Spring): 215–250.

Zartman, I. William, ed. (1995) *Collapsed States: The Disintegration and Restoration of Legitimate Authority.* Boulder, CO: Lynne Rienner Publishers.

Zartman, I. William, and Saadia Touval. (1996) "International Mediation in the Post–Cold War Era." In *Managing Global Chaos: Sources of and Responses to International Conflict,* edited by Chester A. Crocker and Fen Osler Hampson, with Pamela Aall. Washington: United States Institute for Peace, pp. 445–462.

Ziring, Lawrence, Robert Riggs, and Jack Plano. (2000) *The United Nations: International Organization and World Politics,* 3rd ed. New York: Harcourt College Publishers.

Index

563

Henkin, Louis, 37
Hinduism, 416
Hitler, Adolf, 71
HIV/AIDS, 30, 100, 104, 121, 124, 131,
138–139, 226, 264; in Africa, 203, 402,
405, 499–450; as challenge for global
governance, 499–506, 510, 518; and
child soldiers, 502; debate over access to
drug therapies, 503–506; and failed
states, 502; and genocide, 502; government roles, 502; international responses
to, 502–503; NGOs, 502–503, 505; partnerships, 500, 505, 511; peacekeeping,
502; people living with, 421; role of
pharmaceutical companies, 81, 502, 503,
505–506; scope of epidemic, 499–500; as
security issue, 97, 113, 233, 353, 499,
511; UN Joint Programme on AIDS
(UNAIDS), 502. *See also* World Health
Organization
Holocaust, 37, 337, 415, 423, 424, 447
Home Depot, 222
Honduras, 187, 296
Honeywell Corp., 394
Hong Kong, 215, 217; in APEC, 189, 194
Hudson Bay Co., 361
Human development, 267, 355–411, 516;
human development index (HDI), 363
Human Development Reports, 23, 375, 376,
440
Humane Society, 218
Humanitarian crises, 24, 26, 58, 100, 129,
138, 234–235, 243, 280, 291, 306, 423;
Iraq, 301; Kosovo, 450; and peacekeep-
ing operations, 279, 312, 316, 324–325,
444; relief aid, 10, 57, 130, 212, 214,
216, 244, 245, 246, 283, 319, 322, 351,
445, 513; Sudan, 349, 445. *See also*
Humanitarian intervention; Humanitarian
law
Humanitarian intervention, 51, 121–122,
284–288, 444; in Bosnia, 325, 444; criteria for, 287; East Timor, 325, 444; emerging norm 97, 324–327, 353, 444, 512;
International Commission on
Intervention and State Security, 287, 326;
Iraq, 324–325, 444; Kofi Annan on, 286,
287; Kosovo, 325–326, 444; and NGOs,
282, 324; Rwanda, 325, 444; and selectivity, 326, 445; Sierra Leone, 325, 445;
as threats to peace and security, 326
Humanitarian law, 420, 446–447. *See also*
Geneva Conventions
Human rights, 20, 21, 25, 86, 100, 103, 104,
109, 115, 131, 147, 158, 180–181, 193,
201, 226, 227, 242, 251, 261, 264, 268,
273, 274, 353; Asian states, 417–418,

431, 437; campaigns, 419–420, 421, 456;
of children, 415, 417, 421, 423, 429, 432,
438, 456, 511; child soldiers, 413–415,
416, 511; and China, 251, 417, 425, 429,
435, 443, 449, 512; cultural relativism,
417–418; debate on universality,
417–419; and debt relief, 356; and
democracy, 312, 432, 440; and development, 377, 440; disappearances, 420,
421, 431, 437; education, 441; enforcement, 415, 418–419, 432, 441–447, 452,
456; and environment, 432; evolution,
415–419; first generation (political and
civil), 432, 438; genocide, 13, 24, 57, 94,
112, 201, 218, 280, 285, 286, 291, 316,
319, 324, 327; and globalization,
456–457; and humanitarian intervention,
284–288, 324; and humanitarian law,
420; indigenous peoples, 417, 432, 456;
ILO role, 414, 423–424, 433;
International Covenant on Civil and
Political Rights, 284, 429, 434, 455;
International Covenant on Economic,
Social, and Cultural Rights, 429, 454;
law, 284; League of Nations, 421–424;
monitoring, 12, 130, 415, 420, 423,
433–440, 456; and multinational corporations, 31, 222, 408; and NGOs, 10, 59,
212, 213, 216, 218, 219, 224, 226, 233,
245–246, 301, 408, 413, 414–415,
419–421, 432, 433, 435, 437–440, 441,
442, 456; norms, 6, 12, 52, 145, 324,
415–419, 452; and peacekeeping/peace-
building operations, 312–313, 315, 316,
323, 414; philosophical origins, 416–417;
promotion, 440–441, 452, 456; and
refugees, 417, 429, 456; regime, 51,
180–181, 209, 428–433, 454, 455, 456;
and regional organizations, 427, 429,
430, 435–437, 441, 445–446; and religious traditions, 416–417, 428; right to
development, 431, 440; second generation (social and economic), 432, 438;
slavery, 76, 218, 419–420, 421, 429, 511;
standards, 427, 428–433, 452, 454; and
state sovereignty, 280, 286, 416,
418–419, 427, 443, 512; sweatshops,
421; and terrorism, 348; third generation
(group rights), 432, 441; torture, 218,
284, 421, 429, 431, 436, 437, 442, 451;
trafficking, 511; treaty monitoring committees (UN), 434, 439-40; in UN
Charter, 424; UN human rights organizational structure, 425–426; Universal
Declaration on Human Rights, 145, 284,
285, 417, 418, 425, 427, 428, 442, 454;
U.S. role, 454–456; violence against

About the Book

This long-awaited examination of international organizations covers the entire breadth of the subject in a way that will be welcomed by students and teachers alike.

Professors Karns and Mingst trace the evolving roles both of IGOs, NGOs, states, and nonstate actors and of norms, rules, and other pieces of global governance. While they give extensive attention to the UN system, the full range of regional and subregional organizations is also thoroughly covered, as are the activities and influence of a variety of nonstate actors.

Each of four issue-based chapters—on peace and security, economic development, human rights, and the environment—presents a contemporary case study and then examines the issues and the pieces of global and regional governance that are involved. Throughout, the authors highlight questions of the legitimacy, accountability, and effectiveness of global governance.

Margaret P. Karns is professor of political science at the University of Dayton. **Karen A. Mingst** is Lockwood Chair Professor in the Patterson School of Diplomacy and International Commerce and professor of political science at the University of Kentucky. Professors Karns and Mingst are coauthors of *The United Nations in the Post–Cold War Era.*